Leaders
of the Reformation

Leaders
of the Reformation

Edited by Richard L. DeMolen

Selinsgrove
Susquehanna University Press
London and Toronto: Associated University Presses

Associated University Presses
440 Forsgate Drive
Cranbury, NJ 08512

Associated University Presses
25 Sicilian Avenue
London WC1A 2QH, England

Associated University Presses
2133 Royal Windsor Drive
Unit 1
Mississauga, Ontario
Canada L5J 1K5

Library of Congress Cataloging in Publication Data
Main entry under title:

Leaders of the Reformation.

   Bibliography: p.
   Includes index.
   1. Reformation—Addresses, essays, lectures.
2. Reformers—Biography—Addresses, essays, lectures.
I. DeMolen, Richard L.
BR309.L4   1984   270.6'092'2   83-51423
ISBN 0-941664-05-8

Printed in the United States of America

Contents

Preface   7

1 The Interior Erasmus by Richard L. DeMolen   11

2 Luther's Communities by Scott H. Hendrix   43

3 Zwingli: Founding Father of the Reformed Churches by Robert C. Walton   69

4 Lay Religion in the Program of Andreas Rudolff-Bodenstein von Karlstadt by Calvin A. Pater   99

5 The Religious Beliefs of Thomas Cromwell by Stanford E. Lehmberg   134

6 For the Greater Glory of God: St. Ignatius Loyola by John Patrick Donnelly   153

7 Calvin as a Reformer: Christ's Standard-Bearer by David Foxgrover   178

8 Machiavelli, Antichrist, and the Reformation: Prophetic Typology in Reginald Pole's De Unitate and Apologia ad Carolum Quintum by Peter S. Donaldson   211

9 Family, Faith, and Fortuna: The Châtillon Brothers in the French Reformation by Nancy Lyman Roelker   247

10 The Image of Ferdinand II by Charles H. Carter   278

11 William Laud and the Outward Face of Religion by J. Sears McGee   318

Epilogue   345

Notes on Contributors   348

Index   351

Preface

The Reformation was one of the epochal events in the history of early modern Europe. Its causes were multiple and diverse. Political, religious, economic, social, and cultural-intellectual forces intermingled to produce an awesome transformation in the Christian church. In the process itself, the role of individuals remained pivotal. It is the purpose of the following collection of essays to determine how some major figures in the Reformation perceived themselves as reformers.

Once the battle lines were drawn, writers appeared to laud or castigate the leading figures in the Catholic and Protestant phases of the movement; but their interpretations often tell us more about their own confessional positions than about the men they set out to evaluate. The reader of these essays will be struck by the personal piety of the men included. It was a disciple of Philip Melanchthon, Joachim Camerarius, who wisely observed that "those who count it a reproach to great and famous people when anything blameworthy is found in them, have too soft a conception of the position of such people. For only God has this privilege, to be without a fault; human nature is not capable of it." Though Martin Luther's polemics against the papacy (the pope as Antichrist) were matched, for example, by his venemous attacks on Ulrich Zwingli and Erasmus of Rotterdam, he remained a man of singular goodness.

It is of value to note that each of the reformers in this collection found in himself the strength to reform the church; that the reforming ideas of all these men were related to an inward religious experience that changed their exterior lives and gave them the incentive to alter the lives of others. As Gerhard Ritter has observed: "In spite of the many paradoxes and contradictions contained in his writings, and his own at times inconsistent behaviour, what emerges from this work is the final, magnificent unity of Luther's theology—and this, moreover, a unity rooted in religious experience of quite exceptional depth and power. Luther is a religious prophet: his public acts, his militancy, his efforts as organiser of church life—all stem from this. Only those who view Luther in this light can hope to arrive at any understanding of his essential character." What was important to all these men, whether Protestant or Catholic, was the immediate experience of God in the heart of the believer.

The authors of these essays have decided to dedicate the volume to Professor A. G. Dickens, director emeritus of the Institute of Historical

Research in the University of London, whose seminal studies on the Reformation have inspired their own research and whose efforts on behalf of improving contacts between Anglo-American scholars deserve special commendation. To these scholars and to Professors John C. Olin, Albert Rabil, Jr., and James D. Tracy I extend my special gratitude for assistance in the editorial process.

Leaders
of the Reformation

1

The INTERIOR Erasmus

RICHARD L. DeMOLEN

> Though our outward man is corrupted, yet the inward man
> is renewed day by day.
>
> (2 Corinthians 4:16)

Hailed as a classicist, humanist, theologian, and reformer, Erasmus of
Rotterdam has for nearly five centuries attracted the attention of scholars of
every Christian persuasion. What is lacking, however, in this four-
dimensional view of the prince of humanists is his own deep spiritual life—
an interiorization of his philosophy of reform, *philosophia Christi*, which
grew out of his contacts with the *Devotio Moderna* and was activated in the
monastery of the Canons Regular of St. Augustine at Steyn in about 1489
when Erasmus underwent a spiritual awakening of enormous consequences. Marjorie O'Rourke Boyle, on the other hand, has argued recently
that the commonplace view that holds that Erasmus was "spiritually
formed under the tutelage of the "Brothers of the Common Life" can no
longer be supported. She goes on to insist that Erasmus's theological
method of imitation "is grounded in the pedagogy of classical rhetoric
more probably than in the piety of the Modern Devotion as scholars have
previously insisted"; that Erasmus was more clearly indebted to the works
of Cicero than to those of Thomas à Kempis. Boyle sees "very distinct
theological tonalities" in the works of Erasmus that make it impossible for
him to have based his *philosophia Christi* on the *Imitatio Christi* of Thomas à
Kempis, a fellow Augustinian canon.[1] It will be one of the purposes of this
essay to disprove this thesis and to argue that the language of the
philosophia Christi is identical to the undogmatic spirituality of the *Devotio
Moderna* and that Erasmus proposed a way of life rather than a method of
learning.

All of the portraits of Erasmus that were painted during his lifetime have
one thing in common: they show an introspective subject. Albrecht Dürer,
Hans Holbein the Younger, and Quentin Metsys have captured the spirit

11

of Erasmus by revealing his reflective nature. Even the presence of a money pouch, a fur-lined gown, and rings does not detract from the preoccupation with the nonphysical world that is etched on Erasmus's visage. The extensive correspondence of Erasmus, on the contrary, gives a different view of the man. He appears gregarious, industrious, at times peevish and even sarcastic in the pages of his letters. The correspondence shows a man of the world.[2] Reacting to this image, writers have tended to liken Erasmus to a peripatetic scholar in pursuit of honors and revenues or, somewhat more disparagingly, to the offshoot of "a long line of maiden aunts."[3] It is doubtful if very many authors of works about Erasmus would suggest that he was, above all, a man of God or would go so far as to acknowledge that he not only proposed a plan for holiness but actively pursued it as well. In the following pages I hope to show that this two-sided image of Erasmus was deliberately effected in an effort to demonstrate to mankind that sanctity grows out of a persistent struggle with sin and imperfection. Erasmus conveyed through his correspondence and literary labors the image of an adolescent and, later on, of an adult who not only possessed human weaknesses but also committed transgressions against God and man. And yet it was the very same man who would transcend his physical frailties and faults and submerge his personality in the love of Christ.

Writing to Wolfgang Faber Capito at the height of his career, 1517, Erasmus of Rotterdam was profoundly aware that l'uomo universale possessed not only a sound mind in a sound body but also a noble character that reflected inner goodness:

> Aulus Gellius tells us how long ago a good and acceptable proposal was rendered futile by the bad character of its proposer; and in the same way the fruits of study are quite rightly made more attractive by the reputation of the man who recommends it.[4]

During the last quarter of his life Erasmus suffered from the stings of critics who sought to discredit his philosophia Christi by attacking his character. In spite of the severity of these attacks, Erasmus maintaind pious practices during his lifetime as a demonstration of his Christian commitment and as a testimony to the integrity of his program of reform.[5] He emphasized that devotion must show itself in acts or else it is false:

> Perhaps you are wont to venerate the relics of the saints. . . . No veneration of Mary is more beautiful than the imitation of her humility. No devotion to the saints is more acceptable to God than the imitation of their virtues. Say you have a great devotion to St. Peter and St. Paul. Then by all means imitate the faith of the former and the charity of the latter.[6]

The emphasis on imitating virtue remained a consistent theme through-out Erasmus's writings. In his work on Christian marriage, Erasmus ob-served: "The fact is that from the best of parents the worst of children may be born and on the contrary we sometimes see admirable men born from illicit unions."[7] No doubt Erasmus was here thinking of his own parents and the sordid conditions that surrounded his birth and that of his older brother, Peter. Even in the face of adversity he insisted on the pursuit of virtue.

During his adolescence Erasmus endured physical as well as emotional crises. He lost both of his parents in his early teens and was separated from his only brother when the two boys, Peter aged 19 and Erasmus aged 16, were required to enter the religious life for lack of independent finances. It was probably during this time that Erasmus became aware of those circum-stances that surrounded his birth. In Leo X's letter to Andrea Ammonio (26 January 1517), Erasmus was described as "de illicito et, ut timet, incesto damnatoque coitu genitus." Writing in the sixteenth century, J. C. Scaliger spoke of Erasmus as "incesto natus concubitu, sordibus parentibus, altero sacrificulo, altera prostituta." Having been born to unmarried parents, Erasmus faced a debilitating awakening during his formative years.[8]

From an early date, Erasmus reacted strongly to personal attacks on his character. As Jacopo Sadoleto observed in 1530:

> There is one thing, I repeat, that I desire and which I vehemently urge upon you to do, that is, that you restrain yourself from entering into every sort of recrimination and that in your writing you avoid saying things which, although they may not be contrary to true piety, yet are not in accordance with the long-received opinions of the people and aggravate the zeal of certain men and even certain orders whom I deem it of the greatest importance not to oppose. What makes you, a man who excels in the highest degree in all kinds of learning, fight with persons who are not your equal in these altercations and quarrellings of yours?[9]

Though a personal friend, Sadoleto could not understand the importance of a good reputation in furthering the program of reform that Erasmus had clearly developed before he left the monastery at Steyn; nor could he understand that Erasmus was more than a scholar with a reputation. He was the architect of a spiritual life in Christ. In the words of *The Imitation of Christ*: "The life of a good religious man should shine in all virtue and be inwardly as it appears outwardly."[10]

It was while in residence at the monastery of the Augustinian Canons Regular at Steyn that Erasmus, encouraged by Cornelius Gerard, "decided for the future to write nothing which does not breathe the atmosphere either of praise of holy men or of holiness itself."[11] This was in 1489. And for the rest of Erasmus's life—some forty-seven years—he remained true to his promise: an extraordinary achievement indeed! Since Erasmus was pursuing studies for the priesthood at the time, he owed his life's ambition to a spiritual awakening among the Augustinian canons—an indebtedness that recalled his childhood contacts with the Brethren of the Common Life at Deventer and 's Hertogenbosch. At the outset of Book 1 of *The Imitation of Christ*, Thomas à Kempis offered a similar dedication:

> Let all the study of our heart be from now on to have our meditation fixed wholly on the life of Christ, for His holy teachings are of more virtue and strength than the words of all the angels and saints. And he who through grace has the inner eye of his soul opened to the true beholding of the Gospels of Christ will find in them hidden manna.[12]

Although Erasmus spoke disparagingly of the teaching abilities of the Brethren of the Common Life at 's Hertogenbosch, as well as of their zeal in promoting religious vocations, he praised them for their attitude toward religious vows: "For men of this persuasion have one exceptional advantage, which is a vestige of the early days of religion: they are not bound by indissoluble vows."[13] In 1493 Erasmus accepted a secretaryship with the Bishop of Cambrai in order to escape the monastic life at Steyn and to pursue a particular goal.

Soon after Erasmus left Steyn, admiring colleagues were aware of the program of reform that this newly ordained priest had initiated. The learned Robert Gaguin, writing in 1495, insisted that

> I do not write this with the intention of teaching you, for you are fit to be the teacher of others. I only wish to show what hope of glory lies in the journey you have undertaken. For I have come to believe of you that you combine piety with integrity of character. . . .[14]

Those scholars who claim that Erasmus's *philosophia Christi* owed its origins to John Colet ignore the fact that Erasmus had undergone a spiritual renewal before his arrival in England in 1499.[15] He came to England as a committed disciple of Christ as well as a reputable scholar. Colet himself summarized the opinion of English humanists concerning this "truly virtuous man":

> You have already been recommended to me by your reputation and by the evidence afforded by certain of your writings. At the time when I was in Paris the name of Erasmus on the lips of scholars was one to conjure with. . . . But what above all recommends you to me is the fact that the reverend father with whom you are staying, the prior of the house and congregation of Our Lord Jesus Christ, only yesterday described you to me as one who was, in his judgment, a truly virtuous man, uniquely endowed with natural goodness. . . . I hope you may like

our country as much as I think you are capable of benefiting her by your scholarship; while for my part I regard you, and shall continue to regard you, as a person whom I consider to be eminently virtuous as well as eminently learned.[16]

It is clear from this passage that Colet believed that the presence of Erasmus would stimulate English scholarship and spirituality. In 1499 Erasmus was more than a classical scholar in search of a research project. He was a man of deep religious commitment and considerable virtue. Moreover, as a sign of his dedication to Christ, he chose as his friends men of like disposition: John Colet, Sir Thomas More, and Bishop John Fisher[17]—all of whom nurtured and gave direction to his preconceived plan of holiness in the century that followed.

When first applying for a dispensation to hold ecclesiastical offices and to live outside of the cloister at Steyn in 1506, Erasmus acknowledged his illegitimacy but did not refer to the clerical status of his father.[18] Later on he acknowledged the possibility that his father was in holy orders at the time of his birth when he applied for a dispensation from Leo X to hold more than one benefice, to live outside the monastery at Steyn, and to adopt a modified form of the Augustinian habit. The letter granting the dispensation sets forth as the reasons that led the pope to grant it: Erasmus's uprightness of life and character, his exceptional learning, and his outstanding virtues—all of which had been commended to the pope in letters from Henry VIII and Charles V.[19]

In defense of his new mode of life, Erasmus wrote to his superior at Steyn that "I have always regarded as the worst of my misfortunes the fact that I had been forced into the kind of profession which was utterly repugnant to my mind and body alike: to my mind because I disliked ritual and loved freedom, and to my body because, even had I been wholly satisfied to live such a life, my bodily constitution could not tolerate its hardships."[20] The key words are "I disliked ritual and loved freedom." In essence it is a summary of the religious life that Erasmus envisioned not only for himself but for all Christians. Freedom from ritual and dogmatism would enable men to reach the ultimate heights in their progress toward union with Christ—a theme common to *The Imitation of Christ*.

Unable to endure the rigors of community life at Steyn because of physical disabilities, Erasmus followed legal channels in arranging his release from the monastery and its obligations. One is struck by his zeal in effecting the change from the formal religious habit of the canons regular, which resembled that of a bishop, to that of a secular priest. In doing so he sought simplicity. The garb of the canons regular, with its rochet and train, was far too ostentatious for his tastes and contradicted his call for simplicity in dress. Having decided to follow a life of commitment to Christ, he felt certain that his external image had to testify to his interior disposition.

Leo X's letter to Andrea Ammonio insists that Erasmus, "through no desire of his own but under pressure of events at first concealed and later altogether abandoned the habit which the said canons do customarily wear and went about for several years and still goes about in the habit of a secular priest . . . and now wishes for the peace of his soul and the avoidance of greater scandal to continue in the said secular habit.[21]

Erasmus proposed a life style for himself that would be in keeping with his relaxed status as a canon regular:

> I have searched for the kind of life in which I should be least bad; and indeed I believe I have found it. During this time I have lived among men of sobriety, and among literary studies which have kept me away from many vices. I have been able to enjoy the society of such as have the true flavour of Christianity and have been improved by their conversation.[22]

Erasmus here resolved to live the life of a priest-scholar in pursuit of Christ. Furthermore, in a letter to an unnamed monk dated 1527, Erasmus gives us a capsule summary of the kind of life he was actually living then:

> What kind of liberty is that where it is not allowable to say prayers, where it is not permitted to say Mass, where it is not proper to fast, where it is not licit to abstain from meat? Think what could be more wretched than such things even in these times.[23]

Though scholars have frequently cited the importance of liberty or freedom in his life, Erasmus carefully qualified and centered it around those practices which were in keeping with his clerical status. Thus as late as 1527 he pursued a priestly life by offering prayers, saying Mass, fasting, and abstaining from meat. For him pious practices had to involve the whole person, not just the mind.[24] Continuing his advice to the monk referred to above, he reminded the reader:

> May I die if I should not prefer to dwell with you there than to be the highest bishop in the palace of the Emperor, provided that this poor, weak body of mine had strength to live there. . . . If with all your heart you will despise the false attractions of this world; if you will give yourself to sacred literature and to mediating on the heavenly life, believe me, you will find more than abundant solace, and this little weariness of which you speak will vanish like smoke.[25]

It seems certain that by 1527 Erasmus had learned to reject the attractions of this life and had given himself wholly to the cause of sacred literature and to mediating on the heavenly life. The solace that he was offering the monk was already his. He had earned it from a life of withdrawal from the earthly realm and from a life of commitment to spiritual pursuits.

Separated from the monastery at Steyn, Erasmus was forced to seek patronage from a variety of sources. Indeed, subsistence was an almost constant preoccupation with him at the start of his public career. In a gentle admonition Colet cautioned him in 1511 not to be so active in pursuing patrons but to rely more on Divine Providence; and at the same time he observed how much Erasmus hated to act as a beggar for himself.[26] In time Erasmus became far more selective. Though numerous offers of patronage came to him from France, Germany, and Rome, he refused most of them.[27]

In declining the offer to come to the French court, Erasmus remarked that the generous opinion that others had of him laid upon him the burden of a reputation that he could not accept without gross egoism nor live up to without being a different sort of man.[28] Erasmus chose not to mix court politics with his pursuit of holiness. Near the end of his life he observed that "the glory [of an immortal name] moves me not at all, I am not anxious over the applause of posterity. My one concern and desire is to depart hence with Christ's favour."[29]

Following the appearance of *In Praise of Folly* in 1509, which was soon criticized by Maarten van Dorp and other theologians at the University of Louvain, Erasmus confessed that he regretted its attacks on theologians and its apparent mockery of sacred subjects:

> I am almost sorry myself that I published my *Folly*. That small book has earned me not a little reputation, or notoriety if you prefer; but I have no use for reputation coupled with ill will. . . . In all the books I have published my sole object has always been to do something useful by my exertions or, if that should not be possible, at least to do no harm.[30]

Erasmus also reminded Dorp that he had never singled out any theologians by name and that his discussion of faults did not imply a criticism of any particular individual. The real intent of his work was to offer guidance, to show men how to become better. He also sought comfort from the fact that not all theologians reacted so unkindly to his *Folly:*

> how many theologians I could list for you, renowned for holiness of life, eminent for scholarship, and of the highest station, some of them even bishops, who have never given me such a warm welcome as since the publication of my *Folly*, and who think more highly of that small book than I do myself.[31]

Nor was Dorp Erasmus's only critic. Guillaume Budé complained to Erasmus that he wasted his talents on trivial schoolboys. Erasmus responded with reference to his program of reform:

> Again, the risk you display before me that by publishing so many

minor works I shall get myself a bad name does not move me in the least. Whatever in the way of notoriety rather than glory has been won for me by my publications, I would peacefully and willingly dispense with, if I could. . . . For my own part, these superficial subjects are the field in which it suits me to philosophize, and I see in them less frivolity and somewhat more profit than in those themes which the professional philosophers find so pre-eminent. Finally the man whose sole object is not to advertise himself but to help other people, asks not so much Is it grand, my chosen field? as Is it useful?[32]

Erasmus's defense of his reputation was based not on self-conceit but on a desire to protect his reform program, which was directed to every Christian, from schoolboy to king.[33] He was convinced that both the minds and hearts of the young could be soundly molded and directed by good teachers. The wise mentor could teach the intellect and will to know and choose good and the spirit to savor virtue and love God. Of the prince, Erasmus insisted that he be reared "in such a manner that from the example of his life all the others (nobles and commoners alike) may take this model of frugality and temperance."[34]

Later on, Luther launched his barbs at the unyielding reformer. Responding to Luther's 1526 letter of apology, in which he begged Erasmus not to take the abuse that had been piled on his head too seriously (Luther had earlier described him as "Christ's most bitter enemy"), Erasmus retorted:

I am not so simple as to be appeased by one or two pleasantries or soothed by flattery after receiving so many more than mortal wounds. . . . it is *this* that distresses me, and all the best spirits with me, that with that arrogant, impudent, seditious temperament of yours you are shattering the whole globe in ruinous discord.[35]

He insisted on civility and refused to be drawn into an untenable position of friendship when Luther's reform produced only confusion in Christendom. Erasmus saw Christ as the prince of peace and not as the advocate of violent change.[36]

In his *philosophia Christi*, Erasmus stressed the importance of interior spirituality rather than external observances; of the ways of the spirit rather than the letter of the law. Writing to Servatius Rogerus, he observed:

We make Christianity and piety consist in place, dress, diet, and a number of petty observances. . . . How much more consonant with Christ's teaching it would be to regard the entire Christian world as a single household, a single monastery as it were, and to think of all men as one's fellow-canons and brethren, to regard the sacrament of baptism as the supreme religious obligation, and to consider not where one lives, but how one lives.[37]

Erasmus found fault with the monastic life at Steyn because it placed so much emphasis on ritual and form that it ignored the interior spirituality of the canon. It was the quality of one's interior life that truly mattered to Christ, and Erasmus refers to it over and over again.[38]

Erasmus composed his blueprint for holiness in 1503 as the result of a request from a woman who sought help for her wayward husband. He made it very clear at the outset that he wished "to describe a way of life, not a method of learning."[39] Titled *The Handbook of the Militant Christian*, it served as "a shortcut . . . to Christ." It was designed for all Christians. Erasmus was anxious to recall theology, which had fallen into squabbling, to its original simplicity. In the spirit of the *Devotio Moderna*, Erasmus wished to interiorize religion and to bridge the gap between God and man that had been ossified by ritual and structure. Indeed, as he himself stated, he proposed a "path to perfection."

Since Erasmus viewed life on earth as "a type of continual warfare," he armed the Christian who sought true spirituality with the weapons of war. Prayer and knowledge were the two major ones:

> Pure prayer directed to heaven is able to subdue passion, for it is, as it were, a citadel inaccessible to the enemy. Knowledge, or learning, fortifies the mind with salutary precepts and keeps virtue ever before us.[40]

Armed with these weapons, the Christian is prepared for battle with the devil, the world, and himself: "Christ alone grants that peace that the world cannot give. There is but one way to attain it; we must wage war with ourselves. We must contend fiercely with our vices."[41]

Erasmus also insisted that the true Christian must dedicate himself entirely to the study of Scripture. But in order to understand these writings, he was advised to read the classics, where there are countless examples of right living:

> So pick out from pagan books whatever is best. In studying the ancients follow the example of the bee flying about the garden. Like the bee, suck out only what is wholesome and sweet; reject what is useless and poisonous.[42]

The only purpose of the classics was to aid the Christian in his search for Christ. By imitating examples of "right living," the militant Christian would be led to the imitation of Christ Himself. Closer contact with Christ was the object of one's reading.

Moreover, Erasmus recommended the Church Fathers, whose deep piety would help the reader to penetrate some difficult passages in sacred Scripture. What was needed for religious growth was a spiritual rather than literal understanding of the Scriptures. Too many monks, according to Erasmus, failed to understand the word of God because of its hidden meaning: "They [the Church Fathers] will lead you to an inner penetration of the word of God, to an understanding of the spiritual worth it contains."[43] Once the learner had acquired a true knowledge of Scriptures, Erasmus advocated the imitation of spiritual values.

Though Erasmus warned his reader of the evil inclinations inherent in man, he also argued for the efficacy of reason as a means of restraining vice and redirecting the will toward virtue. He saw man as a tripartite creature, composed of spirit, which has the capacity of making men divine, the flesh, and the soul, which distinguishes men from all other creatures. Of the three parts, Erasmus considered the spirit of man to be the most important:

> It is the spirit that gives us the qualities of religion: obedience, kindness, and mercy. The flesh makes us despisers of God, disobedient, and cruel. The soul, on the other hand, is indifferent, neither good nor bad in itself.[44]

According to Erasmus, it was the spirit in man that produced virtue.[45] Virtues that proceeded entirely from natural inclinations had no merit. It was only when the spirit overcame an evil inclination that one acquired true virtue. It was at this point that Erasmus criticized those Christians who out of self-satisfaction or because they believed it would enhance their reputation presumed that they were practicing virtue when they attended daily Mass or made novenas in honor of one of the saints. Divine service was profitable only when it was entered into in the right spirit. If man attended Mass because he loved God and despised his sins, he was practicing virtue. "Leading a virtuous life is accompanied by a certain discipline that the Holy Spirit breathes into those who sincerely aim at godliness."[46]

For entering into "the pure light of the spiritual life," Erasmus proposed a number of fundamental rules or norms that would guide the reader through the labyrinth of this world. These included studying the Scriptures, pursuing the virtue of perseverance, and making Christ the goal of one's life. Erasmus was convinced that there was not a single item in Holy Scripture that did not pertain to man's salvation. Moreover, he was equally convinced that the allurements of this world (whether family, riches, health, or reputation) must not deter one from his goal. Man must "realize that in Christ is the fulfillment of all things."[47]

Erasmus was seen by many of his contemporaries as the supreme teacher and by a few as the "lodestar of all humane studies."[48] As is apparent from his prefatory letter in the *Novum Instrumentum* of 1516, he regarded himself as a teacher of true Christianity. In making the Bible available to the public in a purer form, he wished to draw all men to a more pious life in Christ.

Much of the spirit of the *Imitatio Christi* appeared in the *Enchiridion*. In one passage Erasmus insisted not only that his readers should reject the things of this world but also that they "must be crucified to this world."[49] His outline of a spiritual life was designed for all men, whether lay or religious or cleric: "If you are in the world, you are not in Christ."[50] For those of little fortitude, Erasmus reasoned:

> Even though all of us cannot reach this goal, cannot attain the perfect imitation of the Head, all of us must aim for this goal with all our efforts.[51]

Like the *Imitatio Christi*, the *philosophia Christi* appealed to all Christians and offered a formula for spiritual perfection that was compatible with a career in the world.

Erasmus categorized the principal goals in life and placed them under three headings: (1) actions that are intrinsically evil; (2) actions that are indifferent, morally speaking, such as health, beauty, learning; and (3) Christ-centered actions. No doubt speaking of himself, Erasmus cautioned:

> If you are interested in learning, certainly this is a fine quality, provided you turn your knowledge to Christ. If, on the other hand, you love letters only for the sake of knowledge, you have not gone far enough. . . . Let your study bring you to a clearer perception of Christ so that your love for Him will increase and you will in turn be able to communicate this knowledge of Him to others. You can do this rather easily if you accustom yourself to admiring nothing that is outside yourself, namely things that do not pertain to the inner man.[52]

Despite this quotation, Edmund Colledge has insisted that Erasmus was poles apart from any of the founders or leaders of the *Devotio Moderna*. He turned for support to a quotation from Lubbert ten Busch, a foundation member and procurator of the house at Deventer, on the intellectual life. It is well worth requoting here because of the similarity to the *Enchiridion* in language and objective:

> You should never study anything which does not nourish the soul, for the fruits of study are the strengthening of the soul and the acquisition of virtues. To study for the sake of knowledge, in order to teach others, or for any other end than the sake of the soul does not strengthen but sickens it.[53]

Erasmus's goal in life was the perfection of the "inner man." He came to this realization in the monastery at Steyn. Here he decided that henceforth he would pursue only studies that would lead to greater piety. He rejected the study of literature for its own sake and aimed all of his scholarship at bridging the gap between God and man:

> There are certain detractors who think that true religion has nothing to do with good literature. Let me say that I have been studying the classics since my youth. For me a knowledge of Greek and Latin required many a long, hard hour. I did not undertake this merely for the sake of empty fame or for the childish pleasures of the mind. My sole purpose was that, knowing these writings, I might the better adorn the Lord's temple with literary richness.[54]

The pursuit of the classics and the study of Scripture and the Church Fathers were useful because they gave man a better understanding of Christ and his message to mankind. Erasmus's spiritual awakening shaped his program of reform and gave special direction to his life. Aware of his own infirmities, he exuded confidence in his quest toward greater perfection.

> Our determination to imitate Christ should be of such a nature that we have no time for these [worldly] matters . . . I suffer from infirmity and weakness, but with St. Paul I show forth a more excellent way.[55]

Erasmus's voluminous correspondence is full of examples of his frailties and weaknesses. They are visible testimony to the fact that he was born with many afflictions. But the important thing to keep in mind is that Erasmus sought to overcome these limitations spiritually and to show others that human failings are not a deterrent to sanctity but serve as incentives or spurs: "A pious man who overcomes great sin is all the more pious. What makes a man evil is not that he sins but that he *loves* his sin."[56]

According to Erasmus the figure of Christ was the "only complete example of perfect piety." For this reason he urged all mankind to imitate Him. At the same time he called forth the examples of Christ's saints and advised his readers to "emulate them in such a way that each of them prompts you to eradicate one or another vice, and practice their particular virtues."[57] It was the practice of virtue that constituted the imitation of Christ and the imitation of His saints.

Erasmus also insisted that external acts of penance ("manual works") have little or no value unless they are accompanied by internal piety. God as a Spirit "is appeased by spiritual sacrifices." To the religious, Erasmus directed this advice:

> Of what advantage to you is a body covered by a religious habit if that same body possesses a mind that is worldly?[58]

The true Christian lives inwardly. He rejects the attractions of this world so that he can concentrate his efforts on knowing and pleasing God: "Blessed are they who hear the word of God internally. Happy are they to whom the Lord speaks inwardly, for their salvation is assured."[59]

As early as 1503 Erasmus had committed himself to an internal life of holiness. He would reject the physical attractions of this world in order to love God more fully. At the same time, he vowed to communicate his own concept of greater perfection by composing works specifically for this purpose, works that were in harmony with the spirit of the *Devotio Moderna*. It was the silence of God that Erasmus sought:

> if you make a sincere effort to escape from the chains of blindness with which the love of sensible things has bound you, He will come to you, and you, no longer chained to the things of earth, will be enveloped in the silence of God.[60]

This thought is repeated in the *Imitatio Christi:* "My son, says our Lord. . . . My words are spiritual and cannot be comprehended fully by man's intelligence. Neither are they to be adapted or applied according to the vain pleasure of the hearer, but are to be heard in silence, with great humility and reverence. . . ."[61]

Erasmus chose as his friends men of singular piety and goodness. There is a long list of men of personal holiness who were regular correspondents of his. This fact is not coincidental. Erasmus corresponded with men of sanctity because he wanted to make himself better:

> If people do not think along lines that would make you better, withdraw yourself as much as possible from human companionship and take for companions Christ and His prophets and Apostles.[62]

It was the evil in the world that led Erasmus to speak out so harshly against war in his *Complaint of Peace* and *De bellum inexpertis.*[63] He hated war precisely because it violated Christ's injunction to love one another. But the "war" of which he spoke was not confined to the battlefield. It took place in cities, courts of kings, halls of justice, universities, religious houses, and private homes. Such conflict between human beings was just as un-Christian as military combat because it rejected the example of Christ:

> Consider the whole of his [Christ's] life; what is it, but one lesson of concord and mutual love? What do his precepts, what do his parables inculcate, but peace and charity?[64]

For Erasmus the distinguishing mark of a Christian was charity. Christ will be able to recognize his followers only if they practice charity. Neither religious habits, nor harsh diets, nor special prayers count for anything if one lacks charity.[65]

Erasmus did not confine his blueprint for holiness to the *Enchiridion* but advocated it in all of his works. Take, for example, the following passage from *The Praise of Folly*, which is generally regarded by its critics as a work of satire:

> what is this future life of heaven toward which the pious aspire with so much endeavor? It consists in the first place of an absorption of the body by the spirit, accomplished the more easily as the spirit is now in its own kingdom and is furthermore by reason of its purgations during life adapted to this transformation. Then the spirit will be in a marvelous manner absorbed by the Highest Mind, more powerful than the infinity of its parts. In this way the entire man will be outside of himself, and his happiness will be due to no other fact than that, so placed, he will share in the Highest Good which draws all to Itself. . . . In this mortal life there is, for the pious, a meditation and foreshadowing of this. . . . Even though this is but an infinitesimal drop by comparison with the flowing fountain of eternal happiness, yet it surpasses all corporeal pleasures. . . . And this is why those who are permitted to have a foretaste of this, and they are very few, suffer from something akin to madness. . . . When they return to themselves, they admit they have no knowledge of where they have been, whether in the body or out of it, whether waking or sleeping. They have no memory of what they heard or saw or did. . . . They regret this return to their senses and prefer nothing more than going back to this state of madness. And this is but a small sampling of the future happiness. It seems that I have forgotten myself and transgressed the bounds.[66]

Without question Erasmus was referring to himself in the concluding lines of this quotation. It seems certain that in the guise of Folly the real Erasmus speaks of his own spiritual life with compelling force. Erasmus had by this time experienced an intimate union with God through contemplation.

Moreover, in *The Education of a Christian Prince*, Erasmus repeated his program of reform: "Who is truly Christian? Not he who is baptized or anointed, or who attends church. It is rather the man who has embraced Christ in the innermost feelings of his heart, and who emulates Him by pious deeds."[67]

Some two-and-one-half years before his death in July of 1536, Erasmus composed a treatise at the request of Thomas Boleyn, Viscount Rochford and the Earl of Wiltshire and Ormonde, "teaching how a man ought to prepare himself for death."[68] Erasmus was at the time living in Freiburg. The thought of death was a recurring theme throughout his life of seventy years. His poor health occasioned much concern. In many ways the specter of death conditioned Erasmus's life.[69]

In teaching others how to die in the arms of Christ, Erasmus reinforced the idea that he actively followed a Christ-centered life of detachment. As he himself observed:

> For if with our whole heart we believe the things that God has promised us by his son Jesus, all the delectations of this world should soon be little regarded, and death which sets us ever unto them with a painful (but yet a short) passage, should be less feared.[70]

In a subsequent passage Erasmus carefully clarified the point that "the delectations of this world" included not only material riches, but "honors, pleasures, a wife, children, kinsfolk, friends, beauty, youth, good health." The sincere Christian had to place such earthly goods in perspective and recognize the point that the "more fervently we love a thing, the more painfully we are plucked from it."[71] In rejecting the allurements of physical pleasure for all Christians living in the world, Erasmus was in effect opening up the cloistered cells and bringing into the world what were then regarded as characteristics of the religious life. In calling all men to follow Him, it was assumed that Christ was asking Christians to leave the world and to join a religious community. For Erasmus it was possible to imitate Christ and remain in the world.

To ease the transition from the life of sensual pleasure to that of spiritual growth, Erasmus proposed an interior life of contemplation—an emphasis on things eternal and heavenly rather than temporal and earthly. Erasmus viewed life on earth as "a dark and painful prison."[72] Human life, he suggested, was a series of unpleasant experiences: Birth, infancy, childhood, youth, and old age were painful reminders of man's progression from cradle to grave:

> I stand in doubt whether a man can find any one person so happily born that if God would grant unto him to begin and come up again by the same steps . . . would take this offer.[73]

The unpleasantnesses that he associated with life came not only from without but also from within.[74] As a corruptible entity, man's body habitually encumbered the soul while his earthly habitation depressed the mind. To place life in proper perspective, Erasmus urged his reader to "contemplate and praise his Maker, Redeemer, and Governor."[75] Though physically tied to earth, men of such disposition will learn how to bridge two worlds and enjoy an intimate conversation with God in heaven.

Erasmus's meditation on death had as one of its objects to enrich and extend the faith of the reader. The more frequently the Christian contemplated the life and death of Christ, the easier would be his preparation for death. Faith, together with the virtues of hope and charity, would arm the Christian soldier for battle with the devil and the forces of evil.

Not only did Erasmus counsel frequent meditation on the life of Christ, but he urged his reader to examine his conscience daily and to confess his sins to a priest three or four times a year. Consistency in facing one's shortcomings and faults throughout life would bring much tranquillity to that life and alleviate the fear of a final confession, which was often accompanied by scrupulosity.

After one had confessed his sins to a priest, Erasmus commended to him the frequent reception of the Eucharist, which leads one to spiritual growth: "This shall be if we, our conscience being purged from all affection of sinning, often receive the mystical bread and drink of the mystical cup."[76] According to Erasmus, participation in Communion had two effects: It drew the participant into closer contact with Jesus Christ, the head of the church, and with the other members of the Christian community.[77] It is the participation itself in the mystical body of Christ that conveys goodness to the recipients of Communion.

Erasmus stressed again and again the importance of the individual Christian's relationship to the mystical body of Christ. It should take the form of a lifelong spiritual exercise. In referring to a common practice of requesting prayers for the sick at one of the monasteries of the Carthusians or Friars Observants, he urged the reader to dwell instead on one's spiritual relationship with the whole Christian church and to recognize the enormously beneficial results that can come when an entire church asks God to help a sick man who is approaching the end of life: "The church cannot be poor which is joined to so rich a head . . . nor the member cannot be destitute which is sustained of so many thousands of saints."[78] According to James K. McConica, Erasmus emphasized the active role of the Holy Spirit in maintaining unity—consensus—among Christians as a community of believers. Though Erasmus saw good in Luther's message of reform, he refrained from joining the cause because of its disruptive effect on the ongoing work of the Holy Spirit.[79]

Erasmus saw all baptized men as incorporated members of the church of Christ. The bond of incorporation was enriched and strengthened by the sacraments of penance and Communion. He also recommended the reading of the Book of Hours, "which parted the history of our Lord's death into certain hours."[80] Since, according to Erasmus, examples have great virtue and strength to move men's minds, the actions preceding Christ's passion and death on the cross should serve as the ideal preparation for death:

> But there shall no example be found more perfect than that which the Lord expressed unto us in Himself. For when that last night approached, against the storm of temptation, which was at hand, he armed his disciples with the food of His most holy Body and Blood, monishing us that so often as we fall unto casualty or disease, which threatens death,

forthwith should purge our affections with confession, like as our Lord washed the feet of His disciples, and that done that we take reverently the Body of our Lord, which meat may make our minds strong and unvanquishable against our spiritual enemy. . . . Last of all we must with our Lord all naked ascend upon the cross far from all earthly affections; lift up to the love of the heavenly life that with Saint Paul we may say: "The world is crucified unto me, as I to the world." And there nailed with these nails—faith, hope, charity—we must constantly persevere, fighting valiantly with our enemy the devil, until at last, after we have vanquished him, we may pass into eternal rest through the aid and grace of our Lord Jesus Christ.[81]

The second part of the above passage reveals a side of Erasmus that has been frequently ignored by scholars. Erasmus was more than a humanist or a classical scholar, or even a reformer and theologian. He was an imitator of Christ's life. And as such, he was a man of great interior holiness. It might be useful to draw attention, once again, to his specific language to demonstrate his mystical nature:

Last of all we must with our Lord all naked ascend upon the cross far from all earthly affections. . . . And there nailed with these nails—faith, hope, charity—we must constantly persevere.[82]

If there is one virtue that stands out in the life of Erasmus of Rotterdam, it is that of perseverance to the *philosophia Christi.*

After serving as a priest for thirty-two years, Erasmus composed a treatise on the *Manner and Form of Confession* in 1524. He dedicated it to Francis Moline, the Bishop of London. The contents of the tome were based not only on wide reading but on the reflections of an experienced confessor. This may surprise some readers, since many biographers of Erasmus have claimed that he was an inactive priest who enjoyed all the perquisites of the celibate state but shunned saying Mass or performing other priestly duties. But the record speaks for itself. With regard to his role as confessor, Erasmus interjected this personal account:

For though I do pass over and speak no word, how grievous and how painful a thing it is to a good and well learned priest to spend so much time in hearing the filths and sins of man's life . . . even with the jeopardy of his own integrity, chastity, or health, and to suffer and abide the stinking and unwholesome breaths of them that favor and smell of garlic or which be infected with sickness and disease, namely, seeing that many are diseased and combed with leprosy, which are not yet kept apart, or with the French pocks, which is a spice or kind of leprosy, considering there is no way more sure and undoubted to take infection by than by taking in the breath of the person diseased; so that beside the pain and grief, there is not a little jeopardy also joined thereunto.[83]

Only an experienced confessor could have given us such a detailed account of the hazards of the confessional. And despite the burdens of the confessor, he praised the importance of confession as a means to greater piety.

During the year before this manual on confession was completed, Erasmus suffered from two attacks of gall stones, one in July and the other, more critical, in December. He viewed such rendezvous with death as trial runs for the ultimate meeting with his Maker. As a result of recurring illnesses, Erasmus continually prepared himself for his final end: "I do now diligently and heartily give heed and provide that death may not come upon me, and take me unprepared and unready."[84] One must conclude from this passage that Erasmus remained always in the state of grace so that he would not necessarily need to make a deathbed confession. Thus as early as October 1518 Erasmus could write to Beatus Rhenanus and declare that he was becoming free of the fear of death and of the desire for physical life.[85]

With regard to the sacramental nature of confession, Erasmus was not certain that it had been instituted by Christ or the apostles and therefore it was not absolutely necessary for salvation. Nevertheless he advocated the frequent use of confession because it had been recommended by the popes and prelates of the church "not without the inspiration of the Holy Spirit."[86] Erasmus himself admitted that when he committed a serious sin he confessed to a priest "according to the most common usual custom of the church."[87]

For Erasmus confession was useful because it taught humility. Pride, on the other hand, obstructed the path to sanctity: ". . . the first degree or step unto godliness shall be a mind utterly misliking itself and submitting itself unto God."[88] Having achieved humility, the penitent was prepared to acquire additional virtues. Erasmus pictured Christ as "that mild Spirit" who, being diametrically opposed to "that proud spirit" in man, cannot communicate love without prior submission on the part of the penitent. In the act of confessing one's sins to another man, the penitent acknowledges his dependence on God and the role of the priest as mediator.

In addition to teaching humility, confession led the penitent away from future error, offered comfort, and disentangled doubtful from real evil: "And this thing is never done in better or more convenient season than in sacramental confession."[89] For Erasmus never doubted that confession was a sacrament. He simply did not have enough evidence from Scripture or the Church Fathers to certify to its institution by Christ, though he stood prepared to be shown otherwise.

Erasmus went on in the treatise to elaborate on seven other beneficial results of confession. The third utility concerned ridding the penitent of notions of either rejoicing or despair. Erasmus identified the first group of sinners as those who took special delight in describing every detail of their sin (e.g., "the defiling of a fair and beautiful maiden"), and the second group of sinners as despondents who out of misinformation have despaired of the mercy of God. He cited as an example the fear that nocturnal emissions were in themselves sinful. Criticizing John Gerson for "creating a climate of scrupulosity," Erasmus argued that such emissions were sinful only if they were the result of a "vicious occasion."[90] In the section on the fourth benefit of confession (overcoming scrupulosity), he describes his view of a truly virtuous man:

> A man that is verily virtuous and godly wishes and desires the perfect integrity and cleanness of his body, which he hopes to have in the general resurrection, and therefore he is sorry that his vessel is polluted and defiled with unclean dreams; but it follows not, because it grieves him, and he is sorry for it, that it is therefore straight-away sin. For so good a virtuous man is grieved also, and sorry, that with hunger, with thirst, with sleeping, with fainting or weariness of the body, he is fain to break up the continual fervor of prayer. He is sorry for the rebellious motions of the members against the mind. He sorrows that the flesh does lust against the spirit. But these things are so far off from being sins that they be rather matter and occasion of virtue, if a man does strive against them to the uttermost of his power.[91]

For Erasmus, then, the weaknesses of the body were occasions of virtue. His own frailties of body were prods to virtue and reminders to others that sanctity was not inherited. At the same time, the scrupulous sinner must be taught by the priest how "to love and to fear less," how to distinguish between the occasion of sin and sin itself.

The fifth through the ninth benefits of confession can be condensed below in a single paragraph: sin must be detested and avoided in the future if the penitent expected forgiveness; the shame of having to confess sins was itself beneficial; confession revealed the inner man; the priest in confession prayed that the penitent would receive the grace of the Holy Spirit so that he could resist the devil; and penance restored the individual to fellowship in the mystical Body of Christ. Confession was a vital part of Erasmus's program of reform because it gave direction to the penitent's quest for Christ.

In drawing a conclusion to the section on the beneficial nature of confession, Erasmus reasoned that "though we do grant that the confession, which is made unto a man is not utterly necessary . . . the contumacy and disobedience against the tradition of the church does both offend and displease God and also does hurt the tranquility and quietness of the Christian commonwealth. . . . By confession in due form made unto a priest is increased much light and much grace, which lucre and winning no man who is in very deed virtuous and Godly will despise and make light of."[92] Confession was efficacious because it preserved the tranquillity of the mystical body of Christ and promoted virtue. With Luther in mind, Erasmus directed the following comment at Protestant reaction to the sacramental nature of confession: "I see and perceive that the contempt and setting at nought of confession is a special and principal step . . . unto . . . heathen manner of living, whereunto we do see many men nowadays . . . fall again under the false title and name of evangelical liberty."[93] Though Erasmus agreed with Luther that external rites were not essential for salvation, he disagreed with him on the doctrine of free will and predestination. With regard to the latter, Roland H. Bainton has insisted that "Erasmus would rather give up God's absolute power than to make Him no longer amenable to the canons of human reason and the moral sense."[94]

The second part of his treatise on confession identified nine harmful effects of confession, which critics have much discussed, followed by Erasmus's defense of the sacrament itself. The objections to confession may be easily summarized below: (1) the discussing of sin corrupted innocent children; (2) men who were less sinful than others took comfort from their sins; (3) confession caused many priests to become proud and high-minded because of the power that had been given to them; (4) evil priests made disciples out of their penitents; (5) confession could jeopardize the reputation of the penitent; (6) the disclosing of sin seemed to teach unshamefacedness; (7) the confession of secret crimes and offenses brought weak persons into desperation; and, at the same time, (8) failed to change their living habits so as to avoid future occasions of sin; and (9) confession encouraged some to hypocrisy. Despite these many objections to confession, Erasmus restated his defense of the sacrament and promoted its use by every Christian.

As for the qualifications of the confessor, Erasmus wanted a man who was virtuous, learned, mature, and close of tongue: "It was therefore the part and duty of the bishops or else also of the head officers and rulers to choose out such persons as are meet to take this office upon them, both in age, in living, in learning, in trustiness, in wisdom, in mildness. . . ."[95] It is clear from this section of the treatise that Erasmus did not believe that every priest should be authorized to hear confessions, especially inexperienced ones.

Erasmus's view of what constitutes a true confession is worth repeating. He insisted that a superficial confession was no confession at all; that unless a penitent hated all his sins out of "free love toward God," he was wasting his time and that of the priest. The power to overcome sins comes not from the penitent but from God alone in the form of grace. Furthermore, man must learn how to avoid sin in the future by changing his habits, with God's help, in the present.

Having a practical bent, Erasmus advised the businessman, who might be busy, to examine his conscience at least once a week (rather than once a day), followed closely by confession to an authorized priest, one approved by a bishop or pope. For the priest who is obliged to fast before saying Mass, he proposed common sense. He looked upon the taking of medicine, for example, as a means to fight illness rather than as an infraction of the midnight fast.

Erasmus also insisted that the form of confession should be as simple as possible. Brevity should characterize all confessions. At the same time he cautioned: "And yet venial sins are not to be made light of, especially in the examining and amending of our life. For they, if they be neglected and not taken heed of, do bring men unto greater and more weighty offenses."[96]

Erasmus was especially critical of persons who memorized a confessional formula, thereby accusing themselves of sins of which they were not guilty. Confession must be looked upon as a remedy for sinners, as a specific remedy for the particular sins of the individual, and as a bridge between God and man. Too many people, Erasmus feared, offered too many prayers to the Virgin Mary instead of praying directly to Christ. What began as a simple evening anthem had mushroomed into Mariolatry. Instead of concentrating so heavily on prayers to Mary, Erasmus advised the curate to teach his flock knowledge of the Creed and the commandments of God. This could be reinforced by a prayerbook composed in the vernacular.

Erasmus also instructed his reader on how to increase faith, which he defined as the belief in Scriptures. Faith, for Erasmus, could be "quickened with . . . exercises," such as the study of Scripture, communication with good and virtuous men, holy and devout meditations and thoughts. In the end Erasmus noted that faith and charity were the two rules by which all acts were to be tried and examined.[97]

Erasmus concluded his treatise on confession by recommending various forms of penance for the individual transgressor. Instead of rote prayers, he urged the confessor to prescribe the reading of works by such Church Fathers as Origen, Tertullian, Cyprian, and Chrysostom. For those of tender age he recommended fastings, watchings, or other physical labors. For the wealthy he suggested acts that would succor and relieve the needs of his less fortunate neighbors. At the same time, Erasmus insisted that those penances which involved pain must be coupled with ones that involved charity. As Thomas N. Tentler has pointed out: ". . . the purpose of confession for Erasmus is clear: if it is to be worthwhile it must increase virtue."

In order to increase the piety of a community of Benedictine nuns at Cologne, Erasmus wrote the *Comparison of a Virgin and a Martyr* in 1523. It was offered as a response to gifts of sweets that the nuns had sent him on previous occasions. The nuns had been made aware of Erasmus's reputation for holiness and asked for his advice on how to serve God more faithfully. Erasmus applauded their desire for spiritual reading but described himself as an unsatisfactory source. His image of himself was at odds with the view of these religious women.[98]

The main theme of the *Comparison of a Virgin and a Martyr* was that the life of a martyr and a virgin was pleasing to Christ, who was himself both martyr and virgin. Comparing the two, Erasmus placed the life of a virgin above that of a martyr because virgins "daily conduct a constant warfare of the spirit against worldly enticements." Indeed, Erasmus argued that with Christ's help, the dedicated virgin exceeded human power and assumed a dignity comparable to that of angels.

One is tempted at this point to suggest that Erasmus believed that his own life of virginity was a gift of God and that he took deliberate steps to maintain it throughout his many years as a priest. In advising the nuns at Cologne how to become closer to God, he drew from his own experiences as a religious living in the world. He enjoined the nuns to commit themselves totally to Christ, to be chaste in mind as well as deed, to avoid ornate and costly apparel. Religious virgins must reject the things of this world and seek a life of prayer, fasting, spiritual reading, and pious works, such as helping the poor and needy.

But Erasmus was ever the realist. He drew numerous excerpts from the Bible to emphasize the joy that one will find in following Christ and contrasted them with examples of suffering and humiliation that were also to be found in the life of a true disciple of Christ.

Erasmus ceased to be a member of the Augustinian Canons Regular, who were resident at Steyn, when he received a dispensation from Leo X in 1517, but he was never granted dispensation from the rule or obligations of the order itself. As such, Erasmus spent his entire priestly life as a member of the Canons Regular of St. Augustine. He lived outside the houses of the order and wore a modified habit, but he was in deed as well as in spirit a canon regular.[99]

In offering the nuns at Cologne a blueprint of holiness, Erasmus was keenly aware of the path that his own religious life had taken since his ordination in 1492. Just as he advised these Benedictine nuns to reject riches, honors, pleasures, and a long life, so he himself had rejected such worldly attractions. He went as far as to identify virginity with the true Catholic faith: "Whosoever swerves from the true Faith Catholic, his virginity is defiled."[100]

But Erasmus advised the nuns at Cologne to go farther than just the rejection of earthly pleasures and urged them to "mortify and flee the flesh." He believed that the religious life required such positive action as physical mortification of the body. The lean, gaunt figure of Erasmus in the paintings of Dürer, Holbein, and Metsys reflects this attitude toward mortification. Is it any wonder that Erasmus would exclaim: "I say gladly depart out of this wretched body."[101]

Having rejected the ornate habit of the Canons Regular of St. Augustine, Erasmus chose the simple dress of a parish priest. He continually insisted that "He [Christ] loves a pure spirit, a clean soul, and a well painted mind" rather than the richly arrayed.[102] In his contrast of the apparel of a woman of the world with that of a bride of Christ, there is a hint in it of his own former dress as a canon regular and his concern for virtue:

> For precious stones she is ornated and decked with virtues; instead of purple she has charity; for gold, wisdom; for feigned colors simpleness of mind; for silks chastity and shamefacedness; for broches and jewels, soberness and temperance in all her words and deeds. The fair beauty of chastity cannot be defiled with sluttish garments.[103]

Writing to Thomas Linacre in the summer of 1506, Erasmus shared with the London physician the widespread rumor that he had succumbed to the plague. He noted: "I now have a foretaste, while I am still alive, of what those who survive me will say about me when I am dead!"[104] Since thirty years of his life had not yet gone by when these prophetic lines were written, Erasmus knew only a small share of the criticism that would be his later on in life. Yet there was enough of the sting in the air by 1506 to cause Erasmus more than a little discomfort. Bruce E. Mansfield has concluded that "one doubts if in the historiography of the Reformation, not lacking in uncharitable and perverse notions, any figure has suffered more from unsubtle and anachronistic historical thinking, from priggish and 'holier-than-thou' attitudes, from the malice of his enemies and the naivety of his friends."[105]

Beatus Rhenanus, the first biographer of Erasmus and his personal friend, summed up the last days of the Dutch savant's life with the observation that illness "brought his death with the greatest calm and acceptance as he implored Christ's mercy in his final, oft repeated words."[106] Whether or not Erasmus of Rotterdam actually received the last sacraments on his deathbed remains uncertain. What was important to Erasmus throughout his life and would have been of even greater importance to him in his final hour was that he had lived the life of a Christian to the best of his ability. Having committed himself to Christ after a spiritual awakening at Steyn in 1489, Erasmus took comfort from his lifelong imitation of Christ and from his spiritual link with all Christians in the mystical body of Christ. Surely one can recognize the figure of Erasmus in this passage from the *Imitatio Christi*:

> It is good that we sometimes have griefs and adversities, for they drive a man to behold himself and to see that he is here but as in exile, and to learn thereby that he ought not put his trust in any worldly thing. It also is good that we sometimes suffer contradiction, and that we be thought of by others as evil and wretched and sinful, though we do well and

intend well; such things help us to humility, and mightily defend us from vainglory and pride. We take God better to be our judge and witness when we are outwardly despised in the world and the world does not judge well of us. Therefore, a man ought to establish himself so fully in God that, whatever adversity befall him, we will not need to seek any outward comfort.[107]

No more accurate a portrait of Erasmus exists anywhere than this description of a good man by Thomas à Kempis. Erasmus of Rotterdam died on July 12, 1536, misunderstood or despised by Catholics and Protestants alike. True to his commitment to Christ, he had rejected the plaudits of this world so that he could preserve his interior spirituality, and in this way he truly imitated his Master. It was because of his reputation for holiness among a handful of his admirers that a 1537 primer, printed in England, included the name of Erasmus for July 12 in its calendar of saints.[108] One can only hope that one day the sanctity of Erasmus of Rotterdam will be acknowledged by the whole Christian church.[109]

NOTES

1. Marjorie O'Rourke Boyle, *Erasmus on Language and Method in Theology* (Toronto, 1977), 233 n. 244, and 101. The following writers have adopted a different point of view by maintaining that Erasmus's religious ideas were in harmony with the *Devotio Moderna:* Louis Bouyer, *Erasmus and His Times,* trans. Francis X. Murphy (Westminster, Md., 1959); Lewis W. Spitz, *The Religious Renaissance of the German Humanists* (Cambridge, Mass., 1963); E. E. Reynolds, *Thomas More and Erasmus* (New York, 1965); and John Payne, *Erasmus: His Theology of the Sacraments* (Richmond, Va., 1970).

2. Important biographical information about Erasmus can be found in numerous letters written by him. Especially important are his letters to Servatius Rogerus (8 July 1514) in *The Correspondence of Erasmus* (Toronto, 1974), 2:294–95, and to Lambertus Grunnius (August 1516), *The Correspondence of Erasmus,* 4:8–32. (Hereafter the Toronto edition of Erasmus's correspondence cited as *CWE*.)

3. Preserved Smith, *Erasmus: A Study of His Life, Ideals and Place in History* (New York, 1923), 440. Christopher Hollis went even further and accused Erasmus of being non-Christian: "Any pretense that he ever made that he tried to regulate his own conduct by that of Christ was the most patent insincerity, and on its most fundamental ethical teaching he was at issue with Christian theory." See Hollis, *Erasmus* (Milwaukee, Wis., 1933), 265. Albert Hyma offered another negative view when he insisted that "He [Erasmus] gave no expression to any amount of love for Christ. . . . The Cross, which saves through pain and death, seems to have had practically no significance for Erasmus at Steyn. See Hyma, *The Youth of Erasmus* (New York, 1968), 18.

4. Erasmus to Wolfgang Faber Capito (26 February 1517) in *CWE*, 4:266.

5. For example, in 1501, he sent his patroness, Anna von Borrsele of Veere, a gift of some prayers to the Blessed Virgin and a poem in praise of St. Anne. See *CWE*, 2:17. Moreover, in 1523 he composed a Mass in honor of Our Lady of Loreto at the request of Theobald Bietricius. Both sets of devotion are an indication of Erasmus's fidelity to the mother of Christ. Erasmus also dedicated his *Commentarius in duos hymnos Prudentii* in 1523 to Margaret More Roper, who reciprocated by translating his *Precatio Dominica* into English.

6. Erasmus, *The Handbook of the Militant Christian*, trans. and ed. John P. Dolan in *The Essential Erasmus* (New York, 1964), 66.

7. Erasmus, *Opera omnia*, ed. Joannes Clericus (Leiden, 1703–06), 5: col. 669B. It was first published at Basel in 1526.

8. Leo X to Andrea Ammonio (26 January 1517), CWE, 4:190: "an unlawful and (as he fears) incestuous and condemned union." J. C. Scaliger's accusation is discussed by Christopher Hollis, *Erasmus* (Milwaukee, Wis., 1933), 3. See J. C. Scaliger, *Contra Desid. Erasmum Roterodamum Oratio II* (Paris, 1537). For a discussion of Erasmus's adolescence, see R. L. DeMolen, "Erasmus as Adolescent," *Bibliothèque d'Humanisme et Renaissance* 38 (1976): 7–25.

9. Jacopo Sadoleto to Erasmus (12 February 1530), *Opus Epistolarum Des. Erasmi*, ed. P. S. Allen et al. (Oxford, 1906–47), 8:360. Hereafter cited as EE.

10. Thomas à Kempis, *The Imitation of Christ*, ed. Harold C. Gardiner (New York, 1955), bk. 1, chap. 19, 53.

11. Erasmus to Cornelis Gerard (1489?), CWE, 1:51.

12. Kempis, *Imitation of Christ*, ed. Gardiner, 1. 1. 31.

13. Erasmus to Lambertus Grunnius (August 1516), CWE, 4:12.

14. Robert Gaguin to Erasmus (24 September 1495?), CWE, 1:85.

15. Douglas Bush, *The Renaissance and English Humanism* (Toronto, 1939), 64.

16. John Colet to Erasmus (October 1499), CWE, 1:198–99.

17. After More's death Erasmus confessed: "I feel as if I had died with More so closely were our two souls united." See E. E. Reynolds, *Thomas More and Erasmus* (New York, 1965), 238.

18. Julius II to Erasmus (4 January 1506), CWE, 2:105–06.

19. Leo X to Erasmus (26 January 1517), CWE, 4:197. Indeed, Erasmus was held in high esteem by all the pontiffs between Julius II and Paul IV. Julius II praised Erasmus's zeal for religion, his integrity of life and character, and his uprightness and virtue. See CWE, 2:105. In a letter dated 31 May 1535, Paul III wrote to Erasmus: "We especially exhort you, our son, whom God has adorned with so much talent and learning, to help us in this pious work, which is so much in keeping with your ideals, to defend the Catholic religion both in word and writing before and during the Council. In so doing you will not only crown in the best fashion possible a life of religion and literary productivity, you will also refute your accusers and rouse your admirers." See John P. Dolan, ed., *The Essential Erasmus* (New York, 1964), 23.

20. Erasmus to Servatius Rogerus (8 July 1514), CWE, 2:295.

21. Leo X to Andrea Ammonio (26 January 1517), CWE, 4:191. In the words of *The Imitation of Christ*: "I am He who teaches all the people to despise earthly things, to loathe things that are present, to seek and savor eternal things, to flee honors. . . . See Kempis, *Imitation of Christ*, ed. Gardiner, 3, 43, 166.

22. Erasmus to Servatius Rogerus (8 July 1514), CWE, 2:295. Thomas à Kempis also cautioned his readers to "Keep company with the humble and the simple in heart, who are devout and of good deportment, and treat with them of things that may edify and strengthen your soul." See Kempis, *Imitation of Christ*, ed. Gardiner, 1.8.39.

23. Erasmus to an unnamed monk (15 October 1527), EE, ed. Allen, 7:200.

24. One finds a similar attitude in *The Imitation of Christ*: "The religious habit and the tonsure help little; the changing of one's life and the mortifying of passions make a person perfectly and truly religious." See Kempis, *Imitation of Christ*, ed. Gardiner, 1. 17. 50.

25. Erasmus to an unnamed monk (15 October 1527), EE, ed. Allen, 7:200–201.

26. John Colet to Erasmus (end of September 1511), CWE, 2:175.

27. In declining the offer of a cardinalate from Paul III, Erasmus wrote to Latomus that "I have a friend in Rome who is particularly active in the business: in vain have I warned him more than once by letter that I want no cures or pensions, that I am a man who lives from day to day, and every day expecting death. . . ." Erasmus to Bartholomew Latomus (24 August 1535) in Johann Huizinga, *Erasmus and the Age of Reformation*, trans. Barbara Flower (New York, 1957), 253. Earlier, in 1516, Erasmus had declined a bishopric. See CWE, 4:95–96.

28. Erasmus to Etienne Poncher (14 February 1517), CWE, 4:219.

29. Erasmus to Bartholomew Latomus (24 August 1535) in Huizinga, *Erasmus and the Age of Reformation*, 252.

30. Erasmus to Maarten van Dorp (end of May 1515), *CWE*, 3:112. Beatus Rhenanus expressed the same point: "I do remember him often saying while he was alive that if he had foreseen such an age arising as ours, he would not have written many things or would not have written them in the way he did." See John C. Olin, ed., *Christian Humanism and the Reformation* (New York, 1965), 49.

31. Erasmus to Maarten van Dorp (end of May 1515), *CWE*, 3:123.

32. Erasmus to Guillaume Budé (28 October 1516), *CWE*, 4:104.

33. Erasmus to Paul Volz (August 1518) in Olin, *Christian Humanism and the Reformation*, 112.

34. Erasmus, *The Education of a Christian Prince*, trans. and ed. Lester K. Born (New York, 1936), 210.

35. Erasmus to Martin Luther (11 April 1526) in Huizinga, *Erasmus and the Age of Reformation*, 240–41.

36. In a letter to Archbishop Albert of Brandenburg (1519), Erasmus insisted that he had never been involved in Luther's reforming efforts; that he preferred to have Luther's criticisms of the church corrected but not crushed. He himself stated that "I shall never knowingly teach error or cause confusion; I would endure anything sooner than provoke dissension." Erasmus to Albert of Brandenburg (1519) in Olin, *Christian Humanism and the Reformation*, 145.

37. Erasmus to Servatius Rogerus (8 July 1514), *CWE*, 2:296–97.

38. Kempis made a similar observation about withdrawal: ". . . whoever intends to come to an inward fixing of his heart upon God and to have the grace of devotion must with our Saviour Christ withdraw from the world." Kempis, *Imitation of Christ*, ed. Gardiner, 1. 20. 56.

39. Erasmus, *The Handbook of the Militant Christian*, trans. and ed. John P. Dolan in *The Essential Erasmus* (New York, 1964), 38–9. Erasmus also insisted that "It is my plan to propose a number of fundamental rules or norms that will guide us through the labyrinth of this world into the pure light of the spiritual life." Ibid., 51. 2.

40. Ibid., 28, 35.

41. Ibid., 40.

42. Ibid., 39.

43. Ibid., 64. Likewise, Thomas à Kempis praised the works of the Church Fathers: ". . . do not disdain the parables of the ancient Fathers, for they were not spoken without great cause." Kempis, *Imitation of Christ*, ed. Gardiner, 1. 5. 37.

44. Erasmus, *The Handbook of the Militant Christian*, ed. Dolan, 50.

45. For a fuller discussion of this theme, see Georges Chantraine, *"Mystère" et "Philosophie du Christ" selon Erasme* (Gembloux, 1971).

46. Erasmus, *The Handbook of the Militant Christian*, ed. Dolan, 52.

47. Ibid., 54. *The Imitation of Christ* offers a similar reflection: "How great a vanity it also is to desire a long life and to care little for a good life; to heed things of the present and not to provide for things that are to come; to love things that will shortly pass away and not to haste to where joy is everlasting." See Kempis, *Imitation of Christ*, ed. Gardiner, 1. 1. 32.

48. Ludwig Baer to Erasmus (12 November 1516), *CWE*, 4:127.

49. Erasmus, *The Handbook of the Militant Christian*, ed. Dolan, 55. Kempis reinforced the same theme: "My son, it is profitable to you to be ignorant in many things and to think of yourself as dead to the world and one to whom all the world is crucified." Kempis, *Imitation of Christ*, ed. Gardiner, 2. 44. 167.

50. Erasmus, *The Handbook of the Militant Christian*, ed. Dolan, 55. *The Imitation of Christ* underscored a similar message: "Study, therefore, to withdraw the love of your soul from all things that are visible, and to turn to things that are invisible." Kempis, *Imitation of Christ*, 1. 1. 32.

51. Erasmus, *The Handbook of the Militant Christian*, ed. Dolan, 55.

52. Ibid., 58. In the *Imitatio Christi*, Kempis cautioned the reader against misguided learn-

ing: "Well-ordered learning is not to be belittled, for it is good and comes from God, but a clean conscience and a virtuous life are much better and more to be desired. . . . On the day of judgment we will not be asked what we have read, but what we have done; not how well we have discoursed, but how religiously we have lived." Kempis, *Imitation of Christ*, ed. Gardiner, 1. 3. 35.

53. Edmund Colledge, "Erasmus, the Brethren of the Common Life, and the Devotio Moderna," *Erasmus in English* (1975), 7:3.

54. Erasmus, *The Handbook of the Militant Christian*, ed. Dolan, 93.

55. Ibid., 59, 61.

56. Ibid., 80. Kempis offered a similar reflection on temptation: "And He [God] brings about occasions for such battles so that we may overcome and win the victory, and in the end have the greater reward." Kempis, *Imitation of Christ*, ed. Gardiner, 1. 11. 42–43.

57. Erasmus, *The Handbook of the Militant Christian*, ed. Dolan, 66.

58. Ibid., 69. *The Imitation of Christ* made the same point: "If we place the end and perfection of our religion in outward observances, our devotion will soon be ended. Kempis, *Imitation of Christ*, ed. Gardiner, 1. 11. 43.

59. Erasmus, *The Handbook of the Militant Christian*, ed. Dolan, 70.

60. Ibid., 71.

61. Kempis, *Imitation of Christ*, ed. Gardiner, 3. 3. 105.

62. Erasmus, *The Handbook of the Militant Christian*, ed. Dolan, 92–93.

63. See also Erasmus's eloquent expression of abhorrence of war in his letter to Antoon van Bergen (14 March 1514), *CWE*, 2:280.

64. Erasmus, *The Complaint of Peace. Translated from the Querela Pacis (A.D 1521)* (La Salle, Illinois, 1974), 16.

65. Kempis made a similar reference to charity: "The outward deed without charity is little to be praised, but whatever is done from charity, even if it be ever so little and worthless in the sight of the world, is very profitable before God." Kempis, *Imitation of Christ*, ed. Gardiner, 1. 15. 48.

66. Erasmus, *The Praise of Folly*, trans. and ed. John P. Dolan in *The Essential Erasmus* (New York, 1964), pp. 172–73. For a fuller discussion of the *philosophia Christi* in the works of Erasmus, see R. L. DeMolen, "*Opera Omnia Desiderii Erasmi:* Rungs on the Ladder to the *Philosophia Christi*," in *Essays on the Works of Erasmus*, ed. R. L. DeMolen (New Haven, Conn., 1978), 1–50.

67. Erasmus, *The Education of a Christian Prince*, trans. and ed. Lester K. Born (New York, 1965), 153.

68. Erasmus, *Preparation to Death*, anonymous trans. (London, 1538), [A₂]. The English translation has been modernized by this writer both here and elsewhere in the essay.

69. Roland H. Bainton, *Erasmus of Christendom* (New York, 1967), 17–18, 87.

70. Erasmus, *Preparation to Death*, [A₄].

71. Ibid. Thomas à Kempis would have agreed with Erasmus: see Kempis, *Imitation of Christ*, ed. Gardiner, 1. 11. 43.

72. Erasmus, *Preparation to Death*, [A₆].

73. Ibid., [B₆ᵛ].

74. Kempis underscored the same observation: "And truly, to live in this world is but misery, and the more spiritual a man would be the more painful is it to him to live, and the more plainly he feels the defects of man's corruption." Kempis, *Imitation of Christ*, ed. Gardiner, 1. 22. 61.

75. Erasmus, *Preparation to Death*, [A₆ᵛ].

76. Ibid., [D₃ᵛ]. It is interesting to note that the entire fourth book of *The Imitation of Christ* commends the reception of communion, especially chap. three, titled "That it is very profitable to receive Communion often." See Kempis, *Imitation of Christ*, ed. Gardiner, 4. 3. 209.

77. Erasmus, *Preparation to Death*, [D₄].

78. Ibid., [D$_4$^{v}].

79. See McConica, "Erasmus and the Grammar of Consent," *Scrinium Erasmianum*, ed. Joseph Coppens (Leiden, 1969), 2:77–99.

80. Erasmus, *Preparation to Death*, [D$_5$].

81. Ibid., [H$_2$^{v}, H$_4$].

82. Ibid. Kempis also emphasized the importance of Christ's passion: "And if you flee devoutly to the wound in Christ's side, and to the marks of His Passion, you will feel great comfort in every trouble." Kempis, *Imitation of Christ*, ed. Gardiner, 2. 1. 76.

83. Erasmus, *A Little Treatise of the Manner and Form of Confession*, anonymous translation (London, 1535?), [F$_4$^{v}–F$_5$]. The English translation has been modernized by this writer both here and elsewhere in the essay.

84. Ibid., [A$_3$^{v}].

85. Thomas N. Tentler, "Forgiveness and Consolation in the Religious Thought of Erasmus, *Studies in the Renaissance* 12 (1966): 110–33.

86. Erasmus, *Manner and Form of Confession*, [A$_6$^{v}].

87. Ibid.

88. Ibid., [B$_4$]. *The Imitation of Christ* offered a similar view on humility: "What avail is it to a man to reason about the high, secret mysteries of the Trinity if he lack humility and so displeases the Holy Trinity?" Kempis, *Imitation of Christ*, ed. Gardiner, 1. 1. 31.

89. Erasmus, *Manner and Form of Confession*, [D].

90. Ibid., [D$_4$]. Kempis also warned against scrupulosity: "Sometimes excessive scrupulosity over a sense of devotion or too much doubt about making Confession greatly hinder this holy purpose." Kempis, *Imitation of Christ*, ed. Gardiner, 4. 4. 221.

91. Erasmus, *Manner and Form of Confession*, [D$_6$–D$_6$^{v}].

92. Ibid., [E$_3$^{v}–E$_4$].

93. Ibid., [E$_5$].

94. Bainton, *Erasmus of Christendom*, 187–88, 190.

95. Erasmus, *Manner and Form of Confession*, [G$_4$^{v}–G$_5$].

96. Ibid., [H$_7$].

97. Ibid., [I$_7$].

98. Erasmus's own modesty is reflected in his works: "For it is certain, and many things go to prove it, that they [the Dutch] are not wanting in intellectual power, though I myself have it only in a modest degree, not to say scanty—like the rest of my endowments." Erasmus, "Auris Batava" (1508) in Margaret Mann Phillips, *The Adages of Erasmus: A Study with Translations* (Cambridge: University Press, 1964), 211. *The Imitation of Christ* also stressed the importance of humility: "How much ought I, in my heart, despise myself, even though I am considered ever so holy and good in the sight of the world. . . ." Kempis, *Imitation of Christ*, ed. Gardiner, 3. 14. 125.

99. For a discussion of Erasmus's commitment to the Canons Regular, see R. L. DeMolen, "Erasmus' Commitment to the Canons Regular of St. Augustine," *Renaissance Quarterly* 26 (1973): 437–43.

100. Erasmus, *Comparison of a Virgin and a Martyr*, trans. Thomas Paynell (London, 1537); reprinted. Gainesville, Fla.: Scholars' Facsimiles & Reprints, 1970, 29. The English translation has been modernized by this writer both here and elsewhere in the essay.

101. Ibid., 55.

102. Ibid., 60.

103. Ibid., 60–61.

104. Erasmus to Thomas Linacre (ca. 12 June 1506), *CWE*, 2:117.

105. Bruce E. Mansfield, "Erasmus and the Mediating School," *Journal of Religious History* 4 (1967): 302.

106. Beatus Rhenanus, "The Life of Erasmus" (1540), in Olin, *Christian Humanism and the Reformation*, 52.

107. Kempis, *Imitation of Christ*, ed. Gardiner, 1. 12. 43–44.

108. James K. McConica, *English Humanists and Reformation Politics under Henry VIII and Edward VI* (Oxford, 1965; rev. ed. 1968), 159–60.

109. For a recent examination of Erasmus's spirituality, see M. A. Screech, *Ecstasy and the Praise of Folly* (London: Duckworth, 1980) and my review of the same in *The Sixteenth Century Journal* 13 (1982): 113–14.

SELECT BIBLIOGRAPHY

The full impact of Erasmus of Rotterdam on his contemporaries has yet to be assessed. Andreas Flitner has opened the way in his *Erasmus im Urteil Seiner Nachwelt* (Tübingen, 1952). For useful studies on the influence of Erasmus after his death, see Marcel Bataillon, *Erasme et l'Espagne* (Paris, 1937) and James K. McConica, *English Humanists and Reformation Politics under Henry VIII and Edward VI* (Oxford, 1965; revised ed. 1968). Moreover, Bruce E. Mansfield has examined critical views of Erasmus between 1550 and 1750; see *Phoenix of His Age: Interpretations of Erasmus c 1550–1750* (Toronto, 1979). A second volume by the same author will cover the period from 1750 to 1970, the quincentenary of his birth.

Because of the success of the Protestant Reformation after Erasmus's death there was little need for his *philosophia Christi* in the late sixteenth century. By 1540 conciliarism had given way to entrenched confessional battles. In contrast, the seventeenth century sought to rehabilitate the image of Erasmus. Jean Le Clerc edited his works (which were published at Leiden between 1703 and 1706) and expressed sympathy for him but found that he was too weak to become a Protestant himself. Margaret Mann Phillips has neatly summarized the eighteenth-century view of Erasmus "as a rationalist and precursor of enlightened agnosticism"; the nineteenth-century view of him "as an apostle of liberty and peace"; and the twentieth-century view of him as a "symbol of international understanding."

The historical perception of Erasmus in the nineteenth century, as had been the case in the seventeenth and eighteenth centuries, tended to be manipulated in order to support a particular ideological viewpoint. In the nineteenth century, for example, the liberal tradition characterized Erasmus as the precursor of modern religious attitudes, but it could not understand how the same Erasmus who promoted the liberation of the human spirit could support traditional Catholic doctrine.

In the twentieth century writers have tended to perceive Erasmus in one of three ways: (1) as a precursor of the Reformation, but of too weak a personality to openly commit himself to it; (2) as the spokesman for the middle way, neither fully Catholic nor Protestant; and (3) as fully orthodox and committed to the reform of the Christian church from within. Among those subscribing to the first position are Ephraim Emerton, *Desiderius Erasmus of Rotterdam* (New York, 1900); Preserved Smith, *Erasmus: A Study of His Life, Ideals and Place in History* (New York, 1923); John J. Mangan, *Life, Character and Influence of Desiderius Erasmus of Rotterdam,* 2 vols. (New York, 1927); Albert Hyma, *The Youth of Erasmus* (Ann Arbor, 1931; 2d ed., New York, 1968); Christopher Hollis, *Erasmus* (Milwaukee, Wis., 1933) and Johann Huizinga, *Erasmus and the Age of Reformation,* trans. F. Hopman (New York, 1924). Examples of those adhering to the second position are Augustin Renaudet, *Etudes érasmiennes (1521–29)* (Paris, 1939); Margaret Mann Phillips, *Erasmus and the Northern Renaissance* (London, 1949), and Roland H. Bainton, *Erasmus of Christendom* (New York, 1969). Finally, examples of those taking the third position are Maurice Wilkinson, *Erasmus of Rotterdam* (New York, 1921); Louis Bouyer, *Erasmus and His Times,* trans. Francis X. Murphy (Westminster, Md., 1959); Lewis W. Spitz, *The Religious Renaissance of the German Humanists* (Cambridge, Mass., 1963); and E. E. Reynolds, *Thomas More and Erasmus* (New York, 1965).

Ephraim Emerton's turn-of-the-century biography views Erasmus as a critic of the church who lacked a definite program of reform. According to Emerton, Erasmus was a vain man whose ambition prevented him from siding with Luther. John J. Mangan's psychological insights have led him to the same conclusion as that of Emerton: "There is not the slightest doubt that had Erasmus had the courage to go over to Luther he would have carried with him the greater part of the scholars of Germany at least" (392). Preserved Smith's biographical study of Erasmus endorses this opinion but also insists that Erasmus was a champion of rational Christianity, who saw religion as an ethical concern and who sought to reduce its emphasis on dogma. Erasmus refused to join the Protestant reform because "his interests emphasized the cause of learning and theirs the cause of dogmatic religion, and . . . he both distrusted and feared a popular rebellion, evidently verging more and more toward violence" (325). Given his personality, Smith argues that he could not have done otherwise. For Albert Hyma, Erasmus's character was largely determined by the first twenty years of his life. By the time he left Steyn, Erasmus was the "typical humanist" and "flattery, fame, and honor deteriorated his character" (150, 212). Like Hyma's, Johann Huizinga's portrait of Erasmus is based on an examination of his complex and withdrawn personality. He traces Erasmus's weak character to his illegitimate birth, the death of his parents during his adolescence, his forced entry into the monastery at Steyn, and his rejected craving for love from Servatius Rogerus, a fellow canon. Huizinga concludes that Erasmus simply did not have the courage of a Luther, a Calvin, or a Loyola: "In that robust sixteenth century it seems as if the oaken strength of Luther was necessary, the steely edge of Calvin, the white heat of Loyola; not the velvet softness of Erasmus . . ." (189). Writing from a similar point of view, Christopher Hollis attributes Erasmus's failure to take a more militant stance against Luther to character defects and lack of moral courage. Furthermore, he portrays Erasmus as an insincere flatterer who was motivated by avarice, and as a hypocrite who criticized others for the very vices that belonged to him.

The second view of Erasmus emphasizes his role as the developer of a *via media*. Augustin Renaudet devotes attention to Erasmus's plan for "le troisième Eglise" between 1521 and 1529. He argues that Erasmus was the initiator of a rationalist spirituality and as such was a forerunner of modernism. Like her mentor, Renaudet, Margaret Mann Phillips champions a case for Erasmus as the spokesman of the "middle way," which was not only distinct from Catholicism and Protestantism but separated the mind and heart. She claims that Erasmus was dedicated to "the furthering of one great cause—the setting of the wisdom of the ancients at the service of the interpretation of Christianity and the betterment of man" (44). She also insists that Erasmus held fast to his belief in the *philosophia Christi* during the heated debates with Luther and his followers. Far from exhibiting weakness, Phillips believes that he showed incredible fortitude: "If Erasmus had been weak he would surely have fled for refuge to one camp or the other; as it was he stubbornly maintained his central position to the end." See Phillips, "Some Last Words of Erasmus," in *Luther, Erasmus and the Reformation: A Catholic-Protestant Reappraisal*, ed. John C. Olin (New York, 1969), 91. Like Phillips, Roland H. Bainton pictures Erasmus as the "battered liberal" who stressed an inward religion to such an extent that he interiorized his belief and was not, therefore, fully orthodox. He argues that Erasmus's concern for peace and consensus within the church kept him from becoming a Protestant.

The last group of biographers stress Erasmus's orthodoxy. One of the earliest was Maurice Wilkinson, who writes that "Erasmus never wavered in his Catholicism," even though he refused to "be partisan of a bland obscurantism" (22–23). Nevertheless, Wilkinson sees Erasmus chiefly as a scholar rather than a reformer because he was "constitutionally and intellectually incapable of leading a popular movement" (65). Less critical of the personality of Erasmus is the assessment by Louis Bouyer, who contends that Erasmus's *philosophia Christi* was radically opposed to Protestantism because of its emphasis on faith translated into a life of practical charity. Though opposed to outward forms, on the one hand, and faith alone, on the other, Erasmus held up the ideal of faith and charity, which became the position of the Council of Trent later on in the century. Bouyer also insists that Erasmus's theology "not only in its use of critical methods, but in its realistic application of a sense of history to the thought and the life of primitive Christianity . . . represents . . . for the first time . . . the use of principle and method entirely adequate to effect a really fruitful renewal of Catholic faith and theology" (174). Despite this positive view, Bouyer seems not to understand Erasmus's periods of discouragement or his need for withdrawal and compares him unfavorably with the "saint of humanism," Thomas More. A far more positive view of Erasmus is to be found in the study by Lewis W. Spitz, who presents Erasmus as the developer of an undogmatic Christocentric spirituality that was faithful to the *traditio* of Christian antiquity: "The reform which he envisioned was a reform in the sense of a union of the Scriptures, the Church Fathers, *humanitas* and the *bonae litterae* within the Church. . . . Erasmus was perfectly orthodox and 'correct' on all matters of dogma" (204, 226). Finally, E. E. Reynolds stresses Erasmus's orthodoxy and maintains that his contacts with such saintly men as Colet, Fisher, Warham, and More were proof of his own interior piety.

2

Luther's Communities

Scott H. Hendrix

With his book *The German Nation and Martin Luther*, A. G. Dickens offered to Reformation scholarship a work that accomplished exactly what Dickens himself said historical synthesis should involve: "writing books which form challenges to write better ones."[1] On the subject of Martin Luther and the German Reformation, historians have taken up that challenge with enthusiasm. Amplifying the by-no-means-novel approach of Dickens, they have concentrated on the setting in which Luther's ideas took shape and on the impact of his reforming activity, especially its impact on the urban populations of Germany. Social structures have taken their rightful place alongside personality and intellect in the gallery of historical forces that scholars seek to merge into a coherent and comprehensive picture of the Reformation.

One result of this inclusive method of studying Reformation history has been to render ambiguous the contribution of biography to that study. On the one hand, the story of the Reformation can no longer be told simply as the account of the lives of its most prominent leaders. On the other hand, leaders did exist for the Reformation as indeed they have for other historical movements, and their lives are an essential part of the story. How much influence should be attributed to their persons in reconstructing the story as a whole? Dickens's own solution to this dilemma was to portray Luther, like every hero of history in his opinion, as the product of social forces that swelled into the Reformation movement: "While Luther's own spirit lacked neither charisma nor intellect, it was the surge of forces within the nation . . . which elevated him to one of the rare titanic roles of western history."[2] However great Luther was as a person or as a scholar, it was society that made him a hero.

Such an approach seems to imply a radical disjuncture between biography and social history, but that is not necessarily the case. It was certainly not the case for Dickens himself, who, although he did not incorporate a biography of Luther into his book on the German nation, still paid considerable attention to the intellectual traditions that influenced Luther and to the theological character of his Reformation discovery. Biog-

raphy need not be regarded as the refuge of the intellectual or psychohisto-
rians; instead, biographical studies can serve as case studies that disclose
the interaction of all those forces—social, political, and mental—which
produce historical movements of epochal character like the Reformation.

   In the case of Martin Luther, some of that interaction can be discerned by
considering the various communities to which he belonged: a monastic
community, the university, the town of Wittenberg, the territory of Electoral Saxony, the German nation, and the church. A closer look at the
nature of these communities reveals how difficult it is to distinguish neatly
between social and intellectual forces. For example, as a member of the
monastic community, Luther belonged to concrete institutions, the Augustinian monasteries in Erfurt and Wittenberg, where specific regulations,
communal functions, and contact with individual brothers influenced his
daily life. Within these same walls, however, Luther simultaneously belonged to a larger, extramural, monastic community, the Augustinian Order in particular and the monastic culture in general. From the larger
monastic community Luther absorbed traditions that influenced both his
thinking and his piety; he responded to these intangible currents as well as
to his daily monastic environment. The same distinction applies to
Luther's other communities. He was exposed to a concrete form of that
community as well as to the intellectual currents that undergirded it and
circulated within it. The forces that elevated Luther to the rank of prominent reformer intersected and made their impact upon him as a member of
one or more of these specific communities.

1. The Monastery

   Luther's sudden entry into the Augustinian monastery at Erfurt in July
1505 brought him into contact with the active core of religious intensity that
gripped the later Middle Ages. The monastic tradition had promoted the
cloistered life as the authentically religious life and it was widely regarded
as the most attainable form of Christian perfection. The demonstrable *con-
versio* of the monk epitomized the rejection of secular values that was
enjoined on the populace as a whole but not really expected of it. The
religiosity that laypersons and secular priests could demonstrate only
through the giving of alms, fasting, pilgrimages, and other good works
was surpassed by a total commitment to the religious life such as Luther
made.

   Luther later described his own commitment to that life as involuntary,
claiming that he took the vow under duress while frightened by the threat
of sudden death.[3] Luther was certainly predisposed to use the religious
vow as an escape from his perilous situation; but did this predisposition
result primarily from the religious culture in which he grew up or was
Luther's vow merely the external expression of parentally induced emo-

tions? In his provocative study *Young Man Luther*, Erik Erikson argues forcefully for the latter by depicting Luther's decision to enter the monastery as a reaction against his father's desire that he study law. The religious vow was a convenient way of binding himself to a divinely willed course that not even his father could alter.[4] Most historians, to the contrary, have maintained that Luther's vow was more culturally than parentally induced. In the first place, the hard historical evidence for strong feelings of resentment against his father is lacking in Luther's case.[5] In the second place, the psychological explanation that Erikson offers minimizes the distinctiveness of Luther's epoch and reduces his experience to the level of an ahistorical Everyman.[6]

In the absence of evidence to the contrary, the religious culture of Luther's day offers the most convincing reason for his vow to enter the cloister. Still, it was the sensitive individual, Martin Luther, who made that vow and who then experienced the monastic life in the manner that laid the groundwork for his career as a reformer. Not everyone who entered the monastery found the religious life oppressive, but Luther did. He took his vocation as a monk with utmost seriousness, no matter how involuntarily he may have embarked upon it. Luther summed up the ambivalence of that experience in the following phrase: "I lived as a monk not, of course, without sin, but without fault."[7] Without fault, because of his zeal for piety and his strenuous adherence to monastic discipline, which was not only confirmed by friends like Philipp Melanchthon (d. 1560) but also conceded by critics like Johannes Cochläus (d. 1552).[8] As a monk Luther performed well under pressure. He did not perform without sin, however, because he could find no satisfaction and peace in his performance. He could not conquer his scrupulosity, and this failure, viewed through the lens of his Reformation theology and self-understanding, was his greatest sin.

Luther's scrupulosity was due as much to the formation of his personality, including the influence of his parents, as to the religiousness of his environment. On this point there is no need to pit culture against parental influence in assessing his development. The monastery, however, was the setting in which the traits of his personality and the traits of the culture interacted to produce his unsatisfying experience of medieval religion. In the monastery, a scrupulous and earnest personality encountered the most demanding challenge that medieval religion could offer, and the result was distress and disenchantment. Since the monastery was the stuctured religious setting that served as the catalyst for this conflict, the monastery and not his family was the primary community that contributed to Luther's development as a reformer of medieval religion. A scrupulous Luther in law school might also have led to disenchantment, but hardly to the Reformation.

How much difference did it make that the monastic order that Luther entered was the Order of Hermits of St. Augustine? Judged by Luther's own remarks, it made little difference; the specific order to which he belonged played a small role in Luther's assessment of his monastic career. Some specific features and personalities of the Augustinian Order did, however, have an important effect on Luther's development. The Augustinian houses in Erfurt and Wittenberg belonged to the reformed congregation of the order, which was governed by a new constitution prepared in 1504 by its vicar-general, Johannes von Staupitz (d. 1525). That constitution contained strict regulations that could have reinforced the scrupulosity of Luther and in this way spurred his religious development. By the same token, the houses contained brothers who sought to assuage the dissatisfaction and guilt that disturbed Luther. Among these was Staupitz himself, who consoled Luther with fresh insights into the nature of repentance.[9] And, according to Melanchthon, a senior member of the Erfurt community taught Luther that belief in the forgiveness of sins meant not forgiveness in general but pardon for his own sin.[10]

The Augustinians nurtured a strong appreciation of the study of theology in their order and harbored a theological tradition as well.[11] To what extent their theological school was really a distinct *via* of medieval theology is an issue still far from being settled. If a *via Gregorii* (named after the Augustinian doctor of theology Gregory of Rimini, d. 1358) did exist, as the statutes of Wittenberg University in 1508 indicate, scant evidence exists for determining its exact content or the nature of its influence on Luther.[12] Nevertheless, an acquaintance with Augustine's theology was passed down to Luther through his order. Both in Erfurt and in Wittenberg Luther had opportunity to read the works of theologians, like Gregory, who incorporated strongly Augustinian themes into their work. In preparing his lectures on the Psalms at Wittenberg between 1513 and 1515, he used the commentary of Jacobus Perez of Valencia (d. 1490) as an important resource. Luther could have learned directly from Staupitz more theology than the insights he received on the nature of repentance; but differences in the thought of both men seem to outweigh the similarities, especially at critical points such as their understanding of faith.[13] While late medieval Augustinianism hung heavy around the head of Luther during his years in the cloister, no single Augustinian current has as yet been isolated as the fresh breeze of an incipient Reformation theology.

From his years in the cloister Luther did gain an intimate knowledge of Scripture and stimulation to incorporate examination of the Bible into his study of theology. Luther himself remarked that he learned the Psalter by heart during those years, and Staupitz was credited with encouraging him to pay the closest attention to Scripture in his work.[14] Although Luther's hermeneutical method as a professor of biblical studies eventually differed from that of Staupitz,[15] the example of his Augustinian mentor helped make the biblical text the primary text of his teaching career. Not only his lifelong occupation with interpretation and translation of the biblical text, but also his advice on how to read and study the Bible reflect his monastic beginnings. The *oratio, meditatio,* and *tentatio* that Luther recommended as the access to Scripture in 1539 could have been used equally well by him in his cells at Erfurt and Wittenberg.[16]

Luther the reformer owed much to the monastic tradition, and he did not condemn it in toto. It was difficult for him to discard his monastic identity even after reforms were underway in Wittenberg. He finally stopped wearing the cowl in October 1524, but only after Erasmus had paid him the dubious compliment of not taking advantage himself of the freedom that he preached for others.[17] Monasteries were, affirmed Luther, originally instituted to foster Christian liberty, but that purpose had been undercut in the churches and cloisters of his day by the coercive use of religious ceremonies.[18] Hence his time in the monastery taught him on balance a negative lesson about medieval religion. Luther considered it a lesson worth learning and, typically, he saw the hand of God at work in his entry into the cloister. The Lord wanted him to experience, he said, the "wisdom of the schools" and the "holiness of the monasteries" so that no future opponent could boast that Luther was condemning what he had not known at firsthand. When, therefore, he began, his literary reckoning with monasticism in the treatise *Monastic Vows,* he dedicated it to his father in memory of his personal experience; but, more significantly, he declared his solidarity with all those who were being tormented in the iron furnace of Egypt and the raging fire of Babylon, that is, with all those who were suffering under the tyranny of conscience and sin.[19] Instead of removing him from the people, Luther's time in the monastery taught him all too well what people felt about the religion of their day. Many of these people became his followers.

2. The University

In addition to the holiness of the monasteries, said Luther, he had to learn at firsthand the wisdom of the schools. That side of his education began at the University at Erfurt in 1501 and continued there even after he entered the cloister. As a student he was associated primarily with the University of Erfurt, while as a teacher he spent over thirty-three years on the faculty of the University of Wittenberg. In terms of his occupation, the university succeeded the cloister as Luther's primary community.

Up to 1522, however, the monastery and the university were not so sharply distinguished in Luther's academic life. The impression he made in the Erfurt cloister led him to be selected to study theology in the first place. In Wittenberg, where both the Augustinian cloister and the university were established in the same year (1502), Luther was named *regens studii* of the monastery while simultaneously a member of the theological faculty.

Luther learned and taught theology in both communities, and academic traditions flowed to him through both channels. Nevertheless, the wisdom of the schools was by definition the philosophy and theology taught in the universities, and in that setting it most directly affected Luther's career. Luther learned his scholastic theology well. His philosophy teachers at Erfurt, Jodocus Trutvetter and Bartholomew Arnoldi von Usingen, trained Luther in the *via moderna*. Luther was proud of his Ockhamist skills and on occasion wielded the razor handily himself.[20] His theological study, which did not cease when he began teaching in 1512, acquainted him also with the *via antiqua*, both through primary sources and secondarily through the works of Gabriel Biel (d. 1495), whose book on the canon of the Mass the young Luther considered outstanding. Melanchthon claimed that Luther knew large sections of the works of Biel and of Pierre d'Ailly (d. 1420) by heart.[21] Luther was well-versed and discriminating in his study of scholastic theology. In 1519 he gave trenchant expression to the results of that discrimination: "I know what scholastic theology did for me and how much I owe it! I am glad that I have escaped from it, and for this I thank Christ my Lord. They do not have to teach it to me, for I already know it. Nor do they have to bring it any closer to me for I do not want it!"[22]

Scholastic theology was the target of his first public attack in a set of theses prepared for debate at the university. Prior to this *Disputation Against Scholastic Theology*, which took place on September 4, 1517, Luther had been interpreting for his students the texts of biblical books such as the Psalms, Romans, and Galatians. While he used the terminology of scholastic theology as an aid to explanation, he also sought help in the commentaries of medieval exegetes, in the works of German mystics like John Tauler (d. 1361), and in the works of Augustine, especially the anti-Pelagian writings, which he did not use until his lectures on Romans in 1515–16. These works, in addition to the biblical language that he strove to elucidate, taught him a new form of theological discourse and led him to reject the scholastic *modus loquendi*.[23] He rejected the form of scholastic theology, however, because he discovered that its content, at least on matters of soteriology and revelation, did not conform to the content of the biblical books as Augustine and the mystical writers had helped him to understand it. In 1518 Luther summed up the content of what he had learned: "I teach that men should trust in nothing but Jesus Christ alone, not in prayers and merits or even in their own works."[24] The fresh comprehension of biblical terms like *righteousness, faith,* and *promise* did not fit into the scholastic framework, as Luther discovered most notably while wrestling with Romans 1:17. Although his "Reformation discovery" helped to resolve the tension in his religious life that the monastery had exacerbated, the new theological insight was first and foremost an academic discovery made in the context of his duties as a teacher at the university.

And the immediate consequence was not an attack on monasticism, but on the scholastic tradition in which he had been trained.

The influence of humanism on Luther's development should also be considered in direct relationship to his role as a professor of theology. Luther was never the center of a humanist sodality, but he was well aware of the movement, and its leaders cultivated contact with him. He had been exposed to humanist currents both at the University of Erfurt and through the Augustinian Order.[25] The University of Wittenberg already had a healthy department of humanities before Luther arrived, and Elector Frederick the Wise, founder of the university, remained committed to the humanities in university expansion programs thereafter. In the dedication of his second commentary on the Psalms to Frederick in 1519, Luther wrote: "Who is not aware that Prince Frederick supplies an example to all princes with his promotion of letters? Greek and Hebrew prosper gratifyingly at your Wittenberg; liberal arts are being taught more amply and skillfully than ever before. The pure theology of Christ is victorious; the opinions and questions of men mean practically nothing to teachers or to students."[26] Luther's own use of Greek and Hebrew in his lecture preparation, and his preference for the Bible and the Church Fathers over the scholastic theologians, corresponded to the curricular goals of other humanists and shaped the theological faculty of Wittenberg as well. In correspondence between 1517 and 1519 with friends who had humanist interests, Luther even signed his name in the manner of the humanists as "Eleutherius," a Greek play on words that meant "the free one."[27]

While the linguistic and patristic interests of humanists like Erasmus coincided with his own, their theology and hermeneutical method did not. As early as 1516 Luther criticized Erasmus's interpretation of Romans and divorced himself from Erasmus's preference for the literal sense employed by Jerome over the interpretation of Paul offered by Augustine in his anti-Pelagian writings.[28] When he responded to Erasmus's attack in *The Bondage of the Will* (1525), Luther was reacting to the same theological content that he had found objectionable in scholastic theology, particularly the doctrines of sin, grace, and merit. The debate between Luther and Erasmus in 1525 was not the colossal encounter of humanism versus the Reformation, but another chapter in Luther's attack on the wisdom of the schools. Luther's relationship with the older humanists was parallel to his relationship to the scholastics. While he rejected the content of their theology, he could utilize some of their tools. In both cases, however, Luther tailored those tools specifically to the academic setting where it was his job to teach theology. Anticipating that he would be judged brash for attacking Erasmus, Luther declared that he did so "for the sake of theology and of the salvation of the brothers."[29]

Some of Luther's colleagues at the university rallied to his theological cause, among them Nikolaus von Amsdorf, Andreas Rudolff-Bodenstein von Karlstadt, Melanchthon, and Justus Jonas. Karlstadt, the most enthusiastic devotee of Augustine in the group, and Melanchthon jumped actively into the literary arena so that one could speak of a "Wittenberg University theology"[30] in the earliest years of the Reformation. In 1518 Luther considered the reform of the study of theology the prerequisite for reform of the church.[31] He was wrong. In general, the theological faculties at other universities did not turn Protestant but remained bastions of scholastic theology and steadfast in their opposition to the Wittenberg theology. Not even in Erfurt was John Lang, prior of the Augustinian cloister and one of Luther's earliest pupils, able to convert Luther's former teachers.[32] This fact underscores the uniqueness and importance of Luther's theological *modus operandi* in the academic setting of Wittenberg. The German Reformation was not a case of spontaneous combustion that could have ignited anywhere.

Only in Wittenberg did a university serve as the motor of the Reformation, and it continued to do so after the movement had spread to cities and to the countryside. Many preachers who propagated the message were educated in the new theology at Wittenberg. Compared with 1516, the number of courses on biblical books had increased dramatically by the 1530s and 1540s;[33] among them were Luther's lengthy lectures on Galatians and Genesis and Melanchthon's lectures on Romans. In these lectures, and in disputations, which were reinstated as part of the academic routine, Luther's theology was refined and expanded. Strengthened by the offerings of Jonas, John Bugenhagen, and Caspar Cruciger, theological instruction made a vivid impact on the students of those decades.[34] Luther utilized members of the university community in the team that produced "his" translation of the Bible, and from the university Luther and his colleagues issued countless memoranda on practical matters of reform. The University of Wittenberg remained Luther's most important community and he was proud of it, as he showed in this remark from his later life: "In this school God revealed his word, and today this school and this city can stand up against all others both in doctrine and in life, even though we are clearly not perfect *in via*."[35]

3. Wittenberg

As a member of the university faculty Luther remained a resident of the city of Wittenberg until his death. A striking symbol of the local changes to which the Reformation led was the conversion of the Augustinian cloister into the most famous Protestant parsonage by the gift of Elector John to Martin and his new wife, Katherine, in 1525. With just over two thousand inhabitants, Wittenberg may have looked small to a person who had lived in Eisenach (over four thousand) and Erfurt (sixteen thousand); but, in fact, Wittenberg was a medium-sized city that in population ranked among the top ten percent of the cities in sixteenth-century Germany.[36] Furthermore, Wittenberg was rich enough in institutions—the castle, the university, cloisters, and churches—to provide Luther with contacts with colleagues and with people of the town. Luther, of course, made the city famous just as he did the university. But more important, Wittenberg supplied Luther with an audience for his new theology and a testing ground for his reforms after the break with Rome occurred.

In addition to his brothers in the cloister and students at the university, the people in the town became a sizable segment of Luther's audience because of his frequent preaching. Luther's first preaching post was in the cloister and he preached at the Castle Church, especially on academic occasions and in later years when important visitors stopped over in Wittenberg. Luther also occupied the city preachership, which was financed by the city council and which called for him to preach in the City Church, where he had wider exposure to the people of the town.[37] When he began preaching against indulgences, private Masses, and religious fraternities, he had more than enough targets in Wittenberg itself. By 1519 visitors to Elector Frederick's relic collection could take advantage of almost two million years' worth of indulgences or benefit from one of the nine thousand Masses celebrated annually in the Castle Church.[38] Wittenberg was the prime example of a Reformation setting: a preacher in a publicly-financed pulpit who advocated Luther's theology and initiated reforms in the face of a thriving medieval piety.

Wittenberg fostered not only the spoken word but also the writings of Luther. After 1517 Luther began publishing tracts at an astonishing rate. By the time he was excommunicated in January 1521, as many as one-half million copies of his works may have been in circulation. Many of these were first published in Wittenberg, where by 1523 some six hundred editions of Luther's writings had been printed.[39] The town, which had no export business at all before 1500, became the most productive center of printing in Germany, not least of all due to its publication of Luther's German Bible in eighty-six editions between 1534 and 1626. In 1539 Luther tried to stop the Leipzig printer Nicholas Wolrab from reprinting the Bible because it would "take the bread out of the mouth of our printers."[40] Wolrab's own business of printing anti-Luther tracts had been hurt by the introduction of Protestantism into the Duchy of Saxony.

Through its listeners and its readers Wittenberg supplied the local popular audience to which Luther directed his reforming message. Once the conflict with Rome had flared, Luther took his case to the people as well as to the hierarchy. He defended the *Ninety-five Theses* in Latin for the theologians and he summed up his position in German sermons and treatises for the people. Indeed, he justified his protest against the indulgence practice by stressing the damaging effect it had on the people. They were being

seduced by the lure of cheap forgiveness when they should be driven by a
realistic assessment of their sin to repentance and trust in God. It was this
advocacy of the people that remained the motivating force behind Luther's
opposition to the papacy.[41] In refusing to retract his writings at the Diet of
Worms in 1521, Luther appealed not just to his conscience held captive to
the word of God, but to the consciences of the people as well. They had
been tortured by the laws of the pope and the traditions of men, he said;
and if he were to recant, he would be opening not just the windows but
even the doors to more such godlessness.[42]

The primary purpose of the Reformation in Luther's eyes was to liberate
the people from the burdensome and deceptive practices of the medieval
church and to reeducate these same people to a new religious life based
upon faith instead of upon religious performance. The message of liberation that resounded in Luther's most famous treatises like *The Freedom of A
Christian* was clearly heard, while the call for a new devotion to one's
neighbor, equally stressed in that treatise and in others, did not receive
equal attention. The appeal to be lord of all was more popular than the call
to be servant of all. For that reason, Luther wrote as many edifying works
as he did polemical ones prior to 1522. These guides to the Christian life
appeared as expositions of biblical books and of the Lord's Prayer, the Ten
Commandments, and the Creed, and as sermons on the sacraments. Much
of the material formed the basis for his catechisms of 1529, which were
sparked by the religious ignorance and slackness he had discovered during
the inspection of church conditions in Saxony. Even prior to the wide
distribution of the catechisms, however, Luther had articulated the fresh
view of Christian faith and life that made him the most popular religious
writer in Germany.[43]

In addition to changing people's attitudes, the problem of changing
religious practices and institutions had to be faced. This challenge emerged
first in Wittenberg while Luther was still in hiding at the Wartburg. The
changes that corresponded to the Wittenberg theology seemed obvious:
clerical celibacy, monastic vows, and private Masses should be abolished;
the public Mass should be celebrated in German; the people should receive
both elements during Communion. The initiative was seized by Gabriel
Zwilling in the Augustinian cloister and by Karlstadt in the university and
in the community. Without waiting for approval from Elector Frederick,
Karlstadt and Zwilling began making these changes and Karlstadt wrote a
church order for the city that was passed by the city council. When disorder erupted in the City Church on February 6, 1522, and the council felt
itself caught between the wishes of the elector and the demands of Karlstadt, Luther was recalled to Wittenberg to take charge of the reform.[44] The
strategy articulated by Luther in his Invocavit Sermons of March 1522 was
to make those changes which were absolutely necessary in order for people
to hear the evangelical message but not to force any other changes on the

unwilling. Hence the Mass was once again celebrated in Latin, but without those passages which implied that the Mass was a sacrifice. No one had to receive the wine as well as the bread in Communion. Eventually, Luther provided forms for both a Latin and a German Mass and the reception of both elements by the laity became the common practice. In contrast to Karlstadt, who deemphasized learning and rejected theology as an academic discipline, Luther supported the reopening of the city school of Wittenberg under John Bugenhagen and the reorganization of the university by Melanchthon.

In Wittenberg, Luther was able to demonstrate that his message could change religious practices and institutions without destroying them or the social order. Gradual implementation of reforms without the use of force was indeed possible. Reformation did not have to mean revolution. Luther utilized this argument for his cause against opponents like Duke George of Albertine Saxony who faulted this movement at just this point.[45] Perhaps the favorable outcome in Wittenberg made Luther too optimistic about changes in other cities. The only ecclesiastical institution to offer any real resistance was the All Saints' Chapter still cherished by Elector Frederick and dissolved only after his death in 1525. Plenty of Wittenberg students and teachers did lead the Reformation movement in other German cities, but they did not always find the social and ecclesiastical conditions so amenable to peaceful reform.

The initial success in Wittenberg may also have raised Luther's hopes for the qualitative impact of his movement to an unrealistic level. Luther expected people to change visibly as a result of becoming Protestant. When the people of Wittenberg and the surrounding towns did not commune more often or behave any better than previously, Luther was disappointed and occasionally took out that disappointment on Wittenberg itself. On a trip in July 1545 Luther wrote to his wife that he did not wish to return to Wittenberg and it would be best if they could "get away from this Sodom."[46] Luther frequently preached that doctrine meant more than morals, and for that reason Protestants could rightly claim they were better than the papists.[47] But Luther also hoped he had fathered a more serious and responsible populace. Luther's hopes, however, are less reliable criteria for judging the impact of his movement than the actual role that Wittenberg played as the cradle of his message and the proving ground for reform.

4. Electoral Saxony

The influence that Elector Frederick exercised during the disturbances at Wittenberg illustrated how important territorial authority was for the career of Luther and the German Reformation. Wittenberg was not a free imperial city; it was one residence of a territorial prince who was bent on consolidating his authority and reviving the prestige of his dynasty. Prior

to 1517 the Wettin family of Saxony had lost ground to the house of Hohenzollern, which ruled the neighboring territory of Brandenburg. In 1513
Albrecht, the younger brother of Elector Joachim I of Brandenburg, succeeded the brother of Elector Frederick as Archbishop of Magdeburg and
administrator of the diocese of Halberstadt. One year later, when Albrecht
was also elected Archbishop of Mainz, the Hohenzollern family captured
its second electoral position within the empire. They also gained control
over the city of Erfurt, which lay in the middle of Ernestine lands.

This dynastic competition, which the papal legate Aleander called a
"deadly enmity," played a major role in Frederick's protection of Luther.[48]
Frederick was hardly disposed to surrender Luther because he had
criticized an indulgence promoted by Albrecht, which competed with
Frederick's own relic collection and accrued to the credit of the Hohenzollern. Frederick was strengthening his hand over against the emperor, and
his new university at Wittenberg was a symbol of the centralized control
that he had acquired over Ernestine Saxony. Luther both increased the
prestige of that university and provided Frederick with welcome leverage
in the delicate balancing of power between territory and empire. By the
same token, Frederick's own position as a candidate for emperor after the
death of Maximilian in 1519 gave him considerable freedom over against
Rome in handling the case of Luther. The appearance of Luther before the
Diet of Worms and his secure exile at the Wartburg demonstrated how
adroitly Frederick and his advisers managed Luther's case, even though
they did not win a favorable verdict for Luther. All in all, Luther owed
more to the fact that he lived in Saxony than he did to the person or to the
religious preference of Frederick.

Luther may have sensed that fact. Although he recognized how much he
was indebted to Frederick, he did not always obey him. On his way back to
Wittenberg from the Wartburg against the Elector's wishes, Luther assured
Frederick respectfully that he was going to Wittenberg under a far higher
protection than the Elector's and that he might be able to protect Frederick
more than Frederick could protect him.[49] That attitude was typical of
Luther; he was never a court theologian and always insisted on his independence and his right to comment on political matters. In 1542, for example, Luther defended his intervention in a feud between the two Saxonies
in a letter addressed to both Elector John Frederick and to Duke Maurice of
Albertine Saxony. In the first place, he said, 1 Timothy 2:1–2 commanded
preachers to look out for worldly rulers and to pray for peace on earth. In
the second place, the preacher and theologian must proclaim the word of
God in all situations, whether it be to comfort the sorrowful or to admonish
the stubborn.[50] Earlier, when Maurice's uncle, Duke George, forbade the
sale of Luther's German New Testament in Albertine Saxony, Luther used
a theory of two kingdoms to defend the integrity of the spiritual realm. The
boundary between the two kingdoms was just as real as the boundary
between the two Saxonies.[51] The theory of the two kingdoms was a two-

edged sword, however; it placed the temporal sphere as well as the spiritual realm under the rule of God and justified the political involvement of Christians, including, presumably, preachers. Luther himself commented freely on social and political issues as specific questions arose. He could have remained silent, but it was unlikely, given the fact that his own case was from the beginning a political matter and that his prince also exercised tight control over religious affairs.

Luther's personal involvement in territorial affairs reflected the various stages in his own reforming career and in the progress of the Reformation.[52] Elector Frederick never considered Luther an adviser and did not actively seek his counsel. For Frederick there was officially no new church to oversee, but only the unsettled case of Luther in which Luther himself never played an equal role. Between 1522 and 1525 Luther was involved primarily with the same concrete reforms of worship and Christian life at the local level as had surfaced during the Wittenberg movement. When Elector John took over in 1525, Luther's horizons widened. Unlike his brother, John was an ardent supporter of the new theology and the time called for active leadership in religious affairs. The aftermath of the Peasants' Revolt forced a closer look at religious and social conditions in Saxony itself, and the result was the organization of a territorial church structure. Protestant rulers like John, Philip of Hesse, and Ernest of Lüneburg were willing to take more aggressive action to bring about a resolution of the political status of imperial estates that followed Luther. Political stands were taken at the Diets of Speyer in 1526 and 1529, alliances were formed, and political Protestantism emerged as a force to be reckoned with in the empire. After Emperor Charles V failed to achieve religious reunion at the Diet of Augsburg in 1530, the question of resistance by the Protestant princes to the Emperor had to be faced. Luther was consulted on most of these matters and rendered judgments both political and theological in nature.[53] He might change his mind, as he did on the issue of resistance after the Diet of Augsburg in 1530; but during these crucial years Elector John usually followed Luther's advice, even though he might have to rule against his own chancellor and his son, John Frederick, who became Elector in 1532.[54]

Luther lived out his last years under the conditions of the Peace of Nuremberg (1532), which led to a political stalemate between the Smalcald League and the Empire. These last years mark the period of the older Luther.[55] It has received less attention from Luther scholars than the earlier years, not because Luther was less interesting but because the historical decisions made during these fourteen years seemed less obviously crucial than those made earlier and later. Luther's career was very much tied to the historical role of Saxony in the German Reformation, and that role, apart from Frederick's initial protection of Luther, was more pronounced between 1525 and 1532 and again after Luther's death. There were exceptions, of course, like the Diet of Smalcald in 1537, which was critical to

Protestant unity and perseverance. Here Luther was once again a key figure with his *Smalcald Articles*. As a rule, however, under John Frederick, Luther retreated from direct involvement in territorial politics in favor of Melanchthon.[56] Luther contributed polemical treatises on specific political encounters, especially in the 1540s, when tensions were again increasing, but most of his energy was spent on consolidating the Reformation in Saxony and in surrounding territories.[57]

The attitudes as well as the career of Luther were frequently shaped by the territory in which he spent all of his life after 1521. His firsthand acquaintance with other parts of Germany was slight, not to mention Europe as a whole. Although not isolated in Wittenberg, Luther often spoke in his letters of distant events in a categorical manner typical of one who was not in close touch with them. Rumors about the Turks, the pope, and the emperor, when relayed together, posed an ominous picture that fed Luther's long-held suspicion that the Last Days were at hand. His perception of the Peasants' Revolt might have been influenced by the relatively favorable situation of the peasants in Saxony.[58] In the beginning it may have appeared to Luther than their grievances could be settled without violence. After the unrest erupted, however, and Thomas Müntzer became identified in Luther's area with the cause of the peasants, the uprising assumed much more dangerous proportions in Luther's mind and led eventually to his harsh reaction. Even Luther's negative attitude toward the Jews expressed in his later life may have been related to the edict that Elector John Frederick promulgated in August 1536, forbidding Jews to do business in Electoral Saxony or to travel through his lands.[59]

As the predominantly territorial reformer of his later years, Luther remained in lockstep with the rhythm of the Reformation. In the 1530s territories joined forces to protect and intensify the reform initiated in the 1520s in city and territory alike. In northern Germany a significant expansion of Protestantism occurred around Luther's land in 1539. The conversion of Joachim II of Brandenburg was satisfying in view of the old rivalry between the Wettin family and the Hohenzollern, but the entry of Ducal Saxony into the Protestant camp was especially welcomed. On Pentecost Sunday, 1539, Luther preached in celebration of the occasion at St. Thomas Church in Leipzig. Three years later, when Luther intervened in the feud between the two Protestant Saxonies, he claimed that he was now respected by both sides as a servant of Christ and preacher of the Gospel.[60] Luther had become the reformer of both Saxonies.

5. Germany

"God favored much-celebrated Germany, the true Japhite (Genesis 10), with the imperial majesty, crown and sceptre at the end of the world and sent it a German prophet as well; therefore, Dr. Luther arose and, like a

German prophet, preached and wrote publicly against indulgences, and he taught the true nature of that blessed Christian repentance which makes one righteous in God's sight."[61] In this encomium, Luther's first biographer, Johann Mathesius, applied a label to Luther that had been used earlier by Luther himself: the German prophet. It was not uncommon for Luther to be called a prophet; as early as 1518, in the preface to the first edition of Luther's writings published in Basel, Wolfgang Capito compared Luther with the prophet Daniel.[62] "German prophet" was an ambiguous label, however. Luther's own use of the term was not without reservation. After identifying himself as the German prophet in the *Warning to His Dear German People* (1531), Luther added that he had to assume such presumptuous titles in order to humor the papists.[63] Just a half year earlier, while the Diet of Augsburg was still in session, Luther had written publicly that he was no prophet, but in the next breath he claimed that he had to speak out on behalf of miserable Germany, his dear fatherland.[64]

There was good reason for the ambiguity. Luther was not the prophet of a militant German nationalism, as indeed Ulrich von Hutten and other German nobles like Franz von Sickingen had hoped. Luther shared their resentment of Roman control over German wealth and territory, but he did not share their dreams of a restored German glory or the rehabilitation of the knightly estate. Above all, he rejected the idea that blood might be spilled through his movement as it was in the revolt of the knights. When the failure of the Diet of Augsburg raised for Luther the possibility that Emperor Charles might go to war against the Protestant princes, he could bring himself only with great difficulty to counsel resistance to the emperor. Half seriously he called himself the German prophet because he was convinced that in this case his warning would promote the salvation of the German people and not his own glory.[65]

Luther's identity with Germany was real, but it was tempered by the religious significance of his movement. In his early campaign against scholastic theology he let slip some enthusiasm for German theologians as the "best theologians" when he published the complete *German Theology*, an anonymous mystical work, in 1518.[66] His *Address to the Christian Nobility of the German Nation* two years later was, in Luther's words, more an appeal to the laity against the clergy than an appeal to Germans against Rome. The Saxon advisers who were behind the treatise knew that a responsive patriotic chord would be struck nonetheless. Even Duke George admitted that there was some truth in the treatise, although he agreed not to allow its publication in his territory.[67] The *Address* was Luther's most popular treatise to date, and he benefited from the resentment against Rome already bubbling in the empire more than he contributed to it.

The threats contained in the Edict of Worms made Luther's ultimate reception in Germany uncertain. By 1524, however, when it was clear he had survived and reform had proceeded apace in Electoral Saxony, he addressed an appeal to a different cadre of lay leadership in Germany on behalf of a specific reform proposal that he had mentioned in the address to the nobility: *To the Councilmen of All Cities in Germany That They Establish and Maintain Christian Schools*. Luther now identified his work openly with the land of Germany in a manner that revealed his emerging prophetic self-understanding. God had opened his mouth and commanded him to speak, said Luther, and it had become clear that God was standing beside him because his movement had expanded and grown strong in the face of opposition without Luther's own doing.[68] Confidence in divine direction was not new for Luther. During the initial years of the conflict with Rome he had frequently consoled himself with the thought that the whole affair was in God's hands. Luther wrote to Staupitz in 1519 that God was seizing and moving him and that he had no control over himself.[69] By 1524 Luther was convinced that God had not only vindicated his personal struggle but in addition had visited all of Germany with His word. Germany had never before heard so much of God's word as now, he exclaimed. Buy when the goods are at your door and gather in the harvest while the weather is good, he advised. Use God's gifts and word while they are available, for God's word is like a passing shower that does not return where it once has been. The Jews, Greece, and Rome had all had their chance, and the word would not tarry in Germany forever, either.[70]

Luther was now articulating a view of God's work in history that included a specific German dimension, and he was identifying himself with the coming of the word to Germany. As he put it, the Gospel had gone out from Wittenberg into Germany and to all parts of the world.[71] This interpretation of God's work in history and of his own place in it was a prominent part of his self-understanding as a reformer. That self-perception was aided by the fact that Luther lived in a climate where German self-consciousness was on the rise, but it was predominantly influenced by the success of a new religious movement in German territories that could be played off against an ecclesiastical hierarchy identified with Rome. Luther's original advocacy of the people of the church against the hierarchy, translated into the spatial terms of his spreading movement, became an advocacy of the German people against a Roman papacy, a Roman hierarchy and, if need be, against an emperor more loyal to Rome than to the Gospel and to his own German subjects.

In this sense Luther certainly fulfilled the function of a prophet, even of a German prophet: he interpreted history in terms of God's relationship to his own people. That interpretation was not limited to the contrast between Germany and Rome. The threat the Ottoman Turks posed to the empire in Luther's lifetime was explained by Luther as a sign of God's anger at the German people on account of their unbelief and ingratitude. The Turks became part of the team of forces which, in Luther's eschatological vision of history, opposed the Gospel and signaled that the Last Days were at hand. Nevertheless, Luther did not advocate a crusade against the Turks. Instead, he defended war against them on the ground that peace and order in the empire should be protected.[72] With this reasoning Luther sounded more like a modern theorist than a German prophet.

Whereas Luther hesitated to call himself a prophet without reservation, he unambiguously described himself as a faithful teacher of his fellow Germans.[73] That title reflected more accurately the purpose of his address to the city councilmen of Germany. Luther stressed the opportunity that had come to Germany through the shower of the word in order to convince the councilmen that they should establish "Christian schools," which would teach children languages and good literature for the good of both church and society. Luther eloquently defended the necessity of knowing biblical languages in order to interpret the word of God aright, even though he might have offended his own pastors by distinguishing between simple preachers who did not know these languages and true prophets of the word who could use them. Luther not only helped to shape the modern German language but also upheld the value of classical languages for German society as a whole. Still, he feared that the "foolish" Germans would not be willing to import a valuable commodity like languages, although they purchased all sorts of unnecessary wares from other lands.[74] The pamphlet literature of the sixteenth century described Luther as the educator and enlightener of the people and as the prophet of the Last Days.[75] Perhaps he should stand alongside Philipp Melanchthon as another *praeceptor Germaniae*.

Once Luther realized that his reform movement had spread to other territories, he was convinced that the interpretation of himself as the vehicle of God's work in Germany was true. Luther did not arrive at that self-understanding by himself but was drawn to it by humanists like John Lang, Christoph Scheurl, and Wolfgang Capito, who were impressed by his person and stimulated by his writings.[76] They were not impressed because Luther embodied any quintessential German traits of character. Even in the pamphlet literature Luther was seldom praised as a German, although it was maintained occasionally that Germany could now shake off the yoke of Rome if it would only take to heart the pure Gospel that Luther taught.[77] The Germany that received Luther and that he in turn regarded as the field of his work was the historical community, which responded to him in terms of the concrete circumstances of his age. It was not a spiritual Germany that could make out of Luther a metahistorical character of the German for all seasons.

6. The Church

While Luther's impact on Germany was limited to a geographical community, his relationship to the church involved him with the most extensive community in which he lived. In the first place, the church from which he emerged, the Roman Church, was more widespread than Germany alone, claiming for itself the ancient mark of catholicity. In the second place, the Protestant churches he helped to create were established on the premise that the true church was more extensive than the Roman Church. The true church was ecumenical in Luther's opinion; any institutional form of the church could claim legitimacy only by belonging to that universal community.

That universality already belonged to the view of the church that Luther formulated in his early lectures. True Christians were those who lived by faith in the promises of God. The church was not limited to any one ecclesiastical community but was present wherever people were able to hear the word of God.[78] Applied to the specific situation after 1518, this view asserted that the true church could exist beyond the Roman Church. History supplied examples of non-Roman Christian communities like the Eastern churches, and Luther utilized these examples in his arguments. On the same basis, the continuation of the church apart from the jurisdiction of the Roman bishops was possible after Luther's excommunication. His ecclesiology provided the underpinnings for an ongoing Protestant church structure as well as a bridge over his own break with the papacy. As adapted by other reformers, Luther's ecclesiology was the basic theoretical justification for the separation from Rome and the establishment of new Protestant religious structures.

At first Luther did not worry about what kind of structure might be best suited to his aims. He assured local parishes like Leisnig of their right to bypass the medieval patronage system and call a Protestant pastor.[79] The first concern was to see that local parishes were provided with Protestant preachers. The administration of emerging Protestantism was less important to him. The aftermath of the Peasants' War demonstrated the urgent need for instruction in basic Protestant belief and practice at the local level. Hence Luther agreed to ask Elector John for an official inspection of the parishes in Saxony. This visitation resulted in a territorial church structure in which control of church affairs was vested primarily in the prince and in agencies appointed by him. Historians have debated whether or not this development undermined Luther's original intention and contradicted his view of the church.[80] In the preface to his *German Mass*, Luther did voice, on behalf of those who earnestly desired to be Christian, the desire to assemble for their own worship and study.[81] Moreover, Luther seemed to be critical of the Elector's self-appointed role in the visitation and of new features of the Saxon church like the rite of ordination or the function of the consistory.[82] Did the territorial church gainsay the ideal of small congregations of devoted Christians and nullify Luther's chance of shaping the new church in Germany according to a more independent model?

Luther definitely did not prescribe a structure for Saxon Protestantism as

John Calvin did for the church in Geneva or Martin Bucer for Strassburg. In that sense he did not etch the face of German Protestantism. There is, however, little reason to believe that Luther was fundamentally displeased with the territorial church as he knew it. It did help to provide what Luther considered to be the most important element in an ecclesiastical organization: the educated pastor who could properly instruct his parish in Protestant doctrine and practice. Whether the territorial church conformed in every detail to his ideal, if indeed Luther cherished an ideal form, did not matter as long as the good pastor was supplied. Not the territorial church and certainly not the Lutheran Church, but the Protestant pastor was the visible legacy of Luther to the Reformation.[83] The pastor was critical because he was the vehicle through which the new theology and practice were transmitted to the people. The preacher was the key to the realization of Luther's reforming intention: to liberate and to reeducate the populace. To this extent Luther achieved a modicum of success. At least in his own territory the Protestant clergy were better educated and more responsible in performing their parish duties than the priests of the old church had been.[84]

Whether the new pastors, once they were in place, were able to reeducate the people is another question. The records of visitations in Protestant parishes in the second half of the sixteenth century indicate that Luther succeeded better as a liberator than as an educator. Many people did not learn the catechism, did not attend church regularly, did not treat pastors with respect, did not give up traditional beliefs, and did not behave any better than previously.[85] In other words, Reformation theology even when preached faithfully by good pastors did not necessarily root out popular religion or aversion to formal religion. If accurate, these results are not surprising, even if the records reflect the tendency of official inspectors to record what caused them dissatisfaction instead of what met their high ideals.

Luther was not very different from religious reformers of any age in this regard. In spite of his realistic appraisal of human nature, he still expected people to change both their behavior and their theology. In contrast to many reformers, however, he did not expect to create a perfect church or society. In fact, he regarded his movement as a prelude to the complete reformation of the church that God would effect at the imminent Last Days. The historical movement was more a holding action until the true Reformation should arrive.[86] People could change, but not necessarily become perfect in view of the fact that the end was approaching and evil was stronger than ever. This perspective on his work kept Luther from being naive about preempting God's own Reformation. He did reform the church by changing the worship, rituals, and structure of the medieval institution, but he did not expect to bring about a complete reform of the people in the church.

Martin Luther shaped all the communities to which he belonged and he was in turn shaped by them. It is tempting, but ultimately not very illuminating, to argue which community was the sine qua non for his development as a reformer. Without minimizing his own creative powers and the impact of his personality, one can still appreciate the uniqueness of the historical moment in which the person Luther and all those communities of which he was a part interacted to unleash the German Protestant Reformation. For this reason Luther's biography is not a restriction of perspective, but will remain an essential part of Reformation historiography.

NOTES

1. A. G. Dickens, *The German Nation and Martin Luther* (London: Edward Arnold, 1974), 210.

2. Ibid., 226.

3. *D. Martin Luthers Werke: Kritische Gesamtausgabe* (Weimar: Böhlau, 1883–) (cited as *WA*), 8:573.30–74.4. Cf. *Dokumente zu Luthers Entwicklung*, ed. Otto Scheel, 2d ed. (Tübingen: Mohr [Siebeck], 1929), 68 (no. 175).

4. Erik H. Erikson, *Young Man Luther: A Study in Psychoanalysis and History* (New York: Norton, 1962), 94–95.

5. See esp. Lewis W. Spitz, "Psychohistory and History: The Case of Young Man Luther," *Soundings* 56 (1973): 182–209; reprinted in *Psychohistory and Religion: The Case of Young Man Luther* (Philadelphia: Fortress, 1977), 57–87.

6. Steven Ozment stresses this point in *The Age of Reform 1250–1550: An Intellectual and Religious History of Late Medieval and Reformation Europe* (New Haven and London: Yale, 1980), 224–25. Erikson anticipated this criticism and rejected it, albeit ambiguously, in his discussion of Luther's vow: *Young Man Luther*, 94.

7. *WA*, 8:574.29–31.

8. Scheel, *Dokumente*, 198 (no. 532) and 201 (no. 533).

9. See Luther's letter to Staupitz, dated May 30, 1518: *WA*, 1:525.4–26.14. See also Heiko A. Oberman, " 'Tuus sum, salvum me fac': Augustinréveil zwischen Renaissance und Reformation," *Scientia augustiniana: Studien über Augustinus, den Augustinismus und den Augustinerorden. Festschrift Adolar Zumkeller*, ed. Cornelius Mayer and Willigis Eckermann (Würzburg: Augustinus, 1975), 349–94.

10. Scheel, *Dokumente*, 199 (no. 532).

11. See Adolar Zumkeller, "Die Augustinerschule des Mittelalters: Vertreter und philosophisch-theologische Lehre," *Analecta Augustiniana* 27 (1964): 167–262; idem, "Augustiner-Eremiten," *Theologische Realenzyklopädie* (cited as *TRE*), 4:728–39.

12. See H. A. Oberman, "Headwaters of the Reformation: Initia Lutheri—initia Reformationis," in *Luther and the Dawn of the Modern Era: Papers for the Fourth International Congress for Luther Research*, ed. H. A. Oberman (Leiden: E. J. Brill, 1974), 69–82. For a summary of the views of Luther's relationship to Augustine, see Ulrich Bubenheimer, "Augustin/ Augustinismus III: Augustinismus in der Reformationszeit," *TRE*, 4:718–21. While Oberman is convinced that late medieval Augustinianism was the *occasio proxima* of the new Wittenberg theology ("Headwaters," 82), Zumkeller categorically rejects any anticipation of Luther's theology by medieval Augustinian theologians: "Augustiner-Eremiten," *TRE* 4:731.

13. David C. Steinmetz, "Hermeneutic and Old Testament Interpretation in Staupitz and the Young Luther," *Archiv für Reformationsgeschichte* 70 (1979): 57; idem, "Religious Ecstasy in Staupitz and the Young Luther," *The Sixteenth Century Journal* 11 (1980): 35.

14. Scheel, *Dokumente*, 194 (no. 518); 204 (no. 536).

15. Steinmetz, "Hermeneutic and Old Testament Interpretation," 56–58. For an interpretation of the impact of monasticism on Luther's hermeneutic, see Darrell Reinke, "From Allegory to Metaphor: More Notes on Luther's Hermeneutical Shift," *Harvard Theological Review* 66 (1973): 386–95.

16. *WA*, 50:659.1–4.

17. Heinrich Bornkamm, *Martin Luther in der Mitte seines Lebens* (Göttingen: Vandenhoeck & Ruprecht, 1979), 230.

18. *WA*, 5:39.18–28.

19. *WA*, 8:574.26–29; 8:577.10–13.

20. H. A. Oberman, *Werden und Wertung der Reformation* (Tübingen: Mohr [Siebeck], 1977), 368–71, 425.

21. Scheel, *Dokumente*, 199 (no. 532).

22. *WA*, 5:22.18–21.

23. Leif Grane, *Modus loquendi theologicus: Luthers Kampf um die Erneuerung der Theologie (1515–1518)* (Leiden: E. J. Brill, 1975), 141–43. In 1531 Luther told his students it was still important for them to be acquainted with the scholastic *modus loquendi:* Scheel, *Dokumente*, 65 (no. 168).

24. *D. Martin Luthers Werke: Briefwechsel* (Weimar: Böhlau, 1930–) (cited as *WABr*), 1:160.10–11 (March 31, 1518).

25. Helmar Junghans, "Der Einfluss des Humanismus auf Luthers Entwicklung bis 1518," *Lutherjahrbuch* 37 (1970): 37–101; Oberman, "Headwaters," 69–70.

26. *WA*, 5:20.18–22. See Maria Grossmann, "Humanismus in Wittenberg 1486–1517," *Lutherjahrbuch* 39 (1972): 11–30; Heinz Scheible, "Gründung und Ausbau der Universität Wittenberg," in *Beiträge zu Problemen deutscher Universitätsgründungen der frühen Neuzeit*, ed. Peter Baumgart and Notker Hammerstein (Nendeln: KTO, 1978), 131–47.

27. Helmar Junghans, "Initia gloriae Lutheri," in *Unterwegs zur Einheit: Festschrift für Heinrich Stirnimann*, ed. Johannes Brantschen and Pietro Selvatico (Freiburg and Vienna: Herder, 1980), 313–17.

28. *WABr*, 1:70–71 (October 16, 1516).

29. *WABr*, 1:71.42–43.

30. Karl Bauer, *Die Wittenberger Universitätstheologie und die Anfänge der deutschen Reformation* (Tübingen: Mohr [Siebeck], 1928), 51.

31. *WABr*, 1:170.30–40 (May 9, 1518).

32. Oberman, *Werden und Wertung*, 332–34.

33. Scheible, "Gründung," 142–44.

34. See, for example, Simo Heininen, *Die finnischen Studenten in Wittenberg 1531–1552* (Helsinki: Luther-Agricola Society, 1980), 39–62.

35. *D. Martin Luthers Werke: Tischreden* (Weimar: Böhlau, 1912–) (cited as *WATR*), 4:674.9–11 (no. 5126).

36. Helmar Junghans, *Wittenberg als Lutherstadt* (Berlin: Union, 1979), 73–75.

37. Helmar Junghans, "Wittenberg und Luther—Luther und Wittenberg," *Freiburger Zeitschrift für Philosophie und Theologie* 25 (1978): 107.

38. Ibid., 111.

39. Bernd Moeller, *Deutschland im Zeitalter der Reformation* (Göttingen: Vandenhoeck & Ruprecht, 1977), 62, 193.

40. *WABr*, 8:491 (July 8, 1539).

41. A forceful statement of this advocacy is contained in Luther's *Warning to His Dear German People* (1531): *WA*, 30/3:308.23–16.38.

42. *WA*, 7:833.10–20.

43. Heinz Dannenbauer, *Luther als religiöser Volksschriftsteller 1517–1520: Ein Beitrag zu der Frage nach den Ursachen der Reformation* (Tübingen: Mohr [Siebeck], 1930), 6:30–42.

44. For sources and interpretation, see Nikolaus Müller, *Die Wittenberger Bewegung 1521 und

1522 (Leipzig: M. Heinsius Nachfolger, 1911); James S. Preus, *Carlstadt's Ordinationes and Luther's Liberty: A Study of the Wittenberg Movement 1521–1522* (Cambridge, Mass.: Harvard, 1974); Mark U. Edwards, Jr., *Luther and the False Brethren* (Stanford, Calif.: Stanford University Press, 1975), pp. 6–33.

45. Bornkamm, *Martin Luther*, 541–43.

46. *WABr*, 11:149.7–50.21.

47. For example, *WATR*, 1:294.19–95.5 (no. 624).

48. Paul Kalkoff, *Die Depeschen des Nuntius Aleander vom Wormser Reichstage 1521* (Halle: Verein für Reformationsgeschichte, 1886), 20. See the review of Wilhelm Borth, *Die Luthersache (Causa Lutheri) 1517–1524*, by Günter Mühlpfordt in *Deutsche Literaturzeitung für Kritik der internationalen Wissenschaft* 95 (1974): 897–906.

49. *WABr*, 2:455.75–78 (March 5, 1522).

50. *WABr*, 10:32.8–17 (April 7, 1542). See Eike Wolgast, *Die Wittenberger Theologie und die Politik der evangelischen Stände: Studien zu Luthers Gutachten in politischen Fragen* (Gütersloh: Gerd Mohn, 1977), 285–90.

51. *WA*, 11:263.13–21. See Bornkamm, *Martin Luther*, 108.

52. Wolgast, *Die Wittenberger Theologie*, 290–99.

53. Bornkamm, *Martin Luther*, 538–57.

54. Wolgast, *Die Wittenberger Theologie*, 295.

55. Bornkamm, *Martin Luther*, 9.

56. Wolgast, *Die Wittenberger Theologie*, 296–98.

57. Karl Trüdinger, *Luthers Briefe und Gutachten an weltliche Obrigkeiten zur Durchführung der Reformation* (Münster: Aschendorff, 1975), 142.

58. See Karlheinz Blaschke, *Sachsen im Zeitalter der Reformation* (Gütersloh: Gerd Mohn, 1970), 57–58, 65–67; Junghans, "Wittenberg und Luther—Luther und Wittenberg," 113.

59. See Luther's letter to the Jew Josel of Rosheim, who had appealed to Luther for help against the edict: *WABr*, 8:89–91 (June 11, 1537).

60. *WABr*, 10:33.23–25 (April 7, 1542).

61. In E. W. Zeeden, *Martin Luther und die Reformation im Urteil des deutschen Luthertums*, (Freiburg: Herder, 1952), 2:26.

62. Junghans, "Initia," 304–5.

63. *WA*, 30/3:290.28–30.

64. In an open letter to Archbishop Albrecht of Mainz: *WA*, 30/2:411.22; 412.20–23.

65. *WA*, 30/3:291.7–9.

66. *WA*, 1:379.7–12.

67. *WA*, 6:404.11–16. See *Akten und Briefe zur Kirchenpolitik Herzog Georgs von Sachsen*, ed. Felician Gess, vol. 1:1517–1524 (Leipzig: Teubner, 1905), 139.

68. *WA*, 15:27.12–20.

69. *WABr*, 1:344.8–9 (February 20, 1519).

70. *WA*, 15:31.33–32.14.

71. *WA*, 25:310.18–21. See Wolfgang Günter, "Die geschicntstheologischen Voraussetzungen von Luthers Selbstverständnis," *Von Konstanz nach Trient: Festgabe für August Franzen*, ed. Remigius Bäumer (Munich, Paderborn, Vienna: Ferdinand Schöningh, 1972), 388–94.

72. Bornkamm, *Martin Luther*, 525–26.

73. In the *Warning*: *WA*, 30/3:290.28–32.

74. *WA*, 15:40.14–26; 15:36.9–20.

75. See Andrea Körsgen-Wiedeburg, "Das Bild Martin Luthers in den Flugschriften der frühen Reformationszeit," *Festgabe für Ernst Walter Zeeden*, ed. Horst Rabe et al. (Münster: Aschendorff, 1976), 157, 162–63.

76. Junghans, "Initia," 320–23.

77. Körsgen-Wiedeburg, "Das Bild Martin Luthers," 163–64.

78. See Luther's strong conjunction of the church with the word in an early sermon: *WA*, 1:

13.28–14.3. Compare the implications as drawn out by Luther in 1521: *WA*, 8:491.18–38; in 1539: *WA*, 47:774.15–75.5.

79. *WA*, 11: 411.13–30.

80. The earlier debate has been summarized by Hans-Walter Krumwiede, *Zur Entstehung des landesherrlichen Kirchenregiments in Kursachsen und Braunschweig-Wolfenbüttel* (Göttingen: Vandenhoeck & Ruprecht, 1967), 13–47. For more recent views see Irmgard Höss, "The Lutheran Church of the Reformation: Problems of its Formation and Organization in the Middle and North German Territories," *The Social History of the Reformation*, ed. Lawrence Buck and Jonathan Zophy (Columbus: Ohio State, 1972), 322; Krumwiede, "Reformatorische Theologie und die Selbstverwaltung der Kirchengemeinde," *Jahrbuch der Gesellschaft für niedersächsische Kirchengeschichte* 73 (1975): 211–29.

81. *WA*, 19:75.3–30.

82. The import of Luther's remarks in the introduction to the *Instruction for Visitors* (*WA*, 26:197.12–99.2) has been the subject of considerable debate. See also Trüdinger, *Luthers Briefe und Gutachten*, 82–85; I. Höss, *Georg Spalatin 1484–1545* (Weimar: Böhlaus Nachfolger, 1956), 373–74; Susan C. Karant-Nunn, *Luther's Pastors: The Reformation in the Ernestine Countryside* (Philadelphia: American Philosophical Society, 1979), 56–60, 73.

83. Martin Rade, "Der Sprung in Luthers Kirchenbegriff und die Entstehung der Landeskirche," *Zeitschrift für Theologie und Kirche* 24 (1914): 259–60.

84. Karant-Nunn, *Luther's Pastors*, 19, 72.

85. See Gerald Strauss, *Luther's House of Learning: Indoctrination of the Young in the German Reformation* (Baltimore and London: Johns Hopkins, 1978), 307. Whether or not this means that the Reformation was a failure, as Strauss suggests, depends very much on the criteria for success and failure employed. Strauss's thesis and methodology are being debated at several points and his conclusions should not be uncritically accepted.

86. This perspective of Luther and the "reformation" is elaborated by Heiko A. Oberman, "Martin Luther: Vorläufer der Reformation," in *Verifikationen. Festschrift für Gerhard Ebeling zum 70. Geburtstag*, ed. Eberhard Jüngel, Johannes Wallmann, Wilfrid Werbeck (Tübingen: J. C. B. Mohr [Paul Siebeck] 1982), 91–119.

BIBLIOGRAPHICAL ESSAY

At the First International Congress for Luther Research in 1956, Heinrich Bornkamm warned scholars that they were in danger of losing sight of Luther the person because of their preoccupation with his theology. The same concern was voiced at the Fifth Congress in 1977. On the whole, however, Luther scholarship during the last twenty-five years has shown considerable interest in aspects of Luther besides his theology, and a more comprehensive picture of the man and his significance is emerging. This is due to several factors. First, more attention has been paid to the context in which Luther worked; second, new attempts have been made to assess Luther's impact on modern history; third, historical studies of phases of Luther's career, though not complete biographies, have laid the groundwork for a new, comprehensive, and critical biography of Luther. Add to these developments the continuing interest in Luther's theology, and Luther research has come far enough since 1956 to render the complaint of Bornkamm no longer necessary.

Historians have long recognized that Luther could not be isolated from his context; that was the presupposition of Karl Bauer's groundbreaking study: *Die Wittenberger Universitätstheologie und die Anfänge der deutschen Reformation* (Tübingen: Mohr, 1928). The same perspective has been adopted in such widely varying works as Ernest G. Schwiebert, *Luther and His Times: The Reformation from a New Perspective* (St. Louis, Mo.: Concordia, 1950), and A. G. Dickens, *The German Nation and Martin Luther* (London: Arnold, 1974). Luther's immediate context, the town of Wittenberg, has been closely examined by Helmar Junghans in his book *Wittenberg als Lutherstadt* (Berlin: Union, 1979). The relationship between Luther and his princes, the electors of Saxony, has been the subject of several works: Hermann Kunst, *Evangelischer Glaube und Politische Verantwortung* (Stuttgart: Evangelisches Verlagswerk, 1976), and Eike Wolgast, *Die Wittenberger Theologie und die Politik der evangelischen Stände* (Gütersloh: Mohn, 1977). On a larger scale, Luther's view of the constitution of the empire has been studied by Wolfgang Günter, *Martin Luthers Vorstellung von der Reichsverfassung* (Münster: Aschendorff, 1976). Günter determined that Luther changed his preference from a monarchical to an aristocratic model of imperial authority during the 1530s. This change corresponded to the course of the Reformation but was not determined solely by it. Günter's conclusion is typical of the results produced by all these studies: Luther both influenced and was influenced by the social and political structures in which he lived. The consideration of this reciprocal influence will make future interpretations of Luther more nuanced.

Taken in its broadest sense, context includes the intellectual as well as the political environment. Hence, the search continues for the antecedents of Luther's ideas and, in this connection, the old question of Luther's relationship to the Middle Ages and to modernity has again emerged. A new appreciation of the complexity of the question has led to answers that stress Luther's kinship with both periods. In his address to the Fourth Luther Congress ("Headwaters of the Reformation: *Initia Lutheri—Initia Reformationis*," in *Luther and the Dawn of the Modern Era*, ed. H. A. Oberman [Leiden: Brill, 1974], 40–88), Heiko Oberman emphasized the medieval Augustinian context of Luther's beginnings while denying that this context provided a single answer to the question. Gerhard Ebeling, addressing the same congress, located Luther at a point that transcended both ages and enabled him to be critical of both ("Luther and the Beginning of the Modern Age," in ibid., 11–39). Luther's view of conscience put him in much the same position, according to the analysis of Michael Baylor, *Action and Person: Conscience in Late Scholasticism and the Young Luther* (Leiden: Brill, 1977). Although critical of ecclesiastical authority, Luther adhered to the scholastic idea of the authority of conscience; by tying the conscience to Scripture, however, Luther set the stage for the modern discussion of religious freedom, which depended on the relationship between conscience and religious faith. Works like these, which relate Luther to the larger historical context, manifest a distinct appreciation for the originality of his thought and preclude an easy explanation for that originality drawn from either age.

Although the social theory of Marxist historians has permitted them to overcome the medieval-modern dichotomy, it has locked them into an interpretation of Luther that allows little variation. Luther is associated with the "early bourgeois revolution," a concept that, though disputed, reflects Luther's role both in precipitating the social conflict of the sixteenth century and in preventing this conflict from becoming a thoroughgoing revolution. According to Gerhard Zschäbitz, *Martin Luther: Größe und Grenze* (Berlin: Deutscher Verlag der Wissenschaften, 1967), Luther created a religious ideology for the bourgeoisie as he revolted against the reactionary medieval church. A more intensive application of the theory of class conflict to Luther's early theology by Rosemarie Müller-Streisand, *Luthers Weg von der Reformation zur Restauration* (Halle: Niemeyer, 1964), also stresses Luther's submission to the ruling classes. In spite of this limitation, Luther's economic and social views have received some positive evaluation from Günter Fabiunke, *Martin Luther als Nationalökonom* (Berlin: Akademie, 1963).

The ecumenical character of modern Catholic Luther research was given its stamp by Jospeh Lortz in his book *Die Reformation in Deutschland*, 2 vols. (1939–1940; 4th ed. Freiburg: Herder, 1962). Lortz's regard for the catholicity of Luther's thought increased over the years, even though he continued to fault Luther for his subjectivism and maintained that Luther overcame a Catholicism that was no longer fully catholic. More of a parity between Luther and medieval theology has been discovered by other Catholic scholars, for example, by Otto Pesch in his book *Theologie der Rechtfertigung bei Martin Luther und Thomas von Aquin* (Mainz: Grünewald, 1967). Pesch distinguishes between the sapiential theology of Thomas and the existential theology of Luther and concludes that the different character of the theologies does not represent an antithesis that would justify anathemas. Catholic Luther scholars who have concentrated on the question of authority tend to draw a sharper line between Luther and the medieval period; a case in point is Remigius Bäumer, *Martin Luther und der Papst*, 2d ed. (Münster: Aschendorff, 1971). On the whole, however, the contemporary Catholic interpretation of Luther is quite positive, as exemplified by the appreciative works of Jared Wicks, *Man Yearning for Grace* (Washington: Corpus, 1968) and "Luther," in *Dictionnaire de Spiritualité* (9: cols. 1206–43).

That positive Catholic interpretation has spurred the quest for the distinctive nature and genesis of Luther's Reformation theology. Some scholars have followed Ernst Bizer (*Fides ex auditu*, 3d ed. [Neukirchen: Neukirchener Verlag, 1966]) in designating a new concept of the Word of God as the content, and 1518–1519 as the date, of Luther's Reformation discovery. In his book *Modus loquendi theologicus* (Leiden: Brill, 1975), Leif Grane offered a convincing rebuttal of Bizer's thesis without denying the importance of the initial conflict with Rome in drawing out the implications of Luther's theology for a reformation of the church. At stake is the relationship between that conflict and Luther's early theology in his development as a reformer. This question is still being examined at the level of methodology; see, for example, the essays by Heiko Oberman and Leif Grane in *Archiv für Reformationsgeschichte* 68 (1977): 56–111 and 302–15. A sampling of earlier essays on this subject is contained in *Der Durchbruch der reformatorischen Erkenntnis,* ed. Bernhard Lohse (Darmstadt: Wissenschaftliche Buchgesellschaft, 1968).

The stately figure of Karl Holl looms over that discussion as well as over many others. His essays on Luther, *Gesammelte Aufsätze zur Kirchengeschichte,* vol. 1: *Luther,* 7th ed. (Tübingen: Mohr, 1948), stressed the influence that Luther's religion and theology exercised on all aspects of his life. In spite of important contributions like those of Holl, however, the only comprehensive, critical biography of Luther remains the two-volume work by Julius Köstlin, *Martin Luther: sein Leben und seine Schriften,* first published in 1875, and revised under the same title by Gustav Kawerau, 5th ed. (Berlin: Duncker, 1903). Different phases of Luther's life have been studied since Köstlin. The young Luther was examined by Heinrich Boehmer in *Der junge Luther,* first published in 1925, 4th ed. (Leipzig: Koehler & Amelang, 1951), and Robert Fife published a thorough account of Luther's conflict with Rome up to 1521: *The Revolt of Martin Luther* (New York: Columbia University Press, 1957). Mark Edwards provided well-researched and well-written accounts of Luther's conflict with his Protestant opponents in *Luther and the False Brethren* (Stanford, Calif.: Stanford University Press, 1975). Fortunately, Heinrich Bornkamm helped to make his own earlier complaint obsolete by leaving far enough advanced for posthumous publication his study of Luther's middle years: *Martin Luther in der Mitte seines Lebens,* ed. Karin Bornkamm (Göttingen: Vandenhoeck & Ruprecht, 1979). And the older Luther, the man in his fifties and sixties, has received a colorful treatment from H. G. Haile, *Luther: An Experiment in Biography* (Garden City, N.Y.: Doubleday, 1980). Although not proposing different interpretations of Luther, these studies are dissimilar enough to justify the conclusion that no new and definitive interpretation of the whole Luther has yet emerged out of modern Luther research. The time is ripe for a new comprehensive biography, especially with the five-hundredth anniversary of his birth and the completion of the one hundred year-old Weimar edition of his works at hand.

3

Zwingli: Founding Father of the Reformed Churches

ROBERT C. WALTON

Huldrych Zwingli (1484–1531) was the first Swiss reformer. He began his program of church reform based upon biblical norms in the canton of Zurich on January 1, 1519. Humanist respect for the sources of the Golden Age of Christianity, above all for the Scripture to which even the writings of the Church Fathers were subordinate, was the basis for Zwingli's Bible-centered reform program. His biblicism never led him to jot-and-tittle orthodoxy. True to his early study of Origen, Zwingli remained convinced that the letter killed and only the Spirit gave life.

Only after he had begun to preach reform did Zwingli become fully aware of the significance of Luther's reform movement.[1] Zwingli was encouraged by Luther's example and drew inspiration from his writings but was never a disciple of the Wittenberg reformer; nor can his own theological development be explained in terms of the pattern of Luther's development. He never accepted the fundamental tension between the law and the Gospel that was essential to Luther's theology. From the beginning Zwingli's theology was a unique amalgam of the theology of the *via antiqua*, particularly that of Duns Scotus, and Erasmian humanism. George Potter has summed up Zwingli's uniqueness very well: "Zwingli undoubtedly formed his own opinions by his own independent study of the Bible, and particularly of Erasmus' edition of the New Testament with his notes and paraphrases, before reading any of Luther's writings."[2]

Zwingli, not John Calvin, was the founding father of the Reformed Churches. He, like the later theologians of the international reformed movement, was far more radical than was Luther in his break with the traditions of the old church. This is particularly noticeable in his doctrine of the Lord's Supper, which did not represent mere memorialism, and in his total rejection of the role of music in the worship of the church. Unlike Calvin and many later reformed theologians, Zwingli's consistent "Erastianism" prevented him from ever considering the establishment of a Presbyterian form of church government to preside over a clearly defined ecclesiastical realm. For Zwingli, church and civic community were one indivisible body, a true *res publica christiana*, governed by the spiritual and secular officers who accepted the authority of the Bible and worked in the closest possible harmony. Typical of this cooperation was the Zurich marriage court (*das Ehegericht*, 1525), which was presided over by a mixed commission of councillors and theologians. The court enforced a rigid moral discipline upon the inhabitants of the Zurich commonwealth.

Zwingli is best remembered for his troubled relations with the early *Täufer* (Anabaptist) movement at Zurich, which emerged from the radical wing of his own followers, and for his death in battle on October 11, 1531, during the second Kappel war. He was the only major reformer to die in battle and to frame plans of campaign for the use of the city's soldiers. Zwingli's approach to political problems and his very great success in influencing the policies of the Zurich council can be variously explained. He was certainly the urban reformer *par excellence*. There is no doubt that his Neoplatonist pursuit of purity in the worship of God led him to militancy and fanaticism, which were not always restrained by his great store of peasant shrewdness.

To understand Zwingli and his reformation, it is necessary to place both in the proper context of the upper-German urban society. The publication of Bernd Moeller's *Reichsstadt und Reformation* in 1962 began a flood of literature on the subject. The English historian A. G. Dickens had since concluded that the Reformation was "an urban event." The new trend appeared to culminate in the publication of Stephen Ozment's *The Reformation in the Cities* in 1975,[3] but it did not end there. Thomas A. Brady's careful study, *Ruling Class, Regime and Reformation at Strasbourg*, appeared in 1978. It cast a critical look at Moeller and Ozment and described the Strasbourg ruling class as a part of the lower nobility in Alsace rather than a separate urban ruling class. Brady's work raised questions about the definition of what a late medieval city was and cast the role of the Zwinglians in Strasbourg's Reformation as that of the religion of "the little people," not that of the ruling class. This assertion challenged one of Moeller's basic assumptions about the role of Zwingli and Bucer's theology in the context of the sacral urban community of the South German imperial cities. The volume of essays, entitled *The Urban Classes, The Nobility and The Reformation: Studies on the Social History of the Reformation in England and Germany* (published by the German Historical Institute in London in 1979), was largely a response to Brady's work. As long as Hans-Christoph Rublack's institute continues to devote its energies to the systematic study of the structures that formed the context for the urban Reformation in Germany, there will, no doubt, be further debate about the question of the nature of the Reformation in the South German imperial cities.[4]

Despite Brady's not unjustified skepticism, Moeller's assertion that

Zwingli and Bucer won their greatest following in the Southwest German Swiss imperial cities, the cultural centers of the German empire, has to be taken seriously.[5] Their reformation was from the beginning a movement whose natural context was the city. At least in Zurich a sizable number of the wealthier artisan guildsmen who dominated the corporate oligarchy of the city's government adhered to Zwingli's theology. Between 1970 and 1974, Moeller demonstrated Zurich's significance for the introduction of the Reformation in the other South German cities even more convincingly in a two-part study that appeared in the *Zeitschrift der Savigny-Stiftung für Rechtsgeschichte* under the title "Zwinglis Disputationen. Studien zu den Anfängen der Kirchenbildung und des Synodalwesens in Protestantismus." The main thrust of his argument was that the Zurich disputations of January 1523 marked a new phase in the development of the Reformation. The January disputation ended in the foundation of the "first Protestant church" ("die erste Kirchenbegründung im Bereich des Protestantismus überhaupt"). According to Moeller, the church's form was not clearly articulated because Zwingli conceived of the visible church as coterminous with the structure of the city state. This conception also explains Zwingli's close cooperation with the magistracy, which was obvious since the conflict over the violation of the fast in the spring of 1522. What was done at Zurich became the model for the founding of Protestant churches elsewhere. Moeller refers to these as *Disputation-Reformations* ("Disputations-Reformationen"). In the second part of his study Moeller elaborated his argument with numerous examples and concluded that the disputations all had an urban character and served urban interests by demonstrating that the power exercised by the old church was not supported by the authority of Scripture. This argument gave the city magistrates a long-sought-after justification to take full control of the local church and to exercise fully the *jus reformandi* that they had already begun to claim.[6]

Moeller's conclusions leave no doubt about both the urban character of Zwingli's reformation and the significance of his achievement as a reformer. Zwingli's theology spoke to an urban world and best expressed the religious aspirations of the urban governing classes in the cultural centers of the German empire, which even if Strasbourg is excepted, were the South German imperial cities. In this connection it is interesting to note that Machiavelli greatly admired the Swiss Confederacy and the German imperial cities, because he believed that they achieved true "freedom." For him, as for most late medieval statesmen, the exercise of freedom by a city or a member of the Swiss Confederacy meant it was possible for the city (or the confederate) to act in its own interest vis à vis all other political entities.[7] Zwingli's program of religious reform freed the Zurich council, the delegated authority of the people, to act in its own interest in religious affairs. As an urban theologian, Zwingli was a natural champion of urban liberty.

But two questions remain: (1) What does one mean when one speaks of the city in the sixteenth century? and (2) How "popular" was the participation in the government of those cities which enjoyed liberty? The first question is easy to answer. Quoting Emmanuel Wallerstein's *The Modern World System*, Brady has asserted that the town and land formed "a single society." The answer to question one is: In the sixteenth century a city was a natural part of the landscape. The second answer is more difficult. It depends in part upon the definition of who were the citizens who participated in the government. In Strasbourg Brady has discovered the remnants of a tripartite division: the patricians, the people in the middle *(die Bürger)*, and the *Handwerker (tribus)*, who were the artisan guildsmen.[8] As will be seen, Zurich tended to have a two-tiered structure in which the patricians and members of a few rich guilds dominated; and all members of the guilds were termed "citizens" *(die Bürger* or the *populus)*, although their participation in government was very limited. Just as at Strasbourg, Zurich was governed by an oligarchy as, indeed, was the entire countryside. Consequently, to talk as freely about liberty and popular participation in city government as does Dickens—who depends here on his understanding of Moeller—is not entirely justified.[9] A look at Zwingli's own background should make this clear.

Zwingli was the third son of a rural chief magistrate in the Duchy of the Toggenburg, a territory allied with the Swiss Confederacy through its treaties with Glarus and Schwyz, and since 1488 subject to the Abbey of St. Gall. Zwingli's father had succeeded his grandfather as *Ammann* at the village of Wildhaus in the district of Wildenburg, a part of the upper Toggenburg. The Ammann, or local magistrate, was chosen by the community from the wealthier local farmers and presided over the affairs of the village and the region around it. He was also responsible for maintaining good relations with the Abbey of St. Gall and, when necessary, with the representatives of the cantons of Schwyz and Glarus. Zwingli's lifelong interest in politics and his pride in being a Swiss confederate, even though the Toggenburg was only allied to the confederacy and did not have the authority reserved for the thirteen ruling cantons, were doubtless the product of his home environment. The fact that the first book he purchased while a student in Heinrich Wölflin's *(Lupullus)* Latin school at Bern was Cicero's *De Officiis* indicates how early and deep seated Zwingli's political interest was.[10]

Zwingli's rural background is of particular importance in assessing his role as an urban theologian. Both Zwingli and his successor at Zurich, Heinrich Bullinger, were recruited from the ranks of the well-to-do peasantry.[11] The Zwinglis were far-and-away less rich than the Bullingers, in part because the mountainous fields and pastures that they had inherited in and around Wildhaus were simply not so productive as those of the rolling, rich, and well-watered fields of Bullinger's Aargau, which were part of Switzerland's fertile *Mittelland*.[12] The role the two families played both in local government and in the church was the same. Indeed, in late medieval Switzerland the church offered the children of the well-to-do peasantry their only real chance for social mobility,[13] unless they turned to mercenary service, as had the peasant Hans Waldmann. Even in the country districts of an urban canton like Zurich, the city government relied on the wealthier farmers to serve as assistant district bailiffs *(Untervögte)*. When the rural establishment became disaffected, as it did under the influence of the Anabaptists in 1526 in the Grüninger Amt, the Zurich government could not enforce its policies on the region.[14] The governments of all rural areas depended upon an alliance between the wealthier local peasants and the ruling establishment that governed the region; the wealthier local peasants were really part of the ruling oligarchy.

The local assemblies *(Gemeinden)* in the Toggenburg had the right to choose their own magistrates but they selected them from the wealthy farmers for the simple reason that only representatives of this group had the time to devote to the problems of government.[15] While it is true that the rural society from which Zwingli came was not governed by a self co-opting oligarchy as was Zurich, it was a hierarchical society. The guild oligarchy in Zurich developed for much the same reason. Wealthier peasants were invariably chosen to be district magistrates in the Toggenburg or elsewhere in the confederacy and Southwest Germany because they had sufficient means to be able to devote their time to the affairs of government. Unlike their rural equivalents, the urban councillors used their position to establish an oligarchy. The rural governing class never established an oligarchy but they can be termed a village "patriciate"; they were referred to as the *meliores* or *seniores* in the village, or as the *elteste*, just as the urban oligarchs were.[16] The tendency toward oligarchy was present in their recognized status and in their exclusive employment as local magistrates. Thus Zwingli's early political awareness was deeply and unchangeably conditioned to accept the claims of those possessing wealth to represent and govern "the people."

It is necessary at this point to say something about the corporate tradition of the local assemblies in the countryside. Their traditions rested upon foundations almost as ancient as those of the city and typified the structure of medieval local government.[17] Each of the thirteen Swiss cantons had corporate constitutions of various origins and were allied with each other either by a *Bund* in the case of the eight earliest members of the confederacy or, for the remainder, a *Burgrecht*, sometimes called a *Landrecht*, similar to that which bound the Toggenburg to Glarus and Schwyz. Representatives of the cantons or confederates met in a General Assembly, the *Tagsatzung*, whose decisions, except in questions involving the regions jointly controlled by the confederates, were hardly binding. Up to the time of the Reformation, the confederacy can be viewed as a league of states that had come into being within the German empire and was beginning to show signs of becoming a federal state.[18] This development is best illustrated in the beginning of the separation from the German empire, which took place as a result of the Swabian War (1499). At all levels of the confederacy the forms of representation developed typified the pattern of delegated authority determined by corporate constitutional thinking. Though the constitutions of the cantons are variously classified as "aristocratic" types (*aristokratische Zunftverfassungen*), democratic guild types (*demokratische Zunftverfassungen*), and purely democratic territorial assemblies (*demokratische Landsgemeindeverfassungen*), the differences between them were not very great. Regardless of the nature of their constitution, no Swiss canton claimed to be a democracy in the modern sense; all stressed the fact that their constitutions fulfilled Aristotle's requirements for a stable, mixed constitution in which aristocratic and democratic elements were properly combined. All spoke of themselves as "democratic" in the sense that they had representative institutions, not a system of government based upon one man, one vote. The important point was that the community as a whole was able to delegate its authority to one or another kind of governing body. This was the essence of corporate government. There can be no doubt that in a modern sense the *Landsgemeinden* were somewhat more representative than the urban councils but the tendency toward oligarchic government was apparent at every level. Where the full assembly of citizens (all males over fourteen years of age) met at all, they tended merely to confirm decisions already taken by the recognized leaders of their respective cantons. They accepted the oath of the newly elected, in most cases co-opted, magistrates and renewed their oath to the confederacy every five years. The *Landsgemeinden* permitted the *Dorfgemeinden* a greater autonomy than did the urban cantons. The affairs of the *Landsgemeinden* (Uri, Schwyz, Unterwalden, Glarus, Appenzell, Zug) were directed by the regional bailiff (the *Landammann*); the local bailiffs (*Landvögte*); the standard-bearers (*Pannerherren*, who were responsible for military matters;) the treasurer (*Seckelmeister*); and the secretary. The cantons, dominated by a city such as Zurich, Basel, or Bern, were governed by self-co-opting councils in which the small council dominated.[19] Thus Zwingli's theology can as fairly be termed a theology of territorial oligarchy as an urban theology. In his world his theology, be it rural or urban, was naturally a theology of oligarchy. Such a theology was necessarily republican but the essence of republicanism was inevitably oligarchical.

Zwingli's education was typical of that enjoyed by a wealthy farmer's son. He may at first have attended a German school but at the age of five he was sent to his uncle Bartholomew Zwingli, pastor of Weesen on the Walensee, to begin to learn Latin, the spoken language of the educated. His uncle sent Zwingli at age ten to the young and able George Bünzli in Basel to learn the trivium (grammar, rhetoric, and logic). Bünzli recognized the boy's ability, especially his musical ability, and, when he had taught him all he could, he sent him either in 1496 or 1497 to Heinrich Wölflin in Bern. Wölflin was the city's chief schoolmaster and a figure of importance in the development of Swiss humanism. Under his teacher's direction Zwingli probably gained his first accurate knowledge of Swiss history, though he never became, as did his successor Bullinger, an enthusiastic student of the confederacy's history. His remarkable musical talents continued to develop at Bern and attracted the attention of the Dominicans there. Zwingli apparently seriously considered entering the novitiate but the wiser councils of his uncle and, probably, his father, prevailed. He continued to study at Bern and then at age fourteen entered the University of Vienna in the autumn of 1498 (the winter semester).[20]

It is not known whether Zwingli actually heard Conrad Celtis, the poet laureate of the empire, lecture at Vienna. It is certainly true that he was further introduced to the humanist movement at Vienna and began his close friendship with Vadian, but his intimate contact with humanism dates from a later phase of his development. Both his period of study in Vienna and his years at Basel (B.A., 1504; M.A., 1506) were a time in which Zwingli followed a very traditional pattern of schooling. In Basel, as at Vienna, he listened intently to the representatives of the *via antiqua*, that is, those theologians who adhered to the teachings of Thomas Aquinas and his disciples. At this time the division between the two theological directions was not rigidly adhered to and Zwingli clearly became familiar with the main tenets of both schools. However, the impact of the *via antiqua* upon his thought was far more significant for the development of his theology than was that of the *via moderna*.[21]

It was during his years at Glarus (1506–1516) that Zwingli learned Greek and, through his friend Glarean, was introduced to Erasmus and the humanist circle at Basel.[22] He was not suddenly converted to humanism, nor did his humanist interests cause him to break with scholasticism. Zwingli's very typical criticism of scholastic method and vocabulary actually masks a fusion of various strains of humanist and scholastic thought that broadened his intellectual horizons. Zwingli's enthusiasm for the return to the sources, common to humanists everywhere, was naive and typical. The frequent classical references in his letters and the epithets ("by Hercules"), which become ever more common, were often strained. There are times when one senses the "country boy" in Zwingli, reveling in the new educational program but never quite gaining the sophistication and polish one might expect from an adherent of humanism who so admired Erasmus.

Zwingli later claimed that he began to preach the Gospel in 1516. What he meant by "preaching the Gospel" is difficult to say. If his early preaching at Zurich provides a good sample, Zwingli was the advocate of a biblically based reform program whose inspiration clearly came from Erasmus. English historian George Potter has expressed the essence of humanism and its impact on Zwingli very succinctly. His description probably explains what Zwingli meant when he said that he began to preach the Gospel in 1516:

> And in 1516 he was one of the first to secure the *novum instrumentum* which was the fruit of Erasmus' painful months at Cambridge. . . . having the new original text before him, determined not to accept traditional interpretations but to concentrate upon the meaning of the words themselves. How new this was and how courageous, our literate and incredulous age can appreciate only with difficulty. It is indeed almost impossible to recapture the thrill of this fine folio volume. Here was the very word of God in the original tongue and something he could use and reverence. . . . certain that the key to eternal bliss lay in these pages, the young man turned to Jesus as never before. It was this New Testament, added to study of St. Augustine's treatise on the fourth gospel, that opened his eyes and impelled him to fill his sermons with the new-found glad tidings. . . . It was exactly what he needed. . . . His own knowledge of Greek enabled him to value the discussion of such words as ecclesia, presbyter, *poenitentiam agite*. . . . He could read that Christ, Eternal Wisdom, alone could teach with authority and was the sole mediator for salvation.[23]

European Zwingli scholars generally define Erasmian humanism in terms of a relatively superficial, rationalistic form of biblicism that failed to grasp the depth of the biblical and patristic sources it employed. Its chief characteristic is its optimistic anthropology, which failed to take seriously the Pauline-Augustinian understanding of man's sinful nature. The most recent work on the subject defines Erasmian humanism in terms of Jacob Burkhardt's definition of humanism and then follows Arthur Rich in describing the "deepening" of Zwingli's theological development in the course of 1520, which by 1522 caused him to turn away from the superficialities of Erasmian humanism to a Pauline-Augustinian anthropology.[24] This interpretation is marred by the uncritical application of the assumptions of modern dialectical theology, namely, neoorthodoxy, and a total misunderstanding of what humanism was. American scholars who have read P. O. Kristeller and have been influenced by Charles Trinkaus would recognize in Zwingli the typical humanist who became a student of sacred philology and an advocate of reform by means of a return to the sources.[25] That Zwingli refined and deepened his theology as he continued his study was quite natural, but he never underwent a conversion from Erasmian "rationalism." Neither he nor Erasmus was a rationalist; Erasmus's much criticized anthropology was a typically scholastic anthropology. Thanks to Erasmus and others, Zwingli turned, as Erasmus had done under John Colet's influence, to the sources of western Christian thought; and being a devout as well as very practical man, he set about using the sources to achieve an improvement in the church. His dedication to a program of reform led him to become ever more fanatic about his goal. This fanaticism was no doubt encouraged by his reading of Origen and, above all, Augustine, who had advocated the use of force to bring theological deviants, such as the Donatists, back to the truth, which is what in the end Zwingli also advocated. In his early development Zwingli's theology was no doubt deepened and influenced by his bout with death during the plague in 1519. Anyone who has faced death so intimately can be expected to think about the meaning of his life and his faith. Zwingli's poem the *Pestlied* (1519) reflects the impact of his experience.[26]

While at Glarus, Zwingli was not interested merely in theology. True to his background and training he took an active interest in the politics of the Swiss Confederacy and emerged as the advocate of a papal rather than a pro-French alliance. As his poem *The Ox* reveals, he wished the Swiss mercenaries to serve the church when it was threatened rather than the French. His own experience as a military chaplain in Italy in 1513 and 1515, if not also in 1512, caused him to abandon his enthusiasm for the papal alliance and for the practice of selling mercenaries to the foreign powers on a confederacy-wide basis. This abhorence is clear in his poem the *Labyrinth* (1516), which reflects Zwingli's own experience before and during the disastrous battle of Marignano. It is too much to say that Zwingli advocated complete pacifism in response to what he had experienced, but he came to believe that war was just only when hearth and home were attacked. Therefore he maintained that unless attacked by a foreign power, the confederacy should remain neutral.[27]

Zwingli's revulsion against what he had experienced in Italy and his genuine and forcefully expressed fear that the very independence of the confederacy was being threatened by the system of mercenary service was misunderstood in Glarus. He was viewed as an agent of the Holy See, from which he had indeed for some time received a pension, thanks to Cardinal Matthäus Schinner's good offices. In 1516 the French persuaded the entire confederacy to make an alliance with them and a high tide of pro-French bribes swept the confederacy. Zwingli was one of its victims. The pro-French party at Glarus forced his departure from the town but not his resignation as people's priest. To tide him over until he could return to Glarus, Zwingli was appointed people's priest to the population of Einsiedeln. Einsiedeln was a great Ottonian monastic foundation in the canton of Schwyz. The Benedictine monastery was in decline, though its precious Black Madonna remained the object of veneration for thousands of pilgrims. The number of monks had dwindled to two by the time Zwingli arrived. To become a monk at Einsiedeln one had to come from the nobility and few candidates from this class were willing to enter the monastic vocation in this period of European history.[28]

Zwingli busied himself at Einsiedeln teaching the two monks, the people, and the pilgrims the precepts of a program of Bible-centered reform. He also spent some of his spare time in the company of a loose woman in Einsiedeln, with whom he later admitted having had sexual intercourse. He excused his conduct on the grounds that he was not the first man to have slept with her and had hence done the woman no wrong. The fact that his excuse was accepted as valid tells us a great deal about late medieval attitudes toward sexual morality. It also touches indirectly upon a major factor in the lives of many late-medieval clergymen. It was common for them to live in concubinage. In the bishopric of Constance there were fixed fees that had to be paid to the local bishop to obtain a concubinage license. An additional head tax was due to the bishop's chancery for each child born of such a union. Zwingli later appealed to Hugo von Hohenlandenburg, Bishop of Constance, to permit the clergy to marry (*Supplicatio ad Hugonem episcopum Constantiensem 2 July 1522*). He was informed that if the request were granted, the Bishop's treasury would suffer a considerable loss.[29]

By the time he was compelled to go to Einsiedeln, Zwingli had become known as a humanist reformer, as a champion of a pro-papal alliance, and as an effective preacher and religious councillor. It was not long before he had offers of better positions than his post at either Glarus or Einsiedeln. He rejected an offer of the post as people's priest in Winterthur in 1517. Zurich offered him the same job the following year and, despite objections to his unsavory relations with the woman in Einsiedeln, Zwingli was finally chosen people's priest at Zurich toward the end of 1518. The opposition to his appointment came from the cantons at the Zurich Great Church and their supporters, especially in the *Constaffel*, who were pro-French and received French pensions for their recruiting activities. They feared Zwingli as a humanist reformer and the proponent of a pro-papal alliance.[30]

The objections to Zwingli's appointment reflected a power struggle that had been going on in the city for some years. Since the turn of the century there had been growing opposition to the mercenary system, especially in the countryside, though many countrymen profited from it. In the city itself the pro-French orientation of many of the leading patrician families, like the Göldlis, caused considerable friction within the establishment itself, for Zurich had traditionally been the ally of the Habsburgs and the advocate of close, friendly relationships with the papacy. Both the Holy See and the Habsburgs kept resident ambassadors at Zurich and regarded the city as their ally and friend. The confidence of both the papal resident and the representative of the emperor fed the erroneous assumption that the Zwinglian reform was merely a ruse employed to excuse the city's pro-imperial policy in the eyes of the other confederates and to win Zwingli and his allies in the town council time to consolidate their position in the city to the detriment of the pro-French party. In addition, the mayor of Zurich, Markus (Max) Roist, a close ally of Zwingli, was the titular head of the Swiss guard at Rome. His son Kaspar actually led the guard.[31] This close link to the Roman curia also served to protect the early stages of the development of the Reformation from untimely papal countermeasures.

It was possible to bring Zwingli to Zurich because the pro-French party in the *Constaffel*, the patrician society that enjoyed special representation in Zurich's small council, had already begun to lose its influence as a result of the disastrous battle of Marignano (1515). The defeat of the pro-French party was part of a much more complicated process of social amalgamation between the wealthier representatives of the guilds, especially those in the innkeepers' and spice sellers' guilds, and the old families, whose seat of power was the *Constaffel*—the political club of the knights and merchants, men who were in fact not of unduly ancient origins despite their patrician pretensions. This process had been going on since the final decades of the previous century. The economic and political decline of Zurich in the course of the fifteenth century had actually reduced the wealth of the older patrician families and made an amalgamation between the richer guildmasters and the patricians possible. Here it should be noted that the urban context for the Zwinglian reformation was one of economic decline and shrinking economic horizons, not one of economic prosperity, which Brady claims was the case in Strasbourg. For the most part the wealthier guildmasters had largely local economic and political interests. The process of altering the composition of the governing establishment inevitably divided the old establishment itself. The power struggle made possible Zwingli's appointment but it identified him with a faction within the *Constaffel* that was still a minority.[32] The Zwinglian reformation was destined to hasten the process of change and social amalgamation and to lead to the extinction of some of the old patrician families, but it did not begin it. What is important to remember is that from the very beginning Zwingli was identified with a political faction in the governing establishment. The success or failure of his program of reform at Zurich depended upon the ability of his political supporters to consolidate and expand their power in the city.

Zwingli preached his first sermon at the Zurich Great Church on January 1, 1519. In it he made a radical break with past tradition. He ignored the set text for that Sunday and began to preach a series of sermons based upon the Gospel of Matthew. In the course of time he preached through the whole book. This was the basis of his conception of reform; it had to be based upon what the Scripture said. In typical humanist fashion, Zwingli also laced his sermons with direct and pointed references to the moral failings of members of the congregation. Zwingli knew how to speak to his fellow Swiss and, though some found the import of his sermons frightening and distressing, others delighted in them and began to listen and learn.[33]

The question of just when Zwingli achieved the final break with Rome has been given various answers. Some argue that the final break with the old church took place when the Mass was abolished and replaced by an evangelical Communion service on April 13, 1525. Others, including Moeller, claim that it was when the council called the first disputation (January 26–29, 1523). Zwingli justified the validity of this assembly as a Christian gathering, as well as the council's right to call it, on his interpretation of the council as exercising a Christian magistracy. The summoning of the initial disputation marked the creation of the first Protestant synod, which certainly represented a complete break with the old church. However, in the very formal sense, the final break with the old church came when the council made explicit what had already been implicit in the way in which the disputation was summoned—when it recognized that the authority of Scripture was the sole authority by which religious questions and moral principles were to be judged. The formal recognition of the Bible as the normative authority in all religious matters marked a total break with the claims to authority made by the old church. It was then inevitable that the Mass would be abolished, but its abolition was no longer crucial. Too much attention is paid to the significance of the abolition of the Mass in the Zwinglian reformation. At least in Zurich, recognition of biblical authority, not the abolition of the Mass in April 1525, was the crucial issue. The break with Rome occurred as a result of the first Zurich disputation at the end of January 1523.

After the first disputation at Zurich the story of the Reformation in the city centers around Zwingli's relationship with two groups: the pro-French, pro-mercenary party within the *Constaffel*; and the radical element among his own followers. From the beginning he had faced a formidable opposition within the Zurich establishment. The final defeat and destruction of the leaders of the opposition was symbolized by two events: the beheading of Jacob von Grebel in 1526 and the reduction of the *Constaffel's* position within the constitution of the city to that of another guild in June 1529. After Zwingli's death in the second Kappel war, the *Constaffel* was indeed able to regain its special place in the city's constitution,· but not its old political dominance, which had begun to slip well before Zwingli arrived in the city.[34]

Because of his own family background and his experience in Glarus, Zwingli realized from the first that a successful reform of the church at Zurich would require the help of the council. He was the natural ally of the government, even though many within the government did not wish to embrace him as an ally. From the first Zwingli's relations with the Zurich Council were not easy. When he was chosen people's priest, he was the candidate of those who were pro-papal and not opposed to a closer relationship with the emperor. It is remarkable that he was able to bring many of these supporters around to accept the break with Rome, which also meant an end to the city's pro-papal sympathies. Zwingli knew how to persuade and influence those in power, because he understood how they thought about the exercise of authority. Also, he came from a family accustomed to lead others. This fact needs to be kept in mind when considering Zwingli's actual role in the foreign and domestic affairs of the city in the period between the death of Jacob von Grebel in 1526 and the disastrous second Kappel war of October 1531. The Lucerne chronicler and champion of the old faith, Johannes Salat, lived through the period that ended in Zwingli's death at Kappel in 1531 and described Zwingli's achievement at Zurich in terms of the establishment of a theocracy in which Zwingli, the priest, guided the political and religious policies of the city. Salat's interpretation has found many supporters. It has been assumed that Zwingli was a member of the secret council that really governed Zurich from the period just before von Grebel's death to the beginning of the second Kappel war.[35]

Leonhard von Muralt and his students have called this interpretation into question and have presented convincing evidence that Zwingli did not serve as a priestly dictator to the town's council. They have also discovered that in the formal sense no secret council ever existed at Zurich, though the term was used. A small committee or commission of councillors, whose membership constantly changed, considered crucial issues in times of emergency and guided the decisions reached by the two councils about how to deal with these emergencies. Zwingli's role in the decision-making process of the city's government was usually confined to giving advice. He also helped to frame memoranda and diplomacy and occasionally was appointed to sit on the committee when a specific issue was decided. Zwingli's ability to influence Zurich's policy was based upon his private personal relationship with those who governed, as well as on the impact of his immensely persuasive preaching. It never depended upon a formal position within the structure of the city's government.[36]

With the agreement of the Zurich council Zwingli did not take part in the Baden disputation in 1526, because the council feared for his life. At Baden he might well have been condemned by the Catholic majority of the confederates, and, despite the promise of immunity from punishment offered him, if he took part in the debate he ran the risk of being burned as a heretic. In his recent biography of Zwingli, G. R. Potter has supported Köhler's argument that it would have been better for Zwingli if he had gone to Baden and met a martyr's death. Potter believes that the example of martyrdom would have aided the spread of Zwingli's teaching. He feels that after Baden Zwingli became fatally involved in Zurich's foreign and domestic affairs and that this involvement led to the disastrous second Kappel war, which ended the spread of the Zwinglian Reformation in Switzerland.[37] Zwingli would not have agreed. His basic conception of Christian society naturally involved the reform movement in the realm of politics. Zwingli framed two plans of campaign for Zurich (*Plan zu einem*

Feldzug, between July 1, 1524, and January 4, 1525, and the *Ratschlag über den Krieg,* between May 25 and 29, 1529) and dedicated his later theological works to various princes in the hope of attracting them to an anti-Habsburg alliance in defense of the reform movement. He plotted the secularization of the extensive territories of the Abbey of St. Gall. He was an enthusiastic champion of an alliance with the Landgrave Philip of Hesse and the Lutheran princes. An alliance with Philip was made, but a union with the German princes failed, because Zwingli and Luther were not able to agree on the interpretation of the Lord's Supper. Zwingli favored the introduction of congregational autonomy to ensure the spread of the Reformation in the areas jointly governed by the confederates (which was in fact a violation of the terms of the agreements framed to permit the various cantons to cooperate in ruling these regions). He did not favor the compromise policy of blockading the forest cantons until they permitted the free preaching of the Reformation in their territories. He favored a war. His policy found no great favor with the majority of the Zurich Council and helped to alienate Bern, Zurich's most important ally. Many members of the Zurich Council understood better than did Zwingli the fact that, although Zwingli had helped win Bern to the Reformation at the Bern disputation in 1528, Bern's adherence to the cause of the Reformation did not change her interest in westward expansion and in a continuation of the French alliance. Zwingli's political naiveté with respect to Bern's foreign policy and the death of his ally at Bern, Nikolaus Manuel, who himself had always had doubts about many of Zwingli's foreign policy ambitions, led to his political isolation at Zurich in the months before the disaster at Kappel.[38]

Zurich's defeat and the reformer's death were probably not necessary. The peaceful conclusion of the first Kappel war, which had guaranteed the Zwinglian cantons the freedom to practice their own religion as well as the chance to extend the influence of their religion into the territories jointly administered by the confederacy, should have been sufficient to satisfy the ambitions of Zwingli and his followers, but it was not. True to their own Augustinian view of truth, they desired to spread that truth into the heartlands of the old confederacy, the forest cantons. Among others things, their program of reform called for the end of the practice of sending men to fight abroad for hire. This would have meant an economic disaster for the overpopulated forest cantons, whose cow-based, mountain-farm economy was unable to absorb its own surplus manpower. At the same time, the farm economy was unable to produce enough income to pay for the import of grain, which the mountain farmers needed to avoid starvation. The system of mercenary service provided the foreign exchange necessary to keep the population of the forest cantons from starving. This fact plus the traditional nature of rural life made the original cantons a less fertile field or the proclamation of the Zwinglian reformation than the confederacy's urban cantons.

The economic blockade decided upon by the urban cantons after the first peace of Kappel as a means of persuading the forest cantons to open their parishes to the preaching of the new Gospel served to strengthen the Swiss Catholic alliance with Austria (*Christliche Vereinigung*) and to drive them into the field against the Zwinglians. The Catholic military campaign came just as the tensions between Bern, the major military power of the Zwinglian alliance system, and Zurich were at their height. It also caught Zurich at a time when she was least prepared to wage war. Zwingli's campaign against the *Pensionenherren* had disrupted the command structure of the canton's defense forces. Many of the officers who marched to Kappel were inexperienced and did not enjoy the trust of their men. A great many militiamen preferred to stay at home and never arrived for the muster. In the disaster that followed, Zwingli died fighting in the second rank. His body was later identified by the Catholics, who drew and quartered it before burning. The story that his heart remained untouched in the ashes of the fire is hagiography.[40] The defeat of the Zwinglians in the second war put an end to the spread of the Reformation in German Switzerland. The Zwinglian cantons were compelled to be content with a necessary process of inner consolidation rather than external religious expansion. The Catholic cantons offered moderate peace terms because they were now able to preserve their faith and had no wish to destroy the Swiss Confederacy. Their military supremacy in the confederacy lasted until the early eighteenth century. Bern was also now free to continue her westward expansion, which opened the way for the conquest of Vaud (1536) and brought Bernese troops to the borders of the territory of Geneva—a fact destined to influence directly the course of the Reformation.[41]

Zwingli's dealings with the Anabaptists, now called the *Täufer*, were also far from successful and in recent years have been the subject of intensive research. The father of this mass of modern research and the guide and councillor to scholars who have taken radically different positions on the origin of the Täufer movement at Zurich was the late Fritz Blanke.

Modern Mennonite scholars, led by H. S. Bender and John H. Yoder, are eager to demonstrate that Zwingli originally advocated the establishment of a "free church" at Zurich and then in the autumn of 1523 compromised his position and made a deal with the magistrates. Zwingli's compromise led to the establishment of a state church, which persecuted some of Zwingli's former friends and followers who had formed themselves into a believers' church at Zollikon on January 21, 1525, and practiced believer's baptism. Their attempt to adhere to Zwingli's original teachings doomed them to persecution, exile, and death. The Zurich authorities executed the first Täufer in 1527, not for heresy but for sedition.[42]

Other scholars, including Martin Haas, J. F. Gerherd Goeters, James M. Stayer, and Robert C. Walton, have called this interpretation in question. Haas demonstrated just how much more subversive of public order, that is how seditious, the *Täufer* in fact were, a point modern Mennonite historians are unwilling to admit. Goeters has examined carefully the development of the Grebel circle among Zwingli's followers and concluded that the basis for the break that developed over the question of tithes was clear during the second disputation. When Zwingli accepted the council's refusal to abolish the Mass immediately, both at the end of the second Zurich disputation (October 29–31, 1523) and again when the issue was raised in December 13–19, 1523, the final break took place. Goeters notes that we do not know why adult baptism was pushed to the fore in the final development of the *Täufer* movement up to January 1525. He also observes that Grebel did not seem to have a realistic understanding of what the role of the Zurich Council had to be in any matter of church reform. When the *Täufer* challenged the payment of tithes for the support of the clergy, they challenged the whole basis for civic control over the church, which was a major reason the council had come to support the Zwinglian reformation. Stayer has added appreciably to our understanding of the issues involved in the split between Zwingli and his more radical followers by demonstrating that in the beginning the *Täufer* were not at all opposed to the use of the sword to gain their ends. He has also shown that the *Täufer* played a much more active role in stirring up trouble in canton Zurich during the peasant's unrest than has heretofore been realized. Walton maintains that Zwingli never was the adherent of a separate or free church; from the beginning of his career Zwingli believed in a unified *res publica christiana* and assumed the corporate nature of the city's constitution when speaking of the visible church. He notes that the sermon *On the Free Choice of Foods*, preached after the Lenten fast violations in the spring of 1522, contains warnings to his own enthusiastic followers about the harm that incautious individuals can do to those who are not yet ready for the meat of the Gospel. Walton stresses the extent to which the council permitted the form of the Mass to be altered in response to fresh agitation against the Mass in December 1523. He maintains that throughout his career Zwingli had every reason to work with, not against, the Zurich Council. Goeters' observation that Zwingli sometimes used his own more enthusiastic followers to push the council toward further action merely illustrates how effectively Zwingli was able to work through the council to achieve his goal.[43]

No assessment of Zwingli's significance is possible without some discussion of his theology, but limited space permits only a brief sketch to be presented. Zwingli's career was marred both by the schism among his followers, which led to the rise of a politically and theologically divisive movement, Anabaptism, in canton Zurich, and by the disastrous failure of his hopes to convert the entire confederacy, by force if necessary. As a theologian Zwingli was more successful. He left behind him a theology that was a unique amalgam of biblical, patristic, and scholastic elements.[44] His successor, Bullinger, completed the work that Zwingli had begun and, thanks to his great talents as an international churchman and theologian, guaranteed the survival of the Zwinglian theology as an essential component of what became the international reformed tradition. Zwingli has rightly been called Calvin's direct predecessor.[45]

The best guide to the scope and nature of Zwingli's theology can be found in the major theological treatises that he left behind. They include: *The Defense of the Sixty-Seven Articles* of July 1523 *(Auslegung der Gründe der Schlussreden)*; the *Commentary on True and False Religion (De vera et falsa religione commentarius)* of May 1525, which was dedicated to Francis I of France; *the Confession of Faith (Fidei Ratio)*, sent to the Emperor Charles and the Diet of Augsburg in 1530; and the *Explanation of the Christian Faith (Fidei Christianae Expositio)*, dedicated to Francis I in July 1531.

Other works of major importance include *De Providentia Dei* of August 30, 1530, which bore a dedication to Philip, Landgrave of Hesse, and the *Sermon Der Hirt* (March 24, 1524) first preached on October 28 during the second disputation, in which Zwingli clarified the pastor's function. Zwingli expanded this theme further in his sermon *Von dem Predigtamt* of 1525. His conception of the pastor's role was basic to his idea of the government of a Christian society and the maintenance of church discipline. Zwingli granted the control of excommunication to the magistracy and left the noncoercive function of admonishing the miscreant to the pastor.[46] The pastor was also the flock's biblical instructor. This idea was fundamental to the establishment of the biblical lectures, the *Prophezei*, that is, the "prophesying" at Zurich (1525), which played a major role in providing theological education both to the theological students at the *Carolinum* and later to the city's laity. In time the "prophesying" became a form of instruction that played an important role in the spread of the "reformed" Reformation. Zwingli insisted that all the clergy were bishops and conceived of their function as that of prophetic shepherds.[47] His emphasis upon the shepherd's role as prophet increased after 1528 when he began to expound the prophetic books of the Old Testament in the "prophesying." The books were also translated into German.[48] His understanding of the nature and function of the prophet's office followed logically from his doctrine of the Holy Spirit and the distinction between letter and spirit that was basic to his theology. Zwingli warned that the prophet should never imagine that his words could influence the congregation. When the prophet's preaching was successful, it was because God had blown *(inblasen)* his message into the hearts of the people. The shepherd's words were God's vehicle of communication with men, but they depended upon God's spirit for their effect.[49] The one thing that Zwingli forbade the prophet was the right to participate in the affairs of government: "according to Scripture, it is for-

bidden for the clergy to exercise any authority which either conflicts with
that of the secular arm or is separated from that which the government
possesses, for the exercise of such authority causes disunity." He denied
that Christ had given any of the apostles the power of the keys in Matthew
16:18–19, upon which they could base a claim to secular authority. The
clergy were not even to rule over their congregations but rather were to set
an example for their sheep by their conduct.[50] The prophet served as a
Spartan ephor to prevent, through his preaching, the government and
indeed the whole society from going astray. If his warnings were heeded,
the society would prosper. If they were not, Zwingli believed that the fate
of Sodom and Gomorrah would be repeated. This belief was basic to his
concept of God's eternal covenant, which played a significant role in his
theology, especially his conception of the sacraments. Zwingli applied the
covenant idea to Zurich because it was a Christian city-state.[51] Zwingli's
understanding of the shepherd's role provided future generations of reformed ministers with the model of an educated, morally upright, and
fearless preacher who dedicated his life to proclaiming the Gospel to the
world.

Zwingli viewed the exposition of God's word by the prophet as central to
the religious life of the city. The emphasis upon the preaching of the Word
carried with it an incipient reductionism, which was an Erasmian inheritance and had a direct effect upon his doctrine of the sacraments and of
the church. However, before these questions can be considered it is necessary to understand what Zwingli's doctrine of Scripture was.

Zwingli's conception of biblical authority, his understanding of the role
of the Holy Spirit in leading men to accept the authority of the Bible, and
his view of the relationship among the Scripture, the Holy Spirit, and the
church formed the basis for his theology. He began the *Defense of the Sixty-
Seven Articles* with a discussion of the authority of Scripture, a topic with
which Zwingli had already dealt in his sermon "On the Clarity and Assurance of the Word of God" in September 1522. Zwingli explained that the
Gospel did not depend upon the authority of the church or a church
council for its validation. The ability to understand and to believe God's
word came from God himself, who alone could assure men of the Scripture's authority.[52] In discussing this point he also cited Paul (Romans 8:5) to
demonstrate that a man who is dominated by his flesh and not by his spirit
cannot receive the assurance of the Scripture's authority. The Neoplatonic
dichotomy of spirit and flesh was basic to Zwingli's anthropology. It was
also essential to another distinction that Zwingli frequently made in dealing with the problem of reform: the word of man (i.e., of the flesh) and that
of the spirit (i.e., of God) were basically opposed to each other. The old
church was in error because it was subject to the word of man and not that
of God; therefore it could not be moved by the spirit. The juxtaposing of
human and divine authority in this way was one of the distinguishing

characteristics of Zwingli's theology.[53] Zwingli maintained that God alone brought men to the knowledge of Christ. For Zwingli the Bible was self-authenticating because it depended upon God's authority. The vehicle by which God taught man and authenticated the Bible was the Holy Spirit: "Mark you well: The Holy Spirit will teach you everything . . . he will teach us what we should know of God. . . . Listen here! God himself writes his law so clearly in the hearts of men that no one may learn such things from men. . . . God enlightens and draws the heart to himself."[54] Zwingli's conclusion was obvious: all those who know Christ have been instructed by God. Paul, he continued, came to know the Gospel not from any human sources but rather from "the revelation of Jesus Christ" (Galatians 1:12). The apostles were not commissioned to teach the Gospel by a church council; they were filled with the Holy Ghost at Pentecost.[55] This passage reveals the central role that the Holy Spirit played not merely in moving the hearts of individuals during a sermon but in Zwingli's conception of worship and of the government of a Christian society. All depend upon the unifying action of the Holy Spirit.[56] The third person of the Trinity really served as the instrument by which God asserted his sovereignty on earth and also assured men of hope in the Gospel of Christ. Without the Holy Spirit no visible, earthly institution could function properly.

Any standard summary of the main themes of reformed theology begins with the assertion that reformed theologians were particularly concerned to assert and defend the absolute sovereignty of God. Zwingli was no exception. His supralapsarian doctrine of predestination, as well as his conception of divine foreknowledge reflect this fact. They also reflect how heavily he drew upon Thomas Aquinas (*Summa*, Part 1, question 23) to develop his idea of God's sovereignty.[57] For Zwingli God was the source of all being and was by nature the highest good both in essence (*esse*) and action (*actio*). He had created the world *ex nihilo*. The being and goodness that men possess was derived from God; only God could possess these characteristics *de esse*. Men were therefore dependent upon God for their virtue. Unlike Luther, Zwingli's God was not a hidden God: "For God is near to us, he is not a God who is far away from us." The most famous example of Zwingli's assertion of God's sovereignty can be found in his discussion of the *Blessedness of Elect Heathen (Über die Seligkeit der auserwählten Heiden)*. Here Zwingli argued that God was able in Christ to elect some pagans to eternal blessedness. His sovereignty knew no bounds.[58] This argument is a unique mixture of classical and Christian themes.

Both the doctrine of the sacraments and Zwingli's doctrine of the church served to demonstrate the basic theme of God's sovereignty. Though he established the sacraments and the church as vehicles of communication with men, God was in no way bound to them and, when he so willed, could work outside of them. It was for this reason that Zwingli, certainly by 1524, rejected transubstantiation; and later could not accept Luther's doctrine of consubstantiation; both intepretations limited God's sovereignty.

The sacraments, Baptism and the Lord's Supper, were the successors to circumcision and the feast of the Passover in the Old Testament, and guaranteed the true continuity of God's promise to Abraham. The old signs of Israel's unity had been transformed in Christ. Baptism represented a pledge that one will be a soldier of Christ and follow his commands; participation in the Lord's Supper demonstrated belief in Christ's death and united those who shared this belief. Without the working of the Holy Spirit both were bare signs. It is false to say that Zwingli's doctrine of the sacrament of the Lord's Supper was mere memorialism. As Augustine had said, the sacraments were signs of the "Holy Things." For Zwingli the Lord's Supper was a public thanksgiving for Christ's gift of reconciliation. True to the teaching of Scotus, Zwingli asserted that Christ was physically seated on the right hand of God in Heaven. Only his spirit could be present at the sacrament. The spirit of Christ was present in the hearts of those who believed and they were spiritually strengthened as a result of their participation. What was very important for Zwingli was the common character of the Supper. Those gathered at the table were united in the Holy Spirit and became the true body of Christ.[59] The moving force in his doctrine of the sacraments was the Holy Spirit.

Zwingli later referred to the sacraments as signs of the elect. He could also have said that they were badges of citizenship. Early in his career he had asserted that the term *church* could be employed to refer to all those who were elect. This church was the true church known only to God. The word *church* could also refer to an individual church, such as that of Lyon or Zurich. The members of this church were a mixed body, as Israel had been. It contained both the elect and the reprobate. In the *Fidei Ratio* he argued that visible churches such as the church at Zurich consisted of all those who confessed Christ with their mouths. Only God knew how many also confessed Christ in their hearts. Anticipating Calvin's "judgement of charity," Zwingli said that by a "judgement of men" all the members of the church could be considered elect if they adhered to an external standard of conduct.[60] The standard of conduct was that of human righteousness. This was the standard that God gave to men in the Ten Commandments, one that a magistracy could enforce. It was based on men's essential moral weakness. The standard of human righteousness was constantly challenged by the norms of divine righteousness found in Scripture, which always reminded men that God required more of them. The theme was again one that Zwingli derived from Thomas Aquinas. Zwingli delivered his sermon on *Divine and Human Righteousness (Von der göttlichen und menschlichen Gerechtigkeit)* in June 1523 at the height of the tithe agitation and then printed it at the end of July. It provides the basis for our understanding of how Zwingli believed the magistrate and the pastor should function in this world and what their respective norms should be. It also helps to explain why Zwingli identified the political structure of the community with the visible church, the *corpus permixtum* of saved and damned in this world.[61] Zwingli's letter to Ambrosius Blarer at Constance, written on May 4, 1528, is another vital piece of theological literature. In it Zwingli openly identifies the visible church with the political structure of the Zurich commonwealth. The final consequences of this identification can be found at the conclusion of his introduction to Jeremiah written in March 1531, in which he states that when the prophet and the magistrate cooperate, one can say that "the Christian man is nothing else but a faithful and good citizen and the Christian city nothing other than the Christian church."[62]

Zwingli's theology fitted the context of a city-state like Zurich very well. It was a theology that drew freely from various traditions to develop a set of doctrines able to support and justify the corporate constitution of the city, and the city oligarchy's right to govern all aspects of human life in their society with the advice of the pastor and the guidance of God's spirit. The *Morality Ordinance (Sittenmandat)* of 1530 was the logical consequence of Zwingli's conception of Christian society, as was the second battle of Kappel.

NOTES

1. "Als ich nun im 1519. jar ze Zürich anhub ze predgen . . . Zů anfang des selben jares . . . hatt niemans by und von dem Luter ützid gewüsset, ußgenommen, das vom dem ablas etwas ußggangen was von im, das mich wenig leret;" *Huldreich Zwinglis sämtliche Werke*, ed. Emil Egli and Georg Finsler (Leipzig: M. Heinsius, 1908), 2:145, 21–28; hereafter cited as Z. See also Arthur Rich, *Die Anfänge der Theologie Huldrych Zwinglis* (Zürich: Zwingli Verlag, 1949), 77ff., 93ff.

2. George Potter, *Zwingli* (Cambridge: Cambridge University Press, 1978), 292.

3. Bernd Moeller, *Reichsstadt und Reformation*, No. 180, "Schriften des Vereins für Reformationsgeschichte" (Gütersloh: Gütersloher Verlagshaus Gerd Mohn, 1962). Steven E. Ozment, *The Reformation in the Cities. The Appeal of Protestantism to Sixteenth-Century Germany and Switzerland* (New Haven and London: Yale University Press, 1975). The English edition of Moeller's work is *Imperial Cities and the Reformation: Three Essays*, ed. and trans. H. C. Erik Midelfort and Mark U. Edwards, Jr. (Philadelphia: Fortress Press, 1972). A. G. Dickens, *The German Nation and Martin Luther* ("an urban event") (London: Edward Arnold, 1974), 180, 182, 184, 187, 190, 192, 195, 189, 225; cf. A. G. Dickens, "Intellectual and Social Forces in the German Reformation," *The Urban Classes, The Nobility and the Reformation: Studies on the Social History of the Reformation in England and Germany*, vol. 5, Publications of the German Historical Institute (London, Stuttgart: Ernst Klett Verlag, 1979), 19, 22.

4. Thomas A. Brady, *Ruling Class: Regime and Reformation at Strasbourg. 1520–1555.* vol. 22, *Studies in Medieval and Reformation Thought* (Leiden: Brill, 1978), 3ff., 8–15, 19ff., 84–85, 93–94, 139–140, 237ff., 243ff., 270–72, 291–95, as cited in n. 3. See also, e.g., Rublack's study on the

Reformation in Constance, *Die Einführung der Reformation in Konstanz von den Anfängen bis zum Abschluß*, No. 27, Veröffentlichung des Vereins für KG in der evangelischen Landeskirche in Baden (Gütersloh-Karlsruhe, 1971), and more recently, Ingrid Bátori, *Städtische Gesellschaft and Reformation*, vol. 12, *Spätmittelalter und frühe Neuzeit. Tübinger Beiträge zur Geschichtsforschung* by Josef Engel and Ernst Walter Zeeden (Stuttgart: Ernst Klett, 1980). It is, however, most unfortunate that Brady's basic definition of Zwinglianism is derived from Norman Birnbaum, who knows very little about theology and even less about Zwingli's. Birnbaum's social analysis of the function that the Reformation had at Zurich is simply wrong. Brady, 239. Cf. R. C. Walton, *Zwingli's Theocracy* (Toronto: University of Toronto Press, 1967), 53–54 (n. 11); idem, "The Institutionalization of the Reformation at Zürich," *Zwingliana* 13/2 (1972): 506–8. Brady identifies the use of excommunication by the church as a characteristic of Zwinglianism. As far as Bucer and Oecolampadius are concerned, he may be right. Zwingli did not share this view. Brady, 270–72. Cf. Walton, "The Institutionalization, 498ff., 502–4, 505, 508–14.

5. Moeller, *Reichsstadt und Reformation*, 10ff., 25–26, 29ff., 38–40, 52, 56–58, 61–62, 66–67, 76.

6. Bernd Moeller, "Zwingli's Disputationen, Studien zu den Anfängen der Kirchenbildung und des Synodalwesens im Protestantismus," 2 pts., *Zeitschrift der Savigny-Stiftung für Rechtsgeschichte*, vols. 87, 91; *Kanonistische Abteilung*, 56, 60 (1970, 1974): 275–324, 214–364. Moeller, "Zwingli's Disputationen," 1:306, 309–12, 313–15, 319–23; 2:349ff., 356, 358–61, 362–64.

7. Marcia Colish, "The Idea of Liberty in Machiavelli," *Journal of the History of Ideas*, 32 (1971): 327–28, 330, 334–35; see also Robert C. Walton, "The Institutionalization of the Reformation at Zurich," *Zwingliana* 13, no. 8 (1972): 500–501; idem, "The Reformation in the Cities: Another Look," *Occasional Papers of the American Society for Reformation Research*, 1:142–143.

8. Brady, 93–95, 126–29, 139–40, 291.

9. Brady, 108. See Walton's definition of the citizen in "The Institutionalization of the Reformation at Zürich," *Zwingliana* 13, no. 8 (1972): 500–505, and Dickens, *The German Nation*, 181–82, 184, 187–89, 192, 194, 195.

10. Oswald Myconius, *Vom Leben und Sterben Huldrych Zwinglis. Das älteste Lebensbild Zwinglis*, ed. Ernst Gerhard Rüsch, No. 50 of *Mitteilungen zur Vaterländischen Geschichte* (St. Gallen: Fehr'sche Buchhandlung, 1979), 37. G. R. Potter, *Zwingli* (Cambridge: Cambridge University Press, 1976), 4–7. Martin Haas, *Zwingli und seine Zeit. Leben und Werk des Zürcher Reformators*, 2d rev. ed. (Zürich: TVZ Verlag, 1976), 11–13, 15–17. Eduard Kobelt asserts that for Zwingli the confederacy *(die Eidgenossenschaft)* was his Fatherland *(Vaterland)*, i.e., the larger regional grouping that provided a history for and gave protection to the individual. The Toggenburg was his home *(Heimat)*, the place that he knew best and in which he had spent his youth. His home received its history and protection from the confederacy. Both individually and collectively, the individual and his *Heimat* were subordinated to and received meaning from a larger community, in this case the confederacy. Eduard Jacob Kobelt, *Die Bedeutung der Eidgenossenschaft für Huldrych Zwingli* (Zürich: Buchdruckerei Leemann AG, 1970), 5–8. Haas, 208ff.; Walther Köhler, *Huldrych Zwingli* (Stuttgart: K. F. Koehler Verlag, 1950), 14–17; Haas, *Zwingli*, 21.

11. The Bullingers came from a class of very wealthy *Herrenbauern* who associated and hunted with the aristocracy and played a crucial role in the local government of the Aargau. In using the term *Herrenbäuer* I have employed Jean-Jacques Siegrist's definition. According to Siegrist the *Herrenbauern* were largely descendants of the medieval *Altfreien*. A *Herrenbauer* had enough land and income to live an "idle life." He generally also possessed the right to hunt, a right usually denied to the peasantry. Siegrist observes that very often the *Herrenbauer* were related to the urban upper classes. It was common for a *Herrenbauer* to move to the city when he had achieved a solid level of prosperity but he was often not welcome there. The urban oligarchies were slow to welcome well-to-do outsiders even if they were distant relatives. In the countryside the *Herrenbauern* provided the jurors *(Gerichtssassen)*, the local officials *(Amtsleute)*, and assistant bailiffs *(Untervögte)* who served in the local government. The function of these local officials was particularly important. As in the case of Zwingli's father and

grandfather, they were generally elected officials and served a double function: they governed and were part of the ruling establishment, but at the same time they also represented the interests, or better, expressed the opinion of the governed, the *Untertanen*. They were the link between the authority that came from above and that which came from below as a result of the development of the *Dorfgemeinde*. See Jean-Jacques Siegrist, *Rupperswil. Ein aargausches Bauerndorf im Mittelalter und in der früheren Neuzeit*, 3 vols. (Acrau: Sauerländer AG, 1971), 1:119–21, 91ff., 96, 122–28, 136–37, 185–96. The same structure of local government can be found in the upper German territories of the empire. Peter Blickle, *Landschaften im Alten Reich. Die staatliche Funktion des gemeinen Mannes in Oberdeutschland* (Munich: C. H. Beck, 1973), 449–61. The opinions expressed by the local officials did not bind the *Vogt* (bailiff) or the government he represented, but they were heeded. The function of the *Herrenbauer* illustrates well the corporate nature of late medieval government as well as the extent to which local participation and autonomy were practiced. Bader notes the autonomous origin of most medieval *Dorfgemeinden* (village assemblies). *Studien zur Rechtsgeschichte des mittelalterlichen Dorfes, Dorfgenossenschaft und Dorfgemeinde*, 2 pts. (Weimar: Böhlaus Nachfolger, 1957, 1962), pt. 1:23, 45ff.; pt. 2, 34–37, 60–62, 68–69, 84–85, 96–101, 102ff., 114, 266–68 (the *Dorfgemeinde* as a *Genossenschaft*). Zwingli's entire conception of the independence and right of the church congregation to decide for or against the Reformation, especially in the areas governed jointly by the confederacy, cannot be separated from the nature and function of the largely independent *Dorfgemeinde*, which Zwingli understood all too well. One major cause of peasant unrest that led to the peasants' war was the fact that new forms of central administration were circumscribing the independence of the village assemblies. Hans Rudolph Lavater, "Bauernkrieg 1825—eine Betrachtung," *Reformatio* 24 (1975): 474–76.

12. For the wealth of the Zwinglis, see Walther Köhler, *Huldrych Zwingli*, 7; Oskar Farner, *Huldrych Zwingli*, 4 vols. (Zürich: Zwingli Verlag, 1943–1950), 1:33ff., 43ff., 50–51. Heinrich Bullinger estimated his family's fortune at 1400£ (700 Gulden) in 1527. Young Heinrich's mother, Anna Wiederkehr, who lived in concubinage with Heinrich Bullinger, Sr., was the daughter of a wealthy Bremgarten miller and town councillor. The Bullingers were landowners who had given Bremgarten its richest prebends, which were traditionally held by members of the family. Millers and innkeepers were usually the rural bankers because they had surplus capital. The Bullingers' fortune was large enough for them to be classified as rich. *Heinrich Bullinger Werke*, pt. 2, *Briefwechsel*, ed. Fritz Büsser (Zürich: Theologischer Verlag, 1973), 134–35, n. 176. Otto Sigg, "Bevölkerungs-, agrarund sozialgeschichtliche Probleme des 16. Jahrhunderts am Beispiel der Zürcher Landschaft," *Schweizer Zeitschrift für Geschichte*, (1974), 77–58, 71–72. W. Schnyder, "Soziale Schichtung und Grundlagen der Vermögensbildung in den spätmittelalterlichen Städten der Eidgenossenschaft," *Festschrift für Karl Schib* (Thayngen, 1968); Robert C. Walton, "Heinrich Bullinger, Repräsentant der reichen Bauern und seine Beziehungen zur städtischen Oligarchie," *Reform, Reformation, Revolution* (Leipzig: Karl-Marx Universität, 1980), 134–35.

13. Haas, *Zwingli*, 12.

14. M. Haas, "Täufertum und Revolution," *Festgabe Leonhard von Muralt* (Zürich: Berichthaus, 1970), 291, 293–95.

15. The election had to be confirmed by the Abbot of St. Gall and was usually not for life; the incumbents were often changed, though they all came from the same class. See Blickle, *Landschaften*, 454–55, 461. That Zwingli's father succeeded his grandfather as Wildhaus's *Ammann* is a tribute to their skill and popularity as local magistrates.

16. Siegfried Bader, *Das Mittelalterliche Dorf als Friedens-und Rechtsbereich* (Graz-Wien-Köln: Hermann Böhlaus Nachf, 1967), 2 vols., pt. 2:280–91.

17. For example, see Heinrich Büttner, "Anfänge des Walserrechtes im Wallis," *Das Problem der Freiheit in der deutschen und schweizerischen Geschichte*, vol. 2, Vorträge und Forschungen (Darmstadt: Wissenschaftliche Buchgesellschaft, 1963), 89–102. The village assemblies in the Toggenburg were also part of the larger corporate entity formed by the territory *(Land)* and

people *(Volk)* of the country, which had its own law, though the county was technically the possession of the Abbot of St. Gall. The abbot and the people were subordinate to and bound together by the same law, the *Landrecht.* See Kobelt, 17. Otto Brunner gives the following definition, which Kobelt cites only in part: ". . . eine Genossenschaft landbebauender und landbeherrschender Leute, es ist eine Rechts-und Friedensgemeinschaft, die Grundzüge noch lange bewahrt, die auf die germanische Frühzeit zurückweisen. Landrecht und Landfriede sind ihre Wesenselemente." Otto Brunner, *Land und Herrschaft* (Darmstadt: Wissenschaftliche Buchgesellschaft, 1970), 236–37.

18. Hans Conrad Peyer, *Verfassungsgeschichte der alten Schweiz* (Zürich: Schulthess Polygraphischer Verlag, 1978), 36ff., 39ff., 43–44, 45.

19. Peyer, 48–55: Brady's definition of Swiss or Zwinglian Republicanism does not fit Switzerland. See Brady, 270–72, 291ff.

20. Myconius, *Vom Leben,* 37–39; O. Farner, *Huldrych Zwingli,* 1:160–75; Haas, *Zwingli,* 18–21.

21. Myconius, *Vom Leben,* 39–41; O. Farner, 1:175ff., 178–84, 196ff., 205ff., 210–26; Haas, *Zwingli,* 23–33. For a comparison of Luther and Zwingli's use of the *via moderna* and *via antiqua* respectively, see Walther Köhler, *Zwingli und Luther. Ihr Streit über das Abendmahl nach seinen politischen und religiösen Beziehungen,* vols. 6 and 7, *Quellen und Forschungen zur Reformationsgeschichte* (Leipzig and Gütersloh: Vermittlungsverlag von M. Heinsius Nachfolger Eger and Sivers, C. Bertelsmann Verlag, 1924, 1953), 2:137–38. For some interesting remarks on the importance of the role of the *via antiqua* in the urban Reformation, see Heiko A. Oberman, *Werden und Wertung der Reformation* (Tübingen: J. C. B. Mohr, 1977), 362ff.

22. Myconius, *Vom Leben,* 41–45; O. Farner, 2:45–52, 107ff., 119–24, 127–39, 144 (here Farner stresses the importance of Erasmus's poem on the beginning of Zwingli's Gospel preaching), 152–64, 164ff.

23. See n. 20; Z, 1:256, 14. "Ich hab, vor und ee dheim mensch in unserer gegne ütz von des Luters namen gewüßt hab, angehebt das evangelion Christi ze predgen im jar 1516. . . ." Z, 2:144–45. Potter, 39–40.

24. Gottfried Locher, *Die Zwinglische Reformation im Rahmen der Europäischen Kirchengeschichte* (Göttingen and Zürich: Vandenhoeck & Ruprecht, 1979), 42–54; see especially the summary of the literature Locher used on p. 42; for Locher's summary of Rich, see 88ff. Arthur Rich, *Die Anfänge der Theologie Huldrych Zwinglis* (Zürich: Zwingli Verlag, 1949), 10ff., 21ff., 29ff., 36–37, 38, 40–45, 93–95, 96ff., 119ff., 153–55, 156–60, 170–71; see also Joachim Rogge, *Zwingli und Erasmus* (Berlin: Evangelische Verlagsanstalt, 1962, 25–26. For a typical example of the results of the confused European approach, see Wilhelm H. Neuser, *Die Reformatorische Wende bei Zwingli* (Neukirchen-Vluyn: Neukirchener Verlag, 1977); see also Ulrich Gäbler, "Huldrych Zwinglis Reformatorische Wende," *Zeitschrift für Kirchengeschichte* 89 (1978): 120–35.

25. Paul O. Kristeller, "Studies on Renaissance Humanism," *Studies in the Renaissance* 9 (1962): 10, 14–16, 17, 18–23. For a summary of Kristeller's significance, see Heiko A. Oberman, "Quoscunque tulit foecunda vetustas," *Itinerarium Italicorum. The Profile of the Italian Renaissance in the Mirror of its European Transformations,* ed., Heiko A. Oberman and Thomas A. Brady, vol. 14 of *Studies in Medieval and Reformation Thought* (Leiden: E. V. Brill, 1975), esp. xi–xii, xiv, xxvii; P. O. Kristeller, *Renaissance Thought,* 2 vols., (New York: Harper and Row, 1961, 1965), 2:70, 77–79; Charles Trinkaus, *In Our Own Image and Likeness: Humanity and Divinity in Italian Humanist Thought,* 2 vols. (Chicago, 1970).

26. Rich, 112ff.; Locher, *Die Zwinglische Reformation,* 91–92.

27. Myconius, *Vom Leben,* 43, 45; O. Farner, 2:93, 96ff., 102–7; Potter, 36–40; Haas, *Huldrych Zwingli,* 42–45, 57–59; Rogge notes clearly the limits of Zwingli's pacifism and demonstrates his willingness to defend the Reformation with force. Rogge, 44, 51; R. C. Walton, *Zwingli's Theocracy* (Toronto: University of Toronto, 1967), 32–34.

28. Myconius, *Vom Leben,* 45–47; Haas, 57–60.

29. Myconius, *Vom Leben,* 47; O. Farner, 2:298–306; Potter, 45–46; Haas, 74; Walton, 106–14;

See Z, 1:225, 6 for the exact amounts of the concubinage fees.

30. Haas, 60; Theodor Pestalozzi, *Die Gegner Zwinglis am Großmünsterstift in Zürich, Der erste Teil einer Arbeit über die katholische Opposition gegen Zwingli in Stadt und Landschaft Zürich 1519–1531* (Zürich: Gebr. Leemann & Co., 1918), 41–44, 48, 61–62. Rudolf Pfister, *Kirchengeschichte der Schweiz,* 2 vols. (Zürich: Theologischer Verlag, 1974), 2:60–61.

31. Haas, 69–72; for an example of the erroneous conclusions reached by imperial observers: "Placuit intelligere quod Zurichenseg perserverent boni Papales . . . 24 October 1522. Haus, Hof-und Staatsarchiv, Wien Schweiz 7/137, Ka 100/1921.

32. Haas, 71; Walton, "The Reformation in the Cities/Another Look" *OPASRR,* 1:144–46; Hans Morf, *Zunftverfassung und Obrigkeit in Zürich von Waldmann bis Zwingli* (Zürich: Leemann Ag, 1969) 10–15, esp. 14, 26–27, 28–32, 38ff., 40–42, 75–76. Hans Nabholz, "Die soziale Schichtung der Bevölkerung der Stadt Zürich bis zur Reformation," *Festgabe für Max Huber* (Zürich: Berichthaus, 1934), 10–12, 19–22; Werner Schnyder, "Soziale Schichtung und Grundlagen der Vermögensbildung in den spät-mittelalterlichen Städten der Eidgenossenschaft," *Festschrift für Karl Schib* (Thaynigen: Karl Augustin, 1968), 232–34, 227–40. For the nature of Zwingli's support during the Reformation, see Walter Jacob, *Politische Führungsschicht und Reformation. Untersuchung zur Reformation in Zürich 1519–1523,* vol. 1, *Zürcher Beiträge zur Reformationsgeschichte.* (Zürich: Zwingli Verlag, 1970), 65–66, 67–69, 70–72, 82.

33. Myconius, 47–51, Haas, 86–93; Walton, 36–38.

34. Haas; 191–94, 195–200, 201–2, 204; Potter, 241; Leonhard von Muralt, "Renaissance und Reformation," *Handbuch der Schweizergeschichte,* 2 vols. (Zürich: Berichthaus, 1972), 1:526.

35. Leonhard von Muralt, "Zum Problem der Theokratie bei Zwingli," *Discordia Concors, Festgabe für Edgar Bonjour zu seinem siebzigsten Geburtstag am 21. August 1968,* 2 vols. (Basel and Stuttgart: Verlag Helbing & Lichtenhahn, 1968), 2:369–79. As von Muralt observes, Alfred Farner describes Zwingli as the leader of a "Prophetic theocracy." See Alfred Farner, *Die Lehre von Kirche und Staat bei Zwingli* (Tübingen: J. C. B. Mohr, 1930), 123–28, 129ff., 134. Von Muralt does not agree with the traditional interpretation.

36. Von Muralt summarizes the work of his students in his article, "Zum Problem der Theokratie," *Discordia Concors,* 2:374ff., 377–79, 381–82, 383–85, 387–89, 390. The von Muralt students are: René Hauswirth, *Landgraf Philipp von Hessen und Zwingli,* No. 35, *Schriften zur Kirchen-und Rechtsgeschichte* (Tübingen: Osiandersche Buchhandlung, 1968); Martin Haas, *Zwingli und der Erste Kappelerkrieg* (Zürich: Verlag Berichthaus, 1965); Kurt Spillmann, *Zwingli und die Zürcherische Politik gegenüber der Abtei St. Gallen,* No. 44, *Mitteilungen zur Vaterländischen Geschichte* (St. Gallen: Fehr'sche Buchhandlung, 1965). The works of Morf and Jacob belong to the von Muralt school. Cf. n. 32. Ekkehart Fabian has posed the only challenge to the von Muralt school. Ekkehart Fabian, "Zwingli und der Geheime Rat 1523–1531," *Gottesreich und Menschenreich, Ernst Stäehelin zum 80. Geburtstag* (Basel: Helbing & Lichtenhahn), 151ff., 181ff. See chap. 2, "Zwinglis politische Stellung," in Haas, *Huldrych Zwingli,* 205–15. Helmut Meyer has also added to our knowledge and justifies the use of the term *Secret Council.* Helmut Meyer, *Der Zweite Kappeler Krieg* (Zürich: Hans Rohr, 1976), 68ff., 73–74, 77–80ff., 83.

37. Haas, *Huldrych Zwingli,* 167–74; Potter, 233ff., 239–41; Walther Köhler, 167–69, 170–73, 266–69, 275–76. The standard work on the Baden disputation remains Leonhard von Muralt, *Die Badener Disputation 1526* (Leipzig, 1926).

38. Leonhard von Muralt, "Renaissance und Reformation," *Handbuch der Schweizer Geschichte,* 1:484, 485, 487, 489–91. (*Das Christliche Burgrecht* with Constance, Zwingli's plans for other alliances, the means for spreading the Reformation in the jointly administered territories), 491–92 (the Catholic response: the *Christliche Vereinigung*), 494–96, 497 (majority decisions for the Reformation), the issue of the Abbey of St. Gall) 499 (Bern's policy of westward expansion threatened), 502–4, 506–7. Jean-Paul Tardent, *Niclaus Manuel als Staatsmann (Sonderdruck aus dem Archiv des Historischen Vereins des Kantons Bern,* vol. 51 (1967), 317, 328–36; Spillmann, 80ff., 106–7; Hauswirth, 259; Haas, *Huldrych Zwingli,* 267, 268–71, 272–74.

39. Leonhard von Muralt "Renaissance und Reformation," *Handbuch der Schweizer Geschichte,* 1:500, 507–10, 511–12, 514, 517–18; Haas, *Huldrych Zwingli,* 267; Potter, 36ff.; Meyer,

76, 78, 84, 87–88, 111–12. See also W. Bender, *Zwinglis Reformationsbündnisse* (Zürich: Zwingli Verlag 1970), 177ff.

40. Haas, *Huldrych Zwingli*, 277ff., 280–82, 288; Myconius, *Vom Leben*, 71–74; O. Farner, 4:483ff., 489.

41. Leonhard von Muralt, "Renaissance und Reformation," *Handbuch der Schweizer Geschichte*, 1:526ff; Meyer, 314.

42. Fritz Blanke, *Brüder in Christo. Die Geschichte der ältesten Täufergemeinde (Zollikon 1525)* (Zürich: Zwingli Verlag, 1955). Harold S. Bender, *Conrad Grebel 1498–1526; Founder of the Swiss Brethren.* (Scottsdale, Pa.: Herald Press, 1950), 91–92, 82–83, 85, 252–53; John H. Yoder, *Täufertum und Reformation in der Schweiz, I: Die Gespräche zwischen Täufern und Reformation 1523–1528*, No. 6, "Schriftenreihe des Mennonitischen Geschichtsvereins" (Karlsruhe: H. Schneider, 1962), 164–65, 167–69, 162; idem, "The Turning Point in the Zwinglian Reformation," *Mennonite Quarterly Review* 32 (April 1958): 128–40. Most Mennonite scholars assume that Zwingli abandoned his original free church position. Peter Klassen is an exception. Peter Klassen "Zwingli and the Zurich Anabaptists," *Gottesreich und Menschenreich*, 199ff., 207, 210. Works by Mennonites such as Paul Peachy, *Die soziale Herkunft der Schweizer Täufer in der Reformationszeit. Eine religiöse Untersuchung*, No. 4, "Schriftenreihe des Mennonitischen Geschichtsvereins" (Karlsruhe: H. Schneider, 1954); Guy F. Hershberger, ed., *The Recovery of the Anabaptist Vision* (Scottsdale, Pa: Herald Press, 1957) share this assumption, as do the works of non-Mennonites like Franklin H. Littell, *The Anabaptist View of the Church: A Study in the Origins of Sectarian Protestantism* (Boston: Star King, 1958) and G. H. Williams, *The Radical Reformation* (Philadelphia: The Westminster Press, 1962). *The Mennonite Quarterly Review* is the best journal for Mennonite studies.

43. The best summary of the *Stand der Forschung* is by James M. Stayer, Werner O. Packull, and Klaus Deppermann, "From Monogenesis to Polygenesis: The Historical Discussion of Anabaptist Origins," *MQR* (1975), 83–121. Stayer's *Anabaptists and the Sword* (Lawrence, Kans.: Coronado Press, 1972), 99, 109, demonstrated a theme already developed by Haas, that in the beginning the Täufer were quite willing to consider using force. Haas, "Täufertum und Revolution," *Festschrift Leonhard von Muralt*, 294–95; idem, "Die Täuferkirchen des 16. Jahrhunderts in der Schweiz und in Münster—ein Vergleich," *Zwingliana* 13 (1972): 437–40, 441ff., 449ff., 460ff. Stayer praises Goeter's article "Die Vorgeschichte des Täufertums in Zürich," *Studien zur Geschichte und Theologie der Reformation. Festschrift für Ernst Bizer* (Neukirchen-Kluỳn: Neukirchener Verlag, 1969), 264–70; see esp. 278–79, 280–81, 252–53, 264–65, 272–75. The basis for this work was Goeter's earlier *Ludwig Hätzer, Spiritualist und Antitrinitarier. Eine Randfigur der Frühen Täuferbewegung*, vol. 25, *Quellen und Forschungen zur Reformationsgeschichte* (Gütersloh: C. Bertelsmann Verlag, 1957). Stayer, Packull, Deppermann, 95–97, 99 (on Haas and the *Wildwuchs der Reformation*). Stayer and Haas's contributions to *Umstrittenes Täufertum 1525–1975*, ed. Hans-Jürgen Goertz (Göttingen: Vandenhoeck & Ruprecht, 1977). The articles are: Haas, "Der Weg der Täufer in die Absonderung," 50–78, and Stayer "Die Anfänge des schweizerischen Täufertums im Reformierten Kongregationalismus," 19–49. See also Stayer, "Reublin and Brötli: The Revolutionary Beginning of Swiss Anabaptism," in *The Origins and Characteristics of Anabaptism*, ed. Marc Lienhard, vol. 87. *Archives Internationale l'Histoire des Idées* (The Hague: Martinus Nijhoff, 1977), 84–86, 87–89, 96, 99, 102; Walton, xiff., 60ff., 77ff., 83, 176–208. Anyone wishing to study the Täufer further should use: Claus-Peter Clasen, *Anabaptism: A Social History* (Ithaca, N.Y.: Cornell University Press, 1972). Hillerbrand's bibliography is also essential: Hans J. Hillerbrand, *A Bibliography of Anabaptism 1520–1630* (with supplement), St. Louis, Center for Reformation Research (1975) as well as *Hans-Jürgen Goertz, Die Täufergeschichte und Ihre Deutung.*

44. Fritz Büsser, *Huldrych Zwingli. Reformation als prophetischer Auftrag*, vol. 74/75 *Persönlichkeit und Geschichte*, 35, 36–37, 49–51, 53–54.

45. Büsser, 50–51.

46. Zwingli's conception of excommunication requires further study. The close parallels between his vocabulary in dealing with Matthew 16:18–19 and 18:15–20 and that of Erasmus

in his *Paraphrases* and *Annotationes* need to be examined. For the question of the control of excommunication see Haas, 155–56; Walton, 123, 174–75, 209, 211. For a good discussion of Zwingli's idea of church discipline see Roger Ley, *Kirchenzucht bei Zwingli* (Zürich: Zwingli Verlag, 1948) and Walther Köhler, *Zürcher Ehegericht und Genfer Konsistorium. Das Zürcher Ehegericht und seine Auswirkung in der Deutschen Schweiz und zur Zeit Zwinglis*, 2 vols. (Leipzig: M. Heinsius Nachfolger, 1932 and 1953), 1:28ff.

47. Z, 1:231–32.

48. Büsser, 39–40.

49. Z, 3:22.

50. Z, 3:303; Z, 2:298–99, 300, 301; Z, 3:728, 730, 732–33, 734; Z, 36.

51. For the origins of the idea of the covenant in Zwingli's theology, see Jack W. Cottrell, "Is Bullinger the Source for Zwingli's Doctrine of the Covenant?", *Heinrich Bullinger 1504–1575. Gesammelte Aufsätze zum 400. Todestag*, ed. U. Gäbler and E. Herkenrath, 2 vols. (Zürich: Theologischer Verlag, 1975), 75–81.

52. Z, 2:21–22; cf. Z, 1:294–95.

53. Z, 2:22. Gottfried Locher, *Die Theologie Huldrych Zwinglis im Lichte seiner Christologie* (Zürich: Zwingli Verlag, 1952), 1:78ff.; idem, *Die Zwinglische Reformation*, 202; idem, "Grundzüge der Theologie Huldrych Zwinglis im Vergleich mit derjenigen Martin Luthers und Johannes Calvins," *Zwingliana* 12 (1964–1968): 476–77, 484, 489–93.

54. Z, 2:23.

55. Z, 2:23, 24.

56. For a careful study of the role of the Holy Spirit in Zwingli's theology, see Christof Gestrich, *Zwingli als Theologe. Glauben und Geist beim Zürcher Reformator. No. 20, Studien zur Dogmengeschichte und systematische Theologie* (Zürich: Zwingli Verlag, 1967).

57. Rudolf Pfister, *Die Seligkeit Erwählter Heiden bei Zwingli* (Zürich-Zollikon: Evangelischer Verlag, 1952), 68: "Nam illo elegit nos ante mundi constitutionem." SS, 6:16, 17; O. Farner, 1:211.

58. Pfister, 11, 18–19; Z, 3:641–45; O. Farner, 1:211. Locher, *Die Zwinglische Reformation*, 204–5; Locher, "Grundzüge," *Zwingliana* 12:497–501; Locher, *Die Theologie*, 61ff., 70ff., 78ff.

59. Walton, 213; Büsser, 66–69, Jacques Courvoisier, *Zwingli: A Reformed Theologian* (Richmond, Va.: John Knox, 1963), 72, 75–76, 77. See J. Schweizer, *Reformierte Abendmahlsgestaltung in der Schau Zwinglis* (Basel: Friedrich Reinhardt, n.d.), 80–81. Markus Jenny, *Die Einheit des Abendmahlsgottesdienstes bei den Elsässischen und Schweizer Reformatoren* (Zürich: Zwingli Verlag, 1968).

60. Z, 1:152; Z, 3:56, 58, 682; Z, 3:410; Z, 6/2:800, 801, 802.

61. Haas, *Huldrych Zwingli*, 117–25; Walton, 158ff; Z, 2:484.

62. Fritz Blanke, "Zwingli mit Ambrosius Blarer im Gespräch," *Der Konstanzer Reformator Ambrosius Blarer 1492–1564. Gedenkschrift zu seinem 400. Todestag*, ed. Bernd Moeller (Konstanz and Stuttgart: Jan Thorbecke, 1964); Z, 14:424.

THE SOURCES

The standard English language biography of Zwingli, *Zwingli*, was written by George Potter and published by Cambridge University Press in 1976. With his *Huldrych Zwingli*, which appeared as a volume in the *Documents of Modern History Series*, the two books provide a reliable and up-to-date introduction to the Zurich reformer's life. Potter's *Zwingli* will surely remain the standard work on the subject in English for many years to come. There is really nothing in German to match it. Two other modern Zwingli biographies are available in English: Jacques Courvoisier, *Zwingli:*

A Reformed Theologian (Richmond, Va.: John Knox, 1963), and Jean Rilliet, *Zwingli: The Third Man of the Reformation* (Philadelphia: Westminster, 1959). Both reflect the Zwingli renaissance that has taken place in Swiss Zwingli scholarship during the last fifty years. Courvoisier's study provides a particularly clear statement of Zwingli's doctrine of the sacraments. The reprint of Samuel M. Jackson's *Ulrich Zwingli (1484–1531): Selected Works* by the University of Pennsylvania Press in 1972 makes a small number of Zwingli's writings available to the English-speaking reader. Jackson's larger collection of translations, *The Latin Works of Huldrych Zwingli, Together with Selections from his German Works*, ed. C. N. Heller, 3 vols. (Philadelphia: The Heidelberg Press, 1912, 1929), which was never completed, is extremely useful but is not available in most libraries. G. W. Bromiley's *Zwingli and Bullinger*, vol. 24 of *The Library of Christian Classics* (Philadelphia: Westminster, 1953) is helpful on Zwingli but not sufficiently extensive. H. Wayne Pipkin's translations of Zwingli's major writings, whose publication will be financed by the Emil Brunner Foundation, will fill a very large gap.

In 1897 Georg Finsler published his *Zwingli-Bibliographie. Verzeichnis der gedruckten Schriften* (Zürich: Orell Füssli, 1897). Ulrich Gäbler brought Finsler's work up to date in 1972 with his *Habilitationsschrift*, entitled *Huldrych Zwingli im 20. Jahrhundert, Forschungsbericht und annotierte Bibliographie 1897–1972* (Zürich: Theologischer Verlag, 1975). Each year in the December issue of the Swiss periodical *Zwingliana*, a list of recent works on Zwingli and the Zwinglian reformation is published.

Gäbler's bibliographical study is important, because it provides a fair and accurate guide to the modern literature on the subject of Zwingli research. Henry Meylan offers a more general collection of materials dealing with the Swiss Reformation as a whole in the section "Suisse" of the *Bibliographie de la Réforme 1430–1648* (Leiden: Brill, 1966).

The standard general works that provide the beginner with a necessary background for the study of Swiss history are summarized in volume one of the *Handbuch der Schweizer Geschichte* (Zürich: Berichthaus, 1972) and volume two of Rudolph Pfister's *Kirchengeschichte der Schweiz* (Zürich: Theologischer Verlag, 1974). Von Muralt bibliographical recommendations given at the end of the section on the "Reformation, Counter-Reformation" in the *Handbuch der Schweizer Geschichte* should be followed. Hans Conrad Peyer's *Verfassungsgeschichte der alten Schweiz* (Zürich: Polygraphischer Verlag, 1978) can be read with great profit in conjunction with Andreas Heusler's now quite outmoded *Schweizerische Verfassungsgeschichte* (Basel: Frobenius AG, 1920). The best recent history of canton Zürich remains Anton Largiader's *Geschichte von Stadt und Landschaft Zürich*, 2 vols. (Zürich-Erlenbach: Eugen Rentsch Verlag, 1945). A careful student will also want to read Karl Dändliker's *Geschichte der Stadt und des Kantons Zürich*, 3 vols. (Zürich: Schulthess, 1908). The most reliable work on the beginning of the

Reformation at Zurich remains Emil Egli's *Schweizerische Reformationsgeschichte*, vol. 1 (Zürich: Zürcher & Furrer, 1909). Egli's other works, particularly his *Analecta Reformatoria*, 2 vols. (Zürich: Zürcher & Furrer, 1899, 1901), are still of great value.

There is no space in an essay of this brevity to consider the various source editions that are essential for the study of the Zwinglian reformation. Emil Egli's *Aktensammlung zur Geschichte der Zürcher Reformation in den Jahren 1519–1533* (Zürich: J. Schabelitz, 1879) should be brought up to date, as should J. Strickler's *Die Eidgenössische Abschiede*, vol. 4, (Zürich: Druck von J. Schabelitz, 1873, 1876). The same can be said for Strickler's *Aktensammlung zur Schweizerischen Reformationsgeschichte*, 5 vols. (Zürich: 1878–1883), and the edition of Heinrich Bullinger's *Reformationsgeschichte*, ed. J. J. Hottinger and H. H. Vögeli, 3 vols. (Frauenfeld: Ch. Beyel, 1839), E. Gagliards's edition of J. Stumpf's *Schweizer Reformationschronik*, 2 vols., *Quellen zur Schweizer Geschichte* (Zürich, 1952, 1955) is a model of what could be done, as is E. G. Rüsch's German and Latin edition of Oswald Myconius's *Vom Leben und Sterben Huldrych Zwingli's*, No. 50, *Mitteilungen zur Vaterländischen Geschichte* (St. Gallen: Fehr'sche Buchhandlung, 1979). The new edition of Zwingli's works begun by Emil Egli in 1904 is nearing completion (Zwingli Huldrych, *Huldrych Zwingli Sämtliche Werke*, ed. E. Egli and Georg Finsler, 14 vols. (Leipzig and Berlin: C. A. Schwetschke and Son, 1905–1980. (However, it is still necessary to consult *Zwingli Huldrici Opera*, ed. Melchiore Schulero and Jo. Schulthessio (Turici: Ex Offinia Schulthessiana, 1836). The volumes in the series *Quellen zur Geschichte der Täufer in der Schweiz*, begun by Leonhard von Muralt and L. Schmid in 1952, have been ably continued by H. Fast and M. Haas. They are essential for the study of Zwingli's relationship to the *Täufer*.

The second edition of Martin Haas's *Huldrych Zwingli und seine Zeit*, published by the Theologischer Verlag in 1976, is the best single, short biography of Zwingli and should be translated into English. Though Haas does not summarize Zwingli's theology so succinctly and well as did Fritz Büsser in his *Huldrych Zwingli: Reformation als prophetischer Auftrag*, vols. 74/75, *Persönlichkeiten und Geschichte* (Göttingen, Zürich, Frankfurt: Musterschmidt, 1978), he places it most clearly in the political context of the Zurich reformation and draws upon the important contributions to the history of Zwingli's thought made by Gottfried Locher, particularly in his recent work, *Die Zwinglische Reformation im Rahmen der europäischen Kirchengeschichte* (Göttingen: Vandenhoeck and Ruprecht, 1979). Haas also sums up the general conclusions of the Zwinglian renaissance to which his mentor, Leonhard von Muralt, contributed so much. He has employed Walther Köhler's massive studies of Zwingli and Luther, as well as the *Zürcher Ehegericht*, to explain the differences between Luther and Zwingli, and with the help of Moeller as well as Köhler, Zürich's significance for the Reformation in general (Walther Köhler, *Zürcher Ehegericht und Genfer Kon-*

sistorium, vol. 7 of *Quellen und Abhandlungen zur Schweizerischen Reformationsgeschichte* [Leipzig: M. Heinsius Nachfolger, 1932]; idem, *Zwingli und Luther. Ihr Streit über das Abendmahl nach seinen politischen und religiösen Beziehungen,* 2 vols. (6 vols. and 7 of *Quellen und Forschungen zur Reformationsgeschichte;* for Moeller, cf. nn. 2 and 4). His knowledge of Oskar Farner's work has allowed him to assess the importance of the *via antiqua* in Zwingli's thought and his careful study of Arthur Rich has encouraged him to stress Zwingli's independent development as a reformer, which is one of the major contributions of the Zwingli renaissance. (Oskar Farner, *Huldrych Zwingli,* 4 vols. [Zürich: Zwingli Verlag, 1943–1960]; Arthur Rich, *Die Anfänge der Theologie Huldrych Zwinglis* [Zürich: Zwingli Verlag, 1949].) Haas's biography also presents a clear statement on the conclusions of the works of von Muralt's students, who have demonstrated beyond the shadow of a doubt that Zwingli was not a theocrat. Their work, which has been dealt with in the main body of this essay, represents the second major contribution of the Zwingli renaissance (cf. nn. 35 and 36). Finally, Haas's Zwingli biography has given a clear picture of Zwingli's relationship to his own radical followers who became the *Täufer.* In the biography and other works Haas has added to the work of Goeters, Stayer, and Walton to reject the general Mennonite contention that the *Täufer* were the true followers of Zwingli's original ecclesiology. As has been shown in the essay itself, Haas has demonstrated that the *Täufer* were quite willing to use force as long as they believed that they could achieve the type of Christian commonwealth the Bible required. Only after their political hopes were disappointed did they embrace separatism. This interpretation probably represents the most important contribution of the von Muralt school to Zwingli scholarship (cf. nn. 42 and 43).

Several recent works on the Anabaptists deserve brief mention. Marc Lienhard edited a very useful collection of essays' entitled *The Origins and Characteristics of Anabaptism—Les Débuts et les caractéristiques de l'anabaptisme,* vol. 87 of *Archives internationales d'histoire des idées* (The Hague: Martinus Nijhoff, 1977). Hans Jürgen Goertz, *Die Täufergeschichte und ihre Deutung* (Munich: Verlag C. H. Beck, 1980), also deserves mention. Finally, the reader should not forget Robert Friedmann's *The Theology of Anabaptism* (Scottsdale, Pa.: Herald Press, 1973). This brief essay does not do full justice to the work of such fine Zwingli scholars as Fritz Schmidt-Clausing, Heinrich Schmid, and many others.

4

Lay Religion in the Program of Andreas Rudolff-Bodenstein von Karlstadt

Calvin A. Pater

Traditionally Karlstadt (ca. 1480–1541) has been defined in relation to Martin Luther. Indeed, Karlstadt's career in the University of Wittenberg had fateful consequences for him as well as for the church. He enrolled in Wittenberg in 1505, received his doctorate in theology in 1510, rose to prominence in this new provincial university, promoted Luther to the doctorate in 1512, and later collaborated with Luther and Melanchthon in reforming Wittenberg's curriculum. Luther, however, in his phenomenal rise as a reformer, overshadowed Karlstadt, especially in March 1522, when he sided with Frederick the Elector and "the weak," thus helping to undo Karlstadt's earlier liturgical and social reforms. Karlstadt gradually withdrew to Orlamünde in 1523 and under pressure he resigned his academic and related positions in August of 1524. He seemed to have failed in Wittenberg, and, following a pamphlet war, he was derided in Luther's two-volume work *Against the Heavenly Prophets* (1524–1525).

Karlstadt deserves to be studied in his own right, however, especially since he was influential in the formation of the Baptist movements of the Reformation era. Although he has largely been forgotten by his spiritual descendants in the "free churches," Karlstadt continues to wield his influence in modulated form among the growing number of Protestants outside the now largely static or declining branches of traditional Lutheran and Reformed Protestantism.[1]

Karlstadt distinguished himself from Luther primarily by propagating a biblicism that attempts to dissolve all traditional churchly accretions of Christendom to return to the ideal of a primitive Christianity. Consequently Karlstadt attempted to reinstate early Christian sectarianism by basing the Christian faith on a personal decision, made as an adult, which sets one off from the "world" and which may even rend the ties of the family. Since the distinctions between the clergy and the laity had not been foreseen in the primitive church, Karlstadt's church promoted egalitar-

ianism as a basic principle, which was enacted fully in the church of
Orlamünde from 1523 to 1524.

The church structures that Karlstadt therefore challenged were those of
the medieval church, whether he opposed them fully (as in the case of
Catholicism) or partially (as in the case of Lutheranism). According to the
Council of Florence, one's triumphal entry into the Christian life began as
an infant, and one related to God and his institutional representatives in
childlike fashion. One lived in obedience to *Mother* Church, and one's
salvation depended on the sacramental ministrations of a priest (i.e., pres-
byter, therefore one's senior or superior) or *pfaff* (i.e., *papa* or *pater*).

In Lutheranism the role and function of the highest medieval clergy
(whose jurisdiction was international) disappeared, and the power of the
national clergy was diluted by the assertion of biblical authority and the
doctrine of salvation by faith and grace. However, Luther's principled and
practical indifference toward hierarchical structures allowed the "priesthood of all believers" to remain mere principle. Passivity in the process of
salvation was, in fact, enhanced by the doctrine of salvation by pure grace
and its essential corollary: divine predestination. Of course, predestination
was thought to affect clergy and laity alike, but the quietism this fostered in
classical Lutheranism also bode ill for lay initiative.

Luther was strictly opposed to individualistic religion, and just as the
medieval church stipulated lay subservience to the priesthood with regard
to the sacraments, Luther proclaimed the dependence of believers on the
Word, which he then tied to the structures of his own church. For the
"Word" was not conceived as an independent or purely spiritual entity.
Luther insisted that the Word was always mediated. Faith comes through
hearing, and hearing depends on the proclamation of the pure (i.e., Lutheran) gospel, whether through preaching or the administration of the
sacraments. In this crucial area, therefore, the Lutheran congregation was
dependent on its local cleric, now no longer called "priest" or "father" but
"Lord of the Parsonage" *(Pfarrer)*, and just as a lord could eject a peasant,
so the "Lord of the Parsonage" could excommunicate any member of his
church, without the need for outside consultation.

One significant exception to lay impotence or muteness in the church
should be noted. Since the medieval pattern did not provide for regionally
independent *Landeskirchen*, the regional ruler stepped into the breach as
Notbischof (bishop in emergency), and this emergency became legally permanent with the adoption of the principle of *cuius regio eius religio*. Regional
coordination was in lay hands, but at the local level, and thus for virtually
all the laity, the "Lord of the Parsonage" spoke the divine Word.

Karlstadt repudiated this development altogether. By harmonizing predestination with human choice, an adult decision led now to a rather
sorrowful entry into the Christian life. Karlstadt also leveled the distinction
between "God's little congregation *(heuflein)*" and its congregationally

elected "minister" or "messenger" *(bott)*. This development did not come about hastily, and certainly not as an act of pique toward Luther. Karlstadt's lay Christianity represents the logical culmination of his career as a reformer. Naturally his radical break with the medieval church occurred in dialogue with or polemic against the structures of the church around him. Therefore, despite the inner logic of his own development toward lay reform, the thrust of his polemic changes with his circumstances. Seen from this apologetic perspective, Karlstadt's doctrine of the laity moves through three phases. At first (1517–1520) Karlstadt challenges various trends dominant in the late-medieval church from within, that is, without publicly repudiating the Church of Rome.[2] During this phase he is circumspect in the way in which he formulates his radical ideas, and he protects himself by citing voluminously from the Church Fathers (out of context if necessary), especially Augustine and Jerome. Following his censure by Rome in the bull *Exsurge Domine* (1520) Karlstadt forsakes all pretense and he repudiates Pope Leo X as a heretic. In this second phase Karlstadt coexists uneasily with Luther, and he is prudent enough to acknowledge publicly his "dear father, Doctor Martin Luther" while he addresses "the little congregation" and "the poor lay person who has been cheated and deceived."[3] Karlstadt no longer hides behind the Fathers:

> For Christ does not say "I am the tradition *(consuetudo),*" but "I am the way, the truth, and the life." From this it follows that the teaching of Augustine is in no wise comparable to Scripture to overcome us or others who contradict you. For we may cast down Augustine himself through Holy Scripture, as he himself desires.[4]

During his so-called Invocavit Sermons (9–16 March 1522) Luther denounces Karlstadt's reforms for having been instituted "too hastily." After his preaching has been curtailed, and after his treatise in reply to Jerome Emser has been ordered destroyed by the censors of the university, Karlstadt gradually disentangles himself from Wittenberg and goes to Orlamünde as "neighbour Andreas," the "new lay person," who is learning to farm, doing honest work in preparation for the day when he can support himself like Paul, the tent-maker. His new program of lay reform now assails both "the Old and the New Papists."[5] Karlstadt's later career in Switzerland involved some compromises; thus the years from 1523 to 1525 should be regarded as the third and most independent phase of his career.

Toward a New Outlook (1517–1520)

Having been incited toward the study of Augustine by Luther, Karlstadt purchased a set of Augustine's writings at the Leipzig Book Fair, January 1517. Three months later he published *151 Theses*, which contained many excerpts from Augustine. According to Kähler: "Although Augustine is not the sole Church Father [in Karlstadt's mind], Augustine nevertheless plays the most important role and is the primary model among the Fathers of the Church."[6] Kähler's comment was prompted by Karlstadt's seventh thesis: "Augustine's opinions on ethical matters are not inferior to anyone (*Against the canonists*)." However, Karlstadt had begun his career with a thorough immersion in the intricacies of logic, whether Aristotelian, Thomist, or Scotist, and one should keep in mind that Karlstadt's praise in the seventh thesis restricted itself to the realm of ethics. There is no way of dating his comment, but Karlstadt had reacted angrily when he read of the conferral of the title of "tutelary deity" upon Augustine in the statutes of the University of Wittenberg. The comment that he scribbled in the margin reads: "Blasphemy against God."[7]

Karlstadt was impressed by Augustine's *De spiritu et littera*, especially its principles for the interpretation of Scripture; he lectured on it, and in preparation for his classes he published sections of it, interspersed with his own *scholia*. Soon thereafter, however, Karlstadt occupied himself with the canon of Scripture, and was even somewhat more extreme than Jerome in opposing Augustine's view of the canon.[8] Elsewhere I have shown that Karlstadt quoted Augustine selectively, and in doing so undercut Augustine's doctrines of predestination and baptism.[9] Thus Karlstadt did not only learn from the Fathers; he treated them critically and found them useful to cover up what to some of his contemporaries were shocking statements. In 1518 Karlstadt wrote:

> The text of the Bible is not only to be preferred to one or many doctors of the church, but even to the authority of the whole church. Here the church is to be taken as the congregation or public gathering of all the faithful. [Moreover], where the Lord and his apostles spoke openly, there the Roman pontiff may not proclaim a new law.[10]

Theoretically, Karlstadt was probing the fringes of legitimacy; he did not yet proclaim specific "heresies," but he was provocative. In 1519 he began his treatise *Ausslegung* with a pious affirmation toward Rome, an affirmation that ends with a restriction: "I shall always adjust to, obey, and follow the Roman Christian Church. May a little child lead me. But only according to the dictates and contents of Holy Scripture."[11] Karlstadt posited the possibility of conflict between a council, or a pope, or the Church of Rome in general, and Scripture too often to be thought of as merely delineating a theoretical possibility. In fact, his emphasis on the supremacy of Scripture was a turning point in the development of lay religion, for it gave the laity a weapon to counter the encroachments of a clericalized church.

In *380 Conclusions*, published 9 May 1518, Karlstadt asserts: "It is totally false to argue that God grants grace according to our effort. Consequently we who honour Holy Scripture, together with Augustine, do not know an intermediate state (*medium*) between those who are tormented by everlasting fire and those in whom God will be all in all."[12] This statement as well as its implications is radical. Karlstadt here denies a tradition of long standing in the Eastern and the Western church. He must also oppose the underlying supposition that sins that are forgiven may none the less carry a divinely imposed penalty. Intercessory prayer on behalf of the dead is now useless. With this the traditional doctrine of indulgences also tumbles, even though Karlstadt waited longer than Luther to attack it openly. Finally, and perhaps worst of all, Karlstadt had repudiated one of the most lucrative sources of income for the church, namely, the endowment of Masses for the souls of the dead.

Karlstadt's argument did not yet explicitly involve the financial burdens of the laity or a desire to shrink the profile of the institutional church. He argued on the basis of authority, namely, Scripture versus tradition. Nevertheless, this involved a drastic reduction in the number of priests to be supported by the laity. Perhaps this problem had already entered Karlstadt's mind in relation to indulgences, for this traffic benefited the papacy above all. Karlstadt declares a ruler "to be praiseworthy when he takes care that the lamb is not eaten by the rapacious wolf, or does not enter into the jaws of [Pope] Leo [the lion] (in *Leonis fauces*)."[13]

The denial of a state intermediate between heaven and hell also obliterated the doctrine of limbo; this removed the urgency from the baptism of infants. In fact, Karlstadt's view of baptism at this stage was such that its sacramental efficacy was already eroding. In 1519 Karlstadt claims that as a Christian he must defend the supreme authority of Scripture, and this obligation was incurred in baptism. Significantly, Karlstadt does not appeal to the sacrament of baptism itself, but to the vows then made on the child's behalf.[14]

A central factor in Karlstadt's rejection of a hierarchically organized church was to be the denial of the special status of the saints. Saints are not creatures on whom one should feel dependent; they have value only to the extent that they led Christian lives. Those who "turn humans into gods, calling them saints" are devils (*cacodaemones*), who are guilty of "shameful servility."[15] Karlstadt dismisses the stigmata of Saint Francis, refusing "to be deceived by outward spectres (*externa decipi larva*)." Avoiding the honorific title of "saint," Karlstadt objects: "One wonders why you attribute so much to Francis. Would it not be sufficient that he was a Christian? But you have made an idol out of him."[16] During this debate between the Wittenberg scholars and the tertiary Franciscans, Karlstadt attacks the source of their income (i.e., mendicancy) and objects to the distinction between the common people who must work for a living and the mendicant regulars who do not:

Karlstadt: In addition to [the scriptural texts] that we have already cited, such mendicancy has been voided by divine law, as is shown by the Psalm "Because you eat by the labour of your hands, therefore it shall be well with you" [Psalm 127:2, Vulgate]. "And the work of our hands, O Lord, establish upon us" [Psalm 89:17, Vulgate]. Therefore, work rather than idleness, is required of us. Moreover what reason do you have to spend your life in idleness?
And the Franciscan answered: Because we have forsaken all things.
Karlstadt: Who then has to do the work?
Franciscan: The people of the world (*Saecularibus hominibus*).
Karlstadt: Pshaw! Try to prove that claim! "We have forsaken all things, therefore we need not engage in labour." And, I believe, this would please everyone; forsaking all things to avoid having to work.[17]

Thus far, Karlstadt's ideas for reform merely *implied* changes that would have a beneficial effect on the laity, but his debate with Johann Eck at Leipzig (July 1519) would have consequences far beyond the immediate topic under discussion, namely, predestination. Some statements made in preparation for the debate were condemned by the University of Louvain and rejected as if they were theses emanating from Luther—an indirect warning.[18] A direct warning came when Eck used these theses to have Karlstadt's name appended to the papal bull *Exsurge Domine* in 1520. Just as significant, however, for the development of Karlstadt's theology of the laity was an incident that took place on 2 July 1519 and that was related by Karlstadt half a year later.

According to Karlstadt, Eck made several concessions to anti-Pelagianism, but on the Feast of the Visitation of the Blessed Virgin Mary, Eck boldly preached to the multitudes a "contrary, repugnant, and harmful" doctrine that deviated from his position taken the previous day, when he was debating Karlstadt. Karlstadt confronted Eck with this, and Eck is said to have responded as follows:

Do you imagine that we should divulge to the people the same issues which we treat and explain in the theological schools? The seeds that we cast on the soil of erudition before the learned auditors and their disciples, should not (he said) be foisted on the common people and illiterates. You are not (he said) as tactless (*ineptis*) as all that, that you would treat the Christian populace to the same select doctrines which, in the schools, we derive or elicit from the proclamation of Scripture?[19]

One hesitates to give full credence to Karlstadt's report of this incident, for he had become a bitter opponent of Eck. Karlstadt probably exaggerated Eck's response to clarify the basic issues. Then again, although he reported the incident half a year later, Karlstadt's memory was exact with respect to the time, for the Feast of the Visitation took place on 2 July, and a look at the record of the debate, which was published later, reveals that on 1 July Eck had indeed been trapped by Karlstadt into affirming that the whole good work proceeds from God, and when Karlstadt pointed out that this contradicted one of Eck's earlier assertions, Eck tried to save face by claiming that this involved "the whole good work, but not in its totality" *(totum sed non totaliter)*.[20] Thus, although Eck's response is not a verbatim quotation, he may well have accepted some form of "double truth." At any rate, Karlstadt denounced this notion: "Not only ought they who are seasoned theologians and hooded brothers to search diligently all the documents of Scripture, but even the populace of Christians, even the lads and the youngsters." According to Deuteronomy 4 boys and girls are to be instructed. Moses and Joshua did not have any secrets; their laws were taught to "all the people" of Israel, "men as well as women, little ones, and foreigners."

> Christ moreover says: "What I speak into your ear, proclaim on the roofs"; I [Karlstadt] say, "before whom stand the listeners of the common multitude *(turbae)*." Luke moreover adds: "that which was spoken into the ear in the closet, proclaim from the roofs." Eck does not believe that the laity should be preached to. Why then does he dispute before a great multitude?[21]

The demand that the laity should have complete access to the discussions of the theologians goes even beyond what Lutheranism was to accomplish. The idea of the "clarity of Scripture" meant that all should have access to the Bible, a sharp deviation from medieval notions about the "obscurity of Scripture." In classical Protestantism, however, the authority of the scriptural expert was to be taken much more seriously than lay opinion. At least there loomed a new bondage here, now no longer to the priesthood but to the theologians. Karlstadt is already so egalitarian in 1519 that he must oppose such a development, despite the overtones of anti-intellectualism this produces. The common people are better interpreters of Scripture than the "wise":

> They are the ones of whom the Apostle says: "I shall destroy the wisdom of the wise and I shall judge the prudence of the prudent," etc. God has turned the wisdom of the world to folly, and it pleased him through the folly of preaching to save the believers, namely Jews, Greeks, barbarians, the untutored *(idiotae)*, the simple, the foolish, the illiterate, rustics, women, children, servant girls, the stranger: to them the Word of God is God's power. God calls neither the noble, nor the prudent, nor the wise, but God chooses the fools of the world to confound the wise, and the weak to confound the strong.[22]

Biblical as this message was, Karlstadt was not yet proclaiming its subversive teachings from the roofs. *Verba Dei* (1519–1520) was after all written in Latin, and addressed those who would preach God's Words sincerely. Therefore its primary aim was to make preachers responsive to the needs of the laity, but *Verba Dei* contains a charter of lay rights, the first to be published by any of the reformers.

Finally, Karlstadt's writings during the early years of the Reformation reveal leanings toward mysticism, which have been discussed by Bubenheimer.[23] Unlike Luther, whose earlier praise for the *Theologia Deutsch* was soon muffled, and who began to oppose mysticism, Karlstadt retained a genuine attachment to it, even during his "Reformed" days in Basel.[24] The relationship between mysticism and dissent has been explored by Ozment.[25] When one takes the aim of mysticism seriously, namely, to reach for direct access to God, culminating in bridal union *(Brautmystik)*, then the path to God is purely spiritual, and the structures of the church are silently bypassed. This was crucial for Karlstadt's understanding of Mary. We saw already that "Francis" is best appreciated for having been a Christian. In other words, the saints are not to be venerated for mediating divine grace, or as intercessors, but their value is paradigmatic when they point one toward the better life. Thus saints are no longer out of reach, but any believer can accomplish what they did. When this notion is fused with bridal mysticism, even the Virgin Mary's experience of conceiving the Son of God can be claimed by the believer:

> Therefore they conceive Christ spiritually who diligently and reverently hearing the Word of God also have become mothers of Christ. It is more important to bear Christ in the heart spiritually than physically. The flesh profits nothing but the Spirit gives life. All moreover who adhere faithfully to the word of God, being no strangers to tribulation, bear the Word [Christ] from the word [Scripture]. I do not at all broadcast this because I intend to detract from the honour of the Virgin. She is most holy, for she conceived Christ carnally as well as spiritually. For when she believed the word of the angel, the angel praised her as blessed.[26]

This statement is, of course, contradictory, because Karlstadt's new insight clashes too strongly with his earlier respect for and veneration of the Virgin. Mary's uniqueness is still asserted, for she is *"most* holy," but if one takes seriously Karlstadt's basic thesis that the flesh profits nothing, then how can it profit Mary? The text that the flesh profits nothing (John 6:63) was to haunt Karlstadt later, when he developed his theology of the Lord's Supper. Once that obstacle was overcome, Mary too would lose even this final vestige of her uniqueness.

Karlstadt's Uneasy Alliance with Luther (1520–1522)

During these years Karlstadt publicly clarified several issues like indulgences, purgatory, and the intercession of the saints, issues that had been treated earlier, but then Karlstadt had cautiously preferred the tactic of insinuation. New issues arose as well, and Karlstadt became the first reformer to denounce the entire monastic system and to give the laity independent access to the sacraments. He also deflates the fears of the common people regarding evil spirits; they are also emancipated from the need for angelic and saintly intercession.

More clearly than ever, Karlstadt disavows churchly tradition and institutional authority apart from the Scriptures. The medieval churches base their structures on councils and popes that are fallible and untrustworthy. The Council of Meaux (845) "erred deliberately (perperam erravit)" and since then all councils have fallen. The papacy has similarly been devoid of authority since the pontificate (1254–1261) of Pope Alexander IV.[27] In any case, the pope "is incomparably lower than Scripture."[28] Karlstadt admits that his voluminous quotations from the Fathers during the Leipzig Debate had been designed to ward off accusations of heresy:

> Therefore I based my arguments in Leipzig on the Bible and the books of Augustine, Jerome, Ambrose, Bernard, Gregory, Cyprian, Cyril, and others, to avoid all suspicion of heresy, levelled at me. . . . Nor would the Pope be able to condemn me as a heretic, unless he also condemns the pillars of the Christian church. But as you will notice the angry and violent Pope Leo did not heed this at all, and wants to push me away from the Bible against God, justice, and honour. But he shall not succeed, even if he made a fire that encompassed all the earth.[29]

Also, "The pope should stand only on Scripture, then his decretals will fly into hell,"[30] and "Let there be only one foundation, the canonical and universally accepted books of the Bible. Therefore you should not advance any human law, to bind me with it."[31]

With the doctrine of the sole sufficiency of Scripture established against councils, the papacy, and even the Fathers, Karlstadt now discusses indulgences in greater detail. In responding to Franciscus Seyler, Karlstadt first considers the reasons given for indulgences: They take away God's penalty for venial sins; they remove the penance ordered by a priest during confession; less commonly they are seen as remedy for the defect of less than wholehearted love of God. Karlstadt counters that he cannot find such indulgences in Scripture.[32] Then why did the church invent them? One reason is priestly greed in "emptying the purses of the people with their teaching."[33] Having thus undercut traditional indulgences, Karlstadt still hesitates (August 1520) and wonders whether a biblical interpretation of indulgences is feasible. There are two areas where this doctrine might be reformulated. "Now I let it pass that secret sins are rubbed in by means of a temporal punishment, which indulgences take away. But then I do not know what to reply to Isaiah 29: 'They feared me with human commandments and teachings.' "[34] Indulgences might also serve as a fine for those whose public sins demand public penance, but would it not be better to turn to Christ? When God forgives, he also forgets (Ezekiel 33:16), even if we remember, and "those who use indulgences for the [wrong] purpose detract from God's forgiveness." The best thing to be said for indulgences is that they demand repentance.[35] Perhaps Karlstadt's doubts are wrong, and Franciscus Seyler should then prove to him that indulgences are scriptural. With mock humility, Karlstadt begs Seyler for instruction:

> Similarly I am offering to learn from an untutored child that leads me away from errors and corrects me, not to mention someone who for forty years has worn a cord [seyl, a pun on Seyler] around his navel and can chant the Psalter from memory.[36]

Toward the end of 1520, Karlstadt reaffirms his opposition to the traditional doctrine of satisfaction that supported indulgences, while he expresses concern for the "untrained": "Christ suffered the curse, having been cursed on our behalf. Therefore for believers Christ is justice. Satisfaction, which is a custom in the church, is not a part of penance, according to the divine law. The customary practice of satisfaction has been instituted by the bishops to discipline the untrained (rudibus). Thus with works of satisfaction the bishops impiously burdened those whose consciences were afflicted, contrary to the example of Christ who does not quench the smoking flax, neither does he trample the crushed reed."[37]

Much of the fear and superstition, and the burden of artificially good works, is being removed with the onslaught of reformation. Another area where fear was promoted involved the world of the spirits, where Christian motifs were blended with the substance of the pagan subsoil of medieval Christendom. Scholars might not always take the magic arts too seriously for themselves, but the common people were all affected by them; in Wittenberg, at least, Melanchthon dabbled in astrology, and when Karlstadt's theses on necromancy appeared, Melanchthon was in close contact with the Zwickau Prophets, who claimed familiarity with spirits. Karlstadt moves well beyond a discussion of necromancy. His *48 Theses* (December 1521 to January 1522) radically deny purgatory, Luther's doctrine of soul-sleep, communication with the dead, the intercession of the saints, demon possession, and perhaps the doctrine of infant baptism. Since so many issues are settled here, I quote extensively:

1. On leaving the body, the soul enters heaven or hell at once.
2. "If a tree has fallen the south or the north, where it has fallen, it will be," that is, remain [Ecclesiastes 11:3, Vulgate].
3. Those who have done good, will enter into life eternal, but those who have done evil into eternal fire.
9. It is impious to lustrate a son or daughter, to dissect entrails, to give heed to dreams and omens, and to have regard for familiar spirits.

10. Thus to ask something from the dead is a crime and abomination before the Lord.
11. The apparitions of disembodied spirits are either dreams or diabolical illusions.
12. Therefore their responses are nothing but cunning tricks, deceptions, and the oracles of demons.
13. We know with respect to the spells of enchantresses, that expelled spirits by themselves transform the unwilling hosts.
21. When used in the service of the Devil, God's word is the highest blasphemy.
22. This is the transformation of Satan into an angel of light, by which he would deceive the weak in faith through fakery.
39. Between the place of solace [heaven] and suffering [hell] a deep abyss has been fixed [cf. Dives and Lazarus].
40. Wherefore those who delight in consolation, when they wish to go to those in misery, cannot cross over from there.
41. Neither can the captives cross over from one place to the other.
42. Nor can they return to their own homes.
44. Those who trust the dead, and not the sacred letters, must be blamed for infidelity.
45. Those who believe that in addition to the blessed land, there is a purgatory for immortal souls, are also unfaithful.
46. By this infidelity and superstition regarding the evil spirit, they would entangle the foolish in the faith, and simulate and dissimulate communication. Thus spells and the conjuring of the dead signify idolatry.
48. I stand at the bar of Scripture, where I ought to be judged.[38]

When one considers the potential for fear in religion, Karlstadt's eschatology is far more benign than its medieval predecessors. The fear of purgatory has been removed (1–3, 45) as has the need to purchase indulgences. Heaven is attained directly, and one is not dependent on the saints (i.e., the dead) for intercession (10, 44). Specters are illusions created by the devil. Those who experience a spell, or demon possession, do not seem to be liable for their condition; at least they are "unwilling hosts" (13). Karlstadt does not specify the nature of the fire of hell, whether it is alchemical or spiritual. He does at times use the word *hell* to signify human suffering in a general sense, but one hesitates to introduce this notion from elsewhere to explain what he does not explain here. At any rate, Karlstadt is more benevolent toward the damned than those who accepted the common notion (held by Thomas Aquinas, for example) that one of the joys of the elect in heaven is to watch the sufferings of the reprobate in hell. Karlstadt assumes that the elect would want to help the damned (40).

There is a note of skepticism in Karlstadt's denial of the reality of specters (11, 12) and ghosts (41). Elsewhere Karlstadt denied medieval folklore about a devil with horns.[39] Since those who experience a spell or demon possession are regarded as unwilling hosts, they are not morally liable. This deduction may seem daring, but Karlstadt does maintain the same thing about warlocks and witches, excusing them because they were either deluded or possessed against their will.[40] Theses 21 and 22 seem to be an intrusion at first sight, but in thesis 21 Karlstadt must be reacting very negatively to the preaching of someone who was well versed in the Scriptures. This seems to fit Nikolaus Storch, one of the Zwickau Prophets, whom Melanchthon at first admired for his knowledge of Scripture. When thesis 22 about the devil's transforming himself into an angel of light is read in conjunction with this, the identification seems even more certain, for it was Storch who immodestly claimed to have had a vision in which the archangel Gabriel appeared, saying: "Thou shalt sit on my throne."[41] Karlstadt was negative in his assessment of the Zwickau Prophets, and this shows that his enthusiasm for lay religion was not unbounded. He may, nevertheless, have been impressed by Mark Thomä, who denied infant baptism, provided that Karlstadt's opposition to "the lustration of sons and daughters" (9) is a covert and sarcastic reference to infant baptism. By now Karlstadt's own view of infant baptism was riddled with inner tensions, which may have opened him up to new suggestions.[42]

Mystical terminology reappeared from time to time. *Gelassenheit* (surrender of self to God) involves a pacific stance with respect to armed defense. The pope could well use physical violence, but one may not respond in kind. Only the spiritual sword of Scripture may be taken up in self-defense. If this leads to martyrdom, one surrenders to God's will; however, martyrdom exists for God's, rather than humanity's, glory, and therefore it is not to be aimed for, sought out, or provoked.[43]

The interior nature of the relationship with God liberates one from a too-literal reading of the Bible as well as from the church's institutions. Sacramental observances, which foster lay dependence on the priesthood, are now being sapped of salvific power. God's eternal will does not delight in external sacrifice; therefore liturgical observances have no part in the Ten Commandments, uttered by God. Even in the period of the Old Testament, ceremonies were simply designed to keep the people from drifting into idolatry. Christ did not stand on ceremony either. The Lord's Prayer was very brief, "to deflect inordinate pride."[44]

All external commands of God are temporary, perishable, and of slight value. One can please God's gracious will without performing anything externally *(one alle eusserkeit)*. Nothing is achieved through sensuous or external signs *(antzeich)*. God can even be provoked to anger when the external deed does not signify *(antzeich)* the inner Spirit of God which is lacking, for that is a lie. But what is required, the imperishable and eternal, was created by God internally in the naked soul. . . . You should search the Spirit of Scripture, that is you should search the eternal will of

God, and you should do or avoid what the letter commands or pro-
hibits—not according to the letter, but according to the concealed or
hidden spirit.[45]

Such convictions were bound to erode institutional religion. If taken
seriously, they would do away with all churchly pomp and liturgy and
with the need for a priesthood. Did Karlstadt already draw such inferences? Apparently he did, even when this affected his own authority. On
the title page of *Willen Gottes* (102), Karlstadt's name appeared without the
doctoral title, which in any case had often been omitted, but now a fresh
honorific title had taken its place. The author appears as "Andres Bodenstein von Carolstat, a new Layman." Force of habit, no doubt, had caused
him to overlook another relevant matter. As his name now appears, it still
betrays Karlstadt's noble origins. Many would have coveted such a claim,
and spurious claims to nobility were not uncommon. Had not plain
"Johann Eck" begun to style himself "Johann von Eck" when he embarked
on his career as a doctor of theology? Earlier Karlstadt had dropped the
name Rudolff, which connected him with the nobility through the maternal line, perhaps because it made his name too cumbersome. But a "new
layman" would not merely have to drop his doctoral titles to become a
commoner unto commoners. The paternal name Bodenstein would have to
be amputated. Henceforth his name would be Andreas or, even more
humbly, Andres Carolstat. Only rarely did the doctor's title accompany his
treatises, but one must reckon with a certain amount of liberty on the part
of the printers. Not until Karlstadt lived in Basel was the name Bodenstein
reinstated, but then presumably because he wanted to be identified with
his elder children, who were growing up and could hardly be named after
the town where their father had been born. The name Karlstadt had other
drawbacks. When Karlstadt became minister to the people of Orlamünde,
he could hardly identify with them with a name that proclaimed his foreign
Thuringian origins. During that period he styled himself "Brother" or
"Neighbor" Andres. Luther derided such egalitarianism, and he was especially incensed when Karlstadt dropped his doctor's titles, since one of
Karlstadt's doctoral degrees had been earned in Wittenberg. Karlstadt was
just an unreliable radical, as anyone would have been who actually practiced what the reformers were supposed to teach.

   To cast out the fear that enthralled the common people with respect to
the higher classes, the nobility, the academics, even the papacy, was a feat
of mundane proportions compared to dealing with the fear of pious lay
people in approaching the God-man, newly slain upon their altars, and
miraculously uniting himself with the outer form of the oblations, which
could not be handled by the unconsecrated laity. Luther had trembled with
fear when he celebrated his first Mass, not because of a *peculiar* psychological obsession (though he experienced his share of such), for this was an

obsession that haunted *all* late-medieval Christendom. Not until the Council of Trent was frequent lay Communion reinstated.

Karlstadt realized that the main obstacle to the restoration of frequent lay Communion was feelings of unworthiness, provoked by priestly emphasis on the need for preparation. Therefore he attacks the solemnity of the observance and self-perceptions of unworthiness. The Mass should be joyous *(freudenreich)*.[46] Paul was indeed concerned about the blasphemy of not discerning the body and blood of Christ, but Paul also said that where sin abounds, grace will abound the more.[47] The centurion who confessed to Christ that he was unworthy is often cited as an example, but Christ praised him only for his faith, not for his feelings of unworthiness. In contrast, Zacchaeus received the Lord joyfully, and he is praised without reservation.[48] Some cite Christ to prove that it is better to leave a gift at the altar than to approach after one remembers a dispute with a brother. Karlstadt does not apply this to sins committed in ignorance.[49] Christ calls not the just but sinners; he forsakes the ninety-nine sheep for one that has strayed; like a widow, he searches for a lost penny.[50] The sick should not flee from medicine, nor should sins stand in the way of receiving the flesh and blood of Christ. Traditional preparations for the sacrament "with devotions, fasting, prayer, mourning, acts of penance *(casteyen)*" are wrong if used to cast out sin.[51] Doubts are irrelevant. No one can be absolutely sure. Therefore certainty is no criterion for admission.[52]

In harmony with his colleagues, Karlstadt speaks of the primacy of the Word, which must be received first. His view of the signs and promises reflects the united position of Wittenberg. Luther's treatises of 1519 and 1520 may have been produced in consultation with Karlstadt, who even later conferred with Luther when he had written several tracts on the Lord's Supper.[53] However, Luther, insisting on the primacy of the Word, still joins Word and sacrament. Karlstadt also encourages participation in the sacrament, but Word and sacrament are not so well integrated as they are for Luther. Both men would agree that it is not an honor to Christ to abstain from the sacrament. The sacrament is food and medicine, in traditional Augustinian fashion.[54] Nevertheless, "the sign is less than the word, and the sign is established because of the promise."[55] Like the rainbow in the Old Testament, the element of Communion is "only a sign *(nur ein zeychenn)*" of God's promises.[56] Up to this point Luther might have assented, but then he would have argued that the use of the signs has none the less been commanded in Scripture. Karlstadt is less legalistic here. Since faith is essential, one can be saved without eating the sacrament.[57] Either way, the scrupulous laity need no longer fear the sacrament.

Soon Karlstadt made further progress toward lay equality. The cup had been withheld from the laity, popularly for fear of spilling the Precious Blood, but, since the Council of Constance (1415), officially to challenge the Utraquists in Bohemia. Luther preferred Communion with both elements, but he did not insist on it. Karlstadt's primitivism comes to the fore when he insists that conformity to the Gospel rites is essential. Ever since he wrote *Verba Dei* in 1519, Karlstadt had been concerned about the laity, and as a consequence began to involve himself in such local issues as the use of water and salt in Baptism, issues of lay piety. This concern was not always expressed, however, though often enough to make it significant. Perhaps foremost in Karlstadt's mind was the restoration of Christianity to its pristine form, but his efforts to achieve this guaranteed the development of a theology for the laity; for the practices of the primitive church were simple, had not been beset by more than a millennium of theological reflection, and had not been burdened with the complex heritage of an ever more rampant clericalism. Thus primitivism led Karlstadt to demand the restoration of wine in lay Communion:

On participation in the Lord's Table

9. They are not Bohemians, but true Christians, who consume both bread and wine. 10. One who merely eats the bread, sins in my opinion. 11. It were prcferable not to consume any specie (as they call it) than to consume only one. 12. For that corresponds neither to the ancient allusions nor to the institution of Christ. 13. Behold, the act of consecration is irregular, when, in accord with the Roman Pontifex, the sacrament of bread and wine is foolishly divided. 14. In this wise the recipient of one specie commits an irregular act. 15. It is less of a sin if the consecrated wine is spilled on the earth, than if it were to flow into an unbelieving heart. 16. A sorrowful harlot offends less in eating Christ's flesh than someone who is a just Pharisee, conscious of his justice.[58]

Karlstadt would soon stiffen his demand for Communion with both elements by distinguishing the promises signified by bread and wine. The promise of victory over death is signified by the bread; the promise of forgiveness, by the cup.[59] Since present practice does not conform to biblical injunctions, it is better to abstain than to participate in a rite that offends God. Not participating involves no danger as long as one's faith is strong. Karlstadt cites Augustine: "Believe and you shall have eaten *(crede et manducasti)*." "Therefore," argues Karlstadt, "see to it that you do not lose in eating wrongly what you would have gained in eating rightly [i.e., spiritually]."[60] But how can Karlstadt justify such a procedure when Scripture demands more than that? By using another scriptural text:

For as Christ's [mere] flesh profits nothing [John 6:63], neither does the visible bread. For the Spirit makes alive, the Spirit of faith, whose word is the message of the promise. . . . Therefore, one is justified outside of the consumption of bread and wine.[61]

Ideally, Communion should be shared with others, but what should the laity do, if no proper celebration is practiced? The strong do not need it, but the weak do. They turn to it for spiritual nourishment, medicine for the soul, and consolation in distress. They should not be deprived, and Karlstadt draws the logical inference that they should celebrate by themselves with both elements, if need be:

> Surely one who celebrates mass (as they call it) privately, sins less in the present circumstances than one who divided the sacrament. Truly I do not condemn one who celebrates privately, even though Christ said "Take (plural)" and not "Take (singular)." Otherwise, if one could construe a law and principle of truth out of Christ's Supper, it would follow that lay people could not celebrate privately, nor even receive the sacrament, for only bishops reclined with Christ.[62]

This was a clear instance of lay needs taking primacy even over Karlstadt's principle of primitivism. He now is a strict primitivist when it aids the laity; when it does not, he argues for an exemption.

Karlstadt was acutely sensitive toward words and their connotations, another contrast with Luther. Several times he had modified a reference to specie with the phrase: "as they call it." A reference to the word *Mass* has been similarly modified. Karlstadt was also concerned that liturgical gestures often visualized an interpretation that he now opposed; for example, the priestly elevation of the elements is a feature of sacrifice.

> The priests who are extremely dull, and opposed to the institution of Christ, would conceal the word from the laity, and they elevate the bread and the cup just as a sacrifice is elevated.[63]

These new insights, having been tested during debates in the university, needed to be communicated directly to the laity. The possibility of spilling the Precious Blood interfered with lay acceptance of the cup. Karlstadt had argued that it was less of a sin than dividing the sacrament, but why should one commit even a lesser sin? Now Karlstadt distinguishes between intentional and unintentional spilling of the blessed wine. Intentional spilling shows contempt, but even "if one were to spill a whole cup accidentally, I do not see that that should be punished."[64]

The fear of the bread, wrought by lay misinterpretations of transubstantiation, also was very real. The adoration of the bread, if it is adoration of "the baker's bread," is pernicious. One should adore the bread of heaven, which is Christ. The elements should not be feared. Christ and the bread are united; since this is a miracle, this should not be explained. Karlstadt was now contending with Luther's explanation of Christ's presence as "up, under, and in" the bread, as well as medieval notions of transubstantiation. The elements should not be feared, for they are creatures as we are. "We are all one bread who eat the bread."[65]

Throughout the years 1520 to 1522, Karlstadt retains the traditional parallelism between blessed communion bread and the God-Christ on the one hand, and the human and divine Christ, on the other. Had he been thoroughly consistent then, he would have explained the relationship between the human and divine Christ similarly as a miracle, to be accepted in faith, without further speculation. Such a radically simplified christology would have come close to primitive Christian thought, and it would have been eminently communicable to the laity. Karlstadt, however, did not openly draw such inferences, for his statements on christology as such are traditional. His conservatism in this regard was to be reinforced by another, radical, development. Karlstadt's views of Communion would need further adjustment if true lay equality were to be achieved, for then one could hardly retain a miracle that depended on the priestly act of consecration. Then the objective connection with Christ, the heavenly bread, is severed, allowing Karlstadt to abandon the symmetry between Communion and the doctrine of the incarnation. Thus he retains even the Chalcedonian categories, not just in a treatise for theologians, as Eck and others might have done, but in a sermon to the people at Grossmünster Church in Zurich.[66] For now, however, the battle to restore the cup to the laity is central: "And again I say that the lay people seek in the bread what the bread does not give [i.e., forgiveness of sins], and that for which it has not been instituted. Therefore they receive nothing unless God would have allowed us to establish our own signs, following our own minds."[67]

Karlstadt regards arguments concerning the Precious Blood or the need to oppose the Utraquists as mere masks of clericalism:

> The Pope regarded only his priests as worthy of receiving both forms. He treats the laity as unworthy of receiving the cup, and that from pure spite and arrogance, and (he does not want to concede this) this is done so he and his priests will be esteemed more highly than lay people. He claims that the dividers of the sacrament commit a great and powerful sin because they take one form at a time. Therefore I say: Is it a sin when a priest splits and divides the sacrament in this way? Then it follows that the lay people commit such a grievous sin when they take only one form.[68]

In other words, Karlstadt insists on equal treatment of priests and laity in the administration of the sacraments. If it is a sin for a priest to consume bread without the wine, it is a sin also for the laity. Karlstadt is not merely responding in kind here. He does that too, to confront the traditionists. The argument, though, is also his own, for he was convinced that improper administration of Communion implied unworthy eating. This explains the urgency with which he now began to demand liturgical reform, and the haste with which he wanted theory to be turned into practice.

In December 1521 Karlstadt's encouragement of reform bears premature fruit. He retains the word *sacrament* but drops the word *Mass* without further ado.[69] On Christmas Day he celebrates the first public Protestant Communion service. He faces the congregation, wears unadorned secular clothing, and deletes all sacrificial references from the Mass. Instead of whispering the words *Hoc est corpus meum*, he shouts the phrase in the language of the people, for all to hear and understand. Karlstadt does not require confession before Communion. Even if it could achieve anything, it would detract from Christ's absolution offered in the cup. Unlike Luther, Karlstadt opposes auricular confession. Another area of priestly control over private lives has disappeared. The only requirement for Communion is faith; without it, mere commemoration is offensive.[70]

In Karlstadt's introductory sermon he explained the changes. He pointed to the need for both elements and their specific promises. Later Luther accused him of having introduced changes unexplained, but Luther had been away at the Wartburg. When Luther returned, the changes were undone for the time being. Not till after Karlstadt's death was the elevation of the sacrament abolished. Karlstadt was disgraced in Wittenberg.

One other issue that had surfaced was the problem of images, which were also dreaded by many of the laity. Karlstadt did not regard images important enough to have been worth one of the Ten Commandments. Rather, he regarded the prohibition of "graven images" as a specific application of the First Commandment: "Thou shalt have no other gods before me."[71] Images were not the real issue; it was the use made of them by the laity.[72] Theologians could of course distinguish between proper and improper veneration (*dulia* and *latria*), but the people could not, or perhaps they really had preferred idolatry. The "so-called saints" detract from the devotion owed only to God.[73] Images are not books for the laity, as Pope Gregory claimed.[74] Karlstadt himself continued to have a deep fear of images, from the days of his youth. People called and treated images as saints, while crucifixes were known as Lord-Gods.[75] Similarly, because of their sacrificial connotations, altars should be removed.[76] If not in Wittenberg, the treatise *On the Removal of Images* was influential in Zurich, where Reformed and Anabaptist alike embraced it. This determined the plain interiors of church buildings in these traditions.[77]

A good deal of progress had been made since 1517 in Karlstadt's view of Scripture. Basic developments in that area had been achieved by 1520, by the time he broke with the papacy. Now the relationship of the laity to the sacraments was more significant than the earlier biblical issues. Defending lay rights in this area was of fundamental importance, but not so controversial, because it did not tend to challenge competing structures. I have already referred to a form of anti-intellectualism as a way of overcoming the differences between the laity and the experts. In 1520 Karlstadt gives further evidence of idealizing the natural intuitive ability of the lay mind, drawing a contrast with scholarly complexity and artifice. Lay people have an advantage in understanding the Scriptures:

> From the same blossom both draw sustenance; but the spider transforms what it has savoured into venom, while the bee changes it into honey. This also applies to the law of God. Turning to the law, the naïve and plain soul is sprinkled solely with faith. When a mind filled with human doctrine (and of course with wisdom and good sense) reads and appropriates the same law, however, it turns all the claims of Scripture into something else.[78]

This observation is made in Latin for the benefit of scholars, including Karlstadt. In its German form, *Bucher* is addressed to "all Christians, old and young, consecrated and unconsecrated, men and women." For them Karlstadt ranks the biblical books (minus the Apocrypha) in order of importance, as an incitement to start reading the important books first. Regular reading at home after meals is encouraged: "For the enjoyment and edification of the Christians, I would counsel that they spend some time, more or less, reading or hearing the holy gospels in the morning, and after the noon meal or supper, let them peruse, or better yet thoroughly examine the Holy Scriptures of the Old Law."[79]

The Final Stage (1523–1525)

Karlstadt now identified himself with the problems and aspirations of those whom Luther mocked as "the saints" of Orlamünde, and whom Karlstadt fondly recalled as "the sinners" of Orlamünde. A preacher from Joachimsthal, Wolfgang Kuch, wrote a friendly preface to Karlstadt's sermon *On Purgatory (Fegfeür)*, giving an apt summary of Karlstadt's concerns as he went to Orlamünde:

> Christian reader, although this sermon has not been adorned with courtly, dressed up, painted, and worldly-wise words, it is none the less abundantly endowed with a full, pure, and simple spirit, as well as understanding of the Scriptures. From this you will no doubt learn how far our forefathers and the very learned have striven against God's will, and judge how all their successors have stumbled and erred until now. For there are poor, wretched, unsaved people (the monks and the priests) who devour others and enrich themselves; of whom some are driven by their blind and torn understanding of the false vain light and the high arts. Others are driven by hunger for money and pride; still others, acting from ignorance of the Scriptures or simple-minded good will and cowardice or fear towards the spiritual rulers, followed the wrong conclusions and illusions of the multitude. They believe the status and situation of Christian souls that have passed on to be poor

and miserable. They regard the bosom of Abraham as hard, or the gate of heaven as narrow. They have materialized and heated up purgatory. Consequently the common man was led astray and deceived, and went from consolation to sadness, from Abraham's bosom to the jaws of Lucifer, by means of their vigils, masses for the dead, lighting of candles, sacrifices, all the while reaching and jumping. Would it not have been better, if the priests had consoled the poor and simple who lack understanding? Should they not have comforted them with the Word of God, not to worry about their friends who have died in Christ?[80]

Karlstadt, after once spurning the notion of purgatory, is now recasting it. For all the hellish accretions purgatory had acquired over the ages, and the fear this induced, its original basis had been benign. Purgatory had offered one crucial consolation to the people. If illiterate serfs or peasants, who never even entered the abode of their lord on earth, felt unworthy approaching the courts of the Lord of Lords, or if they had led less than exemplary lives, purgatory was preferable to hell. Now the Reformation attempted to end such fears by declaring all to be unworthy, and by regarding salvation as an act of God's pure grace. For the first generation of Protestants this created another problem, for then they faced questions about the status of their relatives, who had died ignorant of the new faith.

Karlstadt firmly believed that the papal church had been so thoroughly corrupted as to have fallen away from the truth. This made the fate of relatives all the more urgent. In 1520 Karlstadt had penned a moving devotional treatise, *Gelassenheit*, to his mother, who worried about her wayward son who was in danger of excommunication. What about the status of Karlstadt's dead father? Jews or gentiles who became Christians had already faced the same problem. Consequently the early church met the problem by speculating that Christ must have preached to the captive souls when he descended into hell, thus wresting from Satan's dominion the souls of their predecessors; but the idea of a limbo of the Fathers lost appeal as time passed, for Christ had entered only once and that was long ago.

This notion proved useful to Karlstadt, however, when he in fact extended the existence of limbo into a new purgatory, without alchemical fire. He warns against idle speculation, but, armed with biblical texts and a few inferences and extrapolations and aided by an earlier treatise of Wessel Gansfort, he achieved a coherent argument.[81] The soul, placed in the new purgatory, must come to self-judgment, repentance, and decision. At that point the soul is alone before God, hence intercessory prayer is useless:

Is it not a business of the devil that we allow ourselves to be led around by the nose like monkeys, and heed the senseless priests and monks when they bellow: "give money, burning lights, and sacrifice; help the souls, redeem them from purgatory"—as if such aid were of any use to the poor soul.[82]

The souls of those who need remedial exercise are spiritual and cannot be subjected to a sensuous, alchemical fire. Therefore the fire in their souls must also be spiritual; it is a fire of self-judgment, repentance, and an intense longing for God. Where progress is impeded because of ignorance, instruction is provided. Thus purgatory is like a school where the souls receive theological instruction.[83]

This reinterpretation of purgatory proved helpful to those who worried about their relatives. It could have been a new threat to those who had fervently embraced the new doctrine, but who did not want to face a second theological school in the future life. They do not need to worry, for believers are already partakers of eternal life. Heaven for them begins on earth:

The noble and eternal life begins here, for, everyone who believes in Jesus Christ, already partakes of the beautiful, precious, and heavenly life. Thus when one dies bodily in this life, one departs bodily but perseveres in life. Thus for eternity one cannot perish, but one abides and rests in Christ Jesus, and life becomes to such a one like a sweet sleep.[84]

Two points signal other differences between Karlstadt's eschatology of 1520 and his present position. The notion of "soul sleep," rejected earlier by implication, returns as an experience *like* sleep. Karlstadt did not ascribe physical processes to the soul to counter the popular notion of purgatory, based on physical burning. Consequently Karlstadt cannot defend the sleep of the soul outright, because sleep is a bodily function; therefore he modifies it through parallelism. Another difference with 1520 is Karlstadt's somewhat harsher attitude toward the damned. Earlier the elect in the bosom of Abraham would have aided the damned if they could. Now they are totally unconcerned with the damned. It may have occurred to Karlstadt, who never abandoned the notion of a hell for the damned, that if the elect tried to respond to the entreaties of the damned from hell, they would not have accepted the will of God. At least the blessed do not gloat over the torments of the wicked.

Karlstadt's new notion of purgatory also rounded off his doctrine of predestination, which he based on free human choice, and on a God who is loving toward all and not initially partisan. Karlstadt treats personal immortality and resurrection, but he opposes apocalypticism and nearly deletes Revelation from the Bible.[85] In the work that Karlstadt first published, once he settled in Orlamünde, there is an apparent change in perspective, which is also evident in all his writings of the Orlamünde period. As an academic he had, on the whole, attacked only official Catholic teachings, and he was scrupulously honest in this respect. Of course, he had also attacked the opinions of many medieval scholars, but those were permissible attacks on individual teachings. He did not accuse the traditional church of popular misconceptions. Now he no longer cared to draw such distinctions. I assume that he had not suddenly become dishonest. Rather, Karlstadt holds all Catholic and Lutheran "papists" responsible for popular misconceptions, if they are tolerated. The effect of the church on its laity, rather than its theories, becomes the touchstone for judgment.

Another issue that had to be faced anew was popular reverence and superstition involving the saints, angels, and the Virgin. The cult of the saints detracts from the honor that the church owes to God alone. No feasts should be set aside for saints or angels. All of life is a Sabbath, and God created the Sabbath to be devoted to Himself alone. God, rather than the angels, created time.[86] The presence of angels is a comforting, rather than a fearful idea. Angels descend only at the command of God, not whenever they please. Therefore they cannot answer prayer. When they are sent by God, their aid is invaluable. To the perplexed they teach the deeper meaning of Scripture, and they may predict the future, yet in this they are "messengers" and they do not lord it over anyone. Therefore it is folly to prostrate oneself at the feet of angels, or to sacrifice to them, or to celebrate the day of St. Michael.[87]

In his work on the intercession of Mary (Fürbitt Marie), Karlstadt denies Mary an intercessory role. He continues to respect her, but he will not venerate her in unbiblical fashion. Mary would point one to Christ. Not much here is new, compared to Karlstadt's earlier opinions, except that the paradigmatic Mary has disappeared, obviously because she too detracted from Christ. Consequently, the gap between Christ and the believer begins to close. Believers are not just Christ-bearers, but like Christ they also become God-bearers, participating in divine incarnation. Mary had been venerated as a benign creature; there had been far less potential for fear in her cult than in the worship of Christ, the judge of the world. Christ had dramatically sacrificed himself for believers, and thus purchased their redemption. That was benign, but this act was repeated in every Mass with great solemnity and reverence tinged with awe. So great was fear of the host that Karlstadt had been unable to dispel it totally during his Christmas sermon and Communion of 1521. Two oblations had fallen to the ground, and Karlstadt's kind request to the bystanders to pick them up left even the most daring paralyzed. He had to retrieve them himself.[88] That was the situation in Wittenberg, the foremost center of reform. The situation Karlstadt had to confront in Orlamünde was worse. A fresh exposure to popular superstition had marked effects on Karlstadt's view of the Lord's Supper. During his last two years in Wittenberg, Karlstadt had adapted his view of the sacrament to the views of Luther. He showed some originality, but his deviations were such that harmonization and collaboration remained possible. But after Luther's return from the Wartburg there was no longer any hope for even a limited amount of pluralism in Wittenberg. Thus Lutheranism was purified from Karlstadtian taint, and thereby also impoverished.

Karlstadt tried to work out the salvation of the laity in Orlamünde. He spoke and worked freely on his own ideas for reform. But his treatises on the Lord's Supper he did not try to have printed. The dramatic confrontation between Karlstadt and Luther in Jena (22 August 1524) led Luther to challenge Karlstadt; Luther publicly tossed a guilder at him as a sign of open feud, and challenged Karlstadt to publish his works on the Lord's Supper. The money for the venture was raised by the radicals of Zurich, including Felix Manz and probably Andreas Castelberger. Johannes Oecolampadius, censor of Basel, personally approved the publication of seven works, mostly on the Lord's Supper. Karlstadt's dialogue against infant Baptism was rejected, but Manz took it to Zurich, where he turned it into a manifesto, delivered to the council.[89] Thus the breach between the Lutherans and the Baptist and Reformed churches was initiated.

The treatises thus published reflect Karlstadt's preaching activity in Orlamünde. Some issues had to be dealt with again, because Orlamünde was not even Lutheran. Above all Karlstadt defamed the priests of the law, who laid claim to sacrificing Christ anew. Indeed, Christ has been sacrificed by three types of priests: by God the Father, by himself, and by the high priests, Pilate, the bailiffs, and the executioners.[90] The traditional priests (Annas, Caiaphas, the priests who say Mass) have always vented their inner hatred of Christ by wanting to slay him. The priests are guilty of betraying Christ; so are the lay people, who have been their accomplices by paying priests to say Masses. "Had they not offered their money to the clerics, the clerics would not have said masses."[91] Don't pay priests who enrich themselves by saying Masses for the dead for a fee! Instead pay a poor priest who is a real priest! But let this be done voluntarily, for compulsory tithes are an abomination.[92] Christ's sacrifice cannot be repeated. The devil chose a truth (one sins daily) to propagate a lie (one needs a daily sacrifice). Christ's true bread is the bread from heaven; the priests' bread comes from below. The priests make Christ's sacrifice less effective than was the scapegoat of the people of Israel. The priests sacrifice daily to accomplish what a scapegoat did once a year.

Next Karlstadt discussed a theme that was determinative for the stand taken by non-Lutheran Protestants in denying Christ's physical presence in the Supper. If Christ can be brought down at the bidding of a priest, "his glorious ascension would also be destroyed."[93] Karlstadt and Luther believed in a Ptolemaic universe, both having kept abreast of medieval science:

Air and elemental fire above the sky are a form of matter that is rare; therefore they cannot be seen. Even the air is more dense than the spiritual bodies of the angels. We see the sun and the moon, because they are dense, but the vaults of heaven, we do not see.[94]

Ptolemy's ingenious *Almagest* was the bible of the pre-Copernicans and Karlstadt preferred it to the cosmology of the Scriptures. Else sun and moon would not have been dense; they would have been windows (*luminaria*, Genesis 1:16, Vulgate) in the crystalline spheres, through which the heavenly light passed on the way to earth.

The placement of Christ beyond the rarefied regions proved to be a distinct advance over popular conceptions, which subjected Christ to the categories of time and space, with fears of spilling the Precious Blood or biting the Host. Since Christ's resurrection body dwells beyond time and dense space, it is not identical with the body of the historical Christ who suffered on the cross. The body itself, unlike Christ's earthly body, is now immortal and rare. Therefore the priesthood that dealt with physical things has passed out of existence, for Christ's exalted flesh cannot be sacrificed anew.[95] If others do not accept this, they are traditionists, even if they claim to be biblical. Therefore Lutherans have fallen from one papistic trap into another; they are double papists. Do not follow me, Karlstadt urges, or Doctor M. L., but follow Scripture.[96] In 1521 Karlstadt rejected the word *Mass;* now he rejects the word *sacrament.* Christ is the heavenly bread of John 6, not made with human hands. The Lord's Supper fails without faith. Unbelievers receive nothing but bread.[97]

Karlstadt's doctrine of Christ has detached Christ's physical body from the communion meal. Earlier Karlstadt identified Christ's body with the bread, on the basis of an incomprehensible miracle, but the nature of the bread as such had been left unaltered. For a transformation, he looked to Mary as paradigm of one who had borne the Christ. That conflicted with his opposition to the veneration of the saints, so he had to drop that, albeit reluctantly. Now the historical Christ becomes paradigmatic. Just as Christ in his historical body responded to the action of God, so believers partake of Communion as a spiritual response to God: "Therefore the communicants should carefully test themselves before they eat the Lord's bread, that they may respond to the figure of the eternal bread in their own bodies."[98]

In Orlamünde the laity no longer needed to worry about celebrating by themselves to avoid superstition. Now Karlstadt can reappropriate Luther's and probably his own earlier notion of *synaxis,* that is, Communion is Communion with believers as well as God, and therefore is to be practiced communally. Then it becomes a fervent *(inbrünstig)* commemoration and reappropriation of what Christ accomplished historically on the cross.

False practices are worse than suspending the observation of the Supper, for even the Serpent in the Wilderness, which had been made at the explicit command of God, was smashed by King Hezekiah when people began to venerate it.[99] Karlstadt will use rationalistic language to denounce superstition, not because he is a rationalist but because he is dissolving unbiblical accretions. He protects such notions as the Virgin Birth, for example, as scriptural. The elements of Communion, though nothing of themselves, do signify communion with Christ and should therefore be respected, as long as they are not used for superstitious ends. Solomon said that those who eat the King's bread eat it with respect. How much more should the bread of "my Lord Jesus Christ" be respected![100] Despite that, one should not dwell on the bread, but move upward in mind and heart to the bread of heaven, which is the glorified Christ. The pope directs one below to the earthly bread; Christ directs one upward to heaven. One drinks in remembrance of Christ, not of the sacraments.[101] One eats Christ's flesh spiritually; sacramentally it profits nothing.[102] In short, the Lord's Supper is a memorial that is based on faith, and by participating in it one witnesses to the congregation. A lay person or a "messenger" (bott) distributes the elements.[103] Karlstadt's relentless attack on popular superstition led him from the physical elements of the earth to the rarefied regions of the heavens. Thus his own spiritual journey was a counterpart to the Ptolemaic universe. But he prefers the rare elements to those that are dense. Therefore he abandons the old hierarchical conception for an ever-going-upward form of total egalitarianism for believers. This is very evident in the whole of his theology. Images are to be discarded because the saints are greater than their mere representations. The saints are to be discarded because Mary is greater than they, and at least Scripture calls her blessed. Mary is nearly discarded, because Christ is greater than she. And Christ is partially transcended, for although he always is mediator of forgiveness and resurrection, he is also an example of one who in Gelassenheit surrendered himself directly to God, just as the believer does. Therefore, although the Scriptures and Christ give one access of God, direct access to God the Spirit is also assured.

The movement upward is the hallmark of Karlstadt's doctrine of the Lord's Supper. At first he decried going to confession to a priest. For forgiveness one goes to the cup, where Christ's blood is directly accessible. Now Christ's body has ascended to heaven. This leaves Christ's historical body as a model for the believer's obedience and direct communication with God. Thus Christ's life was not a mere event in the irrevocable past. Time can be transcended; one can go backward in time. One can also move forward, as when eternal life is already experienced on earth. Thus the human fetters of the categories of matter, space, and time are discarded. They may imprison the body but the soul has been liberated by God and God's Christ. Finally, this gives one access spiritually, even to the glorified and ascended Christ in heaven, who (as God though not as man) is also accessible on earth. This religion required self-examination, rather than examination by a priest. It required participation rather than observation in worship. It required the discipline of the reading of the Bible at meals. It required the laity to become its own clergy. It demanded a level of under-standing that was high. For the first time a persistent movement had arisen in Germany that proclaimed a church in which all were treated alike as adults, capable of participating in it and governing it, and of following a creed for adults. No wonder Karlstadt was a threat and became a laughingstock to the theologians. It would take a lay historian, Hermann Barge, to rescue Karlstadt from the theologians. In Orlamünde, too, the people fought the authorities when Karlstadt was exiled, but their letters were rebuffed, although Karlstadt published them for posterity.[104] All along, the council had been involved communally, and every church mem-ber had to be involved in church. It was their Reformation as well as Karlstadt's. Nevertheless, although Karlstadt had spiritually liberated them to explore even the vaults of heaven, their bodies remained on earth, bound by time, space, matter, and human oppression. Karlstadt was far from being a gnostic, who would have tolerated such a situation. He had envisaged a society where the ideas of heaven would return to liberate people from the kind of suffering and inequality that was caused by human greed and exploitation. He opposed prostitution, mendicancy, unequal pension payments to widows; he proposed communal dowries for or-phans; he proposed that those whose occupations had become obsolete be retrained at communal expense; he proposed the establishment of a com-munity chest; and there was much more.[105] But all that, having been enacted into law with Luther's temporary approval, was undone—first in Wittenberg, then in Orlamünde.

Others picked up the pieces. The Baptists came closest to preserving Karlstadt's vision, but Oecolampadius similarly preserved the treatises on the Lord's Supper for future generations. In the Reformed tradition Karl-stadt became respectable, though to be respectable the Reformed tradition had to dissociate itself from Karlstadt. Nevertheless, the theology of the Lord's Supper, found in Calvin and the Reformed confessions, comes much closer to Karlstadt than to Luther. A possible link between Karlstadt and Calvin, via Zwingli and Oecolampadius, needs to be explored. Preus, in his study of the Wittenberg movement, noted that Calvin's reform of society bears a striking similarity to the Wittenberg Ordinance, which Karl-stadt had defended. Preus pointed to a possible connection with Basel, where Calvin spent some time, and where an ordinance similar to the one from Wittenberg had been introduced under Oecolampadius. The Re-formed attitude toward images was definitely influenced by Karlstadt. Other correspondences involved Psalm-singing by the congregation, a fairly strict stance on Sabbath observance, and the church's resistance to the magistracy if it interfered with reform. In addition there were a number of inter-Protestant beliefs for which Karlstadt was responsible, including the total rejection of the monastic system, the denial of saintly intercession, and even the Protestant canon of the Bible.

Appearances are sometimes deceiving. Karlstadt himself thought that his efforts had been nullified. However unintentional this was, Luther had given Karlstadt a much broader audience, once he had challenged him to publish. Therefore Luther put the Reformed and the Baptists in his debt, first by starting the Reformation, and then by ensuring that Karlstadt's ideas would get a hearing, even though Luther never even dimly understood why the Most Reverend Lord Professor Doctor Andreas Rudolff-Bodenstein von Karlstadt, Doctor of Theology, Doctor of Canon and Secular Law, Canon of All Saints, was converted into Brother Andy.

NOTES

Karlstadt's works are cited without reference to the author and with brief titles. There follows a number in parentheses, which corresponds with the numerical entry in the standard bibliography of E. Freys and H. Barge, "Verzeichnis der gedruckten Schriften des Andreas Bodenstein von Karlstadt," *Zentralblatt für Bibliothekwesen*, 21 (1904), pp. 153–79, 209–43, 305–31. Karlstadt's treatises are cited by leaf and number; where numbers are lacking in the original, they have been added in brackets. The traditional designation r. (recto) has been discarded, but the v. (indicating verso) has been retained. Thus *Ausslegung* (15), [A4-v] refers to Karlstadt's *Ausslegung und Lewterung*, etc., entered under no. 15 in the bibliography of Freys and Barge, while the page numbers refer to a quotation that runs from leaf A4 recto to A4 verso, a leaf without signatures in the original. The abbreviation th. stands for thesis or theses. Secondary works cited here are often quite rare; therefore they are all cited fully at first, and thereafter simply by name of author with a parenthetical number that refers to the footnote where the full title is cited.

1. See Calvin Augustine Pater, *Karlstadt as the Father of the Baptist Movements* (Toronto: University of Toronto Press, 1983). For the numerical strength of the various branches of Protestantism, see David B. Barrett, *World Christian Encyclopedia* (Nairobi: Oxford University Press, 1982).

2. *Iustificatione* (13), [D4]: "Sacrosancta Romae Ecclesia omnia subjicimus."

3. *Ochssenfart* (90), [Av].

4. Ibid., A2v.

5. *Wider die alte und neüwe Papistische Messen* is the full title of *Messen* (131).

6. Ernst Kähler, *Karlstadt und Augustin, Hallische Monographien*, 10 (Halle, 1952): 12.

7. Walter Friedensburg, *Urkundenbuch der Universität Wittenberg, 1 (1502–1611)*, "Geschichtsquellen der Provinz Sachsen und des Freistaates Anhalt," n.s. 3 (Magdeburg, 1926): 32, 39 n.a.: "Blasphemia contra Deum."

8. *Scripturis* (34) and *Bucher* (46–48).

9. Pater (n.1), pp. 26–29, 94–96.

10. Daniel Gerdes, *Scrinium Antiquarium sive Miscellanea Groningana* (Groningen, 1749), 1:xli, th. 12, 13, 346

11. *Ausslegung* (15), [A]: "Romischer Christenlicher kirchen wil ich in aller gutwilligkeit

alletzeit gewertig, gehorsam, und gevolgig sein. Lasse mich auch ein kindt weyssenn. Doch lawts und inhalts heyliger scriefft."

12. *380 [i.e., 405] Concl.* (3), as cited in Gerdes (n. 10), 1:19, th. 244–45.

13. Ibid., p. 20, th. 365.

14. *Ausslegung* (15), [A]: "Der ich mich in eydes crafft verbunden, und mein pflicht, auf gemeindschafft und gelupt Christlicher Sacramenten betewrt hab."

15. Kähler (n.6), p. 105.

16. "Militia Franciscana seu militia Christi," ed. Gerhard Hammer, *Archiv für Reformationsgeschichte* 69 (1978): 72: "Ast mirum est vos tanta tribuere Francisco. Sufficeretne hominem Christianum eum fuisse?"

17. Ibid., p. 74.

18. For a thorough discussion, see Karel Blockx, *De veroordeling van Maarten Luther door de theologische faculteit te Leuven in 1519, "Verhandelingen van de Koninklijke Vlaamse Akademie voor Wetenschappen, Letteren en Schone Kunsten van België, Klasse der Letteren,"* 31:5–11.

19. *Verba Dei* (26), A2v-3: "Putas tu eadem populo dicenda quae in scholis theologicis tractamus et concludimus? Non sunt, inquit, vulgariis Christianis et illiteratis semina inculcanda quae in eruditam humum doctosque auditores et assectatores iacimus. Tu ne usqueadeo ineptis, ait, qui plebeos christianos e pulpito ecclesiae doctrinis illiusmodi dignitatis, quas in scholis ex scripturae faucibus, vel derivamus, vel elicimus?"

20. Otto Seitz, *Der authentische Text der Leipziger Disputation: Aus bisher unbenutzten Quellen* (Berlin, 1903), p. 28.

21. *Verba Dei* (26), C3.

22. Ibid., Ev.

23. Ulrich Bubenheimer, *Consonantia Theologiae et Iurisprudentiae, Jus Ecclesiasticum* 24 (Tübingen, 1977): 3, 6–7, 10.

24. See Karlstadt's *Loci Communes* (156), pub. 1540.

25. Steven E. Ozment, *Mysticism and Dissent: Religious Ideology and Social Protest in the Sixteenth Century* (New Haven, Conn.: Yale University Press, 1973).

26. *Verba Dei* (26), Cv.

27. See *10 Theses*, reprinted in Bubenheimer (n. 23), 290–91. Unlike Bubenheimer (pp. 172–73), I do not take this date very literally. Karlstadt's date for Alexander's fall (1246) was wrong anyway; he may have relied on memory, and he adjusted the date several times (Pater, 1, p. 48). Bubenheimer's argument that Karlstadt intended to protect Pope Innocent IV in 1520, because he respected the unrecanted opinions of the Fathers, of which Karlstadt approved in 1518, seems too speculative. Innocent's view could only have alienated Karlstadt from him in 1520; see *Gelassenheyt* (38), [A4]. Finally, when Bubenheimer deduces from this that Karlstadt must still approve of most of canon law, I dissent, for this would be far too grave an inconsistency on Karlstadt's part. In *Bucher* (46), [C4] Karlstadt had opposed even the *name* of "canons" for papal decretals, "for they are not rules for Christian believers, but for hypocrites."

28. *Bucher* (46), C3.

29. *Gelassenheyt* (38), B.

30. *Heylickeit* (44), B3: "Derhalben sol [der Bapst] die Biblien teglich lesen, auss der selben alle geystliche sachen mit guttem erkentnis vortragen und vor allen dingen solten alle gottis dienste unnd ehr erbiettung auss der Biblien fliessen und auffgericht werden. Wan das geschee, sso musten seine Decretalis ad infernum fliehen."

31. *Ablass* (28), A2v: "Soll das ein grund sey durch die heylige schrifft, vorstee ich keyn ander denn die in der Biblien als Canonica und Catholica von allen angenummen ist, darumb darfstu mit keyn menschen gesetz furwerffen, mir damit zupinden."

32. Ibid., A3v.

33. Ibid.

34. Ibid., B2v.

35. Ibid., Bv–2v.

36. Ibid., A3v.

37. Th. 3–7 of 7 *Theses,* reprinted in Hermann Barge, *Andreas Bodenstein von Karlstadt,* 2 vols. (Leipzig: Friedrich Brandstetter 1905), 1:473–74: "3 Maledictionem sustulit Christus, factus pro nobis maledictum. 4 Iustitia itaque credentibus Christus est. 5 Satisfactio, cuius usus est in ecclesia, non est pars paenitentiae, iure divino. 6 Sed satisfactio vulgata est instituta ab episcopis pro exercendis rudibus. 7 Proinde impie onerant quidam satisfactoriis operibus adflictas conscientias, alieni ab exemplo Christi, qui linum fumigans non extinguit, et arundinem quassatam non confringit."

38. Ibid., pp. 495–97.

39. Pater (n. 1), p. 23, n. 50.

40. Ibid., pp. 72–73.

41. See Gordon Rupp, *Patterns of Reformation* (London: Epworth Press 1969), pp. 100–101. Rupp connects Karlstadt with the Zwickau Prophets, making purely speculative inferences. Karlstadt, however, distrusted Storch and attacked the docrines of the Prophets, Pater (n. 1), p. 281; cf. p 16.

42. Pater (n. 1), pp. 106–8.

43. *Gelassenheyt* (38), Bv-2, [B4]. Cf. *Gewaldt* (63).

44. *Willen gottes* (102), G3: "gleicher weyss Christus die menschen von der eergeyrikeit tzeucht durch kurtz gebeth."

45. Ibid., G3-v.

46. *Empfahern* (54), [C5v].

47. Ibid., A3-v, [A4v]–B.

48. Ibid., A2v-3. Cf. Matthew 8:8; Luke 19:6.

49. Barge (n.37), 1:480, th. 1–2. Cf. Matthew 5:23–24.

50. *Empfahern* (54), A3v.

51. Ibid., B2.

52. *Christianissimi VVittenbergensis Gymnasii* (described Barge, n. 37, 1:472, Second Collection of Theses), B2, th. 1–5 of *De sacramento panis,* debated on 12 July 1521.

53. Karlstadt refers to Luther's works as "Luther's and my teachings." *Ochssenfart* (90), A2. On leaf [A4v], Karlstadt says: "Derhalben will ich auff das mein sehen, und beken mich auch dartzu, das ich etliche buchlin (die Messe betreffen) hab fur mangerley augen gelegt, wil auch furt mehr lassen furlegen, den Christen tzu gut."

54. Ibid., Bv-2.

55. Ibid., C2: "Sag ich das ein zeychen minder ist dan das wort, und das das zeichen von wegen der zusag furgestelt wurt."

56. Ibid., C2v.

57. Ibid., B4v.

58. *Christianissimi Gymnasii* (n. 52), B3v: "DE participibus mensae Domini. 9. Non sunt Bohemi sed veri Christiani, panem et poculum Christi sumentes. 10. Qui solo pane vescitur, mea sententiae, peccat. Satiusque foret, si nullam, ut aiunt, speciem sumeret, quam unam tantum. 12. Quia neque figuris veteribus, neque Christi instituto satisfit. 13. Sicut consecrans fit irregularis, ut cum Romano Pontifice ineptiam, sacramentum panis et poculi dividens. 14. Ita recipiens unam speciem irregularitatem incurrit. 15. Minus peccatem est, si vinum consecratum in humum defluit per imprudentiam, quam si cadat in cor incredulum. 16. Minus offendit meretrix adflicta, manducando carnem Christi, quam iustus aliquis phariseus suae iustitiae conscius."

59. Barge (n. 37), 1::488, th. 75, 80, 81.

60. Ibid., p. 488, th. 88, 90; p. 489, th. 99.

61. Ibid., p. 489, th. 95–97.

62. Ibid., p. 487, th. 65: "Verum qui solus edit non eatenus peccat, quatenus divisor sacramenti." P. 489, th. 112–13: "Verum non illum condemno qui privatim celebrat, propter hoc quod Christus dicit. Accipite et non dicit accipe. Si ex Christi cena legem et formam veritatis sumere liceret, sequeretur, quod laici non possent privatim celebrare, neque sacramentum accipere, quia cum Christo soli episcopi accubuerunt."

63. Ibid., p. 487, th. 61.

64. *Messe* (71), E: "Aber wan einer angefeer einen kelch vergoss, weiss ich nit das er tzu straffen sey."

65. *Anbettung* (68), B3; cf. A2v, [A4v].

66. Cf. Calvin Augustine Pater, "Karlstadts Zürcher Abschiedspredigt über die Menschwerdung Christi," *Zwingliana* 14, no. 1 (1974): 1–16.

67. *Messe* (71), [E4v].

68. Ibid., [D4]: "Der Bapst hat allein seine Pfaffen beyder gestaldten wirdig gemacht, die leyhen macht er des kelchs unwirdig, und thut das aus lawterem frevel und mutwill. Das er und seine Pfaffen hoher geacht werden dan leyhen, wie wol er das nit gesteen wil. Er spricht das die teiler des hochwirdigen sacraments ein grosse mechtige sunde thun, drumb das sie ein gestalt allein nyessen. Darumb sag ich, sundigt einer darumb das er das sacrament speltet wan ein priester ein gestalt nimbt? Volget ouch das die leyhen solliche greuliche sund thun wan sie ein gestalt allein nehmen."

69. 1 Corinthians 1 (75), [A4].

70. Barge (n. 37), 1:357–62.

71. Hans Lietzmann, *Kleine Texte*, vol. 74 (Bonn: 1911), 4:21–25; 7:17–24.

72. Ibid., pp. 6, 7, 10, 13, 14, 17.

73. Ibid., pp. 4:32–5:11.

74. Ibid., p. 16:9–11.

75. Ibid., p. 19:15–33.

76. Ibid., p. 20:12–20.

77. Pater (n. 1), 130–34.

78. *Scripturis* (34), Bv: "Ex eodem flore apis et aranea sumunt escam, sed haec in venenum, illa in mel, vertit quod carpit. Ita eandem dei legem, vacuus animus adhuc simplex, solaque fide perfusus. Et mens doctrinarum humanarum plena, plena denique sapientiae et prudentiae legit et discit. Verum haec omnes scripturae sententias in alienum humorem commutat."

79. *Bucher* (46), [B4v].

80. *Fegfeür* (95), Av.

81. See John Walter Kleiner, "Andreas Bodenstein von Karlstadt's Eschatology as Illustrated by Two Major Writings of 1523 and 1539." Th. M. thesis, Harvard Divinity School, 1966.

82. *Fegfeür* (95), [A4].

83. Ibid., C2v: "Ich halt es dafur, das sy dort studieren und leren miessen (sein sy anders versehen zur seligkeit) und erkennen alle ware urtail oder sententz welche got will haben erkandt, ee er sy in hymel nymt."

84. Ibid., Bv.

85. *Scripturis* (34), M3v-[4].

86. *Engelen* (122), A2: "Vor alem solt ir wissen das man den engeln keynen tag zumessen kan . . . den sye schaffen keyne zeit." See also Erich Hertzsch, *Karlstadts Schriften as den Jahren 1523–25*, "Neudrucke deutscher Literaturwerke des 16. und 17. Jahrhunderts" (Halle [Saale], 1956–1957), vol. 325 (published in two parts), pt. 1:23–24.

87. *Engelen* (122), [C4-v].

88. Barge (n. 37), 1:361.

89. Pater (n. 1), 159–67, 290–94.

90. *Priesterthum* (112), [B4].

91. Ibid., F-v: "Hetten sie nit den pfaffen gelt angebotten, so hetten sich die pfaffen der messen auch enthalten."

92. Ibid., F-v. Karlstadt first had this subject debated in Wittenberg, January 1522; see Barge (n. 37) 1:494, th. 1–8, 10–15. For the probable impact of the theses in Switzerland, see Pater (n. 1), pp. 129–30.

93. *Priesterthum* (112), D3: "So must die herliche hymelfart Christi auch zu nicht werden."

94. *Engelen* (122), A2v.

95. *Priesterthum* (112), D2.

96. *Leyb* (129), A, [D5].

97. Ibid., [C4v]: "Die gotlosen, so kein forcht gottes haben, kunden das fleisch Christi weder einnemen noch essen. Das aber Thomas von Aquin schreibt. Es nemen es die guten und die bosen. Das ist erlogen."

98. Ibid., D3v: "Der halben solten sich die communicanten wol brufen, ehe sie des herren brodt ässen, auff das sie der figur des eusserlichen brodtes unther sich in irem leyb antworten.

99. Hertzsch (n. 86), pt. 2, p. 8.

100. Ibid., p. 21:25–35.

101. Ibid., pp. 21–23.

102. Ibid., p. 25:5, 14–15: "Geistlich müssen wir des hern fleisch essen. Der leib Christi sacramentaliter ist gar nichts nütz."

103. Ibid., pp. 26–28.

104. Ibid., pp. 56–58.

105. Appended to *Bilder* (87–89); see Lietzmann (n. 71).

106. See the section dealing with Karlstadt in the bibliography of Pater (n. 1), pp. [297]-302.

107. See n. 23.

108. *Andreas Bodenstein von Karlstadt 500-Jahr-Feier, Festschrift der Stadt Karlstadt zum Jubiläumsjahr 1980* (Karlstadt: Michel Druck, 1980), pp. [5]-[58].

109. Cf. Ronald J[ames] Sider, *Andreas Bodenstein von Karlstadt* (Leiden, 1974), pp. [1]-6; Bubenheimer (n. 23), pp. 4–6; Pater (n. 1), pp. 6–8. See also my review of Bubenheimer's and Sider's volumes in *The Catholic Historical Review* 67 (1981): 124–26.

110. Pater (n. 1), 7–8.

111. Rupp (41), pp. 149–53.

112. Barge (n. 37), 2:515–18.

113. Ibid., pp. 386–93.

114. The traditional sources for the Flensburg Debate are W. I. Leendertz, *Melchior Hofmann* (1883) and F. O. zur Linden, *Melchior Hofmann* (1885).

115. Barge (n. 37), 2:466–77.

116. Barge (n. 37), 1:495, th. 11, which has already been cited.

117. James S. Preus, "Carlstadt's *Ordinaciones* and Luther's Liberty: A Study of the Wittenberg Movement 1521–22," *Harvard Theological Studies* 26 (Cambridge, Mass., 1974).

118. Ibid., pp. 78, 80.

119. *The Sixteenth Century Journal* 10, no. 1 (1979): 107.

A NOTE ON THE RECENT LITERATURE

Traditional comments on Karlstadt in English secondary literature are dated and misleading. Since Luther's works were accessible to scholars in the original as well as in English translation, they determined most of the polemic. Modern methods of duplication have made Karlstadt accessible again to those who collect his works. Two volumes (now out of print) contain some of the most significant writings of Karlstadt's Orlamünde period. They were published by Professor Erich Hertzsch of Orlamünde. A small number of writings have been translated into English.[106]

Reviews of the literature have appeared recently. In German, Bubenheimer has published an admirable volume on Karlstadt's career as jurist.[107] In 1980 the largely Catholic town of Karlstadt celebrated the quincentennial of the birth of its wayward native son. A *Festschrift* was published, containing essays of uneven quality, because Bubenheimer's contribution to clearing up Karlstadt's ancestry and early life is outstanding.[108] Since virtually all the literature has been reviewed and is easily accessible, I shall not duplicate those observations.[109] There remain a few contributions that need special consideration. Since there is no biography in English, the portrayal of Karlstadt in Gordon Rupp's *Patterns of Reformation* (London 1969) is frequently consulted. Its inaccuracies may well seem to be offset by Rupp's fluid and engaging style, and by the fact that his sketch fills a definite gap. Elsewhere I was reluctantly forced to challenge Rupp's attempt to debunk Karlstadt's academic degrees.[110] Rupp is willing to make occasional concessions, and his treatment of Karlstadt advances beyond traditional assessments, but Rupp is still so beholden to the tradition that Karlstadt is presented as a foil for Luther.

Rather than becoming embroiled in the assessment of Luther's and Karlstadt's personalities, over which far too much ink has been spilled in the past, I shall discuss Rupp's final chapter, which deals with Karlstadt's escape from Saxony (1529) till his final years in Basel, as professor of Hebrew and dean of the university. Rupp deals with a total of six issues in this chapter, all of which need to be examined. This chapter is entitled "Shallows and Miseries."[111] The title is justified for the period when Karlstadt lived in Saxony from 1525 to 1529; it does not apply to the final years of his life, when he rose to prominence in Basel and worked to reorganize the university, as he had done in Wittenberg. Karlstadt drew a high salary during those final years; it was invested in rental properties to sustain his widow later.[112] Compared to any period after 1522, these years were the most secure and perhaps the happiest of his life. At the beginning of the chapter Karlstadt's final years in Saxony are considered. Karlstadt evaded censorship in Saxony by corresponding with his old friends like Kaspar Schwenckfeld and with the Moravian Baptists, probably to find a route of escape. His family was on the brink of starvation. Luther was putting considerable pressure on Karlstadt, demanding that he attack Oecolampadius's and Zwingli's doctrine of the Lord's Supper. Luther also had written the elector, suggesting that although he did not think that Karlstadt should be executed, there were some who thought that he should be imprisoned for life.[113] These facts are not even mentioned by Rupp—merely the correspondence, which he takes as a sign that "Karlstadt could not resist the temptation to intrigue." After his flight from Saxony, Karlstadt went to Holstein, to a friend, the furrier Melchior Hoffman. Rupp then refers to a debate at Flensburg between Karlstadt and Bugenhagen. The debate, however, never took place, because Bugenhagen feared to debate Karlstadt, induced the crown prince to expel Karlstadt, and then boasted in Saxony that Karlstadt had been afraid to debate him.[114]

According to Rupp, the attempt to confer degrees on the ministers who lectured at the University of Basel was instigated by Karlstadt. However, Barge has shown that Karlstadt acted under intense pressure by the senate and had reservations all along. Karlstadt left behind a statement concerning academic degrees ("The degrees, which they call the Master's and the Doctorate, are to be ranked as least among the things that are intrinsically evil"), not much of an endorsement. The treatises *Axiomata* and *IOB VII*, published in Basel, do not even mention Karlstadt's academic degrees.[115]

Rupp also implies that Karlstadt, while he was still in Orlamünde, may have created Poltergeist phenomena to show that he was called from heaven. Erich Hertzsch had examined the same evidence, used by Rupp, and concluded that it was based on a "gossipy and obviously unbelievable report." Karlstadt, with his attacks on externalized religion, had emphasized that the call from heaven was an *inner* experience. Karlstadt, unlike Luther, did not even believe in the existence of Poltergeists.[116]

Finally, Rupp brings in Karlstadt's wife to testify against him: "the young girl of sixteen, the roses dying from her cheek, as she strove to follow her unpredictable husband." Karlstadt was not unpredictable. He lived steadily in Wittenberg for sixteen years. Even his thought is marked by rigorous consistency. But Rupp, like many others, is unwilling to face the fact that *Saint* Martin Luther might have persecuted anyone; therefore those who flee in fear of their lives are unpredictable. When Karlstadt's wife is presented as "the young girl of sixteen" one makes a modern judgment. Sixteen years was not regarded as an immature age for marriage, and disparities between the ages of husband and wife were a common occurrence. This leaves "the roses dying from her cheek" a claim difficult to contest. However, nowhere else have I encountered the charge that husbands are responsible for the fact that wives grow older. One regrets that Rupp was really too defensive about Luther to do justice to Karlstadt. In my criticism I have confined myself entirely to facts that are known when Rupp wrote. He is, of course, not responsible for the fact that many earlier observations that he made have since been overturned in the latest literature.

Of newer trends, the study of the Wittenberg Movement by James Preus needs attention.[117] Since my work on Karlstadt has been done in areas that did not overlap with Preus's work, I have not dealt with it. This of course does not detract from Preus's study. Preus has carefully examined the program of magisterially oriented reform and legislation, which was instigated chiefly by Karlstadt in Wittenberg. Preus was also concerned with Luther's role in the suppression of the Wittenberg Ordinances, and he is scrupulously determined to do justice to both Karlstadt and Luther. Traditionally Luther was thought to have stood for freedom, while Karlstadt defended legalism. Preus does not take the slogans of "freedom" and "law" at face value. He tests the slogans by relentlessly pursuing such questions as "whose freedom" and "is law automatically oppressive?"

Preus has shown that Luther's concept of freedom granted freedom mostly to the clergy rather than the laity, whereas Karlstadt's ordinances expressed the consensus of a large section of the laity. In his epilogue, Preus summarizes the consequences of Luther's intervention in Wittenberg in March 1522:

> In the name of the freedom of the faith, conscience and the gospel, Luther rejected statutory implementation of reformed public worship at Wittenberg under an ultimatum: either the other must go, or I will recant.
>
> But when the rhetoric of evangelical liberty was translated into reality, we see that its real exercise belonged to the leaders, since a situation prevailed in which evangelical policy was to be set at Wittenberg by Luther himself, and elsewhere by evangelical clergymen, trained and/or certified by the Wittenberg theological faculty. It was an exercise of freedom for him to revert for the time being to the singing of Latin mass and withholding the cup from an "unqualified" laity, just as it was in late 1523 when he announced that the people were now ready for both kinds, and so henceforth it would be implemented in Wittenberg. But where was the liberty of the congregation? Against the wishes of the majority, the cup was withheld at first; then, once both kinds became the practice, one kind was no longer offered.
>
> The principle was that conscience transcends the law, and the law must not coerce conscience. The reality at Wittenberg was that the law became incarnated in Luther, himself functioning freely.[118]

Prues's very perceptive analysis is born out in the history of Protestantism. There is far more than irony in the fact that the spiritual descendants of the "free" Luther have mostly been found in churches that submitted supinely to state control, whereas the "legalistic" Karlstadt's spiritual heirs, whether Baptists, Mennonites, or some of the Reformed, opted for the freedom that comes from the separation of church and state. For Karlstadt demanded the translation of his ideas into churchly political structures that could learn to resist the intrusion of the state. If one grants Preus that Lutheran polity was incarnated in Luther, then one understands how, after Luther's death, the secular rulers could usurp the Lutheran structures. This offered lay control on the top, but because the rulers became tyrants once again. Lutherans who had been conditioned to accept the authorities as instruments of God could offer only pitiful resistance. Preus's work has broken new ground in terms of the political situation in which Karlstadt found himself. Its chief limitation is the assumption that Karlstadt and Luther clashed primarily over political matters. There were deep issues that were separating Luther and Karlstadt, however. They were known better to Karlstadt than they were to Luther. However, Preus concedes that he was dealing with a period of only a few months in Karlstadt's life, and that the trend of Karlstadt's thought may well reveal other issues. All in all Preus made a superb contribution, essential for anyone interested in Karlstadt's political program or Karlstadt's biography.

Finally I note that some years back I wrote my first book review, dealing with Ronald J. Sider's *Karlstadt's Battle with Luther*.[119] Showing my inexperience, I failed miserably, for I injected a bit of humor. But book reviews are a serious matter. Some friends wondered afterward whether my comments were made sarcastically, sarcasm apparently being allowable. My humor was an act of self-defense, for it was directed at the tendency, sometimes actually observed in studies of the German Reformation, of picturing a Ptolemaic Reformation with Luther at the center of the universe. My comments should be read in light of the serious endorsement that I gave to Sider's work. Naturally one has one's differences, but the work of Sider, Bubenheimer, and Preus is of remarkable quality. Moreover, for all the uproar that Barge's work quite unintentionally created at the turn of the century, his work, too, was solid, even if modifications are now necessary. Compared to anything published before Barge, a nearly total revision and reassessment of Karlstadt is being accomplished.

5

The Religious Beliefs of Thomas Cromwell

Stanford E. Lehmberg

There can be no other leader of the Reformation whose religious beliefs remain as obscure as Thomas Cromwell's. Indeed, as is well known, earlier writers often pictured him as a man totally devoid of personal conviction: R. B. Merriman, for example, held that "the motives that inspired his actions were invariably political" and "his religious beliefs, as far as can be discovered, absolutely nothing when disconnected from practical ends."[1] A reassessment, in considerable degree begun by A. G. Dickens, credits Cromwell with genuinely held views, and G. R. Elton's recent retelling of the Tudor narrative describes Cromwell as a clear Protestant imbued with evangelical zeal for the purification of religion.[2] But even for Elton "exactly what he believed remains a debatable point," while one of Elton's own students remarks that the picture of "the new evangelical Cromwell" is unconvincing.[3]

The difficulty is largely of Cromwell's own making. Throughout the whole course of human history few men have left behind such large deposits of correspondence and official papers that reveal so little about private life and inner convictions. Cromwell's acts of state are, of course, well known and require no elaboration here: he drafted the legislation that separated the English church from Rome and confirmed Henry VIII's position as supreme head; he supervised the dissolution of the monasteries; more than anyone else, he was responsible for the authorized dissemination of the English Bible. Such outward acts may imply inward beliefs, but they cannot pierce to the heart of human conviction. Yet the personal position of so important a leader as Cromwell matters a good deal. Can the hints he left us be pieced together so as to tell us something more about the religious beliefs of the man behind the Henrician reformation?

I

A few documents prepared by Cromwell himself bear directly on the issue. They are his will, his Injunctions of 1536 and 1538, his speech opening the Parliament of 1540, and his final utterances from the scaffold.

It was in July 1529 that Cromwell drafted his will: a crucial time in his life, when he could foresee the fall of his patron, Thomas Cardinal Wolsey, but could not predict his own rise with any confidence. (One is reminded of the tearful interview reported by Cavendish, in which Cromwell said, "it is my unhappy adventure, which am like to lose all that I have travailed for all the days of my life for doing my master true and diligent service."[4]) The orthodox, medieval tone of the will is its most interesting feature. Cromwell began by bequeathing his soul

> to the grete god of heuen my meker Creato[r] and Redemer beseching the most gloryous virgyn o[r] blessed ladie Saynct Mary the vyrgyn and Mother w[t] all the holie companye of heuen to be Medyatours and Intercessours for me to the holie trynytee So that I may be able when it shall please Almightie god to call me out of this miserable worlde and transitorie lif to inherite the kingdome of heuen.

Money was left for distribution among poor people to pray for his soul, although these revenues were to be transferred to Cromwell's son Gregory when he reached the age of twenty-five; for payment of a priest "being an honest person of contynent and good lyuyng" to sing masses for his soul for a period of three years; for additional prayers by the five orders of friars in London; for poor maidens toward their marriage; for relief of poor householders; "poure parochanss of the paroche Where god shall ordeyn me to haue my dwelling plac at the time of my dethe," and poor prisoners in Newgate and other jails. His parish church was to receive 20 shillings "for my tithes forgotten," and his funeral was to be performed "w[t] out any erthelye pompe."[5]

At some subsequent date Cromwell revised this testament. By this time he was richer, and he increased most of his charitable contributions, giving his chantry priest £46 13s. 4d. over seven years rather than £20 over three, each order of friars 20s. instead of 13s. 4d., the poor maidens £40 instead of £20, and poor householders £20, not £10. Only the payment to his parish church was deleted; presumably Cromwell was confident that he had not in fact forgotten to pay his tithes. There were also some alterations in bequests to members of Cromwell's family. In particular, all payments to his daughters Anne and Grace were eliminated, no doubt because they had died. If we knew the dates of their death it might help us to fix the date at which the will was changed, but no record seems to survive. It is usually assumed that they were gone after 1529 and that revision followed shortly after the original drafting of the will. If so, one could regard the traditional religious arrangements as normal for the period and not indicative of Cromwell's more mature beliefs. But it is not certain that this is the case; all one can safely say is that the revision occurred before 1536, when Cromwell was made a baron and would no longer have referred to himself

merely as a gentleman of London. How long Cromwell continued to believe in the efficacy of mediators, good works, and prayers for the dead
remains open to question.

The will at least reflects some of Cromwell's personal beliefs at some
stage in his life. It is less clear to what extent the two sets of injunctions to
the clergy can be viewed as revealing his convictions, for they were essentially state documents issued by Cromwell as the king's vicegerent in spiri-
tuals. Still, they were promulgated over Cromwell's name and give every
appearance of having been written by him; they probably demonstrate
inner beliefs as well as external pressures.

The earlier Injunctions of 1536 are closely related to the ambiguous but
moderately Protestant Ten Articles issued by Henry VIII as a first statement of Anglican doctrine. Not surprisingly, Cromwell ordered the clergy
to explain these articles to their parishioners and to preach against the
Bishop of Rome's usurped jurisdiction. It is of greater interest that he
enjoined priests to teach their people the Lord's Prayer, Creed, and Ten
Commandments in English—an early proof of Cromwell's concern for vernacular texts and religious education—and that he spoke disparagingly of
images, cults of saints, and pilgrimages. There may be a glimpse of the
essential Cromwell in the statement that subjects can please God better by
exercising truly their occupations than by traveling to shrines, by giving to
the poor than by offering oblations to relics.[6]

The Injunctions of 1538 are best known because they require the keeping
of parish registers, a sign of Cromwell's tidy administrative mind if not of
his religion. They restate the need for laymen to be taught (by rote) the
Pater Noster and Creed—"euery christen person ought to knowe the same
before they shuld receyue the sacrament of the aulter"—and they carry
farther the campaign against relics, images, and pilgrimages. "Images
serve for no other purpose but as to be bookes of vnlerned men that can no
letters," so no tapers should be burned before them and those which have
been abused by superstition should be removed.[7] But lights may still burn
by the rood loft, "afore the sacrament of the altare," and, presumably at
Easter, "about the sepulchre." Cromwell's concern for preaching "the very
gospell of Christ" is emphasized in what may be the most revealing of the
injunctions: all clergy are to exhort their people to perform works of

> charite marcy and faithe specially prescribed and commaunded in scrip-
> ture, and not to repose there trust of affiance in any other workes de-
> vised by mens phantasies besydes scripture, as in wanderyng to
> pilgremages offeryng of money candelles or tapers to Images or reliques
> or kissing or lickyng the same, sayng ouer a nombre of beades not
> vndrestanded ne mynded or in suche like superstition, ffor the doyng
> wherof ye not only haue no promise of reward in scripture but contrary-
> wise grete threates & maledictions of god, as thinges tendyng to Idolatry
> and superstition which of all other offences god almighty doth most

detest and abhorre for that the same diminisheth most his hono^r and glorie.

Another momentous article requires each parish church to provide an English Bible "of the largest volume" and to set it up where parishioners "may most commodiously resorte to the same"; clergy shall

> expressely provoke stere and exhorte to euery person to reade the same as that which is the very lyvely worde of god, that euery christen person is bounde to embrace beleve and followe, if they loke to be saved, admonyshing them neuertheless to avoide all contention and altercation therein, but to vse an honest sobrietie in thinquisition of the trewe sence of the same, and to referr the explication of obscure places to men of higher jugement in scripture.[8]

This commitment to the English Scriptures and concern about contention are themes recurring throughout Cromwell's later life.

An intense dislike of discord is manifest again in Cromwell's parliamentary "swan song," the speech opening the session of 1540. Here Cromwell purported to be informing the Lords and Commons of the King's concern, in phrases that foreshadow Henry's own famous denunciation of "old mumpsimus and new sumpsimus," but it seems evident that his own views were involved as well when he said that

> the rashness and licentiousness of some, and the inveterate superstition and stiffness of others in the ancient corruptions, had raised great dissensions to the sad regret of all good Christians. Some were called papists, others heretics; which bitterness of spirit seemed the more strange, since now the Holy Scriptures, by the King's great care of his people, were in all their hands, in a language which they understood. But these were grossly perverted by both sides, who studied rather to justify their passions out of them, than to direct their belief by them.[9]

These words deploring faction were almost the last recorded utterance of Cromwell as Vicegerent and Earl of Essex. Within two months after he spoke he had been arrested on a treason charge. The bill of attainder prepared by his conservative enemies obviously cannot be taken as evidence of his beliefs, but it is significant that this propagandistic accusation made much of his supposedly radical views. Here Cromwell is charged with being a "detestable heretic," causing "damnable errors and heresies to be inculcated, impressed, and infixed in the hearts of . . . subjects," spreading heretical literature, setting convicted heretics at liberty, infecting his retainers with heresy, and even threatening to "fight in the field in mine own person, with my sword in my hand," against the king should Henry turn away from the reformed faith.[10] What was perhaps the most extreme charge accused Cromwell of asserting that every Christian man could administer the Sacrament. This has led some historians, including J. J. Scarisbrick, to believe that Cromwell was charged with being a sacramentary, a member of that ultra-radical sect, detested as much by Lutherans as by Catholics, that denied the real presence and preached anarchy.[11] In a letter to the King written from the Tower, Cromwell specifically denied that charge, insisting that "god . . . knowethe" him to be guiltless of holding sacramentary beliefs.[12]

Cromwell's brief address from the scaffold, recorded by John Foxe, is less precise on this point but more vehement in asserting the general orthodoxy of Cromwell's faith.[13] Begging forgiveness of the king and the Holy Trinity—"O Father forgive me! O Son forgive me! O Holy Ghost forgive me! O three persons in one God forgive me!"—he went on to charge all spectators to be his witnesses:

> And now I pray you that be here, to bear me record, I die in the catholic faith, not doubting in any article of my faith, no nor doubting in any sacrament of the church. Many have slandered me, and reported that I have been a bearer of such as have maintained evil opinions; which is untrue; but I confess, that like as God, by his Holy Spirit, doth instruct us in the truth, so the devil is ready to seduce us; and I have been seduced. But bear me witness that I die in the catholic faith of the holy church.[14]

A final prayer, too, is suffused with personal conviction that is at once orthodox and reformed:

> O Lord Jesu! which art the only health of all men living, and the everlasting life of them which die in thee, I, wretched sinner, do submit myself wholly unto thy most blessed will . . . I see and acknowledge that there is in myself no hope of salvation . . . I have no merits nor good works which I may allege before thee. . . .Thou, merciful Lord! . . . sufferedst most grievous pains and torments for my sake: finally, thou gavest thy most precious body and thy blood to be shed on the cross for my sake. . . . Let the merits of thy passion and blood-shedding be satisfaction for my sins. . . . Grant me, merciful Saviour! that when death hath shut up the eyes of my body, yet the eyes of my soul may still behold and look upon thee; and when death hath taken away the use of my tongue, yet my heart may cry and say unto thee, 'Lord! into thy hands I commend my soul; Lord Jesu! receive my spirit.' Amen.

In the difference between these utterances and the preamble to his will one discerns most clearly the ways in which Cromwell's beliefs had changed during his years in office. At the end he made no mention of the Virgin Mary or other intercessors, and he held out no hope that the prayers of the living could benefit his soul. He did not trust in his own good works, such as the charitable contributions he had intended to make, but rather fixed his hope wholly on the salvation offered to believers in Christ's death and passion.

II

Lacking a more precise formulary of faith written by Cromwell himself, we are driven to other sources. In particular, the writings of men with whom Cromwell was closely associated may shed light on his views. We must, of course, avoid the untenable argument that patrons necessarily share all the beliefs of their protégés: even the closest of friends are bound to differ on some issues. But where ideal evidence does not exist, historians are surely justified in doing what they can with what they have, so long as they acknowledge that their conclusions are tentative, probable rather than certain.

In the case of Thomas Cromwell we are fortunate in possessing a wide variety of writing by such associates and protégés as Hugh Latimer, Miles Coverdale, Richard Morison, Robert Barnes, and Thomas Starkey. The mere list of names is suggestive; although Cromwell's followers were independent thinkers, they were all committed to some variety of religious reform. It does not appear that the vicegerent ever threw his weight behind a true conservative or upholder of the ecclesiastical *status quo*.

Cromwell's relations with Barnes and Starkey are especially revealing, for in both cases we know that writings were modified under Cromwell's influence or as a direct result of his criticism. Examination of these works can illuminate—at least by reflected rays—the beliefs of Cromwell himself.

III

Robert Barnes first assumed a position of some importance in the English Reformation on Christmas Eve, 1525, when he preached a notable sermon at St. Edward's Church, Cambridge. A native of Norfolk, Barnes had become an Augustinian friar at Cambridge and, after further study in Louvain, had risen to be prior of the house. It was Thomas Bilney who "converted him wholly unto Christ" (earlier, according to Foxe, he "did not see his inward and outward idolatry"[15]), and his views at this stage seem to have been quite similar to Bilney's. Barnes was not yet a Lutheran, and his ideas were essentially those of Wycliffe and the Lollards.[16] While the most striking single point in Barnes's sermon was his insistence that Christmas should be celebrated with no more festivity than any other days—Barnes deduced this from the biblical text "Rejoice in the Lord *always*"—its real meat lay in an attack on the bishops, who were too rich, too worldly, and too unyielding to permit the true preaching of the Gospel. After a trial of Westminster Barnes adjured his heresies, but he was sent to prison nonetheless. Eventually he fled to the continent, probably arriving at Antwerp in 1528 and Wittenberg in 1530. Here he became friendly with Johannes Bugenhagen and Martin Luther, and here he published his first book, called *Sentenciae ex doctoribus collectae*. This brief work, heavily influenced by Luther, formed the basis of a much more important treatise, *A supplicatyon . . . vnto the most excellent and redoubted prince henrye the eyght*.

Printed at Antwerp in 1531,[17] the *Supplication* was sent to Cromwell by Stephen Vaughan—not once but twice, since the first copy did not arrive in good time and Vaughan surmised that the messenger might have been afraid to deliver it.[18] "I thynke verely the common people haue neuer byn somuche moued to geue credence to any worke that before this, hath byn put forthe in thenglishe tongue as they wilbe vnto this," Vaughan wrote, "by cause he presumeth to proue his lernyng aswell by the scripture, as by the doctours and the Popes law."[19]

By Christmas 1531 Barnes was back in England, having come "at the king's great solicitation."[20] From this time on his career was closely linked with Cromwell's. It was doubtless Cromwell who saved Barnes from Sir Thomas More's attempt to prosecute him as a relapsed heretic.[21] From January 1532 until August 1534 Barnes was again in Germany. We know relatively little about his activities, and we have no specific evidence of contacts with Cromwell during this period. But Barnes was certainly at work on a revision of the *Supplication*, altering its emphasis and striving to make it more acceptable to Henry VIII. It seems probable that conversations with Cromwell in London, and quite possibly later correspondence that does not survive, suggested what these changes should be. In them we may find clues concerning Cromwell's creed.

The second edition of the *Supplication*, printed in London by John Bydell, appeared in November 1534.[22] It reflects major revision in three areas:[23] Barnes moved away from the strictly Lutheran theology of 1531; he made striking changes in his theory of kingship; and he added material arguing that clergy should be allowed to marry.

It is in the section dealing with faith and works that Barnes modified his Lutheran position most significantly. As the first of the eight "comen places which he disputeth" in the first edition Barnes had listed Luther's fundamental doctrine "that Alonlye faith justefyeth before god." Like Luther he relied heavily on Paul's Epistles: "Paule saythe that the Iustificacion of fayth is alonly sufficient. So that if a man/do beleue alonly he is iustifide though there be no workis done of hym at all." Critics of this view "were wont to say that faithe dothe Iustifye/but not alonly and therfore wolde crye/For.Sola.Sola.Sola.only/only/only. [But in St. Paul] haue you also Sola.Sola.Sola.so that you nede not Crye no more for Sola."[24] The 1534 edition did not abandon this belief in justification by faith, but Barnes moderated his discussion by deleting considerable material that denied the efficacy of good works: he eliminated references to the Epistle of James and the papists, whom he had originally castigated as Antichrist for allowing some role in salvation to human works. A more precise statement of Barnes's final position regarding justification can be found in the propositions he laid before Stephen Gardiner in 1540. Here he wrote:

> Theffect of Christes passion hath a condition. . . .
> The fulfilling of the condition requyreth first a knowleage of the condition wch knowleage we haue by faithe. . . .
> I doo well and proufitably to myself to exercise this faith.
> Ergo by the gifte of god I maye doe well bifore I am justifyed towardes the atteyning of iustification.
> There is ever asmoche charitie towardes god as faith and as faith encreaseth soo charitie encreaseth.
> To the attaining of iustification is required faith and charitie. . . .
> ffaith must be assurance to me of the promyses of god made in Christe if I fulfill the condition and love must accomplish the condition whervpon foloweth the atteining of the promes according to goddes truthe.[25]

In acknowledging that good works were a necessary outgrowth of faith and a manifestation of justification before the world, Barnes adopted a more moderate position better suited to the English church.

His political theories were altered even more significantly. Originally Barnes was motivated by his quarrel with the bishops, whom he accused of treason because of their usurpation of worldly power and wealth. He argued that the king enjoyed absolute power in temporal affairs as a direct gift of God, and he claimed that the bishops had falsely assumed a share of this temporal jurisdiction, for instance, by meddling in probate of wills and testaments. The second edition, on the other hand, is less critical and finds episcopacy evil only if the bishops uphold papal supremacy. In another important shift Barnes allowed royal jurisdiction in the spiritual realm as well as in the temporal. He deleted an entire section, "That mennes constitucions which be not founded in scripture binde not the conscience of man vnder the payne of deedlye sinne," which expounded Luther's doctrine of the separate functions of church and state.[26] Obviously this position was incompatible with Henry's role as supreme head of the church and Cromwell's as his vicegerent. In only one matter could subjects be justified in disobeying the sovereign: "It is lawfule for alle maner of men to reade holy scryptur," Barnes insisted, and no one could prevent them from doing so. The tone of his section on the Scriptures was moderated in 1534, however, by the deletion of a long section denouncing the bishops in general and Cuthbert Tunstal of London in particular for their refusal to make the English Bible available to the people.[27] Barnes excised two further sections, "What is holy churche" and "What the keyes of the churche are and to whom they are geuyn."[28] These too denounced bishops and denied that "the auctorite of the pryst be the keyes of heuyn," and they contained references to Christ as the sole head of the church, which Henry might have found distasteful. By 1534 Barnes evidently contemplated an English church whose policies would be determined by the king and put into effect by bishops of his selection, perhaps under the supervision of an agent like Cromwell.

The Supplication of 1531 had contained no discussion of clerical celibacy, rather surprisingly since Luther had taken a wife in 1525. Barnes himself never married, but in his revision he argued that priests who lacked the gift of chastity should be allowed the privilege of marriage. Not one priest in three, he believed, was truly chaste; mandatory celibacy was not grounded on Scripture or the Fathers, but solely on papal whim. Barnes's writing on this topic is particularly forceful.[29] One wonders if Cromwell had suggested that Barnes put the case for a reform that the vicegerent favored, even if the king himself had not been converted to the cause.

A few minor changes are worthy of note. Barnes dropped his insistence that "Alle maner of Chrysten men/ bothe sprytuale and temporalle are bound . . . to receue the sacrament in bothe kyndes vnder the payne of dedlye synne,"[30] presumably not because he no longer believed in the desirability of extending the chalice to the laity but rather because he came to regard this as a thing indifferent, in which subjects might wait for the king's order without endangering their souls. Similarly, he deleted a section arguing that "We ought not to worshupe Sayntes or ymages": its general line accorded well enough with Cromwell's injunctions, but its extreme position probably went farther than Cromwell would have liked.[31] A section on free will was slightly revised, although its basic denial that man of his own strength can do anything but sin remained unaltered. Some of the deleted material was replaced by a refutation of the writings of Sir Thomas More, especially his doctrine of the nature of the church, as was appropriate after More's resignation and imprisonment.

Nowhere does Barnes develop a full eucharistic theory, but it is reasonably clear that he adhered to belief in the Real Presence. A letter from Tyndale to John Frith casts light on Barnes's view. "Of the presence of Christ's body in the sacrament," Tyndale wrote, "meddle as little as you can . . . Barnes will be hot against you [if you deny it]. . . . I would have the right use preached and the presence to be an indifferent thing till the matter can be discussed at leisure."[32] The matter is of some importance in view of the fact that Barnes, like Cromwell, was unfairly accused of being a sacramentarian.[33]

Barnes's final theological position, then, seems to have been a moderate one, founded upon Wycliffe, profoundly tinctured with Lutheranism, but in the end eclectic and peculiarly English in its acceptance of royal supremacy. It is worth emphasizing that Barnes was not just an English disciple of Luther and that his beliefs, however much they might be criticized by conservatives, were essentially moderate. His position was best characterized by Hugh Latimer, who praised one of Barnes's sermons for its "grett moderation & temperaunce" and later wrote, "Seurly he ys alone in handlyng of a pece of scrypture, & in settyng forth of Christe, he hath no felow."[34]

During the years between 1534 and 1539 Barnes was sent on several embassies to Germany: he was involved in Cromwell's unsuccessful attempt to secure Lutheran approval for Henry's divorce and in the later negotiations for Henry's marriage to Anne of Cleves. In 1540, when Cromwell's own power was crumbling, he preached a sermon at Paul's Cross attacking Stephen Gardiner. Barnes recanted, but then returned to his old opinions and was sent to the Tower. With his patron no longer able to protect him, he was condemned to death by an act of attainder.[35] Barnes was burned at Smithfield on July 30, 1540, just two days after Cromwell was executed on Tower Hill.

IV

Barnes was probably recruited to Cromwell's service. As Geoffrey Elton has emphasized, Thomas Starkey was not; rather, he deliberately sought government service under Cromwell's aegis.[36] Educated at Oxford, he spent most of the decade beginning about 1523 on the continent, studying in Avignon and Paris for three years, then joining Reginald Pole's household in Italy.[37] Late in 1534 he returned to England; early in 1535 he wrote to Cromwell, acknowledging that he was "to you a straunger, almost vnknowne" but offering to spend "the rest of my lyfe . . . accordyng to your ordur & dysposytyon."[38]

Cromwell must have been impressed by Starkey's credentials. Perhaps to test Starkey's learning, he asked his new protégé to describe "what thyng yt is aftur the sentence of Aristotyl, & the ancyent perypatetykys, that communly among them ys callyd pollycy."[39] Here Starkey sketched out the basic elements of a general political theory:

> The polytyke body [is] by pollycy rulyd, as euery partycular man ys by reson & vertue. . . . Respecte must be had to all partys Ioyntly, [since all parts of the body politic must function together. As a Christian you must life up your eyes] hyar then nature doth lede you . . . if you wyl put your assurance in the promyssys of Chryst. . . . Then shall you turne thys pollycy, worldly and to you naturall, into Chrystyan pollycy & spiritual.

Evidently Cromwell discussed this argument with Starkey, suggesting modifications. After pondering them Starkey came to "see as hyt were ij polycees, ij maner of lyuyngys, ij dyuerse fascyons of passyng thys pylgrymage, the one cyuyle polytyke & worldly, the other, heuenly, spiritual & godly." Civil and politic law was of necessity established by nature because of man's frailty; men follow it for fear of punishment or hope of reward.

Spiritual or godly life is grounded neither on nature nor on man's reason,
but on "the certayne & true reson of god" as taught by Christ and the
apostles. "Fayth must show hym al the mysterys therin, fayth must lay the
groundys in thys kynd of lyfe as nature dyd in the other. . . . Fayth, loue
and charyte [will] be hys gydys . . . to sure felycyte & . . . true lyberty."
Ecclesiastical order is founded on "mere pollycy," so it is part of the civil
sphere and as such may be governed by the king; even the sacraments may
be regulated by the sovereign, "though they spryng of the word & reson of
god," for they are also "the chefe bondes & knottys, wherby the polytyke
lyfe ys couplyd wyth the spiritual."[40]

It was probably in April 1535 that Starkey sent Cromwell a "little scroll,"
asking him to read it and, if he thought proper, show it to the king.[41] There
is no evidence that Cromwell approached Henry VIII, but he certainly
examined the writing with some care. That he was not entirely satisfied
with it is clear from Starkey's next letter, which provides one of our most
fascinating insights into Cromwell's beliefs.[42] The essence of Cromwell's
criticism was that Starkey had not set out at large the doctrine of the mean,
the *via media* of compromise between the extreme religious positions on
both sides. Like any writer presented with an unfavorable reader's report,
Starkey felt obliged to defend himself: other readers had judged the manuscript in an opposite way, noting it "for a grete faute" that Starkey appeared to be "of nother parte but betwyxt both indifferent." The author
would not try to explain the reason for their view—presumably these com-
mentators were themselves zealots who believed that Starkey did not come
down heavily enough on the side of reform—but he admitted that Cromwell was right. After he had "perused the thyng agayn & weyd y^t wyth my
selfe somewhat more dylygently," Starkey was ready to "confesse vnto
you the truthe . . . that as you haue Iugyd of the mater, so hyt ys
indede. . . . Even lyke as you haue euer touchyd the stryng & knot of the
mater in . . . yor communycatyon . . . so you haue downe vndowtydly in
thys."

Addressing the substance of Cromwell's criticism, Starkey wrote:

The mean wych you requyre, ys not at length set out in my boke nor I
can not tel whether my wyt be suffycyent . . . therto, for thys mean in al
thyng ys a strange stryng, hard to stryke apon & wysely to touch, for by
thys the [h]armony of al thys hole world ys conteynyd in hys natural
course & bewty, by thys al cyuyle ordur & pollycy ys maynteynyd in
cytes & townys wyth gud equyte, by thys mannys mynd wyth al kynd of
vertue garnyshed, ys brought to hys quyetnes & felycyte, and by thys
here in our purpos, al gud & true relygyon wythout impyety or supersty-
cyon, ys stablysh[ed], ye to goddys honoure & glory.

It was not necessary, Starkey believed, to present common people with an exact disquisition, "the wych thung parteynyth to hyar phylosophy." For them, "obedyence . . . to thyngys decred by commyn authoryte [is more necessary] then scruplose knolege." Reverting to his earlier doctrine of worldly policy, Starkey wrote that

> the pepul & body of the commynalty, euery man dowyng hys offyce & duty as he ys callyd & by goddys prouysyon appoyntyd, here in thys worldly pollycy, shold hang apon the commyn ordur in euery cuntre, & leyn ther vnto, wyth sure fayth & expectatyon of euerlastyng lyfe here aftur to be had, by the mere benfyte & gudnes of god.

If any man, moved by scruple, refuses to abide by such common policy and order, he is not fit to live in the commonwealth. Such condemnation applies equally to those—presumably papists—who abhor "al gud ordur & cyuylyte" and to those—obviously radical reformers—"who by arrogant opynyon lyghtly conceyuyd" utterly despise and tred under foot "all rytys & custumys ecclesiastical."

Starkey doubted that his writing could be of such power as to induce these people "of the scrupulose sorte" to be obedient to common authority, but he did promise to do what he could. In fact he modified his writing, probably substantially, along the lines suggested by Cromwell. It was then published by Thomas Berthelet, who did much of Cromwell's semi-official printing, as *An Exhortation to the people, instructynge theym to Unitie and Obedience.*[43]

The *Exhortation* is really little more than a literary expansion of Starkey's letter to Cromwell. It begins with a preface addressed to Henry VIII. Here Starkey says that he was struck, when he returned to England after her peregrinations, by the "disobedience and diuersitie of opinion" that had grown up "by corrupte iugement, to great confusion, and to the great breeche of christian vnitie." A letter to all readers cites the troubles in Germany, "where as by the folyshe avoydyng of superstition they haue slipped into great discorde and sedition, whose example I truste shall be to vs a spectacle, ministringe vnto vs no small instruction." Now, "by the prouidence of god," even the German sects "begynne to fall vnto the meane, that ys to say Christis true religion."[44] Clearly England should do the same.

In elaborating his discussion of the mean, Starkey utilizes the doctrine of things indifferent or, in the Greek word, *adiaphora.* Starkey did not invent this concept, nor, as has been suggested, did he borrow it from Philip Melanchthon. Rather, Starkey picked up a doctrine that had, by 1535, become a commonplace.[45] His definition is simple: "Thynges indifferent I calle all suche thynges, whiche by goddis worde are nother prohibyted nor commaunded, but lefte to worldly polycie, wherof they take their ful authoritie, by the whiche as tyme and place requireth, they are sometymes good, and somtymes yll: as to eate fleshe the fridaye." Among things indifferent is the matter of the pope's superiority, "whiche so troubleth many weake consciences. For as I iuge it not so yll and damnable, that all our forefathers whiche haue ben obedient therto this .vii.C. yeres hertofore be damned, so I iuge it not so good, that obedience therto shal be necessarie to them whiche shulde be saued." So are the ceremonies and traditions of the church. Although these things indifferent are neither good nor bad in themselves, "yet when they be set out with authoritie, by them whiche haue hole rule in any kynd of policie . . . then the people are to them bounde, ye by the vertue of goddis owne worde, who commaundeth expressly his disciples to be obedient to commune policie, whan so euer therby is commaunded any thinge, whiche is not repugnant to his preceptes and doctrine."[46] For Starkey the Nicene Creed sets out all that is necessary for salvation; everything else is indifferent.

So all-encompassing a category of *adiaphora* was possible for Starkey because of his insistence that the religious controversies of learned men need not trouble unlearned subjects. "For menne, the whiche are of lernynge and letters, in suche matters neuer dydde yet accorde nor agree . . . it is ynough that they accorde in the artycles of our feythe: and as for the reste, lette theym proue theyr wyttes after theyr owne pleasure, mynde, and lybertie." Ordinary people "must conceyue if we wyl be true professours of Christis dictrine, a certayne brotherly loue eche one towarde other, iudgynge our selfes to be borne of one father, nouryshed by one mother, membres of one body, hangynge of one heed, lokyng for one reward, promysed vnto vs, lyuyng to gyther in this vnitie."[47] Starkey's distaste for extremists, professed in his letter to Cromwell, is amplified in a section that laments the "corrupt iugement one of an other, by the reson wherof, eche one in hart iugeth other to be, eyther pharisee or heretyke, papist or schismatike." Condemnation of the "vayne superstition" of conservatives, "arrogant blyndenesse" of reformers, foreshadows Cromwell's words to the Parliament of 1540.[48]

Although most of the *Exhortation* is couched in these general terms, Starkey does touch on a few specific issues. He is opposed to the notion that private property should be abolished and all things held in common: "the perfection of Christis religion resteth not so moche in the refuse of all possession, and wylfull pouertie, as it dothe in the streight vse of these worldly thynges, with perfyte charitie."[49] He believes that "bothe faithe & workes . . . be of necessity required to our saluation . . . for thoughe this fastynge, pylgremage, and almesse dede, with all other outwarde dedes of man, be not of them selfe sufficient to mans saluation, yet to testifie the inwarde faithe . . . they haue bene euer iudged conueniente meanes."[50] Monasteries, though often corrupt, could continue to stand if reformed. They should, however, be reduced in size—Starkey's eccentric reason for this is that they have become so swollen that "many cities almoste be left voyde."[51] Similarly, pilgrimages, fastings, observance of holy days, invocation of saints, and prayers for the dead are permissible if purged of excesses.[52] In a passage condemning conservatives Starkey argues in favor of simplified church music, a liturgy in English, and married clergy: only the superstitious would think Christ's religion overturned "if the organes shoulde be plucked oute of the churche, and the curyous syngyng tempered and broughte to a conuenyente meane, ye as yf the prayers commonly sayde amonge vs in temples in a strange tongue, of the people not vnderstonde, shoulde openly be rehersed in the mother tongue . . . and further if to preistes the mynisters of goddis worde, libertye were graunted . . . to marye and take wyues for the auoydynge of Fornycation."[53]

Finally, Starkey returns to the doctrine of the mean; he quotes some of his letter to Cromwell:

> We shalle by this meane soo fourme our affectes, and in some partes soo correcke our iudgementes, that as of the one syde we shall auoyde al blynde supersticion, so we shal of the other syde eschewe all arrogant opinion. . . . For by a certain mean the armonie of this hole worlde is conteyned in this natural order & beautie: by a mean al ciuile order and polycye is mayntayned in cities and townes with good ciuilitie: by a meane mannes mynde with all kynde of vertue garnysshed, is brought to his naturall perfection and lyght: And by a meane all trewe religion without impyetye or superstytion, is stablysshed and sette forthe to goddis honour and glorye in all christian natyons and countreyes: ye and soo by a meane we shall, mooste christyan people, chiefely auoyde this dangerous diuisyon growen in amonge vs, by the reason wherof, somme are iudged to be of the newe fashyon, and somme of the olde.[54]

Starkey's ideas about preaching formed the basis of what appears to be a draft proclamation, probably written in 1536 or 1537.[55] Here he argued that preaching was essential but that preachers should not put forward their own personal interpretations and doctrines. Unfortunately "scrypture in certayn placys, ys somewhat obscure, & not easy to be vnderstond." In these cases "the opynyonys of the precharys . . . are to be dyrectyd & temperyd, by a certayn vnyte in doctryne much necessary, that In al such placys of scrypture wych appere dowteful & obscure, they precharys swarue not at theyr own lyberty from the most commyn & long tyme receyuyd Interpretatyon therof." They should follow the ancient doctors; if these disagree, preachers should "cleue vnto the consent & laudabul custume of the church of Englond," which is "not in any parte repugnant to the truthe of goddys word." Thus discord may be abolished and unity achieved.[56]

The *Exhortation* was the only work of Starkey to be published in his lifetime. His *Dialogue between Reginald Pole and Thomas Lupset*, now better known because it has received two modern editions[57] and considerable scholarly comment,[58] was not printed until the nineteenth century. Since it was written before Starkey's association with Cromwell,[59] it cannot be taken as evidence of the vicegerent's beliefs, however much Cromwell and his circle may have been impressed by its arguments for social reform.

Starkey's service to Cromwell in the years after 1535 seems to have been limited by the perception that he was politically unreliable, perhaps still closely tied to Pole. He did address a long letter to Henry VIII, condemning violence in achieving the Reformation and urging that the wealth of dissolved monasteries be used for the betterment of society, and he himself received a living in the collegiate chapel of Corpus Christe, London.[60] He died in 1538.

V

Drawing on these pieces of evidence, what can we conclude about Cromwell's creed? First, there were clearly several things that Cromwell was not. He was not a Lutheran. His view of the proper relationship between church and state, between the spiritual and the civil polity, was different from Luther's. It is probable, too, that he did not share the Lutheran belief in justification by faith alone. He probably held, like Starkey, that faith must be coupled with love and charity, that both faith and works are necessary for salvation. He was not a "sacramentary."[61] While his own views may have lacked the precision of fully developed theology, he probably believed in the real presence of Christ in the Eucharist. Most likely he favored Communion in both kinds but did not regard it as essential. Almost certainly he would have denied that it could be administered by any save properly ordained priests. He was not an Anabaptist or believer in the abolition of private property. The social disorders arising from radical programs and lack of respect for constituted authority would have been profoundly distasteful to him, and there is no reason to believe that he read the Scriptures as justifying an economic revolution.

To move to positive policies, it is clear that Cromwell believed in making the Scriptures available to all Englishmen in the vernacular. He gave his support to Coverdale and Richard Grafton, the translator and the publisher of the English Bible, and he must have shared Grafton's hope that an authorized translation would end "the whole scisme & contencyon that is in the realme/ which is some callyng them of the olde & some of the new/ now shuld we all folow one god/ one boke & one learnynge."[62] He may well have favored an English-language prayerbook as well, although he was wise enough to know that the Latin Mass was not going to be superseded during Henry VIII's lifetime. Possibly he would have preferred simplification of liturgy and of church music. Certainly he reacted against the abuse of relics, images, pilgrimages, and the invocation of saints, but he inclined to reform in these matters rather than total condemnation. Like

Starkey, he believed strongly in the importance of preaching—it could be a valuable tool in promoting understanding of his policies and gaining support for them—but he acknowledged the necessity of regulating it, so that pulpits not be used for the dissemination of conflicting theologies and interpretations of Scripture.[63] Like his friend Cranmer, he probably held that the clergy should be free to marry, that there was no theological justification for mandatory celibacy.

Above all, he believed, as passionately as he believed in anything, in the mean, the middle way between rival extremes. He probably shared Starkey's position regarding things indifferent. The beliefs and practices necessary to salvation were few and simple; in nonessentials one should be willing to lay aside personal preference and "tarry for the magistrate" (to borrow the Elizabethan phrase) until the time was propitious for change to be mandated by properly constituted authority.

Unsympathetic to extremists at both ends of the religious spectrum, Cromwell took his stand somewhere between Rome and Wittenberg. His personal beliefs, never developed with the logic of a systematic theologian, were eclectic and pragmatic. In this adherence to moderation and "mediocrity," Cromwell did much to launch the Anglican Church upon its unique middle path.

NOTES

1. R. B. Merriman, *Life and Letters of Thomas Cromwell*, 2 vols. (Oxford, 1902), 1:iii, 301.

2. A. G. Dickens, *Thomas Cromwell and the English Reformation* (London, 1959), passim, esp. 197–81; G. R. Elton, *Reform and Reformation: England, 1509–1558* (Cambridge, Mass., 1977), passim, esp. 171–73.

3. Elton, 171; Brendan Bradshaw, "The Tudor Commonwealth: Reform and Revision," *Historical Journal* 22 (1979): 469.

4. George Cavendish, *The Life and Death of Cardinal Wolsey*, in *Two Early Tudor Lives*, ed. Richard S. Sylvester and Davis P. Harding (New Haven, Conn., 1962), 108.

5. SP 1/54, fols. 269–85, Public Record Office, printed in Merriman, 1:56–63. Hereafter s. = shillings and d. = pennies.

6. David Wilkins, *Concilia Magnae Britanniae et Hiberniae*, 4 vols. (London, 1737), 3:813–15.

7. It is interesting to note how quickly this could be done. On August 29 Sir Richard Gresham wrote Cromwell, "By Doctor Barnes I haue perceyvyd yo[r] meynde Consernynge the ymages In [St.] Powlles and by hys adveyse I sent vnto the Busshope of Chechester [Richard Sampson] beynge deane and shewyd hym what Commandement I hade for to take downe the sayd ymages. And he sent me aunswher that he wolld see yt dcon the sawme nyght beynge the xxiij daye of August and In the mornyng I went to Powlles and ther I dyd see that all thynges was doon accordyngly." SP 1/135, fol. 247, P.R.O.

8. Wilkins, 815–17. Quotations here are from the MS, SP 6/3, fol. 1, P.R.O., rather than Wilkins, who took his text from Cranmer's Register.

9. This is a translation of the Latin version of the speech in the *Lords' Journal*, 1:128–29; see Stanford E. Lehmberg, *The Later Parliaments of Henry VIII, 1536–1547* (Cambridge, 1977), 90–91.

10. 32 Henry VIII, c. 62, not printed in *Statutes of the Realm*, 11 vols. (London, 1810–28) but in Gilbert Burnet, *History of the Reformation*, 7 vols. (Oxford, 1865), 4:415–32; cf. Elton,

"Thomas Cromwell's Decline and Fall," in his *Studies in Tudor and Stuart Politics and Government*, 2 vols. (Cambridge, 1974), 1:220–26; Lehmberg, 107–9.

11. J. J. Scarisbrick, *Henry VIII* (London, 1968), 379–80.

12. Quoted in ibid. from Cottonian MS Otho C. X, fol. 247, British Library.

13. John Foxe, *Acts and Monuments*, ed. S. R. Cattley, 8 vols. (London, 1837–41), 5:402–3.

14. J. A. Froude, *History of England*, 12 vols. (London, 1856–70), 3:251–22, suggested that this speech was fabricated by Cromwell's enemies, who wished to have him die "with a lie upon his lips," but there is no reliable evidence that this is the case.

15. Foxe, 415.

16. On this point see William A. Clebsch, *England's Earliest Protestants, 1520–1535* (New Haven, Conn., 1964), 45.

17. The small black-letter volume (no. 1470 in the *Short-Title Catalogue of English Books, 1475–1640*, ed. A. W. Pollard and G. R. Redgrave [London, 1946[) was printed by Symon Cock. The facsimile reprint published by Da Capo Press (Amsterdam and New York, 1973) is actually a copy of this edition, not "1534?" as stated on its title page.

18. Cottonian MS Titus B. I, fol. 373, B.L. (*Letters and Papers of Henry VIII*, 21 vols. [London, 1862–1932, hereafter cited as *L.P.*], 5:533).

19. SP 1/68, fol. 56, P.R.O. (*L.P.*, 5:532).

20. Chapuys to Charles V, in *L.P.*, 5:593.

21. Cf. Foxe, 5:419: "Cromwell was his great friend."

22. S.T.C. 1471. The 1572 edition of *The Works of Tyndale, Frith and Barnes*, ed. Foxe, conflates the two editions, sometimes producing irreconcilable contradictions.

23. The changes have been analyzed by W. D. J. Cargill Thompson, "The Sixteenth-Century Editions of *A Supplication unto King Henry the Eighth* by Robert Barnes, D.D.: A Footnote to the History of the Royal Supremacy," *Transactions of the Cambridge Bibliographical Society*, 3 (1960): 133–42; Clebsch, 58–73; Neelak S. Tjernagel, *The Reformation Essays of Dr. Robert Barnes, Chaplain to Henry VIII* (London, 1963), 96–111.

24. *Supplication*, 1531 ed., fols. i, xli.

25. Cottonian MS Cleopatra E. V, fol. 107, B.L. (*L.P.*, 15:312).

26. *Supplication*, 1531 ed., fols. i, Cxvii–Cxx.

27. Ibid., fols. C–Cxii. Tunstall had allegedly advised a merchant to have his servants read Robin Hood rather than the Scriptures in English.

28. Ibid, fols. lvii–lxxx.

29. Cf. Clebsch, 72–73.

30. *Supplication*, 1531 ed., fols. Cxxiii–Cxxxii.

31. Ibid., fols. Cxxxiii–Clii.

32. *L.P.*, 6:403; *Works of Tyndale, Frith and Barnes*, 435.

33. Cf. Cottonian MS Cleopatra E. V, fol. 397, B.L. (*L.P.*, 9:230), a letter claiming that Barnes taught that "the blessed sacrament of the alter is but a figure and a remembraunce of the passion of Criste."

34. SP 1/122, fol. 254^v, and SP 1/127, fol. 141^v, P.R.O. (*L.P.*, 12:ii, 258, and 1259).

35. Lehmberg, 111–12, 125–26. Before dying Barnes insisted that he was neither a heretic nor an Anabaptist.

36. Elton, *Reform and Renewal: Thomas Cromwell and the Common Weal* (Cambridge, 1973), 46–55. See also Dickens, 83–84.

37. Starkey's studies abroad are considered in detail in Thomas F. Mayer's "The Life and Thought of Thomas Starkey," Ph.D. diss., University of Minnesota, 1983, pp. 9–92.

38. SP 1/89, fol. 175, P.R.O. (*L.P.*, 8:213), printed in S. J. Herrtage, *England in the Reign of King Henry the Eighth* (London, 1878), lxvii–lxviii.

39. SP 1/89, fol. 181^v, P.R.O. (*L.P.*, 8:216 [2]).

40. SP 1/89, fols. 179–80, P.R.O. (*L.P.*, 8:216 [1]).

41. SP 1/95, fols. 59–60, P.R.O. (*L.P.*, 8:95).

42. SP 1/89, fols. 177–78, P.R.O. (*L.P.*, 8:215).

43. S.T.C. 23236, printed before March 1536, not in "1540?" (see W. Gordon Zeeveld, *Foundations of Tudor Policy* [Cambridge, Mass., 1948], p. 148). Facsimile reprint, Da Capo Press (Amsterdam and London, 1973).

44. *Exhortation*, fols. a.ii–iii, 4.

45. Starkey's doctrine of things indifferent is discussed, rather superficially, in Zeeveld, 149–56; the development of the concept is traced in Bernard J. Verkamp, *The Indifferent Mean: Adiaphorism in the English Reformation to 1554* (Athens, Ohio, 1977). Zeeveld's view that Starkey borrowed this concept from Melanchthon has been refuted by Mayer, "Starkey and Melanchthon on Adiaphora: A Critique of W. Gordon Zeeveld," *Sixteenth Century Journal* 11, no. 1 (1980): 39–49.

46. *Exhortation*, fols. 6–7.

47. Ibid, fols. 8, 11.

48. Ibid., fols. 20–28.

49. Ibid., fol. 29.

50. Ibid., fols. 80–81.

51. Ibid., fols. 21, 75.

52. Ibid., fols. 75–79.

53. Ibid., fols. 21^v.

54. Ibid., fols. 82^v–83^r. Zeeveld has pointed out these parallels, 148.

55. See Mayer, "Life and Thought of Thomas Starkey," pp. 94–95. There is no basis for the argument, presented in Joseph Block, "Thomas Cromwell's Patronage of Preaching," *Sixteenth Century Journal* 8, no. 1 (1977): 40, that this document was drafted in preparation for the meeting with the bishops mentioned in *L.P.*, 12:i, 708.

56. SP 1/100, fol. 130 (*L.P.*, 9:1160).

57. J. W. Cowper for Early English Text Society, 1878, in Herrtage, 1–215; ed. K. M. Burton (London, 1948).

58. Elton, "Reform by Statute: Thomas Starkey's *Dialogue* and Thomas Cromwell's Policy," in *Studies* 2:236–58.

59. See Mayer, "Starkey and Melanchthon," 44.

60. SP 1/105, fols. 119–40, P.R.O. (*L.P.*, 9:156), mostly printed in Herrtage, xlviii–lxiii, and discussed by Elton, *Reform and Renewal*, 52–55.

61. Henry VIII himself seems to have been particularly antagonistic to sacramentaries: in the draft of his proclamation prohibiting the publication of religious books without license, the word *sacramentary* was added three times in Henry's own hand, coupled with Anabaptists and such-like heretics. Cottonian MS. Cleopatra E. V, fols. 357–84, B.L.; Paul L. Hughes and James F. Larkin, eds., *Tudor Royal Proclamations*, 3 vols. (New Haven, Conn.: 1964–69), 1:270–76.

62. Cottonian MS. Cleopatra E. V, fol. 340, B.L. (*L.P.*, 12:ii, app. 35).

63. Mayer, "Life and Thought of Thomas Starkey," 125, emphasizes Starkey's interest in preaching, while Block, 37–50, discusses several cases of Cromwell's patronage of reformed preachers, especially Robert Wisdom and Thomas Swynnerton.

SELECT BIBLIOGRAPHY

There is no real biography of Thomas Cromwell; the paucity of material relating to his private life makes is unlikely that one will ever be written. Cromwell's work in government has been examined and evaluated in G. R. Elton's masterful trilogy: *The Tudor Revolution in Government: Administrative Changes in the Reign of Henry VIII* (Cambridge, 1953); *Policy and Police: The Enforcement of the Reformation in the Age of Thomas Cromwell* (Cambridge,

1972); *Reform and Renewal: Thomas Cromwell and the Common Weal* (Cambridge, 1973). There are also important articles on Cromwell in Elton's *Studies in Tudor and Stuart Politics and Government,* 2 vols. (Cambridge, 1974). A. G. Dickens's small volume in the "Teach Yourself History" series, *Thomas Cromwell and the English Reformation* (London, 1959), is an excellent example of sound scholarship and appealing writing for the general reader. B. W. Beckingsale, *Thomas Cromwell, Tudor Minister* (London, 1978) is another good piece of popular history and contains essays dealing with most aspects of Cromwell's career.

Cromwell's correspondence has been published by R. B. Merriman, *Life and Letters of Thomas Cromwell,* 2 vols. (Oxford, 1902); Merriman's life of Cromwell, however, is opinionated and frequently in error. A newer selection of letters is *Thomas Cromwell on Church and Commonwealth,* ed. A. J. Slavin (New York, 1969). Among general accounts of the religious changes under Henry VIII, A. G. Dickens, *The English Reformation* (London, 1964) is outstanding. Cromwell's work in Parliament is discussed in Stanford E. Lehmberg, *The Reformation Parliament, 1529–1536* (Cambridge, 1970), and *The Later Parliaments of Henry VIII, 1536–1547* (Cambridge, 1977). The best modern life of the king is J. J. Scarisbrick, *Henry VIII* (London, 1968). On Barnes see William A. Clebsch, *England's Earliest Protestants, 1520–1535* (New Haven, Conn., 1964), Neelak S. Tjernagel, *The Reformation Essays of Dr. Robert Barnes, Chaplain to Henry VIII* (London, 1963), and James Edward McGoldrick, *Luther's English Connection: The Reformation Thought of Robert Barnes and William Tyndale* (Milwaukee, Wis., 1979); on Starkey see W. Gordon Zeeveld, *Foundations of Tudor Policy* (Cambridge, Mass., 1948), and Thomas F. Mayer, "The Life and Thought of Thomas Starkey," Ph.D. diss., University of Minnesota, 1983.

6

For the Greater Glory of God: St. Ignatius Loyola

JOHN PATRICK DONNELLY, S.J.*

Ignatius Loyola is a central figure, perhaps the prototypical figure of the Counter-Reformation, and the way he has been seen partly reflects the way historians of the early twentieth century have viewed the Counter-Reformation. The word *Counter-Reformation* and its equivalents in all western languages have negative connotations: it has been seen as a movement that revivifies medieval ideals against humanism or that blocks the modernization of the church through the creative, enlightened forces of Protestantism, thereby insuring a sterile period between the Renaissance and the Enlightenment. Increasingly, contemporary historians have abandoned such simple views. Art historians, for instance, have come to a more favorable view of the Baroque and the Jesuit role in art from 1550 to 1700.[1] Historians, such as Jean Delumeau and A. G. Dickens, have tried to study the Counter-Reformation on its own merits, seeing it in relation to the social, intellectual, and cultural development of Catholic Europe and showing how it unleashed forces that remained influential down into the eighteenth century.[2] For Catholic Europe the Counter-Reformation was not so much a reaction against either the Renaissance or the Reformation as a necessary stage in the modernization of medieval religion and society.[3] In this perspective Ignatius Loyola appears no longer as a medieval knight of God but as one of the makers of the modern world.

Iñigo Lopez de Oñaz y Loyola (1491–1556) was the twelfth and youngest child of Don Beltrán, Lord of Loyola Castle.[4] The Loyola family was not wealthy but had played a prominent role since the twelfth century in the remote Basque province of Guipúzcoa. The distinctive world of medieval Spain began to disappear the year after Iñigo's birth. The three great monotheistic religions had met and mingled in medieval Spain, but in 1492 Ferdinand and Isabella completed the conquest of Moslem Granada and

*The author wishes to thank Eugene Donahue and Manuel Ruiz Jurado for their suggestions, which have greatly improved this essay.

expelled the Jews from Spain. Columbus discovered the new world and opened the way for conquest and settlement. A decade later the great captain Gonzalo de Cordoba conquered Naples for Ferdinand and laid the basis for two centuries of Spanish domination of Italy. During Iñigo's youth Spanish might spilled over into North Africa and established a string of bases from Oran to Tripoli. The walls of Loyola Castle echoed with these triumphs: two of Iñigo's brothers fought in the wars for Naples, another helped suppress a Moorish revolt in Granada, and a fourth sailed to America to make his fortune.

Don Beltrán destined his two youngest sons, Pedro Lopez and Iñigo, for the church, and arranged for a tutor to teach them reading and writing. Iñigo received the tonsure but showed so little interest in study that Don Beltrán sent him as a page to the court at Arévalo of Juan Velázquez, High Treasurer of Castile. There Iñigo lived the free and easy life of young courtiers; he wrote sonnets and played the viola; he engaged in tournaments and duels; he wasted his money in gambling and his time in reading romances of chivalry. He became involved in amorous adventures and got into serious trouble when he and his brother Pedro Lopez beat up another man in a nighttime brawl. The judge rejected Iñigo's appeal to his tonsure and clerical immunities, but his court connections seem to have saved him from punishment. After Velázquez unsuccessfully opposed the new king, Charles V, and was forced to retire, Iñigo joined the entourage of the Duke of Nájera in 1517, again as a courtier. Courtiers were not actually soldiers, although they were expected to serve as soldiers in a pinch. The point is worth stressing since Loyola is often wrongly seen as a soldier-saint, and his contribution to the Counter-Reformation is described in military language.[5] In fact, Loyola did only a few months of military service, and these were as a noble volunteer rather than as a soldier. In 1520 the revolt of the Spanish Comuneros broke out against Charles V. The Duke of Nájera, as Viceroy of Navarre, faced the rebels to the south and an invading French army to the north. Iñigo Loyola was among the handful who tried to defend the citadel of Pamplona against the advancing French. A cannonball passed between his legs, wounding the left and breaking the right.

Pamplona fell, and a new life began for Iñigo the courtier. The victorious French provided doctors who set Iñigo's leg and released Spanish soldiers who carried him on the painful journey back to Loyola. At the castle the doctors found that the leg was badly set. Always a man of extraordinary determination, Iñigo insisted that the leg be broken and reset and that a protruding bone be sawed off. To hurry his nine-month convalescence, Iñigo asked for his usual reading, romances of chivalry, but the castle had only Ludolf of Saxony's *Life of Christ* and Jocobo de Voragine's lives of the saints in Spanish translations. Even in his days at court Loyola had a traditional faith, which now became the basis of a conversion experience. The exploits of the saints, particularly the more bizarre and heroic, resonated with his sense of chivalry. He dreamed of turning to God and performing prodigies of austerity. Then his imagination would return to his early dreams of valiant service to some great lady in the tradition of Amadis of Gaul. When he compared his daydreams, he discovered a bitter aftertaste from his reveries on chivalry and a profound inner peace from his fantasies about serving God. This alternation of consolation and desolation was his first experience in what he later termed the discernment of spirits. He was convinced that God was working within him and guiding him to a new life, whose outline he only dimly perceived. He took up the challenge of the saints with characteristic generosity. As yet he could understand holiness only in terms of doing great penances and bearing intense humiliations. For a while he considered joining the strict Carthusian monastery at Seville, but instead he decided to make a penitential pilgrimage to Jerusalem. In February 1522 he set out for the shrine of the Virgin at Montserrat, where he made a detailed confession of his sins, gave away his knightly clothes, and put on beggar's robes. Still seeing his spiritual dedication in knightly terms, he made an all-night vigil within the shrine, where he left his sword and dagger as ex voto offerings.[6]

Before heading to Barcelona and Jerusalem, he stopped for a few days in the nearby town of Manresa to add some notes to the spiritual commonplace book he had started at Loyola. The few days gradually stretched into nearly a year. He lived first at the hospital for the poor, then in a cell at the local Dominican monastery, but more important was a nearby cave to which he retired for prayer. There Iñigo, the generous but rude beginner, was transformed into one of the giants of the Golden Age of Spanish mysticism. Mystical experience—the direct, immediate encounter, different from ordinary sense perception and reasoning, with an object perceived as ultimate—is private and ineffable by its nature. Historians have no way to judge mystical experience directly; some would deny the possibility or validity of such experience on a priori grounds. Yet Loyola himself and his close acquaintances insisted that his mystical experiences gave purpose and drive to his life. Whatever judgment historians make about the transcendent validity of his mystical experiences, they are central to an understanding of his life and impact on his society. At Manresa Loyola spent seven hours daily in prayer on his knees, fasted, and scourged himself to the point of endangering his health. Later in life he discouraged such extreme austerity among his followers. The months at Manresa were anything but unbroken spiritual rapture. Loyola was at times discouraged at the prospect of continuing such a hard life; later he was so tormented by scruples about his past sins that he considered suicide. To rid himself of scruples he determined to give up all food until they went away. After a week his confessor learned about his fast and ordered him to eat. He complied and the scruples disappeared—for a time. Meanwhile he reflected on his experiences. Several, he concluded, were satanic in origin.

Later he claimed that while at Manresa "God was treating him just as a schoolmaster treats a little boy when he teaches him."[7] At Manresa Loyola claimed many mystical visions, sometimes of the Trinity, more often of the humanity of Christ: "he saw with the inner eyes the humanity of Christ . . . but he saw no distinction of members."[8] The greatest illumination came along the banks of the Cardoner river: "He beheld no vision but he saw and understood many things, spiritual as well as those concerning faith and learning."[9] Later he felt that this one experience surpassed all his other spiritual experiences taken together.

Mysticism is sometimes seen as a private road to God that bypasses or lessens the mystic's need for sacraments, traditional dogma, Scripture, and involvement with the life of the Church. This is emphatically not true of Iñigo Loyola nor of the great Spanish mystics of the sixteenth century generally. On the contrary, Loyola's mystical experiences at Manresa reinforced his loyalty to traditional Christianity. His experiences dealt precisely with the Trinity, Christ's humanity, and the presence of Christ in the Eucharist. Later he claimed: "These things which he saw gave him at the time great strength, and were always a striking confirmation of his faith, so much so that he has often thought to himself that if there were no Scriptures to teach us these matters of faith, he was determined to die for them, merely because of what he had seen."[10] Even more than at Manresa, his later mystical experiences at Rome, which are recorded in the surviving fragments of his spiritual diary, center on his daily Mass.[11] His mysticism drew him increasingly to serve God in his fellow men, toward engagement rather than toward withdrawal.

At Manresa Iñigo kept notes of his insights, which he later worked into the main outline of the *Spiritual Exercises*. He did not publish the *Spiritual Exercises* until 1548, after Paul III had approved two Latin translations, but he was giving a primitive form of the *Exercises* as early as 1527.[12] Right down until the time of publication he kept making minor revisions, and he reworked the whole after he finished his studies at Paris in 1535. In a few instances it is possible to isolate late additions to the text; for example, the famous "Rules for Thinking with the Church" obviously reflect his theological studies at Paris and his increasing awareness of Erasmianism and Protestantism, but the main lines of the *Exercises* clearly go back to the Manresa experiences. Partly because few early manuscripts survive, the efforts of scholars to work out a redaction history of the *Exercises* have not yielded striking results. Likewise the search for literary sources has turned up surprisingly little. Loyola had read Ludolf of Saxony and Jacobo de Voragine during his convalescence. At Montserrat his confessor, Dom Jean Chanones, probably gave him a confessional manual and the *Ejercitatorio de la vida espiritual*, which the abbot of Montserrat, García Jiménez de Cisneros, wrote and had printed on the monastery presses in 1500. Despite their similar titles, the *Spiritual Exercises* and the book of Cisneros are very different. Cisneros reprints many passages from earlier spiritual currents, particularly the *devotio moderna;* he is diffuse and theoretical where Loyola is concise and practical. At Manresa Iñigo also read the *Imitation of Christ.* Efforts to find direct verbal borrowings from this handful of sources have produced rather meager results, but they did contribute to a subtle psychospiritual atmosphere whose traces can be found in the *Exercises.*[13]

Most readers find the *Spiritual Exercises* disappointing; a little book of about 160 pages, it lacks literary grace and seems a thicket of rules and directions, a jigsaw puzzle of bits and pieces without coherence. The *Spiritual Exercises* was not written to be read any more than is a cookbook or a manual of physical exercises. Just as only those who have conscientiously gone through the exercises in a physical fitness manual can judge their effectiveness, so only those who have made the *Exercises* can appreciate their spiritual dynamism and psychological impact. The *Spiritual Exercises* were written as a guide for retreat directors. The director was to be an experienced spiritual guide who had already made the *Exercises.* Later supplementary manuals, or directories, were written to give fuller advice to directors. The *Exercises* were designed to help serious Christians reorient their lives into closer conformity with God's will. The full *Exercises* require that the exercitant (the person making the *Exercises*) devote thirty days to religious experiences that are designed to uproot old habits and strengthen the resolve to live a life of dedication to God. Giving the *Exercises* also took a heavy toll on the time and energy of the director, who worked with individual exercitants and tailored the *Exercises* to their precise needs. Loyola primarily intended the *Exercises* for persons who were considering entering religious orders, and many of the earliest recruits were won to the Jesuits through the *Exercises*, but he also gave them to people (for instance to Cardinal Gasparo Contarini) whose vocation in life was fixed and who were seeking spiritual reform.[14] Obviously, the original *Exercises* were intended for an elite. Later they were scaled down in length to eight or even three days and were preached to groups. This dilution of the *Exercises* underlies the retreat movement within modern Catholicism, a work of great religious importance, but such preached, group retreats possess only a fraction of the force of the authentic *Spiritual Exercises.*[15] Loyola himself suggested the possibility of group retreats and urged a shortened version for persons of lesser spiritual promise.

In the *Exercises* Loyola tries to foster in a lower key the experiences and insights that he had at Manresa. The thirty days are split into four "weeks" or stages of growth whose actual length the director can adjust to individual needs. The heart of the first week is a series of meditations on the purpose of human life ("to praise, reverence and serve God"), sin, and hell. In the second week exercitants dedicate themselves to follow Christ the King. To fortify this resolve they meditate on the life of Christ. Toward the end of the second week exercitants are expected to make an election: a choice about a state of life or a resolution to reform themselves in their ongoing state. The third week is more somber, since the meditations center on the passion of Christ. The fourth week, on the resurrection, is joyous, and climaxes in a contemplation for attaining divine love whose tone is at once more philosophical and more open to mysticism. The last two weeks aim at confirming exercitants in their election. Most of the meditations on the life of Christ are bare outlines, which the experienced director shapes to the temperament and mood of the exercitants. In addition to meditations, the exercitants are given rules and directions on such topics as eating habits, the distribution of alms, dealing with scruples, and thinking in conformity with the teaching of the church. The most important set of rules deals with "the discernment of spirits," which helps exercitants understand and deal with their psychoreligious moods and inclinations.[16]

The *Exercises* also teach several methods of mental prayer. The most fundamental sort of meditation involves the application of memory and reasoning powers to various religious truths, followed by efforts to employ the emotions and issuing in practical resolutions for personal reform. Another method is the reconstruction by the imagination of incidents from the Gospels, followed by resolutions drawn from the example of Christ. Another method consists in taking a standard prayer, the Lord's Prayer, for instance, and reflecting prayerfully on it phrase by phrase for an hour. Loyola includes a system of examining the conscience to be used daily for the rest of the exercitant's life. There is a general examination of the day, plus a specific or particular examination on a single virtue that is being cultivated or a single sinful inclination that is being attacked. Exercitants keep notebooks in which they track their daily progress. The general desire for reform of life is thereby given specific focus as one problem area after another is brought under control. It is easy to dismiss such methods as mere bookkeeping, but as A. G. Dickens has observed: "The craving of a troubled but order-seeking century was a craving for precise guidance, and this Loyola offered."[17]

Loyola's teaching on mental prayer made clearer and more precise those methods which were spreading in the late Middle Ages. The *Exercises*, more than any other single source, added to the rise of systematic meditation that became characteristic of reforming Catholicism in the sixteenth and seventeenth centuries. After Loyola's death an hour's meditation became obligatory for Jesuits, and many other religious orders, even monastic orders with rather different traditions, took up the practice. The new Tridentine seminaries taught these methods of prayer to their students. St. Francis de Sales adapted meditation for lay men and women. The *Spiritual Exercises* itself became a great all-time best-seller with nearly five thousand editions, and it has been translated into over twenty languages. Several treatises and manuals of meditation, today remembered only by specialists, outsold Shakespeare and Descartes in the seventeenth century.[18] The growth of systematic mental prayer probably contributed more to real religious reform among Catholics than did the reform legislation of the Council of Trent. A strong influence of the *Exercises* shows up in unexpected places. For example, they were the main source of inspiration for Polish poet Mikolaj Sep Szarzyński.[19] John Donne, the Anglican dean of St. Paul's Cathedral in London, wrote *Ignatius His Conclave,* which describes Loyola's descent into hell, where Satan gladly gives him second place lest the wily Jesuit take over the whole kingdom of hell; but Donne's religious poetry, his greatest achievement, depends in its use of poetic imagination on Loyola's techniques for meditation.[20] Echoes of the *Spiritual Exercises* have been found in René Descartes's *Discourse on Method* and the *Meditations;* indeed, Descartes's choice of the latter title may have derived from Loyola.[21]

In February 1523 Iñigo resumed his pilgrimage to Jerusalem, begging his way via Barcelona and Rome to Venice. He deliberately gave away all money given him beyond his immediate needs, including his fare from Venice to Jerusalem. In Venice he met and captivated a wealthy Spaniard who introduced him to the doge. The doge was so impressed that he provided passage for Iñigo on the Governor's galley bound for Cyprus. From there he traveled to Jaffa and on to Jerusalem, where he spent three weeks visiting the places connected with the life of Christ. He wanted to settle in Jerusalem to pray and work for souls, but the Franciscan provincial, who had direction over all Catholics in Palestine, saw obvious practical problems in the pilgrim's plan and insisted that he return to Venice. Loyola, always respectful to religious authority, reluctantly complied. After barely escaping shipwreck, he reached Venice and decided that if he were to help souls, he would need an education. That decision controlled his life from 1523 to 1535.

The door to education was Latin, the language of instruction in every sixteenth-century university. The once-proud hidalgo, who had taken offense at any slight to his honor, returned to Barcelona and at age thirty-three began to learn the rudiments of Latin with twelve-year-olds. He soon found that his delight in prayer was hurting his progress in memorizing Latin vocabulary, so he deliberately cut down his prayer during his years of study. His Franciscan confessor gave him a copy of Erasmus's *Handbook of the Christian Soldier,* the classic statement of the Christian humanist approach to devout living. Its elegant Latin surely must have stretched Iñigo's ability to the limit, and perhaps that was part of the confessor's purpose, but Loyola soon put Erasmus aside for another reason: "As soon as Ignatius read the book, he observed that it caused the spirit of God within him to chill and his spiritual intensity to wane. Reflecting on this he threw the book away and became so hostile that he refused to read other books by that author and forbade members of our Society to read them."[22]

Several of Loyola's biographers not only have accepted this account of his rejection of Erasmus but also have seen it as foreshadowing the judgment of the Church on Erasmus and the humanist movement.[23] Erasmus was too critical, too skeptical, too ambivalent. The future lay with Luther and Loyola, with men of strong faith and total commitment. Two passages in the *Spiritual Exercises* may echo Erasmus, but Loyola gives them both a twist that they lack in Erasmus. One deals with the end of man: Loyola stresses readiness to accept hardship, poverty, and dishonor.[24] In the other passage Loyola says that Christians must prefer the judgment of the hierarchical church even to the evidence of their senses.[25] But were Loyola and Erasmus really so antithetical? The Jesuit colleges of the late Renaissance provided the framework that spread humanist educational objectives, although in an expurgated version, far more widely than any institutions established by the humanists. The Jesuits would probably not have earned Erasmus's approval, but most of the distinctive innovations of Loyola as a religious legislator deal with those aspects of the older orders which most drew the ridicule of Erasmus. It is significant that many humanist churchmen, such as Cardinal Gasparo Contarini, warmly supported the earliest Jesuits, while many anti-Erasmians, such as Melchor Cano, were also bitter opponents of the Jesuits within the Catholic Church.[26]

After two years in Barcelona Iñigo acquired enough Latin to enroll at the University of Alcalá, where he studied scholastic philosophy for a year while also teaching catechism and giving an early form of the *Spiritual Exercises*. During his student years he always found businessmen and women who were happy to support him and give him alms for distribution to the poor. At Alcalá he gathered around him three disciples: Lope de Cárceres, Juan de Arteaga, and Calixto de Sa. Rumors about Loyola and these companions reached the Inquisition at Toledo. In the middle 1520s the Spanish Inquisition was more concerned with local *Alumbrados* or *illuminati* than with Lutherans or Erasmians. Partly looking back to currents within medieval Islam, the *Alumbrados* put great stress on passive contemplation to the detriment of the sacraments and the Church; those who had reached the stage of enlightenment were no longer bound by conventional Christian morality. The rumors connected Iñigo and his disciples with the *Alumbrados;* but after the inquisitors checked into their life and teaching without finding any errors, they turned the matter over to the local vicar, Juan Figueroa; still they required Iñigo and his companions to give up their distinctive dress since they were not members of a religious order. Figueroa later had Iñigo arrested for forty-two days when he was blamed because a wealthy married woman and her daughter suddenly disappeared on a pilgrimage. After their safe return he was released but was forbidden to discuss religious matters until he completed three more years of study. Rather than forgo giving catechism lessons, Iñigo transferred during the summer of 1527 to the University of Salamanca.

At Salamanca he ran into similar problems. This time it was the Dominicans who suspected the preaching of the half-educated Basque. He was thrown into jail and chained, then called before a tribunal of four professors who questioned him acutely on theology and examined his notes on the *Spiritual Exercises*. After twenty-two days Iñigo and his companions were released; the judges treated them kindly but again laid restrictions on their teaching activity. Later at Paris, Venice and Rome, Loyola had to face charges of either false teaching or scandalous conduct. In fact, he faced such accusations ten times. He always tried to get a public declaration of his innocence from the authorities. Despite this repeated harassment he never rejected the legitimacy of the Inquisition and similar agencies; on the other hand, he did not hesitate to leave their jurisdiction rather than submit to their restrictions, and on several occasions he appealed over their heads to higher authorities.

During his eighteen months at Spain's two most illustrious universities, Loyola had learned very little and suffered great frustration. He determined to leave Spain and head for the world's most famous university, that at Paris. There he hoped to learn faster and suffer less restriction on his activities. He left behind his companions, who planned to rejoin him later at Paris, but they never again figured importantly in his life. At Paris Loyola made new disciples and these formed the nucleus of the nascent Society of Jesus.

Seldom has a less promising student entered a great university. The diminutive Basque (barely over five feet tall) was thirty-seven, walked with a limp, and had a poor academic background and no funds. He enrolled at the Collège de Montaigu, famous for its strict discipline and the conservative theology of its rector, Noel Beda. Erasmus studied there and hated every minute; later he took literary revenge on the college in his *Colloquies*. John Calvin had left Montaigu only four days before Loyola arrived; it is doubtful that they ever met.[27] Since Loyola could not afford to live at the college itself, he stayed at a hospice for the poor and begged for a living. This cost so much study time that he took the the advice of a friend and spent the summers of 1528, 1529, and 1530 begging from rich Spanish merchants in Bruges. There he gained so much that he could devote full time to study during the academic year and even had funds to help other poor students. In 1531 he added London to his begging expedition. At Paris Ignatius Loyola spent one year studying rhetoric and three years on philosophy, receiving his Master of Arts in 1535. He also attended lectures in theology under the Dominicans for two years but never took a degree. By the standards of the time he was well trained, but he was never a scholar like Erasmus, Luther, or Calvin, nor did he pretend to be one.[28]

In September 1529, Loyola transferred from Montaigu to the Collège de Sainte-Barbe, which was much frequented by Spanish and Portuguese students. There he was given a room with two other students, Pierre Favre and Francisco Xavier.[29] Favre was of Savoyard peasant stock, gentle, studious, and pious. Soon he was confiding his religious problems to Loyola, who became his spiritual director and gave him the *Exercises*. In time Favre became the most skilled director of the *Exercises* among the early Jesuits, except for Loyola himself. His simple goodness won people of all kinds, whether the nobles at the court of Charles V or the Italian townsmen who listened to his street preaching. His effect on people is clearest from the case of young Peter Canisius, who heard about him in Cologne and went to Mainz to meet him and then made the Exercises under his direction. Canisius wrote back to a friend: "To my great good fortune I have found the man that I was seeking—if he is a man and not an angel of the Lord. Never have I seen nor heard such a learned and profound theologian nor a man of such shining and exalted virtue. I can hardly describe how the *Spiritual Exercises* transformed my soul. . . . I feel changed into a new man."[30]

Francis Xavier was a Navarese nobleman. He was a gifted student and a skilled athlete, determined to make a career that would restore luster to his family, whose loyalty to the old royal house of Navarre in its struggles against Ferdinand and Charles V had cast them into disfavor. Xavier was not captured so easily as Favre. He seems at first to have resented his eccentric roommate: a Spanish nobleman going about begging for a living! But Loyola was nothing if not persistent in winning men whose natural gifts might make them giants in God's service. By 1533 Francis Xavier had also committed himself completely to God, and the next year he made the *Exercises* with characteristic generosity. His later career as a missionary is too well known to need comment here.

The next two disciples, Diego Laynes and Alfonso Salmerón, came easily: they had heard stories about Loyola at Alcalá where they were students, and had come to Paris partly to seek him out. Both had high intellectual gifts and later served as papal theologians at the Council of Trent. Laynes eventually became Loyola's successor as superior general of the Jesuits and was a major figure in the Counter-Reformation. The little group was soon joined by the suave Portuguese nobleman Simon Rodriquez, who founded the Jesuit province in his homeland and had great influence on King John III. The last recruit was Nicolas Bobadilla, rough-hewn peasant who had already studied at Alcalá and Valladolid. Generous, impetuous, and stubborn, he later made a reputation as a preacher and convent-reformer up and down Italy and live on to give headaches to a succession of Jesuit generals. All the companions that Loyola gathered around him at Paris proved men of extraordinary energy and talent. Loyola possessed a charismatic gift for persuading others to give either themselves or at least their influence and wealth to his goals.

On the feast of the Assumption, 1534, the group climbed Montmarte at the edge of Paris to a small chapel where Favre, the only priest among them, celebrated Mass; before receiving Communion each of the seven made a vow of poverty, chastity, and to go to Jerusalem to live and work for souls. This action was far from constituting the Society of Jesus, but it gave structure to their friendship and their desire to work together in God's service. The idea of working in Jerusalem was, of course, Loyola's old dream in a new form. Since he and his companions were practical men as well as dreamers, they added a clause to their vow: if it proved impossible within a reasonable time to go to Jerusalem or live there, they would go to Rome and ask the pope to use their services wherever he wished. Since the Turks controlled Palestine and were often at war with Venice and Spain, their fall-back clause was only prudent.

Loyola's health had long been uneven. Usually it did not hinder his work but he was subject to recurring problems. The autopsy after his death revealed dozens of stones in his kidneys, liver, and elsewhere, which were probably responsible for excruciating pains that struck him from time to time.[31] In April 1535 he left Paris and returned home to Guipúzcoa, to restore his health through his native air, the sovereign remedy of perplexed sixteenth-century doctors. His companions planned to complete their studies at Paris while Ignatius acted as their agent in Spain and cleared up the temporal responsibilities involved in their vows. They would all reassemble at Venice to seek ship for Jerusalem.

Toward the end of 1535 Loyola reached Venice and devoted most of his time to studying theology in preparation for ordination. He lived at the hospital for the poor and gave the *Spiritual Exercises*, mostly to Spaniards resident in Venice. One such was Diego de Hoces, who had been a penitent of Gian Pietro Carafa, co-founder of the Theatine order and later Paul IV. Carafa seems to have resented his rival, especially since Hoces soon joined Loyola's companions, and may have been behind an investigation into Loyola's orthodoxy in Venice. Loyola wrote Carafa a long letter that criticized several Theatine practices. The letter was probably never sent, but it indicates that Loyola was pondering the direction that a new religious order should take if it were to fit contemporary needs. Later at Rome relations between Carafa and Loyola remained tense.[32] Loyola's companions joined him at Venice in January of 1537. They had added three new members: Claude le Jay, Paschase Broet, and Jean Codure. While they awaited the sailing season, they engaged in menial tasks in the Venetian hospitals, particularly the Hospital of the Incurables, which was filled with the victims of that new scourge, syphilis. The sight of these Masters of Paris caring for the sick caused a minor sensation in the city. In March Ignatius's companions went to Rome for the pope's blessing on their trip to Jerusalem. Intrigued by the strange group, Paul III had them take a turn debating theology at his dinner table, an entertainment that he frequently employed. He was so impressed that he gave them journey money and permission to be ordained by any bishop they chose. Meanwhile diplomatic relations between Venice and the Turks were broken and war followed. There would be no ship to Palestine, but Loyola and his companions did not easily give up their dream of Jerusalem. In June, Loyola was ordained in Venice and then retired with Favre and Laynes to a deserted monastery on the edge of Vicenza for a forty-day retreat. The mystical experiences that had been muted during his student years came flooding back—they were to continue and increase throughout the remaining twenty years of his life. Loyola spent the months following the retreat in street preaching; his Italian was never fluent, and in these early days his preaching was a jumble of Italian, French, Spanish, and Latin that only the sincerity and fervor of the speaker made effective. His companions fanned out to other north Italian cities to preach and help the poor. Loyola suggested at a meeting at Vicenza that if they were asked the name of their little band, they should reply: the Company of Jesus. This was later Latinized to *Societas Jesu* and abbreviated S. J.

Late in November of 1537 Loyola, Laynes, and Favre journeyed to Rome and took up residence near the top of the present Spanish Steps in a villa that a nobleman loaned for their use. Loyola's years of wandering were over; except for short trips he remained in Rome until his death. Early that year a committee of churchmen headed by Cardinal Gasparo Contarini had presented the *Consilium de Emendanda Ecclesia* to Paul III. Armed with a letter from Pietro Contarini, who had befriended him in Venice, Loyola approached Cardinal Contarini, who at once recognized the potential of Loyola and companions in fostering reform. Another key supporter was Pedro Ortiz, the imperial ambassador to the pope and former professor of theology at Paris, where he had known Loyola. Both Contarini and Ortiz made the *Exercises* with enthusiasm under Loyola's personal direction. After Easter, 1538, Ignatius summoned his companions from the north Italian cities, where they had been preaching, to Rome to deliberate about their future. They finally agreed that the Jerusalem pilgrimage could not be realized and that they should put into effect the second part of their vow by putting themselves at the pope's disposal. Paul III authorized them to preach at various Roman churches; Loyola went to a Spanish church and spoke in Spanish, but his younger and more fluent companions preached in Italian. Paul III appointed Laynes and Favre to teach at the papal university, the Sapienza, and arranged for the companions to dispute theology at his table every other week. The winter of 1538–1539 was exceptionally severe and followed bad harvests. Hungry peasants flocked into the city from the countryside, but they could not afford the soaring food prices. Every night starving people froze to death in the piazzas and ruins of the Eternal City. Ignatius and his companions helped over three thousand by turning their residence, now at the Torre del Melangolo, into a hospital and begging for the starving among wealthy churchmen and nobles.

Loyola and his companions had as yet no plans to found a religious order, but in early 1539 Paul III sent Broet and Rodriquez to work in Siena, and other similar missions could be expected. The companions faced a decision: either they must work as so many individual free lances, or they had to devise a flexible structure that combined maximum service to the Gospel with corporate union. To keep their days free for apostolic work, they met frequently by night from March to June and determined to form a religious order, elect a superior, and seek papal approval. Their joint deliberations sketched out many of the distinctive features of the future Jesuit order. Their decisions were based on their three years of work together in Rome and northern Italy and were designed to carry forward the sort of apostolic work that they were already engaged in. Ignatius organized these deliberations into five short chapters and submitted them to Tommaso Badia, the official theologian of the pope. Urged on by Cardinal Contarini, Paul III gave verbal approval to the plans for the Company of Jesus on September 3, 1540. Formal approval did not come so easily. Three cardinals, Contarini, Ghinucci, and Guidiccioni, were charged with drawing up the formal approval of the new religious order. Girolamo Ghinucci, a canon lawyer, objected to many fine points in Loyola's draft, but Contarini gradually brought him around. More serious was the opposition of Bartolomeo Guidiccioni, who was opposed in principle to any new religious orders. Loyola countered by soliciting letters of testimonial from bishops and rulers in northern Italy on the good work done there by his companions. Eventually Guidiccioni capitulated to this bombardment, but he had a measure of revenge: the papal bull *Regimini militantis ecclesiae* (27 September 1540) authorized the Company of Jesus but restricted it to sixty professed members. Subsequent papal decrees lifted this restriction.

The bull authorized the new order to elect a superior general and to draw up constitutions. In April 1541 the companions met in Rome or sent in their ballots to elect a general. All ballots but his own named Ignatius. He refused to accept the office; so, after four days of prayer, there was a second election. The results were the same. Again he refused the office but finally surrendered on the insistence of his confessor. Directing the fast-growing order became the major task of Loyola's last fifteen years.

His other major task was drawing up the *Constitutions* of the order. In March 1541 the companions delegated this job to Ignatius and Jean Codure, but Codure's death five months later left Loyola to carry on alone. He started slowly. His life since his conversion had not been the carrying through of a fixed plan but a continual adaptation to circumstances and what he saw as the will of God. Loyola and his companions had no blueprint when they started their deliberations about founding an order. Their initial sketch, which was incorporated into the bull *Regimini*, was based on their previous experience. Loyola's *Constitutions* themselves grew out of the organic life of the early order as it added members, reached out to new apostolates such as teaching, and consolidated its pattern of living through trial and error. The *Constitutions* could not be written before the Society of

Jesus existed and functioned on a fairly large scale. The written *Constitutions* tried to distill the experience of the early Jesuits into legislation so that their charisma and work could be passed down to later generations of Jesuits.

Loyola began to work in earnest on the *Constitutions* in 1547 and completed the main draft by 1550; two years later this was put into effect on an experimental basis, but revisions based on practical experience were constantly added. Loyola's main work on the *Constitutions* coincided with the appointment of Juan Polanco as his secretary. Polanco, a humanist with experience in the papal curia, not only eased the burden of Loyola's ordinary correspondence but gathered extracts from the rules of Saints Benedict, Augustine, and Francis, from papal legislation on religious orders, and even from the constitutions of medieval universities for Loyola to study. Polanco, a skilled writer, improved the style of the Spanish original and made most of the Latin translation, which was approved as the official text and printed in 1558. Polanco also prepared a series of doubts, or questions that laid out options and reasons for either alternative. Loyola made the choices, but Polanco's spadework helped clarify the options and forced Loyola to sharpen his vision of what was distinctive about the Jesuits by close study of previous monastic legislation and practice. However important Polanco's contribution, the substance of the *Constitutions* was Loyola's work, and their basic spiritual framework again and again reflects the themes of the *Spiritual Exercises*.[33]

The *Constitutions* had still another source: Loyola was convinced that God had called the Society of Jesus into existence and was guiding its progress. More particularly he felt that the Holy Spirit was directing his decisions about the Jesuit *Constitutions*. The surviving fragments of his spiritual diary (2 February 1544–27 February 1545) are mainly notes of his efforts to gauge the will of God regarding the kind of poverty best suited for Jesuit houses.[34]

The Jesuit *Constitutions* are much longer than the rules of earlier religious orders: 275 pages of text in the modern English edition. The disposition of material is not based on abstract themes but follows the dynamic incorporation of an individual into the Society. It begins by reprinting, with minor retouches, the sketch (or *Formula*) contained in the papal bulls that established the order. This is followed by a fuller explanation (the *General Examen*) of Jesuit life that was normally given to men about to enter the novitiate. Finally, there are the *Constitutions* in a narrow sense together with explanatory declarations, which start with a description of the sort of person who should be admitted and of those who should be dismissed from the order. Then comes material on the progress and training of Jesuits together with a discussion of Jesuit colleges and universities. The next section takes up full admission and the vows and discusses the mobility characteristic of Jesuit life. Then follow sections on the general congregation or supreme governing body of the order and on the superior general who runs the ordinary operation of the order. The *Constitutions* close with a section on preserving the fervor and well-being of the Society. While there are many passages that exhort to lofty spiritual ideals, a shrewd practicality is the most striking characteristic of the document: its last sentence directs that colleges should be built in healthy locations with pure air.

What was distinctive about the Jesuits? How did they differ from older orders? The monastic orders such as the Benedictines aimed primarily at self-sanctification by contemplation and withdrawal from the world. The friars tried to mix prayer and some active apostolate. The Jesuit ideal united prayer and apostolate: the ideal Jesuit was *in actione contemplativus*. The whole structure of the religious life and even individual prayer was aimed at the apostolate. The Jesuit's union with God in prayer was to drive him to work for souls redeemed by the labor, death, and resurrection of the God-man. His activity was in turn to feed and inform his prayer. Withdrawal from the bustle of human life was unthinkable: *Benedictus montes, Bernardus valles, Franciscus colles, magnas amavit Ignatius urbes:* Ignatius in contrast to earlier founders loved the big cities, Paris, Venice, Rome. His spiritual odyssey included the cave at Manresa but ended in downtown Rome. Within decades every major city of Catholic Europe had a Jesuit college.

The specific innovations of Loyola as monastic legislator are attempts to fit the religious life for more effective action among people. Obligatory corporal penances and the singing of the office in common were therefore dropped. The Jesuits wore no special religious habit but adapted the ordinary cassock of the secular clergy. Since Jesuits were not isolated in a monastery, monastic discipline had to be interiorized by a more intensive spiritual training: hence the novitiate was stretched from one to two years and a third year of spiritual training (tertianship) was added after the completion of studies. The active life demanded well-educated priests, so a long and rigorous intellectual training was developed. Loyola valued natural gifts, such as health, education, good manners, mental quickness, even noble birth, in candidates to the Society because these could contribute to effective priestly activity. Candidates were to be carefully screened. During Loyola's lifetime a high percentage of those who entered the Jesuits either left or were dismissed. Some of those dismissed, such as Guillaume Postel, were gifted but did not fit the order's other requirements.[35] Loyola instituted a number of grades within the Society partly as a screening process. In most religious orders candidates took solemn perpetual vows of poverty, chastity, and obedience after one year's novitiate. The Jesuit novice took only simple perpetual vows, which could be more easily dispensed if he left the order. After a dozen or so years an elite segment of priests were admitted to solemn profession of the three regular religious vows and usually added a special vow of obedience to the pope. The other priests and the lay brothers took final, simple vows. While all the priests could serve as rectors and superiors, only those with solemn vows could hold higher offices, such as provincial and general.

Although a general congregation was the supreme governing body within the Jesuits, it rarely met except to elect a general, who served for life; appointed subordinate officials; and had complete control of the order's day-to-day operation. Although the structure had some built-in checks, Loyola put unprecedented power into the hands of one man. Certainly it contrasted with the decentralization of the monastic orders and the more democratic capitular government of the friars. Loyola's centralization, perhaps influenced by the development of the new monarchies in his day, had two advantages: it allowed the general at Rome to channel the resources of the Society to maximum apostolic effect, and it gave him power to reform lax houses and practices by direct action in a way that was impossible among the friars. The potential dangers of such centralism are obvious, but in 440 years no Jesuit general has been impeached for misconduct, nor has there been any serious movement to impeach. While there have been many differences over policy and the interpretation of the rule among Jesuits, these have never resulted in schism or the sort of stormy history that has marked the Franciscans. If placid internal history is the mark of good constitution-making, Loyola ranks high.

While many features of the Jesuit *Constitutions* and life-style were foreshadowed by the canons regular of the late Middle Ages and by the Theatines, Barnabites, and Somaschi, Italian religious orders founded shortly before the Jesuits, it was the Jesuit example that had the greatest immediate impact and long-range influence on the evolution of later religious orders and congregations. Hundreds of religious orders and congregations for men and women have sprung up since the sixteenth century. Almost all of them were active congregations and therefore were following in the path opened up by Loyola and his companions. The constitutions of several of these congregations simply took over much of Loyola's legislation.[36] On other congregations his influence is more subtle but very real. Even older orders such as the Dominicans, Franciscans, and Augustinians have evolved into more active orders; the example of the Jesuits has surely conditioned this evolution.

Unlike the other great founders of religious orders, Ignatius did not found a parallel second order for women; indeed, he resisted attempts to do so. This was not because he dismissed the potential of women for spiritual greatness nor the contribution they could make to the Church—on this score his record compares well with contemporary reformers such as Luther and Calvin.[37] But Ignatius Loyola was a practical man. The spiritual care of a second order would have cut down the mobility of his men. His reshaping the religious life toward more intense activity caused misgivings among conservative churchmen. Several popes, Paul IV, for instance, tried to reimpose this or that monastic practice on the new order. Among the Jesuits themselves there were strong currents pushing in the same direction. To have tried to set up a fully active second order for women on the Jesuit model could not have succeeded in sixteenth-century circumstances and might have jeopardized the male order. The Ursulines started as an active order and were quickly cloistered. In the early seventeenth century conservative churchmen frustrated Mary Ward's efforts to start an active order for women on the Jesuit model.

Despite Loyola's stress on quality rather than numbers, the Jesuits grew rapidly, so that there were about one thousand Jesuits at his death in 1556. Foreign missions were the most esteemed apostolate—by 1556 there were Jesuit missions in Brazil, Ethiopia, the Congo, India, Indonesia, and Japan. As early as 1542 the Jesuits began to set up so-called colleges for their own members, but non-Jesuit students were gradually admitted. Soon there were colleges exclusively for lay students. During Loyola's lifetime fifty Jesuit colleges were opened. Half of them had non-Jesuit students, the largest with 900, the average running about 250. After his death the Jesuit colleges grew rapidly in number and size. There were 293 by 1607, but they could not keep up with the demand, even though many Jesuits made education their primary apostolate. Most of the Jesuit colleges corresponded to modern preparatory schools, but a few were full-fledged universities. The Jesuit college system, which spread through southern and eastern Europe and Latin America, became a primary means of spreading Catholic reform to the laity, particularly the upper classes.[38]

The record of Loyola's last fifteen years, which were spent in directing the early growth of the order, is preserved in his vast correspondence; all but twenty-eight items out of 6,795 date after his election as general. While some of his letters are mini-treatises on spiritual topics, most give practical advice to Jesuits who were wrestling with the problems of setting up and running religious houses and colleges throughout Catholic Europe.[39] The correspondence makes a startling contrast with the pages of Loyola's spiritual diary from the same period: his days at Rome externally seem divided between mystical prayer and the bureaucratic routine of running a multinational enterprise. Internally there was no division, since both aspects of his life had a single goal: the greater glory of God.

Despite his burdens as general, Loyola set aside some time for personal apostolic work, which he directed toward those whose spiritual and material need he considered greatest. He brought to these efforts his genius for organization. Rome swarmed with prostitutes. Poverty, sheer hunger, and the practical impossibility of escaping to a respectable life trapped many women in prostitution. Merely to stir up religious repentance in such women would not solve the personal or social problem. Loyola mobilized the help of women of the highest social rank—Margaret of Austria, natural daughter of Charles V, Eleonora Osorio de Vega, wife of the Spanish

Ambassador, Vittoria Colonna, gifted poetess and friend of Michelangelo—to help his work. Eleonora de Vega and her servants went into the streets to talk with potential converts and give them refuge in her palazzo. Since the work required more than generous individual effort, Loyola organized the Confraternity of Grace to enlist the help of the upper classes. Funds were raised and the House of St. Martha was set up as a halfway house under the spiritual direction of a Jesuit. The house helped former prostitutes readjust their lives before reentering the main stream of society. Some of the ex-prostitutes were so moved by the experience that they asked to become nuns; a convent annex at St. Martha's soon became famous for its fervor and austerity.

Prevention is better than cure. There were many young girls who for various reasons were cast adrift in Rome without protection or family. Many drifted into prostitution. Loyola again directed upper-class charity toward this problem; his efforts resulted in the Hospice of St. Catherine, where girls between the ages of ten and twelve received protection and education until they could lead respectable lives on their own. Earlier Gian Pietro Carafa had set up a similar home for abandoned boys, but it needed funds. Ignatius, the master beggar, came to the rescue. Finally he also set up organizations to help Jewish converts and impoverished noblemen.[40]

Reformation meant for Loyola primarily the individual's cooperation with divine initiative toward personal moral and spiritual reform. Here his great legacy was the *Spiritual Exercises*. To the corporative reform of the Church he contributed the Jesuit order and its myriad activities. After the election of Paul III in 1534, Rome became the center of Catholic efforts at reformation. Loyola was closely linked to Contarini and other reforming cardinals. Paul III employed the early Jesuits in many ways both inside and outside Italy: diplomatic missions, preaching, reforming convents. Diego Laynes, Alfonso Salmerón, Peter Canisius, and Claude Lejay served with distinction as theologians at the Council of Trent. The sixteenth-century outburst of missionary activity aimed at winning new lands to the Catholic Church and thereby compensated for Protestant gains in northern Europe; here too the Jesuits played a role disproportionate to their numbers.

Loyola and his followers emphatically rejected the Protestant understanding of reformation: that a fundamental alteration was needed in the doctrine and devotional life of the late medieval Church. Rather the old devotional practices and teaching must be revivified and used with greater fervor and intelligence. Loyola's "Rules for Thinking with the Church" urges Christians "to obey promptly our Holy Mother the hierarchical Church . . . to praise stations, pilgrimages, and indulgences . . . and scholastic theology. We must be careful lest by speaking too much . . . on faith, we give people occasion to become lazy in the performance of good works."

For centuries textbooks and sermons have contrasted Luther and Loyola as prototypes of the Protestant and Catholic reformations. The antithesis between Luther and Loyola had its first major statement in Ribadeneira's biography of Loyola.[41] It finds classic artistic expression in the statue group by Pierre Legros to the right of Loyola's tomb in the Gesu church in Rome: True Faith is assisted by a putto in attacking heresy and destroying books whose spines bear the names of Luther, Calvin, and Zwingli. The Luther-Loyola antithesis rightly implies that the Jesuits were the single most important factor in halting and reversing the Protestant advance, but it wrongly suggests that Loyola founded the Jesuits to serve as papal shock troops against Protestanism. Had a war not intervened, Loyola and his companions would have sailed to Palestine to waste their perfume on the desert air. The first tasks that the papacy assigned the Jesuits were aimed at reviving piety in Italy rather than blocking Protestanism. During Loyola's lifetime Jesuit growth in central and eastern Europe, the main stage of later Jesuit Counter-Reformation activity, was very slow. It was fastest in Portugal and Sicily, the two areas of Europe farthest from Protestant territory, lands where popular concern centered on Islam rather than Protestanism. Loyola considered heresy a secondary problem, but he was still its implacable enemy. His most comprehensive statement on how to deal with Protestanism comes from a letter to Peter Canisius, which gives Canisius suggestions to pass on to Ferdinand of Austria. The kind should deprive Protestants of all offices within his domains, especially schoolmasters and the Protestant professors at the University of Vienna. Protestant books should be combed out of libraries and burned. Booksellers who deal in Protestant books should suffer exile. Priests who incline to Protestantism should be deprived—better that the flock have no pastor than have a wolf for a shepherd. The king should proclaim that Protestant preachers have a month to return to Catholicism. Those who return should be welcomed kindly; the others should be exiled or jailed. Indeed, a few executions might serve as a good example, but Loyola recommends against trying to set up an Inquisition in Germany. The letter is Loyola's most extreme statement against Protestantism; the second and longer part of it returns to his usual themes on how to strengthen Catholic faith and practice.[42]

The quantity and quality of primary material for the life of Loyola easily surpasses that available for earlier founders of religious orders. There is the autobiography for his earlier life and his correspondence for his Roman years. Several friends added their reminiscences. Juan Polanco contributed a detailed chronicle of early Jesuit history.[43] The early Jesuits were acutely conscious of the need for public relations, especially since their expansion and aggressiveness roused protests not only from Protestants but also from loyal Catholics, particularly members of the mendicant orders. Founders of religious orders are usually proposed to the order for imitation. Soon after Loyola's death the Jesuits began to push for his canonization, partly out of genuine veneration, partly to gain honor for the order, partly to secure a vindication of their way of life against their many detractors. An acceptable image of the founder was necessary for both the younger members and the general public. To meet this demand three major biographies were written within twenty-five years of Loyola's death. The most important was that of Pedro de Ribadeneira. Ribadeneira entered the Jesuits at Rome in 1540 and immediately became a special favorite of Loyola. In 1567, the Jesuit general commissioned him to prepare an official biography, and primary materials were put at his disposal. In 1572 a limited Latin edition was circulated for criticism. The Spanish biography of 1583, a masterpiece of Spain's literary Golden Age, incorporated these criticisms. It combined warm personal reminiscences, an eye for the revealing anecdote, and a passion for exact detail; but it lacked objectivity and presented a static image, without development. Juan Polanco, Loyola's secretary during his last eleven years, wrote a Latin biography in 1574 that lacked Ribadeneira's flair and exactness but was more analytic and had a better sense of history. Although not published until the twentieth century, it was used by later Jesuit biographers, notably Gian Pietro Maffei. Not all Jesuits were pleased by Ribadeneira's effort, so Maffei was commissioned to do an alternative biography, which he published in 1589. His book, in brilliant rhetorical Latin, enjoyed considerable popularity in Italy and northern Europe. All three of these early biographies contain valuable details about Loyola, culled from men who knew him well; they present an official portrait, but a fairly honest one.

Loyola was canonized in 1622. This and the baroque stereotype of what a saint should be produced a new image of Loyola as world-historical giant and thaumaturge that dominated the seventeenth century and found expression in masterpieces such as Peter Paul Rubens's paintings of Loyola for the Jesuit church in Antwerp. Still more extreme are the frescoes of Loyola's life done by the Jesuit painter Andrea Pozzo for the Church of St. Ignatius in Rome. These climax in the "Triumph of St. Ignatius," which covers the whole central ceiling: two stories of painted architecture open onto a vision of heaven above, a distant Christ points to Loyola, from whom rays of power go out to Asia, Africa, America, and Europe; each continent is depicted as an area of Jesuit victory over Satan. Several Jesuit poets of the seventeenth century wrote Latin mini-epics in the same spirit. The baroque biography par excellence is that of Daniel Bartoli, published in Italian in 1650 and translated into French, German, Latin, Spanish, and English. It remained standard until well into the nineteenth century. Suffice it to say that the book ends with an account of one hundred miracles attributed to Loyola, some of them decidedly bizarre.[44]

The groundwork for the modern historical understanding of Loyola was laid by the *Monumenta Historica Societatis Jesu*, which was started in Madrid in 1894 and continued in Rome since 1932 by the Historical Institute of the Society of Jesus. All of Loyola's writings and all important contemporary sources for his life have appeared in critical editions. The bibliography of this essay discusses these documents.

The older historiography, whether from Catholic, Protestant, or secularist viewpoints, tended to use the soldier-saint stereotype. The better modern studies have abandoned this to see Loyola as a religious reformer whose distinctive contribution is best seen by comparison with previous founders of religious orders or contemporary Catholic reformers. The full-scale attempts to compare Loyola with the major Protestant reformers, such as Luther and Calvin, have been less successful, largely because they are written in a polemical, pre-ecumenical spirit that does less than justice to the Protestant side of the comparison.[45] So much of the study of Loyola's life and spirituality has come from the pens of Jesuits that it has perhaps discouraged outsiders who could bring new viewpoints. Several Protestant biographies have stressed Loyola's sincerity, zeal, and gift for organization. The best of these are the works of Robert Harvey and Paul Van Dyke.[46]

Hostile studies of Loyola now come mainly from writers of secularist viewpoint who tend to interpret Loyola in terms of Fëdor Dostoevski's Grand Inquisitor. The best example of this sort of interpretation is Ludwig Marcuse's *Soldier of Christ: the Life of Ignatius Loyola*, originally written in German. There are English, French, Spanish, and Portuguese translations. Marcuse combines a grasp of the sources with a brilliant impressionistic style. For Marcuse the hermit of Manresa becomes a dictator of souls, corrupted by the thirst for religious power over man: "Kings, businessmen and the monk imperalist must think only of conquering the world. . . . A cross fertilization of the seed of Assisi and Machiavelli. And Machiavelli was the stronger."[47] Recent Loyola studies can be more conveniently discussed in the bibliography that follows the notes.

NOTES

1. Cf. John Addington Symonds, *Renaissance in Italy* (New York: Modern Library, n.d.), 2:648–50, with the essays in Rudolf Wittkower and Irma B. Jaffe, editors, *Baroque Art: The Jesuit Contribution* (New York: Fordham University Press, 1972).

2. Jean Delumeau, *Catholicism between Luther and Voltaire* (Philadelphia: Westminster, 1977); A. G. Dickens, *The Counter Reformation* (N.P.: Harcourt, Brace and World, Inc. 1969).

3. Wolfgang Reinhard, "Gegenreformation als Modernisierung?" *Archiv für Reformationsgeschichte* 68 (1977): 226–52.

4. Iñigo was the Basque form of Enneco, the name of a saintly Spanish abbot. When Loyola arrived at the University of Paris he Latinized his name to Ignatius. *MHSI* 115:788. For abbreviations used in these notes, see the beginning of the bibliography of this essay.

5. It is true that Loyola later used military metaphors to describe the spiritual life, but these were commonplace, going back to St. Paul, indeed to Job. The title *Company of Jesus* connoted in southern Europe an analogy to religious confraternities, such as the Company of the Blessed Sacrament, rather than to military units. The Jesuit superior general (often shortened

to general) parallels the Dominican master general and the Franciscan minister general—the superior with overall direction of the order—rather than a commander directing armies. Jesuit obedience is often compared to military obedience, but such comparisons are anachronistic, since the modern concept of military obedience largely dates from the eighteenth century. Military metaphors are conspicuous for their absence from Loyola's famous letter on obedience: *MHSI*, 29:669–81. Discipline and obedience were hardly hallmarks of sixteenth-century soldiers. Thomas H. Clancy, "Ignatius Loyola: A Soldier-Saint," *America* 125 (1971): 317–18.

6. Pedro Leturia, *Iñigo de Loyola*, trans. A. J. Owens (Syracuse, N.Y.: Le Moyne College Press, 1949), is the most detailed and authoritative study of Loyola's life up to the Montserrat vigil. The main primary source for his life up to his arrival in Rome in 1537 is Loyola's autobiography, *St. Ignatius' Own Story*, trans. W. J. Young (Chicago: Henry Regnery, 1956).

7. *St. Ignatius' Own Story*, p. 22.

8. Ibid., p. 23.

9. Ibid., p. 24.

10. Ibid., p. 23.

11. San Ignatio de Loyola, *Obras Completas* (Madrid: Biblioteca de Autores Cristianos, 1977), 3d ed., 341–410; *MHSI*, 63:xcv-cxx.

12. *St. Ignatius' Own Story*, pp. 41, 49.

13. For the best scholarly text of the *Exercises*, see *MHSI*, 100; for bibliography dealing with the text, see Jean-François Gilmont, *Les Écrits spirituels des premiers jésuites* (Rome: IHSI, 1961), p. 49.

14. See the bibliography of this essay for works dealing with the *Spiritual Exercises*.

15. Over the centuries more than a hundred million people have made the *Spiritual Exercises* in one form or another. Thus in 1949 more than seven million people made the *Exercises* under the direction of members of religious orders: Giorgio Papàsogli, *St. Ignatius Loyola* (New York: Society of St. Paul, 1959), 150.

16. Piet Penning de Vries, *Discernment of Spirits According to the Life and Teaching of St. Ignatius Loyola*, trans. W. Dudok van Heel (New York: Exposition Press, 1973).

17. *The Counter Reformation*, p. 81.

18. Luis de la Puente's *Meditaciones de los misterios de nuestra santa fe* (1605) has had over seven hundred editions; Alonso Rodríquez's *Ejercicio de perfeccion y virtudes cristianas* (1609) has enjoyed over three hundred editions in twenty-three languages. Both of these are very long works.

19. *AHSI*, (1975), 325–27.

20. John Donne, *Ignatius His Conclave* (Oxford: Oxford University Press, 1969), edited by T. S. Healey; Louis Martz, *The Poetry of Meditation* (New Haven, Conn.: Yale University Press, 1962), 25–56.

21. Walter J. Stohrer, "Descartes and Ignatius Loyola: La Flèche and Manresa Revisited," *Journal of the History of Philosophy* 27 (1979): 11–27.

22. The quotation is from Pedro Ribadeneira's early biography, *MHSI*, 93:174; Juan Polanco, Loyola's secretary, repeats the statement, *MHSI*, 66:585. Loyola does not refer to reading Erasmus in his autobiography.

23. Papàsogli, 95–97; James Brodrick, *St. Ignatius Loyola: The Pilgrim Years, 1491–1538* (New York: Ferrar, Straus and Cudahy, 1956), 156–63.

24. Brodrick, 156–63.

25. Penning de Vries, 178–79.

26. Other scholars, with good reason, have questioned the passages in Ribadeneira and Polanco, who were probably trying to picture Loyola as anticipating the Church's judgment on Erasmus: Marcel Bataillon, *Erasmo y España*, trans. Antonio Alatorre (Mexico City: Fondo de Cultura económico, 1950), 1:248–50; John Olin, "Erasmus and St. Ignatius Loyola," in *Luther, Erasmus and the Reformation*, ed. John Olin et al. (New York: Fordham University Press, 1969), 114–133. These scholars suggest that Loyola read Erasmus later at Alcalá in the Spanish

translation printed by Loyola's friend and benefactor Miguel de Eguía. Although Loyola was inclined to look unfavorably on Erasmus's criticism of traditional religious practices, the *Handbook of the Christian Soldier* has little such criticism. The differences between Erasmus and Loyola are more nuanced than is usually assumed (Olin, 120–27). Ricardo García Villoslada, *Loyola y Erasmo* (Madrid: Taurus, 1965), stresses the differences between Loyola and Erasmus rather more than does Olin.

27. Brodrick, 219.

28. Loyola ranked thirtieth in his licenciate class at Paris in 1532. The exact number in the class in unknown, but Loyola probably ranked near the middle. Ibid., 274.

29. The most detailed treatment of Loyola's life from 1529–1540 is found in Georg Schurhammer's *Francis Xavier: His Life, His Times*, trans. M. J. Costelloe (Rome: IHSI, 1973), vol. 1.

30. Otto Braunsberger, ed., *Beati Petri Canisii Societatis Iesu epistulae et acta* (Freiburg i. B.: Herder, 1896), 1:76–78.

31. Brodrick, 277, 302, 320.

32. Georges Bottereau, "La 'Lettre' d'Ignace de Loyola à Gian Pietro Carafa," *AHSI* 44 (1975): 139–52.

33. For a critical edition of the Jesuit *Constitution,* see *MHSI,* 63–65. For an English translation with introduction and notes, see George Ganss, ed. *The Constitutions of the Society of Jesus* (St. Louis, Mo.: Institute of Jesuit Sources, 1970).

34. See n. 11 of this essay.

35. Henri Bernard-Maître, "Le Passage de Guillaume Postel chez les premier Jésuites de Rome," in *Mélanges d'histoire litteraire de la renaissance offerts à Henri Chamard* (Paris: Librairie Nezet, 1951), pp. 227–43.

36. *MHSI,* 65:lxxxix-cxiii; Arturo Codina lists verbal borrowings from Loyola in the constitutions of later religious congregations, but the Jesuit influence was much more pervasive and subtle than his listings suggest.

37. See Hugo Rahner, *Saint Ignatius Loyola: Letters to Women,* trans. K. Pound and S. A. H. Weetman (Edinburgh: Nelson, 1970).

38. George Ganss, *Saint Ignatius' Idea of a Jesuit University* (Milwaukee, Wis.: Marquette University Press, 1954); Ladislaus Lukács, "De origine collegiorum externorum deque controversiis circa eorum paupertatem obortis," *AHSI* 29 (1960): 189–245; 30 (1961): 3–89.

39. Loyola's correspondence fills twelve large volumes in *MHSI:* 22, 26, 28, 29, 31, 33, 34, 36, 37, 39, 40, and 42.

40. Papàsogli, 234–46.

41. *MHSI,* 93:314, 338, 714. The first to draw out the Luther-Loyola antithesis was Antonio Possevino, *Moscovia et alia opera* (Cologne: Birckmann, 1587), 313. For a discussion of the antithesis, see Mario Scaduto, *L'epoca di Giacomo Lainez* (Rome: Civiltà cattolica, 1974), 2:xxvi–xxviii.

42. *MHSI,* 34:398–404 (letter #4709, 13 August 1554).

43. *Obras,* 5–10; Gilmont, 28–39. The history of the interpretation of Loyola's life is traced in *Obras,* 3–38.

44. Daniel Bartoli, *The History of the Life and Institute of St. Ignatius Loyola, Founder of the Society of Jesus* (New York: E. Dunigan, 1855).

45. Friedrich Richter, *Martin Luther and Ignatius Loyola: Spokesmen of Two Worlds of Belief,* trans. L. F. Zwinger (Westminster, Md.: Newman Press, 1960); André Favre-Dorsaz, *Calvin et Loyola* (Paris/Brussels: Editions Universitaires, 1951).

46. Robert Harvey, *Ignatius Loyola: A General in the Church Militant* (Milwaukee, Wis.: Bruce, 1936); Paul Van Dyke, *Ignatius of Loyola, Founder of the Jesuits* (New York: Scribners, 1926).

47. Ludwig Marcuse, *Soldier of the Church: The Life of Ignatius Loyola,* trans. C. Lazare (New York: Simon and Schuster, 1939), p. 271.

BIBLIOGRAPHY

About eighty books and articles are published every year on Loyola, mainly in English, German, French, and especially in Spanish. This bibliography stresses material available in English. Fortunately, excellent guides are available to this forest of material. A few abbreviations will simplify the entries: The Institutum Historicum Societatis Iesu (IHSI), the Jesuit Historical Institute, has published critical editions of the writings of Loyola and the early Jesuits in the series *Monumenta Historica Societatis Iesu (MHSI)*. It also publishes the *Archivum Historicum Societatis Iesu* (AHSI), a semiannual journal devoted to Jesuit history. The best guide to older Loyola studies is J. F. Gilmont and P. Daman, eds., *Bibliographie ignatienne (1894–1957)* (Paris/Louvain: Desclée de Brouwer, 1958), which lists 2,872 items arranged topically. More recent literature is described with critical comment in *Orientaciones bibliográficas sobre san Ignacio de Loyola* (Rome: IHSI, 1965) by Ignacio Iparraguirre; Manuel Ruiz Jurado has published a second volume of the same work (Rome: IHSI, 1977) covering 1965 to 1976. Still more recent is László Polgár, *Bibliographie sur l'histoire de la Campagnie de Jésus, 1901–1980* (Rome: IHSI, 1981), vol. 1; Polgár publishes an annual bibliography in AHSI.

The *MHSI* contains critical editions of all Loyola's writings: his letters (vols. 22, 26, 28, 29, 31, 33, 34, 36, 37, 39, 40, 42); the *Spiritual Exercises* and related documents (vols. 76, 100); the *Constitutions* and Jesuit rules (vols. 64, 65, 71); biographical material (vols. 66, 73, 85, 93, 115). Loyola's major writings and a selection of his letters are available in handy volumes in Spanish and Italian: *Obras Completas* (Madrid: B.A.C., 1977), 3d ed., ed. I. Iparraguirre and C. de Dalmases; *Gli scritti di Ignazio de Loyola* (Turin: U.T.E.T., 1977), ed. Mario Gioia. Unfortunately, no such volume exists in English. A handy translation of the *Spiritual Exercises* is that by Anthony Mattola (Garden City, N.Y.: Doubleday, 1964). George Ganss has translated and commented on *The Constitutions of the Society of Jesus* (St. Louis: Institute of Jesuit Sources, 1970). William Young has translated both Loyola's autobiography (see n. 6 of this essay) and a selection of his letters: *Letters of St. Ignatius of Loyola* (Chicago: Loyola University Press, 1949).

Good biographies of the earlier part of Loyola's life are given in nn. 6, 23, and 29 of this essay. The best account of Loyola's years in Rome is André Ravier, *Ignace de Loyola fonde la Compagnie de Jesus* (Paris: Desclée de Brouwer, 1974). For the texture of Loyola's day-to-day direction of the early Jesuits, the best source is Pietro Tacchi-Venturi, *Storia della Compagnia di Gesù in Italia*, four large volumes in two (Rome: La civiltà cattolica, 1950–1951). Although dated, the best complete biography remains Paul Dudon, *St. Ignatius of Loyola* (Milwaukee: Bruce, 1949), trans. William Young. Jesus M. Granero in *San Ignacio de Loyola: Panoramos de su vida* (Madrid: Razon y Fe, 1967) presents excellent interpretative essays on key questions in Loyola's life. These studies are all within the Jesuit tradition. For outside views, see the studies mentioned in nn. 46 and 47 as well as Michael Foss, *The Founding of the Jesuits 1540* (London: Hamish Hamilton, 1969), which sees the founding of the Jesuits as a turning point for Catholicism in the Reformation crisis.

Most recent studies of Loyola have not been biographical in the strict sense but rather have investigated the interface of Loyola's life, his spiritual heritage (especially the *Spiritual Exercises*), and the spiritual needs of modern Christians. Ignacio Iparraguirre surveys much of this literature in "Demystificación de San Ignacio: La imagen de San Ignacio en el momento actual," *AHSI* 41 (1972): 357–73. Iparraguirre has also written extensively on the *Spiritual Exercises*, particularly *Historia de los Ejercicios de San Ignacio* (Rome: IHSI, 1946–1948), of which the first volume covers Loyola's lifetime, the second the later sixteenth century, and the third the seventeenth century. Among modern studies of the *Exercises noteworthy are Henri Pinard de la Boullaye, Exercises spirituels selon la méthode de Saint Ignace* (Paris: Beauchesne, 1944–1947), 4 vols.; *Harvey D. Egan, The Spiritual Exercises and the Ignatian Mystical Horizon* (St. Louis, Mo.: Institute of Jesuit Sources, 1976); and Eduoard Pousset, *Life in Faith and Reason: An Essay Presenting Gaston Fessard's Analysis of the Dialectic of the Spiritual Exercises of St. Ignatius* (St. Louis, Mo.: Institute of Jesuit Sources, 1980), trans. Eugene L. Donahue. For an example of how a great modern theologian updates the *Exercises,* see Karl Rahner, *Spiritual Exercises* (New York: Herder and Herder, 1965), trans. K. Baker. Loyola's key role within the whole tradition of Jesuit spirituality is the thesis of Joseph de Guibert's *The Jesuits; Their Spiritual Doctrine and Practice* (Chicago: Loyola University Press, 1964), trans. William Young. Friedrich Wulf has edited a number of excellent studies by German and Austrian scholars in *Ignatius Loyola; His Personality and Spiritual Heritage, 1556–1956* (St. Louis: Institute of Jesuit Sources, 1977). Hugo Rahner, *Ignatius the Theologian* (London: G. Chapman, 1968), trans. Michael Barry, presents part of Rahner's longer German study of Loyola's personality and theological development. Karl Rahner and Paul Imhoff have joined an interpretative essay with old engravings and lavish color photographs in *Ignatius of Loyola* (London: Collins, 1979).

7

Calvin as a Reformer: Christ's Standard-Bearer

David Foxgrover

Introduction

In his reply to Jacopo Sadoleto, Calvin defends his ministry by saying that he was not a deserter of the church, but one who "seeing the soldiers routed . . . and abandoning the ranks, raises the leader's standard, and recalls them to their posts."[1] Although this military metaphor may not seem congruent with Calvin's frequent characterizations of himself as a retiring scholar and lover of privacy,[2] it does provide an accurate description of Calvin's understanding of his role as a reformer, and that in at least three ways: first, Calvin was acutely aware of the ruinous state of the church. Without men to raise "that noble banner" of God, the church would be overwhelmed by superstition, ignorance, and immorality. Second, Calvin viewed the struggles of his time as a continuation of the struggles of the church described in both Testaments. David, Daniel, and Paul were also standard-bearers, and in their words, as in a mirror, Calvin beheld himself and his own times. Finally, Calvin saw himself surrounded by antagonists of all kinds: papists, Anabaptists, Epicureans, and compromisers.

After briefly developing these points, I will show that Calvin's understanding of his role as a reformer must be seen in the context of three themes: Calvin's belief that the world is degenerating in morality and religion, his expectation that the church would always suffer, and his conviction that Christ would return soon to deliver his church.

In one of his most compelling statements about the goals of the Reformation, *The Necessity of Reforming the Church*, Calvin argues that the church of Christ is in "grievous distress and in extreme danger." All the marks of the true church, doctrine, sacraments, and discipline, have been vitiated and obscured:

those heads of doctrine . . . in which the pure and legitimate worship of

God, and those in which the salvation of men are comprehended, were in a great measure obsolete. . . . the use of the sacraments was in many ways vitiated and polluted. And we maintain that the government of the Church was converted into a species of . . . insufferable tyranny.[3]

In other writings Calvin employs a variety of images to describe the church's precarious condition. On Genesis 33:6 Calvin laments that "at this day also the glory of the Church" is covered with a "sordid veil"; and on Genesis 49:18 Calvin remarks that the church of his day "seems to be tossed on a turbulent sea, and almost sunk in the waves."[4] Frequently Calvin speaks of the church's being submerged in the darkness of ignorance, into which the light of the Gospel must penetrate: "the true method of reforming the Church" is to give "sight to the blind and hearing to the deaf." Calvin adds, "We have experienced this in our time, when we have been brought out of the darkness of ignorance and restored to the true light."[5] Elsewhere, the church is described as "mangled and disfigured" by the papal theologians and the pope himself.[6] These "vile errors and abuses" move Calvin to employ a most vivid image of the church's decadence: commenting on Genesis 28:6, he says that a reformation was "absolutely necessary" because the papal theologians were "unwilling that the filth of this Camarine marsh be stirred."[7]

Calvin had no illusions about the magnitude of the work involved in restoring the church to its "pristine condition." Toward the end of his life Calvin remarked that "God has forwarded the restoration of his Church further than I had dared hope,"[8] but he had learned "by experience that it is not the work of one or two years to restore a fallen church to a tolerable state."[9] Calvin often spoke of how "few in numbers" were those committed to the reform when compared to the power and opulence of the papal churches. "Many take us for fools," Calvin wrote on Matthew 24:1, "as if a man should try to pull down the sun from the sky." It is difficult for such "fools" to attract and maintain supporters, for "we know," Calvin adds on 24:5, "how quickly we fall out to join the crowd, especially when we are few in number."[10]

In describing himself as Christ's "standard-bearer," Calvin did not intend to say that he stood alone in reforming the church. In dedicating his Titus commentary to G. Farel and P. Viret, Calvin says that as Titus completed the work began by Paul, so he was the successor of Farel and Viret, "striving to the best of my ability to carry on the work that you had begun so successfully and so well."[11] If Calvin's comparison of himself to Titus and Farel to Paul is inappropriate, it is nonetheless typical of Calvin to compare himself to past standard-bearers of the Lord. "Compare" is too weak a word; Calvin found himself in the lives of David, Daniel, Paul, and others. Of David, Calvin wrote that "it seemed to me that by his own footsteps he showed me the way," and that "in unfolding the internal affections both of David and of others, I discourse upon them as matters of which I have familiar experience."[12] The prophecies of Daniel are a "mirror" in which Christians of Calvin's time can see how God proves his people by trials. The "ancient examples" in this book will guide every "runner" from "the starting post to the goal."[13] The image may shift from standard-bearer to soldier to runner, but in each case Calvin sees the struggles of earlier times as paradigms for himself. Reading Calvin's comments on the pastoral letters, one senses that Calvin is applying all that he says to himself: in these letters we have a "living picture of the true government of the Church,"[14] and a part of that government are Christian teachers, "standard-bearers in Christ's army." The chief things required of a teacher are that "he should hold to the pure truth of the gospel, and that he should minister it with good conscience and honest zeal. Where these two things are present, the rest will follow of themselves."[15] There could be no better description of Calvin's ministry.

Calvin expected the church to be afflicted continually and therefore the struggles of the past will be repeated in the present—and again in the future: "It is then an exercise eminently fitted to comfort true believers to look back to the conflicts of the Church in the days of old, in order thereby to know that she has always laboured under the cross."[16] Because all of the faithful are of "the same body," Calvin says, "it is right and just that our condition should be like that of the fathers."[17] This comment does not go far enough in explaining the correctness of looking to the biblical past to understand the present and future. "It is because," Calvin says on Daniel 8:24–25, "we have fallen upon the fullness of times" that "whatever happened to the Church of old, belongs also to us."[18] The sixteenth century is part of the "fullness of time" and therefore the writings of David, Daniel, and the New Testament authors are relevant to Calvin's circumstances. It is not enough to say that the past struggles of the church are examples or models; the past is being relived in the present.[19]

Finally, as Christ's "standard-bearer" Calvin saw himself surrounded by enemies: papists, Anabaptists, compromisers, hypocritical ministers, and mockers of God. Calvin wrote on Philemon 1: "For although all Christians share in this warfare, teachers are, so to speak, Christ's standard-bearers and ought to be ready to fight harder than the others."[20] Calvin's denunciations of his enemies are severe, but those against compromisers and hypocrites in his own group are even harsher.

It is noteworthy that in spite of the profound differences between his papist and Anabaptist enemies, Calvin says that the "principal weapon with which they assail us is the same": they "boast extravagantly of the Spirit" and "bury the Word of God."[21] The papal theologians are more concerned about "subtle speculations" and "filling their bellies" than teaching "godly doctrine," which "establishes us in the fear and worship of God."[22] Because the Word of God is silent, the papacy has succumbed to superstitions, ignorance, hypocrisy, and immorality. The Anabaptists are repeatedly criticized by Calvin for their perfectionism: they think they have become angels who no longer need the disciplines of the church, and who need not be limited to the bounds of Scripture. Calvin says it is "satanic infatuation which has taken hold of those who speak so much of perfection in holiness." They speak in "magnificent terms of regeneration," but do away with "gratuitous reconciliation," which "God's people are commanded to seek daily."[23] Elsewhere Calvin chides the "illusory belief of the Enthusiasts that those who keep reading Scripture or hearing the Word are children, as if no one were spiritual unless he scorned doctrine."[24]

Calvin knew that the church would always contain true and false members, but that did not stop him from vehemently criticizing compromisers who were weakening the reform efforts. There are many mediators, Calvin says, who want "to reconcile Popery with the . . . Gospel." But God will not endure such a mixture, because "light cannot agree with darkness."[25] Writing on Amos 7:10–13, Calvin excoriates princes who, seeking only peace, want to follow a "middle course." Calvin adds caustically: "we have no enemies more hostile . . . than these domestic traitors."[26] Others begin in the faith with a flourish but do not persevere. On Zephaniah 1:2–3 Calvin laments that "though God now appears to the world in full light, yet few . . . submit themselves to his word; and fewer . . . still there are who sincerely . . . embrace sound doctrine." Surrounded by compromisers and people who do not persevere, Calvin warns

> not to regard ours as the golden age, because some . . . profess the pure worship of God: for many . . . think that . . . mortals are like angels, as soon as they testify . . . their approbation of the Gospel: and the sacred name of Reformation is . . . profaned when any one who shows as it were by a nod only that he is not wholly an enemy to the Gospel, is immediately lauded as a person of extraordinary piety.[27]

Calvin frequently castigates the incompetent ministers who were aligned with the reform. He was so devoted to the restoration of the pastorate that he would not tolerate scandalous conduct from pastors. It was the ignorance and sloth of pastors that destroyed purity of doctrine among the papists, Calvin says on 2 Timothy 2:17.[28] "Sloth, desire for gain, and lust for power" are the vices most common to pastors, Calvin says on 1 Peter 5:1;[29] and on 2 Timothy 1:15 he displays his contempt for those who abuse the pastorate:

> In our day also, there are many who, either because they are not admitted to the ministry here in Geneva, or because they have been expelled . . . because of their wickedness, or because we won't support them in idleness, or because they have committed theft or fornication and have been forced to flee, forthwith wander through France and

beyond and try to establish their own innocence by directing against us all the accusations they can.[30]

Calvin concludes in disgust: "It would be desirable that all these men should have their foreheads branded so that they may be recognized at first sight." Although Calvin wrote to Myconius that his colleagues, with the exception of Farel and Viret, were a "hindrance rather than a help,"[31] he wrote to Sadoleto in defense of the reformed ministry: " . . . even if some ministers be found of no great learning, none is admitted who is not at least tolerably fit to teach."[32]

In dealing with incompetent ministers and compromisers, Calvin faced "internal enemies"; but there was a group of "external enemies" whom he also vilified: the Epicureans and Lucianists. These men were "mockers of God who . . . despise all religion" and who "abandon themselves to every wickedness." Calvin adds: "We see that the world is full of such a rabble of men today."[33] The papists may be the embodiment of Antichrist and may have buried the Word of God, but they affirm God's existence and revere the Scriptures. In *Concerning Scandals* Calvin says these mockers of God desire to "obliterate all fear of God from the minds of men," and allege that "God exists because it pleases men to believe so, that the hope of eternal life has been invented to deceive the simple, and that the fear of judgment is childish terror."[34] The seriousness with which Calvin took the challenge of this enemy is seen in his comments on Habakkuk 2:20, where he says that the evil of superstition is "more tolerable than that gross impiety which obliterates every thought of God." When confronted with the Epicureans, Calvin finds himself defending the papists, for they at least "retain this principle—that honor and worship are due to God."[35]

Portraying Calvin as Christ's "standard-bearer" highlights his intense and uncompromising devotion to the reform. Seen in this perspective Calvin appears as harsh and highly critical—a bilious spirit. But we must not forget that Calvin spoke about joy, love, and hope as often as judgment, hyprocrites, and enemies. His sermon on Ephesians 1:13–14 reveals how he maintained a spirit of joy and hope along with his determination to persevere: "we must determine with ourselves to fight and groan continually and yet, at the same time to rejoice also. . . . To rejoice in our hearts and yet to cry with Paul, 'Alas, wretched creature that I am . . .,' are not incompatible things."[36] Calvin's emotions reflected his belief that redemption was complete in Jesus Christ, but was yet to be completed within the believer. As Calvin says on Romans 8:23: "Paul calls for two kinds of feelings in believers. They are to *groan,* since they are burdened with a sense of their present misery, and yet they are to *wait* patiently for their deliverance."[37]

Calvin's frequent—and at times eloquent—statements on hope, joy, and love enable us to see him as a complex personality who, for the most part, maintained a balance between "groaning" and "rejoicing" in keeping with the dual realities of sin and redemption. A man who had not experienced the "joy of salvation" could not have written these words on hope in Romans 8:20: "From hope comes the swiftness of the sun, the moon and all the stars in their constant course, the continued obedience of the earth in producing its fruits, the unwearied motion of the air, and the ready power of the water to flow." If God has "inwardly implanted the hope of renewal" in the inanimate creation, how much more should his people rejoice and hope, to whom he has given the "earnest of the Spirit."[38]

As Calvin struggled to reestablish the true church in reality as well as in theory, as he fought to proclaim the Word of God and to ward off the attacks of his enemies, he was sustained by three beliefs: first, the world was becoming worse and therefore the external enemies would become increasingly powerful; second, the lot of the church would always be one of struggle; and third, Christ would return to deliver the church. It is to these beliefs that we now turn.

1. The world is "perpetually becoming worse"

Not only did Calvin affirm the depravity of humankind and the fall of creation, but he frequently suggests that the world is continuing to decline in morality and religion. This notion of the world's becoming worse is found in Calvin's commentaries on Genesis and Daniel, in particular, and in other writings as well. Calvin does not develop this idea consistently, but it explains his radical pessimism about the deliverance of the church apart from divine intervention and his near-paranoia about being surrounded by "Epicurean and Lucianist dogs." I shall first consider some of Calvin's general statements of the idea; second, consider how the idea is manifested in Calvin's handling of particular issues; and third, challenge Calvin's consistency on this issue.

On the second chapter of Genesis, Calvin writes that ever since the Fall, "it became necessary that the world should gradually degenerate from its nature." This decline becomes evident immediately in creation itself. The phrase "God created" implies that God created all things that "tend to the lawful and genuine adorning of the world." It is only afterward, Calvin notes, that we find God saying, "Let the earth bring forth thorns and briers." Many things that are now in the world are "corruptions of it rather than any part of its proper nature." In the "existence of fleas, caterpillars and other noxious insects" there is seen "some deformity of the world."[39] Does Calvin intend to speak literally? He must realize that fleas *et alia* were all part of the "good" creation! His point is nonetheless clear: the world is "corrupted, and as if degenerated from its original creation."[40] When he comes to 3:18 ("thorns and thistles"), Calvin repeats the ideas just mentioned, and adds that the earth is not exhausted because of a long succession of time, but the "increasing wickedness of men" gradually diminishes the "remaining blessing of God."[41] Here again is the idea that circumstances are worsening.

The evils of Noah's time indicate the increasing depravity of man and creation. God had for some centuries, Calvin says, invited men to repentance, but "the world . . . nevertheless, was perpetually becoming worse."[42] The fact that the entire world, save Noah and his family, had to be destroyed implies that the world could become no worse. Then, following the Flood and the Noahic covenant, the process of degeneration would begin again. There are periods of decline and renewal, suggesting that Calvin does not see the world on a steady decline from some high point in the past to the abyss of his own era.

The commentaries on Daniel also present the reformer's view that "the world grows worse as it becomes older." The vision of the beast made of gold, silver, brass, iron, and clay leads Calvin to say that even the "profane poets invented fables about the Four Ages, Golden, Silver, Brazen and Iron." Although the vision refers to a specific time in the past, the Babylonian through the Roman empires, Calvin's comments suggest that the process of degeneration continues into his own time: "Experience also demonstrates how the world always degenerates, and inclines by degrees to vices and corruptions."[43] Calvin could be interpreted to mean that there is a gradual decline from the time of Daniel to the sixteenth century. But when we think of Calvin's words about "no moral restraint" and "no distinction between good and evil" in his own time, it is hard to imagine that the decline could get any worse.

That the world is degenerating morally and spiritually is expressed by Calvin on occasion with passages from Horace and Xenophon. In his exposition of Psalm 78:8 ("that they might not be as their fathers"), Calvin says that the "experience of all ages" shows that what Horace writes is "true everywhere": the fathers, inferior to the grandfathers, beget children who are still worse. Calvin asks rhetorically: "what then would be the consequence, did not God succour the world which thus proceeds from evil to worse?"[44] In 4:xii, 22 of the *Institutes,* while discussing the degeneration of clerical discipline, Calvin refers to "a memorable passage in Xenophon where he tells how foully the Persians had degenerated from the ordinances of their forbearers."[45] Here Calvin is ridiculing the papists for their "ridiculous imitation" of the Church Fathers, but his use of the passage reveals the same assumption: the state of affairs within the church and without continues to degenerate. In a particularly scalding criticism of his own times, Calvin writes in *Concerning Scandals:* "since crimes have been sweeping indiscriminately through almost the whole world, must we not say that the complaint of the poet is just as opposite to our own times also?" Then Calvin quotes Horace again.[46]

Calvin took these proverbs seriously, as we see in his sermon on Ephesians 3:1–6 where he says: "we in our time cannot say that we are better than our forefathers . . . For if you have an eye to the general state of things, there was more faithfulness among men fifty years ago than there is today."[47] Our standard-bearer fought under the assumption that conditions overall were worsening; the church is being reformed, but there is little evidence that the condition of the world is improving.

Related to the "thorns and thistles" comments about degeneration revealed in creation is Calvin's explanation of Genesis 12:11 ("thou art a fair woman to look upon"). It is possible for Sara to be beautiful though she is an "old woman," because "there was then greater vivacity in the human race than there is now."[48] Earlier Calvin said that the earth is not exhausted by its age, but here he suggests that humanity has less strength with the passing of time. Often Calvin illustrates the world's decline by descrying the lack of integrity in his own times. In the same story of Genesis 12, Calvin explains how Sara was saved from dishonor. God's protection is the ultimate reason, but it is also true that "perhaps . . . greater integrity still flourished in that age; so that the lusts of kings were not so unrestrained as they afterwards became."[49] Calvin's comments on Amos 1:3–5 also demonstrate his belief that greater integrity existed in times past. Calvin has a difficult time reconciling the idea that Amos's time was a "golden age" compared to the sixteenth century with the fact that people of Amos's time were monstrously wicked. Calvin states:

> when we compare that age with ours, it is certain that greater integrity existed then: all kinds of evils so overflow at this day, that compared with the present, the time of Amos was the golden age; and yet we hear him declaring . . . that the people . . . were monstrously wicked.[50]

The decline in morality is found in marriage customs and the frequency of adultery. On Genesis 24:59, the marriage of Rebekah, Calvin writes that "posterity has greatly degenerated from the pure and genuine method of celebrating marriages used by the fathers."[51] Neither Isaac nor Rebekah was compelled to marry, but each respected the wishes of the parents.[52] Moreover, Rebekah dressed modestly and wore the veil.[53] Greater "simplicity" prevailed in that age, Calvin remarks. On the story of Abraham and Abimelech, Genesis 20:9, Calvin observes that adultery was then called a "great sin," but he rues that "at the present time, Christians . . . are not ashamed jocularly to extenuate so great a crime, from which even a heathen shrinks."[54] The uprightness of ages past is also seen in that people wore jewelry sparingly,[55] a maid could go alone out of the city,[56] common people deferred to their rulers,[57] and "friendly intercourse was then more faithfully cultivated than it is now."[58]

As I have said, there is no consistency in Calvin's treatment of the idea that the world is degenerating. His comments on the beast in Daniel imply a steady decline, whereas his words on the Noahic covenant show that there was an increase in morality after a period of decline. A comparison of Calvin's analysis of Romans 1:24–32 with his sermon on Ephesians 5:15–18 also illustrates that his views fluctuate. Paul's catalogue of vices in Romans 1:26 prompts Calvin to say: "He then enumerates a long catalogue of vices which existed in all ages, but at that time prevailed universally without any restraint at all."[59] In other words, Calvin describes the depravity of Paul's time in exactly the same terms as he describes his own. There cannot be a gradual decline from Paul's time to Calvin's if there is no restraint in either age. The first century is as decadent as the sixteenth! But when we read Calvin's sermon on Ephesians 5:15–18, we find that there was more integrity in Paul's time than in Calvin's: ". . . if St. Paul has said that the days were evil, when there was a hundred times more integrity than there is nowadays, we ought to be the more vigilant in keeping careful watch, according to the increasing evil of the time."[60]

Though Calvin's descriptions of the world's decline are not consistent, they must be taken seriously. They explain Calvin's profound pessimism and his expectation that his work as a reformer would be assailed by enemies without and within. There is no hope for the world if one looks only to the present. The standard-bearer of God awaits divine deliverance.

2. The suffering church: "war under the perpetual cross"

Calvin's call as Christ's "standard-bearer" was to restore the church to its "golden age," and although he sought earnestly to build a true church in Geneva, he had no illusions about creating a church of "earthly splendor." Calvin was convinced that the church is "ordained for this purpose, that as long as it is a sojourner in the world it is to wage war under the perpetual cross."[61] In a series of antinomies so characteristic of his style, Calvin distinguishes the condition of the true church from the wealth and influence of "earthly powers." If the church were "flourishing with wealth and influence, enjoying unbroken peace," it would have the appearance of an "earthly power," and the "spiritual kingdom of Christ" would have to be sought elsewhere. Calvin warns:

> let us remember that the outward aspect of the Church is so contemptible that its beauty may shine within; that it is so tossed about on earth that it may have a permanent dwelling-place in heaven; that it lies so wounded and broken in the eyes of the world that it may stand, vigorous and whole, in the presence of God and his angels; that it is so wretched in the flesh that its happiness may nevertheless be restored for it in the spirit.[62]

The true strength of the church is spiritual, and therefore the well-being of the church cannot be determined by its outward circumstances. In fact, earthly pomp and power may be detrimental to the church's spiritual life. In a revealing allusion to the Schmalkaldic War, 1546–47, Calvin warns of the dangers of a "highly triumphal gospel": ". . . more danger threatens us from our own victory than from that of our enemies, and . . . no disasters are to be feared so much as what I may call a highly triumphal gospel, which would transport us to a state of elation."[63] Christ's standard-bearer is sustained by God alone.

Calvin's view of the suffering church can be seen by examining three topics: first, the church "has always overcome by suffering"; second, proclamation of the Gospel leads to controversy; and third, the ingratitude of men will be punished by God—and punishment begins with the church. It is remarkable that one who labored so consistently for the edification of the church did not envision the establishment of an influential and splendid institution. Instead, Calvin believed that the Gospel would triumph in a weak church so that glory would be ascribed to God alone.

In *Concerning Scandals* Calvin describes the church's victory through suffering by giving a "brief description of all the ages" that he applies to his own time. In each period of suffering the church has been preserved in a remnant. For example, following the fall of Adam and Eve and the slaying of Abel, it was not until the time of Seth that the "name of God began to be invoked." But Cain's descendants were "superior in number and more presumptious," and they "vaunted themselves in a most savage way" against Seth and his people.[64] On Genesis 4:26 Calvin comments that the "face of the Church began distinctly to appear" when Seth begat a son, establishing the worship of God for posterity. A similar "restoration of religion has been effected also in our own time,"[65] Calvin adds, showing that he thought the church was nearly extinct. As the oppression of Seth and his descendants continued, only "one man and his tiny family were left," namely, Noah. Noah, too, was persecuted by "those who were raving like madmen against God." Although Noah and his family were saved and the world preserved, it was not long before they were endangered, and the worship of God was upheld only by Melchizedek and "a few others."

It is not necessary to go through Calvin's entire survey, for the pattern of near destruction and divine deliverance occurs throughout the ages. It is the two lessons of this history that are most significant for Calvin: first, it is beneficial for the church to suffer; and second, God's power is seen more in a suffering than in a triumphant church. Calvin realizes that he has not mentioned "even the tenth part" of the instances of God's deliverance, but his concern is that "my readers grasp this one thing that I want them to know: the more the church has been crushed beneath the cross, the more clearly has the power of God shown itself in raising it up again."[66] Calvin also argues that these two lessons can be "seen under the rule of Christ more plainly,"[67] and in his own time tortures and persecutions display the "royal dignity of Christ," which is in reality the "humiliation of the cross."[68]

Because Christ is the head of the church, the church must expect to "labor under the cross."[69] Calvin frequently alludes to Psalm 129:1–3 and its reference to those who have "ploughed upon my back" to describe the afflictions of the church. The Psalmist, Calvin says, "compares the people of God to a field through which a plough is drawn." The plough is the cross: "the cross has always been planted on the back of the church, to make long and wide furrows."[70] In *Concerning Scandals* Calvin contends that "anyone who is willing to look at the historical records of all the past ages" will see that the church has "encountered such hostile unbelievers that they 'ploughed upon her back, and made long their furrows.' "[71] Calvin uses this same Psalm in his commentary on Daniel 12:1, where he argues that a "more harassing warfare" awaits the church after Christ's appearance than before: ". . . although the church had in former periods been wretched, yet after the appearance of Christ, it should suffer more calamities than before. We remember . . . the Psalmist: The impious . . . have drawn the plow across my back."[72]

Calvin often asserts that when the church is threatened with death and the grave, only then does God intervene to bring life. The story of Joseph's deliverance, Genesis 37:6, prompts Calvin to say that God "brings forth the salvation of the Church, not from magnificent splendor, but from death and the grave."[73] From the example of Joseph, we learn that "God permits us to be cast down in various ways, so that we seem nearer hell than heaven."[74] Writing on Daniel 12:2 Calvin affirms that God will be the "constant preserver of his Church," but not in a carnal sense, for the church "will be like a dead body until it shall rise again." Calvin adds: "As long as we fix our eyes only on this present state of things . . . we shall always be like the dead."[75] Referring to his own time, Calvin says on Exodus 1:17 that when we are "urged to despair," we should remember that the "divine aid appears suddenly and unexpectedly," when "immediate destruction seems to await us."[76]

The church is the "suffering Church" because the Gospel provokes controversy. A significant criticism of the Reformation was that it disturbed the peace of the church. Calvin counters this objection by arguing that whenever the Gospel is proclaimed, conflict between good and evil, between the kingdoms of God and Satan occurs. Calvin concludes his *Reply to Sadoleto* by referring to this charge of controversy. There was peace before the Reformation because Christ was silent: " . . . it appears that, before we kindled the strife, all was tranquility and peace! . . . You cannot . . . take credit for a tranquil kingdom, when there was tranquility for no other reason than that Christ was silent."[77] Calvin also deals with the charge of controversy in *Concerning Scandals* by arguing that controversy results because the Gospel exposes hypocrisy and ungodliness. Calvin admits that "thirty years ago religion was flourishing everywhere, and all were in agreement about the . . . customary worship of God."[78] However, this tranquility was simply a cover-up for ignorance, hypocrisy, and numbness of conscience. Controversy results because, when the "torch of the gospel has been brought in, hypocrisy is routed and ungodliness is made plain to see."[79]

Christians should not be surprised that reform brings controversy, for whenever Christ appears tumults result. Calvin's comments on Daniel assert several times that people were wrong to think that when the Messiah comes, there will be peace. Daniel warns the people that "the Church's state would not be tranquil even when the Messiah came."[80] The people returning from Babylon expected peace, but Daniel "predicts fresh trouble amidst the very commencement of their joy."[81] Controversy and suffering are the perpetual lot of the church, and, Calvin solemnly observes, "the similarity of the times adapts these predictions to ourselves."[82] When Calvin treats Daniel 7:21–22 ("until the ancient of days come"), he shows how the "bitterest conflicts" occur at the coming of Christ. Conflict and controversy are at their height because, with Christ's appearance, the salvation of the world is being carried out and the devil is enraged.[83] In Exodus 5:9 Calvin applies this truth to his own times: "Nowadays the Gospel procures hatred for many. . . and endangers the life of some; in a word, the more God exerts his power, the more is Satan's rage excited."[84] Psalm 2:1–3 offers consolation to the believer, Calvin writes, because he knows that controversy has been predicted: "as often as the world rages . . . we have only to remember that in all this there is just a fulfillment of what was long ago predicted."[85]

Calvin expected the church to suffer not only because of external enemies, but because disobedience and ingratitude are punished by God. God punishes the disobedience and ingratitude of all people, but punishment begins with the church. Just as Calvin provided a history of the church's suffering in the tract *Concerning Scandals,* so he provided a history of the church's disobedience and ingratitude that demonstrates how God uses external enemies to punish the church. Calvin applies this same spiritual dynamic to his own times.

The church is disturbed by "numerous and varied changes," Calvin says, which have their origin in man's rebellion: "man's constant revolts are what have interrupted the otherwise constant and unimpeded course of his [God's] grace."[86] The history of God's punishment of man's rebellion begins with Seth, when true worship was established. After only eight generations, Seth's descendants had "rushed into every kind of sin." They were destroyed in the flood with the rest of the world that they had polluted. The family of Noah was soon reduced to the family of Shem, which "became so degenerate that a large part of it was deservedly renounced by God." The sons of Abraham who were delivered from Egypt "knew no limit to their sin, until they were all destroyed by horrible means in the wilderness."[87] The pattern of rebellion and punishment repeats itself, and Calvin asks: "What is the history of the Jews but a record of one rebellion after another?"[88] Such "desperate stubbornness" and "base ingratitude" cannot go unpunished.

This pattern continues after the coming of Christ—and into the sixteenth century. Since God's blessing in Christ in greater than all previous blessings, God's punishment of ingratitude is more severe. Men would have experienced the happiness of God's kingdom, if they had allowed Christ to remain in their midst. Instead of peace there occurred such "violent storms of wars" as the world has never seen. Why? "God was punishing such great ingratitude" of men who did not accept his Son.[89] God brings salvation, the majority reject it, and then God punishes this ingratitude. In the Reformation this pattern recurs; Calvin writes: "The same thing can be observed in our time. A few years after the remarkable beginnings of the reborn church . . . we then saw them collapse back into ruins."[90] No doubt Calvin sees the enemies that threaten the Reformation as God's means of punishing the "filthy profanations of the gospel" by the many who renounced the papacy only to "abandon themselves to licentiousness of every kind." Such hypocrites are "treading under their feet the incalculable treasure of the gospel," and God will punish such contempt and ingratitude.[91]

Calvin writes on Daniel 8:24–25 that there have been two great restorations of the church: "the first restoration took place when . . . the people . . . returned from exile . . . and the second occurred at the advent of Christ."[92] In both restorations salvation was received by many, but after a time the majority became disobedient and ungrateful. Calvin says of the first restoration: "The return after seventy years was like a second birth for them. But as soon as they were back home they forgot such a great blessing, and once again fell away into various corrupt practice."[93] Although Calvin does not say so explicitly, it is accurate to say that the sixteenth-century Reformation was the third great restoration, in which the pattern of the first two is repeated: salvation is offered, there is initial acceptance by many, and then disobedience and ingratitude, which God punishes.[94]

God punishes the world for its ingratitude,[95] but he deals more severely with the church. Writing on Daniel 9:12 Calvin states that the chastisements of the church are "far more tremendous" than those against others, for the impiety of the church is "the more detestable to God." Members of the church are "doubly impious," for God "shines" upon them, and yet they resist him with "determined wilfulness."[96] Calvin deals at length with the sufferings of the church in his exposition of 1 Peter 4:16–17. He makes three points: first, the church is subject to "the common miseries of men" and that God "puts forth his hand indiscriminately against his own people and against strangers." Moreover, the church suffers more than the wicked: "He seems in a manner to spare the reprobate, in contrast to his severity toward the elect." But, Calvin observes, in fact God "fattens the wicked for the day of slaughter," while "He recalls by corrections His own children . . . to the right way." Calvin concludes: "it belongs especially to Christ's kingdom, that the beginning of the reformation should be in the Church."[97] Finally, though all are subjected to adversities, Christians "look to a different end": they feel that "their guilt is blotted out," and in His judgments God "marks" them with the "personality of His own Son."[98]

Calvin was a faithful standard-bearer because he believed that the church was sustained by the power of God and the message of the Gospel, not because he expected the church to be adorned with pomp and splendor. Given enemies without and ungrateful members within, it is inevitable that the church would be afflicted. But the suffering of the church did not prevent Calvin from being hopeful. In the Daniel commentaries Calvin frequently says that the "sons of God . . . ought always to return to this principle—if those afflictions await us for a time and times, the half time will follow afterwards."[99] The reference to "time" and "times" means that after severe afflictions, worse afflictions often follow. This happened in both restorations. However, the "half time," the time of salvation, *will* come. The respite will come from God, not from the power of the church. Therefore Calvin was hopeful, though the outward condition of the church was hopeless. One can even say that the "hopeless" condition of the suffering church is a *source* of hope. Calvin writes on Psalm 5:9 that David "not only persevered in prayer, but finds ground for hope even from the . . . apparent hopelessness of his outward condition."[100] The ultimate source of hope is the return of Christ.

3. The Second Coming of Christ

Beset by enemies without and within, convinced that the world was degenerating and that the church would always be a suffering minority, Calvin was nonetheless certain that the church would triumph at the last day when Christ returns. We do not understand properly Calvin's view of himself as a reformer unless we take seriously his belief that Christ would come again and accomplish the final "Reformation." In this final section, we first establish the importance of the Second Coming; second, underscore Calvin's contention that no one can calculate the time of Christ's return; and third, show that no one knows the time of Christ's return because all the prophecies of Scripture are fulfilled or are being fulfilled. Nothing remains except for the Second Coming. Finally, I offer two points of interpretation: first, one expects Calvin to say that the "signs" of his own time imply that Christ's return is imminent. However, Calvin shies away from saying this because he is convinced that no one can know the time. Second, Calvin's view of prophecy means that prophecies that were fulfilled in the earliest years of the church continue to be fulfilled in later periods and in Calvin's own time. For example, Christ's statements about wars were fulfilled in the period immediately following Christ's ascension and continue to be fulfilled in the wars and persecutions of the Reformation.

Calvin's statements on I Thessalonians 1:9–10 and II Peter 3:4 show the importance of Christ's Second Coming. Because Christ's standard-bearer finds no hope in the world, he looks to the resurrection and Christ's return:

> Christ is to be awaited from heaven, for we shall find nothing in the world to bear us up. . . .Paul intimates that His resurrection would be of no effect, unless He appears a second time as their Redeemer, and extends to the whole body of the Church the fruit and effect of that power which he displayed in himself.[101]

This waiting gathers up one's whole being: "let all who would persevere in a life of holiness give their whole minds to the hope of Christ's coming."[102] Calvin says on II Peter 3:4 that to attack belief in the last resurrection and Christ's return means "nothing is left of the Gospel, the power of Christ is drained away and all religion is destroyed. Satan directly attacks the throat of the church when he destroys faith in the return of Christ."[103] Although one would not consider the Second Coming the center of Calvin's theology, one should not underestimate its importance.

Calvin's comments on 1 Thessalonians 4, 2 Thessalonians 2, Matthew 24, and Daniel 7, 9, and 12 are the key sources for his understanding of Christ's return. On 1 Thessalonians 4 and Matthew 24 Calvin teaches that no one knows the time of Christ's return, even though these passages sound as if the return is imminent. Calvin says that in 1 Thessalonians 4:15 Paul speaks as if he would live until the last day, but he did this in order to "keep all the godly in suspense, so that they may not promise themselves some particular time."[104] A notable interpretation: Paul spoke as if the end were imminent so that no one would try to calculate the time! Calvin adds that Paul "knew by a special revelation that Christ would come at a somewhat later date."[105] A similar interpretation of Matthew 24:9–14 is given by Calvin. A superficial reading of these verses suggests that one could calculate when the end would come. After persecutions, false prophets, the worldwide preaching of the Gospel, and apostasy, "then shall the end come." However, Calvin says these verses mean that there will be a long period of persecution and trial, and that the character and duration of those trials do not allow one to calculate the end-time. Calvin paraphrases Christ's teaching: "The end of the age will not come until I have long tested my church with hard and wearisome temptations: this is contrasted with the false notion the Apostles had conceived among themselves."[106] Christ's words are not a key to calculate the time of his return; the "lesson" of these words "is that no particular time is fixed, as if the last day were to follow directly upon the outcome of his predictions, for the faithful have long since experienced what we have just read, [and] Christ did not then appear."[107]

Since Christ has taught that no one knows the time of the Second Coming, Calvin warns against vain and curious calculations. The teaching of Matthew 24:36 ("of that day . . . knoweth no one") is that "Christ means to keep the minds of the faithful in suspense, in case by some false notion they might fix a time on the final redemption."[108] The disciples were always "hurrying on to triumph, out of time." What the Lord desires, Calvin says, is that the disciples be vigilant, that his coming would be "so hoped for . . . that yet no one should dare to ask when it will come. He wants his disciples . . . without knowing times with certainty, to expect the revelation with patience. Beware then not to worry more than the Lord allows over details of time."[109] Calvin's warnings on 1 Thessalonians 5:1–3 and 2 Thessalonians 2:1 about the suddenness of Christ's return and "over-curious" calculations about the time are emphatic. On the first passage he says that "anything that is not immediately visible" to men's eyes they "consider to be mythical." Therefore "the Lord, to punish this carelessness . . . casts down the ungodly."[110] The result of speculating about the time of Christ's return, Calvin says on the second passage, is that people become "dispirited, since by nature they are unable to endure a long delay."[111] "Over-curious individuals," such as "Lactantius and the Chiliasts," have unwittingly become the instruments of Satan who, since he could not "openly destroy the hope of the resurrection . . . promised that the day was . . . at hand, in order to undermine it by stealth."[112]

Some in Calvin's day argued that the reference in Daniel 12:11–12 to 1,290 and 1,335 days preceding the end means that 2,600 years must elapse before Christ's return. Since Daniel was prophesying approximately 600 years before Christ's first advent, he is saying that Christ would return in the year 2,000. After saying that in "numerical calculations I am no conjurer," Calvin criticizes those who "expound this passage with too great subtlety . . . trifle in their own speculations, and detract from the authority of the prophecy."[113] To some contemporaries who proclaimed Christ would return in their time, Calvin wrote: "In these days there is a general rumor of impending judgment. But only a few have been taught by God that Christ will come . . . in due time."[114] Calvin interprets literally the teaching that one can neither know nor calculate the time of Christ's return.

My second point explains more fully why Calvin was convinced that no one could calculate the time of Christ's return: all the prophecies about the last times have been fulfilled and are being fulfilled. The "last times" includes all the ages from Christ's resurrection and the worldwide spread of the Gospel. The descriptions of wars, earthquakes, inclusion of the gentiles, and the coming of the Antichrist have been fulfilled. Only the return of Christ is yet to occur. Thus there is no progression of events that will enable one to predict the time of Christ's return. It is as likely that Christ would have come in 1559 as in 476. If Calvin were alive, he would say that Christ is as likely to return today as in 1789. Calvin believed that Christ's standard-bearers are living in the "last times," and therefore they must be vigilant. Writing on 1 Peter 1:5, Calvin says that the "last time" is "the whole period from the coming of Christ,"[115] and on 1 Peter 4:7 Calvin affirms that "from the time when Christ once appeared there is nothing left for the faithful except to look forward to His second coming with minds alert."[116]

Key passages in Matthew 24 and 2 Thessalonians 2 show how Calvin viewed the end-times prophecies as being fulfilled. First, the Old Testament prophecies about the Day of the Lord have been partially fulfilled at Christ's first advent. On Matthew 24:3 Calvin says that "we know there are frequent passages where peace, joy and abundance of all good things" are promised at the coming of Christ. Referring to Isaiah 54:13, Joel 2:18, and Jeremiah 31:34, Calvin comments that these prophecies do not "lack effect, but their fulfillment does not take place at once. It is enough that the faithful receive a taste of these good things now."[117] Second, when Christ predicts, "Ye shall hear of wars," Calvin says that Christ "means here the troubles in Judaea." These troubles, including the destruction of Jerusalem, serve as "the prelude to yet greater disasters." The later references to earthquakes, famines, and signs from heaven were also fulfilled shortly after Christ's ascension—even though Calvin adds laconically: "We have no certain record of these things. It is sufficient that they were predicted by Christ. The reader may find the rest in Josephus."[118] Calvin does not consider that these events may be preludes to Christ's return in the distant future.

Third, on Matthew 24:14 ("This gospel . . . shall be preached in the whole world") Calvin affirms that the Gospel has been preached throughout the world. He writes that some in his own day "object that the Antipodes and other remote nations so far have not even the faintest word of Christ"; but this objection is dismissed, for "Christ is not talking of individual tracts of land or fixing any particular time," but affirming that the Gospel would be preached throughout the world before his return.[119] Other statements in Calvin's writings make the same point about the proclamation of the Gospel throughout the world during the apostolic period. For example, on Matthew 24:6 ("as the lightning . . . from the East"), Calvin writes that Jesus is warning the disciples that the Redeemer is not to be sought only in Judaea, but his kingdom will extend to the corners of the earth. Calvin's final words on this verse are: "The wonderful rapidity with which the gospel flew out to every region of the globe was a shining testimony to the divine power. It could not be the result of human industry that the light of the gospel should flash like lightning and reach from one corner of the world to the other extreme."[120]

Passages from Daniel and Romans also make it clear that Calvin believed the Gospel was preached throughout the world during the apostolic period, thereby showing that another prophecy was fulfilled and is being fulfilled. Calvin objects to those who refer Daniel 7:14 ("all . . . nations . . . should serve him") to the close of Christ's reign and not its beginning: "this [verse] ought properly to be understood as the commencement of the reign of Christ, and ought not to be connected with its final close, as many interpreters force and strain the passage."[121] Calvin's interpretation of Romans 11:25 ("until the fulness of the gentiles") is notable. This verse, too, refers to the worldwide preaching of the Gospel during the apostolic period, not to an event still to come. The word *until*, Calvin says, should be rendered *in order that*; thus Paul is referring to the inclusion of the gentiles that took place during his own time and in later centuries.[122] We cannot help observing that Calvin had a somewhat restricted view of the "world": On Isaiah 24:1 he states that when we speak of "our world," we "almost never go beyond Europe"![123]

Another verse whose prophecy has been fulfilled is Matthew 24:16 ("let them that are in Judaea flee unto the mountains"). These verses do not refer to the return of Christ, but the end of legal worship in Jerusalem and the punishment of the Jews for their rejection of Jesus. Calvin writes: "After Christ teaches by the testimony of the prophet [Daniel], that with the profanation of the temple will shortly come the end of legal worship, He goes on to tell of the terrible and dread calamities that are at hand for all Judaea."[124]

We must still consider the prophecies about the Antichrist, but now I want to elaborate on this idea that prophecies *have been* and are *being* fulfilled. Calvin's comments on Matthew 24:34 ("This generation shall not pass away") give us some insight. In this verse, Calvin says, "Christ simply teaches that in one generation events would establish all that He had said. Within fifty years the city was wiped out, the temple razed, the whole region reduced to appalling devastation, and the world's obstinacy rose up against God."[125] In other words, the predictions about wars, persecutions, the worldwide preaching of the Gospel, and signs in the heavens began to be fulfilled in the earliest years of the church. A few lines later Calvin adds that these predictions continue being fulfilled in the centuries that follow— including his own: "Although the same evils continued without a break for many centuries to follow, Christ still spoke truly, saying that the faithful would actually . . . experience before the end of one generation how true his oracle was, for the apostles suffered the same things as we see today."[126] Because these prophecies have been fulfilled and are being fulfilled, one cannot use them as a basis for calculating Christ's return. Christ's return, from the earliest centuries, has always been imminent.

Calvin's manner of interpreting these prophecies is clearly seen in his comments on Matthew 24:29ff. Calvin says that "the predictions about a prodigious shaking of the heaven and earth should not be tied to the beginning of redemption, for the prophets had included its whole course, till it came to a finishing point."[127] These prophecies include the beginning of the church's existence (and thus the prophecies are fulfilled) and the entire course of her history (and thus the prophecies are being fulfilled). "In other words, Calvin explains, "as long as the Church's pilgrimage in this world lasts, the skies will be dark and cloudy."[128] Calvin's explanation of Matthew 24:4, quoted earlier, applies to prophecy in general: ". . . their fulfillment does not take place at once. It is enough that the faithful receive a taste of these good things now, that they may cherish the hope of their full enjoyment in the future."[129]

We turn now to the important prophecies about the Antichrist in 2 Thessalonians 2:3ff. Here too we see that prophecies have been fulfilled in the earliest years and continue to be fulfilled in Christ's own time. For Calvin 2 Thessalonians 2:3 means that "the day of Christ . . . will not come until the world has fallen into apostasy, and the rule of Antichrist has held sway in the Church."[130] Apostasy means a "treacherous rebellion from God," which will "spread far and wide among a considerably large number." Paul means " 'The Church must be reduced to a ghastly and horrifying state of ruin, before its full restoration is achieved.' "[131] The Antichrist, or "man of sin" as he is called in verse 3, is not "one individual, but . . . a kingdom that was to be seized by Satan for the purpose of setting up a seat of abomination in the midst of God's temple."[132] Apostasy has occurred from the beginning, was greatly intensified by Mohammed, and reached a peak in the papacy.[133] Calvin believes that the establishment of Antichrist's kingdom in the church was "accomplished in popery," but he alleges in 1 John 2:18 that the "mystery of his [Antichrist's] ungodliness" was "working secretly" in the heretics of the apostle's time. Calvin writes: "Properly speaking, Antichrist was not yet in existence, but the mystery of his ungodliness was working secretly."[134] In other words, the prophecy about Antichrist had been fulfilled in the earliest days of the church and was being fulfilled in a preeminent way during Calvin's time in the papal tyranny.

On two occasions Calvin identifies the papacy with the kingdom of Antichrist: 2 Thessalonians 2:4 and 2:9. On the first passage Calvin says that Paul gives a "striking picture of the Antichrist": he will "appropriate to himself those things which belong properly to God, so that he is worshipped in the temple as a divine being." Calvin continues: "To recognize Antichrist we must set him in diametrical opposition to Christ."[135] This principle leads to the conclusion that the pope is the Antichrist: "Now anyone who has learned . . . the things that belong particularly to God, and who on the other hand considers well what the Pope usurps for himself, will not have much difficulty in recognizing Antichrist, even though he were a ten-year-old boy."[136] This principle of contrast is employed again by

Calvin on 2 Thessalonians 2:9: Christ "enlightens our minds to eternal life," while Antichrist "deals destruction . . . by his godless doctrine." Christ "puts forth the power of His Spirit for our salvation, and seals his gospel by miracles," while the "adversary . . . alienates us from the Spirit" and confirms the people in their error by delusions.[137] We must remember that Calvin did not label any individual pope as the Antichrist, but said that Antichrist refers to "a single kingdom which extends throughout many generations."[138] Such a view can lead to the conclusion that the reign of Antichrist may continue for several more generations; if the "last times" has already extended for many centuries, it may continue for many more.

If apostasy has occurred and the Antichrist rules in the church, is the return of Christ imminent? Has the church been reduced to a sufficiently "ghastly and horrifying state of ruin"? Calvin's interpretation of Matthew 24:29–31 suggests that there must be an intensification of apostasy, persecution, and tyranny of the Antichrist before the end can come. Calvin says that "the tribulation of those days" does not refer to the ruin of Jerusalem, but to a "universal gathering-up ($\alpha\nu\alpha\kappa\epsilon\varphi\alpha\lambda\alpha\iota\omega\tau\iota\varsigma$) of all the evils of which Christ had already spoken."[139] Does Christ's standard-bearer believe that the church is "torn apart by Satan's craft, torn by the savagery of the wicked, upset by unholy doctrines, tossed by storms" to such a degree that Christ's return is imminent?

We have seen that Calvin emphasizes that no one knows the time of Christ's return and that prophecies do not constitute a time-table to calculate the Second Advent. Both points lead to the conclusion that Calvin did not think the return of Christ more likely in his own time than in any other. However, there are passages in Calvin's writings that sound as if the return of Christ *is* near. A notable passage in this regard is 1 John 2:18 ("It is the last hour"), to which I referred concerning the presence of Antichrist. Calvin says that John tells his readers that "the last time had already come," and that divisions and disturbances would occur. Calvin paraphrases: "When various errors crop up, you must be aroused . . . For we must infer from it that Christ is not far away." Then Calvin applies this verse to his own times: "We today must similarly bestir ourselves and apprehend by faith that near advent of Christ when Satan causes confusion so as to disturb the Church. For these are the signs of the last time."[140] This interpretation leads one to conclude that Christ's standard-bearer— beholding the suffering church, the tyranny of the papacy, the errors of the Anabaptists, the mockeries of the Epicureans and Lucianists—believed that Christ's return was near.

After warning that John did not "mean to curtail the future course of the Church," Calvin says again that John calls the period from Christ's ascension the "last time" because "all things are being so fulfilled that nothing will remain but the final revelation of Christ." This reasoning should lead Calvin to conclude that Christ's return is no more likely in the sixteenth century than in the first. However, Calvin asserts that "all the marks" of Antichrist appear "clearly in the Pope," compares his own time to that of the Apostle, and concludes that Christ may come soon: "if the Spirit of God even then commanded believers to be on their guard when they saw only distant signs of the coming enemy, much less is it now a time for sleeping, when he holds the Church oppressed under his cruel tyranny and openly triumphs over Christ."[141] These words lead one to think that it is more likely that Christ will return in Calvin's time than ever before.

Calvin's interpretation of Matthew 24:37 ("as were the days of Noah") suggests that Christ will return when religion is held in contempt by the majority and men abandon themselves to sinning without limits. Calvin's descriptions of the moral and religious decline of the world and the ruinous condition of the church may mean that Calvin believed that his times were like those of Noah and therefore Christ's return was imminent. Calvin's comments on 1 Thessalonians 5:3, where he refers to Matthew 24:37, indicate that the phrase "the days of Noah" may be a clue about the time of Christ's return. Calvin writes that there will be "deadly apathy" and obstinacy, and then Christ will return suddenly and unexpectedly. Calvin adds:

> He sometimes gives evidence such as this about his sudden arrival, but the outstanding proof will be when Christ will come down to judge the world, as He himself testifies (Matthew 24:37) when he compares that time with the age of Noah, since all men will abandon themselves to dissipation.[142]

In other words, when the times are as dissolute as Noah's, then Christ will return. However, a more careful reading of Calvin's exposition reveals that he puts as much emphasis on the unexpectedness of the return as he does on its suddenness. This is particularly so in Calvin's exposition of Matthew 24:37. Calvin begins and ends his comments by stressing the uncertainty of the time of Christ's return. At the outset Calvin writes: "He wished them to be so uncertain of His coming, that from day to day, indeed from moment to moment, they should be intently waiting."[143] Following warnings that the "last age of the world will be quite witless, thinking of nothing but the present life," Calvin concludes: "Note that the uncertainty of the time of Christ's coming . . . ought to be a stimulus to our . . . watchfulness. . . . What would be the trial of faith . . . if the faithful . . . set themselves to meet Christ at three days notice."[144]

Our standard-bearer's expositions of 1 John 2:18 and 1 Thessalonians 5:3, his description of the papacy as the Antichrist, his suspicion that the world is degenerating morally and spiritually, and his awareness of the ruinous condition of the church indicate that he should have believed that Christ's return was likely in his own time. However, Calvin never drew that conclusion, because he was convinced that Christ is to be taken at his word that no one knows the time, and that all the centuries from Christ's ascension are the "last times." Moreover, since the prophecies about the "last times" have been and are being fulfilled, they are not future, sequential occurrences that can be "checked-off" to indicate the time of Christ's return.

There is another characteristic of Calvin's interpretations of the "last times" verses that implies that he did not believe that Christ was more likely to return in his own time: Calvin often speaks as if the return of Christ and events associated with it are being fulfilled in the preaching and suffering of the church. Two passages illustrate this point. Expounding 2 Thessalonians 2:8, Calvin says that the phrase "whom the Lord Jesus shall slay," refers to the "destruction of . . . Antichrist," which will be carried out by "the word of the Lord." What is notable is that Calvin is unsure whether Paul is "speaking of the final appearing of Christ." Calvin admits that "the word . . . appears to have this meaning," but he believes that "Paul does not think that Christ will accomplish this in a single moment."[145] It is true, Calvin concludes, that Antichrist will be completely destroyed at the last day; but "in the meantime Christ will scatter the darkness in which Antichrist will reign by the rays which He will emit before his coming, just as the sun, before becoming visible to us, chases away the darkness of the night."[146] The standard-bearer of Christ may not be rescued by the return of Christ, but in his preaching Christ himself is defeating Antichrist. A few lines later Calvin writes that the preaching of true and sound doctrine "is referred to as Christ's coming to us."[147]

The second passage is Matthew 24:29–31, to which I have already alluded. The "tribulation of those days" refers to a "universal gathering-up (ἀνακεφαλαίωτις) of all the evils of which Christ had already spoken." But the darkening of the sun and moon and the falling of the stars are not interpreted literally; Calvin writes: "as long as the Church's pilgrimage in this world lasts, the skies will be dark and cloudy, but as soon as the end of distress arrives, the daylight will break to show His shining majesty."[148] What appear to be signs of the immediate return of Christ are taken to be descriptions of the church's suffering throughout all the centuries, which constitute the "last times."[149]

Did Calvin believe that Christ's return was imminent? Yes. But Christ's return has always been imminent, for all the prophecies of the "last times" have been fulfilled and are being fulfilled. Did Calvin believe that Christ's return was likely in his own time? This question is more difficult to answer. Nowhere does Calvin predict when Christ will return; but his statements about the Antichrist, apostasy, and the decline of religion and morality lead one to think that Calvin may have believed that matters were so desperate that the end must come soon. However, the success of the Reformation and the presence of standard-bearers such as Calvin suggest that the times must become worse before Christ would return.

Conclusion

As Christ's "standard-bearer" Calvin knew that his calling was most demanding. He applies to himself the Lord's admonition of Joshua (1:6 "Be strong and of good courage"): "let us learn that we can never be fit for executing . . . arduous matters unless we exert our utmost endeavors, both because our abilities are weak, and Satan rudely assails us, and there is nothing we are more inclined to than to relax our efforts."[150] We know that Calvin was one who did not relax his efforts, but persevered with utmost endeavor, animated by the hope that God's kingdom would come in its fullness at the last day. Though Calvin knew that he was battling in the "last times" in a world declining in religion and morality, though he lamented the suffering of the church and expected "a universal gathering-up . . . of all the evils" that Christ predicted,[151] he was a man of hope. Calvin knew that the "last times" were a period of "hope," and as he says in the eloquent comments on Romans 8:24, "as long as we live in the world," our salvation resides in hope." It is the order of God that he "does not call His people to triumph before He has exercised them in the warfare of suffering."[152]

NOTES

1. *Sadoleto*, 248–49. Complete bibliographical information is given in "Works Cited" above.

2. Cf. "Preface," *Psalms* I:xliv. *Sadoleto*, 225. *Minor Prophets* (Zephaniah 3:12–13), 4:298, 30. Cf. Charles A. M. Hall, *With the Spirit's Sword. The Drama of Spiritual Warfare in the Theology of John Calvin* (1968).

3. *Necessity*, 185–86. Cf. *Sadoleto*, 241 and *Institutes*, 4. 2. 11, 1051.

4. *Genesis*, 2:209, 463–64.

5. *Isaiah* (39:18), 2:332. Cf. *II Timothy* (3:4), 328. *Sadoleto*, 231.

6. *I Timothy* (1:4), 191.

7. *Genesis*, 2:109–10. Cf. *Scandals*, 83.

8. "Dedicatory Epistle," *Daniel*, 1:lxx.

9. *Titus* (1:5), 356. Cf. *Articles . . . 1537*, 49.

10. *Gospels*, 3:74 and 78. Cf. *Scandals*, 29, *Daniel* (11:33–34), 2:331.

11. *Titus*, 347. Cf. *Sadoleto*, 222 and "Preface," *Psalms*, 1:xlii.

12. "Preface," *Psalms*, 1:xliv, xlvii.

13. "Dedicatory Epistle," *Daniel*, 1:lxiv–v.

14. "Dedication," *I Timothy*, 182.

15. *I Timothy* (1:18–19), 201–2. Cf. 5:19, where the long section of how pastors are maligned may be called autobiographical. *I Timothy*, 263. Cf. *I Thessalonians* (5:7), 344. Cf. *Scandals*, 111, where Calvin reverses the times: Paul "had to undergo the same struggles by which we are exercised today."

16. *Psalms* (129:1), 5:120.

17. *Jeremiah* (51:46), 5:266–67.

18. *Daniel*, 2:129.

19. Cf. *Daniel* (12:8), 2:385–86: " . . . the instruction . . . of the prophets is more useful to us and produces richer and riper fruit in our age than in theirs." Cf. *Psalms* (87:1), 3:394.

20. *Philemon*, 394.

21. *Sadoleto*, 230.

22. *II Timothy* (1–13), 301. Cf. 3:6, 324 and *Titus* (3:9), 386.

23. *Psalms* (143:2), 5:250.

24. *I Thessalonians* (5:20), 377.

25. *Minor Prophets* (Amos 5:4–6), 2:255.

26. *Minor Prophets*, 2:351–2.

27. Ibid., 4:187.

28. *II Timothy*, 315.

29. *I Peter*, 314.

30. *II Timothy*, 303. Cf. *II Timothy* (1:7), 294: "very few of those who are called ministers of Christ today give any sign of being genuine." The *Register of the Company of Pastors* shows that Calvin's complaints were not unfounded; cf. pp. 314, 357.

31. Quoted by T. H. L. Parker, *John Calvin*, 85.

32. *Sadoleto*, 206.

33. "Theme," *II Peter*, 326.

34. *Scandals*, 62.

35. *Minor Prophets*, 4:129.

36. *Sermons on Ephesians*, 77–78.

37. *Romans*, 175.

38. Ibid., 173. T. H. L. Parker and F. L. Battles have reminded Calvin students of the importance of music in Calvin's theology. Cf. Parker, *John Calvin*, 86ff. Battles, *The Piety of John Calvin*, 117ff., 137ff. Note the importance Calvin attached to singing in his reorganization of the church and worship; cf. *Articles . . . 1537*, 48, 53. On Psalm 119:54 ("Thy statutes have been my songs") Calvin wrote that the law of God was David's "special delight," and that David's "singing is an indication of joy." *Psalms* IV, 440.

39. *Genesis* (2:2), 1:104.

40. *Genesis* (2:2), 1:105.

41. *Genesis*, 1:174–75.

42. *Genesis* (6:3), 1:241.

43. *Daniel* (2:31), 1:163–64. Cf. *Daniel* (7:4), 2:13: "the world is always growing worse and worse." Cf. Calvin's Seneca *Commentary:* "that golden age when men needed no laws," p. 35.

44. *Psalms*, 3:234. Calvin quotes Horace, *Odes*, 3. vi. 46ff. "Actas parentum, peior avis, tulit/ Nos nequiores, mox daturos/Progeniem vitiosiorem."

45. *Institutes*, 1249, Cf. 4. ix. 8 (p. 1172): "affairs usually tend to get worse."

46. *Scandals*, 84.

47. *Sermons on Ephesians*, 239.

48. *Genesis*, 1:361.

49. *Genesis*, 1:363. Calvin's inconsistency in describing the world's decline is seen in this passage. After speaking of that age's "greater integrity," he says that corruption in the court of kings is ancient. Cf. 362.

50. *Minor Prophets*, 2:158. Cf. Amos 2:6 "certainly, the world is now much worse than it was then. . . ." *Minor Prophets*, 2:180.

51. *Genesis*, 2:27.

52. Ibid., 2:29.

53. Ibid., 2:22. Cf. *Genesis* (29:4), 2:128. Cf. Exodus 2:18, *Moses*, 1:55–56: the marriage of Moses and Zipporah.

54. *Genesis*, 1:577–78. Cf. *Genesis* (26:8), 2:62: "now licentiousness has so broken . . . all bounds that husbands are compelled to hear . . . of the dissolute conduct of their wives. . . ."

55. *Genesis* (24:22), 2:21.

56. Ibid., 2:22.

57. *Joshua* (9:16), 144.

58. *Genesis* (29:4), 2:127–28. Cf. *Sermons on Ephesians*, 536: "nowadays" there is no "simple and honest dealing."

59. *Romans*, 36.

60. *Sermons on Ephesians*, 537. It is also difficult to make sense of Calvin's comments on Genesis 29:4 and 31:13. Calvin commends the "ancient simplicity," and then laments that the "whole world had apostasized to false gods." *Genesis*, 2:127–8 and 166.

61. *Scandals*, 30.

62. Ibid., 29–30.

63. Ibid., 48.

64. Ibid., 36.

65. *Genesis*, 1:224.

66. *Scandals*, 40.

67. Ibid., 45.

68. Ibid., 47–48.

69. Ibid., 29.

70. *Psalms*, 5:123.

71. *Scandals*, 31.

72. *Daniel*, 2:371. Cf. Psalm 44:22, where Calvin alludes to Romans 8:36 and says that the "condition of the church in all ages is here portrayed. . . . a state of continual warfare in bearing the cross is enjoined upon us by divine appointment." *Psalms* 2:170.

73. *Genesis*, 2:261.

74. Ibid., 2:266.

75. *Daniel*, 2:374.

76. *Moses*, 1:32.

77. *Sadoleto*, 255.

78. *Scandals*, 57.

79. Ibid., 58. Cf. Exodus 1:22. "Antichrist . . . leaves in peace those who by their treacherous silence deny Christ. . . ." *Moses*, 1:38.

80. "Preface," *Daniel*, 1:82.

81. "Dedicatory Epistle," *Daniel*, 1:lxxi. Cf. lxxviii.

82. Ibid.

83. *Daniel*, 2:57. Cf. 7:25, *Daniel*, 2:64.

84. *Moses*, 1:118.

85. *Psalms*, 1:12. Cf. *II Peter* (2:1), 345.

86. *Scandals*, 31–32.

87. Ibid., 32.

88. Ibid., 33.

89. Ibid., 34.

90. Ibid., 35.

91. Ibid., 35–36. Punishments by God occurred during the Reformation because most did not sincerely accept the Gospel; but Calvin suggests in *Sadoleto* that the reformation averted a harsher punishment by God of papal superstitutions. Cf. *Sadoleto*, 192.

92. *Daniel*, 2:129. Cf. *Psalms* (132:14), 5:158: "the advent of Christ was the 'time of Reformation'. . . ."

93. *Scandals*, 33.

94. Cf. *Daniel* (6:3–5), 1:351: "The world is at this day unworthy of the government which God exercises over it."

95. Cf. ibid. (7:5), 2:17.

96. *Daniel*, 2:167.

97. *I Peter*, 310–11.

98. Ibid., 310. Cf. "Preface," *Moses*, 1:xvi. *Gospels* (Mt. 24:9), 3:79.

99. *Daniel* (12:11–12), 2:391.

100. *Psalms*, 1:60.

101. *I Thessalonians*, 340. Berger and Holwerda (see "Works Cited" above) deal with the relation between the immortality of the soul and Christ's return. We must note Calvin's remark on I Thessalonians (1:9), 339: "It is noteworthy that Paul speaks of waiting for Christ rather than the hope of eternal salvation."

102. *I Thessalonians*, 339.

103. *II Peter*, 361–62. Cf *Daniel* (12:2), 2:373–74.

104. *I Thessalonians*, 364–65.

105. Ibid., 365.

106. *Gospels*, 3:83. Cf. *Gospels* (Mt. 24:3), 3:75–76.

107. Ibid.

108. *Gospels* III, 98.

109. Ibid.

110. *I Thessalonians*, 368.

111. *II Thessalonians*, 396.

112. Ibid., 397.

113. *Daniel*, 2:391–92. Although Calvin says he was no "conjurer," he displays his superior historical knowledge in calculating times past. On Daniel 9:25 Calvin says that we can calculate with certainty the years since the creation of the first destruction of the temple (*Daniel*, 2:208). After that, matters are confused; but Calvin is convinced that Daniel, along with the Roman and Greek historians, gives an accurate chronology from the destruction of the temple to Christ's ascension. Cf. *Daniel*, 2:212 for a summary.

114. *Gospels* (Mt. 24:39), 3:101.

115. *I Peter*, 233.

116. Ibid., 303. Cf. *Daniel* (10:4), 2:255; *I Corinthians* (15:52), 344.

117. *Gospels*, 3:76–77.

118. Ibid., 3:78.

119. Ibid., 3:83.

120. Ibid., 3:91.

121. *Daniel*, 2:45. According to Calvin, the prophecies of Daniel refer to events leading up to and immediately following Christ's first advent. Cf. *Daniel* (7:8), 2:26–28. Cf. *Daniel* (7:27), 2:74: ". . . God begins to give the kingdom to his elect people, when . . . the doctrine of the holy gospel was everywhere received in the world."

122. *Romans*, 255.

123. *Isaiah*, 2:166. Calvin should not be taken too literally; the Geneva church did send ministers to Brazil. Cf. *The Register of the Company of Pastors . . .*, 317.

124. *Gospels*, 3:87.

125. Ibid., 3:97.

126. Ibid. Cf. *Jeremiah* (51:46), 5:266.

127. *Gospels*, 3:93–94.

128. Ibid., 3:94.

129. Ibid., 3:76–77. Cf. *Daniel* (7:27), 2:74: "the prophets, in treating of Christ's kingdom . . . extend their meaning further than its first beginnings . . . while they dwell on its commencement."

130. *II Thessalonians*, 398.

131. Ibid., 399.

132. Ibid.

133. Ibid., 400.

134. *I John*, 257. Cf. *I John* (4:3), 286–87: "it [the spirit of Antichrist] was already in the world, because it performed the mystery of its iniquity. But . . . since the tyranny . . . had not yet openly exalted itself, he says that it would come."

135. *II Thessalonians*, 400.

136. Ibid., 401.

137. Ibid., 406.

138. Ibid., 403–4

139. *Gospels*, 3:93–94. Cf. *I John* (2:18), 256: John "foretells a falling away that would spread throughout the whole Church, as a sort of universal evil."

140. *I John*, 255.

141. Ibid., 257.

142. *I Thessalonians*, 368.

143. *Gospels*, 3:100.

144. Ibid., 3:103.

145. *II Thessalonians*, 404–5.

146. Ibid., 405. Cf. *Gospels* (Luke 21:26), 3:106: " . . . we are preserved . . . by the light of heavenly teaching that goes ahead, especially when Christ Himself does office as our Sun."

147. *II Thessalonians*, 405. Cf. *Gospels* (Luke 21:49), 3:108, where Calvin speaks of the "fire of doctrine."

148. *Gospels*, 3:94.

149. Cf. Daniel 12:7 ("to scatter the power of the holy people"): "this was continually fulfilled from that day to the present. How sad is the dispersion of the Church in these days!" *Daniel*, 2:384.

150. *Joshua*, 31.

151. *Gospels* (Mt. 24:3), 3:75.

152. *Romans*, 176.

WORKS CITED

Primary Sources

Calvin, John. *Articles Concerning the Organization of the Church and of Worship at Geneva . . . 1537*, 48–55. In *The Library of Christian Classics. Vol. 22: Calvin: Theological Treatises*. Translated with introduction and notes by J. K. S. Reid. Philadelphia: The Westminster Press, 1954.

————. *Calvin's Commentaries. A Harmony of the Gospels. Matthew, Mark and Luke*. Vol. 3: *The Epistles of James and Jude*. Edited by David W. Torrance and Thomas F. Torrance. Translated by A. W. Morrison. Grand Rapids, Mich.: Eerdmans, 1972.

————. *Calvin's Commentaries: The Epistle of Paul the Apostle to the Hebrews and the First and Second Epistles of St. Peter*. Edited by David W. Torrance and Thomas F. Torrance. Translated by William B. Johnson. Grand Rapids, Mich.: Eerdmans, 1963.

————. *Calvin's Commentaries. The Epistles of Paul the Apostle to the Romans and to the Thessalonians*. Edited by David W. Torrance and Thomas F. Torrance. Translated by Ross Mackenzie. Grand Rapids, Mich.: Eerdmans, 1961.

————. *Calvin's Commentaries. The First Epistle of Paul the Apostle to the Corinthians*. Edited by David W. Torrance and Thomas F. Torrance. Translated by John W. Fraser. Grand Rapids, Mich.: Eerdmans, 1960.

————. *Calvin's Commentaries. The Second Epistle of Paul the Apostle to the Corinthians and the Epistles to Timothy, Titus and Philemon*. Edited by David W. Torrance and Thomas F. Torrance. Translated by T. A. Smail, Grand Rapids, Mich.: Eerdmans, 1964.

————. *Calvin's Commentaries. The Gospel according to St. John 11–21 and The First Epistle of John*. Edited by David W. Torrance and Thomas F. Torrance. Translated by T. H. L. Parker. Grand Rapids, Mich.: Eerdmans, 1961.

————. *Calvin's Commentary on Seneca's de Clementia*. Introduction, translation and notes by Ford Lewis Battles and André Malan Hugo. Leiden: E. J. Brill, 1969.

————. *Commentaries on Daniel*. 2 vols. Translated by Thomas Meyers. Edinburgh: Printed for the Calvin Translation Society, 1852; reprint ed., Grand Rapids, Mich.: Eerdmans, 1948.

————. *Commentaries on Isaiah*. 4 vols. Translated by J. Pringle. Edinburgh: Printed for the Calvin Translation Society, 1850; reprint ed., Grand Rapids, Mich.: Eerdmans, 1948.

————. *Commentaries on Jeremiah and the Lamentations*. 5 vols. Translated by J. Owen. Edinburgh: Printed for the Calvin Translation Society, 1851; reprint ed., Grand Rapids, Mich.: Eerdmans, 1950.

————. *Commentaries on Joshua*. Translated by H. Beveridge. Edinburgh: Printed for the Calvin Translation Society, 1854; reprint ed., Grand Rapids, Mich.: Eerdmans, 1950.

————. *Commentaries on the Book of Psalms*. 5 vols. Translated by J. Anderson. Edinburgh: Printed for the Calvin Translation Society, 1845; reprint ed., Grand Rapids, Mich.: Eerdmans, 1949.

————. *Commentaries on the First Book of Moses (Genesis)*. 2 vols. Translated by John King. Edinburgh: Printed for the Calvin Translation Society, 1851; reprint ed., Grand Rapids, Mich.: Eerdmans, 1948.

————. *Commentaries on the Four Last Books of Moses*. 4 vols. Translated by Charles W. Bingham. Edinburgh: Printed for the Calvin Translation Society, 1854; reprint ed., Grand Rapids, Mich.: Eerdmans, 1950.

————. *Commentaries on the Twelve Minor Prophets*. 5 vols. Translated by J. Owen. Edinburgh: Printed for the Calvin Translation Society, 1846; reprint ed., Grand Rapids, Mich.: Eerdmans, 1950.

————. *Institutes of the Christian Religion*. 1559 ed. Edited by John T. McNeill. Translated and indexed by Ford Lewis Battles. *The Library of Christian Classics*, vols. 20, 21. Philadelphia: The Westminster Press, 1960.

————. *Concerning Scandals*. Translated by John W. Fraser. Grand Rapids, Mich.: Wm. B. Eerdmans Publishing Company, 1978.

————. *Reply by John Calvin to the letter by [Jacopo] Cardinal Sadoleto . . .*, pp. 221–56 in *The Library of Christian Classics*. vol. 22: *Calvin Theological Treatises*. Translated with introduction and notes by J. K. S. Reid. Philadelphia: The Westminster Press, 1954.

————. *Sermons on the Epistle to the Ephesians*. English translation by Arthur Golding first published in 1577. Revised translation first published by the Banner of Truth Trust, 1973. Edinburgh: The Banner of Truth Trust, 1975.

————. *The Necessity of Reforming the Church . . .*, pp. 184–216. In *The Library of Christian Classics*. vol. 22: *Calvin: Theological Treatises*, translated with introduction and notes by J. K. S. Reid. Philadelphia: The Westminster Press, 1954.

The Register of the Company of Pastors of Geneva in the Time of Calvin. Edited and translated by Philip Edgcumbe Hughes. Grand Rapids, Mich.: Wm. B. Eerdmans Publishing Company, 1966.

Secondary Sources

Berger, Heinrich. *Calvins Geschichtsauffassung*. Zürich: Zwingli Verlag, 1955.

Hall, Charles A. M. *With the Spirit's Sword. The Drama of Spiritual Warfare in the Theology of John Calvin*. Basel Studies of Theology, 3. Richmond, Va.: John Knox Press, 1968.

Holwerda, David E. "Eschatology and History: A Look at Calvin's Eschatological Vision," 110–39. In *Exploring the Heritage of John Calvin (Essays in Honor of John Bratt)*, edited by David E. Holwerda. Grand Rapids, Mich.: Baker Book House, 1976.

Parker, T. H. L. *John Calvin: A Biography.* Philadelphia: The Westminster Press, 1975.

The Piety of John Calvin. An Anthology Illustrative of the Spirituality of the Reformer. Translated and edited by Ford Lewis Battles. Music edited by Stanley Tagg. Grand Rapids, Mich.: Baker Book House, 1978.

ANNOTATED BIBLIOGRAPHY

I have devoted nearly as much space to Calvin's writings as to secondary sources, since Calvin scholars have been blessed in recent years with several new translations and editions of Calvin's writings. In particular I have tried to provide a complete list of Calvin's sermons in print, since they are so crucial to understanding the reformer. Faced with an abundance of excellent secondary sources, I have noted older studies that continue to be indispensable and recent works that, I think, will be of abiding help. I have not included journal articles.

BIBLIOGRAPHIES. Because of its completeness, W. Niesel's *Calvin-Bibliographie 1901–1959* (Munich, 1961) continues to be invaluable; but the annotated bibliography of John T. McNeill, "Fifty Years of Calvin Study, 1918–1968" (pp. xvii–lxxvii in the 1969 reprint of W. Walker's biography of Calvin) will be more helpful to those approaching the maze of works by and on Calvin for the first time. D. Kempff's *A Bibliography of Calviniana: 1959–1974* (Potchefstroom, 1975) picks up where Niesel leaves off, while continuing Niesel's thoroughness. In 1972 Peter DeKlerk began publishing an annual "Calvin Bibliography" in the *Calvin Theological Journal,* usually in the November editions. These bibliographies are enormously helpful. Mention should also be made of Edward A. Dowey's reviews of Calvin studies, 1948–1960, in *Church History* 24 and 29.

BIOGRAPHIES. Although Williston Walker's *John Calvin, The Organiser of Reformed Protestantism, 1509–1564* (1906, 1969) has stood the test of time, the best available biography is now T. H. L. Parker's *John Calvin: A Biography* (Philadelphia, 1975). Parker takes up the crucial biographical issues, while showing the balance between the theological and practical concerns in Calvin's ministry. Topics such as worship, congregational singing, and preaching, often neglected in other biographies, are given their due. Particularly helpful is Parker's detailed examination of Calvin's education and his proposal for redating Calvin's early years. Moreover, one quickly senses that Parker is an excellent stylist as well as an eminent scholar.

While considering Calvin's early years, one must mention the meticulous study of A. Ganoczy, *Le jeune Calvin* . . . (Wiesbaden, 1966), whose views on the subject do not always coincide with those of Parker. A translation of this work is needed. John T. McNeill's *The History and Character of Calvinism* (New York, 1954–1967), of which part 2 is an interpretation of Calvin's life, continues to be widely used, especially in American undergraduate courses. However, A. G. Dickens's criticisms of the study (*Journal of Ecclesiastical History* 19:23) are sound. Although *The Piety of John Calvin* (Grand Rapids, Mich., 1978), trans. and ed. F. L. Battles is not a biography, it is a unique presentation in verse form of autobiographical statements from Calvin's writings. Battles had a great interest in contemporary church music, and a portion of this book is devoted to Calvin's metrical psalms. Battles's word-study of *pietas* is excellent. R. Stauffer's *The Humanness of Calvin* (Nashville, Tenn., 1971) should be noted.

Calvin's Writings. The *Calvini Opera* (59 vols., 1863–1900) continues to be available in two forms: reprints by the Johnson Reprints Corporation (New York, 1964), and microfiche by Information Handling Services (Englewood, Col.). The *Opera Selecta* by P. Barth and W. Niesel (5 vols., 1957) is the standard critical edition of the *Institutes* and several shorter works. J. D. Benoit edited a critical edition of the French *Institution* (5 vols., 1957–63). Two superb English translations of the 1559 and 1536 *Institutes* are widely used: the former, ed. J. T. McNeill and trans. by F. L. Battles (*The Library of Christian Classics* 21 and 22, 1960), and the latter trans. and annotated by Battles (Atlanta, Ga., 1975). The annotations and indexes are excellent. Particularly helpful are Battles's notes in the 1536 *Institutes* showing medieval and late medieval examples of doctrines criticized by Calvin. As long as I am lauding Battles, I can mention *Calvin's Commentary on Seneca's "De Clementia"* by Battles and A. M. Hugo (Leiden, 1969). This is a beautiful work, filled with helpful information on Calvin's humanist background. Calvin scholars are indebted to the late Battles for his many contributions to Calvin studies.

Baker Book House has reprinted the commentaries of Calvin (Grand Rapids, Mich., 1979), originally produced by the Calvin Translation Society (1845–). The Old Testament commentaries are available in this edition alone, while a new edition of the New Testament commentaries was edited by D. W. Torrance and T. F. Torrance (Edinburgh, Grand Rapids; 1959–72). T. H. L. Parker is working on a critical edition of Romans: *Commentarius in Epistolam Pauli ad Romanos* (Leiden). Parker has aided greatly the study of the commentaries with his *Calvin's New Testament Commentaries* (London, 1971). A similar work on the Old Testament commentaries is needed.

The editions of A.-L. Herminjard (9 vols., 1878–97) and J. Bonnet (4 vols., reprinted 1972–73) continue to be the primary sources for Calvin's letters (note, too, the edition of R. Schwartz: 1909, 1961). More work needs to be done in this area of Calvin's writings. Several volumes of Calvin's tracts and treatises are available: the 3-vol. Beveridge translation, *Tracts and Treatises*, was reissued by Baker in 1959; Athlone published *Three French Treatises* in 1970; and several important works were included in *Calvin: Theological Treatises*, ed. J. K. S. Reid (*Library of Christian Classics*, 22, 1954). Reid also edited and translated *Concerning the Eternal Predestination of God* (1961). J. W. Fraser has given Calvin scholars a good translation in *Concerning Scandals* (Grand Rapids, Mich., 1978), and F. L. Battles provided an annotated translation of a note, *De Luxu*, in *Interpretation* (1965), pp. 182–202. A critical edition of *Psychopannychia* (1932) by W. Zimmerli is still helpful as scholars continue to be interested in Calvin's early years and in his eschatology.

There has been great interest in Calvin's sermons. Parker has described the difficulties in gathering the sermons ("Calvini opera sed non omnia," *Scottish Journal of Theology* (1965), 194–203). *Supplementa Calviniana* (Neukirchen, 1961–) is the critical edition of the sermons. The following have been issued: *Predigten über das 2. Bach Samuelis*, ed. Hans Rückert (1961); *Sermons sur le Livre d'Esaie*, chaps. 13–29, ed. G. A. Barrois (1961); *Sermons sur le Livre de Michée*, ed. J. D. Benoit (1964); and *Sermons de libris Jérémie, cap. 14–18 et Threnovum, cap. 1*, ed. R. Peter (1971). English translations in print include *John Calvin's Sermons on the Ten Commandments*, ed. and trans. B. W. Farley (Grand Rapids, Mich., 1980), which has an excellent introduction and notes; *Sermons on Ephesians*, a revision of the Golding translation by Banner of Truth Trust, 1975; two editions of sermons on Isaiah 53, one by T. H. L. Parker (*Sermons on Isaiah's Prophecy of the Death and Resurrection of Christ*, 1956) and another by L. Dixon (*The Gospel according to Isaiah*, 1953). L. Dixon has also contributed *Sermons on Job* (Grand Rapids, Mich., 1952) and *Sermons on the Saving Work of Christ* (Grand Rapids, Mich., 1980; reprint of a 1950 work). Sermons on the pastoral epistles, *The Mystery of Godliness* . . . , were published in 1950. T. H. L. Parker and E. Mülhaupt have provided commentary on Calvin's preaching: the former in *The Oracles of God* . . . (London, 1947), and the latter in *Die Predigt Calvins; ihre Geschichte, ihre Form und ihre religiösen Grundgedanken* (Berlin, 1931).

Another essential primary source in Calvin studies is the Genevan register of pastors. Cf. *Registres de la compagnie des pasteurs de Genève au temps de Calvin*, ed. R. M. Kingdon and J.-F. Bergier (Geneva, 1962, 1964, 1969) and *The Register of the Company of Pastors in the Time of Calvin*, ed. and trans. P. E. Hughes (Grand Rapids, Mich., 1966).

SECONDARY SOURCES. François Wendel's *Calvin: The Origin and Development of His Religious Thought* (New York, 1963) continues to be the best one-volume survey of Calvin's thought. Though the bibliography is somewhat dated, the material on Calvin's education and the sources of the *Institutes*, along with the surveys on the heads of doctrine are excellent. I wish that

Wendel's work would be reprinted; it is still available in French. W. Niesel's *The Theology of Calvin* (Philadelphia, 1956) is still widely used, and E. Doumergue's *Jean Calvin: Les hommes et les choses de son temps* (7 vols. 1899–1927) is still a valuable source of Calviniana. A helpful tool for those approaching the *Institutes* for the first time is F. L. Battles's analytical outline, *Analysis of the Institutes . . .* (Grand Rapids, Mich., 1980).

Calvin's education and humanist background are subjects of Q. Breen's *A Study in French Humanism* (2d ed., 1958). Written in 1932, this is still an excellent study. Josef Bohatec's *Budé und Calvin . . .* (Graz, 1950) is a superb book, covering many topics central to Calvin's thought. Charles Partee's *Calvin and Classical Philosophy* (Leiden, 1977) is not limited to Calvin's early period, but covers Calvin's use of philosophy in treating several key doctrines. Although it is nearly thirty years since E. A. Dowey's *The Knowledge of God in Calvin's Theology* (New York, 1952, 1965) was first issued, it remains an excellent study of this topic and of Calvin's theological method. Calvin's anthropology is the subject of T. F. Torrance's study, *Calvin's Doctrine of Man* (Grand Rapids, Mich., 1957). Though some may disagree with his understanding of the *imago dei*, they will recognize the thoroughness of his work. I note too J. P. Donnelly's *Calvinism and Scholasticism in Vermigli's Doctrine of Man* (Leiden, 1976).

R. S. Wallace's *Calvin's Doctrine of the Christian Life* (Edinburgh, 1959), is based on a wide reading of the commentaries and sermons, as well as the *Institutes*. A work deserving of more attention is C. A. M. Hall's *With the Spirit's Sword. The Drama of Spiritual Warfare* (Richmond, Va., 1968). Calvin scholars have succeeded in showing the "humanness" of Calvin, but the themes of "zeal" and "perseverance" cannot be slighted. E. D. Willis's *Calvin's Catholic Christology; the Function of the so-called 'Extra Calvinisticum'* (Leiden, 1966) is an excellent work that should be reprinted. *Prädestination und Verantwortlichkeit bei Calvin* (Neukirchen, 1937) by P. Jacobs not only discusses these perennial concerns but provides an excellent introductory chapter on Calvin's theological method and its "doppelseitig" nature.

Several studies related to Calvin's doctrine of the church and sacraments must be mentioned: *Calvin's Doctrine of the Church* (Leiden, 1970) by B. C. Milner, Jr.; *John Calvin, the Church and the Eucharist* (Princeton, N.J., 1967) by Kilian McDonnell; *Word and Spirit; Calvin's Doctrine of Spiritual Authority* (Stanford, Calif., 1962) by H. J. Forstman; *Calvin's Doctrine of Word and Sacrament* (Edinburgh, 1953) by R. S. Wallace; and *Calvin, théologien de l'Église et du ministère* (Paris, 1964) by A. Ganoczy. Calvin's view of government, law, and economics continues to be of great interest to Calvin scholars and others. The older work of J. Bohatec, *Calvin und das Recht* (Graz, 1934), is still to be taken into account, and the more recent study of W. F. Graham, *The Constructive Revolutionary: John Calvin and His Economic Impact* (Richmond, Va., 1971) has been well received, though some have objected to the book's theological criticisms of Calvin. The works of

A. Bieler in this area are excellent: *La Pensée économique et sociale de Calvin* (Geneva, 1959) and *The Social Humanism of Calvin* (Richmond, Va., 1964). Finally, on eschatology and history I mention *Calvin's Doctrine of the Last Things* (London, 1955) by H. Quistorp and *Calvins Geschichtsauffassung* (Zürich, 1955) by H. Berger.

In the future I hope to see more work done on Calvin's Old Testament commentaries, sermons, and letters. Several of the commentaries should be translated and edited anew: *Genesis, Psalms,* and *Daniel* in particular. Much needed is a work on the Old Testament commentaries such as T. H. L. Parker provided on the New Testament books. It would be instructive to compare the commentaries and the sermons on specific books. Critical editions and translations of more sermon material and letters are desired. Although Jacobs, Dowey, Battles, and others have considered Calvin's theological method as part of their work on other topics, a full-length study of this subject would be a most valuable contribution to Calvin studies. Several studies have presented predestination, the glory of God, or the *duplex cognitio Domini* as the key doctrine in Calvin's thought; it is impossible to name one doctrine as central, but it would be helpful to have a full-length study of love in Calvin's writings.

8

Machiavelli, Antichrist, and the Reformation: Prophetic Typology in Reginald Pole's *De Unitate* and *Apologia ad Carolum Quintum*

Peter S. Donaldson

In the *Apologia ad Carolum Quintum* (1539)[1] Reginald Pole claimed to know, on the basis of a conversation with Thomas Cromwell some ten years earlier and of subsequent research into Cromwell's views, that Machiavelli's *Prince* had been the inspiration behind Henry VIII's decision to break with Rome, declare himself head of the church, and seize the property of the English monasteries. The *Apologia* remained unpublished until A. M. Quirini's edition of Pole's letters appeared (1744–51): after that, Pole's views were influential in fixing the image of the Henrician polity as Machiavellian in character. To A. F. Pollard, for example, Henry VIII was "Machiavelli's prince in action." Since 1905, however, when Paul Van Dyke devoted an appendix to his *Renascence Portraits* to an examination of the *Apologia*, it has been more common for historians to dismiss Pole's claim that Cromwell knew Machiavelli so early and made *The Prince* the basis of his advice to Henry VIII. Many of Van Dyke's arguments were accepted by G. R. Elton in *Tudor Revolution in Government* (1953) and "The Political Creed of Thomas Cromwell" (1956).[2]

Pole's views on Machiavelli appear in a work that, like the closely related *De Unitate* (1536, published 1539), is permeated by a typological vision of history: the events and persons of Pole's own time are seen as fulfillments or partial fulfillments of biblical models. Pole's typology is quite complex and, though it derives from time-honored medieval traditions of biblical exegesis, somewhat original in its method and in the particular place it finds for current events in the biblical sequence of the Last Days. Pole's works have an important place in the history of sixteenth-century apocalyptic thought now being written; and, as Pole's apocalyptic vision undoubtedly colors his report of the facts, it will be useful to examine his view of sacred history, and particularly the role he assigned to himself in the unfolding of scriptural prophecy, in order to assess how his bias might affect his telling of a story like that of his meeting with Cromwell.

Before we proceed to the texts a brief account of the spiritual and political crisis Pole experienced at the time of their composition is in order.[3] Pole had from early childhood a complex and potentially explosive relationship to the king. Pole's mother was the daughter of George, Duke of Clarence, and the niece of Edward IV. Her brother Edward was executed in 1499 because of the potential danger he represented to the Tudor claim to the throne. Pole was born in 1500, and his father, Sir Richard Pole, died in 1505. Henry VIII came to the throne when Reginald Pole was nine; he favored the Poles, and especially young Reginald, whom he generously supported at Oxford, where he was "king's scholar" at Magdalen from 1513, and then at Padua, where he went for an extended period of study in 1521. Pole was very, perhaps excessively, grateful: in the hope of serving his benefactor with the fruits of his study, he devoted himself to his books to the point of injuring his health (*De Unitate*, sig. Bi^r).[4] In this zeal we may, perhaps, see an attempt to resolve ambivalent feelings: Pole was a boy without a father, and the man who, as kinsman and benefactor, in some measure supplied his place, sat on a throne that might have passed to his grandfather, to his uncle (whom Henry VII had killed), to his own brother. Beneath his childhood loyalty lay great bitterness, which comes to the surface in later references to his uncle, as in this passage from the *De Unitate* in which he points up the irony of his own defense of Mary Tudor's right to the succession:

> If your father came back to earth now, if he saw me, the nephew of the man whom he took care to have killed, even though he was completely innocent, as everyone knows, because he seemed to be too close to the throne and capable of later becoming an impediment to his own de-scendants, if he saw me, offspring of that house he considered danger-ous, defend the right of inheritance of her [Mary] against which you, his son, are taking action! What an extraordinary thing it would seem to him. He would then clearly see how weak human reason is when it tries to remove all obstacles to the perpetuity of a dynasty. For what moved him to the murder of my uncle, who was unanimously judged to have been completely innocent all his life (like a one year's child, as Scripture says) was only that he saw in him the nephew of King Edward, the sole living male in the line which could one day be the source of fresh revolts to establish his right to the throne against that of his own family. . . . Could he have imagined that his own son would attack his succession? . . . And it is I, who come of the same family, son of the sister of the man whom he had killed because he feared he could become an obstacle to his children, it is I who take up the defense of his granddaughter against his son's opposition when he himself had thought that that murder would assure the protection of his line. (Sig. Oii^v–Oiii^r)

Even here there is ambivalence: an ironic loyalty to the Tudor succession is present along with bitter anger at the loss of his uncle.

The turning point in Pole's attitude to the king came in 1535, when Thomas More and John Fisher were executed (sig. Sv^v). This action, the climax of a sequence of events (including the king's divorce, his assumption of supremacy over the English church, the desecration of the shrine of Thomas Becket, and the dissolution of the monasteries) by which Henry had moved away from obedience to Rome, precipitated Pole's own crisis of obedience. This was the major crisis of Pole's life, transforming not just his attitude toward Henry, but his whole religious life and his conception of history. Even his Latin style, which loses urbanity and polish and gains in force and vehemence after the crisis, was altered.[5]

Pole's life was first touched by the changes taking place in Henry's England when he returned from Padua in 1527, and had his conversation with Cromwell about Machiavelli's ideas (and their relevance to Henry's intended divorce). In 1529 he left for study in Paris, but while there was asked by the king to act as royal emissary in obtaining an opinion on the divorce from the University of Paris. He later claimed to have resisted this task, and to have delegated it to Edward Fox. What Pole's actual role was remains unclear, but it is evident that bribery was involved, whether Pole knew of it or not. It seems likely that whatever role Pole played in the mission, he could not have then held such an uncompromising view of the divorce as he was later to do. In 1530 Henry VIII offered Pole the See of York on condition that he declare his opinion on the divorce. Pole tried to devise an acceptable compromise, but when the time came to explain it to the king, he became tongue-tied, then found himself, despite his plan, condemning the divorce to the king himself in the strongest of terms. He attempted to conciliate the king afterwards, but as his position had not really changed, he was unsuccessful. He was allowed to leave England again in 1532 because, according to Eustace Chapuys, the imperial ambassador, he threatened to speak his mind publicly if made to stay. Abroad again, Pole retained his various benefices and royal pension, and Henry made further efforts to persuade him of the rightness of his cause; at this time the breach was not permanent. But it soon was to become so. In Italy Pole's studies took a theological turn and, influenced by the intense piety of Gasparo Contarini and his associates in the Oratory of Divine Love, and by other currents of religious feeling in Padua and Venice, Pole experienced something in the nature of a religious conversion. In the words of one member of his circle "Pole is studying divinity and *meteorologizei*, despising things merely human and terrestrial. He is undergoing a great change, exchanging man for God."[6] Thus when Henry VIII set Thomas Starkey the task of getting Pole to declare his views on the supremacy in 1535, it was a far more religiously committed man with whom they had to deal. Pole's answer took the form of a treatise, the *De Unitate*, which was

sent to Henry in 1536. It is a scathing attack on Henry VIII and on his
policies, and it led to a complete break. Pole's family had remained in
England, and in 1538 Reginald Pole's elder brother Henry was executed.
His aged mother was imprisoned and later (1541) she too lost her life as a
result of her son's rebellion. Pole knew of the danger, and in fact this
aspect of his allegiance to Rome—that he had to abandon his family to
likely death to proclaim it—helps explain why his conversion was so thoroughgoing, his position in regard to Henry so uncompromising. The personal stakes were too high to permit of half-hearted solutions. When he
writes of Henry VIII he adopts the role of the zealot and the prophet,
casting earthly attachments aside in favor of identification with biblical
exemplars of selfless devotion. In the *De Unitate* he writes as one who is
cutting ties not only to his king but to his family. Having put them at risk,
he writes very nearly as if he rejected their claim upon him, while the
church becomes his mother:

> I have seen you kill those who were dearer to me for Christ's sake than
> my own parents [More and Fisher]: I see your hand now make every
> effort to destroy the unity of the Church of Christ and to break off, so
> much as lies in your power, a large part of it, that unity which ought to
> be dearer to me than my parents and my country, dearer than the entire
> creation. Now I am not completely silent, but my mother the Church has
> taught me to speak, and in this decisive and perillous moment at which
> she finds herself should I not raise my voice? should I not speak? should
> I not cry out? (Sig. Sv^v)

One thinks of Cyprian's dictum here: he cannot have God for a father who
has not the church for a mother. Henry, by rejecting one, had lost the
other, while Pole, in his own understanding of these events, was drawing
nearer to his heavenly parents by rejecting the king who had been a symbolic father to him, and at the more terrible cost of abandoning his mother
to his revenge. Only recourse to the transcendent, among biblical examples
of martyrdom and sacrifice, could he find solace (and sanction) for the
course of action his conscience thrust upon him.

Dermot Fenlon has written brilliantly of Pole's spiritual life at this time,
relating Pole's experiences to those of the *spirituali* influenced by Juan de
Valdés and to other traditions of piety and meditation. Pole's was an in-
tensely personal "conversion," but it also entailed the adoption of a scriptural attitude toward history and politics:

> At Venice, in the Benedictine setting of S. Giorgio Maggiore, and at
> Padua, in that of S. Justina, Pole now came into contact with the new
> Biblical scholarship, and with a style of exegesis which began profoundly
> to influence his whole cast of mind. He attended lectures on Isaiah given
> by the Hebrew scholar Jan van Kempen (Iohannes Campensis) whom

Contarini had summoned to S. Justina; there, too, he became familiar with the Scriptures as expounded by the Benedictine scholar Isodorus Clarius. From this time forward, we find in his writings a pervasive consciousness of God's continuous dealings with mankind in history. Pole's thought becomes from this date permeated by the Bible. The effect may be described as follows. He learnt to apply the Bible as an interpretative key to history, including the events of his own time. Time became for him the movement of providential history; he began to read events in the light of what the Scriptures yielded.[7]

In consequence of this new scriptural orientation, Pole's works in which English history is dealt with, especially the De Unitate and the Apologia, place current events in the larger sequences of sacred history and relate contemporary persons to biblical (and especially apocalyptic) counterparts. Pole's personal crisis thus came to seem part of a larger historical crisis, as the tragedy of More and Fisher, the suffering of his family, and his own agonies of conscience became part of the universal anguish that marked the coming of the Last Days. Pole's resistance to Henry was like that of the prophets opposing the wicked kings of Israel, his testimony like the witness the church would be called upon to make against Antichrist.

The De Unitate was finished in early 1536 and sent to Henry in May. In the same year Pole was made a cardinal and shortly thereafter was appointed papal legate to England at a time when Henry VIII faced serious domestic resistance. Pole's two legatine missions ended in failure. It was during the second of these (1538–39) that he visited Charles V and attempted to convince him to invade England. The Apologia ad Carolum Quintum was probably written as an elaboration of the verbal arguments Pole had made to Charles in person. Van Dyke dates its composition between August 1538, when Henry VIII was excommunicated, and early 1539, after Pole read Richard Morison's treatise defending the execution of Pole's brother Henry Lord Montague and that of Henry Courtenay, Marquis of Exeter (late January 1539).[8] Charles did not invade England, nor did he share Pole's view of the threat Machiavelli posed to Christendom, for in 1550 he licensed the Spanish translation of The Discourses, and stated, in the text of the privileg, that he considered the book "muy util y provechoso" and had commended it to his son Philip.[9] Pole apparently made subsequent efforts to oppose Machiavellian influence: an English traveler to Italy who met Pole reported to the Privy Council his intention to do all he could to see that the book was banned; he set his nephew Henry Huntington the task of translating portions of Osorio's De nobilitate (1542), which contains the first published attack on Machiavelli; another early critic of Machiavelli, Lancelotto Politi (De libris christiano detestandis, 1551) may have known Pole's views, for his own argument is quite similar; so that it seems quite likely that Pole's anti-Machiavellian opinions had some subsequent influence despite the Apologia's remaining unpublished in the sixteenth century. All of Machiavelli's works were placed on the first papal *Index* in 1559.[10]

Pole's Apocalyptic Typology: Machiavellism as Secret Doctrine

In the *Apologia*, Pole's central argument is that the actions of Henry VIII—his claim to be head of the Church, the desecration of shrines and monasteries, his manipulation of statute to achieve the death of his opponents—all flow from adherence to a secret doctrine, namely, that of Machiavelli's *Prince*, which is satanic in inspiration, and whose influence in England is a sign of the coming of Antichrist. Pole's story of his meeting with Thomas Cromwell (pp. 133–36) is designed to reveal how he came to know about this doctrine, while at the same time demonstrating that Cromwell wanted to keep it secret.

The *Apologia* is structured so that the recital of Henry VIII's enormities builds suspense for the revelation of Machiavelli as the key to his policies:

> But this will be seen more clearly when I reveal the sources of his counsels, from which these actions derive. (P. 111)

> I say what anyone would have said who knew, as I had occasion to know, that one inmost counsel of his, or should I call it a doctrine, which the king, inclining wholly to tyranny, set up as the new pattern for his actions, and upon which the rest of his plans depended. . . . And because I happened to discover this and knew his counsels, and not because I was led by any special prudence, I predicted what has now happened. (P. 114)

> And now I shall reveal, as I promised, the inmost counsel of the only one of the king's ministers who found the king's return to better thoughts painful. (P. 117)

When Henry wavered about seeking a divorce, Satan sent "one of his own privy councillors" with "more ample orders" in order to strengthen the king's intention to gratify his lust. Pole knows "what those orders were, who brought them, and by whom he was sent" (p. 118), but delays many pages before revealing that the *nuncius Satanae* was Cromwell (p. 126) and that it was Machiavelli who wrote the text that he used to corrupt the king (p. 137).

Even in the actual story of the meeting between Pole and Cromwell, the title of *The Prince* and the identity of its author remain concealed, as we shall see. The meeting took place at a time when Henry was seeking advice about his divorce. Pole had just returned from Italy and Cromwell, welcoming him home, drew him into a conversation about the duties of royal councillors, hoping to find out which way Pole inclined on the divorce question. Pole thought one should tell kings what was honorable, honest, and useful. Cromwell thought this naive; such ideas were very well in school debates, but useless and even dangerous at court, for what princes wanted was not always honorable or honest. This fact could not be taught in schools, and so scholars newly come to court were in some danger of bringing trouble upon themselves and those close to them through their lack of experience. Cromwell's own opinion was that the councillor should consider *quo tendat voluntas principis,* and to help assure that the prince got his way without appearing to be irreligious or immoral. Cromwell recommended that Pole read a book (if he read at all; experience was a better teacher) by a perceptive modern writer who based his views on experience rather than on dreams like those to be found in Plato's *Republic.* Pole did promise to read it, but it was never sent because, Pole thought, Cromwell could judge his real reaction from his face. However, when Pole discovered from those familiar with Cromwell's "secret studies" what book was meant, he took no less pains to get a copy than one might to intercept the secret orders of an enemy in hope of discovering his plans.

For Pole, *The Prince* was written by Satan in the same sense in which Scripture was written by God (p. 137). It was a new *ars regnandi* (p. 151), proposing, in its recommendation of the violence of the lion and the wiles of the fox, new *arcana imperii* and rejecting entirely the traditional basis of statecraft in the kingly virtues and the common good. Pole considered the doctrines of *The Prince* quite literally satanic in origin: the book bore the name of a man on its title page, but was "written by the finger of Satan" (p. 137).

Pole also saw Satan's hand in the transmission of the text, for Cromwell, who was to corrupt Henry with Machiavelli's ideas, had first to be corrupted by demons. Indeed, Pole speaks of him as having become wholly inhabited by them, with little of his human identity left, before he could become the conveyer of Machiavellian influence into England (p. 126). This influence was the turning point in Henry's reign. Basing his advice on Machiavelli's supposed rejection of absolute standards of morality and advocacy of the use of religion as an instrument of policy, Cromwell convinced Henry (pp. 118–23) to declare himself head of the church and seize the property of the monasteries. Henry succumbs to Machiavellian (i.e. demonic) influence. Cromwell refrains from mentioning Machiavelli, as indeed from giving any source for his ideas, but he has transmitted the essential core of the doctrine to Henry, who thenceforth embodies it "to the letter" (p. 146) in his policies. The king becomes a "disciple" (pp. 144, 151) who manifests the teachings of his master more exactly than the disciples embodied those of Christ. Thus Machiavelli's ideas are the doctrines or dogmas of Satan (pp. 114–15 and passim) and *The Prince* is treated as an apocryphon or secret book that embodies them, and is kept concealed, not only from Pole, but even from the king, who becomes an adherent of the doctrine without knowing what book it derives from.

Machiavelli could be thought of as the purveyor of a secret doctrine partly because at the time of his purported influence on Henry VIII, *The Prince* existed only in manuscripts. It was published in 1532—but even after it was widely known it was often thought of as a book that dealt with the *arcana imperii* or secrets of rule.[11] In part this view was prompted by Machiavelli's own sense of himself as an innovator (see *Discourses*, preface; *Prince* XV), by his tone of confidential intimacy with his reader, and by details such as the comparison he makes between his own image of the lion and the fox and the ancient myth of Achilles' tuition by the Centaur, implying that the content of the political secrets of the ancients was identical with his own insights into the half-human, half-bestial nature of political life. But Machiavelli's subject matter itself, his insistence upon the utility of deception and dissimulation, also lent credence to the notion that he was revealing the "secrets of rule" hinted at by Aristotle, Tacitus, and other ancient writers. Surely if the Tacitean phrase *arcana imperii* meant anything, it must refer to these teachings of Machiavelli, which seemed, by making ordinary readers party to the moral license by which princes achieved their ends, to disclose the trade secrets of statecraft. In addition, there was a built-in paradox in the publication of such secrets, for if these really were the techniques by which clever men gained power over others, then publishing them for all to read could only weaken their effectiveness. From this paradox grew a tradition of interpretation that saw Machiavelli as the revealer of princely secrets to the masses. For those who followed this line of interpretation, Machiavelli was secretly democratic in his sympathies, and published the *arcana* in order to alert the populace to the deceptions of their rulers.

Cardinal Pole held no such views of Machiavelli's intentions, but his *Apologia* nevertheless provides the first evidence of such an interpretative tradition, for Pole says that on a trip to Florence he was told by Machiavelli's fellow citizens that the author himself claimed that he had written *The Prince* only in order to hasten the downfall of the Medici (p. 151).[12] Pole rejects this story as excuse-making. But if he rejects the idea of an anti-tyrannical Machiavelli, he nevertheless seizes upon the paradox that lies at the heart of this story, and makes it an essential part of his own analysis of Machiavellism. There is an inherent contradiction in the publication of political techniques that would work better if they remained secret. For Pole, this contradiction reflected the opposition between satanic concealment and divine revelation in the workings of the historical process. Machiavellism was a doctrine of secrecy and deception that contained the seeds of its own destruction, for the more widely it was known, the more its secrets would stand revealed. This paradox illustrated, in extreme form, the self-defeating character of all human attempts to hide the truth; what Pole took to be the unprecedented espousal of dishonesty in *The Prince* was a sign of the approach of the biblically predicted time when evil would stand fully revealed. We must follow Pole's attempt to link Machiavelli's text to biblical archetypes of secrecy and concealment in some detail.

Pole's Apocalyptic Typology: Occultation and Revelation in History

Pole saw Machiavellism preeminently as a doctrine of concealment. The "entire doctrine of Cromwell and Machiavelli" was contained in the idea that the prince should serve his own desires "under pretext of religion" (p. 145). Pole's reading of Machiavelli is one-sided and distorted. Only the phrase *via media* (p. 138) suggests any acquaintance with *The Discourses*. Of *The Prince* he knows chapters 15–19 (Cromwell's reference to Plato, p. 135, paraphrases *Prince*, chap. 15; the discussion of how to avoid being hated, p. 147, refers to *Prince*, chap. 19). What Pole knows best about *The Prince* are those passages in which the *appearance* of religion and virtue is said to be more useful than the actualities:

> He who wishes always to follow truth and faith and religion will never live safe from snares. Nor indeed will he who openly neglects religion find a better state. What then is to be done? Holding a middle course, as prudence dictates, you will observe religion when your advantage instructs you; when it dictates otherwise you will not be so scrupulous that you will not swerve from it, nor so rash that you will openly reject it. (Pp. 138–39; cf. *Prince*, chap. 18)

> What he says of religion . . . he expresses in clearer words concerning all the virtues which religion requires to be observed: piety, faith, justice, liberality, clemency; to possess and observe these is most harmful for princes, but to display the appearances of them, and to be able to use them appropriately—that is always profitable. (P. 139; *Prince*, chap. 18)

> Truly that prince will excel who best knows how to simulate and dissimulate, and is cautious not to show that he rejects those virtues about which philosophers wrote their admirable books, and especially to have regard for religion, faith and justice, and to follow them without reluctance . . . for these are sometimes useful; but to be addicted to them, and to show oneself as, and actually to be a persistent observer of them—that was never profitable. (P. 140; *Prince*, chap. 18)

Pole was quite familiar with the eighteenth chapter, and indeed takes it for the whole of Machiavelli's thought.

In the *Apologia* this Machiavellian motif of dissimulation is set in contrast to the biblical theme of revelation. What men most try to hide is often brought to light by providential discovery, or by the very publicity that attends the attempt to conceal. For example, Machiavelli had advised the prince to avoid being hated at all costs (*Prince*, chaps. 17, 19) and yet had also advised the simulation of virtues:

And it did not escape his notice that, if the simulation were known, it would not be possible to avoid hatred, and therefore he diligently warns the prince to be careful lest he be caught simulating the virtues. But that, most foolish and impious of men, lies not within man's power; the matter rests with God who knows all things and reveals them when he wishes to do so. The words of His Son are "there is nothing hidden that will not be revealed, nor can a city on a mountaintop be hidden." Indeed, even if the simulation of a private man may be hidden for a time, how much more difficult it is for a prince, whose every word and deed, even his sighs, groans, and every gesture of his body (which so often express the soul) are noted. It cannot be, and nature herself says that nothing simulated can be eternal. (P. 147)

Henry VIII himself is a fine example of the ironic character of the project of concealment: "the more he labored to hide his lusts and wicked desires, the more divine providence revealed them, to his shame" (p. 148). When he send round to all the universities to obtain support for his divorce, he merely advertised his lust, and made himself a laughing stock for taking such pains to prove himself incestuous (pp. 148–49)! In this case the act of concealment itself is the means of revelation; in others, as in Pole's chance encounter with Cromwell, providence assists; in all cases what is hidden eventually comes to light.

Behind this contrast of occultation and revelation lies the apocalyptic notion that the work of Satan is a secret work, and that as the Last Days approach, Satan's power will greatly increase, while its increase is accompanied by its revelation to all. When Antichrist's power is complete, his revelation will also be complete, and he will be ripe for destruction. The key biblical text for this notion is 2 Thessalonians 2:

He is the enemy. He rises in pride against every god, so called, every object of man's worship, claiming to be a god himself. You cannot but remember that I told you this while I was still with you: You must now be aware of the restraining hand which ensures that he will be revealed only at the proper time: for already the secret power of wickedness is at work [Vulgate: *nam mysterium iam operatur iniquitatis*], secret only for the present until the redeemer disappears from the scene. And then he will be revealed, that wicked man whom the Lord Jesus will destroy with the breath of his mouth, and annihilate by the radiance of his coming.

The God-challenging *motif* of this passage is crucial to Pole's attempt to identify Henry VIII as a precursor of Antichrist, and will be discussed below. For now we are concerned with the relation between concealment and revelation: Antichrist works in mystery, but only until the proper moment when he stands revealed. Pole clearly thought of his own age as the time when the secret works of Antichrist were being revealed, despite themselves, more fully than ever before, and believed that this revelation marked the start of a new phase of sacred history. In Henry VIII's manipulation of English law to secure the death of his opponents Pole saw the

> mystery of evil, if I should call that a mystery which is so openly manifested by anyone who, in the spirit of Antichrist, opposes the servants of Christ and precedes his coming. But if Antichrist is revealed by the open performance of the works of Antichrist, and if the works of Antichrist are those which the prophet Daniel distinctly set forth and Paul enumerated: to proffer speeches against the Most High, and to rise so high in one's pride that one thinks he can change the laws and the times, then who ever displayed the works of Antichrist so openly and less mysteriously? (Pp. 155–56)

Antichrist worked in secret in the past, but in Henry VIII he works openly:

> Who would ever try this except he who worked openly in the spirit of Antichrist, and no longer in mystery? (P. 157)

> For these are not so much mysteries, are they, as open evidence of the operation of Satan and the reign of Antichrist? And could he, if he were revealed, if he had come, could he exalt his seat any higher? I think he could not. (P. 159)

Henry VIII remains a *type* or a *precursor* (p. 169) of Antichrist. But his resemblance to the archetype is exact; he

> so closely expresses the kingdom of Antichrist *in typo* that if I wanted to examine the exact words which are spoken of the reign of Antichrist, I should not find even one word which he does not embody so closely that a painter could never present a more exact image of anyone. (P. 169)

> He so embodies the form of the reign of Antichrist that it has never been seen, these many centuries, in such open form in any other king or tyrant, Christian or infidel. (Pp. 167–68)

This closeness of approximation to type, and the transition from the "in mysterio" of earlier tyrants to the "palam" or "aperte" of Henry is of the greatest importance for the present attempt to define Pole's use of apocalyptic models. For in insisting that Henry is a more open and more complete approximation of the archetype than has been seen before, Pole adopts a progressive or historicist approach to the biblical texts, seeing the events of his own time as part of an unfolding process rather than as static reflections of unchanging biblical realities. According to Firth, such an emphasis was a special mark of sixteenth-century *Protestant* apocalyptic: ("If [an author] asserts that the revelation of such corruption at one time rather than another is particularly significant, or that by its recognition and defeat a new era in history has begun, then we are dealing with the first

signs of the apocalyptic tradition in Protestant historiography.")[13] Pole certainly has just this understanding of his own era.

Thus Pole saw the ironies of Henry's career and the ironies of Machiavellian dissimulation as closely related, and placed both in the context of
Antichrist's self-concealment and eventual revelation. There had been
wicked kings and wicked councillors before: the inescapable power of sin
assured that political life, like the rest of life, would be morally flawed. But
to sin *ex fragillitate* (p. 143), out of human weakness, was one thing; to
embrace sin as a willfully adopted, explicit political principle, was another.
In Pole's view, the explicit commitment to evil of *The Prince* and the manifestation of this principle in Henry's actions were something wholly new in
the world, marking a distinction between Henry VIII and all previous
tyrants and connecting him with Antichrist. The argument Pole makes for
the novelty of Machiavelli's "new art of ruling" is thus also an argument
concerning the chronology of sacred history, which must enter a new
phase as biblical archetypes come closer to fulfillment or are approximated
in radically new ways.

Pole's periodization of sacred history is mercifully free of the numerical
calculations that were so often the stock-in-trade of apocalyptic writers: his
use of Revelation itself, from which most such schemes derive, is very
sparing, and though Daniel provided a variety of numerical sequences as
well, Pole, who uses Daniel frequently, always breaks his citation off just
as the numbers become specific (e.g., the "time, two times and half a time"
of Daniel 7:25). Nevertheless, his view of the character of the era in which
he lived, and of its relative place in the sequence of apocalyptic events, is
clear. The Machiavellian age would be that period, foretold in Revelation
20, in which Satan was released from his bonds for a time, and in which
Antichrist would appear. Before his own age was the period after Christ
came and during which Satan was bound; after it would come the defeat of
Antichrist and the Second Coming. This sequence can be observed in
Pole's extended argument that the desecration of saints' shrines could not
have taken place unless Satan had been released from bondage (p. 101),
because the power of Satan over the bodies of saints had been reined in
since the coming of Christ (p. 102); in his claim that Henry represents
Antichrist in a new way, and in his prediction of Henry's fall (pp. 167ff.),
which will mirror that of Antichrist. The insistence upon the exact similarity between Henry VIII and Antichrist (pp. 157, 159, 167–68) seems to leave
no room for tyrants to come who will be just a bit worse than Henry and
just a bit short of Antichrist, so that we may conjecture that Pole thought
his own period, that of the unbinding of Satan, would be brief, and that
Antichrist would shortly appear (perhaps even Henry would become Antichrist himself, or would be revealed to have been Antichrist himself all
along—Pole's falling short of asserting complete identity may be
scrupulosity). Having begun with the composition of *The Prince*, ("by the

finger of Satan"), this era would end with the full revelation of Antichrist.

Pole thus has a place in the history of the revival of "historicist" exegesis of the apocalyptic material in the Bible. Recent studies (those of Patterson, Firth, Bauckham)[14] have agreed in finding the main medieval tradition a relatively ahistorical one in respect to apocalyptic. Augustine's views dominated, and for him, unlike many of his predecessors who expected an imminent end and saw scriptural prophecy unfolding in their own time, the Last Days are far off, and the archetypes of apocalypse tend to become ideal types rather than historical realities. As such they are still intimately relevant to experience, for every wicked king is in some sense Antichrist, and every man Adam; but the watchful assessment of current events for evidence of the changing of the times falls into disuse. It survives, as the labors of Marjorie Reeves[15] and others have made us amply aware, in the Joachimist tradition and elsewhere; nevertheless, it makes sense to claim, as Patterson, Bauckham, and Firth all do, that historicist exegesis experienced a revival in the sixteenth century. This revival entailed a shift in the apocalyptic chronology, especially in regard to the events of Revelation 20. That passage speaks of a thousand-year period in which Satan is bound, and then he will be set free for a short time. After that (or perhaps not: perhaps the millennium runs concurrently with the binding of Satan) will come the "millennium" or thousand-year period during which the saints will come to life and rule with Christ. For Augustine, and for the "ahistorical" kind of exegesis generally, the millennium or rule of the saints is coterminous with the period of the binding of Satan: it was the period of the ascendancy of the Church, and the time in which he lived. For Joachim, the millennium was a future, but still historical period that would follow the imminent unloosing of Satan. By and large the sixteenth-century apocalyptic writers took the view (deriving from Wyclif's *De solutione Sathanae*) that Satan had already been unleashed and that Antichrist was embodied in the papacy—but they did not expect a future millennium, as some seventeenth-century writers were to do. These sixteenth-century Protestants were historicist in their interpretation of the apocalyptic prophecies, but not millenarian. Reginald Pole's handling of sacred chronology is very similar: there is no indication that he looks forward to a historical rule of the saints, and he sees his own period as one in which Satan had been recently released from his bonds; the mystery of iniquity is rapidly revealing itself, and lacks but little of the full revelation that will signal the defeat of Antichrist by the radiance of the Second Coming. Needless to say, the *dramatis personae* are quite different: for the Protestants the pope played a role like that Pole assigned to Henry, except that Protestants sometimes saw in the papacy a full and complete revelation of Antichrist, rather than a *precursor Antichristi*. The part of satanic Gospel, which Pole assigns to *The Prince*, is sometimes played in Protestant mythology by papal decrees or canon law. But for Pole, as for them, the events of his own time were rapidly fulfilling biblical predictions of a time in which evil would fully manifest itself, and in which the true church would again suffer persecution, martyrdom, and division before the Second Coming.

It is of special interest that one variety of Protestant apocalyptic comes even closer to Pole's exact scheme. Pole was not unique in the sixteenth century in holding that the advent of Machiavelli marked a sacred epoch. Antonio D'Andrea has shown that a very similar view was presented in the 1577 preface to the Latin translation of Innocent Gentillet's *Contremachiavel*.[16] In this work the new era began when John Wyclif and John Hus began to preach the Gospel in modern languages. The open preaching of the word of God was a blow to Satan's power, which he responded to by inspiring the soul-destroying doctrines of Machiavelli. In a separate study I intend to trace the paths by which Pole's anti-Machiavellian campaign may have influenced this conception. At this point it suffices to note that there were other attempts in the sixteenth century to place Machiavelli in the framework of a revived "historicist" exegesis of apocalyptic prophecy.

Super omne quod dicitur deus: Machiavelli and deification

One of the traditional marks of Antichrist was that he should claim divine status. Pole draws on three biblical texts in his association of Henry VIII with the self-deification of Antichrist. First there was the "Lucifer" passage of Isaiah 14:13–14 (cf. *Apologia*, p. 158):

> You said in your heart I will ascend to heaven, above the stars of God I will set my throne on high; I will sit on the mount of assembly in the far north; I will ascend above the heights of the clouds; I will make myself like the Most High.

Another was the "son of perdition" passage of 2 Thessalonians 2, cited earlier: he will "exalt himself against every so-called god or object of worship, so that he takes his seat in the temple of God, proclaiming himself to be God." Since the language of this passage is based upon Daniel's description of the king symbolized by the "little horn" of the fourth beast of his vision (Daniel 12:36), it was natural to read the passages in conjunction with one another, as Pole does. The "little horn" would be a "king of bold countenance, one who understands riddles [. . .] by his cunning he shall make deceit prosper under his own hand, and in his own mind he shall magnify himself." He will "speak words against the Most High, and shall wear out the saints of the Most High, and shall think to change the times and the law" (Daniel 7:25; 8:25; pp. 156, 158, 168–69).

As apocalyptic identifications go, the association of Henry with this composite god-challenging figure was not a strained one; this intelligent and overweening northern king had unquestionably made himself head of the church, and that could be thought of as a kind of deification. Indeed, John Jewel and others who applied these prophecies to the papacy pointed out that the pope's claim to be head of the church entailed invasion of divine prerogative.[17] For Pole, the God-like powers of the papacy were legitimate, and Henry's usurpation of them blasphemous. It was more difficult to make these passages fit Machiavelli; the secular outlook of *The Prince* might well be thought uncongenial to divine pretensions, and indeed Machiavelli's originality has often been thought to lie in his moving politics out of the sphere of the sacred altogether. For Pole, however, the secular world is part of a sacred universe, so that movement in thought away from sacred categories remains enclosed by those categories. Specifically, he holds that there is an implicit claim to godhead—in the relativizing of good and evil in *The Prince*, and that Machiavellian manipulation of religion, morality, or law entails a reversal of the roles of creature and Creator, and therefore fulfills the predicted arrogance of Antichrist.

The speech Cromwell makes to Henry VIII (pp. 118–23) is Pole's link between Machiavelli's text and biblical prophecy. Pole claims that this speech was the result of the satanic influence of Machiavelli on Cromwell. In it Cromwell argues that the limitations placed on Henry's, indeed upon any prince's actions, derive from the undue influence of academic conceptions of statecraft, for scholars "hold that honesty has its foundation in nature, and that if anyone declines from it he should be held to be wicked" (p. 119). But this idea has a leveling effect, for it binds prince and subject to the same standard. In fact moral categories have no absolute sanction:

> experience of affairs, which is the better teacher, teaches that in fact the honest often changes. For if its foundation were fixed in nature, it would not vary so much among us, who live in nature, that what is called wicked among one nation would be called honest among another; what is called honest at one time be called wicked at another. . . . And if the definition of the honest is changed according to human will, whose will can more appropriately change it than that of princes, whose wishes ought to be held for laws?' (P. 120)

The principle that the honest has no basis in nature has two practical consequences: Henry should declare himself head of the church (thus removing the moral authority that has fettered his desires) and should rule according to his will, which the people ought to accept as law.

Pole believed that this speech was the result of the satanic influence of Machiavelli on Cromwell, and that in consequence of it Henry VIII himself became a disciple of Machiavelli (see above). It is clear that Pole takes it to be, self-evidently, a restatement of the argument of *The Prince*. In fact, however, it is much farther removed from genuinely Machiavellian ideas than what Cromwell had said to Pole about *The Prince* (pp. 135–36) and

Pole's own summary (pp. 138–40) of the book—and even those are distortions. Indeed, Machiavelli does say, especially in the chapters Pole knew best, that the prince's conduct must violate moral norms: but this relativism is pragmatic, not philosophical. Machiavelli never claims that morality is an arbitrary human invention, but only that it is sometimes necessary to act immorally to achieve political ends (*entrare nel male, necessitato*). Also, Machiavelli provides no direct support for a politics based upon the satisfaction of the private desires of princes; he is more interested in analyzing the conditions under which political power is acquired and maintained, and these conditions largely rule out the kind of arbitrariness proposed in Cromwell's speech. Thus, even if the speech were a verbatim account, it would not demonstrate specifically Machiavellian influence on Henry VIII, as Pole thought it did. It is not, in any case, a verbatim transcript: Pole admits he was not present, but claims to know its substance (p. 123). He believed that he had verified Cromwell's opinions, but reveals that he took the liberty of collecting together into one speech various things he knew Cromwell thought (p. 124). In recent years it has come to seem likely, on independent grounds, that Pole's account has some basis in fact; that Cromwell may indeed have put before the king a plan that called for autonomy from Rome, and that he may have risen in the king's service because of it.[18] But the connection with Machiavelli the speech itself offers is too tenuous to permit the conclusion that Machiavelli was behind this plan, or that Henry, in following it, became Machiavellian in any meaningful sense.

The significance of the speech for this inquiry is that it distorts Machiavelli by suggesting that he denied any basis for morality and law beyond the will of the individual, and therefore permits Pole to associate his teaching with the God-challenging subordination of law to will that was predicted of Antichrist. Antichrist would "seek to change the times and the law"; in Pole's opinion no heretic or schismatic had ever gone so far as Machiavelli and Cromwell in undermining the basis of law and substituting human will for it (pp. 128, 141–43). Henry VIII's proceedings confirmed the principle, for in acting against internal opposition (especially against Pole's family) he had begun to manipulate statute law in brazen and unprecedented ways. It is precisely this manipulation of the laws of treason and *lèse-majesté* that Pole cites as the working of the "mystery of iniquity" (p. 155). The God-challenging character of such manipulation is also seen in Henry's plan to change the sacraments:

He who revokes these according to the prescriptions of his own will, so that they are changed, corrected or deleted in accordance with the decision of his will, is he not saying in his heart "I shall place my seat in the far north, I shall be like the Most High?" (P. 158)

In fact, Henry had claimed *more* than divine status:

> If we take account of how he has comported himself in his rule over his people, truly he has not been content to assume in his pride the person of God, but has, as the Apostle predicted of Antichrist, exalted himself above all things called god. (P. 158)

This final elevation—above God—is seen in contempt for law rather than in another aspect of Henry's bad behavior because God himself obeyed his own laws, and kept the covenants he had made with Abraham and with the people of Israel. Therefore to change the laws according to one's desires is to "arrogate to oneself a greater dominion than that which the Most High exercises over all his creatures," and is therefore to give "open evidence of the operation of Satan and the rule of Antichrist" (p. 159).

To deny the sacred character of law (moral or statute) is equivalent to asserting the sacredness of the king's will. This line of reasoning associated Machiavelli with the presumptions of Antichrist, and also made of him a supporter of the notions of sacred kingship that were being revived and applied to Henry VIII by Edward Fox, Richard Sampson, and Stephen Gardiner.[19] In fact, many of the arguments Pole uses in the *Apologia* against Henry's self-exaltation are anticipated in the *De Unitate*, in which Henry's corruption is traced not to Machiavelli, but to the inflated conception of the sacredness of kings proposed by Sampson in his *Oratio de dignitate et potestate regia* (e.g., sigs. Piv^r, Vii^r).

Quasi prophetae personam sumens: Pole as Prophet

The assimilation of Henry VIII to the biblical Antichrist is paralleled in the *Apologia* and in the *De Unitate* by Pole's identification with the Prophets. In warning the emperor to combat Henry as well as the Turk, for example, Pole takes on the prophetic office of predicting defeat unless the internal threat to Christendom is taken as seriously as the external:

> If I seem to speak too confidently on this point, as if assuming the role of a prophet pronouncing with certainty on the outcome of battles, it is because God's justice has been set before my eyes and grants me that role for the time. (P. 167)

Pole's principal prophetic role in the *Apologia*, however, is as revealer of concealed truth. Concerning this role he is full of self-reproach:

> Now that I am resisting him I ought to fear only the reproach of having not resisted him strongly enough, of having opposed his impiety too laxly, since although I had it in hand for so many years to reveal his

malicious impiety, by which he deceived many, I was like a guardian of
his honor and a defender, rather than an opponent of his wicked opinions: I did not make public but kept hidden and concealed for the space
of three years what could have destroyed his reputation. (P. 160)

The three years' wait referred to here may be the period between the
completion of the *De Unitate* and the *Apologia* (1536–39); while the "many
years" more likely refers to the time that had elapsed (nine years, perhaps)
since Pole had recognized in Henry's policies the presence of the
Machiavellian influence his talk with Cromwell had prepared him to expect. He promises to make up in diligence what he has lacked in
promptness, and to conceal nothing of Henry's counsels and actions
(p. 160). Despite this promise, however, Pole continued to delay, for the *De
Unitate* was published without his consent, and the *Apologia*, which contains the full account of the role of Cromwell and Machiavelli, saw print
only in the eighteenth century. But whatever second thought may have led
to further suppression of facts that could injure Henry's reputation, at the
time of the writing of the *Apologia* itself Pole held the view that the time for
full revelation had come.

We have seen that several Old Testament prophecies (Isaiah 14, Daniel
7, 8) were central to Pole's association of Henry VIII and Antichrist. These
prophets also provided a model for Pole: there is something of each of
them in Pole's self-presentation—Isaiah's reluctance and his balancing of
internal and external threats; Daniel's confrontation of his king and his
faith in a God who was preeminently a revealer of secrets (2:28–30, 47).
Pole also draws on Ezekiel 14 (pp. 149–50) in predicting Henry's downfall.
But the most explicit identification Pole makes is with Moses and the Levites. Having revealed the king's secrets like Daniel, Pole calls for Holy
War against him, as Moses did against the worshipers of the Golden Calf,
and, like the Levites who responded to the call, takes upon himself the
sacrifices the battle requires. In a particularly elaborate allegory, Pole likens
the golden ornaments of the Israelites to the spiritual ornaments—religion,
piety, and faith—taken away by Machiavelli. When Moses found that his
people had yielded to idolatry, he called for battle, asking those loyal to
him to take the sword and go through the camp killing their own brothers
and friends (Exodus 32:27–29). The Levites answer the call, and Pole
echoes Moses' blessing of them:

If the voice of the prophet said to those Levites: "Blessed be thou in the
Lord who have consecrated your hands in the blood of your relations,"
how much greater blessing will they merit who . . . consecrate their
hands in the blood of those who have visited such ignominious slaughter upon the people? (P. 154)

Then he himself becomes a Levite:

Those princes of tribes to whom I am sent, I, one of those Levites who have said in this cause to father and mother, "I know you not," and to my brothers, "I do not know you," will they listen to me the less when I propose the example of the Levites as an excellent and most pious model for their imitation, will they less obey the voice of Him who sent me because in all his letters to them that predator of the people calls me a rebel and a traitor? (p. 154)

Pole's offer to sacrifice himself for Henry's salvation ("if my death could, by virtue of Christ, work any change in his life, I could wish for no greater benefit on earth than to be made a sacrifice for him," p. 168) echoes Moses' offer of his own damnation ("blot me, I pray thee, out of the book which thou hast written" [Exodus 32:31]) on behalf of the Jews. This kind of offer, made likewise by Paul (Romans 9:3), was also a part of the office of the prophet, who intercedes for the sinning people to the point of offering himself in their stead.

Pole's habit of identification with the prophets is already well-developed in the *De Unitate*, where the precise form this identification takes is somewhat different. In my opinion, the shift in Pole's understanding of his prophetic or quasi-prophetic responsibilities is of immense importance in explaining why he did not reveal what he knew about Cromwell and Machiavelli until the *Apologia*. Van Dyke's major argument against the historicity of Pole's account of Cromwell's Machiavellian reading was that Pole does not mention Machiavelli in the *De Unitate*, and barely mentions Cromwell, even though the *De Unitate* deals with the same events in English history, and is like the *Apologia*, a scathing attack on the king. If Pole thought Cromwell's Machiavellism was the inspiration for Henry's actions, why not say so there? A partial answer is found in Pole's conception of his prophetic mission and its changing exigencies.

In the *De Unitate*, as in the *Apologia*, Pole has had hidden matters revealed to him, and he in turn must reveal them to others. Christ has given him the order to write his book (sig. Vvi^r), has directly entrusted to him what might save Henry (sig. Vvi^v); God himself guided the decision to send the finished book to the king (sig. Aii^r). God also has revealed to Pole the king's intentions (e.g., in seeking a divorce):

Who could have informed me in what spirit you did this? Who indeed except God knew your heart? Even he, to whom God wished to reveal it knew, prince. And I say it was I to whom God revealed your heart in this matter. (Sig. Niii^v)

In the *Apologia*, though, this "revelation" of Henry's motives is tied to the discovery by Pole of Henry's "inmost counsels," which are Machiavellian. Here Pole disavows special knowledge almost as soon as he has claimed it: "God revealed it to me, but not really to me anymore than to anyone else who took the trouble to find out the cause" (ibid.). Then, in a passage omitted from the Public Record Office manuscript, Pole derives Henry's motive from the facts of the case: if Henry's scruples about his marriage to his brother's widow were sincere, he would not have gone on to marry his mistress's sister!

And if the claim to special knowledge is more ambiguous here (see also the discussion of Christ's special commission to Pole at sig. Vvi^r, ff., which turns out to consist in well-known truths of the faith, rather than the mysteries first hinted at), the call to revelation is more ambiguous as well. Pole tells us that his natural tendency, since childhood, was to conceal the sins of others, or to privately find some means of correction (sig. Bi^r); he would rather suffer unjust blame himself than censure others (sig. Vvi^r). Even when he heard of the death of More and Fisher he was silent for a month, dissimulating his reaction to the news. Then he received the Call:

> it was then that the words of the book of Isaiah seemed addressed no less to me than to the prophet: "Lift your voice like a trumpet," let it be heard, if possible, not only in this kingdom, but everywhere on earth where the name of Christ is venerated. (Sig. Sv^v)

Not the moment of the death of More and Fisher, but the moment at which, a month later, he read Isaiah 58:1 (probably in conjunction with his study of this prophet with Van Kempen) was the moment of prophetic call, and he who had "always kept silent" resolved to lift his voice. But when did he lift it? Both internal and external evidence suggests a far more complex intention than this simple call to speak out.[20] His intention to publish is suggested by a letter in which he defends its harshness of tone on the grounds that he wrote for Englishmen, not Athenians (L.P., 10:169 [no. 420]). He wrote to the king of Scots that he wanted it "to see the light" (Epistolae, 1:174) and we have seen that he promises to reveal what he had not made public for three years in the Apologia (p. 160; see also p. 75: "quae nunc edo"). But in a letter to the Privy Council (1537) in which he defends himself against the charge that he meant to defame the king, Pole claims that the book was written only for the king, and had been sent only to him and not shown even to the pope: "never confessor desired to be more secret as I desired to be in that book."[21] The letter to Edward VI, Vergerio's preface to the 1555 edition, and the letter to Damião de Goes all give evidence for the view that Pole never approved of the actual publication of the book, tried to prevent it, and tried to limit circulation of the printed edition when it appeared.[22] As we have seen, the treatise itself repeatedly speaks of Pole's personal aversion to publicity, yet insists on Pole's intention to speak out. The best way of understanding these opposed intentions is the hypothesis that they represent a *conditional* intention to publish. One key to this intention comes at the beginning, when he says that the death of

More and Fisher has set an example for him—if they have given their lives, surely he cannot, from a safe distance, fail to send what he has written to the king:

> Therefore I shall never, with God himself guiding me, hesitate to send it, or even to testify publicly to these things, if the matter comes to that. (Sig. Aii^r)

Pole is ready to speak publicly—certainly, at this time, prepared to publicly condemn the execution of More and Fisher, which the example of Isaiah had so powerfully prompted him to do—but that does not mean that he will instantly declare all he knows, either by publishing the *De Unitate* or by revealing the *full* extent of Henry's degeneration (Machiavellian influence, relation to Antichrist), which is only hinted at even in the *De Unitate*. Part of the reason for this reserve is that it gives the writer power over Henry, and keeps him guessing about what Pole will do with the finished treatise, and about how much more information Pole has. At times Pole seems to be taunting the king, claiming revealed knowledge of his motives, then denying he knows more than anyone else. But this taunting bears a serious relation to Pole's prophetic role itself: his reserve is not merely strategic, but charitable, for his function is to chastise the king (sig. Yiii^v), to set his sins before his eyes (sig. Yiv^r) so that he will repent; and obviously, if he did repent there would be no need to publicize his sins. The complex use Pole makes of Isaiah 58 is most significant in this regard. Isaiah is the prophet with whom Pole most closely identifies his own mission in this treatise. Noëlle-Marie Egretier notes 29 citations of this prophet as against 17 for Psalms and 7 each for Ezekiel, I Kings, and Genesis, the next most cited Old Testament books. Pole was engaged in formal study of Isaiah at the time of composition, and was inspired, as we have seen, by 58:1 in his own decision to speak out. But, as the treatise proceeds, Pole finds a deeper significance in that passage: at first it seems an unconditional call for public revelation of the king's misdeeds, but later it is seen as sanctioning a more personal and private remonstrance:

> What could I have done more pertinent to your salvation than to heed the example of Isaiah and the Jews (in whose acts your own are represented), in that passage where, by divine command, he condemns the people who come to him with questions, covered with sins. And this is his answer: "Cry aloud, without constraint, lift thy voice like a trumpet, *reveal to my people their sins* [emphasis added]." It is that same command which I believe that I have received directly from God in the interests of your salvation. . . . To that sinning nation which demanded to know the divine precepts, Isaiah began by reminding them of their sins before showing them the way to be delivered from them; and as you have set me an identical question, I have used with you the same method as that used by the prophet. (Sig. Yiv^r)

The trumpet voice, then, is to be used to call the king to repentance, and not, or at least not yet, to call for his destruction.

This *conditional* character of Pole's obligation to reveal is also seen in the final set of citations: Ezekiel 33:4–5, which warns that the blood of him who does not heed the trumpet will be upon his own head, and Ezekiel 18:30, which promises safety to the penitent. In keeping with this principle, the example of the penitent King David (sig. Vv^v; Xi^r) plays an important role in the *De Unitate*, and Henry's resemblance to Antichrist is played down. The "Antichrist" passages of Daniel and Thessalonians are absent, and when Pole uses Isaiah 14 in reference to Henry's blasphemous self-elevation, he identifies the figure Isaiah addresses in that passage as the king of Assyria rather than Antichrist. Pole has no intention of euphemizing Henry's sins—indeed he calls him head of the church of Satan (sig. Ov^v): but he does not want to lock him into the role of Antichrist while there is hope that, like David, he would repent.[23]

This call to repentance seems sincere. Both in its evocation of the anguish of spiritual struggle (see especially Pole's moving use of Isaiah 30:19–21; sig. Xiii^r: "He will surely be gracious to you at the sound of your cry; when he hears it, he will answer you. And though the Lord give you the bread of adversity and the water of affliction, yet your Teacher will not hide himself anymore") and in its proferring of a foretaste of the joys of heaven to the penitent (sigs. Yii^v, Yv^r, Ziii^v), Pole's plea for the king's repentance is based on the example of his own very recent and joyful experience of justification. This note, too, is absent from later polemic. A prophet might call for Holy War in the end, but the call to repentance came first; he might reveal the king's secrets and call for his destruction, but first he would use what he knew to call the king back to God. The prophetic role included responsibility for the partial, gradual revelation of the truth. The Old Testament prophets provided a model of reserve as well as revelation for they often kept back part of the truth, or spoke it in mysterious terms, or communicated it privately to disciples, "binding up the testimony" for future revelation.

Thus the *De Unitate* is framed as a private remonstrance that may be made public if necessary. And even in its pages, only part of what Pole knows is told, and the rest is presented in veiled terms. The most important example of this hinting at further revelation is to be found in Pole's account of Henry's actual fall into temptation. The dialectic of prophetic reserve is well illustrated by this passage, which must be cited at length:

> Consider now, if you will, how God has guided the events which led to your dishonor. First he permitted Satan to approach you, to plant in your spirit the desire to augment your renown and the power of your kingdom. He persuaded you that it would come to pass if you claimed the sovereignty of all sovereignties on earth, which is the supreme head-

ship of the church on earth. Now that was the best way to cast you down beneath all mortals on earth. But how did Satan persuade you of this? But why should we ask how it was done, since we have Sampson's book, which was Satan's instrument to persuade you. Does anything remain hidden which Sampson and the other instruments of Satan spoke in your ear, which they preferred not to write down? This, especially is hidden: how Satan took you up upon a high mountain and showed you, not all the kingdoms of the world, as he did to Christ . . . but rather all the property and land of the priests and promised to give them to you if you would publicly declare yourself supreme head of the church: you, who had hardly been the foot of the church before that!— and he succeeded. The rest he left to Sampson, to prove this by Scripture. For it is written—says Satan in the person of Sampson—"Honor the king." This was the theological position of Satan, who then placed you on the pinnacle of the Temple. (Sig. Vii^r)

This pasasage was central to Van Dyke's argument that Pole had not yet formed his views about Cromwell's Machiavellian temptation of Henry at the time of the writing of the *De Unitate*, for it was "psychologically very hard"[24] to believe that Pole could fail to mention Cromwell here if indeed he considered him the main tempter. But this begs the larger question of the role of Sampson in the book: he was not Henry's closest adviser, nor was his book the most significant of the attempts to defend Henry VIII's supremacy. Christopher St. Germain, Edward Fox, and Stephen Gardiner had all written on the subject as well;[25] yet Sampson is singled out by Pole, and much of the *De Unitate* is devoted to refuting him. It is inconceivable that Pole knew so little about Henry's government that he thought Sampson a more important influence than Cromwell. Yet Cromwell is never mentioned. Sampson's book bears no date, but cannot be earlier than 1534, for the Privy Council commissioned it in December 1553.[26] Sampson plays the role of scapegoat in the treatise: if Henry should incline to repentance, Pole's focus on Sampson makes saving face easier, for he was not close to the center of things, and those closer are spared mention. The passage itself does not, on careful reading, give Sampson the leading role either. First, there are *other* instruments of Satan. Second, Sampson, or these others, may have spoken something in Henry VIII's ear that never got on paper. Here Van Dyke mistranslates "An vero aliquid latet, quod Sampson et reliqua Sathanae instrumenta tibi in aurem dixerunt, quod literis noluerunt mandare" as "Is anything hidden which Sampson and the other instruments of Satan said in thy ears, *since they have been willing to commit it to writing*,"[27] implying that here Pole tells all he knows of the matter, but in fact the underlined portion asks whether there remains anything they *did not* write down, which anticipates a positive answer, and, in the portion of the text that follows, not cited by Van Dyke, gets that positive answer: something *does* remain hidden ("how Satan took you up upon a high mountain . . ."). The temptation itself is hidden. It becomes still harder to doubt that Pole is hinting at knowledge he had but chose not to reveal here when one compares this passage with the description of Cromwell's plan for religious "autonomy" in the *Apologia:*

> And with this speech, as upon the pinnacle of the Temple, or upon the highest mountain, he lifted him, whence he might behold all things subjected to the ecclesiastical power—all the monasteries of the king- dom, which were numerous and very rich, and all the bishoprics, then the entire patrimony of the Church, and added: "All this is yours if you will call yourself what you are in fact: the head of the Church." (P. 121)

It is this—the role of Cromwell, and through Cromwell of Machiavelli, in the formation of Henry VIII's religious policies—that remains hidden, though amply hinted at.

The entire position of the *Apologia*—Henry's presumption to divine hon- ors by virtue of his moral relativism, contempt for law, and usurpation of papal prerogatives, and his threat to Christian unity—is implicit in the *De Unitate;* but the explicit identification with Antichrist is not made, and the role of Cromwell and Machiavelli is not mentioned directly. It was only when the attempt to bring Henry to repentance had failed, and Pole's role as prophet therefore shifted from Isaiah's call to repentance to Moses' call for Holy war, that the whole story was told, and even then only in a work whose publishing history testifies to continuing reticence and reserve on the part of its author.

There is no doubt that there was something in Pole's personality that drove him to these complexities of revelation and reserve, that his stance as concealer and revealer of his king's secrets was one that had roots in his profound and troubling ambivalence toward the king who had stirred his anger as well as his gratitude since childhood. But the energies of this personal conflict took on archetypal significance for Pole at the time of his crisis or "conversion." He began to see himself as in some sense a prophet, and to relate his own spiritual struggle and the events of his time to the complex model of prophetic history. In the "historicist" typology Pole adopted, the prophet, like the historical process itself, reveals part of the truth, and conceals the rest or expresses it cryptically. Indeed, though Pole longed for full disclosure, for the trumpet voice of Isaiah, he knew that the prophets themselves had "bound up the testimony," that their public role had often been ambiguous, the full import of their message being reserved for future revelation, when the times would be ripe. Indeed, the entire typological tradition of exegesis, whether historicist or not, was based upon the notion that no prophet spoke only to contemporaries or could be fully understood by them, for the full significance of prophecy lay in its anticipations of Christ's life and doctrine and beyond that in its relation to the events of the Last Days. Then—in the radiance of the Second Coming and the revelation of the *mysterium iniquitatis*—all would be clear, but until then, that is to say while historical time continued, prophecy retained its mystery, and the reflection of biblical truth in current events continued to be a source not only of illumination, but of anguish as well.

This Cardinal Pole keenly felt, for though he firmly believed that he had been called by God to speak out against the English schism and the tyranny of Henry VIII, and had been entrusted with providentially revealed knowledge concerning the Machiavellian inspiration of these events, he received no revelation concerning when and how he should reveal what he knew, and he never solved the problem of the timing of his prophecy.

APPENDIX: PROPHECY AND FACT

Study of Pole's prophetic typology has suggested that the absence of Cromwell and Machiavelli in the *De Unitate* and their appearance in the *Apologia* are to be explained on the basis of Pole's conception of prophecy: he would reveal what he knew in stages, as Scripture did. This answers one of Van Dyke's objections to the historicity of Pole's story of his meeting with Cromwell, which he explained as resulting from Pole's reading back into the events of 1528 conclusions about the demonic character of Cromwell and Machiavelli he had only come to in 1538. As his analysis continues to be influential, it needs to be addressed in fuller detail here. In summary, Van Dyke argued that:[28]

1. Manuscripts of *The Prince* were scarce, so Cromwell was unlikely to have known Machiavelli at this early date. In 1539 Lord Henry Morley offered Cromwell a copy of the book as something as yet unknown to him.[29]

2. *The Prince* does not deal with the question of the responsibilities of councillors towards princes, as the book recommended to Pole by Cromwell did. Castiglione's *Courtier* does deal with that subject, and was available in 1528.

3. If Pole had thought Cromwell demonic from 1528, he would not have continued polite relations with him for another ten years, nor would he have failed to mention his Machiavellian temptation of Henry in the *De Unitate*, which was finished in 1536; therefore:

4. Pole had neither read Machiavelli nor come to the conclusion that Cromwell played the role of demonic tempter to Henry VIII until after 1536. Sometime after that, perhaps on a trip to Florence mentioned in the *Apologia*, Pole read *The Prince*, and at about the same time (1538) Cromwell began the persecution of Pole's family. These two factors made him re-

member a conversation he had had with Cromwell ten years earlier, and interpret it in the light of the wickedness he now perceived in Cromwell and in *The Prince.*

Van Dyke believed *some* book was actually offered to Pole by Cromwell: "The subject of the conversation and the offer to lend him the book are facts that would be apt to remain in a man's mind. There is not the smallest reason to accuse Pole of inventing them" (p. 400). But that book must have been *Il Corteggiano,* not *Il Principe.*

Manuscripts of *The Prince* were in fact plentiful, however,[30] and Cromwell had lived in Florence, where the chances of hearing of this writer and acquiring a copy of his as yet unpublished work must have been better than in most other places. Besides, Lord Morley's letter does not show that Cromwell did not know Machiavelli, but only that Morley supposed he did not:

> This Boke off Machiavelle de Principe ys surely a very speciall good thing for youre Lordschip which are so ny abought oure Soveraigne Lorde in Counsell to loke upon for many causys, as I suppose youre self schall judge when ye have sene the same. (Henry Ellis, *Original Letters,* ser. 3, 3:66)

Morley certainly assumes that Cromwell will like the book when he does see it.

The Courtier is a mild book in comparison with *The Prince,* and there are no parallels in its publication history with the surreptitious treatment Cromwell gives the book he offers Pole. But *The Prince* was, from the start, thought of as something to be kept secret or handled with caution. Bernardo Giunta, publisher of the 1532 edition (this was the second edition of *The Prince,* appearing several months after the Blado edition of the same year)[31] expected trouble, and tried to ward it off in a defensive preface.[31] The contents were plagiarized, translated into Latin, and published with a careful palinode by Agostino Nifo even before the book itself was printed (*De regnandi peritia,* 1523),[32] and the history of its influence in the sixteenth century and after offers many examples of the kind of surreptitious transmission Pole tells of:[33] it was a shocking book, and one that seemed to reveal secrets of getting and keeping power. Cromwell's treatment of it— keeping it secret but making it the basis of advice to the king—is analogous to William Thomas's use of Machiavelli in his letters of political advice to Edward VI and to Stephen Gardiner's borrowings from it in his *Ragionamento,* which was intended to help Philip II retain power in England.[34] It is easy to see why Cromwell would not want to send it when he found Pole shocked by its ideas; why would anyone need to keep *The Courtier* secret?

The Courtier is, as Van Dyke said, more explicitly a book of advice *for councillors,* whereas *The Prince* addresses a prince. But this is an insignificant difference. As the Morley letter shows, in company with innumerable other examples, a book that tells a prince how to rule is also profitable for councillors to read: "a very speciall good thing for youre Lordschip which are so ny abought oure Soveraigne Lorde in Counsell to loke upon. . . ." In addition, Pole's memory of Cromwell's speech about the book includes a paraphrase of *Prince,* chapter 15, which contrasts the practical truths of experience *(verità effettuale)* with imaginary republics such as the republic of Plato. There is nothing like this in *The Courtier,* which is in fact a work in the Platonic tradition. Pole might have put the words in Cromwell's mouth later, but there can be no question that the description as we have it fits *The Prince* and does not fit *The Courtier.*

Van Dyke is right that Pole's assessment of Cromwell underwent drastic revision, and that Cromwell did not have in 1528 the mythic significance he was later to acquire. But Pole's crisis of obedience, and its resolution in biblical terms may be taken as the catalyst that deepened the archetypal significance of Thomas Cromwell, as it did for all events and persons, in Pole's mind. It was in 1535, when Pole was studying Scripture, and finding in it a key to his own experience, that Henry's descent into evil took on the apocalyptic character it has in the *Apologia.* Cromwell's role in this is not mentioned in the 1536 *De Unitate,* nor is *The Prince* identified with the *mysterium iniquitatis* of Antichrist. But Pole still hoped Henry would reform, and therefore adopts the rhetorical strategy of blaming as much as he can on Richard Sampson while at the same time making it clear that there were "other instruments of Satan" and affirming that the exact manner of Satan's temptation "remains hidden."

If one agrees with Van Dyke that Cromwell offered some book to Pole at that meeting in 1528, it is unreasonable to suppose that that book, whose identity Pole claims to have checked with Cromwell's associates, was anything other than Machiavelli's *Prince.* That does not mean, however, that Machiavelli's ideas were the inspiration for the Supremacy, much less for the Henrician Reformation as a whole. Reading Machiavelli may have strengthened Cromwell's resolve to find both solutions to church and state relations; *The Prince* may be subtly present in the vigor and freedom from tradition of Cromwell's intellectual style; Machiavelli, who had a profound respect for law despite Pole's view to the contrary, may even have influenced Cromwell's persistent use of legislation to effect his reforms. But there were far more immediate influences on Cromwell: Marsiglio of Padua and conciliar theory, for example, and these, not the works of Machiavelli, can be shown to have directly influenced the legislation and official propaganda of the Cromwellian state.[35] The restoration to credibility of Pole's story about Cromwell suggests that Machiavelli was a genuine intellectual presence at Henry's court, and therefore helps correct, as much recent research has done,[36] the once common view the Machiavelli was unknown except by reputation in early Tudor England. But it does not permit us to connect him with any specific course of action or policy.

As to the spirit in which Cromwell recommended the book to Pole, A. G. Dickens, who must not be taken to share the view of the present author that the book in question actually was *The Prince*, has written best:

> Concerning its broad tenor one need not feel totally skeptical, since it is easy to believe that Cromwell, in a characteristic mood of sardonic worldly wisdom, was guilty of baiting the young humanist.[37]

Indeed, we may be reasonably certain that Cromwell's view of *The Prince* was more worldly, and less apocalyptic than that of Reginald Pole. Pole's attempt to come to terms with this radically secular thinking, in combination with other elements of the personal and religious crisis he experienced in 1535, led him to a prophetic, almost dualistic vision of the history of his own time, as he came to see Henry VIII as a precursor of Antichrist and the Machiavellian texts as expressions of the *mysterium iniquitatis*. He met Machiavelli's challenge by reasserting sacred archetypes with new vigor, commitment, and literal-mindedness. But for Cromwell the sacred and the secular realms were not uncompromisingly at odds. If this essay has made it easier to believe that Cromwell offered Pole a copy of *The Prince*, it remains impossible to see in this gesture the apocalyptic significance Pole attributed to it, or to think that Cromwell, even if he accepted Machiavelli's hard teachings about the need to decline from virtue when politics demanded it, ever thought of himself as a satanic tempter.

NOTES

1. The *Apologia* is printed in Angelo M. Quirini, ed., *Epistolarum Reginaldi Poli S.R.E. Cardinalis et aliorum ad ipsum collectio* (Brescia, 1744–57), 3:66–171. Translations from this work and from the *De Unitate* are my own.

2. Albert F. Pollard, *Henry VIII* (London, 1905; reprint ed. 1951), 353; Paul Van Dyke, *Renascence Portraits* (New York, 1905), 377–418; Geoffrey R. Elton, *Tudor Revolution in Government* (Cambridge, 1953), 66ff., 125; "The Political Creed of Thomas Cromwell," *Royal Historical Society Transactions*, ser. 5, 6 (1956): 69–92. See also T. M. Parker, "Was Thomas Cromwell a Machiavellian?" *Journal of Ecclesiastical History* 1 (1950): 63–75.

3. My account is based partly on Wilhelm Schenck, *Reginald Pole: Cardinal of England* (London, 1950), 1–86, and Dermot Fenlon, *Heresy and Obedience in Tridentine Italy: Cardinal Pole and the Counter Reformation* (Cambridge, 1972) 24–44, and partly anticipates the analysis of Pole's use of prophecy made later in this paper. The view taken here of the psychological roots of Pole's crisis is my own.

4. References to the *De Unitate* are to the Blado edition (1539), *Reginaldi Poli Cardinalis Britanni, ad Henricum octavum Britanniae regem, pro ecclesiasticae unitatis defensione, libri quatuor*. For the date of this edition, an account of its differences from the P.R.O. MS sent to Henry, and arguments concerning the need for a critical edition, see Thomas F. Dunn, "The Development of the Text of Pole's *De Unitate Ecclesiae*," *Papers of the Bibliographical Society of America* 70 (1976); 455–68.

5. On Pole's style see Noëlle-Marie Egretier, ed., *Défense de l'unité de l'Eglise* (Paris, 1967), pp. 36–41 and refs., but see also Dunn, "The Development of the Text," 464–67.

6. Fenlon, *Heresy*, p. 36, citing a letter of John Friar to Thomas Starkey, in J. S. Brewer, James Gairdner, R. H. Brodie, eds., *Letters and Papers, Foreign and Domestic, of the Reign of Henry VIII* (London, 1862–1910), vol. 9 (no.917). This collection will be cited hereafter as *L.P.*

7. Fenlon, *Heresy*, 30–31.

8. Paul Van Dyke, *Renascence Portraits*, 387–88.

9. Adolph Gerber, *Niccolò Machiavelli: Die Handschriften, Ausgaben and Ubersetzungen seiner Werke im 16. und 17. Jahrhundert* (Gotha, 1912–13, reprint ed. Turin 1962), 2:4.

10. Letter of John Legh to Privy Council, *L.P.*, 15:337 (no.721); Hieronymus osorius, *De nobilitate civili, libri duo* (Lisbon, 1542), 98ff.; Letter of Pole to Catherine Pole, Bodleian Library MSS Carte 78, fo. 251ʳ; Ambrosius Catharinus [Lancelot Politi], *De libris christiano detestandis, et a christianismo penitus eliminandis* [printed as coll. 339–44 of the *Disputationes* appended to the author's *Enararationes in quinque priora capita libri Geneseos* (Rome, 1551–52). Franz Heinrich Reusch, *Die Indices librorum prohibitorum des sechzehnten Jahrhunderts* (Tübingen, 1886, reprint ed. Nieuwkoop, 1970), 198.

11. Anna Maria Battista, "Direzioni di ricerca per una storia di Machiavelli in Francia," *Atti del convegno internazionale su il pensiero politico di Machiavelli e la sua fortuna nel mondo* (Florence: Istituto nazionale di studi sul Rinascimento, 1972), 63n.; Hermann Hegels, *Arnold Clapmarius und die Publizistik über die arcana imperii im 17. Jahrhundert* (Bonn, 1918), 49.

12. The notion of Machiavelli as a hater of tyranny who wrote with the secret intention of harming the Medici is also found in Giovanni Matteo Toscano, *Peplus Italiae* (Paris, 1578), 52, in Alberico Gentili's *De legationibus libri tres* (London, 1585).

13. Katherine R. Firth, *The Apocalyptic Tradition in Reformation Britain 1530–1645* (Oxford, 1979), 7.

14. Firth, *The Apocalyptic Tradition;* Lloyd Patterson, *God and History in Early Christian Thought* (London, 1967); Richard Bauckham, *Tudor Apocalypse* (Abingdon, 1978). For fuller discussion of the terminology employed in this paragraph and its application to the sixteenth century, see especially Bauckham's introduction and chap. 1 ("The Medieval Heritage").

15. See esp. Marjorie Reeves, *The Influence of Prophecy in the Later Middle Ages: A Study in Joachimism* (Oxford, 1969).

16. Antonio D'Andrea, "Machiavelli, Satan, and the Gospel," *Yearbook of Italian Studies* 1: (1971): 156–77, citing Innocent Gentillet, *Commentariorum de regno . . . adversus Nicolaum Machiavellum Florentinum* (Geneva, 1578), pref.

17. Bauckham, *Tudor Apocalypse,* chap. 5 ("The Antichrist").

18. Geoffrey R. Elton, *Reform and Reformation: England 1509–1558* (Cambridge, Mass., 1977) 136–37.

19. Edward Fox, *De vera differentia regiae potestatis et ecclesiasticae* (London, 1534); Richard Sampson, *Oratio; qua docet hortatur admonet omnes potissimum Anglos, regiae dignitati cum primis ut obediant . . .* (London, n.d.), cited as *Oratio de dignitate et potestate regia;* Stephen Gardiner, *De Vera Obedientia* (London, 1535), also printed in Pierre Janelle, ed., *Obedience in Church and State: Three Political Tracts by Stephen Gardiner* (Cambridge, 1930).

20. Cf. Dunn, "The Development of the Text," 460–62; Egretier, *Defense,* 24–25.

21. *L.P.*, 12 (1): 213 (no. 444). Cf. Latin version printed in *Epistolae*, 1:179–85: "Ad eum certe solum misi; quocum ita egi, ut nemo umquam a confessionibus illi secretior esse potuisset" (p. 181). Pole also says that love for the king and respect for his honor kept him from publishing (p. 182).

22. *Epistolae,* 4:340; *Pro ecclesiasticae unitatis defensio,* ed. Pier Paolo Vergerio (Strasbourg, 1555); *Epistolae,* 3:39.

23. The call to repentance and the example of David (as well as that of Solomon) appear also in the "instructions" Pole sent to Henry with the treatise. These are calendared in *L.P.* 10:403 (no. 974) and printed in Gilbert Burnet, *The History of the Reformation of the Church of*

England (Oxford, 1865), 6:172–76, from British Library MS Cotton (Cleopatra) E₆, fol. 334. Indeed, these instructions bear out the hypothesis of a conditional intention to publish: e.g., "my full purpose and mind was, touching the whole book that never no part thereof should a come abroad in any man's hands, afore his grace had seen it" (p. 174); Pole's recollection of these instructions in *Apologia* (p. 75) was that he had written to the king that he would suppress the book *(librum hunc me suppressurum)* while any hope of reform remained.

24. Van Dyke, *Renascence Portraits*, 411.

25. Christopher St. Germain, *A Treatise concernynge the division betwene the spiritualtie and temporaltie* (London, 1532?); and see n. 19 above.

26. Egretier, *Defense*, 22, citing British Library MS Cotton (Cleopatra) E₆, fol. 317.

27. Van Dyke, *Renascence Portraits*, 411.

28. Van Dyke, *Renascence Portraits*, 377–418.

29. Van Dyke, *Renascence Portraits*, 413–14. Text printed in Henry Ellis, *Original Letters illustrative of English History*, ser. 3, 3 (London, 1846): 63–67 (no. 278).

30. Adolph Gerber, *Handschriften*, 1:82–97; Pasquale Villari, *Niccolò Machiavelli e i suoi tempi* (Florence, 1877–82), 2:405–8; William Gordon Zeeveld, *Foundations of Tudor Policy* (Cambridge, Mass., 1948), 77n., cites unpublished work of Garrett Mattingly showing that in the 1520s at least three Italian booksellers employed professional copyists to produce copies of the book.

31. Niccolò Machiavelli, *Il Principe* (Florence, 1532), prefatory letter of Bernardo Giunta to Giovanni Gaddi.

32. Agostino Nifo, *De regnandi peritia* (Naples, 1523).

33. Felix Raab, *The English Face of Machiavelli* (London, 1964), 40–48. Peter S. Donaldson, ed., *A Machiavellian Treatise by Stephen Gardiner* (Cambridge, 1975); G. M. Bertini, "La fortuna di Machiavelli in Spagna," *Quaderni ibero-americani* 2 (1947): 9, 21–22, 25–26, discovered a proposal for an expurgated edition of Machiavelli's works, translated into Spanish and with the name of the author changed, made to the Inquisition by the Duke of Sessa's secretary in 1584; Dennis B. Woodfield's 1964 Oxford diss., "Books surreptitiously printed in England before 1640 in Contemporary Foreign Languages," deals at length with the London editions of Machiavelli's works published by John Wolfe under false imprint, 1584–88.

34. Raab, *The English Face of Machiavelli*, 40–48; Donaldson, *A Machiavellian Treatise* 1–39.

35. Elton, "The Political Creed of Thomas Cromwell"; Graham D. Nicholson, "The Nature and Function of Historical Argument in the Henrician Reformation," Ph.D. diss., Cambridge, 1977.

36. Raab, *The English Face of Machiavelli*; Donaldson, *A Machiavellian Treatise*, introduction; "Bishop Gardiner, Machiavellian," *Historical Journal* 23, no. 1 (1980), 1–16; Christopher Morris, "Machiavelli's Reputation in Tudor England," *Machiavellismo e antimachiavellici nel cinquecento: Atti del Convegno di Perugia 30-IX-1-X, 1969* (Florence, 1970), 88–105. David S. Berkowitz's work on Richard Morison, *Humanist Scholarship and Public Order* (Washington, D.C., and London, 1984), adds to the evidence now available.

37. A. G. Dickens, *Thomas Cromwell and the English Reformation* (London, 1959), 77.

BIBLIOGRAPHICAL ESSAY

Pole's Works

Pole's first published work was the *Vita Longolii,* a life of the humanist Christopher Longolius (or Longueil), appended to an edition of Longolius's letters and orations (*Orationes duae . . . Longolii vita* [Florence,

1524]). In "Did Pole write the *Vita Longolii?*", *Renaissance Quarterly* 26 (1973): 274–85, George B. Parks argues that this work was revised by a hand other than Pole's. The *"De Unitate"* (this is the commonly used title for *Reginaldi Poli Cardinalis Britanni, ad Henricum octavum Britanniae regem, pro ecclesiasticae unitatis defensione*) first appeared in print in Rome, probably in 1539. The relation between the printed text and the manuscripts is discussed in an important and on the whole convincing article by Thomas F. Dunn: "The Development of the Text of Pole's *De Unitate Ecclesiae," Papers of the Bibliographical Society of America* 70 (1976): 455–68. Dunn argues that the printed editions derive from the Vatican MS, which had been corrected and rewritten by someone else, probably Daniel the Penitentiary. None of the changes thus introduced were "alterations or modifications of the content of *Ven.*" (Dunn, p. 467), so that the printed text can be taken as an accurate reflection of Pole's meaning, though the need for a critical edition based upon the Venetian manuscript is clear. The Public Record Office (London) MS was the one actually sent to Henry VIII, and is an authorial revision of the Venetian MS, omitting the passages accusing Henry of having had relations with Mary Boleyn and attacking him for weakening the succession. Other editions of the *De Unitate* appeared at Strasbourg, 1555, ed. Pier Paolo Vergerio, and Ingolstadt, 1587. There is an English translation by Joseph G. Dwyer, *Pole's Defense of the Unity of the Church* (Westminster, Md., 1965). Some errors in this translation are noted in a generally favorable review by Germain M. Marc'hadour, *Moreana* (May 1967), 99–102. A French translation by Noëlle-Marie Egretier, *Défense de l'unité de l'Église* (Paris, 1967) includes a useful introduction. The *Apologia ad Carolum V Caesarem*, written in 1539 as a preface to the *De Unitate*, is printed in *Epistolarum Reginaldi Poli S.R.E. Cardinalis et aliorum ad ipsum collectio*, ed. Angelo M. Quirini (Brescia, 1744–57), 1:66–171. This five-volume collection contains not only letters to and from Pole, but also several of Pole's shorter works and prefaces, and Beccadelli's life of Pole (to be discussed in the next section of this essay). Though his exact role in the writing of the document cannot be ascertained, Pole was one of the ten clerics (others were Cardinals Carafa, Sadoleto, and Contarini) who prepared the *Consilium delectorum Cardinalium . . . de emendanda ecclesia Romana, jussu Pauli III Papae conscriptum* (London, 1609), which is also printed in *Concilium Tridentinum: diariorum, actorum, epistolarum, tractatuum nova collectio*, ed. S. Merkle (Freiburg im Bresgau, 1901–), 12:131–45. This report, commisioned in 1536, recommended wide-ranging, nondoctrinal changes in church governance. Several of Pole's works were occasioned by the Council of Trent, in the early sessions of which he took part. The *De concilio liber* (Rome, 1562) was composed in 1545, before the opening of the Council in December. It is partly a treatise on the authority and responsibilities of general councils, partly an exhortation to penitence addressed to the participants in the Council, and partly an attempt to reconcile his own views concerning the role of faith in justification with the requirements of Christian unity. At the Council itself, Pole delivered the *Admonitio atque hortatio legatorum sedis apostolicae ad patres in Concilio Tridentino*, printed in Cracow, 1546, and in *Concilium Tridentinum*, 4:548–53. *A Treatie of Justification Founde emong the writinges of Cardinal Pole of blessed memorie* (Louvain, 1569) is a statement and explanation of the Council's decree on justification, although its authenticity has been questioned; see Wilhelm Schenk, *Reginald Pole* (London, 1950), p. 122. Other works of Pole include a treatise on the authority of the Pope, *De summo pontifice* (Louvain, 1569); the *Discorso di pace* addressed to Charles V and Henry II in 1555, published in Rome, probably in the same year and reprinted in *Epistolae*, 4:402–27, and the *Reformatio Angliae*, printed with the *De concilio* in 1562, and in *Epistolae*, 5:230–33. The Gregg Press (Farnborough, Hants) has issued a number of Pole's works in facsimile editions (*De concilio* and *Reformatio Angliae*, 1962; *De Unitate*, 1965; *Epistolae*, 1967; *A Treatie of Justification*, 1967; *Vita Longolii*, 1967; *De summo pontifice*, 1968.)

Pole's Life

There is a wealth of information concerning Pole's life in the *Letters and Papers, Foreign and Domestic, of the Reign of Henry VIII*, ed. J. S. Brewer, James Gairdner, R. H. Brodie (London, 1862–1910), 21 vols. Letters of Pole written during the reign of Henry VIII are calendared in this work. For Pole's role at Trent, the *Concilium Tridentinum: diariorum actorum, epistolarum, tractatuum nova collectio*, ed. S. Merkle (Freiburg im Bresgau, 1901–), prints relevant documents. For other primary sources, printed and manuscript, see Dermot B. Fenlon, *Heresy and Obedience in Tridentine Italy: Cardinal Pole and the Counter Reformation* (Cambridge, 1972) and the bibliography and note on sources appended to Wilhelm Schenk, *Reginald Pole: Cardinal of England* (London, 1950). Fenlon and Schenk are both essential reading for any student of Reginald Pole; Schenk's is the standard biography. It is too brief a treatment, however, so that one often needs to supplement Schenk with one of the older biographies (Thomas Phillips, *The History of the Life of Cardinal Pole* [Oxford, 1764]; Athanasius Zimmerman, *Kardinal Pole, sein Leben und seine Schriften* [Regensburg, 1893]; Martin Haile, *The Life of Reginald Pole* [2d ed., London, 1911]). Fenlon's book is a masterly study of Pole and his circle, of the intellectual and spiritual influences that shaped their distinctive and precarious blend of obedience to Rome and "faith alone" theology, and of the effect on this group of the Council of Trent. There is much excellent discussion of Pole's own role at Trent in Hubert Jedin's *Geschichte des Konzils von Trient* (Freiburg im Bresgau, vols. 1 and 2, 1957; vol. 3, 1970. English translations of vols. 1 and 2 were prepared by Ernest Graf: *A History of the Council of Trent* (Edinburgh, 1957, 1961). F. A. Gasquet's *Cardinal Pole and his Early Friends* (London,

1927) is still useful for the early part of Pole's life, and Rex Harley Pogson's Ph.D. diss., "Cardinal Pole: Papal Legate to England in Mary Tudor's Reign" (Cambridge University, 1972), sheds light on the work of Pole's late years (1554–58). James Gairdner's entry on Pole in the *Dictionary of National Biography*, ed. Leslie Stephen and Sidney Lee (London, 1949–50), provides a convenient and almost wholly accurate overview of the life. The work of Lodovico Beccadelli, Pole's secretary and first biographer, appeared in Italian: *Vita del Cardinale Polo, inglese* (Venice, 1560; also printed in *Epistolae*, 5:355–91) and a Latin version, *Vita Reginaldi Poli, britanni, S.R.E. Cardinalis et Cantuarensis archiepiscopi*, was published at Venice in 1563. Another associate of Pole's, Thomas Starkey, composed *A Dialogue between Reginald Pole and Thomas Lupset*, printed as part 2 of *England in the Reign of Henry VIII*, ed. E. Herrtage (London, 1878), and also available in an edition by K. M. Burton (London, 1948). Starkey knew Pole well, but had badly misjudged the depth of his break with Henry in the period during which the *De Unitate* was composed and Pole had lost favor with the king when his predictions turned out wrong. It remains difficult to assess the value of the *Dialogue*, but the opinions "Pole" expresses in it are often consistent with what we know from other sources, and, used with caution, it rounds out the picture of Pole as a political thinker.

Apocalyptic and Machiavellian Influences in Tudor England

There is a rich literature on the subject of postbiblical prophetic and apocalyptic thought. Essential general works include Norman Cohn, *The Pursuit of the Millennium*, 2d ed. (New York, 1961), LeRoy Froom, *The Prophetic Faith of Our Fathers* (Washington, D.C., 1946–54), 4 vols., and Sylvia Thrupp's collection of articles *Millennial Dreams in Action* (The Hague, 1962). Lloyd Patterson's *God and History in Early Christian Thought* (London, 1967) argues that the historicist variety of apocalyptic fell into disuse after Augustine, while the work of Marjorie Reeves, *The Influence of Prophecy in the Later Middle Ages: A Study in Joachimism* (Oxford, 1969) discovers a varied and powerful reemergence of historicist apocalyptic in a later period. Of special interest is her *Joachim of Fiore and the Prophetic Future* (London, 1976; reprint ed. New York, 1977), particularly chaps. 4–6 ("Joachimist Expectation in the Renaissance Period"; "Joachim and the Catholic Visionaries"; "Joachim and Protestantism"). The literature on prophecy in the English seventeenth century is copious: here I shall mention only Bryan Ball, *A Great Expectation: Eschatological Thought in English Protestantism to 1660* (Leiden, 1975) and Paul Christianson, *Reformers and Babylon: English Apocalyptic Visions from the Reformation to the Eve of the Civil War* (Toronto, 1978), because though their focus is the later period, they deal substantially with the sixteenth century as well, and because their bibliographies will guide students to the seventeenth-century materials;

and Christopher Hill, *Antichrist in Seventeenth Century England* (Oxford, 1971), who traces the later form of the Antichrist legend, central to the present study. On the general history of the Antichrist theme see Wilhelm Bousset, *The Antichrist Legend: A Chapter in Christian and Jewish Folklore*, trans. A. H. Keane (n.p., 1896). All applications of Scripture to current events imply principles or habits of biblical exegesis, and the collection of essays by Olivier Fatio and Pierre Fraenkel, *Histoire de l'exégèse au XVIe siècle* (Geneva, 1978) provides (though its scope is actually far short of its title) an apposite introduction to the wide variety in sixteenth-century hermeneutics. James Samuel Preus's *From Shadow to Promise: Old Testament Interpretation from Augustine to the Young Luther* (Cambridge, Mass., 1969) argues that medieval principles of typology were a more powerful influence on Luther than hitherto recognized. On medieval exegesis generally, the researches of Henri de Lubac, *Exégèse medievale: les quatre sens de l'Écriture* (Paris, 1959–64), unwieldy though they are, remain essential. The books of Richard Bauckham, *Tudor Apocalypse* (Abingdon, 1978), and Katherine Firth, *The Apocalyptic Tradition in Reformation Britain 1530–1645* (Oxford, 1979), treat apocalyptic in Tudor England in more depth and detail than anything that went before. The focus of both studies is Protestant apocalyptic, and both argue for a special link between Protestantism and historicist modes of exegesis.

The study of Machiavelli's influence in England remains deeply indebted to (and sometimes distorted by) the labors of the late nineteenth and early twentieth centuries. Pasquale Villari's *Niccolò Machiavelli e i suoi tempi* (Florence, 1877–82), 4 vols., contains extended discussion of Machiavelli's followers and critics. This material is usefully summarized and added to by L. Arthur Burd in his edition of *Il Principe* (Oxford, 1891; reprint ed. 1968), introduction, pt. 3, "Early Criticism of *The Prince* before the Publication of Christ's Book," pp. 31–69. In 1897 a decisive and still influential error was given wide currency by Edward Meyer, whose *Machiavelli and The Elizabethan Drama* (Weimar) advanced the view that Elizabethans knew Machiavelli only in Innocent Gentillet's distorting summaries. Antonio D'Andrea showed, in 1971 ("Machiavelli, Satan and the Gospel," *Yearbook of Italian Studies* 1:156–77), that the English version of Gentillet, on which Meyer rested much of his case, was not itself in circulation until the early years of the seventeenth century. Long before D'Andrea, however, evidence had been steadily accumulating indicating fuller knowledge of Machiavelli's work in Tudor England. Adolph Gerber's important article "All of the Five Fictitious Italian Editions of Writings of Machiavelli and Three of those of Pietro Aretino Printed by John Wolfe of London (1584–1588)," *Modern Language Notes* 22 (1907): 2–6, 129–35, 201–6, showed that Machiavelli's principal works were available in London in the 1580s, and Gerber's masterpiece of scholarship, *Niccolò Machiavelli: Die Handschriften, Ausgaben und Übersetzungen seiner Werke im. 16. und 17. Jahrhundert* (Gotha,

1912–13; reprint ed. Turin, 1962) testified to the variety of ways in which Englishmen might have come to Machiavelli. John Wesley Horrocks's London D.Lit. diss. of 1908, "Machiavelli in Tudor Opinion and Discussion," provides copious evidence of the serious discussion of Machiavelli in the period and has been of great use to later scholars. Felix Raab's *The English Face of Machiavelli* (London, 1964) is, perhaps, the most useful introduction to English Machiavellism, though its earlier chapters depend heavily, without giving proper credit, upon Horrocks, as shown by Sidney Anglo in "The Reception of Machiavelli in Tudor England," *Il Politico* 33 (1966): 127–38. As Raab's book appeared posthumously, however, too much ought not to be made of its oversights. The work of N. W. Bawcutt, "Some Elizabethan Allusions to Machiavelli," *English Miscellany* 20 (1969): 53–74, continues Horrocks's labors. Émile Gasquet's *Le Courant machiavelien dans la pensée et la littérature anglaises du XVIe siècle* (Lille, 1971) is a large volume, and sums up research to that point. Christopher Morris's excellent article "Machiavelli's Reputation in Tudor England" in *Machiavellismo e antimachiavellici nel cinquecento: Atti del Convegno di Perugia, 30-1X—1 X 1969* (Florence, 1970), 88–105, is original and stimulating, and ought to be widely read. My own edition of Stephen Gardiner's dialogue on English history and politics, *A Machiavellian Treatise by Stephen Gardiner* (Cambridge, 1975), and "Bishop Gardiner, Machiavellian," *Historical Journal* 23 (1980): 1–16, offer evidence that Gardiner had, by the mid 1550s, made a very full study of Machiavelli and had applied what he learned to the questions of how Philip of Spain might best rule England as Mary Tudor's consort or heir.

On the more specific question of Machiavelli's influence at Henry VIII's court, Paul Van Dyke wrote at length on the difficulties Pole's account of the matter presents (*Renascence Portraits* [New York, 1905; reprint ed. 1951]). His strictures were not accepted by T. M. Parker, "Was Thomas Cromwell a Machiavellian?", *Journal of Ecclesiastical History* 1 (1950): 63–75, or by William Gordon Zeeveld, *Foundations of Tudor Policy* (Cambridge, Mass., 1948). Geoffrey R. Elton's *Tudor Revolution in Government* (Cambridge, 1953) and "The Political Creed of Thomas Cromwell," *Royal Historical Society Transactions*, ser. 5, 6 (1956): 69–92, while immensely extending our knowledge of the relationship between ideas and policies in the Henrician period, follow Van Dyke somewhat too closely in the matter of Pole's credibility. The pages of these works that deal with Pole's *Apologia* should be read in conjunction with Elton's later views in *Reform and Reformation: England 1509–1558* (Cambridge, Mass., 1977). David S. Berkowitz's *Humanist Scholarship and Public Order. Two Treatises by Richard Morison against the Pilgrimage of Grace* (Washington, D.C.: Folger Shakespeare Library, 1983) contains valuable information on Morrison's debt to Machiavelli.

On continental "Machiavellism," the literature is too vast to be encompassed here. Villari and Gerber have been already mentioned; Friedrich

Meinecke's *Machiavellism* (London, 1957; trans. D. Scott of *Die Idee der Staatsräson in der neueren Geschichte*) is indispensable and exciting, though later work has not always confirmed his insights. Rodolfo De Mattei's researches in the field were published over a fifteen-year period (1949–64) in the *Rivista Internazionale de Filosofia del Diritto* and in his *Dal premachiavellismo all'antimachiavellismo* (Florence, 1969). Giuliano Procacci explored many new and hitherto-unexplored connections between Machiavelli and other currents of thought in *Studi sulla fortuna del Machiavelli* (Rome, 1965). John G. A. Pocock's *Machiavellian Moment* (Princeton, N.J., 1975) traces the influence of Machiavelli on republican political theory, English and American.

9

Family, Faith, and *Fortuna:*
The Châtillon Brothers in the French Reformation

NANCY LYMAN ROELKER

In a magisterial essay, "France: the Holy Land, the Chosen People and the Most Christian King," Joseph R. Strayer analyzes the mystique of the monarchy and people in the high Middle Ages.[1] It was based on a chain of historical facts: from the leadership of Western Christianity by the bishops of Roman Gaul after the fall of North Africa to the Vandals, through the conversion of Clovis to Roman Catholicism when other barbarian conquerors were Arians, to the Carolingian protection of the papal states ca. A.D. 750, a centuries-long cooperation between the papacy and the French kings had evolved. Moreover, medieval French society was permeated with Roman Catholicism at every level; the peasants regulated their lives by the church calendar and the cathedral school of Notre Dame grew into the University of Paris and became the recognized guardian of orthodoxy for generations. Despite endemic anti-clericalism and a series of spectacular heresies, the linkage of French identity with the Roman Church persisted and movements perceived as foreign found few supporters and many articulate opponents. In the late Middle Ages, ecclesiastical nationalism was codified as "the Liberties of the Gallican Church," by which it was understood that, except in strictly doctrinal matters, the French Church was autonomous. Administrative control was in France and not in Rome; some thought in the hands of French bishops (ecclesiastical Gallicanism); others in those of the king (royal Gallicanism). The prereformers of the early sixteenth century suffered, under the label *luthériens,* charges of following a foreign doctrine, and even the Catholic revival at the end of the century was not generally accepted until formulated by Frenchmen.

Under these circumstances, reaction to the ideas of John Calvin was inevitably ambivalent. While he had a quintessentially French mind—logical, analytical, classifying—and while all of his associates were also French, he had been forced to flee the country and was operating from foreign soil, in Geneva. From the outset his goal was the conversion of his native land, whose nationalist, royalist, and xenophobic character he thoroughly understood. During the lifetime of Henri II, who boasted that he would exterminate heresy, there was no chance of influencing the royal family. His death in 1559, leaving weak heirs and a widow prey to rival factions, which revived the prestige of the Princes of the Blood, seemed to give Calvin his chance. Indeed, Louis de Bourbon, Prince de Condé, had already visited Geneva and seemed open to suggestion, but his older brother, Antoine de Bourbon, King of Navarre, was the prime target. Antoine later repudiated the reform, but his death left his son Henri de Navarre as First Prince of the Blood, and he was being brought up by his uncompromisingly Calvinist mother, Jeanne d'Albret. Yet Henri was still a child (nine years old at his father's death) and there were three Valois sons younger than François II, who had succeeded Henri II. The Queen-Mother, Catherine de Medici, would flirt with the reform for political reasons, but no more. The Protestant cause might have been lost in advance had not *Fortuna*—Calvin would say Divine Providence—brought to its aid the three Châtillon brothers: Odet (1517–1571), Gaspard (1519–1572), and François d'Andelot (1521–1569).*

The Châtillon Brothers before 1560: Ambition, Opportunity, Challenge

The career of Gaspard de Coligny shows how a well-placed noble of more than average ability might attain the status most to be desired in sixteenth-century France—close associations with the king.[1] Military experience in the earlier Italian wars earned him a command in François I's victory at Marignano and he later accompanied the king to the meeting with Henry VIII called by contemporaries the "Field of Cloth of Gold." He died fighting the Spaniards (1552), with the reputation of having always served his king well, "because he had a good head and a good arm."[2]

Even more advantageous to his sons than his own services was Gaspard's marriage (1514) to Louise de Montmorency, sister of Anne de Montmorency, first baron and constable of France. The Montmorencys were the greatest landowners in the country and stood at the apex of the social hierarchy, outranked only by the royal family. After their father's death the Châtillon brothers came under the supervision of their maternal uncle, and for more than thirty years this would be their greatest asset, raising them

---

*This interpretative essay, synthesizing recent scholarship, is particularly indebted to the latest studies of the two elder brothers.

See Junko S. Shimizu, *Conflict of Loyalties: Politics and Religion in the Career of Gaspard de Coligny, Admiral of France, 1519–1572* (Geneva, 1970); Lawrence S. Metzger, "The Protestant Cardinal: Odet de Coligny, 1517–1571" (Ph.D. diss., History, Boston University, 1979). There is, unfortunately, no full-scale study of d'Andelot.

above other nobles at court and offering opportunities at the highest level, because Montmorency enjoyed the favor of François I for most of his reign and was the special councillor of his successor, Henri II.[3] The Châtillons had considerable talent among them, military, political, diplomatic, intellectual, and they were well able to make the most of the favors conferred. Yet their ambitions exceeded their opportunities, and expectations aroused in their youth—of exercising power comparable to their uncle's—would never be realized.

While Montmorency assumed responsibility for the public aspects of their education—their political apprenticeship, as it were—their mother directed the private aspects, moral and spiritual. What is known about Louise de Montmorency is tantalizingly little but it is significant: she was a member of the circle of Marguerite de Navarre, sister of François I, patroness and leader of the humanist-reform at court. These women combined intellectual activity in the "new learning" with intense piety and desire to reform the church—from within. Their lay piety included some unorthodox ideas, such as rejection of purgatory and of the veneration of saints and relics, and the refusal to have a priest present when they were dying, an action attributed to Louise de Montmorency. While this is mere speculation, there is no doubt that her daughter by an earlier marriage (and *her* daughters) openly joined the reform and made important contributions to "the Cause." It is also a fact that Louise entrusted the education of her sons to Nicolas Béraud, a well-known humanist with reforming leanings, whose wife and son became Protestants.[4] The sources are silent on their childhood years, but as adults each of the brothers made a distinct impression on contemporaries: François d'Andelot was forthright, almost foolhardy, "plein de feu," "chevalier sans peur," in contrast to Gaspard, "grave," "taciturn," "prudent," and Odet, known for his good nature, "aimable avec un peu de nonchalance." Odet got on easily with people of all sorts and he repeatedly smoothed the way for his less flexible brothers, while advancing his uncle's interest and building a brilliant career for himself.[5]

As the eldest, and through his gifts as a diplomat, it was natural that Odet should reap the harvest of the constable's favor earlier and more prominently than his brothers. In 1533, during the ceremonies accompanying the marriage of François I's second son, Henri, to the niece of Clement VII, Catherine de Medici, the pope conferred the red hat on Odet, who was sixteen years old. Within two years he was Archbishop of Toulouse and Count-Bishop of Beauvais, the most prestigious of his collection of benefices, which included sixteen abbeys and yielded impressive revenues. The young Cardinal de Châtillon was representative of the Renaissance hierarchy; his offices were conferred by the crown through family influence as political favors and the recipient never took orders. Ironically, in view of his later career, Odet exemplified some of the most conspicious abuses of the Roman hierarchy that stimulated the reform: absenteeism, pluralism, and secularism.

On the positive side, Odet was a major patron of scholarship, letters, and the arts in the decades before all such matters would be swallowed up in civil strife. He subsidized Ronsard, who honored him in many poems; Rabelais dedicated to Odet the *Quart Livre* (1552), and owed to the cardinal not only his permit to publish but also protection when his unorthodox ideas brought him under the censorship of the parlement of Paris. Clouet painted Odet's portrait several times; Ramus was both a friend and a protége.[6] While his luxurious Parisian residence was the scene of most of these activities, Odet's humanist orientation was also a factor in the intellectual life of Toulouse, a city whose attractions included a university with a famous law school and leading families with contacts in Italy, especially at the University of Padua. A number of humanist-jurists active in the latter part of the century were associated with Odet de Châtillon through his Toulousian patronage, notably Michel de L'Hôpital, Arnauld du Ferrier, Paul de Foix, and members of the Du Faur Family. They all held unorthodox ideas and several experienced persecution at the hands of Henri II in the final, most repressive years of his reign. They came into their own much later, as *politiques* in the counsels of Catherine de Medici, and especially Henri IV.[7]

The receptivity of Toulouse to new ideas is particularly striking in contrast to the climate of opinion in Paris in these same years. Repressive edicts, such as imposition of the death penalty for the mere possession of Calvin's *Institutes*, had been issued pell-mell since the mid-1530s, often overlapping or contradicting one another. The Faculty of Theology at the University of Paris anticipated the measures of the papacy itself by drawing up a list of twenty-five articles of faith (1543), the violation of any one of which constituted heresy, and then by issuing a list of proscribed books.[8]

If Odet's achievements were more conspicious, the younger Châtillons were not marking time in the last years of François I. They both fought with distinction against the Habsburgs in Italy and were knighted on the field of Cérisoles (1547). Gaspard was then appointed to the office of Colonel-General of the Infantry and joined an expedition against England, while d'Andelot was sent to Scotland to defend the interests of the French party* before returning to Italy, where he had the misfortune to be captured and imprisoned by the enemy in 1551.[9]

François I died on March 31, 1547, and was succeeded by Henri II, whose chief councillor and companion was Anne de Montmorency, Constable of France. The signal honor of escorting the new king to the altar at his coronation that was conferred on his nephew, Odet de Châtillon, drew

---

*The religious questions as such are discussed in section 3.

wide comment. Subsequently Odet was entrusted with delicate assign-ments at the papal court, where the defense of French policy and of Mont-morency interests both required unusual skill.[10]

At the accession of Henri II, Odet was thirty years old, Gaspard twenty-eight, d'Andelot twenty-six. For the next ten years Montmorency's in-fluence waxed and his nephews scaled the heights of their careers as his protégés. D'Andelot's suffered a five-year interruption because of his im-prisonment, but Gaspard distinguished himself by recovering Boulogne from the English. He was given the office of admiral—the title by which he would be known in history—and later became governor of the Île de France and Picardy as well. In the 1550s Gaspard also became involved in international affairs, and in 1556 he led a delegation to Brussels, where he participated in the negotiation of the Treaty of Vaucelles, the last great accomplishment of the Montmorency faction. It was a fragile truce, hastily put together because the Emperor Charles V was preparing to abdicate, but it was favorable to France in that she retained all the gains from recent fighting.

Even as the Montmorency efforts were successful, however, the avenues of advancement were being blocked off. The Châtillon fortunes had peaked, both at court—where the factional struggle with the Guises was becoming acute and the balance shifting against the constable—and within the Montmorency party, where the former unity between uncle and nephews was giving way to divisions. The constable's sons were now of age, and their careers had priority. The Châtillons were too ambitious to take second place to their cousins, though they would collaborate during the civil wars. Moreover, the apprenticeship was over, as we see in a letter from Coligny to the constable in 1556, in which he complains of insufficient recognition and hints at ulterior motives for his uncle's precious favor.[11]

When the conversion of François d'Andelot to the reform* became known after his release from prison in 1556, the divisions became sharper and more visible, impossible to paper over. D'Andelot's action was abso-lutely unacceptable to his uncle, a conservative Catholic of the traditional stamp, and it posed a problem for his brothers. Without the favor of Mont-morency and that of the king, they had nothing but their native ability, while the other contenders had more valuable assets—the Bourbons, for example, were Princes of the Blood, and the Guises had a vast and varied clientage. These realities could not be ignored by Odet and Gaspard.

Whatever religious posture might be assumed by the Châtillons, or by the constable himself in the late 1550s, it could not appear so ardently Catholic as that of the Guises, self-appointed champions of the Roman Church against heresy. Here also were brothers, François Duc de Guise, a

---

*The Queen, Mary Stuart, was at the French court; Marie de Guise was acting as regent for her daughter.

great captain, and Charles, Cardinal de Lorraine, equally gifted in politics, advancing their personal and family interests as they gained royal favor, at the expense of both the Bourbons and the Montmorencys. Whereas the constable stood for peace, the Guises worked for the renewal of war, and the circumstances in 1557 and 1558 favored them. Fighting, after but a few months of truce, was resumed only a few miles to the northeast of Paris. Montmorency was disastrously defeated at the battle of St. Quentin (1557), and Coligny, after a valiant defense of the town, was captured and imprisoned. Many French nobles were killed; panic swept the capital. The military situation was saved by the Duc de Guise's following a lightning march from Italy, and he shortly surpassed this feat with still another, even more spectacular one—the recapture of Calais from the English, who had held it for two hundred years. François de Guise thus became a national hero in France by the very act that broke Mary Tudor's heart in England.

The efforts of Henri II to procure Montmorency's release, in which Odet de Châtillon took a leading part, contributed to the shift in 1558 to a policy of peace. Furthermore, both France and Spain were facing bankruptcy, and the new Spanish king, Philip II, was willing to make peace also. After six months of negotiations, the Treaty of Cateau-Cambrésis, ending sixty-five years of intermittent conflict between the Habsburg and Valois dynasties, was signed in the spring of 1559. But mutual agreement to suppress heresy was a feature of the document, so that the Guises could press their advantage even though the war was over, especially since they had succeeded in marrying their niece Mary Stuart, Queen of Scots, to the Dauphin in May 1558. In that same spring d'Andelot moved from mere adherence to the reformed faith to active proselytizing when he traveled through the provinces, accompanied by two Calvinist ministers, founding new churches and strengthening others. This could not fail to bring royal displeasure, increase the pressure on his brothers, and widen the breach between them and the constable.

Calvinism was attracting adherents in other influential milieux as well, including the parlement of Paris, the highest court in France. The king was increasingly angry and apprehensive. In a history-making session of the parlement, on June 10, 1559, he had several councillors suspected of heresy arrested and swore to see the most outspoken of them, Anne Du Bourg, "burn with his own eyes." Exactly a month later, during the celebration of the royal marriages that were part of the treaty, he was injured in the eye by the lance of an opponent in the joust. The wound proved fatal.[12]

The death of Henri II brought young François II, husband of Mary Stuart, to the throne. During the seventeen months of his reign the royal couple, the court, and the country were dominated by the queen's uncles, the Duc de Guise and the Cardinal de Lorraine, with consequences momentous for the history of France. One immediate result of the eclipse of the Montmorency party was that it became urgent for the Châtillon brothers to find a substitute for Montmorency's support.

New Means to Old Ends; 1560–March 1562

At least the Châtillons were not isolated in their opposition to the Guise regime. Hostility to the king's "foreign" uncles—Lorraine was not part of the royal domain—grew rapidly in all segments of the population but especially among the nobles who, like the Montmorencys, had been displaced or, like the Bourbons, were excluded by the Guise monopoly. According to tradition, the Princes of the Blood were the king's natural councillors and belonged at his side. The fast-growing Protestant population, in every class, was also prominent among the Guise opponents, for the suppression of heresy was their battle-cry. It was natural that these groups should reach out to each other, and although they never succeeded in organizing a really solid bloc, elements of the nobility and the pastors eventually formed a politico-military coalition under the banner of the reform, the Huguenot party. It did not happen overnight, however, but was gradually hammered out in the events of 1559–1560.

The Guises lost no time in exploiting their advantage. Special commissioners were appointed to search every house for heretics, houses suspected of harboring illicit meetings were razed, and there were massive arrests. Pamphlets, which would multiply in 1560, denounced the Guises as usurpers and tyrants, and called upon the Princes of the Blood to redress the situation and to convoke the Estates-General. The Guise response, embodied in an edict the following November, extended the death penalty to anyone who knew of illicit meetings and did not report them to the authorities. Informers, on the other hand, were to be rewarded and protected. Many people fled the country. Violence became endemic in Paris as Anne Du Bourg was burned at the stake in a dramatic fulfillment of at least part of the late king's vow. Although aimed at heretics, this widecast net of repression caught many orthodox Catholics as well. In the words of one contemporary historian, there were those who were moved by true zeal to serve God and their king, those who were moved by ambition and saw their opportunity, and those who vowed vengeance for injuries inflicted by the Guises. In each of these categories were devout Catholics as well as followers of the reform.[13]

These circumstances enabled the Châtillons not only to survive the fall of the constable, but also to survive the Guise regime. Their obvious course was to add their voices to those appealing to the Princes of the Blood. In the strict sense they never abandoned this strategy,* though coming events would show that the Bourbons were unable to deliver the remedies needed, and in addition would bring forward two more satisfactory sources of support, the queen-mother and the Huguenot party.

---

*Condé was the titular head of the Huguenot party and army until his death in March 1569. He was then officially succeeded by his nephew, Henri de Navarre, then sixteen years old, though the admiral was the *de facto* commander.

Odet de Châtillon could now stand on his own. Unlike the constable, he was not in disgrace, not even much in eclipse. He again escorted the king at the coronation, and he kept his seat on the royal council. During the reign of François II, moreover, the Châtillons were careful not to make any overt challenge to the king's uncles. They cooperated in the French expedition to aid Scotland against the English, for instance, and the Spanish ambassador could say in January 1560 that Coligny and Odet were "following the Guises as they had once followed the constable." By March the government was reported "reduced to" the Guises, the admiral and the cardinal. Catherine de Medici played an important part in this outcome, for she needed to use any available support to mitigate the Guise hegemony.[14]

Under the pressure of persecution, the Huguenots were divided on how to remedy their situation. They believed that if the king understood that they were loyal subjects, persecution would cease and they would be permitted to worship freely. There were several schools of thought and no clear leadership on the question of the removal of the "evil councillors," however. While Calvin and the pastors felt that only spiritual and "constitutional" means were justifiable in resisting tyranny, some others, especially in the lower ranks of the nobility, conspired to "rescue" the king by seizing the Guises and placing François II in the hands of the Bourbons, prior to presenting a petition with their grievances and demands. The conspiracy was betrayed just as it was on the point of execution, at Amboise, in March 1560. The Châtillons joined in the general condemnation, credibly because of their previous prudence.[15] At the same time, Catherine, with their help, capitalized on anti-Guise sentiment to moderate the status of nonviolent dissenters in order to calm the situation pending a general resolution of the religious question.* Amnesty for Protestants who were not rebels and provisional religious toleration were embodied in the Edict of Amboise, March 8.

The Princes of the Blood were not able to provide the necessary leadership. The King of Navarre was playing an ambiguous role, shifting from the Roman Church to the reformed, and giving contradictory impressions to different people—*ondoyant*, in the apt phrase of Montaigne. He would be increasingly unreliable until his death in November 1562, although some would never understand that his only serious commitment was to the recovery of his wife's lost kingdom of Navarre, and would hope in vain for him to become a sincere Protestant leader.[16] Condé was impetuous, and equally lacking in judgment. The Guises could exploit the vulnerability of the Bourbons (Condé was accused of being the "silent chief" of the Conspiracy of Amboise) and expected to turn the meeting of the Estates-General demanded by their enemies to their own purposes.

---

*The Council of Trent had been suspended since 1552. Efforts to reconvene it were hampered by conflicts among the powers over both procedures and matters of substance.

Catherine's counterstrategy in the summer of 1560 was to build a middle party in the council. The most important member was the new chancellor, Michel de L'Hôpital, a protégé of the Guises but a moderate, who had friendly associations with the Châtillons dating back to Toulouse. An Assembly of Notables at Fontainebleau in August 1560 witnessed a confrontation between the Guises, who took extraordinary security measures and prepared to defend themselves, and a large company of which the Châtillons were a part, led by the constable. Some of this group would form the nucleus of the Huguenot party, but the hour had not yet struck. Coligny, notably, acted "more as a mediator than as an advocate" of the reform at Fontainebleau, as we shall see when tracing the course of his religious development.[17] Catherine and the moderates carried the day when the Notables endorsed a convocation of the Estates-General, a suspension of persecution, and a national council pending the resumption of a general one.

With L'Hôpital acting as liaison, the Châtillions had successfully transferred their dependence from the Princes of the Blood to the crown—at least temporarily. But the hope that the Guises had been outflanked was destroyed by the revelation of another conspiracy—to seize Lyon—in which the Bourbons were implicated.[18] The Guises quickly recovered the initiative, and the Montmorency clan, including the Châtillons, withdrew from court. In November Condé was arrested, charged with treason, and condemned to death. His mother-in-law, Madelaine de Mailly, Comtesse de Roye, who had been the chief intermediary for the Huguenots with Catherine de Medici the previous year—half-sister of the Châtillons—was also arrested. They did not venture to help her and they did not get off scot-free themselves. Throughout the autumn accusations of heresy circulated against them, spread by the papal nuncio, among others. The alleged reason was their advocacy of religious toleration, but the real reason was probably their influence with Catherine and her refusal to withdraw her favor from the brothers.[19]

Nevertheless, the outlook was bleak for the anti-Guise cause until, suddenly, toward the end of November, the young king suffered a severe ear infection and died on December 5. His mother was not caught unawares; she prepared to move into the central position while François II was dying, and she accomplished this within a few weeks, chiefly by outmaneuvering Antoine de Bourbon, so that her claim to the regency as Queen-mother would prevail over his, as First Prince of the Blood. There was no doubt that there would be a regent, Charles IX was just ten years old when he came to the throne.[20]

Seldom has a natural death had more dramatic consequences; the power of the Guises was again reduced to that of one among several rival factions. Catherine took pains to placate them; both the duke and the cardinal retained their seats on the council, but at the same time some of Condé's

allies were added, the Constable was invited to return to court and d'Andelot regained the office of colonel-general of the infantry. Catherine did
not intend to be at the mercy of the factions and she continued to depend
on the middle party, loyal to the crown and favorable to reconciliation.
Several noblewomen were especially helpful in this, Renée de France,
Duchess of Ferarra, and Marguerite de France, Duchess of Savoy, both of
royal blood, and Jacqueline de Longwy, Duchess of Montpensier, a special
confidante of Catherine's, influential in the release of Condé and Madame
de Roye, an impressive accomplishment of the moderates.[21]

From our perspective, the two elder Châtillons at this time represent a
via media, advocating some concessions to the Huguenots and a degree of
toleration, but not the replacement of the old faith by the new. At the time,
however, given a Roman Church on the defensive and the position of the
Guises, the Châtillons were perceived as proto-Protestants themselves.
Specifically, their championship of concessions scandalized Montmorency,
who began to draw closer to the Duc de Guise, a rapprochement for-
malized as the "Triumvirate," with Marshal de St. André as the third
member, when Montmorency joined with them in celebrating Mass on
Easter Sunday in a separate service, apart from the royal chapel, where the
Bishop of Valence (Monluc) was preaching a liberal doctrine to the royal
congregation. If Theodore Beza could write at this time that "the admiral
has abandoned idolatry," it is understandable that the constable felt betrayed—although Coligny had made no statement on the matter. Montmorency accused his nephews of ingratitude, in public, and declared that his
past favors to them lay on his conscience. His anger was fueled also by the
fact that his nephews had retained influence with Catherine while he had
not.[22]

Even with reinforcements, Catherine's middle party would never be as
strong as the emerging ultra-Catholic party, which could count on the
support of Spain and the papacy. She would more than once be obliged to
alter a preferred policy in order to appease them, and this imbalance would
grow with the years.*

In the meantime, it was the season of the Protestant flood tide, to the
point where some hoped, while others feared, that the royal family itself
might change over. For several years informal congregations had been
proliferating, and the demand for ministers for regularly constituted
churches exceeded the supply in Geneva.[23] In the summer of 1561 public
attention was attracted by students demonstrating, nuns leaping over convent walls, and people of all classes singing the Psalms of Marot and

---

*The "Holy League" almost succeeded in preventing Henri de Navarre from coming to the
throne; it did succeed in assassinating him eventually (1610), as it had his predecessor, Henri
III, last of the Valois, in 1589.

praying in the vernacular. The most spectacular news concerned the converts at court, and the fact that the queen-mother permitted them to worship in their own fashion—though the doors were supposed to remain closed. The child-king was being taught by unorthodox tutors, the sermons of Jean de Monluc, already accused of heresy, were rivaled by those of Theodore Beza, who had been sent by Calvin to counsel the Huguenot nobles. The court ladies in particular were swept up in the "fad" of the reform, reading and discussing books printed in Geneva and lionizing Beza—and Jeanne d'Albret, when she arrived in late July. Of this period, Marguerite de Valois, later wife of Henri IV, wrote in her *mémoires*, ". . . in order to keep my religion . . . when all the court was infected with heresy, I had to resist the powerful persuasion of several lords and ladies [even of] . . . my brother Anjou, who has since become king of France [Henri III] . . . who threw my Hour Books in the fire and forced me to carry Huguenot Psalms in their place." These accusations should be taken in the context of Marguerite's later bitter feud with Henri III, but there was genuine alarm over the Calvinist upbringing of Henri de Navarre.[24] With Henri, his mother, and Condé leading the reform party while enjoying Catherine's highest favor, the three sources of support available to the Châtillons were briefly united in the summer of 1561, with the Princes of the Blood serving as the link between Catherine and the Huguenots. This was a fleeting moment that would not be repeated.

Of the three policies agreed on at Fontainebleau the previous summer, two had been carried out, with evident, if ephemeral success, that is, persecution had been suspended and the reformed were profiting from provisional toleration. There remained the third: a "national council" on the religious question. Catherine and L'Hôpital hoped that the Colloquy of Poissy (September–October 1561) would produce the desired solution by marking out areas of agreement between the two religious camps instead of emphasizing their differences, so that neither side would feel justified in resorting to violence. The two elder Châtillon brothers gave their full support to this objective. (D'Andelot is not mentioned in this connection.) Coligny appears as a sponsor of Royal policy, that is, of any viable compromise. Shimizu concurs with foreign ambassadors who failed to detect any strong doctrinal opinion on his part, for instance, apropos of the Augsburg Confession: "*I think one or the other is the same to him* [he wants] to assure the agreements with the Germans" (emphasis added). Odet performed the functions of stage-manager for Catherine, welcoming the reformed delegates in the name of the crown, providing them with housing and chaplaincies. He virtually commuted between Poissy and St. Germain, to keep Catherine informed, and she had no more skilled or appropriate advisor for this task. When the original assembly broke up over the interpretation of the Eucharist, the Queen-Mother tried to salvage something in a series of small conferences, only to fail again. In these, and especially in direct talks with papal representatives, Odet was the principal spokesman of the French crown.*[25]

As the fateful year 1562 opened, the Huguenots felt that in order to preserve recent gains they must obtain legal recognition, in a royal edict registered by parliament, of their rights as loyal subjects, including freedom of worship. Catherine and L'Hôpital were convinced that only by such concessions could civil war be averted. Their formula for civil administration was peaceful coexistence of the two rival faiths pending a settlement of the doctrinal issues by a general council of the church. The Edict of January was the most favorable to dissenters of all the edicts that punctuated the civil wars prior to the Edict of Nantes (1598), for which it was the model.[26] Predictably, it provoked a violent reaction. A policy of toleration in a kingdom traditionally unified in religion shocked public opinion and galvanized the ultra-Catholic party into an all-out offensive to block registration of the edict and to discredit the policy it represented. Although they could not prevent registration, after a desperate struggle the ultras succeeded in rendering the edict unenforceable and in pressuring the crown to reorient itself in the opposite direction.

Their chief instrument was the seduction of Antoine de Bourbon (through a promise by Philip II of another kingdom to substitute for the mirage of Navarre). Antoine's defection finally destroyed Huguenot illusions and fatally weakened the moderate party as well, because Catherine also was obliged to submit to the ultras temporarily. Once turned, the Protestant tide receded even faster than it had risen. Catherine reinstated the king's orthodox tutors, banned heretical books and discussions of doctrine at court, and carried out to the letter repressive edicts against iconoclasts. The papal nuncio, who had described France as "half-Huguenot" only a few weeks before, now predicted jubilantly that "the sect" would soon disappear and declared that "the faithful" had taken a new lease on life.[27]

The Huguenot movement had indeed passed its peak. For a few months it had seemed possible either that a degree of toleration could be maintained without violence or that some compromise similar to that of Henry VIII might be worked out; but in opposition to the crown, the Huguenot party was reduced to a dissident, rebellious minority, and the tide of conversions would henceforth flow in the opposite direction.[28]

Nothing could speak more eloquently of the changed policy and atmosphere than the departure of the Châtillons from court and the return of the Guises in mid-February 1562. Six months after the triumphal arrival of Jeanne d'Albret, the winning combination (for the Châtillons) of the Princes of the Blood, the queen-mother and the Huguenots, broke up and

---

*See below, p. 272.

could never be reconstituted. Catherine was in the hands of the Triumvirs; with the defection of Antoine, Condé was obliged to embrace the Huguenots if he were to have any constituency at all; the Châtillons had lost their position as close allies of the crown so that the reform party was the only possible vehicle for their individual and family fortunes.

These political considerations do not fully explain their actions, however. Important questions arise: what place did religion play in their future careers? what motivated their conversions? what is the significance of the timing? what was the nature of their beliefs? did they all have the same priorities? how did they influence one another in this regard?

The Question of Religion

So sharp were the contrasts between the Roman Catholic and the reformed camps in the last part of the sixteenth century, and so dramatic the events of their desperate struggle in the political and diplomatic sphere as well as in several theaters of war, that it is not easy for the twentieth-century student to understand the very different mental climate of 1560. To be sure, the two principal leaders of the rival camps, Philip II in Spain and Elizabeth I in England, had already assumed power, but only just, and their relations would be cordial for some years to come. Representatives of the Emperor Charles V, and of the papacy, had met with Lutheran leaders to discuss compromise on such issues as the use of the vernacular, marriage of the clergy, and Communion in both kinds. Although the results were so far negative, many people still hoped that the Council of Trent would be reconvened on terms acceptable to all the major powers and that some accommodation could be achieved.

The political dichotomies of the latter part of the century (Guise versus Montmorency, Anglo-Spanish rivalry on the seas) developed quickly and visibly, but the religious dichotomies were defined only after the appearance of two new forces, one on each side of the confessional divide: militant Calvinism in Geneva, and in Rome a new leadership determined to fight back by suppressing heresy in regions where it was spreading rapidly but had not become established, like France and the Netherlands, and by vigorously reaffirming Roman Catholic doctrine.

Under the impact of these two forces, the European religious climate was drastically changed. A fluid continuum of degrees of reform opinion in which it was easy to move from one position to an adjacent one—and by the same token, difficult to define heresy—was replaced by a deep chasm, virtually impossible to bridge. Before the emergence of militant Calvinism, reform was a unifying idea, from the Brethren of the Common Life through the Christian humanists like Erasmus and Sir Thomas More, to the liberal cardinals like Gasparo Contarini and Reginald Pole. The scandal of the "abuses" was widely recognized by devout Catholics, and in educated circles firsthand knowledge of the Gospels grew with the study of Greek. Some current practices were condemned because they were not found in the Gospels, and many sincere religious leaders refused to condemn as un-Christian persons whose offense was doubt about the efficacy of relics or refusal to abstain from meat during Lent. Before the final session of the Council of Trent (January 1563), Queen Elizabeth could take over the throne from Mary Tudor and leave her subjects in doubt about her religious beliefs (except for the repudiation of the papacy), and even the Cardinal de Lorraine could conceive of a compromise along the lines of the Confession of Augsburg.

In this atmosphere of religious positions hard to differentiate, the connotation of the word *conversion* was quite different from what it would become when rival institutions were defending their own belief by blackening that of others and trying to swell their numbers at others' expense. Conversion in the earlier period usually meant a specific spiritual experience, often a sudden revelation, resulting in a "commitment to Christ." Sometimes this included doctrines unacceptable to the church, of course, but often it only meant an upsurge of personal, inner piety, replacing a more conventional piety.

These are considerations relevant to the interpretation of the career of the Châtillons, whose spiritual and moral formation had been in the hands of persons following the lead of Marguerite de Navarre. The "pre-reformers" were not pioneer Protestants, but rather *Erasmians,* deeply concerned about the future of the church, anxious to purge it of abuses, and convinced that reform was necessary "in the head" as well as "in the members," and willing to accept a number of changes.[29] As young men growing up in court circles, the Châtillons were certainly exposed to this point of view and probably shared it, although none of them attracted attention with respect to religion until the late 1550s.

Eventually, however, all three were "converted," that is, they adhered to the French Reformed Church in some way, but not all in the same way, nor at the same time, and probably not for precisely the same reasons. François d'Andelot, the youngest, was the first to take the step. Unfortunately, no record of the conversion experience itself has come down to us. Brantôme's is one of the more informative near-contemporary accounts, based on hearsay circulating after d'Andelot's release from prison in 1556:

There was not much supervision of books in his Milan prison, for the Inquisition was not as tight as it has since become. Thus he took up the new religion beyond the smoke he had already sniffed when he was in Germany for the Protestant wars.*

---

*". . . oultre qu'il en avoit senty quelque fumée estant allé en Allemagne a la guerre des protestants."

Possibly because of new factional struggles and the resumption of war, d'Andelot's action escaped public notice for about two years. Like his brother Gaspard, d'Andelot fought and was captured at St. Quentin, but he escaped and rejoined the French army. His performance at the siege of Calais brought extravagant praise from the Duc de Guise, according to Brantôme—that if he had only d'Andelot, Strozzi, and d'Estrées under his command, he could conquer the world.[30] Even greater favor followed from the king, for which d'Andelot paid a stiff price. Coligny, of course, remained a prisoner of the Spaniards and d'Andelot sent him one or more books to "console" him, as he himself had been consoled as a prisoner of war. Contemporaries believed that the youngest brother led both of his elders to the reform, and all accounts of their connection with it begin with Coligny's imprisonment.[31]

After so many months of discretion on d'Andelot's part, in April 1558 he made the bold move that amounted to an unmistakable declaration of his new allegiance when he took two Calvinist ministers* with him, and under armed escort, sponsored their preaching in Orleans, Tours, Angers, and especially Brittany, where the reform was "planted" during this journey.[32] The pastor of the Paris church, Jean Macar, reported to Calvin that in the Norman town of St. Lo, where "they were greeted like angels," a majority of the inhabitants had abandoned the old church "to live according to our custom," to which Calvin replied euphorically that the fire would leap from province to province and burn so strongly that "all the drops in the ocean could not extinguish it."[33]

The Guises had already been antagonized by d'Andelot's conspicuous favor with the king, and they were thought to be seeking a chance to discredit him. However much he might have wished to, Henri II could not afford to overlook d'Andelot's Breton "mission." He summoned him to court and interrogated him personally, charging him with ingratitude, and made several specific accusations beyond responsibility for spreading heresy in the provinces: that he had not attended Mass since the siege of Calais (four months earlier); that he had sent books printed in Geneva to Coligny, and that he had been among those present at recent illicit Protestant assemblies at the Pré-aux-Clercs, a field on the left bank near St. Germain-des-Pres. D'Andelot replied with dignity that he had spared nothing of his own for the king's service, but that he had now to think of his salvation:

The doctrine I admit sponsoring [in Brittany] is good and holy, derived

---

*Jean Carmel, sometimes called Fleury, was the nephew of Guillaume Farel, founder of the reform in Geneva, and Pierre Loiseleur, Sieur de Villiers, was the rector of the Rouen church until the massacre, when he fled to Germany. He was also the author of important theological treatises.

from the New and Old Testaments, approved by the ancient councils of the primitive Church. . . . I happen not to have been at the Pré-aux-Clercs, but if I had I would not consider that by so doing I had done any injury to God, or to Your Majesty. I confess that it is a long time since I have attended Mass, a decision not lightly taken, but on the advice of the most learned men in your kingdom. . . . [I thank God] who has lifted the veil of my ignorance . . . and I am certain that with His Grace, I will never go there [to Mass] again. I did send a book to my brother, the Admiral, to console him in prison, where he is on account of his services to you. . . . I pray you, Sire, leave my soul alone and make any use you wish of my body and my earthly goods, which are entirely yours.

The king was transported with anger. Some say he threw a tantrum and broke a precious plate. Others say that he had to be restrained from physically attacking d'Andelot. Meanwhile, the Cardinal de Lorraine, who could scarcely conceal his satisfaction, taunted the accused. To him d'Andelot retorted that he was very sure of his own beliefs, and called upon the Cardinal's own conscience as his witness, that "worldly honors and ambition have turned you from [pure doctrine] to the point of persecuting members of Jesus Christ."[34] François de Châtillon was then arrested and imprisoned in the chateau of Melun.

Up to the spring of 1558, François d'Andelot, nephew of the Constable and special favorite of the king, was the most prominent convert so far recruited. It is not surprising that the Calvinist leadership reacted strongly. Calvin wrote d'Andelot: "God has brought you forward as witness to His Truth in a place that has so far been closed to it . . . [if your sufferings] were ten times more cruel, the Master you serve deserves that you persist right to the end, not yielding for any reason whatever." D'Andelot subsequently wrote to the King expressing the core of his belief: "[I will accept instruction] from the Word of God only, in which faith and confession I will live and die." He ceased going to Mass because "it did not seem to represent either the primitive supper of Christ with His apostles, or His voluntary, pure and unique sacrifice on the Cross for the redemption of man."[35]

No secular voice joined the reformed clergy in urging d'Andelot to stand fast. As a far-from-neutral nineteenth century commentator puts it: "In the absence of the glorious head of the Châtillon house, still a captive of the Spaniards and himself beginning to become suspect, nobody dared speak in defense of the prisoner of Melun, who was feebly supported by his brother the Cardinal." Odet was in fact using his influence toward a different end: reconciliation with the King, as was d'Andelot's wife, Claude de Rieux, herself prominent in the party. Others urged d'Andelot to recant. Their emissary* cleverly did not press for a retraction, but persuaded him

---

*Identified only as "Dr. Ruzé," but characterized by the Huguenots as "a true disciple of Satan and Loyola."

that he could attend Mass, without compromising his own beliefs, as a gesture to the King, "who asks nothing more." On July 7 d'Andelot consented. In a letter to the Paris church, he explains with evident embarrassment that he had agreed "to attend their sacrifices, submitting to the will of the King, as God has commanded." Macar's response was a carefully balanced blend of sympathy with a stern reminder of his duty. Although the pastors regarded d'Andelot's token attendance at Mass as a defeat, it appears more important in the light of history that he remained a member of the Reformed Church and died fighting to establish its rights. Beza himself says "he made no verbal abjuration of his faith and condemned the Mass for the rest of his life."[36]

It may be that the scandal of the d'Andelot affair was partly responsible for holding back his brothers' commitment to the reform in 1558 and 1559, but it seems more likely that it provided them with a convenient excuse to postpone a decision. The ambiguity of their posture is reflected in the perceptions of contemporaries. In 1557 Beza said cautiously of Coligny only: "he is not our enemy," and Odet was serving as "inquisitor of the Faith" by papal appointment.* The Admiral may have been preparing to follow his younger brother's lead, but Calvin's letter of September 1558 suggests rather that the reformer was trying to recruit him:

> I hope you will not be displeased by my writing, as it is testimony to my concern for your salvation. . . . I pray God to lead you by the Holy Spirit, to fortify you in all the virtues and to save your soul soon.[37]

Every few months diplomatic dispatches would report that Odet was "tainted with heresy," but in February 1559 Calvin described him as unsympathetic to the reform, and Coligny, reappearing at court that spring, absented himself from Mass but kept silent on the subject. When Henri II died in July 1559, leaving a country torn apart over religious policy, the allegiance of the Châtillon brothers could still be interpreted in contradictory ways. Nor was the commitment noticeably greater in the reign of François II, the Guise regime. The impression that the admiral emerged at Fontainebleau in the summer of 1560 as the leader of the party, which is echoed by the latest study,** is correct if interpreted to mean that the Huguenots had begun to seek leadership from him at that time, and to make demands appropriate to the role. Analysis of his words and actions, however, show rather, as Shimizu points out, a mediator's posture. It is particularly telling that he made no effort to help his own half-sister, Madelaine de Mailly, when she was arrested on grounds of encouraging heresy. The two elder brothers were not "Protestants" at this time. Not

---

*In spite of elaborate machinery to repress heresy, there was never an Inquisition subject to Rome in France, as in Italy and elsewhere. The powers of the "Inquisitors of the Faith" were circumscribed by the crown and the Parlement of Paris.

**N. M. Sutherland, *The Huguenot Struggle for Recognition*.

only were they actively cooperating with the liberal Catholics, but they took pains to downplay their opposition to the Guises, as the report quoted above indicates, although it is surely an exaggeration to describe them as "following" the Guises.

After the death of François II, the Châtillons were obliged to make choices. The religious choice—whether to take a more explicit stand, and if so which—was complicated by the political situation. The King of Navarre's unreliability, and especially his loss of the regency to Catherine, made it desirable for the Châtillons to move closer to her. At the same time, they lacked an independent power-base and the Huguenots alone could provide one. Already in January 1561 foreign observers refer to the Châtillons as the leaders of the Reformed party. In February Coligny's son was baptized by Jean-Raymond Merlin, his Calvinist chaplain; not long afterward Beza could say that he had "abandoned idolatry."[38]

Thus with no announcement, "confession of faith" or renunciation, did Gaspard de Coligny, who would be acclaimed from then on as a devout Calvinist, head of the party, and often "martyr," indicate membership in the Reformed Church, by having his son baptized according to its rites. Whether or not this action represented any special spiritual experience or change in belief, we do not know. The probability is against it, in 1561. Such a change, if any, seems more likely to have occurred much earlier, perhaps in prison, in which case we must assume that, for some of the reasons suggested, he felt it prudent to keep it secret. From his overt statements and actions we may plausibly assume that "reform" to Coligny meant primarily elevation of the moral tone of the church and removal of the abuses, rather than any specific doctrines. A further possibility would be a hope, even expectation, of "the reunion of the churches" as the sixteenth-century ecumenical movement was called.

This latter was probably the position of Odet, whose course diverged in several respects from that of the Admiral, and in the spring of 1561 he seemed more "Protestant" than Gaspard. During the "Protestant Lent," Paris had witnessed meat being sold, and eaten, in unusual quantities, while at court Calvinist services in the apartments of Condé, Coligny, and the Queen of Navarre—with all the doors open—were thronged by curious courtiers. Two events occurred on Easter Sunday, April 6, that exacerbated the polarization. While at Fontainebleau the members of the Triumvirate dissociated themselves from the crown by holding a Mass apart from the royal chapel; in Beauvais the Cardinal-Count-Bishop was distributing Communion in both kinds to the laity. Even more scandalous, it became known that he had signed a Calvinist confession of faith in the presence of witnesses.* Violence erupted in Beauvais on Easter Monday. Catholic mobs demonstrated, ran wild, and murdered one of Odet's protégés, an

---

*Destroyed in the French Revolution.

apostate priest named Adrien Fourré. Others barely escaped by taking refuge in the episcopal palace. Then the local magistrates—long at odds over administrative and fiscal matters with their bishop—sympathized with the rioters and condemned the victims, and the Cardinal realized that the situation was dangerous. He appealed to Catherine to send his cousin François de Montmorency, in his capacity as governor of the Île de France, to restore order. The response was immediate and the situation soon under control. After this, it was not surprising to see the Cardinal de Châtillon appearing at the young king's coronation with his "wife,"* but his participation in the coronation Mass was puzzling, and disturbing to some on both sides.[39]

One obvious difference between Gaspard's situation and Odet's was that for the Cardinal a definitive separation from the Roman Church would mean the loss of his numerous benefices, with their revenues. Without denying the importance of so major a factor, there is persuasive evidence that Odet was a sincere irenicist, who thought a compromise between the two confessions possible.

At Poissy the differences between the brothers drew comment. Whereas the Admiral is called "the chief" of the party,** Odet is described as "cooler to the Cause" than formerly. Both brothers continued close association with the middle party, but Coligny confined himself to support for royal policy while Odet took an active part in discussions of doctrine.[40] The pattern persists in the following year. Coligny was reluctant to follow Condé and take arms when the break finally came, but he finally did so (legend has it that he was persuaded by his wife, Charlotte de Laval), while the Cardinal, dressed in black to emphasize his civilian status, continued to play the role of mediator. He was the mainstay of Catherine's last-ditch efforts to stave off disaster and would have carried his neutrality even farther if the Duchess of Savoy had granted his request to pay her a visit. Her own position was not sufficiently secure to oblige him, and in the late summer of 1562 Odet had no alternative but to join his brothers in the Huguenot party and army.[41]

Between the fall of Montmorency and the outbreak of civil war, the Châtillon brothers had each developed a religious posture. D'Andelot was an orthodox Calvinist, despite the temporary compromise of 1558 by which he escaped a heretic's fate. Gaspard's conversion was probably a long-drawn-out and deliberate affair, as Shimizu has concluded, joining his fate to that of the Huguenots in gradual stages that led ultimately to his becoming their greatest leader.[42] His character was Calvinist, responsible, pru-

---

*Odet and Isabelle de Hauteville were not married in the Reformed Church until 1564, but he called her his wife and treated her as such some years earlier.

**It is significant that he had a greater following than Condé, who was the official standard-bearer and later commander-in-chief of the army.

dent, highly disciplined, and little inclined to make allowance for human weakness. The historical consensus on Coligny's Protestant belief is understandable, even if frustrating in its lack of substance. His inner spiritual life was not penetrated by contemporaries, nor by anyone else.

As for Odet, the concessions he tried to wrest from spokesmen for the papacy after the end of the Colloquy probably represent at least some of his personal beliefs. Conceivably he would have gone farther but was constrained to limit himself to the minimum program that he judged within the realm of possibility. The administration of the sacraments in both kinds, for instance, often provided a kind of litmus-test of reformed opinion. In the years before Trent many liberal Catholics seemed willing to accept this modification. Odet had participated with other liberal prelates in such an "opposition Mass" during the conference of bishops that preceded the Colloquy. If the moderates had been able to keep the initiative, the utraquist position might become the basis of some doctrinal agreement, but Beza and the other strict Calvinists refused to accept the Lutheran formula.*[43]

After the collapse of the Colloquy, the Queen did not give up. Odet, with her backing, made a reform-proposal to the papal representatives that included, beyond the abolition of pluralism, reform of the monastic orders and other such conventional matters, use of the vernacular, reduction of the number of Masses, removal of images, Communion in both kinds, some simplification of the baptismal service, and toleration of Protestant worship outside the cities. The Cardinal of Ferarra agreed to send these proposals to Rome, but by the time the pope received them, the Council of Trent was reassembling—with no French bishop in attendance.[44] This move was not one to win papal support for French policy. Catherine was forced—once again—to assume the initiative and to deal with the problem as a national, administrative issue only. The immediate result was the Edict of January. Its rejection by the ultra-Catholic leaders, together with the Queen's dependence on them, led to the ultimate result—civil war. Odet de Châtillon, champion of the middle way, was also a victim when he fled south to join the Huguenot forces near Lyon.

Ecclesiastical questions were often the focus of Reformation disputes and French Protestantism did not escape such divisions within its small constituency. As in Geneva, the French Church was presbyterian, without bishops, and the pastors had the upper hand over the lay elders in the consistories and synods. In the period of the early civil wars this system was challenged by Jean-Baptiste Morély, who advocated greater decentralization, in the direction of congregationalism, and especially greater lay

---

*As early as 1529, at the Colloquy of Marburg, conflicting views of the Eucharist had blocked unity between Lutherans and the Swiss reformers, of whom Zwingli was then the spokesman.

participation. Either of these changes would reduce the control of the pastors, so the leadership condemned Morély unconditionally and repeatedly, leaving him no quarter in their single-minded pursuit over a ten-year period.[45] Odet and Gaspard de Châtillon were among Morély's supporters in the early years of the controversy, as was the Queen of Navarre. In light of what we know or surmise of the religious beliefs of the brothers—moral rather than doctrinal concern on the part of Coligny and an irenicist view on the part of Odet—it is probable that they found the inflexibility and authoritarianism of the pastors irritating and frustrating. Greater power to the laity, as advocated by Morély, on the other hand, would be advantageous for the noble *seigneurs*.

As for Jeanne d'Albret, there is no doubt that she believed strongly in the supremacy of the secular power and she had created an ecclesiastical establishment in her "sovereign" kingdom of Béarn as Erastian as that of England. It was not any theoretical position that made her hold out longest against Geneva in support of Morély, however; it was her high opinion of him as a teacher of her son. She said several times that Henri had learned more in three months from Morély than from "good old La Gaucherie" (the former tutor) in three years. She retained him in her service even after he had been officially condemned and excommunicated in Geneva. It took the persuasive powers of Theodore Beza himself to bring her to accept the "discipline" of Morély.[46] The Châtillons were also brought into line by means of special emissaries from Geneva. Morély's movement was not ultimately destroyed until the massacre, but in the years after 1566 he was deprived of high noble sponsorship.

Controversies over the relationship of church and state constitute the most important legacy of French Protestantism to European political thought. The post-massacre Huguenot pamphleteers have been thoroughly and repeatedly studied by distinguished scholars, but pre-massacre Huguenot political thought has not often been considered as a corpus. The Châtillons, Condé, and Jeanne d'Albret were concerned with action; their "political theory," such as it was, is embedded in their manifestos—often only implicitly.[47] In the petition presented by Coligny at Fontainebleau on behalf of the Huguenots of Normandy, he argued that as loyal subjects of the king they had a right to worship as they pleased provided they did so in peace. The suggestion that religion and politics, church and state, could be thus separated was revolutionary. Historically it is associated with L'Hôpital, justifiably since it became the policy of the crown. On several occasions between December 1560 and the Edict of January 1562—its institutional embodiment—the chancellor elaborated the argument that religious dissent was not *ipso facto* tantamount to sedition.[48]

Catherine's espousal of this notion shows how desperate she was, because it was diametrically opposed to the deep-seated feeling of most Frenchmen that there could be no religious divisions within a state like the

French monarch. *Un roi, une loi, une foi . . .* , the slogan that encapsulates it, occurs again and again in speeches and in the debates of *parlementaires*. Its hold on the majority of Frenchmen was the basic reason for the failure of the Edict of January and of all subequent edicts. Catherine, Coligny, and L'Hôpital could count on support from liberal Catholics who did not believe that consciences should—or could—be forced. Some were highly placed, like Jean de Monluc, but they were a small minority and never able to carry the day against the ultras. The parlement was "purged" as early as June 1562, and in 1568 L'Hôpital would be driven from office.[49]

Contribution of the Châtillon Brothers

The contributions of the Châtillon brothers to the Huguenot cause are featured in every narrative account of the first three Wars of Religion. D'Andelot was active in the field almost constantly, sometimes negotiating, successfully, with German princes or Swiss cities, and otherwise fighting. He was so bitter an enemy of the Huguenots that the ultra-Catholic Claude Haton calls him "one of the ablest soldiers in France."[50] D'Andelot usually followed the lead of Gaspard, but on occasion he took issue with the cautious Admiral. Two significant instances are on record. In late March 1562 the newly assembled Protestant leaders at Orléans debated whether to take arms immediately. D'Andelot advocated such a course, while Gaspard expressed reservations, although he went along with the majority in the end. Odet was trying to avert war, collaborating with the queen-mother at this eleventh hour. This behavior was indicative of their respective temperaments: d'Andelot impatient for action, Gaspard slow to commit himself, Odet mediating, working for accommodation even when it seemed hopeless. The same contrast between François and Gaspard marked the discussions preceding the Huguenot attack on Meaux that started the Second Civil War. D'Andelot was the chief advocate of immediate attack while the Admiral urged restraint, ". . . in such grave matters, which could bring about many evils, one should be moved by necessity only, not by will."[51] Odet, who did not join the Huguenot army until six months into the first war, was one of the principal negotiators of the Peace of Longjumeau, ending the second, in March 1568.

D'Andelot's career lay wholly within the confines of the Huguenot movement, whereas his brothers were major figures in national politics after 1557 and on the European scene when the Protestant coalition took shape in the late 1560s. Odet was admired by contemporaries. Brantôme regrets his adherence to "the Cause," because it deprived the court of his presence, and subtly reproaches his critics: "[He had] a noble and generous heart, incapable of deceit, wherever he might be, whatever garb he might wear." Jacques-Auguste de Thou, *politique* historian of the end of the century, said that "in the greatness of his soul, his integrity, his good faith—a rare virtue in our century—and in his understanding of human affairs, he had few equals."[52] If Catherine had been able to fend off the ultras, it is conceivable that Odet might have performed for her a function comparable to that of Richelieu for Louis XIII. He had many of the same gifts combined with a much more subtle mind and winning manner. As matters stood, the sovereign who most appreciated his talents was Queen Elizabeth of England.

Odet arrived at Dover after a precipitous flight in September 1568 at the same time that Condé, Coligny, Jeanne d'Albret, and Henri de Navarre took refuge at La Rochelle in order to escape capture. Elizabeth showered favors on the Cardinal, renovating a palace for his residence, endowing him with a large pension, and embracing him whenever they met.[53] He overcame her well-known reluctance to spend money and her passionate disapproval of rebellion to persuade her to support the Huguenots against their common enemies. Elizabeth responded, but not openly. Camouflaged as a commercial transaction between the Merchant Adventurers of London and the city of La Rochelle, she sent supplies and money for "the Cause," receiving local products in return. The Cardinal maintained close contact with the Queen of Navarre (and through her, with Coligny, at the front), and was active in implementing the plan to unite the Huguenots and the crowns of England and France against Spain by aiding the Dutch rebels, as Metzger says, through skillful diplomacy: "Odet was a major catalyst in the emergence of England as the leader of Protestant Europe."[54] At times Elizabeth's attitude would cool, when the tide of events shifted against England's interests as she perceived them, but Odet was able to make corresponding shifts and to counteract Catherine's ambassador, La Mothe-Fénelon, until peace talks began in France in the winter of 1570.

Despite their understandable distrust of Catherine's sincerity, the Huguenots agreed to sign the Peace of St. Germain the following August. The French crown needed peace even more than they because of divided leadership and shortage of funds. This explains some important concessions, such as the restitution of property, offices, and titles to the Huguenot leaders, who then sought to follow up their gains by securing a permanent alliance with England. The Cardinal was involved in arranging royal marriages between the partners as he prepared to return to France in the summer of 1571. His sudden death left the Admiral as the only surviving brother; d'Andelot had died in the spring of 1569, shortly after the murder of Condé on the field of Jarnac. In the remaining months of the Third Civil War, Coligny had come into his own as party leader and military commander.

The restraint that differentiated Gaspard from d'Andelot made him a rare kind of war leader, one who never faltered in pursuit of the enemy, but whose piety and conscience made him willing to lay down arms when peace seemed possible. Although he was reputed a strict disciplinarian (Brantôme says "he could be cruel when necessary," I suspect in our sense of the word "tough"), he was ordinarily *bon, doux, gracieux*. He had a great hold on the respect and loyalty of his men, even the German mercenaries, through his ability to inspire trust. "One word of his could make them do what he wished . . . a private word from him was valued as if from the King himself." His simple high-mindedness often touched the hearts of observers, as on the occasion when some of the captains were complaining, to which he replied: "If we have our religion what else do we need?" The general impression of Coligny is summed up in words like *gravité, droiture, homme de bien*.[55]

At the same time, there is no doubt that pride and ambition were also strong motivating forces in the Admiral's makeup, as Shimizu repeatedly points out. "[Coligny's] modesty . . . and moderation in advancing the demands of the Huguenots . . . were not unrelated to his ambition to be the first adviser of the French crown." Through successive identifications with his family, his party and his king, Coligny could fulfill his ambitions by serving ends that embraced his interests as part of a greater whole. The last phase of his life was devoted to the final, supreme thrust in this direction—the Netherlands enterprise. "[His] plan of a Protestant coalition, which included England, Dutch nobles and German princes was intended essentially for the secular interest of France," says Shimizu.[56] France? To the Châtillons "France" could be neither the Holy Land of the medieval mystique, nor the idealized entity of General de Gaulle's *certaine idée*. Yet something of both may have figured in the minds of these brothers, representatives of an aristocracy on the defensive and about to lose its power, who seem nevertheless to be more than champions of a lost cause because of the intelligence, the energy, and the principle with which they tried—in defiance of *fortuna*— to temper the fate of their class as well as their party.

NOTES

Since the studies of Shimizu and Metzger are fully documented in the bibliography below, in the interest of conserving space these notes will not ordinarily repeat the content of theirs, but will refer to them. Where a point is controversial, or for some other specific reason, however, the original sources will also be cited.

1. Joseph H. Strayer, "France, the Holy Land, the Chosen People and the Most Christian King," in Theodore K. Rabb and Jerald E. Siegel, eds., *Action and Conviction in Early Modern Europe* (Princeton, N.J., 1969) 3–16.

2. Pierre de Bourdeille, Signeur de Brantôme, *Oeuvres Completes*, ed. L. Lalanne, 11 vols. (Paris, 1864–1882), 3:187–89. Hereafter cited as Brantôme. Works dealing directly with the Châtillons are listed and analyzed in the bibliography.

3. F. Decrue de Stoutz, *Anne de Montmorency, grand maître et connétable de France, à la cour, aux armées et au conseil du roi François I* (Paris, 1885).

F. Decrue de Stoutz, *Anne, duc de Montmorency, connétable et pair de France sous les rois Henri II et Charles IX* (Paris, 1889).

4. The women of some ranking noble families were leaders in the early stages of the reform; see N. L. Roelker, "The Role of Noblewomen in the French Reformation," in *Archiv für Reformationsgeschichte* (1972), 63:169–95. Hereafter cited as Roelker, "Noblewomen." On Béraud see Ernest and Eugéne Haag (in the bibliography), article Béraud; *Dictionnaire biographique française*, vol. 5, col. 1473. Hereafter cited DBF. Junko S. Shimizu, *Conflict of Loyalties: Politics and Religion in the Career of Gaspard de Coligny, Admiral of France, 1519–1572* (Geneva, 1970, *Travaux d'Humanisme et Renaissance* 114) 22, n. 39. Hereafter cited as Shimizu.

5. DBF, vol. 2, col. 837.

6. Lawrence S. Metzger, *The Protestant Cardinal: Odet de Coligny, 1517–1571* (Ph.D. diss., Boston University, 1979), 72. Hereafter cited as Metzger.

M. Christol, "Odet, Cardinal de Châtillon," in *Bulletin de la Société de l'Histoire du Protestantisme français* 107 (1961) 1–12. Hereafter cited as *BSHPF*.

François Rabelais, *Le Quart Livre*, ed. R. Marichal (*Textes littéraires français* [Paris, 1947]) vols. 16–17, dedication letter to Odet de Châtillon.

M. Thomas, "Odet de Chastillon et la prétendu disgrace de Jean du Bellay en 1549," in *François Rabelais, Quatrième centenaire de sa mort, 1553–1953* (Geneva, 1953), 253–63. Although it was not on the scale of the cardinal's and it involved less prominent persons, Coligny's patronage has also drawn the attention of scholars. See Shimizu, 13–14, n. 2; C.-E. Engel, "La Figure de Coligny dans la littérature," in *Actes du Colloque, l'Amiral de Coligny et son temps* (Paris, 1974), 377–87; J. Pineaux, "Coligny et les poètes," *BSHPF* 118 (1972).

7. On Toulouse, see R. de Boysson, *Un Humaniste touloussain, Jehan de Boyssin, 1508–59* (Paris, 1913). The Cardinal was much interested in education. In Toulouse he patronized the municipal *collège*, defending its interests, subsidizing it when funds were short, and securing the services of well-known teachers. See I. Q. Brown, "Politics and Renaissance Educational Reform: Toulouse and the Founding of its Municipal Collège, 1500–1565," Ph.D., Harvard University, 1969. Later he provided scholarships for one hundred students at the short-lived Calvinist theological school attached to the Reformed Church in Orléans. See G. Bonet-Maury, "Le Protestantisme dans les universités d'Orléans, de Bourges et de Toulouse," *BSHPF* 38 (1889).

8. N. M. Sutherland, *The Huguenot Struggle for Recognition* (New Haven, Conn., 1980), 35–36. Hereafter cited as Sutherland, *Huguenot Struggle*.

9. Shimizu, 15–16; Metzger, 52, n.55.

10. Metzger, 45, n.66; 51.

11. Shimizu, 20; Metzger, 65–67.

12. For an overall interpretation of events between 1557–1559, see Robert M. Kingdon, *Geneva and the Coming of the Wars of Religion in France* (Geneva, 1956). Hereafter cited as Kingdon, *Geneva and the Coming*; Sutherland, *Huguenot Struggle*; H. LeMonnier, "La Lutte contre la maison d'Autriche; la France sous Henri II," vol 5, pt. 2 of E. Lavisse, ed., *Histoire de France illustrée*, 18 vols. (Paris, 1903–1910).

13. Sutherland, *Huguenot Struggle*, chap. 3 (La Planche cited, 84); see also Kingdon, *Geneva and the Coming*; Le Monnier, as cited above.

14. Sutherland, *Huguenot Struggle*, 103–5; Shimizu, 34, n.6; Metzger, 73; see also Lucien Romier, *Catholiques et Huguenots à la cour de Charles IX* (Paris, 1924).

15. On the conspiracy of Amboise, see Sutherland, *Huguenot Struggle*, 81–90; Shimizu, 35–36; Kingdon, *Geneva and the Coming*, 69 ff.

16. The contrast between Antoine, King of Navarre, and Jeanne d'Albret, Queen of Navarre, struck all observers of the scene. See N. L. Roelker, *Queen of Navarre, Jeanne d'Albret, 1528–1572* (Cambridge, Mass., 1968) 145–48. Hereafter cited as Roelker, *Queen of Navarre.*

17. Shimizu, 37–41; Metzger, 80; Sutherland, *Huguenot Struggle*, 110–18; see also below, sec. 3.

18. A. Dufour, "L'Affaire de Maligny, in *Cahiers d'Histoire*, publiés par les Universités-Clermont-Lyon-Grenoble, 8 (1963): 269–83.

19. Shimizu, 43, 45 nn. 71, 72; Metzger, 81, n.5.

20. On Catherine and Antoine, see Roelker, *Queen of Navarre*, 150, where all the sources are cited.

21. On Catherine and the Châtillons, see Shimizu, 39, 54, 57, 60, n. 57; Metzger, 92, 93; on Jacqueline de Longwy, see Roelker, "Noblewomen."

22. Shimizu, 57; Metzger, 103.

23. Kingdon, *Geneva and the Coming*, passim.

24. On this phenomenon, see all the treatments of 1561, e.g., Roelker, *Queen of Navarre*, 165–66.

25. On the Châtillons at Poissy, see Shimizu, 62–64, especially n. 9; Metzger, 119–24, 126–29; see also Donald Nugent, *Ecumenism in the Age of the Reformation: the Colloquy of Poissy* (Cambridge, Mass., 1974) 122, 125.

26. On the Edict of January and the policy of L'Hôpital, see Sutherland, *Huguenot Struggle*, 120, 128, 133, and J. H. Mariéjol, "La Réforme et la Ligue," vol. 6, pt. 1, in Lavisse; see also Quentin Skinner, *The Foundations of Modern Political Thought*, 2 vols. (Cambridge, 1978) 2:250–52, 256–57.

27. On the Catholic counter-offensive, see Sutherland, *Huguenot Struggle*, 133–36, also N. M. Sutherland, *The Massacre of St. Bartholomew and the European Conflict, 1559–1572* (London, 1973). Hereafter cited as Sutherland, *Massacre*. On the ambitions and intrigues of Antoine de Bourbon with Spain, see A. de Ruble, *Antoine de Bourbon et Jeanne d'Albret*, 4 vols. (Paris, 1881–1886), esp. vol. 4: Roelker, *Queen of Navarre*, chaps. 4 and 6.

28. The best analysis of why no solution like that of Henry VIII was possible is in P. Geisendorf, *Théodore de Bèze* (Geneva, 1949); see also Roelker, *Queen of Navarre*, 163, 167, and sources cited.

29. The scholarly literature, notably works of George Williams, deals chiefly with the Italian evangelicals (who were far more numerous and diversified). The best interpretation through a French lay figure is C. J. Webb (Blaisdell), "Between Royalty and Reform: the Predicament of Renée de France, Duchess of Ferrara, 1504–1574" Ph.D. diss., Tufts University, 1969.

30. Brantôme, 6:27.

31. Shimizu, 22–31, including notes.

32. Jules Bonnet, "Jean Macard, un an de ministère à Paris sous Henri II," in *BSHPF* 26 (1877). Hereafter cited as Bonnet.

33. DBF, vol. 2, cols. 835–38; the correspondence of Calvin with Macar(d) can be found in *Calvini Opera Omnia*, ed. Baum, Cunitz, Reuss, 59 vols. (Brunswick, Germany) vol. 17, col. 179 (May 1558). Hereafter cited as *CO*.

34. Bonnet, 56–57.

35. Ibid., 57–59.

36. Ibid., 60, 107, 109–11. The comment is that of Bonnet, p. 60.

37. *CO*, 17, no. 2950, Calvin to Coligny, September 1558.

38. Shimizu, 55; Metzger, 99–100.

39. Metzger, 105–8.

40. Ibid., 116–20.

41. Shimizu, 76; Metzger, 142–48.

42. Shimizu, 29.

43. See Donald Nugent, *Ecumenism in the Age of the Reformation: the Colloquy of Poissy* (Cambridge, Mass., 1974). Sutherland, *Huguenot Struggle* and *Massacre*; also H. O. Evenett, *The Cardinal of Lorraine and the Council of Trent* (Cambridge, 1930).

44. Metzger, 125–29; Nugent.

45. Robert M. Kingdon, *Geneva and the Consolidation of the French Protestant Movement: 1564–1572; a contribution to the History of Congregationalism, Presbyterianism and Calvinist Resistance Theory* (Geneva, 1967), 70–96.

46. Roelker, *Queen of Navarre*, 250–53.

47. For the manifestos of Coligny, Condé, and some of Jeanne's, see Jules Delaborde, *Gaspard de Coligny*, 3 vols. (Paris, 1879–1882), vol. 3.

48. See esp. Vittorio de Caprariis, *Propaganda e pensiero politico in Francia durante le Guerre di Religione* (Naples, 1959), 1:1559–1572 (only the first volume has been published).

49. On L'Hôpital, see the general works cited. Studies of the Parlement in these years are in preparation by N. L. Roelker and Linda Taber.

50. C. Haton (1534–82), *Mémoires contenant le récit des événements accomplis de 1553 à 1582*, ed. L. F. Bourquelot, 2 vols., (Paris, 1857), 1:311.

51. Shimizu, 124.

52. Brantôme, 3:187–89.

53. Metzger, 236, 237, 242, 238.

54. Roelker, *Queen of Navarre*, 305–9; Metzger, 252.

55. Brantôme, 2:280, 296; 6:18; 4:323.

56. Shimizu, 30, 41, 67, 80, 83, 84, 94, 155, and esp. 177.

BIBLIOGRAPHY

Very few studies of the Châtillons exist: three full-scale biographies of Coligny, one recent; two partial biographies and one recent and full-scale of the Cardinal. D'Andelot has yet to find his biographer. Scholarly interpretation is less thin than this would suggest, however, because of two categories of works in which the Châtillons are important, even though they may occupy few lines of print:

(1) serious historial treatments of national politics in France in the third quarter of the sixteenth century;

(2) articles on many aspects of sixteenth-century French Protestantism in the rich and varied collection of the *Bulletin de la Société de l'Histoire du Protestantisme français*, continously published since 1852. In relation to a particular topic, a reader may survey the latter easily using the excellent analytical *Tables* of the *Bulletin* (to 1965, another to appear in 1980). Articles whose main subject is the Châtillons will be included in this bibliography, as will major twentieth-century works on the early Wars of Religion.

The range of primary sources is extensive. Correspondence and dispatches of every agent (official and unofficial) and of every western European state, including the papacy, posted either to France or to any state involved with French affairs in these years are relevant, in addition to French public documents and the correspondence of Catherine de Medici. Other major categories are: the abundant *mémoires* of leaders at court, in the government, and in the nobility; the correspondence of the reformers, especially Calvin and Beza; near-contemporary histories such as the *Histoire Ecclésiastique* (much influenced by Beza) and those of Agrippa d'Aubigné (Calvinist of the second generation of the wars); and Jacques-Auguste de Thou, the leading *politique* historian of the last sixteenth-century generation; and *Receuils* (collections) of miscellaneous documents compiled in the later sixteenth or early seventeenth century. The most important of these for the years up to 1572 is *Mémoires de Condé*, especially the 6-vol. ed. (London, 1743). (The various editions differ considerably;

1743 is the fullest. *Mémoires*, a term often used for these collections, is very misleading.) There is also a biographical dictionary of French Protestantism, containing articles on most of the associates and retainers of the brothers. The article on the Châtillon family is in vol. 4 of the first edition, vol. 6 of the second. Ernest and Eugène Haag, *La France Protestante*, 1st ed. 10 vols. (Paris, 1846–1850); 2d ed. (Bordier) is incomplete, 6 vols. (Paris, 1877–1888).

For all bibliographical detail, readers are referred to the notes and bibliography of Junko S. Shimizu, *Conflict of Loyalties: Politics and Religion in the Career of Gaspard de Coligny, Admiral of France, 1519–1572* (Geneva, 1970). There is considerable variety in the alphabetical manner of listing the Châtillon brothers in the scholarly literature: while the Cardinal is usually listed under *Châtillon*, both he and d'Andelot are also found under *Coligny*, along with the Admiral. The latter is sometimes listed as Gaspard de *Châtillon*. In a few cases d'Andelot is listed separately, sometimes under "D," sometimes under "A."

Studies of the Châtillons, in order of publication

Odet, Cardinal de Châtillon
Leon Marlet, "Odet de Coligny, Cardinal de Châtillon," *Annales de la Société historique et archéologique du Gatinais*, vol. 1 (1883).

E. G. Atkinson, "The Cardinal of Châtillon in England," *Proceedings of the Huguenot Society of London*, vol. 3 (1888–1891).

Lawrence S. Metzger, "The Protestant Cardinal, Odet de Coligny, 1517–1571," Ph.D., Boston University, 1979, sees the Cardinal as representative of the noble class, trying to adjust to the pressures and challenges of the times, with considerable success under the circumstances.

Articles
G. Bonet-Maury, "Les Origines de la réforme à Beauvais, 1532–1568," *Bulletin de la Société de l'Histoire du Protestantisme français* (BSHPF) 23 (1874): 73–88, 124–37, 217–32; G. Bonet-Maury, "Le Protestanisme dans les universités d'Orleáns, de Bourges et de Toulouse," *BSHPF (1889)*.

M. Thomas, *"Odet de Châtillon et la prétendue disgrace de Jean du Bellay, 1549";* in *François Rabelais, Quatrième Centennaire*, Travaux d'Humanisme et Renaissance (Geneva, 1953), 7:223–63.

M. Christol. "Odet de Coligny, Cardinal de Châtillon," *BSHPF* 107 (1961): 1–12.

Gaspard, Admiral of France
Jules Delaborde, *Gaspard de Coligny*, 3 vols. (Paris, 1879–1882). Very full on documents, thin on interpretation. Insufficient analysis of Coligny's relations with the Guises, Catherine de Medici, Jeanne d'Albret, and the French Reformed Church. Skips lightly over the two controversies involving Coligny's "honor"; see below, Shimizu.

A. W. Whitehead, *Gaspard de Coligny, Admiral of France* (London, 1904). Emphasizes religion. Fuller than Delaborde on foreign aspects, but still inadequate on relations with England, 1562–63 and role in the Netherlands Enterprise, 1571–72, owing to over-dependence on *Histoire Ecclésiastique* and failure to include many other sources.

Junko S. Shimizu, *Conflict of Loyalties: Politics and Religion in the Career of Gaspard de Coligny, Admiral of France, 1519–1572* (Geneva, 1970). Deals fully with political and diplomatic aspects previously neglected. Believes political ambition the most important force in career. Scholarly contribution lies in examining all the sources. Devotes a chapter to each of the two controversies: Coligny's responsibility for (1) the clause in the Treaty of Hampton Court, September 1562, by which the Huguenots yielded Le Havre to England pending the return of Calais, chap. 6; and (2) for the assassination of François de Guise by Poltrot de Méré, 1563, chap. 7. On the Le Havre question, Shimizu sees four interpretations by historians (p. 86), ranging from outright treason to total innocence. After full analysis, she concludes that the offending clause was inserted by Huguenot agents in London on the insistence of Queen Elizabeth, *after* Coligny and Condé had signed (pp. 94–95). On the larger question of the Admiral's responsibility for introducing English troops into France, she finds that he did everything possible to minimize English influence and rallied to the French crown, thus disappointing hopes raised in England.

Coligny "never favored calling on foreign military assistance (especially English) . . . tried to separate [England's] assistance to the Huguenots, on religious grounds, from her territorial ambitions . . . limited his request to financial assistance absolutely necessary to continue the war . . . made clear his position *before* he received the loan from England." Moreover, Catherine de Medici tacitly absolved the Hugenots, on condition that they deny the English demand, as they did (p. 103).

On the assassination of Guise, Shimizu notes that those modern historians who believe Coligny guilty are very inimical to Protestantism. "So far as I have discovered . . . there is no evidence or relatively objective document which pronounces Coligny guilty" (p. 110). In this case the Admiral's reputation for honesty proved a two-edged sword. He freely admitted to Catherine de Medici that he did not regret the removal of Guise from the scene, "because I consider it the best thing that could happen to this kingdom, to the church of God, and especially to me and my family, and also . . . the best means to pacify the realm." But at the same time he also said that although he would be willing to kill the Duke in battle, ". . . on his life and honor, it is not true that he has ever sought, induced or asked anyone, to do this by words, money, or rewards, by himself or others, directly or indirectly" (p. 59).

Articles

Nathanaël Weiss, "La Prétendue Trahison de Coligny," *BSHPF* 49 (1900): 37–47.

H. Patry, "Coligny et la Papauté en 1556–57," *BSHPF* 51 (1902): 577–85.

François d'Andelot:

The *Dictionnaire Biographique française*, vol. 2, cols. 835–38, recapitulates the brief biographical notices in the *Biographie Universelle* and Haag (lst ed., vol. 4, cols. 230–37; 2d ed., vol. 6 cols. 557–63). Primary sources, such as Brantôme and the correspondence of Calvin and Beza for 1558–1569, contain various mentions, but, as noted earlier, the greatest number of references are in the *BSHPF*, where there are also about a dozen letters. Even so, there is only one title in which d'Andelot's name figures, a group of articles relating to his captivity in Italy (vol. 3, 1854). The only treatment of his religious-political crisis of 1558 is in the article of Jules Bonnet on Jean Macar (d), in vol. 26 (1877), cited in nn. 32, 34, 35, 36.

Twentieth-Century studies in which the Châtillons figure significantly
(Listed in order of publication by author in each category)

FRANCE, 1550s–1572

Lucien Romier, *Les Origines politiques des guerres de religion,* 2 vols. (Paris, 1913–14).

L. Romier, *Le Royaume de Catherine de Médicis, la France à la vielle des guerres de religion,* 2 vols. (Paris, 1922)

L. Romier, *La Conjuration d'Amboise* (Paris, 1923).

L. Romier, *Catholiques et Huguenots à la cour de Charles IX* (Paris, 1924). Romier's work, especially in the diplomatic sources of the lesser Italian states, was a watershed in the study of factional struggles at court and foreign policy. Although some more recent work (notably Sutherland's) has challenged his interpretations of some events and personalities, no scholar can ignore his contributions.

J. R. Major, *The Estates-General of 1560* (Princeton, N.J., 1951); idem, "Crown and Aristocracy in Renaissance France," *American Historical Review* 69 (April 1964). Major's work has been very influential in revising our understanding of the true relationship of the crown to the nobility, replacing older views that tended to characterize the situation anachronistically as "absolute monarchy."

Vittoris de Caprariis, *Propaganda e pensiero politica in Francia durante le Guerre di religione I, 1559–1572* (Naples, 1959). Vol. 2 has never been published. Little on the Châtillons, fuller on the thinkers of the period. Controversial in several respects not relevant to this essay.

Donald Nugent, *Ecumenism in the Age of the Reformation: the Colloguy of Poissy* (Cambridge, Mass., 1974). The only new study of the politico-religious situation; except for being somewhat too concerned to make parallels with the 1960s, a valuable study that brings out important points formerly overlooked, but not in relation to the Châtillons.

Actes du Colloque: l'Amiral de Coligny et son temps, published by the Société de l'Histoire du Protestantisme français (Paris, 1974). The colloquy was held in Paris in 1972, on the occasion of the four hundredth anniversary of the Massacre of St. Bartholomew. Scholars from fourteen nations participated in a week-long conference.

J. H. M. Salmon, *Society in Crisis: France in the Sixteenth Century* (New York, 1975). The first overview in many years; embodies new scholarship and questions. Sees need for a change in periodization of early modern France, with coherence from 1559 to 1669, instead of more traditional breaks at 1598, 1610, or 1625. The first work anyone new to the field should consult.

French Protestantism to 1572

P-F. Geisendorf, *Théodore de Bèze* (Geneva, 1949).

Robert M. Kingdon, *Geneva and the Coming of the Wars of Religion in France* (Geneva, 1956).

R. M. Kingdon, *Geneva and the Consolidation of the French Reformed Movement: a contribution to the History of Congregationalism, Presbyterianism, and Calvinist Resistance Theory* (Geneva, 1967). Kingdon's studies, together with Geisendorf and the multi-volume collection of Beza's correspondence, ed. Henri Meylan and Alain

Dufour (Geneva, 1960–), are the most important works on the connections between Geneva and France.

N. L. Roelker, *Queen of Navarre: Jeanne d'Albret, 1528–1572* (Cambridge, Mass.,
1968). Useful for the relations of Coligny with the Queen during the Third Civil
War, and for the diplomatic activities of the Cardinal as they affected La Rochelle,
and vice-versa.

N. M. Sutherland, *The Huguenot Struggle for Recognition* (New Haven, Conn., 1980).
In this most recent of her many studies, this major specialist in the field
straightens out the edicts dealing with heresy for the first time. See also her
articles, as listed in Shimizu, p. 210.

There is very little scholarly work on the Catholic side to balance these studies up to
1572; more attention has been paid to the period of the League in the 1580s and 90s.
One should, however, consult H. O. Evenett, *The Cardinal of Lorraine and the Council
of Trent*, (Cambridge, 1930). A new study of Lorraine is much needed; meanwhile,
see Sutherland's articles.

International Repercussions of French Protestantism, 1559–1572

Conyers Read, *Mr. Secretary Walsingham and the Policy of Queen Elizabeth*, 3 vols.
(N.Y., 1925). Masterful analysis of the relationship of England to both the French
and the Netherlands Wars of Religion.

Wallace T. MacCaffrey, *The Shaping of the Elizabethan Regime*, vol. 1 (Princeton, N.J.,
1972). Important new contribution on the English involvements.

N. M. Sutherland, *The Massacre of St. Bartholomew and the European Conflict, 1519–
1572* (London, 1973). Important in correcting the traditional misinterpretations of
Catherine de Medici and in finally resolving the problems of "premeditation" of
the Massacre, distinguishing it clearly from the assassination of Coligny. Somewhat revisionist on the Admiral's relationship to Charles IX and to the Netherlands Enterprise.

Alfred Soman, ed. *The Massacre of St. Bartholomew: Reappraisals and Documents* (The
Hague, 1974). Includes contributions of several major scholars, Sutherland on
impact in Spain; Kingdon on Geneva and Rome, Arthur G. Dickens on England,
and Lewis W. Spitz on the Germanies. These papers were given at two interna-
tional commemorative conferences of the Massacre in 1972, one at the Folger
Shakespeare Library in Washington and one at the Newberry Library in Chicago.
The volume contains a number of other important studies less relevant to the
Châtillons.

10

The Image of Ferdinand II

Charles H. Carter

The aging and ailing Emperor Matthias died in March of 1619, but with the Bohemian government overthrown, the rebels attacking Vienna, and a host of other troubles demanding attention, his successor, Ferdinand of Styria, only got around to his formal election and coronation as the Emperor Ferdinand II in early September. A ceremony of such predictable splendor was always of widespread interest, added to in this case by the turbulent political context, and no doubt whetted by its being scheduled, deferred, and scheduled again. Naturally it was widely covered by Europe's burgeoning public press.[1] One particularly detailed account of it seems a good place to begin a survey of Ferdinand's image in his own time, of its sources, and of the problems involved. Being in English, it also allows one to keep the original language, though radically abridged and paraphrased here.

Ferdinand decided to follow Matthias's precedent (this account begins) and be crowned in Frankfurt. He ordered "the Banners, Robes and other ornaments of the empire" sent there from Aachen (for Charlemagne's sword, *inter alia*) and Nuremberg; they arrived in due course. As the time approached, officers and dignitaries of the Empire streamed into the city. Heavy security was laid on, especially along the procession routes: "The gates were opened to none, the garison souldiers stood in the valley, and the citizens in armes were set in every corner of the streets, but most of all from the Court to the College of Electors, and from thence on both sides of the bridge even to the Church of Saint Bartholomew."

On election day the three ecclesiastical electors functioned as electors, but for the coronation they would function as archbishops—Mainz as consecrator, Trier and Cologne in subordinate clerical roles. Early that morning they went separately to the church and "there putting off their Electoral habits, attired themselves like Bishops as they were, and . . . waited for Ferdinand's coming":

> about 8 of the clock, mounted on a gallant horse, [he] rode unto the Temple in this prince-like order: There went before him on foot a great

train of officers, counsellors, and other noble personages [including] the Ambassadors of the three secular Electors [not present in person], who carried before Ferdinand the Globe, Scepter and Sword of the Empire. Ferdinand himself apparelled like an Elector, and having a crowne upon his head, was carried on horseback under a canopy, which was borne up by [six Frankfort dignitaries]. As soon as they were come to the Church, the Ecclesiastical Electors, in their Pontificalibus, together with their Suffragenes and some others of the Clergy, advanced forward to meet Ferdinand, from the Quire even to the door of the Temple, and having received him honorably, they lead him to an Altar situate at the entrance of the Quire or Chancell: There he entered into a seat appointed for prayer, placed before the Altar, made of cloth of silver, and a Canopy of the same costly stuff let down from the roof of the Church over the seat. The two Archbishops also went into their several seats, on the right hand Triers, on the left Colein, prepared for them and richly hung with red Scarlet cloth. Ferdinand took up a little book which was layd in that seat, and composed himself to prayer, the secular Ambassadors seated also near him. The Chantors meanwhile sang that song, *Glory be to God on high.* The Elector of Mentz began Mass, and in the saying of it the other Electors and Ambassadors lead away Ferdinand to the high Altar, and from thence (after Benediction) unto a royal Throne, which was placed a step or two above the seat where Ferdinand prayed; continuing their observancy and ceremonies he came to the Altar again, and there fell upon his knees, the Electors and the Ambassadors kneeling by him till the Litany was said over him. This done, [the Consecrator] propounded to him the usual Questions. *Whether he would steadfastly keep the Christian and Catholique Religion, defend the Church, administer justice to all, encrease and enlarge the Empire, maintain the widows and fatherless children, render due honour to the Bishop of Rome.* Ferdinand answered affirmatively to every of these, and confirmed his affirmation with a solemn oath. The Consecrator turned himself to the Electors, Ambassadors, and all the people standing roundabout, demanded of them, whether they would submit themselves to Ferdinand, establish his kingdom, and perform obedience to his commandments: when they had testified their consents to all those motions, and cryed with a loud voice, *That he ought to be their King,* he was unclothed in certain places of his body, and then the Consecrator came to him, and taking oil annointed the crown of his head, his neck, his breasts, his right arm and his hands, adding these words at each severall parts he annointed: *I annoint the with holy oyle, in the name of the Father, the Sonne, and the holy Ghost.*

The Unction finished, the Ecclesiasticall Electors, with their Suffragenes lead Ferdinand through the Quire into the Conclave or College of Election, and having wiped off the oil, they put upon him the ancient Emperiall and Pontificall Robes brought from Norimbergh; that is, the Boots and long Surplisse, and Gown let down from his neck by his Brest in parts and so thrown over his shoulders, they put also Gloves upon his hands, and thus attired as it were a Deacon, they bring him forth again from the Chancell to the seat where he first prayed, and there the Consecrator liberally bestowed upon him a new blessing; prayers said, Ferdinand ascends into the Imperial Throne, and the Electors of Triers and Colein take down the Sword of Charles the Great from the Altar, where together with the Crown and Scepter it was layd; draw it forth, and give it into Ferdinand's hands, the Consecrator speaking these words: *Take this Sword by the hands of Bishops.* And when he comes to these words: *Be thou girt with the Sword, etc.* Then the sword is put up into the sheat again, and girt unto his side by the Ambassadors of the Emperiall Electors.

Moreover, after the Consecrator takes the Ring from the Altar, and pronouncing certain words put it upon his finger, from the same Altar he takes the Scepter and Globe of the Empire, and gives them into his hand; the Scepter into his Right hand, the Globe into his Left, with these words: *Take the rod of virtue and Equity;* last of all, the Emperiall Crown is lifted off the Altar and set upon his head by the three Spiritual Electors jointly, with these words: *Take the Crown of the Kingdom,* and then they array him with the golden cloak of Charles the Great. Those Ceremonies observed, he comes down from his Throne, and delivers back these things to the Ambassadors of the Temporal Electors, that is to say, the Globe to the Palatines Ambassador, and the Scepter to Brandenburghs, and so of the rest; then again he makes toward the altar, and there takes a solemn oath, that he will do all those things which belong to a good Emperor.

The oath taken, the Mass goes on, Ferdinand betaking him to his throne the while, and here is exquisit music played by the Quire: from the throne he is once more led to the Altar, the Sacrifice of the Mass first offered, He receives the Sacrament at the hands of the Consecrators; the Sacrament, prayers and other service fully finished, the Consecrator Mentz goes out first, Triers and Colein after him, and between them goes Ferdinand to a stately theater, a stage raised up aloft toward the South, hung on all sides with rich tapistry and Stamell cloth, being layd over the floor thereof: before him are carried the Arms of the Empire by the Ambassadors of the Secular Electors; the Suffragenes and others of the Clergy following after: there the Spiritual Electors place him in a Princely Throne, elevated somewhat above the rest of the stage, covered over with cloth of gold, and hung with a Canopy of red velvet, the chanters at the time singing the Song of Saint Ambrose. The music ceasing, the Archbishop of Mentz draws near to Ferdinand, and in his own name, and in the name of the other Electors, congratulates to him this happy Inauguration, and with all, excellently and carefully commends to him the whole Empire.

At this point the clergy returned to the chancel and the Archbishops of Trier and Cologne changed back into electoral garb, while the new emperor, still in his chair of state, created knights by striking them with

Charlemagne's sword. Then Ferdinand rose and left the theater, and the entire train, with the electoral bishops added, began its elaborate return procession, Ferdinand now "with the Crown on his head, and the Emperiall robes on his back!"

> Thus go they along forwards straight to the Court over the bridge covered over with Stamell [cloth]: there followed a little after three of Ferdinands chaplains on horseback which cast abrode money to the people, gold and silver. . . .

> The casting of this money made such a hurly burly among the common people, that the chaplains could scarce make way for the greatness of the press, though they were on horseback: the cloth on the bridge as soon as the Emperor passed, was cut, torn and rent in pieces by the people.

At the palace "the tables were set and royally furnished for himself and the Princes Electors" at separate tables—those of the secular electors, for example, covered with red velvet—facing the open courtyard and an elaborate artificial well for wine, with the public kitchens at a distance, out of sight. "The Well before the Court, made in the manner of a rock," had the Habsburg symbol as its centerpiece, "an Eagle with two heads crowned," from the two mouths of which red and white wine were to flow, "placed between two lions bearing the Ornaments of Empire, the Scepter, the Globe and Sword." In the kitchen an elaborately stuffed bull had been roasted. The secular rituals of Empire continued; the disorders had only begun:

> When Pappenhemius the hereditary Marshall of the Empire mounted his horse, and being brought with a measure [made] of silver to a heap of oats, being laid together in the open yard, before the Court, between the Well of wine and the kitchen, filled his measure, and struck it with a rod of silver, and then gave [them] to a servant to keep, the people after snatching them away.

> After him appeared one of the Delegates of Brandenburgh riding also on horseback from the Court, and took up a Basen of Silver with a Ewer of Gold, and a Towell, set upon a Board by the kitchen where the Bull was roasted, and carryed it with him to the Court.

> Last of all, the Delegate of the Elector Palatine, Server hereditary, . . . took certain dishes of the Bull roasted in the public kitchen, covered with four silver platters, and bore them with him to the Court.

> This being done, the rude multitude breaking into the kitchen by main force carryed away with them the Bull which was roasted whole, with the head, feet, hooves, tail and horns, and stuft full of Hares, Conies, Lambes, geese, and diverse other sort of birds and fowls, pulling it by piece-meal, and cutting it ascunder with their knives and which is more rude, they defaced the kitchen, and took away all the timber of it.

Meanwhile, Ferdinand and his court were dining on the same fare, apparently unaware of the riot in the kitchen, and the well in the courtyard began to flow with red and white wine from the mouths of the two-headed eagle:

> Now the wine ran out of this Eagle in great abundance for three hours together, being received into two vessels of exceeding great quantity, as many as would having the liberty to draw and drink of it as much as they would, till at last, by the rage of the giddy multitude, they in vain striving against them who were appointed to keep it, the Well was borne down, and the Eagle with the Lions, and all other ornaments of it were carried away.

> The Royal Dinner continued till 5 of the clock in the afternoon with great solemnity and joy. The Emperor at last departed [for home], the Electors [doing likewise] some few days after. There were public tiltings for joy of this Coronation.

> After it the Ambassadors of the Palatine and Brandenburgh, and last of all, of the Duke of Saxony returned home to their Severall Princes, many wishing all prosperitie and good success to the Emperor, and expressing their prayers for him in verse.

Thus did the public press report the affair:[2] a mixture of sacred rite, secular pomp, and anarchic event running out of control of either of those spheres.

The picture is prophetic of Ferdinand's reign. It conformed also to the long war, already beginning, that was to occupy the whole of his eighteen years as emperor, a conflict historians have variously seen as the last of the great religious wars, a set of secular struggles, or a collapse of order, of established structures, of traditional bonds and restraints.

And if historians, who usually treat it as the central event of the early seventeenth century, present a contradictory picture of the Thirty Years' War,[3] they present an equally contradictory one of Ferdinand II, the central figure in that central event. The picture is usually also very simplistic. Ferdinand is either a religious zealot bent on recapturing Germany for the Church or an ambitious political figure bent on establishing absolute rule first over the Habsburg patrimony and then over all of the empire. The goals and the personal characterizations are apparently inseparable.

A cogent argument is sometimes made for the secular view,[4] but particularly in the English-speaking world it is the Counter-Reformation figure we are offered, especially in the broad-stroke version[5] one finds in general works on the period. When Ferdinand arrives on the scene we are offered minor variations on the same swift characterization: "a rabid Catholic, educated and counseled by the Jesuits."[6] This is apparently self-demonstrating: since the latter part of the statement is true, he *of course* was a rabid Catholic. One is inclined to fret at the built-in bigotry, with all

Jesuits treated as interchangeable, and the like. But the non sequitur alone makes it bad history. People from William the Silent to Alfred Hitchcock have been educated by Jesuits without becoming rabid Catholics. In Ferdinand's own time, the Archduke Albert of the Netherlands and Philip III of Spain had Jesuit educations and Jesuit councillors without being noticeably rabid about anything. One must go beyond facile assumptions and make more than facile connections to sort the matter out.

Ferdinand was indeed a firm Catholic who followed a policy of putting down heresy in his own lands when he could. But if we draw a conclusion based on that policy and those actions, we surely have to do the same for France, where a prince of the Church, no less, was concurrently doing more actual destruction of Protestantism than Ferdinand could ever hope for; yet historians seldom even speak of Cardinal Richelieu as a Catholic at all.

And that of course is the problem at hand: to what degree should we speak of Ferdinand in religious or in secular terms? If associations prove nothing by themselves, if actions are ambiguous, and if modern historians are contradictory at best, it is perhaps well to look at how contemporaries perceived him and how he presented himself to them. How he got to that point—the context for such a discussion—is briefly told.

Charles V came to the imperial throne in 1519, Ferdinand II in 1619. This exact century—from the beginning of the Lutheran revolt to the beginning of the Thirty Years' War—is most conspicuously characterized by religious struggle, the old creed first losing vast areas to the new, then beginning a recovery in southern Germany and Bohemia in the 1550s, led by the redoubtable Peter Canisius and the Jesuits. But it is also characterized by an ongoing political struggle between crown and estates, nowhere more hotly than in the various parts of the Austrian Habsburg patrimony. This dichotomy underlies the problem that this essay attempts to explore.

Early in his reign, Charles V turned over administration of that patrimony to his younger brother Ferdinand, who increased it substantially in 1526 when in his own right he became king of Hungary and of Bohemia, with the latter's appendages of Moravia, Silesia, and Lusatia. Eventually succeeding Charles as emperor (1556–64), he divided administration of the family lands among his sons, of whom the Archduke Charles received the much-troubled "Inner Austria": Styria, Carinthia, Carniola, and Goricia, strung out southward along the Hungarian border almost to the Adriatic Sea. There the Archduke Charles twice had to sign "pacifications" with Protestant dissenters, but in the circumstances can be said to have held his own. He died in 1590, and his son Ferdinand, born in 1578, assumed the administration in 1595, while still in his teens. He made steady inroads over the next dozen years until Protestantism was put down and the situation brought under control as effectively as anything could be that close to the rebel havens in Turkish territory.

Meanwhile, Ferdinand I was followed on the imperial throne by his son Maximilian II (1564–76) and Maximilian's son Rudolph II (1576–1612), who died at age sixty without a son. As affairs increasingly got out of hand in Rudolph's later years, he was forced to accept early succession to the Hungarian and Bohemian thrones by his brother Matthias (a gradual hand-over was customary, but the Hungarian throne was transferred as early as 1608; the brothers were almost at war). On Rudolph's death Matthias succeeded to the imperial throne as well (1612–19), with a rather similar end. Sixty-two when he died, he also had no son, also lost control of events (particularly in Bohemia but also in Austria), and also had an early hand-over forced on him.

Matthias's surviving brothers, Maximilian, Grand Master of the Teutonic Order, and Albert, co-sovereign of the Southern Netherlands, also aging and also without sons, cleared the way by yielding their lineal claims. The family agreed (the Spanish Habsburgs concurring in a controversial family treaty) to pass on both the patrimony and the imperial throne to cousin Ferdinand of Styria, who was the same generation as they in terms of distance from Ferdinand I but was two decades younger, had more than proved his ability to cope with difficult times, and, not least, had two sons to resume hereditary continuity.

Matthias duly (if not happily) abdicating, Ferdinand was elected to the Bohemian throne in 1617, the Hungarian in 1618, and by early 1619 was already acting in place of the ailing emperor. Matthias died in late March, by which time the Defenestration of Prague was a year in the past, Bohemia was in rebel hands, and Austria itself seemed in danger. It was from this crisis that Ferdinand's public image emerged—whatever it was to be.

The coronation account quoted earlier gives a satisfactorily objective treatment of the public Ferdinand, but the man does not really emerge from the event. Another type of publication, however, is far more fertile in distinct impressions and, aimed at the encyclopedia market, is at least as factual in intent as a news sheet. Those marvelous compendia of information about a given state or region that one associates especially with the Elzivier publishing house in the United Provinces (but were published by others as well) reached their full development about this time, including a particularly well done *Status Particularis regiminis S. C. Majestatis Fernandi II,* published right at the end of his reign.[7] With more historical detail than the genre usually has, along with the usual topographical, institutional, and other descriptions, it is agreeably rich in pertinent anecdote. For example, a detailed description of Vienna's defenses (and their sorry state) includes an account of Count Thurn's attack on the city, wherein

> a Bohemian souldier . . . did shoot some bullets, from the suburbs . . . into the Imperiall Court or Archducall Castle, and even into the great

Chamber of the Knights and Nobles, and into the Antechamber; and drove his Imperiall Majesty, then King of Hungary and Bohemia, out of his owne Chamber.[8]

Interesting sidelights on Ferdinand's capital sometimes also provide interesting sidelights on his attitudes, here considerably more liberal than could be found in the inhospitable governments of England, Spain, and other places:

The suburbs on the other side of the Danube are inhabited by Iewes, as an Iland apart, and in the Towne they have a place of commerce, where by day they sell their commodities: but it is not lawfull for them to lie all night in Towne. But because they bring great profits to the Imperiall Court, and for other causes and reasons, they are not onely tollerated in the City, but they enjoy many great priviledges and liberties.[9]

But a capsule religious history of the city presents a progressively hardening Ferdinand with regard to Protestants:

The Evangelical Lutheran Religion . . . being heretofore brought into this City, did afterwards so increase under the Emperour Maximilian the Second that the said Evangelicks, amongst other priveledges, had the exercise of their religion in the City it selfe, even in the Minimes Temple, at the Provincial House. And although the Emperor Rudolph the Second, and before him Ferdinand the first, did resolve . . . to abolish the exercise of that religion, and began likewise a great reformation, and advanced the businesse so farre that under the Emperor Rudolph the second the Evangelicall State of Lower Austria lost the exercise of their religion in the City of Vienna, and it seemed as if an universall deformation and a totall suppression and exterpation of all the Evangelicks in those Countries would have followed. Yet the Emperor Mathias the first, for divers great causes, did most graciously grant the Evangelicall state of Lower Austria the exercise of their religion in the Village called Hoernals, about a quarter of a German League from the City, and granted them his high Imperiall and Archducall Protection, nothwithstanding [that] the Catholickes, especially the Cleargy, (whom the exercise of that religion did vehemently offend) perswaded themselves that the Sermons of Cardinal Clozel would have induced the Emperour againe to prohibit the exercise of the Evangelicks of Hoernals. And that he would not permit them Evangelicall Matrimony, nor the administration of the Sacraments of Baptisme, and the Lords Supper.

But when the Emperour Ferdinand the second tooke the raines of the Roman Empire, and had taken the City of Prag, a Priest did seriously inculcate to his Majesty, that where as since the states of the Evangelicall Provinces had beene permitted the exercise of their religion in the Village of Hoernals . . . they had multiplyed that in that congregation there were sometimes twenty, thirty, even forty or fifty thousand persons, and therefore hee earnestly petitioned that the Exercise of that religion might be abolished by publike command. And thereupon it came to passe, that a reformation of religion was directed in the City of Vienna, by an Imperiall Mandate, and the exercise of the Augustan [*sic*; i.e., Augsburg] Confession in the Village of Hoernals (which was afterwards given to the Cathedrall Church of St. Steven in Vienna) was quite suppressed . . . and all the Evangelicall Preachers were forbidden to enter the City upon grievous punishments. But yet in Austria they were suffered, for their persons, as heretofore, and some of the Citizens and inhabitants had leave to go out of the Towne, unto Sermons and Sacraments after the Evangelicall manner, at Intzerrdorff . . . a Mile from the City.

But at the last, Anno 1627, his Imperiall Maiesty severely required all Ecclesiasticall Evangelicks by publike Imperiall and Archducall Proclamations and Mandates, to void by a certaine time, all the Country of Austria and all other his Imperiall Majesties hereditary Dominions, with prohibition under his highnesse pleasure and unpardonable punishments, never to returne, or to remaine there upon any termes.[10]

The Ferdinand that emerges here is neither a hard-hearted authoritarian nor a fiery-eyed zealot, but the description of his habits of worship is harder to interpret:

Now for the person of his Imperiall Majesty, he was of fifty yeares of age, of a midling stature and corpulent, of an excellent complexion, strong and healthfull; his haire and beard somewhat gray, of a gracefull presence; of a Kinde, meeke, bounteous, and liberal disposition, and of a singular understanding, eloquence and memory; Temperate in meate and drinke, and moderate in sleepe, he seldome went to bed till ten at night, and sometimes not till one, and he ordinarily did rise at foure in the morning, and on his bended knees commend himselfe by prayer to God. On festivall and solemne daies principally of the Apostles daies, he did confesse and heare Masse. The thursday before Easter he used to receive the holy Sacrament from the hands of the Popes Nuncio, in company of the Empresse, the King, and the Queene of Hungary, the Archduke, and the Archduchesse, and other principall persons of the Court, according to the rule of the Church of Rome. Before his Imperiall Majesty went to Church, he did appoint Two Masses to be said in the chapell or closet, one for himselfe another for his late wife, who was sister to Maximilian the present Duke of Bavaria, and sometimes at the same time hee did receive the Sacrament. And then he went to Church, where hee commonly did heare a Sermon in Dutch of one of the Iesuits who is the ordinary preacher of the Court, of about an houre long. The Sermon ended, high Masse is celebrated with great devotion, and most sweet Musicke, which lasts at least an houre. After dinner he did use to heare an Italian Sermon by the ordinary Court Italian Preacher, and after that the vespers, which are sung with great solemnity. And in this manner his Imperiall Majesty spent almost the whole Sunday on holiday.

And sometimes he did visit other Churches both within and without the City, [such] as the Dominicans, the Capuchins, the Iesuits, or the Carmelites, and in these Colledges and Convents he sometimes did dine.

In the time of Advent his Imperiall Majesty did commonly rise very early to frequent certaine Mattins, like singing Masses, called *Rorate* because at his entry is sung the said *Rorate Coeli,* which is followed with Musicke of instruments and voices, almost an houres space, which time the people imploy in their prayers and devotions. The same Office is likewise solemnely celebrated with great concourse in all the Churches.

During the time of Lent his Imperiall Majesty was most diligently wont to heare Sermons, in his Court chappell, and in the Augustines Church which is near the Castle, and on Holidaies in the Chappell of the Minimes, especially in the time of the penitentiall processions, and every day in Lent are sung the Vespers at large in the Imperiall Oratory.

On Maunday thursday before noone his Imperiall Majesty publikely, and before all there present, did wash the feet of thirty poore men, then feede them and serve them in his owne person, at table. After he gave to every one a gowne, and a peece of gold to the valew of a double Hungarian ducat.

At the same day and time, in another place apart, the Empresse performes the same out of humility, to thirty poore women.

The last Sunday before Easter his Imperiall Majesty was wont to visit all the Churches of the Towne on foot after the Catholicke Roman manner, and to pray before the Tombs erected in them. This last yeare a coach did ease his feet of that penance.

During the weeke of Holy Crosse, beginning from Sunday to the feast of the Ascension of Christ, his Imperiall Majesty was used to be at the accustomed Processions, at which this yeare his weakenesse hath not suffered him to be present.

On Corpus Christi day, when the great Procession is celebrated, his Imperiall Majesty did use to assist all the Court on foot, bare headed, and to pray on bended knees at all the altars by the way. And the sunday following, he was used to attend the Procession of the Iesuits, and the next sunday to bee present with great devotion at the generall Procession which is very populous, and continues from morning untill noone.[11]

The serious historian who is familiar with the period, or is sensitive to customs and cultures, or who reads for precise meaning and not just impressions, will recognize quickly that there is considerably less here than meets the eye. This long, eventually tiresome account of religious observation is really a great mass of particularities about a few major celebrations spread over the year: the great quantity of detail derives simply from

variations in the repeated items (different churches, etc.), from his attend-
ing services with family and friends, and so forth. Such occasions of course
were not stinted at any major Catholic court; in an age that had not yet
developed secular holidays (a significant misnomer), the major religious
celebrations were the major *public* celebrations.

The foot-washing ceremony, a mark of devotion, was presumably sincere but—though it may seem an excessively graphic performance to mod-
erns—was not an unusual thing for a Catholic monarch to do.[12] It is
perhaps harder to put a *public* act of *humility* into proper perspective, but an
inference of hypocrisy or cant rather undercuts an assumption of zealotry.

And the more one considers what events are actually described here, the
harder it is to avoid a pertinent question: How would a present-day music
lover respond to an opportunity to spend an hour listening to baroque
church music as performed for the imperial court in Vienna three decades
into the seventeenth century? And if one accepted such an opportunity,
would it be a measure of one's religiosity? Since Ferdinand loved music,
surrounded himself with the best musicians, and lived in an exceptionally
good musical period, it seems best not to draw conclusions from his hang-
ing around church choirs.

But the concern at the moment is public perception, not reality, and the
cumulative effect of such a description is great. No amount of content
analysis dispels the reader's sense of a sincerely devout man. And the
religious aura is further heightened by citing the laudatory assessment of a
not-wholly-disinterested observer:

> For this cause [as described above], the Popes Nuncio Cardinall Palatto
> in his relation made to Pope Urban the eight doth testifie (to the great
> commendation of his Imperiall Majesty) the Emperour Ferdinand the
> second may well be stiled a holy Prince, a man after Gods owne heart, as
> was King David, and that for the candor of his conscience, and his firme
> faith in God, the protection of the Almighty hath beene so constant, on
> his Imperiall person, that as the Lords annoynted he never hath or could
> be oppressed or hurt by any as plainely appeareth by his Imperiall mag-
> nanimity, in the very beginning of his raigne, and some following yeeres
> after, when three Regal Offices and Counsellors of the Kingdome of
> Bohemia being throwne out of the window at Prag, in the yeare 1618.
> The 25. of May (The Emperour Mathas the first being yet alive) all his
> hereditary Provinces and Countreys were destroyed with fire and
> sword, and his sacred person (as it were) in the misdst of his ennemies,
> having nothing remaining but onely the City of Vienna, it was not possi-
> ble to force him from his Residence, but on the contrary hee was alwaies
> most miraculously preserved by God.

> The same Nuncio reports also that his Imperiall Majesty hath said, in
> greates dangers, that the divine providence had abundantly manifested

its strength and power in his sacred person, above the reach and understanding of man.

And for matters of religion or conscience, when his Imperiall Majesty did
depute a Counsellour or Commissioner to that end, he did not precipi-
tate a ratification, but first remit all to his Confessour, who is most acute
and prudent father, whose counsell and judgement his Imperiall Majesty (as the sheep his sheepheard) did constantly follow with a willing
and ready mind and heart; and to cleare himselfe from all scruples of
conscience, he did referre unto him all, even the least things.[13]

But the picture is again modulated, as

on other daies, (except the Lords day) having heard two Masses and
dispatched his private Consultations, for every day, or at least every
other day, he did hold a Counsell, unlesse there were something of
greater moment to dispatch, his Imperiall Majesty used to goe out of
Towne to take the aire, or to hunt (in which kind of exercise he did most
delight) and commonly returned not till night: whence the proverb
grew, that his Imperiall Majesty in three things was indefatigable; to wit,
his devotion, in counsell, and in hunting. And although sometimes he
did returne somewhat late and tired from hunting, yet did hee never
refuse or forbeare to signe with his own hand forty, fifty or three score or
more severall things at one time, concerning the businesse of the Empire, and other matters, and without the least shew of displeasure or
impatience, and then hee did sit downe to meate. So that his Imperiall
Majesty did never returne from Counsell, from hunting, or from audience (as they term it,) without prescribing or signing somewhat, or reading memorials, or being otherwise imployed. And for as much as his
Imperiall Majesty by reason of the many businesses of the empire, and
others of great consequences, could not himselfe read the least part of
them; if there was any thing presented to himselfe, or to the [master?] of
his Chamber, hee did command it to be sent by a waiter or huisher of the
chamber unto the Counsell proper for the businesse, that it might be
speedily dispatched.

His Imperiall Majesty was most of all delighted in hunting (as is said)
and in Musicke; and did keepe all kind of dogges, and strange birds, for
hunting and hawking. Of Huntsmen and falcners, hee had about 150.
But besides these, his Imperiall Majesty, in all his hereditary Kingdomes,
and Provinces, had a chiefe Huntsman with divers others, and dogges
without number.

He did use a peece very skilfully; but his chiefest pleasure was to moose
[?] his game, and with his own hand to kill wild boares, which he
afterwards sent for presents of honour to forraine Ambassadours and
Agents, and to the officers of the Court. And he was wont to keepe a

catalogue of the annual number of the Deere he killed, and sent to the Electour of Saxony.

His Imperiall Majesty was likewise very curious to get exquisite Musitians, and to these two kind of men, Musitians and Huntsmen, he did give very liberally, and spend much money on them. Musicke, he said, is profitable, and fit for the praise and honour of the Almighty: and to make the heart of man merry.[14]

In various other states there existed an Ecclesiastical Court of High Commission (England), a Junta of Theologians (Spain), or some other formally constituted body staffed by clergy that in some manner impinged upon the secular government, sometimes with a veto power over policy. So too in the present case:

The Ecclesiasticall Counsell was instituted by the Emperour Maximilian the second, that Ecclesiasticall matters and those which concerne Religion, as well in the Empire, as in his Imperiall Majesties hereditary Kingdomes and Dominions, might be therein resolved and deliberated. This Counsell hath neither a President, not a set number of Counsellours; the one halfe whereof is of Ecclesiasticall persons, and the other of Politique.

The Counsell of Conscience consists only in the meeting of Ecclesiasticall persons, which are more or less according to the occasion.

When his Imperiall Majesty treated the peace of Prag in the yeare 1635. with the Electour of Saxony, and his conscience was much perplexed, whether he might any longer suffer the Evangelicks to enjoy the possessions of Ecclesiasticall goods in the Empire; for the recovery whereof, the warre had so long continued, and so much blood had been shed: This question of conscience, of so great a consequence, was refer'd to the Counsell of Divines, that thereupon they might declare their judgement. Hereupon divers Ecclesiasticall persons were assembled from divers places in the City of Vienna: the Counsell was composed of two Cardinals, two Bishops, two Prelates, two Cannons, two Fathers of every Society and order, (amongst which were also two Iesuits.) And they deliberated and consulted thereon for divers weekes, and at last delivered an opinion, whereupon his Imperiall Majesty did afterwards agree of Articles with the Electour of Saxony, and thereupon the peace was published.

And this Assembly of Ecclesiastiques was then called, the Counsell of Conscience; because the matter touched the conscience of his Imperiall Majesty.[15]

The image that emerges from this end-of-career account could be described as that of a ruler who saw to the defense of his particular faith, definitely a "Counter Reformation figure," though definitely not a

Counter-Reformation ogre. Perhaps predictably, the many eulogies published at his death also emphasize that role, but such things run so heavily
to formula that they tell little about the individual or even what his image
otherwise was: those for Ferdinand are virtually interchangeable with
those for his predecessors, a fact emphasized when one finds his and
Matthias's eulogies actually published in the same tract. And Matthias,
pace the cant of his eulogists, was considered a washout as paladin of the
church. And as a matter of fact, during Ferdinand's lifetime both the man
and the issues were often viewed in very different terms.

In 1620, for example, an Antwerp publisher celebrated the Battle of the
White Mountain and the subsequent rout of the Bohemian forces with a
series of verses devoted to Ferdinand and other principals in the affair:[16]
the event is presented not as a Catholic victory but as a Habsburg one. The
introductory stanza, with the Low Countries in mind, takes a swipe at "the
rebellion of the perverse" in general, then cites Ferdinand's victory as
proof not that he was on God's side but that God was on the side of the
House of Austria:

> Ce rencontre est augure certain
> Que dieu preste a l'Autrice sa main.

The verse on Ferdinand refers to numerous aspects—all secular:

> De Boheme la Capitale a rendu les clefz
> Et voz soldas o Cesar y son heureusement entrez
> Reprens le Sceptre & la couronne
> Et a ce peuple nouvelle loix ordonne
> C'este un pays entierment conquis
> Gaigne par le sang, et tant d'armes
> Grandz fraiz, & mil allarmes.

Prague recaptured, crown retaken, new laws to be given, total conquest,
blood, arms, expense and alarms, but religion nowhere in sight.

The ecclesiastical electors, with one verse for all three, are praised for
raising money for the Emperor's cause: "C'est le vray nerf & appuy de
Mars"—rather than, as one might expect, the emperor's being the "vray
nerf & appuy" of the church. True, in his stanza, the Duke of Bavaria, head
of the Catholic League, is praised for being the "soustien de la foy," but
there are after all not many words that rhyme with "Bucquoy." There is
left-handed praise for the Duke of Saxony's finally siding with "Cesar"
(one would not expect a Lutheran to do so on religious grounds); the
victorious general Bucquoy appears not as a crusader but as "servant of the
House of Austria"; and though "Protestans" are mentioned obliquely in
the gloating stanza on Frederick V, he appears mainly as a hapless loser
("Adieu Fredericq Prince Palatin . . ."). A closing Latin inscription refers to

Ferdinand in heavily religious terms ("Cath. Fidem propagaverit/ Maledictum Calvinistarum . . ."), but this publication clearly celebrates the restoration not of the true religion but of the rightful ruler.

Newspapers in Protestant countries were more apt to find that battle a religious defeat as well as a political one, but most war coverage was handled as either straight military news or news of the doings of famous people. In an age that had to make do without movie stars, rock musicians, and the jet set, war leaders on both sides were celebrities and rather avidly treated as such by the press; the emperor, of course, was one of the superstars. But there was a difference. Generals became famous on the basis of success in the field, and at least get characterized as able soldiers—though they are not *greatly* differentiated—as well as having their actions described. With Ferdinand, however, one is normally just told what he did: little in the way of personal image comes through.[17] This leaves one, mainly, with partisan publications, and the relevant questions to pose:

(1) Did Ferdinand seek to present himself—and his propagandists and other supporters to present him—as paladin of the Church or as aggrieved secular ruler?
(2) Did he and his supporters see and/or present the issues as religious or secular ones, his enemies as religious or political threats?
(3) Did his opponents and critics attack him as a threat to the Reformed Religion or as a secular tyrant: actual in Bohemia, potential in Germany as a whole?
(4) Did he and others, for and against, perceive in religious or secular terms his actions, motives and goals, and the nature of the events, issues and conflicts he was involved in?

There was a great deal of miscellaneous literature about that would fall under the partisan heading. Most of the satirical verse (mostly Latin, mostly wooden), dramatic spoofs (heavy-handed), and various fey conceits such as letters from Parnassus, were usually anti-Ferdinand. The pro-Ferdinand miscellany ran to long and ambitious flights of "scholarship," often bristling with citations, that were typically so swarming in classical allusions as to make it nearly impossible to tell what reality they are supposed to relate to. One can say somewhat vaguely that both kinds of image can be found on both sides of this mish-mash, but this sort of material seems far too ephemeral to bear any substantial conclusions.[18] For that one must turn to issues of substance and what was written about them, beginning with the beginning of the troubles.

The most vocal of Ferdinand's opponents viewed the Bohemian rebellion as a religious matter, not a political one, and many of his more systematic critics also perceived it as basically a struggle for religious freedom. The argument is put particularly well in *A clear demonstration that Ferdinand is by his own demerits fallen from the Kingdome of Bohemia.*[19] Published early and circulated widely, it begins by laying out a theoretical basis that manages to state what is in effect the much-debated doctrine of tyrranicide (or its currently usual religious version), without referring either to the conventional authorities or to recent protagonists:[20]

> It is apparent out of holy and humane Histories, and the examples of all Kingdomes and Provinces: That the safety and prosperitie of all Empires and States doth consist especially in two things. The first is, when the Lawes, covenants, priviledges, and immunities of the Kingdome are religiously observed and kept. And secondly, when the free exercise of true Religion, is allowed and maintained, and all persecution and cruelty utterly abrogated. On the other side, whensoever the priviledges of a State are uniustly undermined, and weakened, & the Orthodoxe Religion sharply persecuted and banished; It cannot chuse, but such a Government must needes degenerate into a most outragious tyrannie, and that all bonds of faith, love, and obedience, which doe tye the Magistrate and Subiects to one another, must needes be dissolved. For as the observance of the Lawes and the liberty of true Religion are the foundations, upon which must be laid a Christian and lawfull rule allowed of God: so on the contrary, where these are wanting, it is evident that that rule, is neither lawfully constituted, nor can long continue. . . . And therefore hath it alwayes beene the greatest care and endeavour of Christian subiects, that these two pillars of their safety; to wit, the liberty of their consciences and of their Country, should be kept firme and unmoved.

> Hence it hath grown a custom that Christian Provinces may (the honour of God, and integrity of Conscience alwayes prescribed) lawfully cast off such tyrannie, and depart from under the yoke of such savage Rulers.[21]

Most of the argument to make this principle apply to the Bohemian case[22] is constitutional, legal, and so forth, but the *problem* is a religious one. The author brushes aside the question of whether Ferdinand was elected legally: he says he was not, but even if it is supposed that he was, "Yet hath Ferdinand after his Election and Coronation so miscarried himselfe that it may be truly said, that hee is fallen from the Kingdome, and hath forfeited it by his own misdemeanour."[23] The two-count indictment the author began with has a secular part (at least nominally) as well as a religious part, but the nature of the misdemeanor is clearly religious.

Or at least the solution is. The Bohemian Estates now desire to bring in "a Conscience untoucht and untainted"—Frederick V—and now pray to God to "stretch out his Almighty arme, against all the enemies of his Church, professing the Gospell of Christ Iesus, and against those Murtherers that so vehemently thirst for Christian blood, and that he will roote them out in the middle of their courses of tyrannie and cruelty unlesse they repent."[24]

"And the same States," he adds, "rest in good expectation, and full assurance" of help from "Christian Princes which professe the Gospell." The goal is the restoration of the true church, and the Estates hope that Frederick, just elected King of Bohemia, "will labor to effect it with all his endeavour. That this new government may tend to the praise and glory of Almighty God, to the propagation of the trueth of the Gospell, to the encrease and commodity of Christes Church: and lastly to the stable and perpetuall peace of all these Countries. Amen."[25]

Ferdinand's supporters met such charges of religious oppression in three identifiable ways: they derided them, they finessed them—two approaches that are discussed later on—or they simply reversed the accusations. According to a nineteen-page *Lettre de Wenselaus Meroschowa Bohemois,* of 1620 but before the Battle of the White Mountain, allegedly written from the Count Palatine's own army in Bohemia, religion was ten times as free under Ferdinand, while now *"le cruel et felon Calvinisme,"* a hundred times worse than *Papisme,"* held them "crushed under an abominable superstition," and they might as well expect "Mohammedanism and circumcision, with a hard servitude" next. By contrast:

> the Elector of Saxony with his adherents, and several imperial towns, judged their religion more assured under the Emperor than under the Calvinists and Turks. They put themselves in his protection, and in conformity with Holy Scripture they render unto Caesar the things which are Caesar's, and unto God the things that are God's. We, on the contrary, have ravished Caesar of that which was Caesar's and offered to the Turk the things that are God's.[26]

In the nature of things, attacks that branded Ferdinand a religious oppressor defended the cause of religious freedom. But in the process they also defended the specific act of rebellion—the defenestration of Ferdinand's ministers and the subsequent election of Frederick as king—and that could be done in two ways: not only by condemning his rule, which was done in religious terms, but by attacking the way he acquired the throne in the first place, a purely political matter.

The struggle between crown and estates was of long standing in Bohemia, and was very much in the air in Europe at the time, so this was a natural tack to take. It was, of course, the other of the two classic grounds on which a ruler could be declared a tyrant and thus subject to legitimate dethronement. But it was a two-edged sword that cut mostly against the rebels. It shifted the focus away from charges of oppression, which was ideal propaganda material, to a complicated scholars' debate that was often mired in constitutional nitpicking and was only rarely capable of stirring emotions. It removed the motive for religion-based support from fellow-Protestant states. It grounded their case on an issue—the right to depose a monarch—that rulers elsewhere were not apt to sympathize with. And it rested on a constitution that the Habsburgs had had the greater hand in shaping.

In the process, of course, the prism through which Ferdinand's image appears shifts from religious to secular. Where before he was presented as a paladin of the Counter-Reformation accused of religious offenses, now he is merely a ruler whose claim to the throne is challenged. Under the old ground rules the attacks were against him as a person, for his actions: mostly now they are just against the validity of his claim to the throne. Even when the attacks are against his actions, there is a considerable improvement. Where before his opponents painted him as a ruthless tyrant oppressing the Reformed Religion, here they can manage nothing worse than a conniving politician.

But the Fernandines finessed this line of attack simply by making it irrelevant: they argued that the Bohemian throne was hereditary anyway. A particularly thoroughgoing case for this was made in 1620 by Augustin Schmid von Schmiedebach, published in German as *De Statu Bohemico*[27] and in Latin as *Informatio Fundamentalis super hodierno Bohemiae statu.*[28] The work is solid enough to appeal to scholars, clearly written enough to be accessible to the average reader. It is long enough to be taken seriously, short enough not to be forbidding (forty-five pages in the German edition, thirty-seven pages in the Latin). About 60% of this ample space is spent on a systematic argument that rests on three principal constitutional pillars, the 1356 Golden Bull of Charles IV, King Wladislai's Disposition of the throne in favor of his daughter Anna, and Ferdinand I's Letter of Majesty, plus pertinent modern writers, with the rest of the space used to publish those documents and sum up Schmiedebach's arguments based on them.[29] There is even a sting in the tail as with a nice bit of irony he ends by drawing support from the Count Palatine's own minister, Philip Cammerarius.[30]

It is little wonder that Ferdinand readily took up the role of aggrieved monarch when the constitutional documents could be made to support his case so neatly. And when all the changes had been rung with respect to the *kingship* of Bohemia, one could start out on the *electorship* that went with it. As a 1619 English edition of the Golden Bull puts it:

> We ordaine, and by our Imperiall authority commaund, this present Law perpetually to be observed and kept; That whensoever the said temporall Princes, Electors, or any of them shall leave their right, voyce, and power of election aforesayd, the same shall iustly, lawfully and freely escheat and fall to the eldest sonne and heire of him or them, being a Temporall person, without any contradiction whatsoever: And if the said eldest sonne shall die without lawful temporall heires male, by vertue of this our Imperiall Edict the right, voyce, and power aforesaid, shall fall to the next brother, being a Temporal person, rightly descend-

ing from his father; and after him to his eldest sonne, being a Temporall Prince: And such succession shall from time to time perpetually be observed.[31]

But his opponents could be just as weighty. *Evidentia causae Bohemieae, qua Ferdinandi II. Caesaris legitima abdicatio et Frederici Palatini justa electio,*[32] published the same year as Schmiedebach's work and about twice as long, makes an exhaustive legal-constitutional-historical case, packed with marginal notes and citations, and numerous cross-references to the sixty-seven backnotes that fill pages 46–76. Just before these the author ends his text with a classical FINIS and a rebellious biblical quote:

No exercetote perversitatem in judicio: ne accipito personam tenuis, neque honorem exhibeto personae magni: juste judicato proximum tuum.

Or, as the brand-new King James translation had it:[33]

Yee shall doe no unrighteousness in Iudgement; thou shalt not respect the person of the poore, nor honour the person of the mighty: but in righteousnesse shalt thou iudge thy neighbor. (Leviticus 19:15)

Leviticus 19 is headed "A repetition of sundry Lawes," which is consistent with the pervasiveness of individual biblical strictures, including this one to judge men and their claims on their own merits regardless of rank: the King James passage, typically, has five cross-references (to Exodus 23:3, Deuteronomy 1:17 and 16:16, Proverbs 24:23, and James 2:9), ample grist for a propagandist in a religious age, even on a political subject, as is frequently shown in Protestant propaganda against Ferdinand. The aged cliché is true, of course, that Scripture will support both sides of most any argument: render unto Caesar, and all that. But both sides could also go to the historical well, and even the constitutional one: Protestants cited constitutional documents right back. Fought with those weapons, the crown began with an advantage in a crown-estates contest, since the key documents were the work of former monarchs, such as a Bohemian king's declaring the throne to be hereditary through the act of disposing of its inheritance in favor of a particular heir. Something like the Letter of Majesty of Ferdinand I was literally a family document: a Habsburg declaring that a throne he held was hereditary, and in the Habsburg family. But the rebels could cite another kind of Habsburg family document on their side.

Of all the documentary and historical support the Fernandines cited, quoted, and published in full, they never mentioned "Letters of Reversal." Their opponents, however, mentioned them all the time. There is a recurring ring of, in effect, "What about the Reversals?" Getting no adequate response, eventually they published them. A thirty-five-page *Briefve Information Des affaires du Palatinat,* for example, leads off with a twelve-page section on "The acceptance of the Crown of Bohemia" that includes the Reversals of both of Ferdinand's two immediate predecessors, Rudolph II and Matthias, complete with key passages in italics. That for Matthias includes:[34]

> *The Estates have unanimously elected us of their good and free will as Expectant and King of Bohemia*, etc., and further down: . . . we promise for all, our heirs and successors, etc. . . . *that this free election of our person, etc.* will not convey any prejudice now nor ever in future times, and will not derogate from their rights, ordinances, privileges, franchises, etc. etc. . . . But in case that we [neglect our duties toward the kingdom]: *The Estates will . . . not be further obligated to us in any way.*

From which the author concludes:

> Since the eldest son of Queen Anne, and his two eldest sons [i.e., Maximilian II, Rudolph II, and Matthias] have one after the other received and accepted the Crown of Bohemia solely from the pure will and free Election of the Estates, and not by any hereditary succession, there is not any reason at all [a *triple* negative in the French!], nor appearance, that the modern Emperor Ferdinand, issue of the next eldest son of the said Queen Anne, should have any more right and claim to the said Crown than they had.

This seems a telling point, and a damning document. It is hard to see how it could lose as propaganda. If it did not decisively settle the dispute (an ideal result hardly to be counted on), it might cancel out the other side's similar documentation, and if hammered hard enough and long enough it might at least discredit all such documentation. But the author apparently could find no way to build a fuller argument upon it. Or perhaps, with only a dozen pages to work with, he wanted to deliver a quick one-two punch. In any case, he left a good argument for a strangely quixotic one:

> To which one must add that after the death of the Emperor Matthias, in the year 1619, when it was a question of electing a new emperor, the Elector of Mainz, Archchancellor of the Empire, called the Emperor Ferdinand (who was not yet raised to the Imperial Dignity) to the Diet of Frankfort to attend the imperial election as King and Elector of Bohemia, *elected, received, annointed* and crowned by the said Estates, as he has expressly declared in his written Apologetique . . . on encountering the complaint that the Ambassadors of the said Estates made at that time of such a convocation, which they alleged to have been done to their prejudice since they were in controversy [with] and had legitimate exceptions [to make] against the said Ferdinand. It would seem that the other Electors received him in the Electoral Conclave, not in virtue of any heredi-

tary right but only following his Election, reception and coronation by
the said Estates. All this demonstrates well enough that the Crown of
Bohemia must be held as Elective and not hereditary. As to the limitation
that the Emperor. . .

This is a tortuous, tenuous argument. That what is eased into the argument as "seemingly" the case in one sentence is escalated to sufficiently
"demonstrated" in the next is an old trick of rhetoric; so it is not necessarily
faulty reasoning. Nor need one quibble overmuch about what an imperial
electoral conclave has to do with the constitutional nature of the Bohemian
crown: in such a dispute one takes support where one finds it, or where
one can pretend to find it. But the conclusion itself makes no sense. The
only real thrust it has is that the electoral conclave formally recognized the
electoral nature of the Bohemian throne by the form of words the chancellor used in calling Ferdinand to the conclave. Yet to accept that requires
accepting the actions of the conclave as decisive in Bohemian constitutional
matters, and the conclave's proceeding with the imperial election with
Ferdinand still in his electoral seat would, in this strange line of reasoning,
just as clearly demonstrate that he was *still* the validly elected king of
Bohemia and his alleged deposition null.

But that was in 1624, well after the Battle of the White Mountain and
Ferdinand's subsequent victories, purges, and confiscations, when his
Bohemian opponents were thoroughly beaten and groping for any kind of
argument they could find (to get any kind of help they could find). When
their situation was better—during the nearly two-and-a-half years between
the Defenestration (early 1618) and the White Mountain (late 1620), when
the anti-Ferdinand forces were in control, ousting Jesuits, besieging
Vienna, and all the rest—their propaganda was better too. Perhaps win-
ners can think better, for they analyzed the situation to far better effect in
those palmy days. In the year that was to end in the White Mountain
disaster *An answere to the question, Whether the Emperor that now is can bee
Iudge in the Bohemian Controversie or no?*[35] presented, like the *Briefve Information,* a two-part argument, but here both parts are effectively done; the first
even has a fall-back position.

First, the author asserts that the standard pro-Ferdinand argument concerning the Bohemian throne is not actually based on his rights as King of
Bohemia but on his position as *emperor,* on his alleged imperial power to
dispose of that particular part of the Empire. This is a telling point, especially because accepting it does not depend on agreement concerning
whether the throne is elective or hereditary. The author's partisanship
almost muddies the waters—he says the pro-Ferdinand arguments are
based upon his supposed imperial power and prerogative and not on his
rights as *duly elected* king of Bohemia—but he clears up any possible confusion about the point he intends:

For it is more than world-notorious, and more then manifest out of all Writings, edictall cassation, and Mandate set forth and published by his Imperiall Maiestie [that he] neither pretendeth nor groundeth his complaint upon any wrong done to the holy Roman Empire, by [Frederick V's] accepting of the said Crowne of Bohemia: But altogether and alone upon this, that namely the . . . Crowne of Bohemia appertayneth onely and alone unto the House of Austria, as being an onely Inheritance of the same.

In sum, if Bohemia *is* Ferdinand's, it is his as an Austrian Archduke (an individual person), not as emperor; Ferdinand *qua* emperor has no say in the matter.

If his reader does not accept this argument, clinging to the notion that an emperor has the right to dispose of thrones within the empire, it does not change anything, because Bohemia is not part of the empire anyway, and the author publishes an extract from the Acts of the Diet of Augsburg to show that this was established in law as long ago as 1548.

The author's second point rests not on specific legalities but on a basic principal of law, and appeals in the process to one's sense of justice. The tract's title poses the question: whether it is proper for Ferdinand, a principal in the matter, to decide the Bohemian controversy as emperor. The answer is predictably "no," but a good case is made for it, and one cannot get around the central fact, that to do so Ferdinand would be "both partie and Iudge."

Nor was there any getting around the 1548 Diet of Augsburg, which had ratified the disposition that Charles V, looking ahead to death or abdication, was making of the Habsburg patrimony currently within the empire. Most historians have apparently forgotten this, which would explain why on textbook maps for later periods the thick red line that indicates the extent of the empire continues to include the Low Countries—the former but no longer Burgundian Circle. So the Fernandines met this argument in the only way they could, by agreeing with it:

It is very true that the Bohemians are not immediately subjects of the Empire, but they are subjects of the King of Bohemia, who is subject to the Emperor, holding the Kingdom of Bohemia in fief, with the right and voice of Electorat.

This of course is disingenous to a fault, and makes the tract's title seem a bit cynical: *Discours Tres-veritable touchant les droicts de la Couronne de Boheme.*[36] But the author spends half his seventeen pages of text arguing this and related matters, and later appends excerpts "Touching the election and succession of the Kings of Bohemia" from that old standby, the Golden Bull. He spends the other half of his space refuting other accusations against Ferdinand. Most pro-rebel tracts confined themselves to a couple of points, but this list totals a startling seventeen specific complaints—and this was still only 1620, before the Battle of the White Mountain, turning the universities of Prague and Heidelberg over to the Jesuits, the executions and confiscations in Bohemia, et cetera. The author responds to them by the numbers, averaging about half a page, but some are dealt with almost out-of-hand, while others get a quite full reply. The treatment, however, is not uneven in all respects, being consistently accrimonious throughout. The critic he is particularly answering is uniformly "this liar," when it is not improved, with redundant overkill, to "this false liar"; his accusations "lies," his arguments "pure fables and dreams." It is perhaps the best brief overview of this ongoing debate to be had in one place:

1. A comparatively long response in the dispute over what Ferdinand promised in his Letters of Reversal.
2. A similarly long explanation of the arrest of Cardinal Klesl.
3. "They say moreover that the Serene King, through the Fathers of the Company of Jesus, has troubled the public repose of the Kingdom of Bohemia, and has filled it with troubles and confusions." He denies this.
4. He denies succinctly that Ferdinand turned over the government to foreigners, a frequent complaint that recurs later.
5. Also briefly, he denies that Ferdinand "has troubled the confederations of the Estates founded in defense of the privileges."
6. Ferdinand, he says, did not force anyone to attend Mass.
7. Ferdinand is accused of having had temples "destroyed and demolished." The author asks: "But I beg you, when and where was this done?"
8. Another religious complaint, concerning a bishop of Prague.
9. They claim that Ferdinand brought force and violence into Bohemia; but the rebels did so first.
10. They claim that Ferdinand's election was improper because all the areas under the Bohemian crown—Moravia, Silesia, Lusatia—were not there. This gets a *long* and innocent explanation.
11. A related, specific accusation, that Ferdinand stalled until most of the Protestants had gone home, is also explained away.
12. The 1617 treaty with Spain is considered suspect. The response—that it is a simple treaty that does not affect the Bohemian succession—is vintage doubletalk.[37]
13. Bohemians have complained of the cruelty and barbarism of Ferdinand's soldiers. The author admits the problem, adds that it is done on both sides, and gives rather unconvincing assurance that Ferdinand has punished his soldiers whenever their guilt has been proved.
14. "To which one adds the protestation of the said Estates that they were stirred and constrained by their own conscience to deliver and protect

the kingdom from tyranny. But this is . . . all rebels' usual way of going about it, thus to make solemn protestations where they lack right, to fall back on consciences, alleging that by inevitable necessity they are constrained to do this [i.e., rebel], and pretend to these specious *noms* of deliverance from tyranny; yet there is nothing in all this, for never was there greater tyranny and oppression in the kingdom than during their directorate, they deprive the innocents of their means of livelihood and possessions with no due process of law nor of justice."

15. Responds concerning alleged actions by Ferdinand against the Estates.
16. "More, this false liar says that King Ferdinand is governed by the turbulent spirits of the Jesuits, and by the Ministers of Rome and Spain, full of pride, envy and cruelty: That is to talk very differently than the said Estates did when they received him as King in their response given to the proposition that was made them, by which they so lauded his virtues and so many diverse talents that were in truth in him.

"But one should not be astonished if, having changed their faith, they now change language, and if they strive today to spread things manifestly false from envy of the King.

"His Majesty has never given the charge of any part of the Kingdom to fathers of the Company of Jesus, nor has he ever made use of their counsels, except for the case of his own conscience. [Neither] the Ministers of Rome nor of Spain have any voice nor seat in his Councils, and when that should be [i.e., if that ever should be the case in the future] there is nothing evil, cruel, bad to expect from their advice and counsels, on the contrary His Holiness and the Most Serene King of Spain, in the hope that they always have of some sort of accommodation of affairs, have not sent during this year but very little aid to His Majesty, having nothing so at heart as the conservation of the House of Austria and the peace of the Provinces."

17. Concerning the difficulty of negotiating with Ferdinand, which of course is denied.

But if Ferdinand's defense of his rights in Bohemia was purely political—rather than defending his religious policies he tried to dissociate himself from the Jesuits and other symbols of the Counter-Reformation—polemically he approached the problem of the *imperial* throne very differently.

In early June of 1619 the Bohemian forces were in the suburbs of Vienna. Though it was poorly defended they failed to take the city and soon withdrew, but this clearly was not going to be a tranquil year. Ferdinand left for Frankfurt later that month to prepare for his election and coronation as emperor. And there was a lot of preparing to do: the ceremonies, intended for July, did not take place until September because Christian of Anhalt had a move afoot to elect the Count Palatine emperor.

The most optimistic scenario for the scheme involved talking the Lutheran Elector of Saxony into joining the Calvinist Elector of Brandenburg
and the Elector Palatine in voting for Frederick. But this, of course, would
only match the votes of the three ecclesiastical electors, which were sure to
be cast for Ferdinand, so a majority would require the vote of the elector of
Bohemia. The only way to take that vote away from Ferdinand—who could
be counted on to vote for himself—was to replace him as *king* of Bohemia
(and thus as elector) with someone who would vote for Frederick for emperor. The former had already been done to this cabal's satisfaction, and
they were of course in the process of putting Frederick himself on the
Bohemian throne, but they still had not done so. For one thing, Frederick
and his backers were as slow as usual in getting their act together. For
another, the smart rebels preferred John George of Saxony to Frederick and
used up a great deal of time trying to convince him. As a result, Ferdinand
might no longer be King of Bohemia, but they did not get a new king
installed in time to try to insist that he be seated as elector instead of
Ferdinand. So it would do them no good to claim that Ferdinand was not
the legitimate elector since they had no one to put in his place. To add a
touch of irony, the Bohemians *did* finally get Frederick elected king two
days before the imperial election, word of which reached Frankfurt just
after the imperial election was over. But John George, who had declined the
Bohemian throne, had already declined to take part in the scheme anyway.
So with the advantage of historical perspective, including having a more
accurate assessment of Saxony's judgment and Anhalt's abilities than
Anhalt probably had, we can say that Ferdinand was certain to be elected
in any case. But with the experience of numerous modern elections that the
challenger could not possibly win but won anyway, we can understand
Ferdinand's treating the challenge as a serious threat.

Ferdinand's response in this wider arena was not constitutional argument but an appeal for support from fellow Catholic rulers, outside of
Germany as well as within, couched in straightforward religious terms.
The Protestants were bringing ruin to Germany and to the Faith; and while
Ferdinand was the natural one to oppose them, he could not do it without
help. This is the principal burden of *Le Manifeste de Ferdinand duc de Baviere*
[sic], *Roy des Romains. Envoyé a tous les Roys, Princes & Republiques Chrestiennes & Catholique, pour la conservation des droits des Princes Catholiques à l'Empire; contre les desseins des Protestans,*[38] a rather vigorous ten-page production
addressed especially to Louis XIII of France and published in Paris as early
as May 29, 1619, just two months after Matthias's death, and just before
the Bohemian attack on Vienna and Ferdinand's later departure for Frankfort. Written for Ferdinand, of course, and in the third person, the *Manifeste* gets off to a fast start: Ferdinand was elected King of the Romans in
June 1617

by the suffrages of all the princes of his house, of two electors, and of many princes, dukes lords and officers of the Empire although Protestants, Lutherans, and others, had been elected King of the Romans. . . . Nevertheless, as the pretentions of other Protestant Princes *heretiques, Calvinistes and Lutheriens* were for some one of them [to be] on the Imperial Throne, to the prejudice of the said noble and ancient house of Austria, numerous and various uprisings, seditions and preparations for war were made in Germany on the subject of the election of the said Ferdinand [and] for the same occasion caused the revolt of several States the one against the other, of subjects against their princes, tumults and emotions civil and intestine in the provinces and in the imperial cities; thus the sedition of Prague, the cruelties exercised at Vienna and in the country of Austria, and the final war raised in Bohemia against the Emperor and his, by the strong league and association of the forces of the United Princes and of several other Protestant republics who had reduced the affaires of the Empire to such an extreme that [Matthias, now deceased, had to retire to Vienna, etc.].

The argument throughout is extremely repetitive, returning again and again to *tradition* that was in danger of being violated—not constitutional precedent, however, but the simple fact that there had never been a Protestant emperor. But the repetitiveness is relieved by a free-swinging polemical style, the author making the Protestants seem not only dangerous and destructive but unworthy in their unseemly haste to take over:

Matthias no sooner had his mouth closed when, *voila* Germany more troubled than before, and while the princes his relatives and friends were mourning his death and regretting his person, *voila* all the imperial towns shut up and in revolt. [Other disorders are cited, and] the provinces are covered with soldiers, the Protestants' troops seem increased by more than half of what they were before the death of Matthias. So much so that *voila* they want to take away by force that which right and reason gave to Ferdinand, designated successor to the Empire: and the more affairs are stirred up in the States the more arms are raised, and from two parties that there were only, more than four are found, all aspiring ambitiously to the reign. And meanwhile the Eagles of the Empire pluck each other, the strength is weakened, and hearts are altered so much that if one time the common enemy of Christianity turned the prideful horns of his Crescent on the rest of Hungary, not only could he invade it, but he would do it at his ease [*donneroit à l'aise*], and without much difficulty up to the gates of Vienna.

Ferdinand, seeing so far ahead in affairs, closed in on all sides by the arms of the Protestant Princes, who would like to take from him the Crown of Hungary and of Bohemia, and *desceptrer* him of the Scepter of the Romans. . . . and seeing . . . the conspiracies[39] that meanwhile one makes all over Germany to enfeeble the party of the Catholic princes and families . . . King Ferdinand exhorts and begs, all and each, the Christian and Catholic Kings, Princes and Republics to contribute in this whatever credit and authority they may have, to prevent that a party so violent and so prejudicial in the Christian Republic should hold the premier rank and the premier Crown of Europe, and give law to all the rest of the Princes.

Now the author addresses Louis XIII directly, asking him to use his authority (including against foreign princes) to keep Protestants from the imperial throne:

> and that His Majesty call to mind, if it please him, that since the Christian Empire was established, no heretic prince has ever sat on the Imperial Throne: [that] he not suffer that in his reign, which is the most glorious in Europe, to the general scandal of the universal Church, of which he is the eldest son, one place a heretic or a Protestant prince between the Eagles to ruin in so doing what little remains of vigor and force of the ancient and true Religion among the peoples of Germany; and that the errors of Luther, of Calvin, and so many others, should pullulate incessantly in the Empire, to the ruin of so many thousands of souls. He begs the King of Spain, his good relatives, friends, and allies also to employ their arms and their power, since it goes to the glory of the Religion, and to the honor of his house and of his particular interest. He further begs the other Catholic Princes, the Bishop Electors, Dukes and Lords (and) Officers of the Empire, the Archdukes of Flanders, the Grand Duke of Tuscany, the Dukes of Savoy and of Lorraine, and all other Catholic States to favor this laudable aim, along with His Holiness, and all the Church in general, to contribute to it their prayers to God, for the advancement of the Catholic faith, to the prejudice of heresy in the Empire, to [which end] may it please his divine Majesty to so unite the wills of the Christian Princes to the management of political affairs that everything succeed to his glory and to the increase of the Christian and Catholic faith and Religion.

This is distinctly religious drumbeating, but the impression of religious motivation is blurred in two ways. First, the manifesto is addressed to an audience outside Germany, where there was no hope of getting support from any Protestant rulers or governments. With his audience effectively limited to Catholics, pleading on the basis of religion was the most promising approach: certainly appealing to the king of France to keep the Habsburgs strong was an unlikely tack. So it seems an open question whether presenting Ferdinand as a defender of the faith is a matter of belief or of policy or both.

Second, just as the author gently asks Louis to consider the Protestants' pretentions *se ressouvenant* the history of the "Christian Empire" (making the point, a cynic might say, that no Calvinist was ever emperor during the Middle Ages), the present author asks the present reader to consider the beginning of this excerpt, calling to mind that that is not the way one elected a king of the Romans. Ferdinand's predecessors had been duly elected king of the Romans, understood to make one emperor-elect, when the incumbent seemed to be in decline; Ferdinand I, for example, arranged this for Maximilian II two years in advance, which seems about par. But one soon notices in the literature on Ferdinand II that even historians who date just about everything never get around to mentioning *when* he was made king of the Romans, nor how. In June 1617—a busy month—the family talked it over and decided that Ferdinand should take over the Bohemian throne from Matthias, and he was elected and crowned that same month; the family also decided that he should succeed Matthias as emperor, but not until Matthias's death; and the Spanish branch of the family agreed to all this in a formal treaty. It was widely assumed—most firmly by the family, but by others as well—that Ferdinand would be the next emperor. He was already acting as emperor during Matthias's last days, perhaps from January on, and after Matthias died he was routinely referred to by that title, though the election and coronation were still months away.

What is surprising is not that his election as emperor was considered a foregone conclusion (even Anhalt must have known that Frederick's candidacy was a forlorn hope), but that over his name in a manifesto written to be circulated internationally one finds this bald description of his idea of a proper election as king of the Romans, which traditionally was tantamount to election as emperor; he was elected by the "suffrages" of all the princes *of his own house,* of just two of the same electors, and of many, not all, of the "princes, dukes, lords and officers of the Empire." One is astounded by the constitutional implications, by his apparent contempt for legalities and legality, and by his oddly confident (given his concurrent Bohemian problems) assumption that others would value such things as lightly as he. The Bohemian rebels' perception of his threat as being to the political institutions seems rather nakedly confirmed in his own manifesto. But Louis XIII, of course, would not be alarmed by that.

What Louis would more predictably be concerned about was what made James I of England disapprove of his son-in-law's accepting the Bohemian throne from rebel hands and what had earlier made his predecessor Elizabeth distinctly cool toward Dutch rebels, support them though she did: the wave of rebellion that seemed to be sweeping monarchical Europe. Although, unlike the "Red scare" of the early twentieth century, it was not identified with a single, coherent ideology, republicanism as such was perceived as a serious menace. This was, of course, just a monarch's way of looking at that "crown versus estates" struggle so common at the time, though that label is a trifle too narrow. The crown's rival *was* the estates in England, where the struggle was just warming up, and had been in the Netherlands, where each side ended up with half the region; in France it was the separate Huguenot institutions (not the Estates General), and in

Ferdinand's domains, especially in Austria and Bohemia, it was the *Protestant* Estates. There is obvious religious content in all this, but it was also possible to see a universal threat to legitimate monarchs.

Though the *Manifeste* touches that matter briefly, it does not muddy the waters by making a big thing of it in a tract focused on sounding the *religious* alarm against *Protestants* and a general Protestant threat. But elsewhere Ferdinand's supporters take that other tack, sounding the *political* alarm against *rebels* and a general republican threat.[40] This argument too is particularly addressed to Louis XIII, which underlines the problem of sorting out how these issues were perceived, or at least how the contestants *wanted* them to be perceived. Here one does not even have two versions for two audiences; the same monarch is separately given a purely religious argument *and* a purely secular one, and virtually invited to pick the one that suits him best.

The serious historian, not allowed so idiosyncratic a choice, is faced with the lack of a *single* distinct impression. One gets the impression that contemporaries lacked any distinct impression at all. At the end of the reign *The Particular State of the Government of the Emperour Ferdinand the Second,* quoted at length in this essay, found a good deal to say, but that was a rare exception.

Contemporary historians had viewpoints, of course, but do not help very much concerning the man. Everhard Wassenberg begins his *Commentarium de Bello,* written shortly after Ferdinand's death, with the rather interesting comment that plotting, including plotting among Catholics, could have destroyed Germany (noticeably not Catholicism); Bohemian "heretics" were a problem but he seems mainly to object to their being "tumultuosi." When the death of Ferdinand arrives at almost the very end of the book—a fine climax to the narrative, one would think—Wassenberg summarizes his reign and assigns him a brief catalogue of conventional virtues, all in about seventy words![41]

When Gualdo Priorato's *Historia delle Guerre*[42] arrives at the same point, he says almost exactly the same things, but expanded to nearly four pages. After describing his death briefly but affectingly he says that Ferdinand "truly was the most religious emperor of Christianity" and "always put the interest of *la Religione* before that of his own State," and later that "Non potevasi tollerare dal riverente della sua conscienza il disdicevole dell'Eresia." But the intervening three pages are given over to a description of his person (sanguine complexion, medium height) and qualities (generosity of spirit, etc.) and a summary of his acts (principally wars), with religion mainly forgotten.

This is nothing if not typical. Ferdinand was spoken of both by his admirers and by his detractors in rather conventional terms as a religious figure, one who saw the issues as religious ones and who, in contesting those issues, was pursuing religious goals. Yet both his supporters and his

enemies almost always debated those issues, even celebrated their outcome, in purely secular terms.

Faced with this contradiction, one is tempted to fall back on a summation
Gualdo Priorato makes at one point: "He was emperor for 18 years, during
which time he constantly maintained six wars. He won five."

NOTES

1. A NOTE ON CITATIONS. There is no satisfactory form established for citing early tract-
length publications. They have some of the characteristics of books and one important one of
manuscript documents: the scarcity of copies of a given item and the uncertainty of where to
find one. So I have combined the two forms, citing them like books and also giving the
"archival location" by citing the British Museum shelf mark; for technical reasons this rather
complicated number is given first. Where length is indicated it is in pages of actual text,
excluding title page and blanks. Where unpaginated items have signature markings, I have
used these as "folio" references.

2. BM 9930.bbb.41: *A Relation containing the Manner of the Solemnities at the Election and
Coronation of Ferdinand the Emperour, in Francford, the 30 of August last past, 1619. With other
occurrences in Bohemia, and divers parts of Germany, etc.* (London, 1620); TP + pp. 1–43. The
title's Old Style date for the coronation is also given N.S. as September 9 in text, with the
election on September 7. The election account, of technical interest to historians, is at 22–23;
the coronation account is at 33–43. Necessarily abridged here, it contains an impressive
amount of detail (the names of the canopy carriers, for example), no doubt partly made
possible by its being published some months after the event. For a shorter but earlier account
see BM 1193.m.1/15: *Descrittione della Gran Solennita, et Festa a fatta nella Incoronatione del Re de
Romani. & Imperatore Ferdinando secondo. L'anno 1619. alli 9. Settembre in Francoforte* (Milan &
Viterbo, 1619), "per i Discipoli," "con Licenza de' Superiori"; TP + 3 pp. See also BM
1199.e.15/1: *De Parentela, Electione, Coronatione Ferdinandi II. Ungariae et Bohemiae Regis . . . in
Regem Romanorum Libri Tres. Cum Stirpibus Consanguineis Augustae Domus Bavaricae et Lotharing-
icae, etc.* (Cologne, 1621).

3. With nationalism in the air and the Thirty Years War (especially French manipulation of
it) the standard explanation of Germany's failure to have achieved political unification,
nineteenth-century German historians concentrated heavily on the secular side. Without
attempting to discuss the literature at length—this essay is concerned more narrowly with the
man, and with contemporary views, not modern—one may note here that the most widely
read works in English, from which generations of English and Americans, apparently including writers of textbooks and general histories, have received their perceptions of the subject,
vary from the Whiggish S. R. Gardiner (freedom-loving Protestants vs. absolutism-prone
Catholics) to the magisterial C. V. Wedgwood (whose 1930s position could be called common-
sense pacifist) but are united in giving Ferdinand a bad press, usually with religion the source
of the evil; one gets the Czech vantage point from Anton Gindely and the Franco-European
one from Georges Pagès (as if by law, all are entitled *The Thirty Years War*). The more recent,
multi-faceted treatments of the war and aspects of it by Joseph V. Polišensky, T. K. Rabb,
Henry Kamen, and others seem not yet to have penetrated the more general level of writing.

4. Hans Sturmberger's brief (44 pp.) *Kaiser Ferdinand II. und das Problem des Absolutismus*
(Munich: Österreich Archiv, 1957), has a chapter (15–23) "Die Gegenreformation als Triebkraft
zum Absolutismus," very pertinent to this dichotomy.

Of Matthias's death Morritz Ritter says, "Es trat damit eine Katastrophe . . . welche auch
unsere Betrachtung von den Abwegen der Pfalzisch-savoischen Entwurfe wieder zum Mittel-
punkt der gewaltsamen Bewegungen zurückführt." *Deutsche Geschichte im Zeitalter der Gegen-*

reformation und des dreissigjahrigen Krieges, 1555–1648. 3 vols. (1889–1908), 3:23. For a key source of religious dispute in Bohemia see Anton Gindely's *Geschichte der Ertheilung des böhmischen Majestätsbriefs von 1609* (Prague, 1858): his treatment (1–181), the document (182–89), and 243 useful notes (195–213). On religious friction in Germany at the time see Felix Stieve, *Der Ursprung des dreissigjährigen Krieges, 1607–1619* (Munich, 1875); this first book (apparently all published) is an exhaustive treatment of "Der Kampf um Donauwörth" (484 pp. of text, 152 of nn.). For a Bavarian's view see his *Ferdinand II., Deutscher Kaiser*, in *Allgem. deutsche Biographie* 6 (1877).

For Ferdinand's involvement with theologians see also Jan Kvačala, "Thomas Campanella und Ferdinand II," in *Kaiserlichen Akademie der Wissenschaften—Sitzungberichte—Philosophisch-Historischen classe* (Vienna, 1908), 159:1–48 (contributions are separately paginated), which is half text, half documents, and *Thomas Campanella, ein Reformer der ausgehenden Renaissance* (Berlin, 1909), chap. 5, pp. 131–51, for Kvačala's brief treatment of Counter-Reformation involvements.

Two examples may illustrate the difficulty the literature poses. Gindely's *Geschichte der Gegenreformation in Böhmen* (Leipzig, 1894), 532 pp., devotes a chapter (136–93) to religious differences in the University of Prague and deals elsewhere with the march of the Counter-Reformation, but begins (chap. 1, 1–82) with the 1619 confiscations of lands of the rebels, *qua* rebels, deals in the latter part (e.g., chap. 9, 427–532) almost entirely with land, and has as its narrative climax the emperor's return to Prague (512ff.), a political act; it is hard to tell whether this is the Counter-Reformation or not. Johann Peter Silbert, *Ferdinand der Zweite, Römischer Kaiser un seine Zeit,* (Vienna, 1836), in 459 pp. of text, spends most of the early pages on the coming of the Bohemian crisis and still has Ferdinand on that throne by p. 43: virtually no attention is paid to his early life; his education and Styrian background are touched only in passing (Silbert is rather compromised anyway by an obsequious dedication to the current emperor).

To this one might add the inchoate: Friedrich E. von Hurter Ammann, *Geschichte Kaiser Ferdinands II . . . und seiner Eltern*, 10 vols. in 5 (Schaffhausen: Hurtersche Buchhandlung, 1850–61), totaling over 5,300 pp. of text plus ca. 840 pp. of erratically organized documents, would hardly have been in "publishable form" for any other publisher.

5. The Age of Counter-Reformation definitely has its quota of two-dimensional cartoon figures, those simplistic caricatures produced with a few brush strokes in primary colors, creating a basically one-characteristic image—coward, simpleton, bigot, or whatever—that subsequent generations of historians have followed without, apparently, much thought. Fortunately, the situation continues to improve. The traditional James I is apparently dead, R. J. W. Evans has shown us a Rudolph II who is not merely bonkers, and the ongoing work of Peter Pierson on Medina Sidonia, William Maltby on Alva, and David Lagomarsino on Philip II and the Netherlands promises to restore those figures to three dimensions.

6. Richard S. Dunn, *The Age of Religious Wars. 1559–1689,* Norton History of Modern Europe (New York, 1970), 70. The wording, of course, varies, as when Roger Lockyer, *Habsburg and Bourbon Europe, 1470–1720* (London, 1974), 340, has him "a rabid Catholic, educated and counseled by the Jesuits." The American Dunn and the English Lockyer, writing mostly and entirely (respectively) about continental Europe, exhibit the anglocentricity typical of both nations' historians by applying English-style dates to events on the continent, where the Julian calendar had been abandoned decades before. E.g., the imperial election was on September 7, 1619, not the parochial August 28 as per Dunn, 70, and Lockyer, 344.

7. BM 8073.a.b: *Status Particularis regiminis S. C. Majestatis Fernandi II.* ([Amsterdam], 1637); 364 pp. in-16°. The title piece goes to 293, plus an appendix *re formulae* (294–96); chap. 3 (32–48) is on Ferdinand's qualities, virtues, piety, etc. This is followed by *Iter Germanicum* by "Danielis Eremitae, Belgae" (a 1609 letter), 297–364.

Quotations are from BM 591.c.24/3: *The Particular State of the Government of the Emperour Ferdinand the Second, as it was at his decease in the yeere 1636. Translated out of Latin by R.W.* (London: Thomas Nichols, 1637); 91 pp. in quarto (unpaged); because Ferdinand died in 1637 the year is apparently given here in Old Style, with the year beginning March 25. The main item has its own title page: *The State of the Imperiall-Court of the Emperour Ferdinand the Second. Wherein is treated, Of all higher and lower Officers* [etc.] . . . *As it was MDC. XXXVI.* "Printed by E.G. [elsewhere Anne Griffin] for Thomas Nichols and are to [be] sold at his shop at the Signe of the Bible in Popes head Alley"—somewhat amusing in context.

This type of publication is described in C. H. Carter, *The Western European Powers*, in *The Sources of History*, ed. G. R. Elton (London, 1971), 214–19. For an example four decades earlier (whose title suggests the kind of content involved) see BM 591.c.24/1: *The Estate of the Germaine Empire, with the description of Germanie. 1. Declaring how the Empire was translated from the Romains to the Germaines: with divers and sundrie memorable accidents following there-upon. Written certain yeeres past as the estate then stood. 2. Describing the scituation of every Countrie, Province, Dukedome, Arch-bishoprick, Bishoprick, Earledome and Cittie of Germanie: The Princes and chief officer of the Empire in their severall places: who have their seates & voyces at the election of the Emperour and at the Imperiall Parliaments: and who are the Electors of the Emperour: and also what companies of Soldiers (both horsse-men and foote-men) every Prince, Arch-bishop, Bishop, Nobleman and Cittie, is bound yeerely to finde against the Turke. Newly set forth for the profite and pleasure of all Gentlemen and others, that are delighted in travaile or knowledge of Countries* (London: Ralph Blower, 1595); item 1 is 12 pp., item 2 is 36 pp.; trans. William Fiston, who says (introduction) that one item was in Italian, one in Latin, but does not say which.

8. *Particular State*, f° B3v°.

9. Ibid., f° C. See also G. Wolf, *Ferdinand II. und die Juden. Nach Aktenstücken in den Archiven der k.k. Ministerien des Innern und des Aussern* (Vienna, 1859). Wolf (1–2) asks, with Ferdinand, "Bienamen 'der Katholische,' " so active against Protestants, "Wie war Ferdinand II. gegen die Juden?" His answer (1–27) and thirteen supporting documents (28–63) entail considerable toleration. The documents include grants of privileges and related items concerning Jews in Frankfort, Prague, etc.; #12 (59–62) is "Wienerisch Judenschaft Jurisdiction" (Vienna, 23 Nov., 1632). On the Catholic-Protestant face-off, see Henry Kamen's perceptive (and determinedly optimistic) *The Rise of Toleration* (London, 1967).

10. *Particular State*, ff. C-C2.

11. Ibid., ff. C4v°-D2.

12. It was one of numerous staples of the Spanish press in the period. E.g., BM 593.h.17/46 describes a similar "Christianissimo Lavatorio" in Barcelona during Holy Week 1626.

13. *Particular State*, ff. C4v°-D2.

14. Ibid., D2–D3.

15. Ibid., F4–G.

16. BM PP. 3444.af/154: *A Son Alteze, sur les nouvelles venues le 23, Novembre 1620, Veille de la Feste de St. Albert* (Antwerp, [1620]); 5 pp. (3–7). The verses, in rhyming couplets, are of six or eight lines each, except for Ferdinand's, which oddly is seven. As the title indicates, the date the news arrived strengthens the occasion for dedicating the effort to the sovereign of the Southern Netherlands, but the author is also unblushingly chauvinistic ("Et vous Bucquoy de la Race Belgique . . ."); Tilly was also of that race and enjoyed a similarly good press in that region. The attitudes shown in two of the verses are of particular interest:

> Au Ducq de Saxen
> Les Bienfaicts vous n'escrivez a Londe
> Tiltre d'ingrat ne vous convient au monde
> C'est a vous que la voix s'adresse
> Prince Sasson qui laisse
> A tous germains la constante conue
> Voz ditz & la foy a CESAR impollue.

> Au Palatin
> Adieu Fredericque Prince Palatin
> Dans Prage iamais verrez festin

> Faictz sagement retire toy
> Pour eschapper les retz du Comte de Bucquoy
> Tenduz par tout chemin
> Qui tire vers le Rhin
> Lequel coule par vos terres
> Ou les Protestans ont mille guerres.

Doggerel, of course, does not lend itself to translation in the sense of reproducing it as verse: even if the rhyme is dropped, it still requires not only translating the meaning but reproducing both that ebullient doggerel bounce and the variable specific tone, which is here by turns gleeful, sardonic, I-told-you-so, etc. But it may be useful to note that "les retz" refers to snares set for birds and other small game.

17. I am currently engaged in a fairly wide examination of what was published and read in the popular press in the period, of the sort described in n. 1, which of course cannot be attempted here.

18. Many bound volumes of printed material of the period have examples of this miscellany. BM 1054.a.5, for example, has two ten-page sets of Latin verses (items /5 and /5*), a five-page imaginary "dialogue" (/19), and (/18) *Senatus Deorum de Praesentibus Afflictissimae et Periclitantis Germaniae Miseriis, & reducenda pace, Hilusus seria ducunt*, (n.p., 1627) (the author signs off with a 1625 date); TP + pp. 3–51, so heavy in classical references and metaphors (rafts of marginal citations) that it is hard to winnow out any specifics regarding current affairs.

19. BM 1054.h.26 (another copy: BM C.55.d.15/1): *A clear demonstration that Ferdinand is by his own demerits fallen from the Kingdome of Bohemia and the incorporated provinces. Written by a nobleman of Polonia, and translated out of the second edition enlarged* (Dort, [1619]); 25 pp. For the United Provinces, the publisher, George Waters, was well placed to serve an English audience. One notes that the original had already had an expanded second edition.

20. This extended and widespread debate, in which Robert Bellarmine, Francisco Suarez, and James I of England are the best known of many participants in this period, is only now beginning to get proper historical attention with respect to its impact on practical affairs.

21. *Clear demonstration*, 1–2.

22. Ibid., 4–23.

23. Ibid., 9–10.

24. Ibid., 24.

25. Ibid., 24–25.

26. BM 8079.e.26/2: *Lettre de Wenselaus Meroschowa Bohemois, Escrite de l'Armée de Frederick Conte Palatin en Boheme, à Ioan Traut de Nuremberg. En laquelle sont par un tres-bref discours referées bien particulierment les vrayes causes des adversitez & pertes dupuis advenues audit Conte Palatin. Encores, la Iustice de la cause de l'Empereur Ferdinand, & l'iniustice de ses ennemis. On y void aussi les feintises, faussitez & impietez dont se servent les Heretiques & Politiques, & par lesquelles ils penseroient empescher l'Election du susdict Emperor Ferdinand. N'agueres venue en lumiere. Discours digne d'estre leu & remarque* (n.p., [1620]); TP + pp. 2–20: 5. I have used the King James wording for Matthew 22:21, adjusted to the author's paraphrase.

See also, e.g., BM 1054.a.5/2: *Relatio nuperi itineris proscribtorum Iesuitarum ex Regnis Bohemae & Ungariae missa ex Helicone justa Parnassum* (Prague, 1619): TP + pp. 3–45; and BM 1054.h.9/7: *Falsae originis Motuum Hungaricorum, succincta Refutatio* (Recusa Augustae Vindelicorum [apud Sarem Mangiam Viduam], 1620); TP + 29 pp. (unpaged). The latter defends Ferdinand against criticism of him in the Hungarian case.

One Jesuit-oriented attack is almost verbatim the modern version referred to earlier. BM 1054.h.9/14: *Luitkonis Thomsonii Carlomontii Dissertatio de Causis nuper motae Bohemiae. Nunc primùm consensu Autoris, in hicem, publico bono data*, (n.p., 1623); TP & v° + pp. 3–39. At 14 he refers to ". . . Consiliarios: . . . quomodo Hispani stipendarios, sic Jesuitarum discipulos." At 38:

Qui altiùs jam immanem hominis, ex improbo divinitusque damnato *coitu* nati: (vide Chemnit. in locis, titulo de conjugio fol. mihi 223.) In Jesuitarum latibulis educati; illis institutoribus, omnibus perfidiae praeceptio imbuti; in hac statim ab obitu Patris, domi forisque exercitate animum; ac nullo obsequio flexilem saevitiam repetentes: ubi ad factiosam ambitionem conscientiarum triste imperium, sui peripsum in ditionem Hispani per *clandestina illa pacta* tentatam concessionem, comminationes diras, caetera item impotentis animi ante biennium, ut dixi, prodita indicia, & jurarae *Cautionis* per tot recentia facinora violationem ventum: Officii sui esse putarunt, non pati ejus tyrannidem per scelus, ac servitutem suam, per socordiam crescere. Quocirca nolverunt ei Imperium concedere, quo indignum se reddiderat, dum non-dum-rerum potens, perversè consulendo quò Status oppressiores forent, eo se munitiorem reddere cuperet, nec ulla benignitate ac clementia amiabilis, ab omnibus; praeterquam pessimis quibusque, formidaretur.

He ends his text (39) with another quotation from Tacitus:

Fato & sorte nascendi ut caetera, ita Principum inclinatio in hos, offensio in illos: An sit aliquid in humanis consilijs, liceatq populo, inter abruptam contumaciam, ac deforme obsequium, pergere iter ambitione ac periculis vacuum.

BM 1054.h.9/15 is a 1624 edition.

27. BM 1193.1.42/3 (also 8073.ccc.22): [A. Schmid von Schmiedebach], *De Statu Bohemico das ist: Der Röm. Kayser auch zu Hungarn und Böhaim Koniglichen Majestät Ferdinandi Secundi, Fundamental Deduction und Gründliche Aussführung der Erbgerightigheit und Erblichen Succession, welche die . . . Kays. May . . . zu dem Königreich Böhmen gehabt und noch haben . . .* (Frankfurt: T. Schönwetter, 1620): TP + pp. 3–47.

28. BM 8073.b.45: [Augustin Schmid von Schmiedebach], *Informatio Fundamentalis super hodierno Bohemiae statu: ubi et successionis iura liquide deducuntur, et ad oculum describuntur, quae Invictissimus & Gloriosissimus Imperator Ferdinandus II et Sereniss. Domus Austriaca in dicto regno habent, Daniae et Norwegia, &c. regi Christiano IV. necnon in superiori & inferiori circulo Saxonico, Imperii statibus, communicata a Sacrae Caesareae Maiestatis suae Legatis DD. Henrico Iulio Saxoniae, Angariae & Westphaliae Duci. . . ,* Cum Priviligio S. Caesareae (Frankfurt: I. T. Schonwetterum, 1620); 3–39.

29. *Informatio Fundamentalis,* 36:

Haec [aurea] Bulla inter Regni Bohemiae potissima privilegia asservatur. Atque Rex Ferdinandus ex regio Bohemico sanquine, utpote Ferdinando I auo, & Anna Regina avia sua in linea recta descendenti procedit. Erg non fuit necesse illum eligere, quia casus electionis nondum venit.

30. *De Statu Bohemica,* 47:

Dis ist im Original der Böhmischen Historien Æneae Sylvii im 57. cap. besindlich. Eben disses wird auch von Doct. Philippo Camerario in seinen Meditationib. histor. Cent. 2. cap. 45 (was alhie geschrieben stehet) angezogen.

31. BM 591.C.24/2: *The Golden Bull: or, The Fundamental Lawes and Constitutions of the Empire. Shewing, The Persons and Priviledges of the Princes Electors, the manner of the Election, the forme and Ceremonies thereof, with other politique Orders to be observed by the States and Subiects of the Empire, which shall be assembled at Francford (for the Election of the now next Emperor) the tenth day of July next ensuing. 1619* (London: T. S. for Nathanaell Newbury, 1619); TP + 54 pp. (unpaged); f° D. As the title notes, this was published in response to widespread interest in the imperial election (which eventually occurred in early September, not July), not with reference to the Bohemian throne; it is quoted here for its English text.

See also, e.g., BM 1054.h.9/6: *Bohemica Iura Adversus Informatorem defensa. Hoc est Responsio ad falsò dictam* INFORMATIONEM *contra scripta Ad Ordinibus* BOHEMIAE *edita,* Typis clanculum vulgatam, 1620; TP + pp. 1–34. The "Responsionis ad Informationem, contra Ordinun Bohemiae Apologias & Scripta," 3–23, poses a similarly historical argument that Bohemia is hereditary, referring back to Charles IV, Ferdinand I, et al. A family table (p. 24), traces the descendants of Charles IV who include Ferdinand II (and previous emperors), but interestingly also Frederick V *and*, through a different line, Elizabeth of Bohemia, through her mother Anne of Denmark. The last page has a catchword (PACTORVM), in caps, suggesting that a half title was to follow.

32. BM: 8073.ccc.23: *Evidentia causae Bohemieae, qua Ferdinandi II. Caesaris legitima abdicatio et Frederici Palatini justa electio, breviter & succincte demonstrata* (n.p., 1620); 74 pp. (3–76)

33. Ibid., 45. The King James quotation is from the first quarto edition (London: Bonham Norton and John Bill, 1625).

34. BM 1054.h.9/17: *Briefve Information Des affaires du Palatinat, Lesquels consistent en quatre Chefs principaux, qui sont: I. L'acceptation de la Couronne de Boheme. II. Le different qui en est survenu entre l'Empereur Ferdinand, & le Roy Frideric. III. La Proscription & sanglante Procedure qui s'en est ensuyvie. IV. Et l'Entremise du Roy de la Grande Bretagne, avec ce qui s'est passé pendant icelle* (n.p., 1624); TP + pp. 3–37; 9–10. Part 1 is at 3–14; "Extraict des Reversales de l'Empereur Rudolph" at 8. I have abridged the remarkably mild circumstances that would free the Estates from their acceptance of the king; the French is somewhat stronger than I have managed in translation.

35. BM Burney 2/2 (also 1054.a.5/4): *An answere to the question, Whether the Emperor that now is can bee Iudge in the Bohemian Controversie or no? Together with the Extract taken out of the Acts of the Dyet at Augspurghe in . . . 1584: Concerning the Kingdome of Bohemia* (n.p., 1620); TP + 22 pp. (unpaged). In this matter of international concern partisan tracts on both sides were published in foreign languages, sometimes in several; the British Museum, presumably with some grounds, cites the place of publication as [Prague?]. The 1584 of the title, a typo, is correctly 1548 elsewhere. The dual argument described goes to f° C3v°, and is summarized along the way at f° A4v°; the quote is at f° A3v°. The Augsburg extract is at ff C4-Dv°.

36. BM 8026.de.11/4: *Discours Tres-veritable touchant les droicts de la Couronne de Boheme* (Paris, 1620); TP + pp. 3–24. The text is at 3–19, the quotation at 9, the 17 points, numbered, at 9–17; the Golden Bull excerpt "Touchant l'Election & succession des Roys de Boheme" at 20–24.

37. Ferdinand's Bohemian enemies constantly claimed that in the "succession treaty" with Spain he had bartered away the Bohemian throne to the Spanish Habsburgs. This makes sense as a reflection of their anti-foreign feelings and their distrust of Ferdinand personally, but not when they claim, as they occasionally did, that it was in exchange for Spanish military aid against their rebellion, since the treaty was agreed to in June and formally signed in October 1617, well before the rebellion began the following March. Portions of the treaty were published, presumably to quell the rumors (routine publication would be *in toto*). See BM 1054.h.9/4: *Pactorum de perpetua Successione in Regnis Hungriae & Bohemiae ac Provinciarum ad ea pertinentium, Instrumenta VI & XV. Mensis junij, Anno DCXVII* (Prague, n.d.; TP + 10 pp. (unpaged). At bottom of TP: "In Catholicae Religionis & Maiestatis Domus Austriacae salutem atque incolumitatem." It is in three parts, all signed 7 October 1617 (by the Count of Oñate for Spain), entitled:

—Phillippus III, Hispaniarum Rege, Iuri suo renunciante, & Matris Suae Annae, Maximiliani II. Imp. Filiae, cessionem ratificante, necnon pro resignatione tam Sibi Compensationem, quam Haredibus Suis, cumprimum in linea recta Ferdinandi Austriae Archiducis series legitima Masculina abrupta fuerit, Restitutionem stipulante.

—Ferdinando, Austriae Archiduci, haec acceptante, grata rataque habente, & iuxta Compensationem, etiam in casu masculorum recta a Se linea serieque non interrupta legitime descendere cassantium, restitutionem promittente.

—Mathia II. Rom. Imp. Pacta haec non solum intercessione Sua procurante, sed etiam Caesare a pariter atque Regia Authoritate confirmante.

38. BM 9200.aa.35/2: *Le Manifeste de Ferdinand duc de Baviere* [sic], *Roy des Romains. Envoyé a tous les Roys, Princes & Republiques Chrestiennes & Catholique, pour la conservation des droits des Princes Catholiques à l'Empire; contre les desseins des Protestants* (Paris, 1619); TP + pp. 3–12. The quotes are from 3–12, abridged. The usual "Privilege du Roy," dated 29 May 1619, conveniently establishes the date but, of course, does not imply agreement.

On a subject that crops up regularly in these debates, see Dorothy M. Vaughan, *Europe and the Turk: A pattern of alliances, 1350–1700* (Liverpool, 1954), esp. chap. 4.

39. *Monopoles:* The modern dictionaries, checked to confirm whether this word has retained its other meaning, offer only business and government monopolies and related metaphors as definitions. *A Dictionary of the French and English Tongues,* comp. Randle Cotgrave, 1st ed. (London, 1611; fac. ed., intro. William S. Woods [Columbia: University of South Carolina Press, 1950], almost exactly contemporary with the *Manifeste,* offers: "Monopole: f. A. Monopolie; a private conspiracie, factious combination, uniust confederation; hence also, the sale of a marchantable commoditie challenged by one, or few; th'ingrossing thereof into one, or few mens hands, by Patent from the Prince, or packing with others." I.e., the word at that time still embraced political conspiracies.

40. This fear of rebellion and a general republican willingness to do without monarchs was fairly common currency of the time, as was the widespread belief in Protestant areas in a Habsburg, especially Spanish, aim to establish a "universal monarchy." See, e.g., on the occasion at hand, BM 8026.b.19: *A Letter written by a French Gent: of the King of Bohemia his Army: concerning the Emperour Ferdinand his Embassage into France,* trans. from French (Flushing, 1620); TP + pp. 1–13. He refers (p. 1) to "the insatiable ambition of the House of Austria, in both branches thereof, which all Christendom shortly will not bee anough to content," but of course has the same solution as Ferdinand: "the assistance and Protection that Kings owe one another" (6–7). But people concurrently saw things in religious terms, as in BM P.P.3444.af/ 155 (another copy 1480.aa.15/52): *Catalogue ande coningen, Princë, graven, ende andere vorsten, met den Keyzer Ferdinandus II, openlÿck houdende teghen de Unie de Calvinisten ende alle adherente Protestanten* (Antwerp, Dec. 5, 1620).

41. As with such works, successive editions bring the narrative up to a later date. The earliest I have consulted is a 1639 Frankfort, 2d ed. Quotations here are from *Florus Germanicus, Sive Everhardi Wassenbergii. Embricensis. Commentariorum de Bello, Inter invictissimos Imperatores Ferdinandos II. & III. Et eorum hostes . . . Ad Annum 1641 . . .* (Hamburg, 1641): 420 pp. (+ a long index); quotations are at 2, 5; Ferdinand's death at 390.

42. Conte Galeazzo Gualdo Priorato, *Historia delle Guerre di Ferdinando II e III Imperatori e del Re Filippo IV di Spagna contro Gostavo Adolfo Re di Suetia e Luigi XIII Re di Francia. Successe dall'anno 1630 sino all anno 1640* (Venice, 1642); 1,110 pp. + alphabetical table of contents; 839–42. The original edition went to 1636, later ones to 1649; the author's treatment of Ferdinand had not changed by the Venice 1653 edition.

A NOTE ON SOURCES.

For the past couple of decades I have repeatedly been impressed by the amount of publicly consumed printed material floating about in the age of Reformation and Counter-Reformation, with a substantial upsurge in the early seventeenth century: religious tracts, of course, but also encyclopedias, newsletters, histories, travel accounts, anecdotal collections, even historical documents. Most of these present problems as sources of historical fact, but I have long wished for an occasion to examine them as "historical facts" in their own right, as evidence of what information was available

to people, or foisted on them, or whatever. The invitation to do an essay on
Ferdinand II for this memorial volume provided that occasion, for the
image of him that I had so frequently encountered in modern histories,
besides being inconsistent, never seemed to jibe with the situations he was
in nor with most of the actions he took. The problem seemed to call for
leap-frogging the modern historians, getting back to fundamentals, and
trying to examine his public image in his own lifetime. This seemed also a
possible step toward an answer to that near-subliminal question that nags
at many historians of the period: whether this olio of religious and political
elements should be considered so distinctly one of *religious* conflict as it
usually has been; again, one sought contemporary perceptions.

Miscellany.

The various types of publication that do not fit either of the first two
categories above are treated in text as a group ("miscellaneous forms")
because no type among them contributes much to the present problem.
Some examples are cited (n. 18), and some verses (n. 16) and a variation on
a type of reference work (n. 7) are given fuller attention in text; a 1619
English-language edition of the Golden Bull is also cited (n. 31).

The essay is therefore based on a systematic examination of some hundreds of publications during Ferdinand's reign now at the British Museum:

(1) pro- and anti-Ferdinand propaganda, and unofficial material of that
    sort by supporters and opponents;
(2) periodical and nonperiodical newspapers;
(3) miscellaneous products of the public press.

Most are quartos (roughly the page size of a present-day octavo book),
most frequently 16 pages, though often 24, 48, or some similar multiple of
8. They are extremely well preserved, allowing one something approaching the "feel" they would have had when read by contemporaries, though
they have been archivally bound, ranging from a few to 150+ items per
volume (quite often with precisely 47, apparently the number of 16-page
items that would fit one of the standard-size bindings).

This special survey was not extended beyond the British Museum because the "sample" one managed to dredge up there (a) was very large,
probably a low four-figure number, (b) was consistent with materials seen
at other European repositories over the years, and (c) was extremely varied
in origin, with the most pertinent areas well represented: Bohemia and
Germany (more in Latin than in German), France (French, some Latin),
England (English, much Latin, some French), the United Provinces
(Dutch, Latin, English—especially for the English market), Italy (Italian,
Latin), and Spain (mostly Spanish, occasional Latin). The languages used

also reflect reality in two corollary ways: Latin was often used always by the Bohemians—to reach an international audience across vernacular language barriers, while something published either in Latin or the language of the place of origin—something published in Vienna in German, for example—would often be published locally in French in France, in English in England, and in Spanish in Spain; the sample is consistent with this.

Proto-newspapers.

One-shot newsletters devoted to some single event—ceremony, battle, natural disaster—had been around in substantial numbers for some time, but near the beginning of the Thirty Years War regular periodical newspapers, weeklies, began to be established in various parts of Europe. The basic bibliographical work on these was done a generation ago by Folke Dahl, librarian of both the city and University of Goteborg, beginning in 1938–39 with his "Short-title Catalogue of English Corantos and News-books, 1620–1642," *Transactions of the Bibliographical Society,* 2, 19:45–95, and ser. 2, 19:44–98. After the war he published two elegant folio volumes with substantial descriptive essays and great quantities of facsimile reproductions, mainly of front covers (which headline the contents: *Dutch Corantos, 1618–1650* (The Hague, 1949) (334 facsimiles from 1618–25), and *A Bibliography of English Corantos and Periodical Newsbooks, 1620–1642* (London: Bibliographical Society, Publications Series, 1952), an outgrowth of his short-title catalogue. In between, with two co-authors, came *Les Débuts de la presse française: nouveaux aperçus,* vol. 4 (Paris: Acta Bibliotecae Gotoburgensis, 1951), which destroyed the claims made for Theophraste Renaudot as publisher of the first French periodical newspaper and placed France more realistically in step with others, in four essays: Dahl, "Les Premiers Journaux en français" and "Découverte d'un journal parisien antérieur à la Gazette de Renaudot;" Fanny Petibon, "Les Précurseurs de Renaudot à Paris: Martin et Vendome"; and Marguerite Boulet, "Le Plagiat de Renaudot." Along the way Dahl also comments on periodicals in other places such as Frankfurt. But periodicals proved not very helpful with the problem at hand, for the reasons cited in text and because the kind of evidence they provide (which supports the thrust of this essay) is too diffuse to be brought effectively into the essay. However, several one-shot news accounts are included, beginning with the description of Ferdinand II's coronation (n. 2).

Propaganda

Long ago E. A. Beller started work on this subject in this period, but instead of pursuing the matter to hard conclusions, useful to historians, he followed the editorial track, producing, for example, a collection of *Carica-*

tures of the "Winter King" of Bohemia (1928), a "fine edition" that would honor any historian's coffee table, but perhaps not his library. Heinrich Ritter von Srbik, *Wallensteins Ende: Ursachen, Verlauf und Folgen der Katastrophe* (Vienna, 1920) (xvi + 408 pp.), very usefully devotes the last half of the book to government propaganda, but it is too specifically focused on the Wallenstein matter to be directly applicable to this essay. But—without criticizing other contributions to the subject by omission—the specific propaganda literature that this essay ultimately rests upon focuses so squarely upon specific issues that the label *propaganda,* though accurate, is perhaps too pejorative a term. Though it was conducted hammer-and-tongs, it was much more a public debate than a discrediting of the enemy through falsehood, so the literature of Big Lie techniques is not really applicable.

All the same, two examples of pertinent modern propaganda might usefully be mentioned, both from World War II. Ernest Sommer, *Into Exile: the History of the Counter Reformation in Bohemia, 1620–1650,* trans. Victor Groue (London, 1944) (154 pp.), was written by a Czech exile in England who readily admitted his purpose of making the Czechs' history of resistance to "foreign" oppression known in the English-speaking world, using the generation after the Battle of the White Mountain as his example. Friederich Stieve, *Wendepunkte europäischer Geschichte vom Dreissigjährigen Kreig bis sur Gegenwart . . .* (Leipzig, 1941) (245 pp.), is less candid but no less transparent. In chap. 1, "Das 'politische Testament' Richelieus," Germany's fate was the political testament: "versank Deutschland—den französischen Dolch in der Flanke—in die endlossen Wirren des Dreissigjährigen Krieges" (p. 13).

The survey also included book-length items. Some of the contemporary histories and other types are mentioned in this essay, but it should be noted that disputations by major controversialists (Lodovicus Camerarius, Gaspar Scoppius, Martin Becanus, et al.) have been omitted from this discussion because the concern is not with debates among scholars and such, but with the public image presented in widely distributed and widely read publications. Beyond the matter of images *presented,* one hopes to provide at least a tentative foundation for corollary inferences concerning (1) public perceptions that may have been derived *from* such publications, and (2) already-held perceptions that at least the commercial publishers may have tailored their material to in given markets. Both (and especially the latter, slippery though it may be) seem important routes to pursue if we are to gain an adequate understanding of mentalities in the period.

The present essay does not attempt to deal with the question of these materials' reliability as sources of fact. Yet I must thank Radomir V. Luza (who, besides being a historian of central Europe, has a Czech's interest in the matter) not only for reading and commenting most usefully on the manuscript, but for pointing out to me the significance of an imperial reference to the Letter of Majesty of Ferdinand I (n. 29).

The focus of this essay is on contemporary publications. Because modern works are dealt with only as a point of departure, the essay does not pretend to comprehensiveness concerning them, though it should perhaps be noted that this essay was written before encountering Johann Franzl, *Ferdinand II.: Kaiser im Zweispalt der Zeit* (Graz, 1948), which does not seem to provide any advance over the traditional views described in the text.

11

William Laud and the Outward Face of Religion

J. Sears McGee

"To think well of the Reformed Religion is enough to make the Archbishop one's enemy."[1] So wrote Algernon Percy, tenth Earl of Northumberland, to a friend whose appointment to a high post in Charles I's government in 1639 had been opposed by the Archbishop of Canterbury, William Laud. From Laud's student days at Oxford to his death on the scaffold as a traitor in 1645, he preached against controversy and, in seeking to suppress it, provoked it. He loved unity, order, and peace but created division, tumult, and war. Hating disputation, he attracted clouds of disputants, and the judgments of historians have varied as widely and as passionately as those of his contemporaries. The Earl of Clarendon thought "that his learning, piety and virtue have been attained by very few, and the greatest of his infirmities are common to all, even to the best men."[2] Yet to the Puritan printer, Michael Sparke, Laud was "that little high-spirited bishop" who endeavored to destroy "all such as would not bow to his Baal, for which he spilt the blood of the innocent, for which the just hand of God was upon him."[3] The eighteenth-century Whig historian John Oldmixon criticized the work of the Tory Laurence Echard: "The reader will find so many panegyrics on Bishop Laud that if he had really been a saint and a martyr, as he represents him, he could not have said more of him; whereas there's nothing so certain in his character as pride, cruelty, bigotry and invincible obstinancy."[4] The illustrious Macaulay found Laud "by nature rash, irritable, quick to feel for his own dignity, slow to sympathize with the sufferings of others, and prone to the error, common in superstitious men, of mistaking his own peevish and malignant moods for emotions of pious zeal."[5] W. H. Hutton, however, praised him as "an ecclesiastical statesman" who strove to "carry out the principles of toleration" and "had no desire to persecute."[6] C. H. Simpkinson eulogized him as "the reformer *par excellence* of his own day, the chief advocate of the working classes, the defender of the poor, the leader of the educational movement, an administrator who endeavored to exterminate the corruptions of the civil service, and an ecclesiastic who proposed to widen the boundaries of the English church."[7]

The object of this extreme adoration and withering contempt was the son of a Reading clothier. The period of his education and rise to power, sketched in this section, contains incidents that adumbrate the three main themes of his thought and career—a strong distaste for doctrinal controversy, a deep love of ceremony, and a fervent commitment to the high mission of the priesthood. At age sixteen he matriculated as a commoner at St. John's College, Oxford, in 1589 and became a fellow in 1593 (B.A. and M.A., 1594; B.D., 1604; D.D., 1608). His tutor was John Buckeridge, who was elected president of the college in 1605.[8] When Buckeridge became bishop of Rochester in 1611, Laud succeeded him as head of St. John's. By the time Laud's Oxford studies began, the "reaction against Geneva . . . was gathering force amongst a party of avant-garde divines in Cambridge," and "this nascent English 'Arminianism'" was finding adherents such as Buckeridge in Oxford as well.[9] One important Cambridge avant-gardiste was Lancelot Andrewes, and Buckeridge and Laud made the first complete edition of his sermons.[10] For much of Elizabeth's reign, a Calvinist school of divines had been the leading theologians in both the universities. The Calvinists were virtually unchallenged until the 1590s, and during those years they put down the handful who espoused more liberal doctrines of grace and free will rather easily. Archbishop Whitgift himself endorsed an essentially predestinarian position in the Lambeth Articles (1595). His quarrel with a Presbyterian Puritan such as Thomas Cartwright was over ecclesiological rather than soteriological issues. In general, Elizabethan Puritans who did not go to the extreme of advocating Presbyterianism differed with the conformists more over matters of liturgy, ministry, and discipline than doctrine.[11]

Laud's Oxford career was punctuated by disputes with the Calvinists. The positions he took and the strength of the Calvinist hold on the universities is demonstrated by the ferocity of the reaction to the ideas of Laud and those with whom he associated.[12] Peter Heylyn, his chaplain and first biographer, wrote that it "were better" in Oxford "to have been look'd upon as a heathen or publican than an anti-Calvinist." Laud, however, was undaunted. In 1603 he "maintained the constant and perpetual visibility of the Church of Christ through the Church of Rome, derived from the apostles to the Church of Rome, continued in that Church . . . till the Reformation." He was answered and sharply criticized by George Abbot, then vice-chancellor of the university. This was the beginning of a long and bitter feud between the two men. In 1604 Laud upheld "the necessity of baptism" and that "there could be no true church without diocesan bishops." In a sermon at St. Mary's in 1606 he took exception to Henry Airey's treatise condemning the practice of bowing at the name of Jesus. This so offended the university authorities that Laud narrowly missed being forced into a public recantation: "he was so openly branded . . . a papist, or at least very popishly inclined, that it was almost made an heresy . . . for anyone to be seen in his company, and a misprision of heresy to give him a civil salutation as he walked in the streets."[13]

His long association with Richard Neile began when Neile as bishop of Rochester in 1608 chose Laud as his chaplain. Neile and Laud presided over the examination of the last heretic to be burned in England (one Edward Wightman in Lichfield in 1612).[14] Neile was the political and Andrewes the spiritual leader of the weak but slowly growing anti-Calvinist party in the Jacobean church, and their cause suffered a major check when Archbishop Bancroft died in November 1610. Bancroft had been sympathetic to their views, and many thought that Andrewes would succeed him. Instead, King James chose Laud's old nemesis, George Abbot. Abbot soon opposed Laud's bid for the presidency of St. John's, but James refused to overturn the disputed election. Laud wrote in his diary that "the Archbishop of Canterbury was the original cause of all my troubles."[15] In 1614 Robert Abbot, master of Balliol, regius professor of divinity and the archbishop's elder brother, denounced the president of St. John's for having preached that the "Presbyterians were as bad as the papists." With Laud in attendance, Abbot asked, "What art thou, Romish or English? Papist or Protestant? . . . A mongrel or compound of both?"[16] When the show-trial known as the Synod of Dort convened in Holland in 1618 to condemn the teachings of Arminius, James sent a strongly Calvinist delegation to join in flaying those who held out for an element of free will in salvation.[17]

It is significant that Laud and other English Arminians continued to win preferment despite the Calvinism of James and Abbot. They did not take over the Church of England but neither were they harried from it. Andrewes, the dean of Westminster, became bishop of Chichester (1605), then Ely (1609), and finally Winchester (1618). Neile was his successor as dean and then successively bishop of Rochester, Lichfield and Coventry, Lincoln and, from 1617, Durham. His London residence, Durham House, became the "party headquarters" of the Arminian movement.[18] Laud owed several positions to Neile directly or to his influence with the king: he became rector of Cuxton in Kent (1610), prebend of Buckden and royal chaplain (1614), archdeacon of Huntingdon (1615), dean of Gloucester (1616). Laud, as a chaplain, was a member of the royal delegation to Scotland in 1617. The Scots were aghast when he wore a surplice to a funeral, and Miles Smith, the venerable and learned Calvinist bishop of Gloucester, was aghast when he had the cathedral chapter move the Communion table from the choir to the east end. S. R. Gardiner thought that "this affair at Gloucester clearly exhibits the causes of Laud's failure in late life. If he had authority on his side, he considered it unnecessary even to attempt to win over by persuasion those who differed from him."[19]

But first he had to get authority over more than a cathedral chapter (he had resigned the presidency of St. John's when he accepted the deanery, despite royal leave to retain it). To do so required the talents of a persuasive courtier. The door to his future greatness was opened by James's favorite, George Villiers. Tuesday, August 27, 1616, may have been the day that their association began. The court was at Woodstock and heard Laud preach that morning on Miriam's leprosy, God's punishment for the temerity she showed when she "spake against Moses." That same day James joyously made Villiers Viscount Buckingham.[20] A year later he was an earl and in another year a marquess. Laud, wrote Bishop Hacket, "had fasten'd on the Lord Marquess to be his mediator, whom he had made sure by great observances." Archbishop Abbot, muttering about Laud's "unsoundness in religion," continued to oppose his promotion, and the king repeatedly refused Buckingham's suits for Laud. Lord Keeper Williams, however, anxious to assist Buckingham, agreed to intercede in Laud's behalf for the bishopric of St. David's in Wales. Williams reminded James that Laud "had deserved well when he was a young man in his zeal against the Millenary Petition" at Hampton Court in 1604. "You have pleaded the man a good Protestant, and I believe it," responded the king. Finally he revealed his most important objection to Laud: "I find he hath a restless spirit, and cannot see when matters are well, but loves to toss and change, and bring things to a pitch of reformation floating in his own brain, which may endanger the steadfastness of that which is in good pass, God be praised." He based this shrewd perception on a quite specific episode. He had in 1617–18 persuaded a General Assembly of the Scottish Church to accept certain changes in worship (the Five Articles of Perth) that were to bring his subjects there into closer "correspondence with this Church of England. I gave them promise . . . that I would try their obedience no further anent ecclesiastical affairs, nor put them out of their own way, which custom had made pleasing unto them, with any new encroachments." Despite this politic restraint, Laud had "pressed me to invite them to a nearer conjunction with the liturgy and canons of this nation." When the king rejected what he called his chaplain's "frivolous draught," the persistent man had "assaulted me again with another ill-fangled platform . . . . He knows not the stomach of that people."[21]

Never were James's powers of prophecy better displayed, but even he could not have imagined that Laud's ignorance of the Scots' digestive capacity would cost his own heir his head as well as Laud's. And, as in other cases where Villiers' wishes were involved, James did not stick to his guns. Williams assured him that Laud, having a "great and tractable wit," would cure himself of such errors. "Then take him to you, but on my soul you will repent it," said the king. "And so went away in anger using other fierce and ominous words, which were divulged in the court, and are too tart to be repeated."[22] Perhaps it was precisely the new bishop of St.

David's persistence that James remembered when he summoned him on April 23, 1622, to save Buckingham's mother from the siren song of a Jesuit known as Father Fisher. She later deserted the Church of England, but her son was so deeply impressed that he made Laud his chaplain. Although the favorite played a double game with his Calvinist and Arminian clients, he and Laud were close from 1622 on. Indeed, Laud came to be known as "the Duke's earwig."[23] Williams had hoped that Laud's diocesan responsibilities would keep him far from the court, but he was disappointed. St. David's was his for five years, but Laud made only two trips there for a total of about four months.

By the time James died in March 1625, Laud had labored long to achieve his relatively secure place in the confidence of the duke and the new king. He had survived the darts of the Calvinists, darts sharpened in response to his own truculence. He had escaped the net with which his wily rival, Lord Keeper Williams, had tried to hold him down. Laud's diary never ceased to record his fears about the permanence of his influence, but these all proved groundless. Charles chose the bishop of St. David's over the Lord Keeper to preside at his coronation and to preach at the opening of parliaments. Laud provided a list of clerics labeled O for orthodox and P for Puritan for the king and the duke to use in appointing clerics.[24] Abbot later wrote that he was not consulted about appointments and knew no more than if he had "dwelt at Venice and understood them by some gazette." From October 9, 1627, to June 24, 1628, Laud and four other bishops were commissioned to exercise Abbot's jurisdiction. He was sequestered for refusing to license the printing of Robert Sibthorpe's sermon asserting that subjects should pay taxes whether voted by Parliament or not. Laud advocated printing the sermon, and he and his cohorts were already thought too ready to defend the king's interpretation of his prerogatives.[25] Laud became bishop of Bath and Wells in mid-1626, a privy councillor in 1627, and bishop of London in 1628. Although he had to wait until Abbot's death in 1633 to ascend to the archbishopric of Canterbury, he was the architect of Charles's ecclesiastical policy almost from the beginning of the reign. His mentor Neile was promoted to the archbishopric of York in 1632. Under James the Arminian party picked up crumbs under the king's table. Under Charles they sat down to a fifteen-year feast.

William Laud was a brusque, businesslike administrator, not an intellectual or a theologian. Supported by a king who admired his tenacity and loyalty and who shared his zeal for order and decency in "the external worship of God," Laud carried out a reform program with an agenda and direction already established by Richard Hooker, Lancelot Andrewes, and others. He published little in the way of systematic justification of his program. Indeed, his usual preference was to let his actions speak for themselves without printed apologia. Star Chamber was a bully pulpit. Historians have therefore tended to describe and analyze his program as he practiced it and for theory to look to his younger and more prolific associates from Durham House days. Their rapid promotions imply his approval of their views. Richard Montagu and John Cosin, on theological and liturgical matters respectively, are indeed essential for an understanding of "English Arminianism" or "Laudianism." Montagu's sharply polemical prose and Cosin's colorful innovations have been seductive—but the king's confidence was in the dull, phlegmatic little archbishop. In this essay, therefore, an attempt will be made to study his outlook as much as possible through his own words. As suggested above, that outlook had three central features. He set himself firmly against public theological controversy and believed deeply in the benefits of ceremony. Underlying and informing these was his deep conviction that the Reformation had deprived clergymen of authority and influence that was essential to the health of religion, monarchy, and society. Restoration of the clerical estate to its rightful place was absolutely necessary, and those who hindered it were no less seditious than sacrilegious. Each of these three themes will be considered in theory and, more briefly, in practice.

Laud was reluctant to publish his *Conference with Fisher*, but James insisted. "I had not hitherto appeared in print. I am no controvertist," he wrote in his diary when the work appeared early in 1624.[26] Reformers and counter-reformers struggled in endless disputations in and out of print, to little purpose as far as he could see. Indeed, their usual result, if carried on in public, was disorder. His role in the hottest theological controversy of the 1620s, the Montagu furore, is instructive. The first attack in the House of Commons on theological Arminianism came in 1624. John Pym objected to the insufficiently vigorous anti-Romanism of Richard Montagu's book against the Romanists. While opposing many Roman Catholic doctrines, Montagu (then an Essex clergyman), backed away from maintaining many that English Calvinists held dear. Pym, like many knowledgeable members of the Church of England, believed deeply that the doctrine of predestination to eternal life for the elect and reprobation for others was at the core of Protestantism and of the legally established doctrine of the Church of England.[27] Pym, like them, thought that the Thirty-Nine Articles, amplified by the Lambeth Articles and the findings of the Synod of Dort, were the very basis of the reformed religion and that the Church of England was and ought to remain a defender of these truths. Montagu, however, contended that only "some" Protestants held such beliefs. Although they were entitled to do so privately, "these are opinions, and defended, but not of all Protestants, not of the Church of England." Lutherans, for example, did not agree, and in any case the use of Scripture, the Fathers of the Early Church, and reason were to be preferred to modern divines. Such opinions "are fitter for schooles then popular discourses: and may be held or not held, without heresie either way."[28] Montagu's views did not in 1624 create the storm that they would in later parliaments. Since the Calvinism of

James and Abbot seemed firm and since some members were uncertain about Commons' jurisdiction "in so deep points of religion,"[29] it was decided to refer the whole business to the archbishop. By the time Charles's first parliament met in 1625, Montagu had written his *Appello Caesarem,* a book more offensive to conservative opinion than the first. The Calvinist counterblasts sprang from the presses. One of them was by a bishop, George Carleton of Chichester, who had been one of the English representatives at Dort. Abbot had been unable to restrain Montagu, who was claiming that the late king had approved his views. "It was becoming steadily clearer in 1625," writes Conrad Russell, "that the issue of Arminianism against predestination was one which had split the court and the bench of bishops down the middle." In July 1625, when the Commons prepared to imprison Montagu for contempt, Charles protected him by making him a royal chaplain, an unmistakable sign "that he was ready for a confrontation on the issue of Arminianism."[30]

Charles may well have been more ready to take on the Calvinists than Laud was. On August 2, 1625, Laud and Buckeridge wrote to urge Buckingham to reinforce Montagu's defense. They argued that when the Church of England "was reformed from the superstitious opinions" of the Church of Rome, it rejected "the apparent and dangerous errors, and would not be busy with every particular school-point." The great mistake of the Council of Trent had been to require subscription to doctrines that were better "left at more liberty for learned men" to examine, as long as they "distract not the church." A cardinal principle of the English Reformation, based upon "the ordinance of Christ, and the continual course and practice of the church," was that doctrinal differences were to be settled by "the king and the bishops," after the former had given specific permission for debate. The Arminian bishops thought that both religion and "civil government" would suffer "if such fatal opinions, as some which are opposite and contrary to those delivered by Mr. Montagu, are and shall be publicly maintained." The bishops reminded Buckingham that "the contrary opinions" in question "were treated of at Lambeth, and ready to be published but then Queen Elizabeth, of famous memory, upon notice given of how little they agreed with the practice of piety and obedience to all government caused them to be suppressed; and so they have continued ever since." True, the Synod of Dort revived them—but that was a "foreign synod," fortunately without authority in England. Nowhere in the letter were the contrary opinions specified—but it was well known that the Lambeth Articles and the Synod of Dort had upheld Calvinist predestinarianism. This letter, a private one after all, rejected Calvinism directly, while espousing Arminianism only obliquely.[31]

Laud's strategy for protecting Montagu, hinted at in the August letter, was stated clearly in another letter to Buckingham early in 1626 (also signed by Neile, Andrewes, Buckeridge, and George Montaigne, bishop of

London). The king had asked these Arminian bishops to examine Montagu's opinions, and they pronounced that "he had not affirmed anything to be the doctrine of the Church of England, but that which in our opinions is the doctrine of the Church of England, or agreeable thereunto." The bishops did not, however, make what might appear to be the recommendation that would follow logically from this conclusion, namely, to encourage public expression of Montagu's opinions while suppressing the contrary opinions of the Calvinists. Instead, they urged the king "to prohibit any further controverting of these questions by public preaching or writing."[32] This thinking is apparent in Charles's proclamation "for the establishing of the peace and quiet" of the church. No subject was to write, preach, or print "any doubts" about "the doctrine and discipline of the Church of England heretofore published and happily established by authority" (16 June 1626).[33] Laud was also behind the king's November 1628 order, printed in the Book of Common Prayer, proscribing public glossing of any of the Thirty-Nine Articles. "Further curious search" was to end, and the subject was not to "put his own sense or comment to be the meaning of the Article, but shall take it in the literal and grammatical sense." That the doctrines of predestination caused special concern is evident from the reference to "disputes shut up in God's promises." By emphasizing "that all clergymen within our realm have always subscribed" to the articles, and that "even in those curious points, in which the present differences lie . . . men of all sorts" accept them, the declaration pretended to ignore the fact that the Arminian interpretation was thought heterodox by many churchmen and laymen. Nor were these men likely to miss the statement that the king intended to call upon the bishops and clergy "from time to time in convocation . . . to deliberate of, and to do all such things as . . . shall concern the settled continuance of the doctrines and discipline of the Church of England now established."[34] Nothing was said about consulting Parliament.

Laud's campaign to suppress the preaching and publication of Calvinist and Puritan doctrinal polemic is well known. What should be noted here is that he also muzzled Arminians, albeit without branding any of their cheeks. Montagu himself chafed when required to abide by the 1626 proclamation and remain silent while books appeared against him.[35] When the master of Trinity College, Cambridge, completed fifteen years of labor on an Arminian treatise of predestination in 1630, Laud indicated a polite interest in reading it (if it "be not too long") and approved of the author's plan to show it to learned friends. "Nevertheless I am yet where I was, that something about these controversies is unmasterable in this life." He thought it unlikely that publication would be licensed, because the king did not want "to have these controversies any further stirred, which now . . . begin to be at more peace." In May 1630 Laud disciplined an Oxford preacher who had defended Arminian tenets and criticized the Synod of

Dort.[36] As Hugh Trevor-Roper put it, Laud believed that "the way to secure orthodoxy was not . . . to prove the true doctrine but to enforce it, and to silence all disputation which tended to reopen a closed question."[37]

The Arminians' critics in and out of Parliament were becoming convinced by 1628–29 that their real goal was the reintroduction of Roman Catholicism. The Calvinists' world was sharply divided between light and darkness, true religion and "popery." In their context Laud's effort to silence controversy could have only one motive—the silencing of those who preached truth as a preparative to unleashing the false prophets of Romanism. They held a parallel suspicion of his liturgical program, for ceremonialism, not preaching, was at the center of it. The first churchman of the Neile-Laud group to undergo attack for what were called "popish" liturgical innovations was Samuel Harsnett—in 1624 the bishop of Norwich—but in that year no connection was made with Arminian doctrine.[38] The appearance early in 1627 of *A Collection of Private Devotions* by John Cosin, followed in 1628 by slashing attacks on his liturgical innovations at Durham Cathedral, made certain that the 1628 Parliament would take unfavorable notice. Only royal pardons saved Montagu and Cosin from punishment and their books from the flames, and members of Parliament were so infuriated that they set out to impeach Neile for his role in their issuance.[39]

We shall never know what Laud thought about some doctrinal issues, but there is no doubt about his admiration for the liturgical ideas of Andrewes, Cosin, and others. The source of his antipathy to public disputation was his conviction that it led society away from unity and order and that the way back was through ceremonies. Dignified ceremonies conducted by properly adorned priests in properly consecrated and decorated churches and chapels were not ends in themselves for Laud any more than the hearing of "godly sermons" in churches, free of the remnants of "popery," were for his critics. Each saw these as the means to greater ends. In Laud's view, society could not progress until the liturgy and the churches were repaired from the deterioration caused by an excess of Protestant zeal. At the beginning of his trial in 1645, he stated that for his whole career he had "labored nothing more, than that the external worship of God (too much slighted in most parts of this kingdom) might be preserved" in as much "decency and uniformity" as possible. He continued to believe "that unity cannot long continue in the church, where uniformity is shut out at the church door." The "public neglect of God's service in the outward face of it, and the nasty lying of many places dedicated to that service, had almost cast a damp upon the true and inward worship of God; which, while we live in the body, needs external helps . . . to keep it in any vigor."[40]

Laud dedicated the 1639 edition of his *Conference with Fisher* to the king, and the preface contains another statement on uniformity and ceremony. Historians have rightly seen Laud as the leader of a party theologically opposed to the Calvinist doctrine of absolute predestination—but they have been less aware how little evidence there is that the leader himself was deeply interested in the alternatives to that doctrine. The 1639 preface, like the 1645 speech, can be read as a retrospective on his career. It is concerned with authority and ceremony, not doctrine. "No one thing hath made conscientious men more wavering in their own minds, or more apt and easy to be drawn" away from the Church of England, wrote Laud, than the lack "of uniform and decent order in too many churches of the kingdom." Generations of Calvinist prelates had winked at Puritan altera-tions of the liturgy and at failures to maintain the fabric of church buildings because they had preferred preachers to priests. The churches had decayed until the Romanists sneered that "the house of God could not be suffered to lie so nastily . . . were the true worship of God observed in them." The truest worship was inward, "but the external worship of God in his church is the great witness to the world, that our heart stands right in the service of God." Without "decency and an orderly settlement of the external wor-ship of God in the church," there can be "no example to men," and "no external action in the world can be uniform without some ceremonies." The difficulty was that the particular ceremonies he set out to enjoin ap-peared, at least in their "outward face," Roman Catholic, and his critics hated them because the example they set was evil. They believed that symbols and examples were important too and that the wrong ones would destroy spiritual vigor. Laud's diagnosis of the disease of his times was "an opinion in too many men, that because Rome had thrust some unnecessary and many superstitious ceremonies upon the church, therefore the Refor-mation must have none at all." Men of that opinion failed to realize "that ceremonies are the hedge that fence the substance of religion from all the indignities which profaneness and sacrilege too commonly put upon it." What held for religious ceremonies applied to others. After Laud's election as chancellor of Oxford, he was grieved to learn that members of the university had been neglecting the "formalities" (wearing of caps, gowns, and academic regalia according to rank). He was appalled that strangers to Oxford "have scarce any mark by which they know they are in a univer-sity. If this go on, the university will lose ground every day at home and abroad." The formalities were "the hedge and fence of those things, which are of far greater consequence."[41] If students and fellows did not dress traditionally, they would lose respect for themselves and the people lose respect for learned men. Similarly, thought Laud, the people would not respect the inward part of religion, the greater part, if the "outward face" were neglected.

In his first diocese, St. David's, Laud acted to create a satisfactory setting for worship by building, adorning, and consecrating a chapel in the episcopal residence, Abergwili House. He continued to take pleasure in refurbishing churches and chapels and consecrating them where necessary. Because the Book of Common Prayer lacked a service for the purpose, he used one that Andrewes had devised.[42] His visitation articles evince his desire to protect not only the church itself and all the things "consecrated for holy use" within it, but also the churchyard. The churchwardens were to report whether "the whole consecrated ground [was] kept free from swine and all other nastiness." His reports to the king contain numerous reports of the horrendous physical condition of many churches and of episcopal efforts to restore them.[43] Laud poured his energies into a campaign for ways and means to repair the "decayed and ruinous estate" of St. Paul's Cathedral in his diocese of London. Resistance to rebuilding was due partly to its cost and partly to iconoclastic attitudes like those of Lord Brook. Early in the Civil War, Brook was killed when a musket ball hit him in the eye as he prepared an assault near Lichfield Cathedral: "Thus was his eye put out, who about two years since said, he hoped to live to see at St. Paul's not one stone left upon another," noted Laud, doubtless with some satisfaction, as he sat in the Tower.[44] Puritans like Brook may have feared that the completed St. Paul's would be similar to the Oxford and Cambridge chapels already completed by Laudians. There were altars, crucifixes, and stained glass and statuary with quite medieval iconography (the Virgin Mary, angels, cherubim). "All in all," writes Horton Davies, "the university chapels (especially Peterhouse in the Puritan stronghold, Cambridge) were a bold and beautiful tribute to the new respect for reverence, the sense of the primacy of the Eucharist over preaching, and the sheer aesthetic sensibilities of the upholders of the Laudian tradition."[45]

Along with reedification of the fabric of the churches, Laud's ceremonialism required reform of the worship services, especially the Holy Communion. "In all ages of the church," he said at his trial, "the touchstone of religion was not to hear the word preached, but to communicate. . . . I call the holy table the greatest place of God's residence upon earth." While defending himself against the charge of belief in transubstantiation, he stated that "the altar is . . . greater than the pulpit; For there 'tis *Hoc est corpus meum*, This is my body; but in the other it is but *Hoc est verbum meum*, This is my word: and a greater reverence is due to the body, than the word of the Lord."[46] His visitation articles inquired whether each parish had "a decent communion table" with silk and linen coverings that was protected from unholy use ("as by sitting on it, throwing hats on it, writing on it") out of service time. The churchwardens were to report if the minister did not cleave to the prayerbook and preside "in his surplice and hood."[47] Requiring the surplice was a venerable bone of contention with many Puritans, as was Laud's insistence on bowing whenever the name of Jesus was read and kneeling to receive Communion. While reawakening these old arguments, Laud created new ones with his "innovations" about Communion tables. The 1559 Injunctions permitted movement of the table from the east end into the chancel when there was no Communion service, and the 1604 Canons said it could be moved anywhere in the church. But when Bishop Williams employed these rules while settling disputes in his diocese, Laud told him that the king did not want the table "to be in the body of the church . . . because the people usually sit in their seats, and [it] cannot be discerned whether they kneel or no while they receive."[48] When parishioners at St. Gregory's in London protested an order from dean and chapter of St. Paul's to place their Communion table at the east end, Laud took care to have the case removed from the Court of Arches to the Privy Council. There the king overruled earlier policy and ordered an "altarwise" (north-south) placing of the table in the east end in the manner of the cathedral. Laud's injunction requiring that the table be so oriented and protected by rails was being enforced in the northern province by Archbishop Neile by 1635 along with the other ceremonial requirements. Elsewhere the rate of progress in enforcing innovations varied.[49]

Laud disliked the forcing of consciences in all but the most essential matters of discipline, while at the same time he felt compelled to apply force in matters of ceremony. He made no attempt to prevent the individual from believing that election and reprobation were absolutely predestined while making every effort to force him to kneel to receive Communion. Right worship was the way to right belief and therefore to social and political order under the sacred king. It was the way to "godly rule." Beliefs need not be uniform as long as behavior was. As Gardiner wrote, "the liberty which he claimed for men's minds, he denied to their actions. Here, at least, order must prevail."[50] Laud had come to lead a school of churchmen that held an Erasmian-Arminian theological position between the free will of Rome and the absolute predestination of Geneva. Richard Hooker and Lancelot Andrewes were prominent English settlers on this middle ground that attracted moderate people throughout Christendom. They emphasized the Scriptures and the Fathers as antidotes to the dogmatism of both Trent and Dort. The high-water mark of what Trevor-Roper has called this "ecumenical movement" came during the three relatively peaceful decades after the defeat of the Spanish Armada in 1588. These were the years of Laud's education and rise to power, and they formed "an interlude between the frontal struggles of Catholic and Protestant, a last ineffective dream before the final, painfully won realization that Christendom was now irremediably plural."[51] The renewal of confessional conflict in the Thirty Years' War rendered hopeless the dream of uniting moderate Protestants and moderate Catholics in a loose confederation of tolerant national churches. Laud recognized this fact and set himself to work to bring the blessing of uniformity to all of Charles I's subjects— English, Welsh, Scots, Irish, immigrant French and Dutch, and emigrant soldiers, merchants, and colonists.

What Laud tragically failed to recognize about the international situation was that it greatly increased fears that his ritualism was a Trojan horse filled with popery. This is not to say that the "innovations" would have been innocuous against a different European background. Puritans believed that the fulfillment of God's will required the widest possible dissemination of doctrinal principles. The Christian had to understand the meaning of the Scriptures and the application of them to his world. This could not be done without cadres of educated, zealous preachers able to explain the most fundamental principle of all, the doctrine of salvation by faith alone, and its numerous corollaries. If the listener could grasp why he might hope that he was among the segment of humankind chosen to receive the unmerited gift of saving faith, he could begin to search his experience for evidence to buttress his hope. With right understanding would come right behavior. Every person had to become a theologian, at least in a rudimentary way. Therefore the hearing of God's word read and preached had to be the heart of the liturgy. Laud's use of a preacher's refusal to wear the surplice as a tool to silence him was a hideous perversion from this perspective. Surplices, altars, and images were not evil in themselves, but they were associated in the popular mind with the Mass. They would hinder the penetration of the Word by reinforcing traditional erroneous beliefs in the automatic efficacy of the sacraments and the magical powers of the priest. As John S. Coolidge has put it, "the preaching of the Word is the original sacrament of Puritanism, without which the Lord's Supper itself is a dead ritual."[52] Right worship and behavior could not possibly issue from wrong belief.

There were churchmen who shared much of Laud's theological outlook without supporting his insistence on ceremonies. His godson, William Chillingworth, preached against "zeal for ceremonies" as well as "zeal against them," and John Hales chided those who "stood so much upon state and ceremony in the church."[53] There were Arminians on whom Charles's favor might have fallen who would not have placed such heavy weight on the frail reed of ritual. Laud did not earn his leadership of the Arminian party by his intellectual or spiritual gifts. It was an accident caused by the king's choice. They were quite different men, but something in their differing rigidities proved sympathetic. Charles was a lazy aesthete short of self-confidence. Laud's dogged industry saved him work, his loyalty gratified the royal ego, and his ceremonialism appealed to the royal sensibilities. All this might have been less dangerous politically had Laud, like Andrewes, promoted "the beauty of holiness" by way of example rather than mandate from High Commission or Star Chamber. If he had contented himself with building a Maginot line against theological controversy in pursuit of the Erasmian vision of unity, he and his master and many others might have died in their beds. The ban on disputation would have troubled the moderate Puritans less than one might think. They could have done their preaching without explicit public discussion of the "deep points" of theology, which had been debated in the universities since the 1590s and more publicly since the Montagu controversy. To be sure, Laud used his authority to stop the distribution of the radical screeds written by men like Alexander Leighton and John Bastwick. But Puritan sermons continued to resound from the pulpits and tumble from the presses filled with what their authors considered the practical consequences of Calvinist divinity.[54] Puritans would still have suspected Laud of a subtle intention to insinuate popish doctrine but, without the pain caused by his zealous imposition of ceremonies, the reaction against him would have been much less powerful.

The Puritan desire for theological understanding was in one of its most important dimensions a laicizing drive toward actualization of the "priesthood of all believers." The rejection of medieval Catholic ceremonialism was a rejection of a special power and authority deriving from the rite of ordination and by it the creation of a separate class in society. Puritans viewed medieval sacerdotalism as a massive ruse designed to divert material resources, political power, and moral influence into the hands of a priestly caste that preserved itself by keeping the laity in theological darkness. Puritanism was thus a continuation of the Protestant drive toward a spiritual self-mastery in which the role of the minister was more pastoral than sacerdotal. It aimed at transferring doctrinal and disciplinary decision-making, which had formerly resided in convocations, church courts, and confessionals, into venues more subject to lay influence (and sometimes to lay control).[55] Laud's dislike of disputation and love of ritual derived from his belief that God's plan for human society had been undermined by the weakening of the clergy's power and influence. Since clerical power supported the monarchy, its decline was injurious to the king. Opposers of Laud's program were enemies no less to church than state. In the struggle against the excesses of Rome, he believed that the Reformation had gone too far. Greedy laymen had seized control of too much of the church's wealth, and they were using part of it to maintain a hypocritical, hireling clergy as a bulwark to defend their booty.

Unifying and inspiring the extraordinary sweep of Laud's labors was his passionate desire to roll back the tide of laicization and restore the clerical estate. The ceremonies that were the means to reorder true religion and social hierarchy would be useless if the priesthood that conducted them was not respected by all the king's subjects, regardless of social rank. Because bishops led the clergy, Laud held a particularly high notion of their calling, and he did not hesitate to use the Court of Star Chamber to mete out cruel punishments to such attackers of the episcopacy as Leighton, Bastwick, Burton, and Prynne.[56] When he noted Andrewes's death in his diary in 1626, he described him as "the great light of the Christian world," and only a few months later he was urging the king to have printed the late bishop's papers "concerning bishops, that they are *jure divino.*" "My tenet was, and is still," he wrote in 1644, that *"Episcopatus* is *jure divino."*[57] This assertion went against not only Elizabethan tradition and Presbyterian doctrines of parity among ordained men, but a broader opposition to clerical meddling in civil matters as well. Laud and Neile were privy councillors from 1627, active in all sorts of business in addition to spiritual and ecclesiastical concerns. Laud scored a major victory against his enemies at court when in 1636 he convinced the king to appoint the bishop of London, William Juxon, to the Lord Treasurership. "No church-man had it since Henry VII's time," chortled the archbishop in his diary. Portland, the former treasurer, had been in Laud's view the epitome of the grasping courtier who used his office for private gain instead of public good. The Juxon appointment seemed a great blow for "thorough" administrative and moral reform of the king's government and a turning point in the clericalist struggle against the excesses of the Reformation. "And now if the church will not hold up themselves under God, I can do no more," he concluded.[58]

The clergy's position could not be restored and maintained without money. As Laud wrote in 1637, "poverty draws on contempt, and contempt makes clergymen unserviceable to God, the church and the commonwealth."[59] Laudian visitation articles bristled with detailed questions designed to enable ministers to discover to the square inch and the last farthing what lands and other assets their parishes had. Higher clergy especially were heavily pressed not to lease property for long periods or for low rents or otherwise alienate what the church still possessed. Laud supported and admired his great friend Wentworth's high-handed successes in recovering former church property in Ireland.[60] The archbishop encouraged fear of the evil consequences of sacrilege in order to persuade holders of impropriated resources to return them to the church. Aware that persuasion would not succeed in more than a few cases, he intended to begin purchasing impropriations once the enormous financial drain caused by the repair of St. Paul's ceased. His courts issued numerous orders that created expenses for laymen, but he was always suspicious of voluntary lay contributions that had or might have strings attached. When a group of prominent Puritan laymen and ministers set up an organization to buy impropriated tithes and advowsons in order to finance preaching, Laud branded them "the main instruments for the Puritan faction to undo the church" and got an Exchequer court order to dissolve them and confiscate the money. When the inhabitants of Hammersmith raised money to build a chapel and pay a minister, Laud approved, but insisted that the nomination of the minister be in the bishop's hands, not theirs. Only so could he be confident that the chapel would be served by an "honest and painful man" and not a "busy-headed" disturber of the peace.[61] The same hostility to lay choice of preachers is apparent throughout his campaign to regulate lectureships. Lectureships were often financed by laymen who chose the preachers, an arrangement that would have troubled Laud even if none of the lecturers had been "busy-headed" men.[62]

Bitter clashes with common lawyers were an inevitable side-effect of Laud's revivification of the church courts and the clerical estate generally. "As for the church," he wrote gloomily to Wentworth, "it is so bound up in the forms of common law, that it is not possible for me, or any man, to do that good which he would, or is bound to do." He saw the law as a hedge protecting private ends against the unifying, centralizing methods of "thorough" reform, and he allegedly said that he "would prohibit the entry into the kingdom of heaven of all who granted prohibitions to the disturbance of the church's right." His success in reducing prohibitions addressed to ecclesiastical courts helped swell the ranks of the civil lawyers.[63] Several concerns close to Laud's heart appeared in the arguments presented by Edward Bagshawe, Lent Reader at the Middle Temple, just before the Short Parliament opened in 1640. In his view, Parliament could pass bills whether the bishops were present or not, and clergymen should neither serve as justices of the peace nor be prevented from appealing to common law courts when deprived of their benefices by the Court of High Commission. At Laud's urging, the king ordered Bagshawe's reading ended, an unprecedented intervention that made the lawyer a popular hero.[64]

Bagshawe was by no means the only common lawyer to suffer for opposing Laudian clericalism. When Chief Justice Richardson disobeyed royal instructions to revoke orders prohibiting churchales, Laud decided to defend the diocesan's jurisdiction over such matters. At a session of the Privy Council with the king present in 1633, the judge received a tongue-lashing that prompted him to say he was "like to be choked with the Archbishop's lawn sleeves." The triumph over Richardson afforded Laud the opportunity to reissue James's Book of Sports, require the reading of it from pulpits, and use refusals by Puritan incumbents as a weapon against them.[65] Earlier in the same year, Henry Sherfield, the recorder of Salisbury, received a similar treatment. He had destroyed a painted-glass window he considered idolatrous and defended himself partly on the ground that the parish vestry had authorized its replacement with plain glass. Censuring Sherfield in Star Chamber, Laud said that vestries ("made and suffered by negligence") lacked the authority to make alterations where spiritual matters were involved. The bishop should have been consulted. The offense was magnified in Laud's eyes because the defendant was a lawyer and justice of the peace. "Thus much let me to say to Mr. Sherfield, and such of his profession as slight the ecclesiastical laws and persons, that there was a time when churchmen were as great in this kingdom as you are now; and let me be bold to prophesy, there will be a time when you will be as low as the church is now, if you go on to contemn the church."[66]

In 1636, three years after his confident prophecy to Sherfield, Laud noted a libel pinned up at St. Paul's: "that the government of the Church of England is a candle in the snuff, going out in a stench." The anonymous libeler proved a better prophet than Laud. The attempt of king and archbishop to extend their liturgical program to Scotland precipitated a rebellion that demonstrated that neither man understood "the stomach of that people." Mobs attacked Lambeth Palace in May 1640, and the bishops were the most hated men in the kingdom. In the Tower less than a year later the archbishop noted with horror the Parliament's decision to establish a "Committee for Religion" in which laymen would have twice as many votes as clergy. "This Committee will meddle with doctrine as well as ceremonies . . . to the great dishonor of the church."[67] Despite his honesty and industry, Laud's attempt to reestablish "the ecclesiastical law and persons" and repair "the outward face of religion" crashed into rubble. We have already considered the reasons for Puritan opposition to Laudianism, but by no means all of the opposition in 1640 derived from theological principles. It remains to consider briefly why the resistance, Puritan or non-Puritan, was so extensive and so effective. The monarchy and episcopacy, restored two decades later, bore only a superficial resemblance to the absolutist and clericalist dreams of Charles I and Laud.[68] Ironically, bishops would stand highest in public esteem when in 1688 they stood in the dock, accused by James II of seditious libeling.

In 1688 the bishops appeared to be defending the religion "by law established" and the traditional rights of Englishmen against a king with centralizing and Romanizing tendencies. But in 1640 the Laudians appeared to be leading the nation in the direction James II was later to take. Both James II and Laud opposed the entrenched leaders of rural and urban society, and both failed. The parochial roots that Laudianism needed in order to prosper were virtually nonexistent. As Patrick Collinson has put it, the Laudians operated under the debatable assumption that "by working with the grain of provincial society, the church placed itself at risk."[69] Instead, they worked against that grain, and the price was high. As late as 1639, Laud's reports to the king contain statements that indicate that orders were not being obeyed. A group of parishioners had "indicted a minister, because he would not come down from the communion table to give them the sacrament in their seats," and "some of the vulgar sort in Suffolk are not conformable enough, especially in coming up to receive at the steps of the chancel, where the rails are set."[70] In fact, disobedience and disaffection were a great deal more widespread than Laud knew, because there were many places where his enemies supplied the information he received. Matthew Wren was the most efficient and committed of his bishops—but the records of his 1639 Ely visitation show no Puritan lay opinion in villages from which many signatures for petitions against episcopacy came in 1640. The visitation returns showed no Puritanism because, as comparison of the names shows, the churchwardens who answered the questions were often Puritans.[71] When the questions had to do with the need for expenditure, the distortions were even more palpable. In Sussex in 1636, Bishop Montagu surveyed twenty-one churches on which the churchwardens had reported only a few weeks before: "The visitors reported 202 items amiss in these churches, only a single one of which, the decay of the shingling of St. Botolphs steeple, had been mentioned by parish officers."[72] Conspiracies of silence were a greater danger to Laud than the conspiracies of radicals he feared. A recent study of Kent noted that the diocesan orders about altar rails, Communion tables, and kneeling were widely disobeyed, and a survey of factionalism in villages found that "the enforcment of Arminianism was provocative even where no more than a moderate puritanism was the established creed."[73]

If Laudians had remained in power long enough for a new generation of "Arminianized" clerics and landowners to emerge from the universities and take their places in Stuart society, they might have succeeded. Over time many more parish ministers would have jumped aboard the Laudian bandwagon because they found promotion attractive financially and the new clericalism satisfying socially.[74] In the short term, however, success for Laud would have required, as Paul Seaver has said, "a frontal attack on the system of lay patronage." This "would have placed him in conflict not only with the aspirations of vestries, merchant companies, and town corporations, of powerful aristocrats, gentry, and merchants, but also with the fundamental property rights of the laity."[75] The maintenance of order in too many towns depended on established Puritan leaders of institutions. Too many gentlemen and lords owned too many advowsons and had patronized too many Puritan preachers whom they intended to defend for rural religion to be changed rapidly with the tools in Laud's hands. Moderate Puritans were extremely adept at avoiding deprivation or suspension from Laud, even while they worked hard to undermine him. The combination of Puritan principle with anticlericalism and anti-Catholicism made for a resilient and resourceful resistance. John T. Evans's conclusion for Norwich holds for many other places: "the roots of the political and religious unrest of the 1630s lay not so much in the innovations and agitations of militant Puritans as in an aggressive episcopal effort to extirpate an already entrenched puritanism."[76]

In a sense, Laud's failure was the result of his conception of the Protestant Reformation. For him the Reformation was over and its work done before he came to power. The doctrinal and liturgical errors and excesses of Rome had been undone to his satisfaction in the Church of England, and he saw his own task as the undoing of the errors and excesses of the

Reformation. For the Puritans who resisted him, however, the Reformation was still very much in progress, and its beachhead on the continent of ignorance and superstition was threatened on all sides. Many of them had grown up in parishes where Communion tables were never placed altarwise, surplices seldom seen, and "godly preaching" seldom lacking. The religion they had experienced was what Laud called "puritan." In doctrinal terms, Laud was in fact a moderate Protestant. One of his explanations for his dislike of doctrinal controversy describes the dynamic that ruined him: "I cannot persuade myself that such a fiery spirit will be quenched by any answer; and then we shall have reply upon reply, till at last moderate men themselves be overheated and all hopes lost."[77] The archbishop himself applied the flame by elevating clerics and their ceremonies against a background of Catholic advance both abroad and at the court of Charles I.[78] By insisting upon what appeared to be a Catholic ritual and priesthood, he ensured that his doctrinal protestations would not be credible. The result was what Robert Ashton has recently called a "logic of polarization," in which the political and religious center was "squeezed by both extremes." There was no shortage of moderate Puritans, men who had long expected that monarchs and bishops would lead the nation to completion of the Reformation. These moderates were as much the victims of Laudianism as the non-Puritan advocates of "reduced" or "primitive" episcopacy.[79] Laud could not tell one Puritan from another, nor imagine how opposition to his endeavors could arise from conscience. Perhaps it is poetic justice that his critics misinterpreted him as badly as he did them. Each saw in the other nothing but greed and lust for power covered by a scab of hypocrisy. The fault for the catastrophe that befell the Church of England was less his than the king's. For as A. G. Dickens wrote, it was under Charles that "the monarchy declined into an instrument of the Laudian minority-group." Elizabeth had had the wisdom not to permit "the monopolizing of that church by the puritan spirit," but Charles was foolish enough to let the Laudians "attempt a counter-monopoly."[80] And so moderate men were overheated and all hopes lost.

NOTES

1. Quoted in Hugh Trevor-Roper, *Archbishop Laud*, p. 376. Where details of publication are provided in the critical bibliography, they are omitted in the footnotes. I am most grateful for suggestions on an earlier draft of this essay made by Esther Cope, Richard Greaves, Caroline Hibbard, John Morrill, Paul Seaver, and Kevin Sharpe.

2. *History of the Rebellion and Civil Wars* (Oxford: University Press, 1849), 3:485–86 (viii, 208). Cf. E. R. Adair, "Laud and the Church of England," *Church History* 5 (1936): 121–27.

3. *Crumms of Comfort. The Second Part* (London, 1652), sig. § 8 (verso).

4. Quoted in R. C. Richardson, *The Debate on the English Revolution* (London: Methuen, 1977), p. 38.

5. *History of England* (New York: Harper & Row, 1879), 1:91.

6. *A History of the English Church from the Accession of Charles I to the Death of Anne* (London: Macmillan, 1903), 43–44, 46.

7. "Laud's Personal Religion," in W. E. Collins, ed., *Lectures on Archbishop Laud*, 1st ed., 1895 (New York: Burt Franklin, 1969), 124. This is the sort of thing that Hugh Trevor-Roper must have had in mind when he remarked that Laud's "clerical biographers, since they approach him on their knees, are naturally unable to see very far." *Archbishop Laud*, 6.

8. Unless otherwise indicated, the source of purely biographical data is the *Dictionary of National Biography* essay by Samuel Rawson Gardiner, 11:626–35.

9. Patrick Collinson, *The Elizabethan Puritan Movement*, 434.

10. P. A. Welsby, *Lancelot Andrewes, 1555–1626*, 193. The sermons were published by order of Charles I in 1629.

11. Collinson, *Elizabethan Puritan Movement*, 43. See also 37, 236–37, 434–35, 460–61. This is not to say that there were no doctrinal differences or that the nondoctrinal differences alone defined Elizabethan Puritanism. See Peter Lake, *Moderate Puritans and the Elizabethan Church*, esp. chaps. 6 and 9.

12. Nicholas Tyacke, "Puritanism, Arminianism and Counter-Revolution, 120. Similarly, Dewey Wallace, Jr., *Puritans and Predestination*, chaps. 2 and 3.

13. Peter Heylyn, *Cyprianus Anglicus* (London, 1668), pp. 52–54.

14. Trevor-Roper, *Laud*, p. 43. One of Neile's chaplains had, like Laud, attended a college whose head was thought "popishly affected" by the Calvinists. The chaplain was John Cosin, the college Gonville and Caius, Cambridge. J. G. Hoffman, "John Cosin, 1595–1672: Bishop of Durham and Chaplain of the Caroline Church," Ph.D. diss., University of Wisconsin-Madison, 1977, 4–5. See also Andrew Foster, "The Function of a Bishop," 33–54.

15. *The Works of . . . William Laud*, Library of Anglo-Catholic Theology (Oxford: John Henry Parker, 1847–60) 3:135. See Trevor-Roper, *Laud*, for an account of the election, 42–43.

16. Heylyn, *Cyprianus Anglicus*, 66–67. For Laud's attitude toward this incident, see *Works*, 7:3–4.

17. On the Synod of Dort and its significance for England, see Tyack, "Puritanism, Arminianism and Counter-Revolution," 128, and his Oxford D.Phil. diss., chap. 4; T. M. Parker, "Arminianism and Laudianism in Seventeenth-Century England," *Studies in Church History* (1964), 1:20–34; Carl Bangs, " 'All the Best Bishoprics and Deaneries': the Enigma of Arminian Politics," *Church History* 42 (1973); 5–16; Wallace, *Puritans and Predestination*, 80ff. On James I's purposes at Dort, see the essays by Christopher Grayson and John Platt in Derek Baker, ed., *Reform and Reformation* (Oxford: Ecclesiastical History Society by Basil Blackwell, 1979), 195–219, 221–43.

18. Trevor-Roper, *Laud*, 56. "With Laud," according to S. R. Gardiner, "the authority of Andrewes was conclusive . . . His whole life was an effort to carry out in a hard practical way the ideas which cast a gleam of poetry over the unworldly bishop." *History of England, 1603–1642* (London: Longmans, 1899), 7:243. Cf. Arthur Kautz, "The Selection of Jacobean Bishops," in Howard S. Reinmuth, Jr., ed., *Early Stuart Studies* (Minneapolis: University of Minnesota Press, 1970), 152–79, and D. E. Kennedy, "The Jacobean Episcopate," *Historical Journal* 5 (1962): 175–81. Kennedy opposes Trevor-Roper's characterization of the Jacobean appointees as "indifferent, negligent, secular," and he concludes that the growth of the Arminian party "was a Jacobean phenomenon; its triumph was a Caroline consummation" (181).

19. *D.N.B.*, 11:627. Laud's version of the Gloucester altar controversy is in *Works*, 6:239–41. Elizabeth gave free rein to Puritan preaching in areas still strongly Catholic. James here seems to have used the same principle in reverse by unleashing a ritualist to combat indifferences to ceremony.

20. D. H. Willson, *James VI and I* (London: Jonathan Cape, 1963), 383. There is no definite indication of a friendship between Buckingham and Laud until 1621. Roger Lockyer, *Buckingham*, 96–97.

21. John Hacket, *Scrinia Reserata* (London, 1693), 63–64. Without giving a reason, Gordon Donaldson doubts Hacket's story. *The Making of the Scottish Prayer Book of 1637* (Edinburgh:

Edinburgh University Press, 1954), 39. Hacket and Williams may have embroidered it in order to discredit Laud—but it remains possible that the story is true. At Hampton Court in 1604, James told the bishops that "if you should walk in one street in Scotland with such a [square] cap on your head, if I were not with you, you should be stoned to death with your cap." Collinson, *Elizabethan Puritan Movement*, 462. For the background to and nature of the Five Articles, see Donaldson, "The Scottish Church, 1575–1625," in Alan G. R. Smith, ed., *The Reign of James VI and I* (New York: St. Martin's Press, 1973), 40–56.

22. Ibid.

23. Conrad Russell, *The Crisis of Parliaments*, 214. Laud's diary (June 9, 1622) has the teasing entry: "Being Whitsunday my Lord Marquis Buckingham was pleased to enter upon a near respect to me. The particulars are not for paper." *Works*, 3:139. Buckingham leaned toward the Arminians at the York House Conference in February 1626 and away from them when impeachment threatened in March. On these maneuverings, see Russell, *Parliaments and English Politics, 1621–1629*, 297–99 (cf. 167–68); Tyacke diss., 172 and chap. 6; Christopher Hill, "The Political Sermons of John Preston," in *Puritanism and Revolution* (London: Panther, 1968), 237–43; Lockyer, *Buckingham*, 276, 305–8; Irvonwy Morgan, *Prince Charles's Puritan Chaplain*, chap. 8. Morgan argues that Laud's power was really based on his influence with Charles, not Buckingham. This is entirely possible.

24. Laud, *Works*, 3:159. On Williams's failure to maintain the lead he appeared to have in 1623, see Trevor-Roper, *Laud*, 58ff. Trevor-Roper conceals neither his admiration for Williams nor his dislike of Laud.

25. P. A. Welsby, *George Abbot: the Unwanted Archbishop, 1562–1633*, 122, 126–31.

26. *Works*, 3:147–48. Cf. 6:37. On the continuities and discontinuities between the generation of Hooker and Andrewes and that of Laud, see Wallace, *Puritans and Predestination*, 75ff.

27. Conrad Russell, "The Parliamentary Career of John Pym, 1621–1629," in Peter Clark, Alan G. R. Smith and Nicholas Tyacke, eds., *The English Commonwealth, 1547–1640* (New York: Barnes and Noble, 1979), 159–61. See also the Tyacke diss., chap. 5, and Hillel Schwartz, "Arminianism and the English Parliament, 1624–1629," *Journal of British Studies* 12 (1973): 41–68. On the conservative character of moderate Puritanism, see Robert Ashton, *The English Civil War* (London: Weidenfield and Nicolson, 1978), 100–103.

28. *A Gagg for the New Gospell?* (London, 1624), 157. The quotations are from his response to the doctrine "that faith once had cannot be lost." For similar statements about free will, election, and reprobation, see 107, 179. Among the other statements that enraged the Calvinists were: "Whether the Pope bee that Antichrist or not, the Church resolveth not. . . . I am not of opinion, that the Bishop of Rome personally is that Antichrist . . . [or] that the Bishops of Rome successively, are" (74–75); "Life, begun in Baptisme by the Laver of Regeneration, is confirmed and sustained in the holy supper by [Christ's] body and blood. How? I cannot explicate." (252).

29. Sir Simonds D'Ewes, quoted in Schwartz, "Arminianism and the English Parliament," 41.

30. Russell, *Parliaments and English Politics*, 232, 233. Russell argues, however, that the clash was not primarily with Parliament. The "developing confrontation remained, for several years, a struggle fought out in the first instance within the court, and between Parliaments as much as in Parliaments. Arminianism was not a court-country issue before 1629, and in 1625, most members still regarded it as merely one branch of the general attack on popery."

31. *Works*, 6:244–46. John Howson, bishop of Oxford, also signed. On the context in which this important letter was written, see Lockyer, *Buckingham*, 258–59.

32. Ibid., 249.

33. The text is in J. P. Kenyon, ed., *The Stuart Constitution* (Cambridge: Cambridge University Press, 1969), 154–55. Cf. Williams's much less restrictive proclamation, the "direction about preachers" (1622) in G. W. Prothero, ed., *Select Statutes and Other Constitutional Documents, 1558–1625* (Oxford: Clarendon Press, 1913), 422–24.

34. This declaration is in S. R. Gardiner, ed., *Constitutional Documents of the Puritan Revolu-*

tion, 1625–1660 (Oxford: Clarendon Press, 1906), 75–76. For examples of Anglican hostility to "curiosity" about divine mysteries, see J. Sears McGee, *The Godly Man in Stuart England*, 102–3.

35. Schwartz, "Arminianism and the English Parliament," 56. The ban on controversy was, however, selectively enforced, and the Arminians got the advantage. See Wallace, *Puritans and Predestination*, 91–97, for a discussion of the Arminian books that were published.

36. *Works*, 6:292; 5:49.

37. Trevor-Roper, *Laud*, 85. Cf. 112–13.

38. Laud, *Works*, 3:152–53; Schwartz, "Arminianism and the English Parliament," 45. The innovations included "approval of images in churches" and "praying toward the east." Apparently no one remembered that in 1584, Harsnett had preached at St. Paul's Cross against the doctrine of double predestination. Collinson, *Elizabethan Puritan Movement*, 501n, and Wallace, *Puritans and Predestination*, 66.

39. S. R. Gardiner, *History of England*, 7:45–57. The debate included Oliver Cromwell's maiden speech in the Commons. Cosin had defended Montagu at the York House Conference, and they had long worked together closely.

40. *Works*, 4:60.

41. Ibid., 2:xvi; 5:16, 19. According to Heylyn, "the habits of priests, by which they were distinguished from other men . . . [were] so much despised, and laid aside, that Doctor Reynolds had the confidence to appear in the Conference at Hampton Court in his Turky gown, and therefore may be thought to have worn no other in the university." *Cyprianus Anglicus*, 52. See Kevin Sharpe, "Archbishop Laud and the University of Oxford." Sharpe notes that Laud's visitation articles and Oxford statutes demonstrate his "primary concern with externals" rather than theological disputes (161).

42. *Works*, 3:171; 4:198ff. Cf. Welsby, *Lancelot Andrewes*, 130–34.

43. Ibid., 5:422, 319, 329, 351, 359, 366. For an account of the allegations about his "bowing and cringing" while consecrating the rebuilt City church of St. Catherine Cree, see Gardiner, *History*, 7:242–44. For Laud's defense of consecration, see *Works*, 4:202–3.

44. *Works*, 6:344; 3:249. On St. Paul's, see Trevor-Roper, *Laud*, 121–26, 346–47, 350–51, and Gardiner, *History*, 7:307–8.

45. *Worship and Theology in England*, 2:39. Matthew Wren and John Cosin were the masters of Peterhouse while the chapel was being built. This style was in sharp contrast to the Cambridge of 1620: "None then dared to commit idolatry by bowing to, or towards, the altar, the communion table, or the bread and wine." J. O. Halliwell, ed., *Autobiography and Correspondence of Sir Simonds D'Ewes* (London, 1845), 1:142.

46. *Works*, 4:284–85.

47. Ibid., 5:401, 405, 421.

48. Ibid., 6:350. Cf. Laud's 1630 visitation articles for Bath and Wells in Margaret Stieg, *Laud's Laboratory*, 358–73. Article 2 asks whether the minister receives the elements kneeling and administers only to those who do likewise. Article 19 requires the surplice and hood. For presentments before the consistory court of persons who refused to bow at the name of Jesus, see 292–95, 300, 303.

49. The St. Gregory's ruling is in Gardiner, *Constitutional Documents*, 103–5, and also in Edward Cardwell, ed., *Documentary Annals of the Reformed Church of England* (Oxford, 1844), 237–41. Cardwell notes that Laud's drive to have altar rails in parish churches did not begin to bite until 1636. See Article 2 in Wren's 1636 visitation articles (Cardwell, p. 252) and the Canons of 1640 (Laud, *Works*, 5:625) for this requirement. On altar rails, see R. A. Marchant, *Puritans and the Church Courts in the Diocese of York*, 56, 192–96; Stieg, *Laud's Laboratory*, 296 (and 297–301 on the celebrated Beckington dispute on placement of the table); Anthony Fletcher, *The Outbreak of the English Civil War*, 109–10, 345. In the diocese of Lincoln, the reorientation of the table had to await Williams's fall from power in 1637. Clive Holmes, *Seventeenth-Century Lincolnshire*, 121.

50. Gardiner, *History*, 3:244. On the differing meanings given to the potent phrase, *Godly Rule*, see William Lamont's book with that title.

51. "The Church of England and the Greek Church," *Studies in Church History* 14 (1978): 218.

52. *The Pauline Renaissance in England*, 142. Such a view could lead to a "high" doctrine of the Eucharist, although by a route Laud could not have understood. See Davies, *Worship and Theology in England*, 2:308–22, and E. B. Holifield, *The Covenant Sealed* (New Haven, Conn.: Yale University Press, 1974), chap. 4. For an argument that the preaching of the Reformed *ordo salutis* is more central to Puritanism than "doctrinaire notions of the right biblical polity," see Wallace, *Puritans and Predestination*, 54–55.

53. Hales, *Works* (New York: AMS, 1971), 2:299; Chillingworth, *Works* (New York: AMS, 1972), 3:31. On Laud's relations with these men, see Trevor-Roper, *Laud*, 337–38, and William Haller, *The Rise of Puritanism* (New York: Columbia University Press, 1938), chap. 6. On the continuing role of moderate episcopalianism, see Ian Green, "Career Prospects and Clerical Conformity in the Early Stuart Church," *Past and Present*, no. 90 (February 1981), 108–15.

54. See, for example, John Preston, *The Breast-Plate of Faith and Love* (London, 1631, and later eds.); William Gouge, *Gods Three Arrowes* (London, 1631); Richard Sibbes, *The Saints Cordialls* (London, 1637); Jeremiah Burroughs, *The Excellency of a Gractious Spirit* (London, 1638); Thomas Goodwin, *A Child of Light Walking in Darkness* (London, 1636). For perceptive remarks on Charles I's temperament, see Fletcher, *Outbreak of the English Civil War*, 232.

55. Patrick Collinson, "Towards a Broader Understanding of the Early Dissenting Tradition," in C. Robert Cole and Michael E. Moody, eds., *The Dissenting Tradition* (Athens: Ohio University Press, 1975), 11; Anthony Fletcher, "Concern for Renewal in the Root and Branch Debates of 1641," *Studies in Church History* (1977), 14:279–86.

56. The most thorough study of these famous cases is Stephen Foster, *Notes from the Caroline Underground*.

57. *Works*, 3:196, 199–200, 262. Cf. 6:43.

58. Ibid., 3:226. For nearly a year after Portland's death, Laud had served on the commission that conducted the treasury's affairs. A biography of Juxon by Thomas Mason is in press.

59. *Works*, 7:375.

60. Trevor-Roper, *Laud*, 351–52, 241–44. Cf. C. V. Wedgwood, *Thomas Wentworth, First Earl of Strafford*, 180–87. See Felicity Heal, "Archbishop Laud Revisited: Leases and Estate Management at Canterbury and Winchester before the Civil War," in R. O'Day and F. Heal, eds., *Princes and Paupers in the English Church*, 129–49.

61. Trevor-Roper, *Laud*, 95–96, 450–53; Laud, *Works*, 3:255, 216; 7:26.

62. The best study of this important institution is Paul Seaver, *The Puritan Lectureships*. For the Hammersmith case, see 48–49 and 323n. (for an indication that Laud did not get his way there). See also Peter King, "Bishop Wren and the Suppression of the Norwich Lecturers," *Historical Journal* 11 (1968): 237–54; Patrick Collinson, "Lectures by Combination: Structures and Characteristics of Church Life in Seventeenth-Century England," *Bulletin of the Institute of Historical Research* 48 (1975): 182–213; G. E. Gorman, "A Laudian Attempt to 'Tune the Pulpit': Peter Heylyn and His Sermon Against the Feoffees for the Purchase of Impropriations," *Journal of Religious History* 8 (1975): 333–49.

63. *Works*, 6:310, 103; Brian P. Levack, *The Civil Lawyers in England, 1603–1641* (Oxford: Clarendon Press, 1973), 80–81. See 190–93 for a discussion of the St. Gregory's case mentioned above.

64. W. J. Jones, *Politics and the Bench* (New York: Barnes and Noble, 1971), 44, 135; Esther S. Cope, "The Short Parliament of 1640 and Convocation," *Journal of Ecclesiastical History* 25 (1974): 171–72; Wilfrid R. Prest, *The Inns of Court under Elizabeth I and the Early Stuarts* (London: Longmans, 1972), 214–15.

65. T. G. Barnes, "County Politics and a Puritan Cause Célèbre: Somerset Churchales, 1633," *Transactions of the Royal Historical Society*, 5th ser. 9 (1959): 103–22.

66. *Works*, 6:14, 20; 4:239. For a sensitive account, see Paul Slack, "Religious Protest and Urban Authority: the Case of Henry Sherfield, Iconoclast," *Studies in Church History* 9 (1972): 295–301. One of Laud's reasons for punishing Sherfield was that in his church a bishop's tomb

had been removed, "his bones taken up, his skull made a mazer in an apothecary's shop . . . his dust thrown about, and all to bury a tanner's wife." *Works*, 6:20.

67. *Works*, 3:229, 241.

68. R. A. Beddard, "The Restoration Church," in J. R. Jones, ed., *The Restored Monarchy* (Totowa, N.J.: Rowman and Littlefield, 1979), 155–75.

69. *Archbishop Grindal*, 292. Cf. Collinson, *Elizabethan Puritan Movement*, 201, 209.

70. *Works*, 5:364.

71. Margaret Spufford, "The Quest for the Heretical Laity in the Visitation Records of Ely in the Late Sixteenth and Early Seventeenth Centuries," *Studies in Church History* 9 (1972): 223–30. Cf. Stieg, *Laud's Laboratory*, 291.

72. Anthony Fletcher, *A County Community in Peace and War*, 85.

73. Peter Clark, *English Provincial Society from the Reformation to the Revolution*, 367; Anthony Fletcher, "Factionalism in Town and Countryside: the Significance of Puritanism and Arminianism," *Studies in Church History* 16 (1979): 295. See also Peter Clark, "'The Ramoth-Gilead of the Good': Urban Change and Political Radicalism at Gloucester, 1540–1640," in Peter Clark, Alan G. R. Smith, and Nicholas Tyacke, eds., *The English Commonwealth* (New York: Barnes & Noble, 1979), 167–88.

74. "A large majority" of the strongly anti-Arminian members of Parliament in the 1620s "had completed their educations before 1600." Russell, *Crisis of Parliaments*, 341. On the attractions of Laudianism for clerics of humble social origins, see Fletcher, *A County Community*, 79, and the Tyacke diss., 249ff.

75. *The Puritan Lectureships*, 265–66. See Kenneth W. Shipps, "Lay Patronage of East Anglian Puritan Clerics in Pre-Revolutionary England," Ph.D. diss., Yale University, 1971, for detailed information about both urban and rural patronage.

76. *Seventeenth-Century Norwich*, 102. For a good example of Puritan agility, see Seaver, *The Puritan Lectureships*, 255–56. On gentry anti-Arminianism in Sussex, see Fletcher, *A County Community*, 90–93, and in Kent, Clark, *English Provincial Society*, 366–69. On order in the towns, see the essays by Clark (n. 73 above) and Slack (n. 66 above).

77. *Works*, 7:87–88.

78. Caroline M. Hibbard, "Early Stuart Catholicism: Revisions and Re-Revisions," *Journal of Modern History* 52 (1980): 28–32, and more fully, in her *Charles I and the Popish Plot*.

79. Robert Ashton, *The English Civil War* (London: Weidenfeld and Nicolson, 1978), 122–23. Cf. Clark, *English Provincial Society*, 369.

80. A. G. Dickens, *The English Reformation* (London: Batsford, 1964), 315, 320. On the tragic failure of Charles I to understand his opponents' purposes (and vice-versa), see Fletcher, *Outbreak of the English Civil War*, 411–18. He concludes that there "is a real sense in which the English civil war was a war of religion."

CRITICAL BIBLIOGRAPHY

Laud himself once referred to the "great bugbear called Arminianism," and indeed anyone interested in the story of Archbishop Laud must begin by wrestling with terminology. *Arminian*, like *Puritan*, is a term fraught with problems—yet early Stuart Englishmen used it so extensively that the word cannot be avoided. The reaction against absolute predestination was under way at Cambridge in the 1590s, before Arminius himself spoke up in the Netherlands. The ceremonial, ecclesiological, and political associations with which the term came to be freighted during Laud's career were not present among the Dutch. The most thorough account of the theological debate in Elizabethan England is by H. C. Porter, who states that "the Cambridge quarrels . . . were one of the tributaries which were to feed the ever-broadening stream which, by circumstance, took its name from the professor at the University of Leiden": *Reformation and Reaction in Tudor Cambridge* (Cambridge: Cambridge University Press, 1958; reprint ed. 1972, with additional bibliography), p. 389. Dewey Wallace, Jr., *Puritans and Predestination* (Chapel Hill: University of North Carolina Press, 1982) is now the best guide to developments in the theology of grace in Tudor-Stuart England, and he argues against Porter's view that the English Arminians represented a "normative Anglicanism" reasserting itself against a "temporarily ascendant Calvinism."

Developments in Elizabethan church history must be studied in two books by Patrick Collinson, *The Elizabethan Puritan Movement* (Berkeley and Los Angeles: University of California Press, 1967) and *Archbishop Grindal* (same press, 1979). Equally essential is Peter Lake, *Moderate Puritans and the Elizabethan Church* (Cambrdige: Cambridge University Press, 1982), a brilliant evocation of Puritan thought that manages to define Puritanism in terms of what it was for rather than what it was against. Lake's broader concept of Puritanism is also discussed in his articles, which include "The Dilemma of the Establishment Puritan: the Cambridge Heads and the Case of Francis Johnson and Cuthbert Bainbrigg," *Journal of Ecclesiastical History* 29 (1978): 23–35, and "Matthew Hutton—A Puritan Bishop?" *History* 64 (1979): 182–204. The subtitle of the article on Hutton suggests a problem that is not entirely solved in an important revisionist essay by Nicholas Tyacke, which extends the discussion up to the Civil War. "Puritanism, Arminianism and Counter Revolution," in Conrad Russell, ed., *The Origins of the English Civil War* (New York: Barnes and Noble, 1968). The essay is based on his 1968 Oxford D.Phil. thesis, "Arminianism in England in Religion and Politics, 1604–1640," some of the conclusions of which are in Russell, *The Crisis of Parliaments: English History, 1509–1660* (New York: Oxford University Press, 1971), 210–17. Charles H. and Katherine George, *The Protestant Mind of the English Reformation, 1570–1640* (Princeton, N.J.: Princeton University Press, 1961), argues that there was no sharp Anglican-Puritan dichotomy, while John F. H. New argues that there was in *Anglican and Puritan* (Stanford, Calif.: Stanford University Press, 1964). J. Sears McGee, *The Godly Man in Stuart England* (New Haven, Conn.: Yale University Press, 1976), defines the terms *Anglican* and *Puritan* for the 1620–70 period on the basis of differing interpretations of the Decalogue, and John S. Coolidge, *The Pauline Renaissance in England* (Oxford: Clarendon Press, 1970) has a searching analysis of Puritan and conformist understandings of the authority of the Bible. Keith Thomas, *Religion and the Decline of Magic* (New York: Scribner, 1971) presents a splendid examination of the popular mentality to which Laud and his enemies sought to speak.

H. R. Trevor-Roper, *Archbishop Laud* (London: Macmillan, 1940) is the best biography, although its emphasis is on the political and social rather than the religious matters. In the preface to the second edition (1962), Trevor-Roper lists relevant works published in the 1950s and recognizes that he could have "dealt more carefully with . . . the real religious leaders of the laity." His essay "The Church of England and the Greek Church," *Studies in Church History* 14 (1978) expands on Laud's "intellectual liberalism." Kevin Sharpe, "Archbishop Laud and the University of Oxford," in Hugh Lloyd-Jones, Valerie Pearl, and Blair Worden, eds., *History and Imagination* (London: Duckworth, 1981), is a lively, stimulating study that stresses Laud's "*silence* on questions of theological controversy" and doubts that Laud was a theological Arminian at all. Much about Charles I's and Buckingham's relations with the Arminians can be learned from Conrad Russell, *Parliaments and English Politics, 1621–29* (Oxford: Clarendon Press, 1979) and Roger Lockyer, *Buckingham* (London: Longman, 1981). Caroline Hibbard, *Charles I and the Popish Plot* (Chapel Hill: University of North Carolina Press, 1983) carefully studies court Catholicism and Laud's relation to it in an international context.

Biographies of churchmen associated with or opposed to Laud include P. A. Welsby, *Lancelot Andrewes* (London: S.P.C.K., 1958) and *George Abbot* (same press, 1962); Andrew Foster, "The Function of a Bishop: the Career of Richard Neile, 1562–1640," in Rosemary O'Day and Felicity Heal, eds., *Continuity and Change: Personnel and Administration of the Church of England, 1500–1642* (Leicester: Leicester University Press, 1976); Irvonwy Morgan, *Prince Charles's Puritan Chaplain* (London: George Allen and Unwin, 1957). William Lamont, *Marginal Prynne* (London: Routledge & Kegan Paul, 1963), depicts Laud's most durable adversary. Stephen Foster, *Notes from the Caroline Underground: Alexander Leighton, the Puritan Triumvirate and the Laudian Reaction to Nonconformity* (Hamden, Conn.: Archon Books, 1978), presents Laud as a "Caroline Samson, pulling down the temple on his enemies as well as himself." Studies of Laud's associates on the Privy Council are helpful in grasping the political context of his career: C. V. Wedgwood, *Thomas Wentworth, First Earl of Strafford* (London: Macmillan, 1975); Martin Havran, *Caroline Courtier* (same press, 1973); Barbara Donagan, "A Courtier's Progress: Greed and Consistency in the Life of the Earl of Holland," *Historical Journal* 19 (1976); R. M. Smuts, "The Puritan Followers of Henrietta Maria in the 1630s," *English Historical Review* 93 (1978).

Topical studies that throw light on Laud and Laudianism are numerous. In *Economic Problems of the Church from Archbishop Whitgift to the Long Parliament* (Oxford: Clarendon Press, 1963) and *Society and Puritanism in Pre-Revolutionary England*, 2d ed. (New York: Schocken, 1964), Christopher Hill used a wide array of printed sources to study such subjects as church courts, tithes, lectureships, patronage, and Sabbatarianism. Felicity Heal and Rosemary O'Day have edited collections of essays that make more use of manuscript sources in some of these areas: *Church and Society in England: Henry VIII to James I* (London: Macmillan, 1977); *Continuity and Change* (cited above); *Princes and Paupers in the English Church, 1500–1800* (Leicester: Leicester University Press, 1981). The most detailed account of the Laudian program and its enforcement in a particular diocese is Margaret Stieg, *Laud's Laboratory: the Diocese of Bath and Wells in the Early Seventeenth Century* (Lewisburg, Pa.: Bucknell University Press, 1982). William Lamont, *Godly Rule* (London: Macmillan, 1969), and Paul Christianson, *Reformers and Babylon* (Toronto: University of Toronto Press, 1978), explore the millenarian motif in religious thought and its political impact. A comprehensive guide to liturgical developments is Horton Davies, *Worship and Theology in England from Andrewes to Baxter and Fox, 1603–1690* (Princeton, N.J.: Princeton University Press, 1975), and the struggle over "idolatry" is depicted by John Phillips, *The Reformation of Images* (Berkeley and Los Angeles: University of California Press, 1973). Paul Seaver's *The Puritan Lectureships* (Stanford, Calif.: Stanford University Press, 1970) is a work of meticulous scholarship with much to say about Laud. For the actual workings of the Laudian program at the provincial level, there are sections in a number of recent books heavily based on archival sources: on Kent, Peter Clark, *English Provincial Society from the Reformation to the Revolution* (Hassocks: Harvester Press, 1977); on Sussex, Anthony Fletcher, *A County Community in Peace and War* (London: Longmans, 1975); John T. Evans, *Seventeenth-Century Norwich* (Oxford: Clarendon Press, 1979); and Robert Ashton, *The City and the Court* (Cambridge: Cambridge University Press, 1979); on the Durham region, Mervyn James, *Family, Lineage and Civil Society* (Oxford: Clarendon Press, 1974); John S. Morrill, *Cheshire, 1630–1660* (Oxford: Oxford University Press, 1974); Ronald A. Marchant, *The Puritans and the Church Courts in the Diocese of York* (London: Longmans, 1960); and Clive Holmes, *Seventeenth Century Lincolnshire* (Lincoln: History of Lincolnshire Committee, 1980). Anthony Fletcher, *The Outbreak of the English Civil War* (New York: New York University Press, 1981) has intriguing discussions of the impact of Arminianism in localities as reflected in petitions sent to the Long Parliament.

Epilogue

The sixteenth-century Reformation sprang in part from humanism's quest for personal freedom against a background of dogmatic disputations and church abuses. It also owed some of its vitality to the *Devotio Moderna*, whose spirit had encircled northern Europe and was best expressed in the *Imitatio Christi*. Erasmus's own vision of a *Christianismus renascens* was intended as a response to the philosophy of humanism. In choosing Christ as the authoritative human model he turned his *philosophia Christi* into an educational movement. *Ad fontes* was a call to the realities of life.

Writing in the last months of the fifteenth century, Erasmus was conscious of the need to return to the teachings of the early church, especially to the reading of St. Paul and the synoptic Gospels; he wished to emphasize the human and historic incidents rather than the symbolic and prophetic. He himself lamented that

> nowadays practically no one devotes himself to the study of theology, the highest branch of learning, except such as, having sluggish or disordered wits, are scarcely fit for letters at all.

Erasmus went on to praise John Colet for undertaking to do battle "with this invincible tribe, for the sake of restoring to as much of its early splendour and dignity as you can that ancient true theology, overgrown as it is with the entanglements introduced by the modern school."[1]

The course of the Reformation produced men who combined great piety with hot-tempered fervor and self-righteousness. Luther thought of himself, for example, as an instrument of God because he felt more acted upon than acting:

> Let us put our trust in Christ. Whether God wishes to take me hence now or tomorrow, I want to leave this bequest, that I desire to acknowledge Christ as my Lord. This I have not only from Scriptures but also from experience, for the name of Christ often helped me when nobody else could. So I've had words and deeds in my favor, Scriptures and experience, and God gave me both in abundance.[2]

Unlike many of their Catholic counterparts, the Protestant reformers underscored the primacy of scriptural evidence over ecclesiastical tradition. By the end of the sixteenth century the doctrinal positions of the two camps had hardened into uncompromising stances, spawning diatribe after diatribe.

Over and against the historical background the reader is asked to reconsider the significance of each of the essays in this commemorative volume. In the opening chapter the editor argues that Erasmus of Rotterdam conceived of his philosophy of reform, *philosophia Christi*, as a way of life rather than as a method of learning. Moreover, he attempts to demonstrate that Erasmus not only proposed a plan for holiness but actively pursued it as well—a way of life that freed the individual from ritual and dogmatism so that he could reach the ultimate heights in his progress toward union with Christ.

Scott Hendrix thereafter explores the effects of the following communities on Luther's reforming efforts: a monastic community, the university, the town of Wittenberg, the territory of electoral Saxony, the German nation, and the church itself. He concludes that the forces that elevated Luther to the rank of a prominent reformer intersected and made their impact upon him as a member of one or more of these communities. In chapter 3 Robert Walton insists that Zwingli's theology was from the beginning a unique amalgam of the theology of the *via antiqua*, particularly that of Duns Scotus and Erasmianism. He reasons, furthermore, that Zwingli's theology addressed an urban world and reflected the religious aspirations of the urban classes. As an urban theologian Zwingli became the champion of urban liberty.

Calvin A. Pater examines the radical element of the Reformation in the succeeding chapter. He demonstrates that Karlstadt distinguished himself from Luther by promoting a biblicism that sought to return to the ideal of a primitive Christianity by abandoning traditional church practices. Karlstadt's insistence that Christian faith must be based on the personal decision of an adult helped to influence the formation of the Baptist movements.

In chapter 4 Stanford Lehmberg searches the correspondence and official papers of Thomas Cromwell to discover the religious beliefs of the man behind the Henrician Reformation. He concludes that Cromwell (most probably) believed that faith and works were necessary for salvation; that Christ was present in the Eucharist; that Communion in both kinds was favored but not regarded as essential; that Scripture should be translated into the vernacular; and that clergy should be free to marry. But, above all, Lehmberg argues that Cromwell believed in the middle way between rival extremes—somewhere between Rome and Wittenberg.

Considering the contributions of the Counter-Reformation, J. Patrick Donnelly, S.J., identifies Ignatius Loyola in chapter 5 as, perhaps, the prototypical figure of the Counter-Reformation who viewed the idea of reformation in terms of the individual's cooperation with God. At the same time, Donnelly notes that Loyola and his followers rejected the Protestant view of reformation, which insisted that a fundamental alteration was needed in the doctrine and devotional life of the late medieval church.

David Foxgrover in the next essay interprets Calvin's understanding of his role as a reformer against a background of three themes: Calvin's belief that the world is degenerating in morality and religion; his expectation that the church will always suffer; and his conviction that Christ will return again to deliver his church from its enemies. It is clear from Foxgrover's essay that Calvin saw himself as a defender of Christ in a hostile environment—the image of the military standard-bearer.

Peter Donaldson sets out to prove in chapter 7 that Reginald Pole not only believed that Machiavelli's *Prince* had been the inspiration behind Henry VIII's decision to break with Rome, to declare himself head of the church, and to seize the property of the English monasteries, but that Pole's views on Machiavelli were permeated by a typological vision of history—that the events and personages of Pole's own time were seen as fulfillments of biblical models. Nancy Lyman Roelker devotes chapter 8 to an exploration of the contributions of the three Châtillon brothers, Odet, Gaspard, and François d'Andelot—a cardinal, an admiral, and a devotee of Calvin—to the success of the Huguenot cause in France. She sees them as representatives of an aristocracy on the defensive because its members are about to lose power to the Catholic majority.

In chapter 9 Charles Carter analyzes the public image of Ferdinand II as revealed in contemporary publications that are found in the British Library. Both his admirers and his detractors characterized Ferdinand as a religious figure who saw the major issues of his day in religious terms and, in contesting those issues, pursued purely religious goals. Finally, J. Sears McGee discusses William Laud in terms of three main themes: his strong distaste for doctrinal controversy, his deep love of ceremony, and his fervent commitment to the high mission of the priesthood. The archbishop sought to undo the errors and excesses of the Reformation without altering the basic tenets of the magisterial reformers who were being attacked by very determined Puritans.

There we have it: beginning with the call for moderation by Erasmus of Rotterdam at the start of the Reformation to Archbishop Laud who called for a return to the past at the end of the movement. The enduring success of the Reformation in its Catholic, Protestant, and Radical expressions owed much to the determination of the above leaders. These reformers brought to the fore the strength of their convictions and their unyielding devotion to the souls of Christ's flock.

NOTES

1. Erasmus to John Colet (October 1499) in *The Collected Works of Erasmus,* trans. R. A. B. Mynors and D. F. S. Thomson (Toronto: University of Toronto Press, 1974), 1:204.

2. Luther, "Table Talk," No. 518, *Luther's Works,* 54.

Notes on Contributors

CHARLES H. CARTER is professor of history at Tulane University. He was awarded a Ph.D. in history by Columbia University in 1961. His two major books are *The Secret Diplomacy of the Habsburgs, 1598–1625* (Columbia University Press, 1964) and *The Western European Powers, 1500–1700* (Hodder and Stoughton, 1971).

RICHARD L. DeMOLEN is secretary/treasurer of the Erasmus of Rotterdam Society and editor of its *Yearbook*. He received a Ph.D. in history from the University of Michigan in 1970. Yale University Press published his last book, *Essays on the Works of Erasmus*, in 1978.

PETER S. DONALDSON is an associate professor of humanities at the Massachusetts Institute of Technology. He earned a Ph.D. in English from Columbia University in 1974. He has edited *A Machiavellian Treatise by Stephen Gardiner* (Cambridge University Press, 1975) and *George Rainsford's 'Ritratto d'Ingliterra' (1556)* for the Royal Historical Society (1979).

JOHN PATRICK DONNELLY, S.J., is an associate professor of history at Marquette University. He completed a Ph.D. in history at the University of Wisconsin in 1972. His principal work is *Calvinism and Scholasticism in Vermigli's Doctrine of Man and Grace* (E. J. Brill, 1976).

DAVID FOXGROVER is chaplain of the Fisher Memorial Chapel at Rockford College (Illinois). He was awarded a Ph.D. in the history of Christian Thought by the Claremont Graduate School. The subject of his 1978 dissertation was "Calvin's Understanding of Conscience."

SCOTT H. HENDRIX is an associate professor of church history at the Lutheran Theological Southern Seminary. He obtained a doctor of theology degree from the University of Tübingen in 1971. E. J. Brill published his *Ecclesia in Via: Ecclesiological Developments in the Medieval Psalms Exegesis and the Dictata Super Psalterium (1513–1515)* of Martin Luther in 1974.

STANFORD E. LEHMBERG is professor of history at the University of Minnesota. He received his Ph.D. in history from the University of Cambridge in 1956. The same university published his books on *The Reformation Parliament, 1529–1536* (1970) and *The Later Parliaments of Henry VIII, 1536–1547* (1977).

348

J. Sears McGee is an associate professor of history at the University of California at Santa Barbara. He earned a Ph.D. in history from Yale University in 1971. Yale published his major work on *The Godly Man in Stuart England: Anglicans, Puritans, and the Two Tables, 1620–1670* in 1976.

Calvin A. Pater is professor of church history at Knox College of the University of Toronto. He completed a Ph.D. in history from Harvard University in 1977. *Karlstadt as the Father of the Baptist Movements: the Emergence of Lay Protestantism* was published by the University of Toronto Press in 1983.

Nancy Lyman Roelker is professor emerita of history at Boston University. She was awarded a Ph.D. in history from Harvard University in 1953. Harvard University Press published four of her books in 1958, 1963, 1963, and 1968—the last one titled *Queen of Navarre, Jeanne d'Albret, 1528–1572*.

Robert C. Walton is professor of modern church history and theology and director of a seminar for the Protestant faculty at the University of Münster. He obtained a Ph.D. in history from Yale University in 1964. His major publication is *Zwingli's Theocracy* (University of Toronto Press, 1967).

Index

Aachen, 278
Abbot, George (archbishop of Canterbury), 319, 320, 324
Abel, 187
Abraham, 88, 118, 119, 185, 189, 227
Adam, 187, 223
Adriatic Sea, 283
Africa, 172, 237
Airey, Henry, 319
Albert of the Netherlands (archduke), 283
Albrecht of Brandenburg (archbishop of Magdeburg and Mainz), 54
Albret, Jeanne d' (queen of Navarre), 248, 257, 258, 264, 267, 269
Alcalá, University of, 160, 162
Aleander, Girolamo, 54
Alexander IV (pope), 107
Alsace, 70
Amboise, Conspiracy of, 254
Ambrose, Saint, 107
America, 172
Ammonio, Andrea, 13, 16
Amos, 185
Amsdorf, Nikolaus von, 50
Anabaptists, 70, 73, 83, 84, 116, 148, 178, 180, 181, 197
Andrewes, Lancelot (bishop of Chichester, Ely, and Winchester), 319, 320, 322, 324, 326, 328, 329, 330, 331–32
Angers, 261
Anglican Church. See England, Church of
Anglo-Spanish rivalry, 259
Anhalt, 302
Anna of Bohemia (empress), 297
Anne of Cleves, 143
Antichrist, 7, 182, 193, 196, 197, 198, 199, 211–46
Antwerp, 140, 172, 291
Apostles, 27, 28, 86, 192, 198, 227
Apostles' Creed, the, 31, 52, 136
Arians, 247
Aristotle, 74, 102, 143, 218

Arminians, 320, 322, 323, 324, 325, 326, 329, 330, 335
Ashton, Robert, 336
Asia, 172
Augsburg, Confession of, 257, 260, 286
Augsburg, Diet of, 55, 57, 85, 299
Augustine, Saint, 48, 49, 50, 76, 77, 82, 101, 102, 103, 107, 112, 113, 166, 223
Augustinians, 44, 46, 47, 49, 50, 139, 168
Austria, 83, 169, 283, 284, 285, 286, 291, 299, 303, 306
Avignon, 143

Babylon, 47
Babylonians, 184
Baden, 81
Badia, Tommaso, 165
Bagshawe, Edward, 333
Bainton, Roland H., 30
Bancroft, Richard (archbishop of Canterbury), 320
Baptism, 83, 84, 88, 103, 108, 110, 113, 285, 319
Baptists, 99, 124, 125, 346
Barcelona, 155, 159, 160
Barnabites, 168
Barnes, Robert, 139, 140, 141, 142, 143
Baroque, the, 153, 172
Bartoli, Daniel, 172
Basel, 57, 74, 75, 106, 111
Bastwick, John, 331
Bauckham, Richard, 223
Bavaria, duke of, 291, 302
Béarn, 267
Beauvais, 249, 264
Beda, Noel, 161
Belgian Congo, 169
Bender, H. S., 83
Benedict, Saint, 166
Benedictines, 31, 32, 77, 167, 214, 215
Béraud, Nicolas, 249
Bern, 72, 74, 75, 82, 83
Bernard, Saint, 107, 167

351

Berthelet, Thomas, 145
Beza, Theodore, 263, 264, 266, 267
Bible. See New Testament; Old Testament; Scripture
Biel, Gabriel, 48
Bilney, Thomas, 139
Bishops, 319, 325, 331, 332, 334, 335, 336
Blanke, Fritz, 83
Blarer, Ambrosius, 89
Bohemia, 112, 278, 283, 284, 285, 288, 291, 292, 293, 294, 295, 297, 298, 299, 300, 301, 302, 303, 305
Boleyn, Thomas, 24
Book of Common Prayer, 325, 328
Book of Hours, 26
Bora, Katherine von, 50
Boulogne, 251
Bourbon, Antoine de, 255, 258, 259
Bourbon, Louis de (prince de Condé), 248, 251, 254, 255, 256, 257, 259, 264, 265, 267, 269
Bourbons, 251, 252, 253, 254, 255
Bourdeille, Pierre de (signeur de Brantôme), 260, 261, 268, 270
Brady, Thomas A., 70, 72, 79
Brandenburg, 54, 56, 281, 282, 302
Brantôme. See Bourdeille, Pierre de
Brazil, 169
Brethern of the Common Life, 11, 14, 259
Britanny, 261
British Library, the, 347
Broet, Paschase, 163, 164
Bruges, 161
Brussels, 251
Bubenheimer, Ulrich, 106
Bucer, Martin, 61, 70, 71
Buckeridge, John, 319, 324
Budé, Guillaume, 17
Bugenhagen, John, 50, 53
Bullinger, Heinrich, 72, 75, 85
Bünzli, George, 74
Burgundy, 299
Burkhardt, Jacob, 76
Burton, Henry, 331
Bydell, John, 140

Cain, 187
Calais, 252, 261
Calvin, John, 61, 69, 85, 88, 124, 161, 168, 171, 173, 178–210, 247, 248, 250, 254, 261, 262, 263, 304, 347. Works: Concerning Scandals,

182, 184, 187, 188, 189; Institutes of the Christian Religion, 184, 250; The Necessity of Reforming the Church, 178; Reply to Sadoleto, 188
Calvinism, 252, 257, 259, 261, 264, 265, 266, 292, 294, 302, 303, 319, 320, 322, 323, 324, 325, 327, 331
Cambrai, bishop of, 14
Cambridge, 76, 139, 325, 328
Camerarius, Joachim, 7
Canons Regular of Saint Augustine, 11, 13, 14, 15, 16, 19, 32, 33
Canterbury, 318, 320, 322
Capito, Wolfgang F., 12, 57, 59
Capuchins, 287
Carafa, Gian Pietro, 163, 170
Carleton, George (bishop of Chichester), 324
Carmelites, 287
Carolingians, 247
Carter, Charles H., 347, 348
Carthusians, 26, 155
Cartwright, Thomas, 319
Castelberger, Andreas, 121
Castiglione, Balthasar, 235, 236, 237
Castile, 154
Catholic Church, 102, 158, 171, 247, 251, 259, 265, 292, 304, 306, 323, 324, 326, 327, 331, 335, 336
Catholic League, 291
Catholics, 7, 32, 34, 81, 83, 100, 120, 138, 153, 159, 167, 169, 170, 171, 173, 247, 253, 256, 258, 259, 264, 266, 282, 283, 288, 302, 303, 345, 347
Cavendish, Thomas, 135
Celtis, Conrad, 75
Chanones, Jean, 156
Chapuys, Eustace, 213
Charlemagne (Holy Roman emperor), 278, 280, 281
Charles I (king of England), 318, 322, 324, 328, 329, 330, 334, 336
Charles IV (Holy Roman emperor), 295
Charles V (Holy Roman emperor), 15, 55, 56, 57, 85, 154, 162, 169, 211, 215, 251, 259, 283, 299
Charles IX, (king of France), 255, 270
Châtillon brothers, 247–77, 347
Chilasts, 193
Chillingworth, William, 330
Christ, Jesus, 11–15, 17–29, 32–34, 48, 49, 56, 76, 86–88, 101, 102, 106, 108, 110, 112–16, 118–24, 136, 138, 139, 141–47, 156–58, 172,

178, 183, 186–88, 190, 191–200, 214, 217, 220, 223, 229, 230, 233, 235, 260, 262, 287, 293, 319, 324, 328, 345–47
Christian of Anhalt, 301, 302
Christianity, 16, 18, 21, 69, 99, 101, 108, 112, 113, 247, 303, 306, 329, 346
Christians, 7, 12, 13, 15, 18–20, 23–26, 29, 30, 33, 34, 44, 47, 52, 55, 57, 59, 60, 76, 80, 81, 85–87, 89, 99, 100, 103, 105, 106, 113, 115, 117, 137, 143, 157, 160, 170, 180, 185, 189, 221, 234, 259, 293, 304, 330, 332, 346
Church, the, 59–62, 69, 80, 85–89, 100–103, 107, 113, 124, 134, 138, 141, 153, 154, 158, 160, 168, 170, 178–80, 183, 185, 186–91, 192, 196, 197, 214, 223, 224, 225, 234, 249, 260, 262, 282, 283, 293, 294, 304, 346
Church Fathers, 20, 22, 28, 31, 49, 69, 101, 102, 107, 142, 184, 323, 329
Cicero, 72
Cisneros, Garcia Jiménez de, 156, 157
Cities, 70, 71, 74
Clarendon, earl of, 318
Clarius, Isodorus, 215
Classics, 22, 49, 59, 75, 87
Clement VII (pope), 249
Clovis (king of the Franks), 247
Cochläus, Johannes, 45
Codure, Jean, 163, 165
Colet, John, 14, 15, 17, 76, 345
Coligny, Gaspard de, 248, 249, 252, 256, 257, 261–70, 347
Coligny, Odet (cardinal de Châtillon), 248, 250–52, 254, 257, 258, 262, 264–66, 269, 347
Colledge, Edmund, 21
Collège de Montaigu, 161
Collège de Sainte-Barbe, 161
Collinson, Patrick, 334
Cologne, 31, 32, 278–80
Colonna, Vittoria, 170
Columbus, Christopher, 154
Communion, Holy, 26, 53, 69, 80, 82, 88, 106, 112, 113–17, 120–23, 142, 148, 156, 162, 257, 259, 264, 266, 285, 320, 328–29, 330, 335, 336, 346
Condé, prince de. See Bourbon, Louis de
Confession, 28–31, 286
Constaffel, 79, 80
Constance, 78, 89
Constance, Council of, 112
Contarini, Gasparo Cardinal, 157, 164, 165, 170, 213, 215, 259

Contarini, Pietro, 164
Coolidge, John S., 330
Copernicus, Nicolaus, 122
Cosin, John, 323, 326
Counter-Reformation, the, 153, 154, 162, 171, 282, 290, 291, 295, 301, 346
Courtenay, Henry, 215
Coverdale, Miles, 139, 148
Cranmer, Thomas (archbishop of Canterbury), 149
Cromwell, Thomas, 134–52, 211–13, 216, 217, 225, 226, 228, 229, 233–38, 346
Cruciger, Caspar, 50
Cyprian, Saint, 31, 107, 214
Cyprus, 159
Cyril, Saint, 107

d'Ailly, Pierre, 48
d'Andelot, François (Châtillon), 248–52, 256, 257, 260–63, 265, 268, 269, 347
D'Andrea, Antonio, 224
Daniel, 57, 178–80, 189, 195, 221, 222, 224, 228
David, King, 178–80, 232, 288
Davies, Horton, 328
de Gaulle, Charles (president of France), 270
Delumeau, Jean, 153
DeMolen, Richard L., 346, 347
Descartes, René, 158, 159
d'Estrées, Jean, 261
Deventer, 14
Devotio Moderna, 11, 19, 23, 157, 345
Dickens, A. G., 7, 43, 70, 72, 134, 153, 158, 238, 336
Dominicans, 75, 155, 160–61, 168, 287
Donaldson, Peter S., 347, 348
Donatists, 77
Donne, John, 159
Donnelly, J. Patrick, 346, 348
Dorp, Maarten van, 17
Dort, Synod of, 320, 323, 324, 326, 329
Dostoevski, Fëdor, 173
Du Bourg, Anne, 252, 253
Duns Scotus, 69, 88, 102, 346
Dürer, Albrecht, 11, 32
Durham, 320, 326
Dutch. See Netherlands, The

Echard, Laurence, 318
Eck, Johann, 104, 105, 111, 115
Edward IV (king of England), 212
Edward VI (king of England), 230, 236

Egretier, Noëlle-Marie, 231
Egypt, 47, 189
Einsiedeln, 77, 78
Eisenach, 50
Elizabeth I (queen of England), 149, 259, 260, 269, 305, 319, 324, 336
Ellis, Henry, 236
Elton, G. R., 134, 143, 211
Elzivier publishers, 284
Emser, Jerome, 101
England, 238, 252, 267, 285, 290, 320; cities of, 70; under Elizabeth I, 259, 269, 305; and Erasmus, 14–15, 34; under Henry VIII, 140, 145, 213–16, 235; history of, 75, 229; language of, 136, 137, 147, 166, 172, 173, 230, 278, 282, 295; laws of, 221; and loss of Boulogne, 251; and loss of Calais, 252; monasteries of, 347; and Reformation, 139, 270
England, Church of, 134, 141–42, 149, 213, 319, 320, 321, 322, 324, 325, 327–35
Enlightenment, the, 153
Epicureans, 178, 182, 183, 197
Erasmians, 76, 86, 156, 160, 260, 329, 330, 346
Erasmus, Desiderius, 7, 11–42, 49, 69, 75, 76, 159–61, 259, 345–47. Works; Colloquies, 161; Comparison of a Virgin and a Martyr, 31, 32; Complaint of Peace, 23; De bellum inexpertis, 23; Education of a Christian Prince, 24; Enchiridion, 19, 24, 159; Manner and Form of Confession, 27; Novum Instrumentum, 21, 69, 76; Praise of Folly, 17, 18, 24
Erastianism, 69, 267
Erfurt, 44, 46, 47, 50, 54
Erfurt, University of, 47–49
Erikson, Erik, 45
Ernest of Lüneburg, 55
Estates General, 253–55, 305
Ethiopia, 169
Eucharist, the. See Communion, Holy
Europe, 7, 56, 153, 167, 169–72, 259, 268, 269, 278, 294, 304, 330
Evans, John T., 335
Eve, 187

Farel, Guillaume, 179, 182
Favre, Pierre, 161, 162, 164
Fenlon, Dermot, 214
Ferarra, 266
Ferdinand I (Holy Roman emperor), 283, 284, 295, 296, 305
Ferdinand II (Holy Roman emperor), 153, 154, 162, 171, 278–317, 347

Fernandines, 296, 299
Ferrier, Arnauld du, 250
Firth, Katherine R., 221, 223
Florence, 218, 235, 236
Foix, Paul de, 250
Fontainebleau, 255, 257, 263, 264, 267
Fourré, Adrien, 265
Fox, Edward, 213, 227, 233
Foxe, John, 138, 139
Foxgrover, David, 347, 348
France, 181, 239; and Châtillon brothers, 247–70, 347; and Erasmus, 17; language of, 164, 172, 173, 297; and Louis XIII, 304; and Richelieu, 283; and Roman Catholicism, 247; and Swiss Confederacy, 77–80, 82
Francis de Sales, Saint, 158
Francis of Assisi, Saint, 103, 106, 166, 167, 173
Francis Xavier, Saint, 161, 162
Francis I (king of France), 85, 248–50
Francis II (king of France), 252, 254, 263
Franciscans, 103, 104, 159, 168
Frankfurt, 278, 297, 301, 302
Frederick V (king of Bohemia), 291, 293, 294, 302
Frederick the Wise (elector of Saxony), 49, 53–55, 99
Freiburg, 24
French civil wars, 268, 269
French Reformation, 247–77, 260, 266
Friars Observants, 26
Frith, John, 142

Gabriel, Archangel, 110
Gaguin, Robert, 14
Gallicanism, 247
Gansfort, Wessel, 118
Gardiner, S. R., 320, 329
Gardiner, Stephen, 141, 143, 227, 233, 236
Gaul, 247
Gellius, Aulus, 12
Geneva, 61, 83, 181, 248, 256, 259, 261, 266, 267, 319, 329
Gentillet, Innocent, 224
George of Albertine Saxony (duke), 53, 57
Gerard, Cornelius, 13
German Historical Institute, 70
Germany, 17, 53–59, 140, 143, 260; cities of, 50–53, 70–71, 285; and Ferdinand II, 278–307; language of, 85, 172, 173, 295; local government of, 73–74, 82, 268, 270; nation of, 346; and Protestantism, 59–62, 124, 171; and Reformation, 43–44, 48, 50

Gerson, John, 29
Ghinucci, Girolamo, 165
Giunta, Bernardo, 236
Glareanus, Henricus, 75
Glarus, 72–75, 77, 78, 80
Gloucester, 320
God, 12, 18, 22–24, 28–32, 34, 47, 50, 52, 55, 57, 58, 61, 85, 87, 89, 100, 103–7, 109–11, 113, 117–20, 123, 124, 141, 153, 155–57, 163, 165–67, 169, 179–84, 186–90, 200, 213–15, 220, 221, 224, 226, 227, 231, 232, 253, 262, 263, 293, 321, 322, 325–28, 330, 331, 345, 346
Goes, Damião de, 230
Goeters, J. F. Gerherd, 84
Grafton, Richard, 148
Granada, 153, 154
Grebel, Jacob von, 80, 81, 84
Greek language, 49, 75, 76, 145, 260
Gregory I, Saint, 107
Gregory VII, Saint, 116
Gregory of Rimini, 46
Guidiccioni, Bartolomeo, 165
Guipúzcoa, 153, 163
Guise, Charles de (cardinal de Lorraine), 252, 260, 262
Guise, François de (duc de Guise), 251, 252, 256, 261, 263
Guises, 251, 252–56, 259, 261, 264

Haas, Martin, 84
Habsburgs, 78, 82, 252, 281–84, 291, 295, 296, 299
Hacket, Bp. John, 321
Hales, John, 330
Hampton Court, 321
Harvey, Robert, 173
Haton, Claude, 268
Hebrew, 49, 214
Heidelberg, 300
Hendrix, Scott, 346, 348
Henry II (king of France), 248, 250, 252, 261–63
Henry III (king of France and Duc d'Anjou), 257
Henry IV (king of France and King of Navarre as Henry III), 250, 257, 269
Henry VII (king of England), 212, 332
Henry VIII (king of England), 15, 134, 136–38, 140–44, 148, 212–18, 220–22, 224–30, 232–35, 237, 238, 248, 258, 346, 347
Hercules, 75
Heylyn, Peter, 319
Hitchcock, Alfred, 283
Hoces, Diego de, 163

Hohenlandenburg, Hugo von, 78
Hohenzollern, 54, 56
Holbein, Hans, the Younger, 11, 32
Holy Land, 270
Holy Roman Empire, 278–317
Holy Spirit, 26, 28, 85–88, 138, 166
Hooker, Richard, 322, 329
Horace, 184
Huguenots, 253–56, 258, 259, 263, 265–70, 305, 347
Humanists, 14, 27, 49, 69, 75, 76, 78, 79, 153, 159, 160, 166, 249, 259, 345
Hungary, 283–85, 303
Huntington, Henry, 215
Hus, John, 224
Hutten, Ulrich von, 57
Hutton, W. H., 318

Ignatius Loyola, Saint, 153–77, 346. Works: *Spiritual Exercises*, 156–62, 163, 164, 166, 170
Île de France, 251, 265
Imitation of Christ, The (Thomas à Kempis), 11, 13–15, 21, 23, 33, 157, 345
Index of Forbidden Books, 216
India, 169
Indonesia, 169
Indulgences, 54, 103, 106, 107, 109
Inquisition, Spanish, 160, 161
Isaac, 185
Isabella, Queen (of Spain), 153
Isaiah, 228, 234
Islam, 160, 171, 294
Israel, 88, 215
Italy: cities of, 164; language of, 286; and Loyola, 164–65, 170–71; and R. Pole, 143, 213, 215, 216; Spanish domination of, 154, 250; and Zwingli, 77

James I (king of England), 296, 305, 320–22, 324, 325, 333
James II (king of England), 334
Japan, 169
Jay, Claude le, 163
Jerome, Saint, 101, 107
Jerusalem, 155, 159, 163, 164, 194
Jesuits, 157–59, 161–73, 282, 283, 287, 290, 298, 300, 301, 322
Jewel, John, 225
Jews, 56, 58, 105, 118, 154, 170, 190, 229, 285
Joachim I (elector of Brandenburg), 54
Joachim II (elector of Brandenburg), 56
Joachimist tradition, 223
John Chrysostom, Saint, 31

John Fisher, Saint, 15, 213–15, 230, 231
John III (king of Portugal), 162
John Frederick of Saxony (elector), 55, 56
John George I (elector of Saxony), 302
John the Constant (elector of Saxony), 50, 55, 60
Jonas, Justus, 50
Josephus, 194
Joshua, 105
Judaea, 194, 195
Juxon, William, 332

Kähler, Ernst, 102
Kappel War, 70, 80–83, 89
Karlstadt, Andreas von, 50, 52, 53, 99–133, 346. Works: *Verba Dei*, 105, 106, 113
Kempen, Jan van, 214
Kempis, Thomas à, 11, 14, 34
Klesl, Melchior Cardinal, 285, 300
Kristeller, Paul O., 76
Kuch, Wolfgang, 117

Lactantius, 193
Lambeth Articles, 319, 324
Lambeth Palace, 323, 334
La Mothe-Fénelon (ambassador), 269
Lang, John, 50, 59
La Rochelle, 269
Last Days, 56, 58, 61, 192, 211, 215, 223, 235
Latimer, Hugh, 139, 143
Latin, 53, 72, 74, 106, 148, 159, 164, 166, 172, 213, 224, 291, 292, 295
Latin America, 169
Laud, William (archbishop of Canterbury), 318–44, 347
Laval, Charlotte de, 265
Laynes, Diego, 162, 164, 170
Legros, Pierre, 171
Lehmberg, Stanford, 346, 348
Leighton, Alexander, 331
Leipzig, 51, 56, 101, 104, 107
Lejay, Claude, 170
Leo X (pope), 13, 15, 16, 32, 101, 103, 107
Levites, 228, 229
L'Hôpital, Michel de, 250, 255, 257, 258, 267, 268
Linacre, Thomas, 33
Lollards, 139
London, 8, 27, 33, 70, 135, 136, 141, 148, 159, 161, 269, 322, 325, 328, 329, 332
Longwy, Jacqueline de, 256
Lord's Prayer, 52, 110, 136, 158
Lorraine, 253, 260, 304
Louis XIII (king of France), 269, 302, 304–6

Louvain, University of, 17, 104
Low Countries, 291, 299
Lucerne, 81
Lucianists, 182, 183, 197
Ludolf of Saxony, 154, 156
Lupset, Thomas, 147
Lusatia, 283, 300
Luther, Martin, 7, 18, 26, 29, 30, 43–68, 69, 87, 88, 99, 101, 103, 104, 106, 108, 112, 114, 121, 122, 124, 125, 140, 142, 160, 161, 168, 170, 171, 173, 304, 345, 346. Works: *Address to the Christian Nobility*, 57, 58; *Against the Heavenly Prophets*, 99; *The Bondage of the Will*, 49; Catechisms (of 1529), 52; *The Freedom of a Christian*, 52; *German Mass*, 60; *German Theology*, 57; *Invocavit Sermons* (March 1522), 52; *Monastic Vows*, 47; New Testament, 54; *Ninety-five Theses*, 51; *Smalcald Articles*, 56; *Warning to his Dear German People*, 57
Lutherans, 61, 82, 99, 100, 120–22, 138, 139, 143, 148, 160, 259, 266, 283, 285, 291, 302, 303, 323
Lyon, 88, 255, 266

Macar, Jean, 261, 263
Macaulay, Thomas Babington, 318
McConica, James K., 26
McGee, J. Sears, 347, 349
Machiavelli, Niccolò, 71, 173, 211–46, 347. Works: *Discourses*, 218, 219; *The Prince*, 211, 216–19, 222, 223, 225, 235–38, 347
Madrid, 172
Maffei, Gian Pietro, 172
Mailly, Madelaine de (Madame de Roye), 255, 256, 263
Mainz, archbishop of. See Albrecht of Brandenburg
Mainz, 162, 278–80, 297
Manresa, 155–57, 167, 173
Mansfield, Bruce, 33
Manuel, Nikolaus, 82
Manz, Felix, 121
Marcuse, Ludwig, 173
Margaret of Austria, 169
Marguerite de France (duchess of Savoy), 256, 257, 265
Marguerite de Navarre, 249, 260
Maria Anna of Bohemia (empress), 287
Marignano, battle of, 77, 79, 248
Marot, Clément, 256
Marsiglio of Padua, 237
Mary, Virgin, 12, 31, 104, 106, 120, 123, 135, 138, 155, 328

Mary I (queen of England), 212, 252, 260
Mary Stuart (queen of Scots), 252
Mass, 16, 20, 27, 31, 48, 51–53, 80, 84, 103, 111, 112, 116, 121, 122, 135, 148, 156, 162, 261–63, 279, 280, 286, 287, 289, 300, 330
Mathesius, Johann, 57
Matthias (Holy Roman emperor), 278, 284, 285, 288, 291, 297, 302, 303, 305
Maurice of Albertine Saxony (duke), 54
Maximilian I (Holy Roman emperor), 54
Maximilian II (Holy Roman emperor), 284, 297, 305
Meaux, 268
Meaux, Council of, 107
Medici, 218
Medici, Catherine de, 248–50, 254–59, 265, 266, 268, 269
Melanchthon, Philipp, 7, 45, 46, 50, 53, 56, 59, 99, 108, 110, 145
Melchizedek, 187
Mennonite scholars and historians, 83, 84
Merlin, Jean-Raymond, 264
Merriman, R. B., 134
Metsys, Quentin, 11, 32
Metzger, Lawrence S., 269
Michael, Saint, 120
Michelangelo Buonarotti, 170
Middle Ages, 44, 61, 107, 121, 153, 158, 160, 166, 168, 170, 247
Milan, 260
Millennium, 223
Moeller, Bernd, 70, 71, 80
Moline, Francis, 27
Monastery, 44–47, 347
Monluc, Jean de, 257, 268
Montagu, Richard (bishop of Chichester), 323–26, 331, 335
Montague, Lord Henry, 214, 215
Montaigne, George (bishop of London), 324
Montaigne, Michel Eyquem de, 254
Montmorency, Anne de (constable of France), 248–52, 254, 256, 262
Montmorency, François de, 265
Montmorency, Louise de, 248, 249
Montmorencys, 251–53, 255, 259, 265
Montserrat, 156
Moravia, 283, 300
Morély, Jean-Baptiste, 266, 267
Morison, Richard, 139, 215
Morley, Henry, 235–37
Moses, 105, 228, 229
Müntzer, Thomas, 56

Muralt, Leonhard von, 81
Myconius, Friedrich, 182
Mysticism, 106, 155, 169

Nantes, Edict of, 258
Naples, 154
Navarre, 154, 162, 254
Neile, Richard (bishop of Rochester), 320, 322, 324, 326, 329
Neoplatonism, 70, 86
Netherlands, The, 259, 269, 270, 284, 286, 305, 320, 329
New Testament, 76, 178, 180; 2 Corinthians, 11; Ephesians, 182, 185, 186; Galatians, 48, 50, 87; James, 296; 1 John, 106, 122, 196–98; Matthew, 79, 86, 179, 192–95, 197–99; 1 Peter, 181, 190, 194; 2 Peter, 192; Philemon, 181; Revelation, 119, 222, 223; Romans, 48, 50, 86, 182, 183, 186, 195, 200; 1 Thessalonians, 192, 193, 198; 2 Thessalonians, 193, 194, 196, 197, 199, 220, 224; 1 Timothy, 54; 2 Timothy, 181; Titus, 179. See also Scripture
Nicene Creed, 146
Nifo, Agostino, 236
Noah, 184, 186, 187, 189, 198
Normandy, 267
Nuremberg, 278, 279
Nuremberg, Peace of, 55

Oecolampadius, Johannes, 121, 124
Oldmixion, John, 318
Old Testament, 85, 88, 110, 112, 178, 194, 228, 231, 232, 262; Amos, 181; Daniel, 180, 183–85, 188–91, 193, 195, 222, 224, 228; Deuteronomy, 105, 296; Ecclesiastes, 108; Exodus, 188, 189, 228, 229, 296; Ezekiel, 108, 228, 231, 232; Genesis, 50, 56, 122, 179, 183, 185, 187, 231; Habakkuk, 182; Isaiah, 107, 194, 195, 214, 224, 228, 230, 231; Jeremiah, 89, 194; Joel, 194; Joshua, 200; 1 Kings, 231; Leviticus, 296; Proverbs, 296; Psalms, 46, 48, 49, 104, 184, 188, 189, 191, 231; Zephaniah, 181. See also Scripture
Olin, John C., 8
Oratory of Divine Love, 213
Origen, 31, 69, 77
Orlamünde, 99, 100, 111, 117, 119, 120, 124
Orleans, 261
Ortiz, Pedro, 164
Oxford, 143, 212, 318–21, 325, 327, 328
Ozment, Stephen, 70, 106

Padua, 212–14, 250
Palatine, 281, 282, 291, 296, 301, 302
Palestine, 159, 163, 164, 171
Pamplona, 154
Papacy, 77–79, 107, 141, 190, 225, 247, 250, 255, 286
Papists, 178, 181, 182, 320, 326
Paris, 14, 143, 156, 161–63, 213, 250, 252, 253, 261, 264
Paris, University of, 213, 247, 250
Parliament, British, 134, 137, 146, 322–24, 326, 333, 334
Parnassus, 292
Pater, Calvin A., 346, 349
Patterson, Lloyd, 223
Paul, Saint, 12, 22, 27, 49, 87, 101, 112, 140, 178, 179, 182, 186, 192, 195, 196, 199, 221, 345
Paul III (pope), 156, 163–65, 170
Paul IV (pope), 163, 168
Pauline-Augustinian tradition, 76
Peasants' Revolt, 55, 56, 60
Pelagius, 48, 49, 104
Percy, Algernon (earl of Northumberland), 318
Perez, Jacobus, 46
Persians, 184
Perth, 321
Peter, Saint, 12
Peter Canisius, Saint, 162, 170, 171, 283
Pharisee, 113
Philip II (king of Spain), 215, 236, 252, 258, 259
Philip III (king of Spain), 283
Philip of Hesse, Landgrave, 55, 82, 85
Philosophia Christi, 11, 12, 14, 21, 27, 345, 346
Philosophy, 48
Picardy, 251
Piety, 7, 11, 20, 22–24, 113, 171, 181, 260, 269, 324
Pilate, 121
Plato, 217, 219, 237
Poissy, Colloquy of, 257, 265, 266
Polanco, Juan, 166, 171, 172
Pole, Reginald Cardinal, 143, 147, 148, 211–46, 259, 347. Works: Apologia, 215, 216, 219–21, 224, 227–30, 234, 235, 237; De Unitate, 211–15, 227–37; Epistolae, 230
Polish language, 159
Politi, Lancelotto, 215
Pollard, A. F., 211
Popes, 7, 28, 31, 52, 56, 58, 77, 78, 104, 107, 110, 113, 163, 165, 167, 171, 179, 180, 196, 198, 216, 249
Portugal, 171
Postel, Guillaume, 167
Potter, George, 69, 75, 81
Pozzo, Andrea, 172
Prague, 284, 285, 288, 298, 300, 303
Predestination, 324, 325, 327
Presbyterians, 70, 319, 332
Preus, James S., 124
Priesthood, 122, 142, 331, 347
Priorato, Gualdo, 306, 307
Privy Council, 215, 216, 230, 233, 329, 333
Protestantism, 71, 99, 105, 153, 156, 171, 266, 283, 323
Protestants, 7, 30, 34, 50, 53, 55–57, 60, 61, 71, 80, 99, 121, 125, 134, 136, 170, 171, 173, 221–24, 248, 249, 254, 256, 258, 260, 261, 263, 266, 268–70, 285, 291, 294, 296, 300, 302–4, 306, 320, 323, 329, 331, 335, 336, 345–47
Prynne, William, 331
Ptolemy, 121–23
Public Record Office, 230
Purgatory, 109, 118, 119
Puritans, 318–44; 347
Pym, John, 323
Quirini, A. M., 211
Rabelais, François, 250
Rabil, Albert, Jr., 8
Ramus, Peter, 250
Rebekah, 185
Reeves, Marjorie, 223
Reformed Churches, 69–98, 260, 263, 264, 292, 295, 318
Renaissance, the, 153, 249
Renée de France (duchess of Ferarra), 256
Rhenanus, Beatus, 28, 33
Ribadeneira, Pedro de, 171, 172
Rich, Arthur, 76
Richelieu, Cardinal, 269, 283
Rieux, Claude de, 262
Ritter, Gerhard, 7
Rochester, 319, 320
Rodriquez, Simon, 162, 164
Roelker, Nancy Lyman, 347, 349
Roist, Markus, 78
Romans, 184, 247, 250, 305
Rome, 17, 51, 54, 57–60, 79, 80, 101, 102, 134, 149, 159, 161, 163, 164, 165, 168–70, 172, 213, 214, 259, 286, 301, 319, 329, 346, 347
Ronsard, Pierre de, 250
Rubens, Peter Paul, 172

Rublack, Hans-Christoph, 70
Rudolph II (Holy Roman emperor), 284, 297
Russell, Conrad, 324

Sacraments, 52, 86–88, 103, 107, 112, 115, 116,
   121, 122, 138, 142, 156, 160, 286, 330
Sadoleto, Jacopo, 13, 178, 182
St. André, Marshal de, 256
Saint Gall, Abbey of, 72, 82
St. Germain, Christopher, 233
Saint Germain, 257, 261, 269
Saint Lo, 261
Saint Quentin, battle of, 252, 261
Salamanca, University of, 160
Salat, Johannes, 81
Salmerón, Alfonso, 162, 170
Sampson, Richard, 227, 233, 237
Sara, 185
Satan, 109, 118, 159, 172, 188, 189, 192, 197,
   200, 217, 221–24, 232, 233, 237, 238
Savoy, 304
Saxony, Duchy of, 44, 51, 52, 54–57, 60, 282,
   290, 291, 302, 346
Scaliger, J. C., 13
Scarisbrick, J. J., 138
Scheurl, Christoph, 59
Schinner, Matthäus, 77
Schmalkaldic War, 187
Schmiedebach, Augustin Schmid von, 295,
   296
Scholasticism, 48–50, 75, 85, 160, 170
Schwyz, 72–74, 77
Scotland, 254; and Laud, 320–21, 329, 334
Scripture, 14, 19, 20, 22, 28, 31, 46–50, 52, 56,
   58, 59, 69, 71, 75–80, 83–88, 100–110, 113,
   116–25, 134, 136–43, 147, 149, 156, 158, 165,
   179–82, 187–95, 212–15, 220, 223, 224, 233–
   37, 260, 294, 296, 323, 329, 330, 345, 346
Seaver, Paul, 335
Second Coming, 191–93, 197, 222–24, 235
Seth, 187, 189
Seville, 155
Seyler, Franciscus, 107, 108
Shakespeare, William, 158
Shem, 189
Sherfield, Henry, 333, 334
's Hertogenbosch, 14
Shimizu, Junko S., 248, 257, 263, 265, 270
Sibthorpe, Robert, 322
Sicily, 171
Sickingen, Franz von, 57
Siena, 165
Silesia, 283, 300

Simpkinson, C. H., 318
Smalcald, Diet of, 55
Smith, Miles (bishop of Gloucester), 320
Sodom and Gomorrah, 86
Somaschi, 168
Spain, 285; and Coligny, 248; and Catherine
   de Medici, 256; under Ferdinand and Isa-
   bella, 153–54; and Ferdinand II, 284, 300–
   301; and Loyola, 153–73; under Philip II,
   252, 259, 261, 269; under Philip III, 304
Spanish Armada, 329
Sparke, Michael, 318
Speyer, Diets of, 55
Star Chamber, Court of, 322, 330–33
Starkey, Thomas, 139, 143–49, 213. Works:
   *Dialogue between Reginald Pole and Thomas
   Lupset*, 147, 148; *Exhortation*, 145–47
Staupitz, Johannes von, 46
Stayer, James M., 84
Steyn, 11, 13–15, 17, 19, 22, 32, 33
Storch, Nikolaus, 110
Strasbourg, 70–72
Strassburg, 61
Strayer, Joseph R., 247
Strozzi, Pierre, 261
Sussex, 335
Swabian War, 74
Swiss Confederacy, 71, 73–75, 77
Switzerland: and Châtillon brothers, 268; and
   Karlstadt, 101; medieval, 73; and Zwingli,
   69–89
Szarzyński, Mikolaj Sep, 159

Tacitus, 218
Täufer movement, 70, 83, 84
Tauler, John, 48
Ten Commandments, 52, 88, 110, 116
Tentler, Thomas N., 31
Tertullian, 31
Theatines, 163, 168
Theologians, 17, 27, 69, 71, 85, 105, 116, 149,
   162, 170, 179, 180, 322
Theology, 7, 11, 19, 46, 48–50, 70, 74, 76, 77,
   84–89, 99, 106, 164, 170, 250, 323, 330, 331,
   345, 346
Thirty-Nine Articles, 323, 325
Thirty Years' War, the, 282, 283, 329
Thomä, Mark, 110
Thomas Aquinas, Saint, 75, 87, 88, 102, 109
Thomas Becket, Saint, 213
Thomas More, Saint, 15, 140, 142, 213–15,
   230, 231, 259

Thomas, William, 236
Thou, Jacques-Auguste de, 268
Toggenburg, 72, 73
Toledo, 160
Toulouse, 249, 250, 255
Tours, 261
Tracy, James D., 8
Transubstantiation, 88
Trent, Council of, 112, 159, 170, 259, 260, 266, 324, 329
Trevor-Roper, Hugh, 326, 329
Trier, 278–80
Trinity, Holy, 87, 138, 156
Trinkaus, Charles, 76
Trivium, 74
Trutvetter, Jodocus, 48
Tudor, House of, 212, 213, 238, 252
Tunstal, Cuthbert, 141
Turks, 56, 58, 59, 163, 227, 283, 294
Tuscany, 304
Tyndale, William, 142

Urban VIII (pope), 288
Ursulines, 169
Usinger, Bartholomew Arnoldi von, 48
Utraquists, 112

Vadian, 75
Valdes, Juan de, 214
Valladolid, 162
Valois, 252
Valois, Marguerite de, 257
Van Dyke, Paul, 173, 211, 215, 229, 233, 235–37
Vaucelles, Treaty of, 251
Vaughan, Stephen, 140
Vega, Eleonora Osorio de, 169, 170
Venice, 159, 161, 163, 164, 213, 214, 322
Vergerio, Pietro Paolo, 230
Via antiqua, 75, 346
Via moderna, 75
Vienna, 75, 278, 284–88, 298, 301, 303
Vienna, University of, 75, 171
Villiers, George (duke of Buckingham), 321–24

Viret, Pierre, 179, 182
Virtue, 12, 20, 21, 219, 220, 269
Voragine, Jacobo de, 154, 156

Waldmann, Hans, 73
Wales, 321, 322
Wallerstein, Emmanuel, 72
Walton, Robert C., 84, 346, 349
Ward, Mary, 169
Wartburg, 52, 54, 116
Wassenberg, Everhard, 306
Wentworth, Thomas (earl of Strafford), 332, 333
Wettin family, 54, 56
White Mountain, battle of, 291, 294, 298, 300
Whitgift, John (archbishop of Canterbury), 319
Wightman, Edward, 320
Williams, Lord Keeper John, 321, 322
William the Silent, 283
Winchester, 320
Wittenberg, 44, 46, 47, 50–58, 69, 99, 112, 116, 120, 124, 140, 149, 346
Wittenberg, University of, 46, 47–53, 54, 99, 101–3, 111
Wittenberg Ordinance, 124
Wladislai (king of Bohemia), 295
Wölflin, Heinrich, 72, 75
Wolrab, Nicholas, 51
Wolsey, Thomas Cardinal, 135
Worms, Diet of, 52, 54, 57
Wren, Matthew, 334
Wycliffe, John, 139, 142, 223, 224

Xenophon, 184

Yoder, John H., 83
York, 213, 322

Zurich, 69–89, 115, 116, 121
Zwickau Prophets, 108, 110
Zwilling, Gabriel, 52
Zwingli, Huldrych, 7, 69–98, 124, 171, 346